# VICE & VIRTUE IN EVERYDAY LIFE

*Introductory Readings in Ethics*

# VICE & VIRTUE IN EVERYDAY LIFE

*Introductory Readings in Ethics*

CHRISTINA SOMMERS
Clark University

FRED SOMMERS
Brandeis University

Under the general editorship of
Robert J. Fogelin, Dartmouth College

HARCOURT BRACE JOVANOVICH, PUBLISHERS
San Diego   New York   Chicago   Austin   Washington, D.C.
London   Sydney   Tokyo   Toronto

Cover: Pieter Brueghel, *Peasant Dance*,
 *c.* 1566–67. Panel, 44⅞ × 64½".
 Kunsthistorisches Museum, Vienna.

ISBN: 0-15-594891-1

Library of Congress Catalog Card Number: 88-81037
Printed in the United States of America

## PREFACE

In the nineteenth century, moral philosophy was the most important course in a student's college career. The course was taken during the senior year and typically was taught by the college president. Now, after many years, normative ethics is flourishing again. Philosophy departments are attracting unprecedented numbers of students to courses in contemporary ethical problems, business ethics, medical ethics; ethics for engineers, nurses, and social workers. We find dozens of journals, hundreds of texts and anthologies, and, according to a survey by the Hastings Center, 11,000 courses in applied ethics. It is too early to venture more than a suggestion as to what has occasioned the renaissance of normative ethics. Undoubtedly, the unsettling effects of rapid social and technological change are somehow implicated. But if we cannot confidently identify the cause of the renaissance, we can describe it and comment on its significance for moral education in America and Great Britain. And, without looking a gift horse in the mouth, we are permitted to criticize its direction. For not all is cause for self-congratulation.

In reading the articles selected for a course in applied ethics, students encounter arguments by philosophers who take strong stands on such important social questions as abortion, euthanasia, capital punishment, and censorship. By contrast, students may find little to read on private individual virtue and responsibility. Many college ethics courses are concerned primarily with the conduct and policies of schools, hospitals, courts, corporations, and governments. Again, the moral responsibilities of the students may be discussed only occasionally. Because most students are not likely to be personally involved in administering the death penalty or selecting candidates for kidney dialysis, and because most will never conduct recombinant DNA research or even undergo abortions, the effective purpose of such courses in applied ethics is to teach students how to form responsible opinions on social policies—a purpose that is more civic than personal. "Applying" ethics to modern life involves more than learning how to be for or against social and institutional policies. These are important goals, but they are not enough.

This anthology brings together classical and contemporary writings on such matters as courage, pride, wisdom, compassion, generosity, honor, and self-respect. The anthology also includes essays on such moral foibles as hypocrisy, self-deception, jealousy, and narcissism. More standard materials are included, among them chapters on theories of moral conduct, moral education, and contemporary social issues. The collection thereby seeks to combine the virtues of current texts on applied ethics with the virtues of more traditional survey texts. In addition, the selections address lively and important issues in personal morality.

Social ethics is only half of normative ethics. Private ethics, including the theory of virtue, is the other half. We believe we need more balanced and traditional fare. Hence, this anthology.

## ACKNOWLEDGMENTS

For their review of the second edition manuscript, we express our appreciation to Julien M. Farland, Middlesex Community College; George A. Graham, University of Alabama, Birmingham; Mark Lance, Syracuse University; Peter L. Trier, California State University, Fresno; and William Davie, University of Oregon. For their excellent editorial advice, we extend a special thanks to Robert J. Fogelin, Bill McLane, and Robert C. Miller. And for their valuable contributions, we are grateful to Kim Turner, Linda Wild, Chris Nelson, and Eleanor Garner.

CHRISTINA SOMMERS
FRED SOMMERS

# CONTENTS

Preface  v

Introduction  1

*Indicates a selection new to this edition.

Contents

# INTRODUCTION

Why, in novels, films, and television programs, are villains so easily distinguishable from heroes? What is it about, say, Huckleberry Finn or the runaway slave Jim that is unmistakably good, and about Huck's father Pap and the Duke and King that is unmistakably bad? For generations children have loved Cinderella and despised her evil stepsisters. Our moral sympathies are in constant play. We root for the moral heroes of the prime-time shows and eagerly await the downfall of the villains they pursue.

   The moral dimension of our everyday experience is a pervasive and inescapable fact. In an important sense we are all "moralizers," instinctively applying moral judgment to the fictional and real people of our acquaintance and, in reflective moments, to ourselves as well. Moral philosophy seeks to make sense of this moral dimension in our lives. One objective is moral self-knowledge and self-evaluation. This is notoriously difficult. It is one thing to recognize good and evil when we encounter it in literature or in our friends; it is quite another to recognize good and evil in ourselves. The philosophical study of morality, by its reasoned approach to the concepts that figure centrally in our moral judgments, can help us be more objective. In particular, it can help by alerting us to some of the characteristic deceptions that prevent us from seeing our own moral virtues and defects.

The philosopher's approach to such concepts as good and evil or vice and virtue differs in important ways from that of the social scientist or theologian. A sociologist or an anthropologist, for example, describes and interprets a society's mores and, in contrast to the moral philosopher, usually is careful to keep the account morally neutral. A theologian will call on us to act in a particular way and to avoid certain sinful practices. By contrast, the moral philosopher, though not neutral, usually does not exhort to action. Instead, the moral philosopher will explain what makes an act right or a person virtuous. In discussing criteria of right action and virtuous character, the philosopher will try to show why certain traits, such as honesty, generosity, and courage, are worthy, and others, such as hypocrisy, selfishness, and cowardice, are not. More generally, the moral philosopher seeks a clear and well-reasoned answer to the question: "What is it to be moral?"

Moral philosophers have viewed this central question in two distinct ways. Some construe the question as asking what we, as responsible agents confronting decisions of right and wrong, ought to do. These moral philosophers, then, see it as their task to formulate general principles of behavior that define our duties by distinguishing right actions from wrong ones. A theory that emphasizes moral duties and actions is *action based*. A second approach—called *virtue based*—takes the central question of morality to be: "What sort of person should I be?" Here the emphasis is not so much on what to *do* as on what to *be*. For virtue-based theorists, the object of moral education is to produce a virtuous individual. They therefore have much to say about moral education and character development. By concentrating attention on character rather than action, the philosopher of virtue tacitly assumes that a virtuous person's actions generally fall within the range of what is right and fair.

In the modern period—beginning with David Hume and Immanuel Kant—moral philosophy has tended to be action based. The reader will learn some of the reasons underlying the recent neglect of virtue and character from selected essays by Bernard Mayo, Anthony Quinton, Bernard Williams, and Alasdair MacIntyre, who are among the growing number of philosophers who view an exclusively action-based approach as inadequate. We have attempted to give equal space to virtue-based theories.

2

The nine chapters of this second edition are distinguished thematically. The opening essays highlight the crucial importance of character and of the capacity for sympathy and compassion. These essays, together with several other selections, suggest that being moral is never simply a matter of knowing how one should act. Sociopaths may be well aware of the right thing to do but, because they lack human sympathy, simply not care enough to be moral except where a display of moral behavior serves their individual purpose. All the same, knowing how to act is essential to being moral. The essays in Chapter Two are devoted to the exposition and criticism of several action-based theories such as act and rule utilitarianism and Kantianism.

The selections on virtue and vice in Chapters 3 and 4 range from classical to contemporary. Aristotle's (and Plato's) thesis that happiness is tied to the moral virtues is a central theme. The religious and philosophical discussions of vice and virtue differ in characteristic ways. For a theologian such as Augustine or Abelard, vice is sin construed as rebellion against the decrees of God. For a philosopher such as Aristotle or Plutarch, vice is more akin to physical illness or deformity. The selections contain representative analyses of such virtues as generosity and wisdom, and such vices as envy and self-deception.

Human beings are variously moral; the amoral personality and the supermoral personality are extreme types. Not very long ago the former type would have been called "nihilistic," but today the more usual label is "sociopathic" or "psychopathic." The moral philosopher who is disposed to argue that amoralism is untenable naturally prefers to condemn the amoralist as a pathological character type. But the philosophers in Chapter Five are keenly aware that more than name calling is required if one is properly to answer the serious question "Why be moral?" The other extreme type—the supermoralist—sometimes is characterized as saintly; the latter half of Chapter Five examines the personality of "The Moral Saint." Oddly enough, some moral philosophers are averse to moral saintliness as an ideal to be pursued. Chapter Six, "Moral Education" continues the discussion of moral character, focusing on training and development. We present several views on how best to educate children to become morally sensitive and mature. Aristotle's classic position that moral education uses reward and other reinforcements to habituate the child to virtuous activity is followed by a contemporary theory (Lawrence

Kohlberg's) inspired by Plato's idea that morality is innate and that moral education proceeds by eliciting it in stages. In this chapter, we also consider the question of how to distinguish an effective but legitimate approach to education from an approach that wrongfully interferes with the child's autonomy through "indoctrination" and "thought control."

Part of being moral is respecting ourselves as well as respecting others. Respect for others is bound up with self-respect since we cannot respect ourselves as moral beings unless we value our respectful treatment of others. Chapter Seven includes discussions of the place of self-respect and dignity in the development of moral character.

The essays in Chapters Eight and Nine pertain primarily to that part of moral philosophy called applied ethics. The student will encounter philosophers arguing different sides of topical moral issues such as divorce, rearing of children, and duties to one's parents, as well as more general social issues such as the morality or immorality of United States foreign policy. Here, where moral issues touch politics, the discussions become familiarly acrimonious. In these controversies, as in many others throughout the book, each student undoubtedly will locate his or her individual position.

What, finally, may the open-minded and careful reader of a comprehensive text on moral philosophy expect to gain? First, if not foremost, the reader will acquire a great deal of knowledge of the classical approaches to moral philosophy and, with this, some sense of the moral tradition of Western civilization as Greek and Judeo-Christian thought have influenced it. Second, the reader will become aware of some of the central problem areas in ethics and will be in a better position to approach them with the confidence that comes with historical perspective and a sharpened moral insight. Social change and novel technologies bring about new problems, each with its moral dimension. Yet morality itself is not really changed in any radical way. There will always be a right and decent way to cope with the new situations that confront us.

# Chapter One

# GOOD AND EVIL

Much of moral philosophy is a disciplined effort to systematize and explain our most common convictions about good and evil and right and wrong. Proper ethical philosophy takes the simplest moral truths as its starting point. Almost no one doubts that cruelty is wrong. But philosophers differ on how to explain what is wrong about acting cruelly and even about the meaning of right and wrong. So we have various systems of moral theory. Inevitably we have the possibility that a philosopher may devise a pseudo-ethical doctrine that loses sight of basic intuitions about human dignity and elementary decency. When such a doctrine achieves currency and popular respectability, it becomes a powerful force for evil. For then, what passes as conventional wisdom allows the average person to behave in reprehensible but conventionally acceptable ways.

In Chapter 1 we find examples of the ways the moral intuitions of the individual may conflict with publicly accepted principles that are not grounded in respect for human dignity. In the first two selections, "From Cruelty to Goodness" by Philip Hallie and "The Conscience of Huckleberry Finn" by Jonathan Bennett, the moral failure of principle is easy to diagnose. A dominant group adopts a philosophy that permits it to confine its moral concern to those inside the group,

5

treating outsiders as beyond the moral pale; their pain, their dignity, even their very lives merit no moral consideration. Huckleberry Finn, being white, is within the moral domain. His mentors have taught him that he does not owe moral behavior to slaves. Yet Huck treats Jim, the runaway slave, as if he too deserves the respect due a white person. And therein lies Huck's conflict. Everything he conventionally believes tells him he is doing wrong in helping Jim elude his pursuers.

Mark Twain's account of the conflict between official "book" morality and the ground-level morality of an innately decent and sympathetic person is one of the best in literature. Usually the conflict is embodied in two protagonists (Victor Hugo's novel *Les Misérables* is an example), but Huck Finn's conflict is within himself. And we are glad that his decency is stronger than his book morality. Both Jonathan Bennett and Philip Hallie quote the Nazi officer Heinrich Himmler, one of the fathers of the "final solution," as a spokesman for those who advocate suspending all moral feeling toward a particular group. Interestingly, Himmler considered himself all the more moral for being above pitying the children and other innocent victims outside the domain of moral consideration. Indeed, we hear stories of Germans who were conscience-stricken because—against their principles—they allowed some Jews to escape.

Our dismay at man's inhumanity to man is qualified by the inspiring example of the residents of the French village Le Chambon-sur-Lignon who acted together to care for and save 6,000 Jews, mostly children, from the Nazis. Le Chambon is said to have been the safest place in Europe for a Jew during the Second World War. From his studies of the village, Hallie concludes that Le Chambon residents successfully combatted evil because they never allowed themselves to be blind to the victim's point of view. "When we are blind to that point of view we can countenance and perpetrate cruelty with impunity." The true morality of Le Chambon drives out false and hypocritical Nazi "decencies" that ignore the most elementary moral intuitions and that permit and encourage the horrors of Himmler's and Hitler's Germany.

The example of Le Chambon is the proper antidote to the moral apathy that is the condition of many people today, and which Martin Gansberg dramatically describes in "38 Who Saw Murder Didn't Call Police." In sharp contrast to the residents of Le Chambon, the spectators who witnessed the murder of Kitty Genovese were literally demoralized. Not only did they fail to intervene; they did not even call for help.

In his selection, Josiah Royce defends a morality that respects human dignity. Beginning from the axiom that we owe respect and decency to our neighbor, Royce confronts the question that the Nazi and all those who ignore the humanity of special groups pervert: Who, then, are our neighbors? Royce answers that our neighbors include anyone with feelings: "Pain is pain, joy is joy, everywhere even as in thee." Royce calls this the Moral Insight. He points out that treating strangers with care and solicitude is hardly unnatural; for each of us, our future self is like a stranger to us, yet we are naturally concerned with the welfare of that stranger.

The moral blindness that is the opposite of Royce's moral insight has tragic consequences for the victims whose humanity is ignored. The point is taken up by Hallie who complains that some moral philosophers who concentrate on the motives and character of evildoers often fail to attend to the suffering of the victims. Hallie argues that it is not the character of evildoers that is the crucial element of evil; but rather that evil mainly consists in the suffering caused by the perpetrators of evil. For Hallie, evil is what evil does. He therefore takes sharp issue with Bennett for saying that the Nazi who professes to be affected by the suffering he causes is in some respects morally superior to theologians like Jonathan Edwards who never actually harmed anyone but who claim to have no pity for the sinner who would suffer the torments of the damned.

Do we punish people for the evil they do or for what they are? Melville's *Billy Budd* is a classic on this question. Billy Budd is an exceptionally pure and good person who has committed a crime. We are tempted to say that Budd's fine character exculpates his crime. But this could be a dangerous doctrine if applied generally, since it challenges the principle that moral agents—including those of especially superior moral character—must be responsible to society for the consequences of their acts.

Nietzsche challenges the tradition of Western morality with its moral insights and its golden rule to refrain from doing to others what you would not want them to do to you. He characterizes this tradition that enjoins us to protect the weak and whose origins lie in the teachings of Judaism and Christianity as "sentimental weakness" and a "denial of life." According to Nietzsche, the tradition emasculates those who are strong, vital, and superior by forcing them to

7

attend to the weak and mediocre. Nietzsche was especially effective in suggesting that morality often is used in hypocritical ways to stifle initiative. Yet, on the whole, philosophers have rejected Nietzsche's heroic morality as tending to encourage a morally irresponsible exercise of power. This is perhaps unfair, since Nietzsche himself almost certainly would have looked with contempt upon such self-styled "heroes" as the leaders of Nazi Germany. Another reason seems more valid: Nietzsche's own ideal does in fact denigrate sympathy with the weak and helpless, and so fails to convince those of us who see moral heroism in the likes of Huckleberry Finn and the people of Le Chambon.

# From Cruelty to Goodness

PHILIP HALLIE

Philip Hallie (b. 1922) is a professor of philosophy at
Wesleyan University. His published works include *The
Paradox of Cruelty* (1969) and *Lest Innocent Blood Be Shed*
(1979).

Hallie considers institutionalized cruelty and finds that,
besides physically assaulting its victims, it almost always
assaults their dignity and self-respect. As an example of
the antithesis of institutionalized cruelty, Hallie cites the
residents of the French village of Le Chambon who, at
grave risk to their lives, saved 6,000 Jews from the Nazis.
For him the opposite of being cruel is not merely ceasing
to be cruel; nor is it fighting cruelty with violence and
hatred (though this may be necessary). Rather, it is epit-
omized in the unambiguous and unpretentious goodness
of the citizens of Le Chambon who followed the positive
Biblical injunctions "Defend the fatherless" and "Be your
brother's keeper," as well as the negative injunctions
"Thou shalt not murder or betray."

I am a student of ethics, of good and evil; but my approach to these
two rather melodramatic terms is skeptical. I am in the tradition
of the ancient Greek *skeptikoi*, whose name means "inquirers" or

FROM CRUELTY TO GOODNESS © Institute of Society, Ethics and the Life Sciences, 360 Broadway,
Hastings-on-Hudson, NY 10706. Reprinted by permission of the copyright holder.

"investigators." And what we investigate is relationships among particular facts. What we put into doubt are the intricate webs of high-level abstractions that passed for philosophizing in the ancient world, and that still pass for philosophizing. My approach to good and evil emphasizes not abstract common nouns like "justice," but proper names and verbs. Names and verbs keep us close to the facts better than do our highfalutin common nouns. Names refer to particular people, and verbs connect subjects with predicates *in time,* while common nouns are above all this.

One of the words that is important to me is my own name. For me, philosophy is personal; it is closer to literature and history than it is to the exact sciences, closer to the passions, actions, and common sense of individual persons than to a dispassionate technical science. It has to do with the personal matter of wisdom. And so ethics for me is personal—my story, and not necessarily (though possibly) yours. It concerns particular people at particular times.

But ethics is more than such particulars. It involves abstractions, that is, rules, laws, ideals. When you look at the ethical magnates of history you see in their words and deeds two sorts of ethical rules: negative and positive. The negative rules are scattered throughout the Bible, but Moses brought down from Mount Sinai the main negative ethical rules of the West: Thou shalt not murder; thou shalt not betray. . . . The positive injunctions are similarly spread throughout the Bible. In the first chapter of the book of Isaiah we are told to ". . . defend the fatherless, plead for the widow . . ." The negative ethic forbids certain actions; the positive ethic demands certain actions. To follow the negative ethic is to be decent, to have clean hands. But to follow the positive ethic, to be one's brother's keeper, is to be more than decent—it is to be active, even aggressive. If the negative ethic is one of decency, the positive one is the ethic of riskful, strenuous nobility.

In my early studies of particularized ethical terms, I found myself dwelling upon negative ethics, upon prohibitions. And among the most conspicuous prohibitions I found embodied in history was the prohibition against deliberate harmdoing, against cruelty. "Thou shalt not be cruel" had as much to do with the nightmare of history as did the prohibitions against murder and betrayal. In fact, many of the Ten Commandments—especially those against murder, adultery, stealing, and betrayal—were ways of prohibiting cruelty.

Early in my research it became clear that there are various approaches to cruelty, as the different commandments suggest. For instance, there is the way reflected in the origins of the word "cruel." The Latin *crudus* is related to still older words standing for bloodshed, or raw flesh. According to the etymology of the word, cruelty involves the spilling of blood.

But modern dictionaries give the word a different meaning. They define it as "disposed to giving pain." They emphasize awareness, not simply bloodshed. After all, they seem to say, you cannot be cruel to a dead body. There is no cruelty without consciousness.

And so I found myself studying the kinds of awareness associated with the hurting of human beings. It is certainly true that for millennia in history and literature people have been torturing each other not only with hard weapons but also with hard words.

Still, the word "pain" seemed to be a simplistic and superficial way of describing the many different sorts of cruelty. In Reska Weiss's *Journey Through Hell* (London, 1961) there is a brief passage of one of the deepest cruelties that Nazis perpetrated upon extermination camp inmates. On a march

> Urine and excreta poured down the prisoners' legs, and by nightfall the excrement, which had frozen to our limbs, gave off its stench. . . .

And Weiss goes on to talk not in terms of "pain" or bloodshed, but in other terms:

> . . . We were really no longer human beings in the accepted sense. Not even animals, but putrefying corpses moving on two legs. . . .

There is one factor that the idea of "pain" and the simpler idea of bloodshed do not touch: cruelty, not playful, quotidian teasing or ragging, but cruelty (what the anti-cruelty societies usually call "substantial cruelty") involves the maiming of a person's dignity, the crushing of a person's self-respect. Bloodshed, the idea of pain (which is usually something involving a localizable occurrence, localizable in a tooth, in a head, in short, in the body), these are superficial ideas of cruelty. A whip, bleeding flesh, these are what the journalists of cruelty emphasize, following the etymology and dictionary meaning of the word. But the depths of an understanding of cruelty lie in the depths of an understanding of human dignity and of how you can maim it without bloodshed, and often without localizable bodily pain.

11

In excremental assault, in the process of keeping camp inmates from wiping themselves or from going to the latrine, and in making them drink water from a toilet bowl full of excreta (and the excreta of the guards at that) localizable pain is nothing. Deep humiliation is everything. We human beings believe in hierarchies, whether we are skeptics or not about human value. There is a hierarchical gap between shit and me. We are even above using the word. We are "above" walking around besmirched with feces. Our dignity, whatever the origins of that dignity may be, does not permit it. In order to be able to want to live, in order to be able to walk erect, we must respect ourselves as beings "higher" than our feces. When we feel that we are not "higher" than dirt or filth, then our lives are maimed at the very center, in the very depths, not merely in some localizable portion of our bodies. And when our lives are so maimed we become things, slaves, instruments. From ancient times until this moment, and as long as there will be human beings on this planet, there are those who know this and will use it, just as the Roman slave owners and the Southern American slave owners knew it when—one time a year—they encouraged the slaves to drink all the alcohol they could drink so that they could get bestially drunk and then even more bestially sick afterwards, under the eyes of their generous owners. The self-hatred, the loss of self-respect that the Saturnalia created in ancient Rome, say, made it possible to continue using the slaves as things, since they themselves came to think of themselves as things, as subhuman tools of the owners and the overseers.

Institutionalized cruelty, I learned, is the subtlest kind of cruelty. In episodic cruelty the victim knows he is being hurt, and his victimizer knows it too. But in a persistent pattern of humiliation that endures for years in a community, both the victim and the victimizer find ways of obscuring the harm that is being done. Blacks come to think of themselves as inferior, even esthetically inferior (black is "dirty"); and Jews come to think of themselves as inferior, even esthetically (dark hair and aquiline noses are "ugly"), so that the way they are being treated is justified by their "actual" inferiority, by the inferiority they themselves feel.

A similar process happens in the minds of the victimizers in institutionalized cruelty. They feel that since they are superior, even esthetically ("to be blonde is to be beautiful"), they deserve to do what they wish, deserve to have these lower creatures under their control. The words of Heinrich Himmler, head of the Nazi SS, in Posen in the year 1943 in a speech to his SS subordinates in a closed session, show how institutionalized cruelty can obscure harmdoing:

> . . . the words come so easily. "The Jewish people will be exterminated," says every party member, "of course. It's in our program . . . extermination. We'll take care of it." And then they come, these nice 80 million Germans, and every one of them has his decent Jew. Sure the others are swine, but his one is a fine Jew . . . Most of you will know what it means to have seen 100 corpses together, or 500 to 1000. To have made one's way through that, and . . . to have remained a decent person throughout, that is what has made us hard. That is a page of glory in our history. . . .

In this speech he was making a sharp distinction between the program of crushing the Jews and the personal sentiments of individual Germans. The program stretched over years; personal sentiments were momentary. He was pleading for the program, for institutionalized destruction.

But one of the most interesting parts of the speech occurs toward the end of it:

> . . . in sum, we can say that we fulfilled the heaviest of tasks [destroying the Jews] in love to our people. And we suffered no harm in our essence, in our soul, in our character. . . .

Commitment that overrides all sentimentality transforms cruelty and destruction into moral nobility, and commitment is the lifeblood of an institution.

## Cruelty and the Power Relationships

But when I studied all these ways that we have used the word "cruelty," I was nagged by the feeling that I had not penetrated into its inner structure. I was classifying, sorting out symptoms; but symptoms are signals, and what were the symptoms signals *of*? I felt like a person who had been studying cancer by sorting out brief pains from persistent pains, pains in the belly from pains in the head. I was being superficial, and I was not asking the question, "What are the forces behind these kinds of cruelty?" I felt that there were such forces, but as yet I had not touched them.

Then one day I was reading in one of the great autobiographies of western civilization, Frederick Douglass's *Life and Times*. The passage I was reading was about Douglass's thoughts on the origins of slavery. He was asking himself: "How could these whites keep us enslaved?" And he suddenly realized:

> My faculties and powers of body and soul are not my own, but are the property of a fellow-mortal in no sense superior to me, except that he has the physical power to compel me to be owned and controlled by him. By the combined physical force of the community I am his slave—a slave for life.

And then I saw that a disparity in power lay at the center of the dynamism of cruelty. If it was institutional cruelty it was in all likelihood a difference involving both verbal and physical power that kept the cruelty going. The power of the majority and the weakness of a minority were at the center of the institutional cruelty of slavery and of Nazi anti-Semitism. The whites not only outnumbered the blacks in America, but had economic and political ascendancy over them. But just as important as these "physical" powers was the power that words like "nigger" and "slave" gave the white majority. Their language sanctified if it did not create their power ascendancy over the blacks, and one of the most important projects of the slave-holders and their allies was that of seeing to it that the blacks themselves thought of themselves in just these powerless terms. They utilized the language to convince not only the whites but the blacks themselves that blacks were weak in mind, in will power, and in worth. These words were like the excremental assault in the killing camps of the Nazis: they diminished both the respect the victimizers might have for their victims and the respect the victims might have for themselves.

It occurred to me that if a power differential is crucial to the idea of cruelty, then when that power differential is maintained, cruelty will tend to be maintained, and when that power differential is eliminated, cruelty will tend to be eliminated. And this seemed to work. In all kinds of cruelty, violent and polite, episodic and institutional, when the victim arms himself with the appropriate strength, the cruelty diminishes or disappears. When Jews joined the Bush Warriors of France, the Maquis, and became powerful enough to strike at Vichy or the Nazis, they stopped being victims of French and Nazi cruelty. When Frederick Douglass learned to use the language with great skill and expressiveness, and when he learned to use his physical strength against his masters, the power differential between him and his masters diminished, and so did their cruelty to him. In his autobiography he wrote:

> A man without force is without the essential dignity of humanity. Human nature is so constituted that it cannot honor a helpless man, though it can pity him, and even this it cannot do long if signs of power do not arise.

When I looked back at my own childhood in Chicago, I remembered that the physical and mental cruelties that I suffered in the slums of the southwest side when I was about ten years old sharply diminished and finally disappeared when I learned how to defend myself physically and verbally. It is exactly this lesson that Douglass learned while growing up in the cruel institution of slavery.

Cruelty then, whatever else it is, is a kind of power relationship, an imbalance of power wherein the stronger party becomes the victimizer and the weaker becomes the victim. And since many general terms are most swiftly understood in relationship with their opposites (just as "heavy" can be understood most handily in relationship with what we mean by "light") the opposite of cruelty lay in a situation where there is no imbalance of power. The opposite of cruelty, I learned, was freedom from that unbalanced power relationship. Either the victim should get stronger and stand up to the victimizer, and thereby bring about a balance of their powers, or the victim should free himself from the whole relationship by flight.

In pursuing this line of thought, I came to believe that, again, dictionaries are misleading: many of them give "kindness" as the antonym for "cruelty." In studying slavery in America and the concentration camps of central Europe I found that kindness could be the ultimate cruelty, especially when it was given within that unbalanced power relationship. A kind overseer or a kind camp guard can exacerbate cruelty, can remind his victim that there are other relationships than the relationship of cruelty, and can make the victim deeply bitter, especially when he sees the self-satisfied smile of his victimizer. He is being cruelly treated when he is given a penny or a bun after having endured the crushing and grinding of his mental and bodily well-being. As Frederick Douglass put it:

> The kindness of the slave-master only gilded the chain. It detracted nothing from its weight or strength. The thought that men are for other and better uses than slavery throve best under the gentle treatment of a kind master.

15

No, I learned, the opposite of cruelty is not kindness. The opposite of the cruelty of the overseer in American slavery was not the kindness of that overseer for a moment or for a day. An episodic kindness is not the opposite of an institutionalized cruelty. The opposite of institutionalized cruelty is freedom from the cruel relationship.

It is important to see how perspectival the whole meaning of cruelty is. From the perspective of the SS guard or the southern overseer, a bit of bread, a smile is indeed a diminution of cruelty. But in the relationship of cruelty, the point of view of the victimizer is of only minor importance; it is the point of view of the victim that is authoritative. The victim feels the suffering in his own mind and body, whereas the victimizer, like Himmler's "hard" and "decent" Nazi, can be quite unaware of that suffering. The sword does not feel the pain that it inflicts. Do not ask it about suffering.

## Goodness Personified in Le Chambon

All these considerations drove me to write my book *The Paradox of Cruelty*. But with the book behind me, I felt a deep discontent. I saw cruelty as an embodiment, a particular case of evil. But if cruelty is one of the main evils of human history, why is the opposite of cruelty not one of the key goods of human history? Freedom from the cruel relationship, either by escaping it or by redressing the imbalance of power, was not essential to what western philosophers and theologians have thought of as goodness. Escape is a negative affair. Goodness has something positive in it, something triumphantly affirmative.

Hoping for a hint of goodness in the very center of evil, I started looking closely at the so-called "medical experiments" of the Nazis upon children, usually Jewish and Gypsy children, in the death camps. Here were the weakest of the weak. Not only were they despised minorities, but they were, as individuals, still in their non-age. They were dependents. Here the power imbalance between the cruel experimenters and their victims was at its greatest. But instead of seeing light or finding insight by going down into this hell, into the deepest depth of cruelty, I found myself unwillingly becoming part of the world I was studying. I found myself either yearning to be viciously cruel to the victimizers of the children, or I found myself feeling compassion for the children, feeling their despair and pain as they looked up at the men and women in white coats cutting off their fingertips one at a time, or breaking their slender bones, or wounding their internal organs. Either I became a would-be victimizer or one more Jewish victim, and in either case I was not achieving insight, only misery, like so many other students of the Holocaust. And when I was trying to be "objective" about my studies, when I was succeeding at being indifferent to both the victimizers and the victims of these cruel relationships, I became cold; I became another monster who could look upon the maiming of a child with an indifferent eye.

To relieve this unending suffering, from time to time I would turn to the literature of the French resistance to the Nazis. I had been trained by the U.S. Army to understand it. The resistance was a way of trying to redress the power imbalance between Hitler's Fortress Europe and Hitler's victims, and so I saw it as an enemy of cruelty. Still, its methods were often cruel like the methods of most power struggles, and I had little hope of finding goodness here. We soldiers violated the negative ethic forbidding killing in order, we thought, to follow the positive ethic of being our brothers' keepers.

And then one gray April afternoon I found a brief article on the French village of Le Chambon-sur-Lignon. I shall not analyze here the tears of amazement and gladness and release from despair—in short, of joy—that I shed when I first read that story. Tears themselves interest me greatly—but not the tears of melancholy hindsight and existential despair; rather the tears of awe you experience when the realization of an ideal suddenly appears before your very eyes or thunders inside your mind; these tears interest me.

And one of the reasons I wept at first reading about Le Chambon in those brief, inaccurate pages was that at last I had discovered an embodiment of goodness in opposition to cruelty. I had discovered in the flesh and blood of history, in people with definite names in a definite place at a definite time in the nightmare of history, what no classical or religious ethicist could deny was goodness.

The French Protestant village of Le Chambon, located in the Cévennes Mountains of southeastern France, and with a population of about 3,500, saved the lives of about 6,000 people, most of them Jewish children whose parents had been murdered in the killing camps of central Europe. Under a national government which was not only collaborating with the Nazi conquerors of France but frequently trying to outdo the Germans in anti-Semitism in order to please their conquerors, and later under the day-to-day threat of destruction by the German Armed SS, they started to save children in the winter of 1940, the winter after the fall of France, and they continued to do so until the war in France was over. They sheltered the refugees in their own homes and in various houses they established especially for them; and they took many of them across the terrible mountains to neutral Geneva, Switzerland, in the teeth of French and German police and military power. The people of Le Chambon are poor, and the Huguenot faith to which they belong is a diminishing faith in Catholic and atheist France; but their spiritual power, their capacity to act in unison against the victimizers who surrounded them, was immense, and more than a match for the military power of those victimizers.

But for me as an ethicist the heart of the matter was not only their special power. What interested me was that they obeyed *both* the negative and the positive injunctions of ethics; they were good not only in the sense of trying to be their brothers' keepers, protecting the victim, "defending the fatherless," to use the language of Isaiah; they were also good in the sense that they obeyed the negative injunctions against killing and betraying. While those around them— including myself—were murdering in order presumably, to help mankind in some way or other, they murdered nobody, and betrayed not a single child in those long and dangerous four years. For me as an ethicist they were the embodiment of unambiguous goodness.

But for me as a student of cruelty they were something more: they were an embodiment of the opposite of cruelty. And so, somehow, at last, I had found goodness in opposition to cruelty. In studying their story, and in telling it in *Lest Innocent Blood Be Shed,* I learned that the opposite of cruelty is not simply freedom from the cruel relationship; it is *hospitality*. It lies not only in something negative, an absence of cruelty or of imbalance; it lies in unsentimental, efficacious love. The opposite of the cruelties of the camps was not the liberation of the camps, the cleaning out of the barracks and the cessation of the horrors. All of this was the *end* of the cruelty relationship, not the opposite of that relationship. And it was not even the end of it, because the victims would never forget and would remain in agony as long as they remembered their humiliation and suffering. No, the opposite of cruelty was not the liberation of the camps, not freedom; it was the hospitality of the people of Chambon, and of very few others during the Holocaust. The opposite of cruelty was the kind of goodness that happened in Chambon.

Let me explain the difference between liberation and hospitality by telling you about a letter I received a year ago from a woman who had been saved by the people of Le Chambon when she was a young girl. She wrote:

> Never was there a question that the Chambonnais would not share all they had with us, meager as it was. One Chambonnais once told me that even if there was less, they still would want more for us.

And she goes on:

> It was indeed a very different attitude from the one in Switzerland, which while saving us also resented us so much.
>
> If today we are not bitter people like most survivors it can only be due to the fact that we met people like the people of Le Chambon, who showed to us simply that life can be different, that there are people who care, that people can live together and even risk their own lives for their fellow man.

The Swiss liberated refugees and removed them from the cruel relationship; the people of Le Chambon did more. They taught them that goodness could conquer cruelty, that loving hospitality could remove them from the cruel relationship. And they taught me this, too.

It is important to emphasize that cruelty is not simply an episodic, momentary matter, especially institutional cruelty like that of Nazism or slavery. As we have seen throughout this essay, not only does it persist while it is being exerted upon the weak; *it can persist in the survivors* after they have escaped the power relationship. The survivors torture themselves, continue to suffer, continue to maim their own lives long after the actual torture is finished. The self-hatred and rage of the blacks and the despair of the native Americans and the Jews who have suffered under institutional crushing and maiming are continuations of original cruelties. And these continuations exist because only a superficial liberation from torture has occurred. The sword has stopped falling on their flesh in the old obvious ways, but the wounds still bleed. I am not saying that the village of Chambon healed these wounds—they go too deep. What I am saying is that the people I have talked to who were once children in Le Chambon have more hope for their species and more respect for themselves as human beings than most other survivors I have met. The enduring hospitality they met in Le Chambon helped them find realistic hope in a world of persisting cruelty.

What was the nature of this hospitality that saved and deeply changed so many lives? It is hard to summarize briefly what the Chambonnais did, and above all how they did it. The morning after a new refugee family came to town they would find on their front door a wreath with *"Bienvenue!"* "Welcome!" painted on a piece of cardboard attached to the wreath. Nobody knew who had brought the wreath; in effect, the whole town had brought it.

It was mainly the women of Chambon who gave so much more than shelter to these, the most hated enemies of the Nazis. There was Madame Barraud, a tiny Alsatian, who cared for the refugee boys in her house with all the love such a tiny body could hold, and who cared for the way they felt day and night. And there were others.

But there was one person without whom Le Chambon could not have become the safest place in Europe for Jews: the Huguenot minister of the village, André Trocmé. Trocmé was a passionately religious man. He was massive, more than six feet tall, blonde, with a quick temper. Once long after the war, while he was lecturing on the main project of his life, the promotion of the idea of nonviolence in international relations, one of the members of his audience started to whisper a few words to his neighbor. Trocmé let this go on for a few moments, then interrupted his speech, walked up to the astonished whisperer, raised his massive arm, pointed toward the door, and yelled, "Out! Out! Get out!" And the lecture was on nonviolence.

The center of his thought was the belief that God showed how important man was by becoming Himself a human being, and by becoming a particular sort of human being who was the embodiment of sacrificially generous love. For Trocmé, every human being was like Jesus, had God in him or her, and was just as precious as God Himself. And when Trocmé with the help of the Quakers and others organized his village into the most efficient rescue machine in Europe, he did so not only to save the Jews, but also to save the Nazis and their collaborators. He wanted to keep them from blackening their souls with more evil—he wanted to save them, the victimizers, from evil.

One of the reasons he was successful was that the Huguenots had been themselves persecuted for hundreds of years by the kings of France, and they knew what persecution was. In fact, when the people of Chambon took Jewish children and whole families across the mountains of southeastern France into neutral Switzerland, they often followed pathways that had been taken by Huguenots in their flight from the Dragoons of the French kings.

A particular incident from the story of Le Chambon during the Nazi occupation of France will explain succinctly why he was successful in making the village a village of refuge. But before I relate the story, I must point out that the people of the village did not think of themselves as "successful," let alone as "good." From their point of view, they did not do anything that required elaborate explanation. When I asked them why they helped these dangerous guests, they invariably answered, "What do you mean, 'Why'? Where else could they go? How could you turn them away? What is so special about being ready to help (*prête à servir*)? There was nothing else to do." And some of them laughed in amazement when I told them that I thought they were "good people." They saw no alternative to their actions and to the way they acted, and therefore they saw what they did as necessary, not something to be picked out for praise. Helping these guests was for them as natural as breathing or eating—one does not think of alternatives to these functions; they did not think of alternatives to sheltering people who were endangering not only the lives of their hosts but the lives of all the people of the village.

And now the story. One afternoon a refugee woman knocked on the door of a farmhouse outside the village. The farmers around the village proper were Protestants like most of the others in Chambon, but with one difference: they were mostly "Darbystes," followers of a strange Scot named Darby, who taught their ancestors in the nineteenth century to believe every word of the Bible, and indeed, who had them memorize the Bible. They were literal fundamentalists. The farm-woman opened the door to the refugee and invited her into the kitchen where it was warm. Standing in the middle of the floor the refugee, in heavily accented French, asked for eggs for her children. In those days of very short supplies, people with children often went to the farmers in the "gray market" (neither black nor exactly legal) to get necessary food. This was early in 1941, and the farmers were not yet accustomed to the refugees. The farm-woman looked into the eyes of the shawled refugee and asked, "Are you Jewish?" The woman started to tremble, but she could not lie, even

21

though that question was usually the beginning of the end of life for Jews in Hitler's Fortress Europe. She answered, "Yes."

The woman ran from the kitchen to the staircase nearby, and while the refugee trembled with terror in the kitchen, she called up the stairs, "Husband, children, come down, come down! We have in our house at this very moment a representative of the Chosen People!"

Not all the Protestants in Chambon were Darbyste fundamentalists; but almost all were convinced that people are the children of God, and are as precious as God Himself. Their leaders were Huguenot preachers and their following of the negative and positive commandments of the Bible came in part from their personal generosity and courage, but also in part from the depths of their religious conviction that we are all children of God, and we must take care of each other lovingly. This combined with the ancient and deep historical ties between the Huguenots and the Jews of France and their own centuries of persecution by the Dragoons and Kings of France helped make them what they were, "always ready to help," as the Chambonnais saying goes.

## A Choice of Perspectives

We have come a long way from cruelty to the people of Chambon, just as I have come a long way in my research from concrete evil to concrete goodness. Let me conclude with a point that has been alternately hinted at and stressed in the course of this essay.

A few months after *Lest Innocent Blood Be Shed* was published I received a letter from Massachusetts that opened as follows:

> I have read your book, and I believe that you mushy-minded moralists should be awakened to the facts. Nothing happened in Le Chambon, nothing of any importance whatsoever.
>
> The Holocaust, dear Professor, was like a geological event, like an earthquake. No person could start it; no person could change it; and no person could end it. And no small group of persons could do so either. It was the armies and the nations that performed actions that counted. Individuals did nothing. You sentimentalists have got to learn that the great masses and big political ideas make the difference. Your people and the people they saved simply do not exist . . .

Now between this position and mine there is an abyss that no amount of shouted arguments or facts can cross. And so I shall not answer this letter with a tightly organized reply. I shall answer it only by telling you that one of the reasons institutional cruelty exists and persists is that people believe that individuals can do nothing, that only vast ideologies and armies can act meaningfully. Every act of institutional cruelty—Nazism, slavery, and all the others—lives not with people in the concrete, but with abstractions that blind people to individuals. Himmler's speech to the SS leadership in 1943 is full of phrases like "exterminating a bacillus," and "The Jewish people will be exterminated." And in that speech he attacks any German who believes in "his decent Jew." Institutional cruelty, like other misleading approaches to ethics, blinds us to the victim's point of view; and when we are blind to that point of view we can countenance and perpetrate cruelty with impunity.

I have told you that I cannot and will not try to refute the letter from Massachusetts. I shall only summarize the point of view of this essay with another story.

I was lecturing a few months ago in Minneapolis, and when I finished talking about the Holocaust and the village of Le Chambon, a woman stood up and asked me if the village of Le Chambon was in the Department of Haute-Loire, the high sources of the Loire River. Obviously she was French, with her accent; and all French people know that there are many villages called "Le Chambon" in France, just as any American knows that there are many "Main Streets" in the United States. I said that Le Chambon was indeed in the Haute-Loire.

She said, "Then you have been speaking about the village that saved all three of my children. I want to thank you for writing this book, not only because the story will now be permanent, but also because I shall be able to talk about those terrible days with Americans now, for they will understand those days better than they have. You see, you Americans, though you sometimes cross the oceans, live on an island here as far as war is concerned . . ."

Then she asked to come up and say one sentence. There was not a sound, not even breathing, to be heard in the room. She came to the front of the room and said, "The Holocaust was storm, lightning, thunder, wind, rain, yes. And Le Chambon was the rainbow."

Only from her perspective can you understand the cruelty and the goodness I have been talking about, not from the point of view of the gentleman from Massachusetts. You must choose which perspective is best, and your choice will have much to do with your feelings about the preciousness of life, and not only the preciousness of other people's lives. If the lives of others are precious to you, your life will become more precious to you.

**STUDY QUESTIONS**

1. Distinguish between positive and negative moral injunctions. Do you agree with Hallie that we need both for moral decency?
2. Do you agree with Hallie that cruelty is prevalent when a serious imbalance of power exists among people? Can we be cruel to our equals?
3. Why does Hallie deny that kindness is the opposite of cruelty? What does he consider to be cruelty's opposite?
4. What does the writer Terence des Pres mean when he says of Le Chambon, "Those events took place and therefore demand a place in our view of the world"?
5. With whom do you agree more: (a) the person from Massachusetts who wrote and called Hallie a "mushy-minded moralist" who has failed to realize that the Holocaust was like a geological event that could not be stopped or modified, or (b) Hallie, who claims that Le Chambon teaches us that goodness can conquer cruelty?

# The Conscience of Huckleberry Finn

## JONATHAN BENNETT

Jonathan Bennett (b. 1930) is a professor of philosophy at Syracuse University. He is the author of several books, including *Rationality* (1964) and *Linguistic Behavior* (1976).

In this article Bennett considers the moral consciences of Huckleberry Finn, the Nazi officer Heinrich Himmler, and the Calvinist theologian Jonathan Edwards. He is interested in how each, in his own way, resolves the conflict between his human sympathies and the moral doctrine he is following that requires him to override those sympathies. Huck Finn develops a deep attachment to Jim, the runaway slave, but the official morality of his community does not allow for fellow feelings towards slaves. When forced to choose between his kindly feelings and the official morality, Huck gives up on morality. Himmler set his sympathies aside. Jonathan Edwards's case represents a third way out: he allowed himself no sympathies at all. Bennett finds Edwards's solution to be as bad as Himmler's, if not worse. Bennett concludes that while we should not give our sympathies a "blank check," we must always give them great weight and be wary of acting on any principle that conflicts with them.

## I

In this paper, I shall present not just the conscience of Huckleberry Finn but two others as well. One of them is the conscience of

THE CONSCIENCE OF HUCKLEBERRY FINN From *Philosophy* 49 (1974), pp. 123–134. Reprinted by permission of Cambridge University Press.

Heinrich Himmler. He became a Nazi in 1923; he served drably and quietly, but well, and was rewarded with increasing responsibility and power. At the peak of his career he held many offices and commands, of which the most powerful was that of leader of the S.S.— the principal police force of the Nazi regime. In this capacity, Himmler commanded the whole concentration-camp system, and was responsible for the execution of the so-called "final solution of the Jewish problem." It is important for my purposes that this piece of social engineering should be thought of not abstractly but in concrete terms of Jewish families being marched to what they think are bathhouses, to the accompaniment of loud-speaker renditions of extracts from *The Merry Widow* and *Tales of Hoffmann,* there to be choked to death by poisonous gases. Altogether, Himmler succeeded in murdering about four and a half million of them, as well as several million gentiles, mainly Poles and Russians.

The other conscience to be discussed is that of the Calvinist theologian and philosopher Jonathan Edwards. He lived in the first half of the eighteenth century, and has a good claim to be considered America's first serious and considerable philosophical thinker. He was for many years a widely renowned preacher and Congregationalist minister in New England; in 1748 a dispute with his congregation led him to resign (he couldn't accept their view that unbelievers should be admitted to the Lord's Supper in the hope that it would convert them); for some years after that he worked as a missionary, preaching to Indians through an interpreter; then in 1758 he accepted the presidency of what is now Princeton University, and within two months died from a smallpox inoculation. Along the way he wrote some first-rate philosophy; his book attacking the notion of free will is still sometimes read. Why I should be interested in Edwards' *conscience* will be explained in due course.

I shall use Heinrich Himmler, Jonathan Edwards, and Huckleberry Finn to illustrate different aspects of a single theme, namely the relationship between *sympathy* on the one hand and *bad morality* on the other.

## II

All that I can mean by a "bad morality" is a morality whose principles I deeply disapprove of. When I call a morality bad, I cannot prove that mine is better; but when I here call any morality bad, I think you will agree with me that it is bad; and that is all I need.

There could be dispute as to whether the springs of someone's actions constitute a *morality*. I think, though, that we must admit that someone who acts in ways which conflict grossly with our morality may nevertheless have a morality of his own—a set of principles of action which he sincerely assents to, so that for him the problem of acting well or rightly or in obedience to conscience is the problem of conforming to *those* principles. The problem of conscientiousness can arise as acutely for a bad morality as for any other: Rotten principles may be as difficult to keep as decent ones.

As for "sympathy" I use this term to cover every sort of fellow-feeling, as when one feels pity over someone's loneliness, or horrified compassion over his pain, or when one feels a shrinking reluctance to act in a way which will bring misfortune to someone else. These *feelings* must not be confused with *moral judgments*. My sympathy for someone in distress may lead me to help him, or even to think that I ought to help him; but in itself it is not a judgment about what I ought to do but just a *feeling* for him in his plight. We shall get some light on the difference between feelings and moral judgments when we consider Huckleberry Finn.

Obviously, feelings can impel one to action, and so can moral judgments; and in a particular case sympathy and morality may pull in opposite directions. This can happen not just with bad moralities, but also with good ones like yours and mine. For example, a small child, sick and miserable, clings tightly to his mother and screams in terror when she tries to pass him over to the doctor to be examined. If the mother gave way to her sympathy, that is to her feeling for the child's misery and fright, she would hold it close and not let the doctor come near; but don't we agree that it might be wrong for her to act on such a feeling? Quite generally, then, anyone's moral principles may apply to a particular situation in a way which runs contrary to the particular thrusts of fellow-feeling that he has in that situation. My immediate concern is with sympathy in relation to bad morality, but not because such conflicts occur only when the morality is bad.

Now, suppose that someone who accepts a bad morality is struggling to make himself act in accordance with it in a particular situation where his sympathies pull him another way. He sees the struggle as one between doing the right, conscientious thing, and acting wrongly and weakly, like the mother who won't let the doctor come near her sick, frightened baby. Since we don't accept this person's morality, we may see the situation very differently, thoroughly disapproving of the action he regards as the right one, and endorsing the action which from his point of view constitutes weakness and backsliding.

Conflicts between sympathy and bad morality won't always be like this, for we won't disagree with every single dictate of a bad morality. Still, it can happen in the way I have described, with the agent's right action being our wrong one, and vice versa. That is just what happens in a certain episode in Chapter 16 of *The Adventures of Huckleberry Finn,* an episode which brilliantly illustrates how fiction can be instructive about real life.


## III

Huck Finn has been helping his slave friend Jim to run away from Miss Watson, who is Jim's owner. In their raft-journey down the Mississippi river, they are near to the place at which Jim will become legally free. Now let Huck take over the story:

> Jim said it made him all over trembly and feverish to be so close to freedom. Well I can tell you it made me all over trembly and feverish, too, to hear him, because I begun to get it through my head that he *was* most free—and who was to blame for it? Why, *me.* I couldn't get that out of my conscience, no how nor no way. . . . It hadn't ever come home to me, before, what this thing was that I was doing. But now it did; and it stayed with me, and scorched me more and more. I tried to make out to myself that *I* warn't to blame, because *I* didn't run Jim off from his rightful owner; but it warn't no use, conscience up and say, every time: "But you knowed he was running for his freedom, and you could a paddled ashore and told somebody." That was so—I couldn't get around that, no way. That was where it pinched. Conscience says to me: "What had poor Miss Watson done to you, that you could see her nigger go off right under your eyes and never say one single word? What did that poor old woman do to you, that you could treat her so mean? . . ." I got to feeling so mean and miserable I most wished I was dead.

Jim speaks his plan to save up to buy his wife, and then his children, out of slavery; and he adds that if the children cannot be bought he will arrange to steal them. Huck is horrified:

> Thinks I, this is what comes of my not thinking. Here was this nigger which I had as good as helped to run away, coming right out flat-footed and saying he would steal his children—children that belonged to a man I didn't even know; a man that hadn't ever done me no harm.
>
> I was sorry to hear Jim say that, it was such a lowering of him. My conscience got to stirring me up hotter than ever, until at last I says to it: "Let up on me—it ain't too late, yet—I'll paddle ashore at first light, and tell." I felt easy, and happy, and light as a feather, right off. All my troubles was gone.

This is bad morality all right. In his earliest years Huck wasn't taught any principles, and the only one he has encountered since then are those of rural Missouri, in which slave-owning is just one kind of ownership and is not subject to critical pressure. It hasn't occurred to Huck to question those principles. So the action, to us abhorrent, of turning Jim in to the authorities presents itself *clearly* to Huck as the right thing to do.

For us, morality and sympathy would both dictate helping Jim to escape. If we felt any conflict, it would have both these on one side and something else on the other—greed for a reward, or fear of punishment. But Huck's morality conflicts with his sympathy, that is, with his unargued, natural feeling for his friend. The conflict starts when Huck sets off in the canoe towards the shore, pretending that he is going to reconnoiter, but really planning to turn Jim in:

> As I shoved off, [Jim] says: "Pooty soon I'll be a-shout'n for joy, en I'll say, it's all on accounts o' Huck I's a free man . . . Jim won't ever forget you, Huck; you's de bes' fren' Jim's ever had; en you's de *only* fren' old Jim's got now."
>
> I was paddling off, all in a sweat to tell on him; but when he says this, it seemed to kind of take the tuck all out of me. I went along slow then, and I warn't right down certain whether I was glad I started or whether I warn't. When I was fifty yards off, Jim says:
>
> "Dah you goes, de ole true Huck; de on'y white genlman dat ever kep' his promise to ole Jim." Well, I just felt sick. But I says, I *got* to do it—I can't get *out* of it.

In the upshot, sympathy wins over morality. Huck hasn't the strength of will to do what he sincerely thinks he ought to do. Two men hunting for runaway slaves ask him whether the man on his raft is black or white:

> I didn't answer up prompt. I tried to, but the words wouldn't come. I tried, for a second or two, to brace up and out with it, but I warn't man enough—hadn't the spunk of a rabbit. I see I was weakening; so I just give up trying, and up and says: "He's white."

So Huck enables Jim to escape, thus acting weakly and wickedly— he thinks. In this conflict between sympathy and morality, sympathy wins.

One critic has cited this episode in support of the statement that Huck suffers "excruciating moments of wavering between honesty and respectability." That is hopelessly wrong, and I agree with the perceptive comment on it by another critic, who says:

> The conflict waged in Huck is much more serious: He scarcely cares for respectability and never hesitates to relinquish it, but he does care for honesty and gratitude—and both honesty and gratitude require that he should give Jim up. It is not, in Huck, honesty at war with respectability but love and compassion for Jim struggling against his conscience. His decision is for Jim and hell: a right decision made in the mental chains that Huck never breaks. His concern for Jim is and remains *irrational*. Huck finds many reasons for giving Jim up and none for stealing him. To the end Huck sees his compassion for Jim as a weak, ignorant, and wicked felony.[1]

That is precisely correct—and it can have that virtue only because Mark Twain wrote the episode with such unerring precision. The crucial point concerns *reasons,* which all occur on one side of the conflict. On the side of conscience we have principles, arguments, considerations, ways of looking at things:

> "It hadn't ever come home to me before what I was doing"
> "I tried to make out that I warn't to blame"
> "Conscience said 'But you knowed . . .'—I couldn't get around that"
> "What had poor Miss Watson done to you?"

---

[1] M.J. Sidnell, "Huck Finn and Jim," *The Cambridge Quarterly*, vol. 2, pp. 205–206.

"This is what comes of my not thinking"

". . . children that belonged to a man I didn't even know."

On the other side, the side of feeling, we get nothing like that. When Jim rejoices in Huck, as his only friend, Huck doesn't consider the claims of friendship or have the situation "come home" to him in a different light. All that happens is: "When he says this, it seemed to kind of take the tuck all out of me. I went along slow then, and I warn't right down certain whether I was glad I started or whether I warn't." Again, Jim's words about Huck's "promise" to him don't give Huck any *reason* for changing his plan: In his morality promises to slaves probably don't count. Their effect on him is of a different kind: "Well, I just felt sick." And when the moment for final decision come, Huck doesn't weigh up pros and cons: he simply *fails* to do what he believes to be right—he isn't strong enough, hasn't "the spunk of a rabbit." This passage in the novel is notable not just for its finely wrought irony, with Huck's weakness of will leading him to do the right thing, but also for its masterly handling of the difference between general moral principles and particular unreasoned emotional pulls.

## IV

Consider now another case of bad morality in conflict with human sympathy: the case of the odious Himmler. Here, from a speech he made to some S.S. generals, is an indication of the content of his morality:

> What happens to a Russian, to a Czech, does not interest me in the slightest. What the nations can offer in the way of good blood of our type, we will take, if necessary by kidnapping their children and raising them here with us. Whether nations live in prosperity or starve to death like cattle interests me only in so far as we need them as slaves to our *Kultur;* otherwise it is of no interest to me. Whether 10,000 Russian females fall down from exhaustion while digging an antitank ditch interests me only in so far as the antitank ditch for Germany is finished.[2]

---

[2]Quoted in William L. Shirer, *The Rise and Fall of the Third Reich* (New York, 1960), pp. 937–938. Next quotation: ibid., p. 966. All further quotations relating to Himmler are from Roger Manwell and Heinrich Fraenkel, *Heinrich Himmler* (London, 1965), pp. 132, 197, 184 (twice), 187.

But has this a moral basis at all? And if it has, was there in Himmler's own mind any conflict between morality and sympathy? Yes there was. Here is more from the same speech:

> I also want to talk to you quite frankly on a very grave matter . . . I mean . . . the extermination of the Jewish race. . . . Most of you must know what it means when 100 corpses are lying side by side, or 500, or 1,000. To have stuck it out and at the same time—apart from exceptions caused by human weakness—to have remained decent fellows, that is what has made us hard. This is a page of glory in our history which has never been written and is never to be written.

Himmler saw his policies as being hard to implement while still retaining one's human sympathies—while still remaining a "decent fellow." He is saying that only the weak take the easy way out and just squelch their sympathies, and is praising the stronger and more glorious course of retaining one's sympathies while acting in violation of them. In the same spirit, he ordered that when executions were carried out in concentration camps, those responsible "are to be influenced in such a way as to suffer no ill effect in their character and mental attitude." A year later he boasted that the S.S. had wiped out the Jews

> without our leaders and their men suffering any damage in their minds and souls. The danger was considerable, for there was only a narrow path between the Scylla of their becoming heartless ruffians unable any longer to treasure life, and the Charybdis of their becoming soft and suffering nervous breakdowns.

And there really can't be any doubt that the basis of Himmler's policies was a set of principles which constituted his morality—a sick, bad, wicked *morality*. He described himself as caught in "the old tragic conflict between will and obligation." And when his physician Kersten protested at the intention to destroy the Jews, saying that the suffering involved was "not to be contemplated," Kersten reports that Himmler replied:

> He knew that it would mean much suffering for the Jews. . . . "It is the curse of greatness that it must step over dead bodies to create new life. Yet we must . . . cleanse the soil or it will never bear fruit. It will be a great burden for me to bear."

This, I submit, is the language of morality.

So in this case, tragically, bad morality won out over sympathy. I am sure that many of Himmler's killers did extinguish their sympathies, becoming "heartless ruffians" rather than "decent fellows"; but not Himmler himself. Although his policies ran against the human grain to a horrible degree, he did not sandpaper down his emotional surfaces so that there was no grain there, allowing his actions to slide along smoothly and easily. He did, after all, bear his hideous burden, and even paid a price for it. He suffered a variety of nervous and physical disabilities, including nausea and stomach-convulsions, and Kersten was doubtless right in saying that these were "the expression of a psychic division which extended over his whole life."

This same division must have been present in some of those officials of the Church who ordered heretics to be tortured so as to change their theological opinions. Along with the brutes and the cold careerists, there must have been some who cared, and who suffered from the conflict between their sympathies and their bad morality.

## V

In the conflict between sympathy and bad morality, then, the victory may go to sympathy as in the case of Huck Finn, or to morality as in the case of Himmler.

Another possibility is that the conflict may be avoided by giving up, or not ever having, those sympathies which might interfere with one's principles. That seems to have been the case with Jonathan Edwards. I am afraid that I shall be doing an injustice to Edwards' many virtues, and to his great intellectual energy and inventiveness; for my concern is only with the worst thing about him—namely his morality, which was worse than Himmler's.

According to Edwards, God condemns some men to an eternity of unimaginably awful pain, though he arbitrarily spares others— "arbitrarily" because none deserve to be spared:

> Natural men are held in the hand of God over the pit of hell; they have deserved the fiery pit, and are already sentenced to it; and God is dreadfully provoked, his anger is as great toward them as to those that are actually suffering the executions of the fierceness of his wrath in hell . . . ; the devil is waiting for them, hell is gaping for them, the flames gather and flash about them, and would fain lay hold on

them . . . ; and . . . there are no means within reach that can be any security to them. . . . All that preserves them is the mere arbitrary will, and unconvenanted unobliged forebearance of an incensed God.[3]

Notice that he says "they have deserved the fiery pit." Edwards insists that men *ought* to be condemned to eternal pain; and his position isn't that this is right because God wants it, but rather that God wants it because it is right. For him, moral standards exist independently of God, and God can be assessed in the light of them (and of course found to be perfect). For example, he says:

> They deserve to be cast into hell; so that . . . justice never stands in the way, it makes no objection against God's using his power at any moment to destroy them. Yea, on the contrary, justice calls aloud for an infinite punishment of their sins.

Elsewhere, he gives elaborate arguments to show that God is acting justly in damning sinners. For example, he argues that a punishment should be exactly as bad as the crime being punished; God is infinitely excellent; so any crime against him is infinitely bad; and so eternal damnation is exactly right as a punishment—it is infinite, but, as Edwards is careful also to say, it is "no more than infinite."

Of course, Edwards himself didn't torment the damned; but the question still arises of whether his sympathies didn't conflict with his *approval* of eternal torment. Didn't he find it painful to contemplate any fellow-human's being tortured for ever? Apparently not:

> The God that holds you over the pit of hell, much as one holds a spider or some loathsome insect over the fire, abhors you, and is dreadfully provoked . . . he is of purer eyes than to bear to have you in his sight; you are ten thousand times so abominable in his eyes as the most hateful venomous serpent is in ours.

When God is presented as being as misanthropic as that, one suspects misanthropy in the theologian. This suspicion is increased when Edwards claims that "the saints in glory will . . . understand how terrible the sufferings of the damned are; yet . . . will not be sorry

---

[3]Vergilius Ferm (ed.), *Puritan Sage: Collected Writings of Jonathan Edwards* (New York, 1953), p. 370. Next three quotations: ibid., p. 366, p. 294 ("no more than infinite"), p. 372.

for [them]."[4] He bases this partly on a view of human nature whose ugliness he seems not to notice:

> The seeing of the calamities of others tends to heighten the sense of our own enjoyments. When the saints in glory, therefore, shall see the doleful state of the damned, how will this heighten their sense of the blessedness of their own state. . . . When they shall see how miserable others of their fellow-creatures are . . . when they shall see the smoke of their torment . . . and hear their dolorous shrieks and cries, and consider that they in the mean time are in the most blissful state, and shall surely be in it to all eternity; how they will rejoice!

I hope this is less than the whole truth! His other main point about why the saints will rejoice to see the torments of the damned is that it is *right* that they should do so:

> The heavenly inhabitants . . . will have no love nor pity to the damned. . . . [This will not show] a want of spirit of love in them . . . for the heavenly inhabitants will know that it is not fit that they should love [the damned] because they will know then, that God has no love to them, nor pity for them.

The implication that *of course* one can adjust one's feelings of pity so that they conform to the dictates of some authority—doesn't this suggest that ordinary human sympathies played only a small part in Edwards' life?

## VI

Huck Finn, whose sympathies are wide and deep, could never avoid the conflict in that way; but he is determined to avoid it, and so he opts for the only other alternative he can see—to give up morality altogether. After he has tricked the slave-hunters, he returns to the raft and undergoes a peculiar crisis:

> I got aboard the raft, feeling bad and low, because I knowed very well I had done wrong, and I see it warn't no use for me to try to learn to do right; a body that don't get *started* right when he's little, ain't got

---

[4]This and the next two quotations are from "The End of the Wicked Contemplated by the Righteous: Or, The Torments of the Wicked in Hell, No Occasion of Grief to the Saints in Heaven," from *The Works of President Edwards* (London, 1817), vol. 4, pp. 507–508, 511–12, and 509 respectively.

no show—when the pinch comes there ain't nothing to back him up and keep him to his work, and so he gets beat. Then I thought a minute, and says to myself, hold on—s'pose you'd a done right and give Jim up; would you feel better than what you do now? No, says I, I'd feel bad—I'd feel just the same way I do now. Well, then, says I, what's the use you learning to do right, when it's troublesome to do right and ain't no trouble to do wrong, and the wages is just the same? I was stuck. I couldn't answer that. So I reckoned I wouldn't bother no more about it, but after this always do whichever come handiest at the time.

Huck clearly cannot conceive of having any morality except the one he has learned—too late, he thinks—from his society. He is not entirely a prisoner of that morality, because he does after all reject it; but for him that is a decision to relinquish morality as such; he cannot envisage revising his morality, altering its content in face of the various pressures to which it is subject, including pressures from his sympathies. For example, he does not begin to approach the thought that slavery should be rejected on moral grounds, or the thought that what he is doing is not theft because a person cannot be owned and therefore cannot be stolen.

The basic trouble is that he cannot or will not engage in abstract intellectual operations of any sort. In chapter 33 he finds himself "feeling to blame, somehow" for something he knows he had no hand in; he assumes that this feeling is a deliverance of conscience; and this confirms him in his belief that conscience shouldn't be listened to:

> It don't make no difference whether you do right or wrong, a person's conscience ain't got no sense, and just goes for him *anyway*. If I had a yaller dog that didn't know no more than a person's conscience does, I would poison him. It takes up more than all of a person's insides, and yet ain't no good, nohow.

That brisk, incurious dismissiveness fits well with the comprehensive rejection of morality back on the raft. But this is a digression.

On the raft, Huck decides not to live by principles, but just to do whatever "comes handiest at the time"—always acting according to the mood of the moment. Since the morality he is rejecting is narrow and cruel, and his sympathies are broad and kind, the results will be good. But moral principles are good to have, because they help to protect one from acting badly at moments when one's sympathies happen to be in abeyance. On the highest possible estimate of the role one's sympathies should have, one can still allow for principles as embodiments of one's best feelings, one's broadest and keenest sympathies. On that view, principles can help one across intervals when one's feelings are at less than their best, i.e. through periods of misanthropy or meanness or self-centeredness or depression or anger.

What Huck didn't see is that one can live by principles and yet have ultimate control over their content. And one way such control can be exercised is by checking of one's principles in the light of one's sympathies. This is sometimes a pretty straightforward matter. It can happen that a certain moral principle becomes untenable—meaning literally that one cannot hold it any longer—because it conflicts intolerably with the pity or revulsion or whatever that one feels when one sees what the principle leads to. One's experience may play a large part here: Experiences evoke feelings, and feelings force one to modify principles. Something like this happened to the English poet Wilfred Owen, whose experiences in the First World War transformed him from an enthusiastic soldier into a virtual pacifist. I can't document his change of conscience in detail; but I want to present something which he wrote about the way experience can put pressure on morality.

The Latin poet Horace wrote that it is sweet and fitting (or right) to die for one's country—*dulce et decorum est pro patria mori*—and Owen wrote a fine poem about how experience could lead one to relinquish that particular moral principle.[5] He describes a man who is too slow donning his gas mask during a gas attack—"As under a green sea I saw him drowning," Owen says. The poem ends like this:

> In all my dreams before my helpless sight
> He plunges at me, guttering, choking, drowning.
> If in some smothering dreams, you too could pace
> Behind the wagon that we flung him in,
> And watch the white eyes writhing in his face,
> His hanging face, like a devil's sick of sin;

---

[5]We are grateful to the Executors of the Estate of Harold Owen, and to Chatto and Windus Ltd. for permission to quote from Wilfred Owen's "Dulce et Decorum Est" and "Insensibility."

If you could hear, at every jolt, the blood
Come gargling from the froth-corrupted lungs,
Bitter as the cud
Of vile, incurable sores on innocent tongues,—
My friend, you would not tell with such high zest
To children ardent for some desperate glory,
The old Lie: Dulce et decorum est
Pro patria mori.

There is a difficulty about drawing from all this a moral for ourselves. I imagine that we agree in our rejection of slavery, eternal damnation, genocide, and uncritical patriotic self-abnegation; so we shall agree that Huck Finn, Jonathan Edwards, Heinrich Himmler, and the poet Horace would all have done well to bring certain of their principles under severe pressure from ordinary human sympathies. But then we can say this because we can say that all those are bad moralities, whereas we cannot look at our own moralities and declare them bad. This is not arrogance: It is obviously incoherent for someone to declare the system of moral principles that he *accepts* to be *bad,* just as one cannot coherently say of anything that one *believes* it but it is *false*.

Still, although I can't point to any of my beliefs and say "That is false," I don't doubt that some of my beliefs *are* false; and so I should try to remain open to correction. Similarly, I accept every single item in my morality—that is inevitable—but I am sure that my morality could be improved, which is to say that it could undergo changes which I should be glad of once I had made them. So I must try to keep my morality open to revision, exposing it to whatever valid pressures there are—including pressures from my sympathies.

I don't give my sympathies a blank check in advance. In a conflict between principle and sympathy, principles ought sometimes to win. For example, I think it was right to take part in the Second World War on the allied side; there were many ghastly individual incidents which might have led someone to doubt the rightness of his participation in that war; and I think it would have been right for such a person to keep his sympathies in a subordinate place on those occasions, not allowing them to modify his principles in such a way as to make a pacifist of him.

Still, one's sympathies should be kept as sharp and sensitive and aware as possible, and not only because they can sometimes affect one's principles or one's conduct or both. Owen, at any rate, says that feelings and sympathies are vital even when they can do nothing but bring pain and distress. In another poem he speaks of the blessings of being numb in one's feelings: "Happy are the men who yet before they are killed/Can let their veins run cold," he says. These are the ones who do not suffer from any compassion which, as Owen puts it, "makes their feet/Sore on the alleys cobbled with their brothers." He contrasts these "happy" ones, who "lose all imagination," with himself and others "who with a thought besmirch/Blood over all our soul." Yet the poem's verdict goes against the "happy" ones. Owen does not say that they will act worse than the others whose souls are besmirched with blood because of their keen awareness of human suffering. He merely says that they are the losers because they have cut themselves off from the human condition:

By choice they made themselves immune
To pity and whatever moans in man
Before the last sea and the hapless stars;
Whatever mourns when many leave these shores;
Whatever shares
The eternal reciprocity of tears.[6]

## STUDY QUESTIONS

1. What does Bennett mean by a "bad morality"?
2. Does Bennett think principles play an important role in moral life? Can you suggest occasions where one's principles *should* overrule one's sympathies?
3. What are the consequences of Bennett's arguments for ethical relativism?
4. Why does Bennett claim that Jonathan Edwards's morality was even worse than Himmler's? Do you agree?
5. What are the implications of Bennett's position for the view that we must always follow our conscience?

---

[6]This paper began life as the Potter Memorial Lecture, given at Washington State University in Pullman, Washington, in 1972.

# The Evil That Men Think—And Do

## PHILIP HALLIE

A biographical sketch of Philip Hallie is found on page 9.

Philip Hallie summarizes and criticizes several recent theories of evil. In particular he objects to the views of Jonathan Bennett in "The Conscience of Huckleberry Finn," where Bennett claims that eighteenth-century theologian Jonathan Edwards, who killed no one, has a "worse morality" than Heinrich Himmler, who sent millions to their deaths but who appears to have suffered somewhat because occasionally he sympathized with those he tormented.

Hallie believes that Bennett can reach this odd conclusion only by perversely overlooking the truly horrific aspect of evil—its victims. On the contrary, it matters greatly that Edwards never actually killed or meant to kill anyone, and that Himmler tortured and killed millions. "Victims are as essential to morality as the presence or absence of sympathy. . . ."

Hallie claims that Bennett and others trivialize the notion of evil by concentrating too heavily on the psychology of evildoers and by paying scant attention to the fate of their victims. Hallie concludes with an excerpt from the official transcripts of the Nuremberg Trials, an excerpt he believes exemplifies the "wholeness of evil": it

THE EVIL THAT MEN THINK—AND DO From *Hastings Center Report*, December 1985. Reprinted by permission of the author.

reveals not only what a Nazi war criminal says he thought but, more significantly, it details what he did and the suffering it caused.

In a cartoon by Edward Kliban, a mechanic is waving his tools and pointing at what he has discovered under the hood of his customer's car. There, where the motor should be, squats a massive monster, a wicked grin revealing his terrible teeth. The mechanic is triumphantly proclaiming to his customer: "Well, *there's* your problem."

In her book, *Wickedness*, Mary Midgley writes that evil must not be seen as "something positive" or demonic like Kliban's monster. If evil were a demon we could only exorcise it, not understand it. To do so, she writes, one must see the various types of wickedness as *mixtures* of motives, some of which can be life-enhancing in themselves but are destructive in certain combinations. For instance, a rapist-murderer can be motivated by power and sex, but his way of combining these often healthy drives is destructive. For Midgley wickedness is "essentially destructive," not the way a terrible-toothed monster can be destructive but the way a person acting under various motives can fail to care about the feelings or even the lives of others. For her, evil is an absence of such caring, "an emptiness at the core of the individual. . . ." It is a negative, not a positive, demon.

This is a sensitive analysis, but the demon Wickedness is a straw demon: very few, if any, modern thinkers on the subject believe in the demonic. For most of them another cartoon would be more apt. A mechanic is waving his tools triumphantly before a customer and is pointing to what he has found under the hood of the car. There, where Kliban's demon was, is a mass of intricately intertwined pipes, and the mechanic is pointing to *this* and announcing, "Well, *there's* your problem." And the customer is as bewildered by this phenomenon as Kliban's customer was.

Many of the people who are writing about wickedness (or immorality or evil, call it what you will) are making it a very complicated matter, like those twisted pipes. Judith Shklar in her quite often brilliant book *Ordinary Vices* is more concerned with various ethical and political puzzles than she is with the ordinary vices she promises to talk about in her introduction and in her title. Usually the unique perplexities of unique people like Robert E. Lee, Richard II, Socrates, and Colonel Count Claus von Stauffenberg interest her more than any single idea of vice does. Her skeptical, energetic mind seeks out mine-fields, not highways: contradictions, not a monster.

My version of Kliban's cartoon applies also to the lucid, careful book *Immorality* by the philosopher Ronald D. Milo. Milo takes Aristotle's all-too-pat distinction between moral weakness and moral baseness, and refines it into a range of kinds and degrees of blameworthiness. In the seventh book of his *Nichomachean Ethics* Aristotle said that the weak (or "incontinent") person is like a city that has good laws, but that does not live by them: the vicious (or "base" person) is like a city that has bad laws by which it *does* live. The zealous mass murderer is vicious without remorse; while the weak, penitent adulterer or drunkard knows he is doing wrong, but does nothing about it. Milo refines and develops this rather crude distinction, so that Aristotle's baseness is no longer a simple contrast between two kinds of cities. Like Shklar, Milo is too perceptive and too circumspect to join the simplifiers that Midgley deplores.

And yet, despite their perceptiveness and circumspection, many of our analyzers of evil have grossly simplified the idea of immorality. In their scrupulous examinations of complexities they have left out much of the ferocious ugliness of Kliban's monster. They too are negligent simplifiers.

For instance, Jonathan Bennett has written an essay entitled "The Conscience of Huckleberry Finn," in which he proves to his satisfaction that the morality of the eighteenth-century American theologian Jonathan Edwards was "worse than Himmler's." He insists that Heinrich Himmler, head of the SS and of all the police systems of Nazi Germany, and responsible for all of the tortures and the deaths perpetrated upon noncombatants by Nazi Germany, was not as wicked as Jonathan Edwards, who never killed or meant to kill anyone.

Why? Because Jonathan Edwards had no pity for the damned, and Himmler did have sympathy for the millions of people he tortured and destroyed. Bennett contends that there are two forces at work in the consciences of human beings: general moral principles and unreasoned "emotional pulls." One such "pull" is sympathy, and Jonathan Edwards's sermons showed no sympathy for the sinners who were in the hands of an angry God, while Himmler's speeches to his Nazi subordinates did express the emotional pull of sympathy. In the mind, the only place where "morality" dwells for Bennett, Himmler is no heartless ruffian, but a decent fellow who had a wrong-headed set of principles and who felt the pangs of sympathy for human beings he was crushing and grinding into death and worse.

## The Central Role of the Victim

In Lewis Carroll's *Alice's Adventures in Wonderland* Tweedledee recites to Alice "The Walrus and the Carpenter." In the poem, the Walrus and the Carpenter come across some oysters while they are strolling on the beach. They manage to persuade the younger oysters to join them in

> A pleasant walk, a pleasant talk
> Along the briny beach

After a while they rest on a rock that is "conveniently low," so that the two of them can keep an eye on the oysters and can reach them easily. After a little chat, the Carpenter and the Walrus start eating the oysters.

The Walrus is a sympathetic creature, given to crying readily, who thanks the oysters for joining them, while the Carpenter is interested only in eating:

> "It seems a shame," the Walrus said
> "To play them such a trick.
> After we've brought them out so far
> And made them trot so quick!"
> The Carpenter said nothing but
> "The butter's spread too thick."

Then the Walrus, out of the goodness of his heart, bursts forth:

> "I weep for you," the Walrus said:
> "I deeply sympathize."
> With sobs and tears he sorted out
> Those of the largest size,
> Holding his pocket-handkerchief
> Before his streaming eyes.

and they finish off all of the oysters.

Bennett, with his concern for the saving grace of sympathy, might find the "morality" of the Walrus better than the morality of the cold-blooded Carpenter, but Lewis Carroll, or rather Tweedledee and Tweedledum, are not so simple-minded:

> "I like the Walrus best," said Alice: "because he was a *little* sorry for the poor oysters."
> "He ate more than the Carpenter, though," said Tweedledee. "You see he held his handkerchief in front, so that the Carpenter couldn't count how many he took: contrariwise."
> "That was mean!" Alice said indignantly. "Then I like the Carpenter best—if he didn't eat so many as the Walrus."
> "But he ate as many as he could get," said Tweedledum.

Then Alice gives up trying to rank the Walrus and the Carpenter and gives voice to a wisdom that is as sound as it is obvious:

> "Well! They were both very unpleasant characters. . . ."

What Lewis Carroll saw, and what Bennett apparently does not, is that the victims are as essential in morality as the presence or absence of sympathy inside the head of the moral agent. And he also sees that sympathy, or rather expressions of sympathy, can be a device for eating more oysters by hiding your mouth behind a handkerchief—it certainly needn't slow your eating down.

Milo never violates the morally obvious as boldly as Bennett does, but when he ranks immoralities he too disregards the essential role of the victim in evil. His conclusions contradict Bennett's. For Milo, apparently, Himmler's would be "the most evil" kind of wrong-doing, just because of his scruples:

> . . . we think that the most evil or reprehensible kind of wrongdoing consists in willingly and intentionally doing something that one believes to be morally wrong, either because one simply does not care that it is morally wrong or because one prefers the pursuit of some other end to the avoidance of moral wrongdoing. . . .

This is a more subtle analysis of evil than Bennett's, but it too ranks evils without the wisdom of Tweedledum and Tweedledee. It too flattens out or ignores the central role of victims in the dance of evil.

## Where Eichmann's Evil Lay

The most distinguished modern philosophic treatment of evil is Hannah Arendt's *Eichmann in Jerusalem, A Report on the Banality of Evil.* Like most of the philosophers who came after her she believed that the evil person is not necessarily a monster. In her report on the Eichmann trial as she witnessed it in Jerusalem in 1961 she shows us a man who did not act out of evil motives. She shows us a man, Adolf Eichmann, whose main trait was to have no interesting traits, except perhaps his "remoteness from reality." His banality resides in his never having *realized* what he was doing to particular human beings. Hannah Arendt tells us that, except for personal advancement, "He had no motives at all." He was an unimaginative bureaucrat who lived in the clichés of his office. He was no Iago, no Richard III, no person who wished "to prove a villain."

There is truth in this position. Eichmann was a commonplace, trite man if you look at him only in the dock and if you do not see that his boring clichés are directly linked with millions of tortures and murders. If you see the victims of Eichmann and of the office he held, then—and only then—do you see the evil of this man. Evil does not happen only in people's heads. Eichmann's evil happened in his head (and here Arendt is not only right but brilliantly perceptive) *and* (and the "and" makes a tight, essential linkage) in the freight cars and in the camps of Central Europe. His evil is the sum-total of his unimaginative head and his unimaginable tortures and murders. And this sum-total is not banal, not flat, not common-place. It is horrific.

As one of the most powerful philosophers of our time, Arendt was conscious of leaving something out by concentrating her attention upon the internal workings of the mind of a bureaucrat. Early in her book she wrote: "On trial are his deeds, not the sufferings of the Jews."

As if "his deeds" could be neatly peeled away from what he did to the Jews! *Her separation* of the mental activity of Eichmann from the pain-racked deaths of millions that this mental activity brought about made Eichmann's evil banal. Without these actual murders and tortures Eichmann was not evil; his maunderings were those of a pitiable, not a culpable man. His evil lay in his deeds, as Arendt says, but not only in his mental "deeds": it lay in all that he intended and all that he carried out, in his mind and in the world around him.

## The Morality of Seeing

In Saul Bellow's novel *The Dean's December*, the narrator, Dean Albert Corde, makes a plea for seeing what there is to be seen:

> In the American moral crisis, the first requirement was to experience what was happening and to see what must be seen. The facts were covered from our perception. . . . The increase of theories and discourse, itself a cause of new, strange forms of blindness, the false representations of "communication," led to horrible distortions of public consciousness. Therefore the first act of morality was to disinter the reality, retrieve reality, dig it out from the trash, represent it anew as art would represent it. . . .
>
> We were no longer talking about anything. The language of discourse had shut out experience altogether. . . . I tried to make myself the moralist of seeing. . . .

The dynamic of passions, moral principles, and perceptions within the heads of moral agents is a dynamic that is part of evil, but those of us who want to face and to understand evil as best we can must, it seems to me, try to live up to Corde's "morality of seeing." We must do our best to see not only what is happening in the inward polities of the doers of evil but *also* what is happening in the lives of the sufferers of evil.

For instance, to write about Himmler requires not only the reading of a few carefully crafted speeches; it also demands learning about the context of these speeches. It is true that at least once Himmler looked as if he felt queasy at an execution, and it is also true that he wrote about this queasiness in terms not entirely unlike those of the Walrus. But even a superficial study of what was actually happening within Fortress Europe in those days makes quite clear that he was coping with a particular problem by talking about "damage in . . . minds and souls" and "human weakness."

Look at almost any volume of the record of the 1947 Nuremberg Trials—for example Volume IV, especially pages 311–355—and it will become plain that the efficient murdering of children as well as other defenseless human beings was being hindered by the depression and even the nervous breakdowns of the people who were herding together and executing these people. Himmler, in order to minimize inefficiency, needed to prepare his followers to deal with such scruples. At least he needed to do this to carry out the project of exterminating the Jews of Europe as well as the majority of the Slavs.

Talking about these scruples was not a *cri du coeur*. He was not opening his heart to his subordinates, as Bennett suggests: he was preparing them for dealing with the psychological problems of the executioners. He was holding up a handkerchief before his eyes, to go back to the imagery of Tweedledee's poem, so that he and his followers could murder more and more helpless human beings.

## A Monster in Action

Even such vigorously human books as *Ordinary Vices* by Judith Shklar and *Wickedness* by Mary Midgley do not meet the obligations laid upon us by a morality of seeing. Shklar provides lurid and deep insights into the implications of making cruelty *summum malum,* the most indefensible and unforgivable evil, and into many other subjects, but she hastens into perplexities and puzzles before she carefully observes the factual contexts of her examples.

Midgley is memorably illuminating in her efforts to clear away the obstacles that keep us from taking wickedness seriously. For instance, very few readers of her book, if they are attentive, will ever describe a mass-murderer and a mass-rapist as "sick" after reading her truly remarkable analysis in the chapter entitled "The Elusiveness of Responsibility." One of her key arguments against replacing the words "wicked" and "evil" by the words "sick" and "ill" is that doing so *distances* us from the destruction that has been done. It removes the "sick" destroyers from blame and from anger (how dare you blame a person for being ill?). It "flattens out," to use her powerful phrase, the distinctions between murderers and kleptomaniacs, between those who make us defensibly angry, when we see what they have *done,* and those who engage only our compassion and help.

Still, so scrupulous is she in removing the obstacles to an awareness of wickedness that she does not reveal much about what evil is. Her description of wickedness as "negative" like darkness and cold (an absence of caring being like an absence of light or heat) is useful but difficult to understand in terms of examples, especially when she tells us that "evil in the quiet supporters [of, for example, a Hitler] is negative," and then tells us that what they do is "positive action." This is a confusing use of metaphysical terms that do not have a plain cash value in relation to observable facts. These terms bring us close to the medieval soup and its casuistical arguments about whether evil is a "privation of good" or something "positive."

Milo's *Immorality* offers a scrupulously lucid and sustained argument about the types and blameworthiness of immorality. It is especially adroit at understanding the relationships between moral weakness and deep wickedness. But he, like these other recent writers on evil, is reluctant to face the full force of evil. He, like them, does not look deeply and carefully at examples, at the terrible details in history and the arts.

These writers are, perhaps, too timid to look hard at Kliban's monster and say, "Well, *there's* your problem." Evil is thick with fact and as ugly as that grinning monster. It is no worse to see it this way than it is to see it as an internal dynamic in a moral agent's head, or a set of carefully honed distinctions, or an array of puzzles and perplexities (as Shklar seems to see it). Many of the insights of these writers are useful for understanding the monster, or rather the many monsters that embody evil, but there is no substitute for seeing the harshness and ugliness of fact.

Here is a monster in action: he is Otto Ohlendorf who was, among other roles, head of Group D of the Action Groups assigned to exterminate Jews and Soviet political leaders in parts of Eastern Europe. To learn more about him, read pages 311–355 of the Fourth Volume of the transcript of the Nuremberg trials of the major war criminals. Here is part of his testimony:

| | |
|---|---|
| COLONEL POKROVSKY (for the Tribunal): | Why did they (the execution squads) prefer execution by shooting to killing in the gas vans? |
| OHLENDORF: | Because . . . in the opinion of the leader of the Einsatzkommandos [Action Groups], the unloading of the corpses was an unnecessary mental strain. |
| COL. POKROVSKY: | What do you mean by "an unnecessary mental strain?" |
| OHLENDORF: | As far as I can remember the conditions at the time—the picture presented by the corpses and probably because certain functions of the body had taken place, leaving the corpses lying in filth. |

| | |
|---|---|
| COL. POKROVSKY: | You mean to say that the sufferings endured prior to death were clearly visible on the victims? Did I understand you correctly? |
| OHLENDORF: | I don't understand the question; do you mean during the killing in the van? |
| COL. POKROVSKY: | Yes. |
| OHLENDORF: | I can only repeat what the doctor told me, that the victims were not conscious of their death in the van. |
| COL. POKROVSKY: | In that case your reply to my previous question, that the unloading of the bodies made a very terrible impression on the members of the execution squad, becomes entirely incomprehensible. |
| OHLENDORF: | And, as I said, the terrible impression created by the position of the corpses themselves, and by the state of the vans which had probably been dirtied and so on. |
| COL. POKROVSKY: | I have no further questions to put to this witness at the present stage of the Trial (p. 334). |
| COLONEL AMEN (for the Tribunal): | Referring to the gas vans which you said you received in the spring of 1942, what order did you receive with respect to the use of these vans? |
| OHLENDORF: | These gas vans were in future to be used for the killing of women and children. |
| COL. AMEN: | Will you explain to the Tribunal the construction of these vans and their appearance? |
| OHLENDORF: | The actual purpose of these vans could not be seen from the outside. They looked like closed trucks, and were so constructed that at the start of the motor, gas was conducted into the van, causing death in 10 to 15 minutes. |
| COL. AMEN: | Explain in detail just how one of these vans was used for an execution. |
| OHLENDORF: | The vans were loaded with the victims and driven to the place of burial, which was usually the same as that used for the mass executions. The time needed for transportation was sufficient to insure the death of the victims. |

| | |
|---|---|
| COL. AMEN: | How were the victims induced to enter the vans? |
| OHLENDORF: | They were told that they were to be transported to another locality. |
| COL. AMEN: | How was the gas turned on? |
| OHLENDORF: | I am not familiar with the technical details. |
| COL. AMEN: | How long did it take to kill the victims ordinarily? |
| OHLENDORF: | About 10 to 15 minutes; the victims were not conscious of what was happening to them (p. 322). |
| | |
| OHLENDORF: | I led the Einsatzgruppe, and therefore I had the task of seeing how the Einsatzkommandos executed the orders received. |
| HERR BABEL (for the Tribunal): | But did you have no scruples in regard to the execution of these orders? |
| OHLENDORF: | Yes, of course. |
| HERR BABEL: | And how is it that they were carried out regardless of these scruples? |
| OHLENDORF: | Because to me it is inconceivable that a subordinate leader should not carry out orders given by the leaders of the state (pp. 353–354). |

I urge you to read the above extracts more than once. The wholeness of evil is there, and if Ohlendorf is not monstrous to you, you are the problem.


## STUDY QUESTIONS

1. Do you agree with Hallie's critique of Bennett? In particular, do you think Hallie is right in saying that Heinrich Himmler's attitude does not exculpate him and that Jonathan Edwards' attitude counts for less than Himmler's deeds?
2. Explain Hallie's reference to Lewis Carroll's *Alice's Adventure in Wonderland*. Do you find the morality of the walrus better than the morality of the carpenter? Do you agree with Alice's assessment? Explain.
3. Explain Hannah Arendt's phrase "the banality of evil." How does Hallie criticize Arendt's view?
4. In what respect does the testimony of Nazi war criminal Ohlendorf exemplify the "wholeness of evil"? Explain.

# 38 Who Saw Murder Didn't Call Police

_____ ♪♪♬━

## MARTIN GANSBERG

Martin Gansberg (b. 1920) is on the staff of the _New York Times_. He taught journalism at Fairleigh Dickinson University from 1947 to 1973.

In 1964, the American public was stunned by reports from Kew Gardens, Queens: Kitty Genovese was brutally stabbed while her neighbors passively witnessed the murder. Gansberg describes the incident in detail without overtly judging the bystanders.

For more than half an hour 38 respectable, law-abiding citizens in Queens watched a killer stalk and stab a woman in three separate attacks in Kew Gardens.

Twice their chatter and the sudden glow of their bedroom lights interrupted him and frightened him off. Each time he returned, sought her out, and stabbed her again. Not one person telephoned the police during the assault; one witness called after the woman was dead.

That was two weeks ago today.

Still shocked is Assistant Chief Inspector Frederick M. Lussen, in charge of the borough's detectives and a veteran of 25 years of homicide investigations. He can give a matter-of-fact recitation on many murders. But the Kew Gardens slaying baffles him—not because it is a murder, but because the "good people" failed to call the police.

"As we have reconstructed the crime," he said, "the assailant had three chances to kill this woman during a 35-minute period. He returned twice to complete the job. If we had been called when he first attacked, the woman might not be dead now."

This is what the police say happened beginning at 3:20 A.M. in the staid, middle-class, tree-lined Austin Street area:

Twenty-eight-year-old Catherine Genovese, who was called Kitty by almost everyone in the neighborhood, was returning home from her job as manager of a bar in Hollis. She parked her red Fiat in a lot adjacent to the Kew Gardens Long Island Rail Road Station, facing Mowbray Place. Like many residents of the neighborhood, she had parked there day after day since her arrival in Connecticut a year ago, although the railroad frowns on the practice.

She turned off the lights of her car, locked the door, and started to walk the 100 feet to the entrance of her apartment at 82–70 Austin Street, which is in a Tudor building, with stores on the first floor and apartments on the second.

The entrance to the apartment is in the rear of the building because the front is rented to retail stores. At night the quiet neighborhood is shrouded in the slumbering darkness that marks most residential areas.

Miss Genovese noticed a man at the far end of the lot, near a seven-story apartment house at 82–40 Austin Street. She halted. Then, nervously, she headed up Austin Street toward Lefferts Boulevard, where there is a call box to the 102nd Police Precinct in nearby Richmond Hill.

She got as far as a street light in front of a bookstore before the man grabbed her. She screamed. Lights went on in the 10-story apartment house at 82–67 Austin Street, which faces the bookstore. Windows slid open and voices punctuated the early-morning stillness.

Miss Genovese screamed: "Oh, my God, he stabbed me! Please help me! Please help me!"

From one of the upper windows in the apartment house, a man called down: "Let that girl alone!"

The assailant looked up at him, shrugged, and walked down Austin Street toward a white sedan parked a short distance away. Miss Genovese struggled to her feet.

Lights went out. The killer returned to Miss Genovese, now trying to make her way around the side of the building by the parking lot to get to her apartment. The assailant stabbed her again.

"I'm dying!" she shrieked. "I'm dying!"

Windows were opened again, and lights went on in many apartments. The assailant got into his car and drove away. Miss Genovese staggered to her feet. A city bus, 0–10, the Lefferts Boulevard line to Kennedy International Airport, passed. It was 3:35 A.M.

The assailant returned. By then, Miss Genovese had crawled to the back of the building, where the freshly painted brown doors to the apartment house held out hope for safety. The killer tried the first door; she wasn't there. At the second door, 82–62 Austin Street, he saw her slumped on the floor at the foot of the stairs. He stabbed her a third time—fatally.

It was 3:50 by the time the police received their first call, from a man who was a neighbor of Miss Genovese. In two minutes they were at the scene. The neighbor, a 70-year-old woman, and another woman were the only persons on the street. Nobody else came forward.

The man explained that he had called the police after much deliberation. He had phoned a friend in Nassau County for advice and then he had crossed the roof of the building to the apartment of the elderly woman to get her to make the call.

"I didn't want to get involved," he sheepishly told the police.

Six days later, the police arrested Winston Moseley, a 29-year-old business-machine operator, and charged him with the homicide. Moseley had no previous record. He is married, has two children and owns a home at 133–19 Sutter Avenue, South Ozone Park, Queens. On Wednesday, a court committed him to Kings County Hospital for psychiatric observation.

When questioned by the police, Moseley also said that he had slain Mrs. Annie May Johnson, 24, of 146–12 133d Avenue, Jamaica, on Feb. 29 and Barbara Kralik, 15, of 174–17 140th Avenue, Springfield Gardens, last July. In the Kralik case, the police are holding Alvin L. Mitchell, who is said to have confessed that slaying.

The police stressed how simple it would have been to have gotten in touch with them. "A phone call," said one of the detectives, "would have done it." The police may be reached by dialing "O" for operator or SPring 7–3100.

Today witnesses from the neighborhood, which is made up of one-family homes in the $35,000 to $60,000 range with the exception of the two apartment houses near the railroad station, find it difficult to explain why they didn't call the police.

A housewife, knowingly if quite casual, said, "We thought it was a lover's quarrel." A husband and wife both said, "Frankly, we were afraid." They seemed aware of the fact that events might have been different. A distraught woman, wiping her hands in her apron, said, "I didn't want my husband to get involved."

One couple, now willing to talk about that night, said they heard the first screams. The husband looked thoughtfully at the bookstore where the killer first grabbed Miss Genovese.

"We went to the window to see what was happening," he said, "but the light from our bedroom made it difficult to see the street." The wife, still apprehensive, added: "I put out the light and we were able to see better."

Asked why they hadn't called the police, she shrugged and replied: "I don't know."

A man peeked out from a slight opening in the doorway to his apartment and rattled off an account of the killer's second attack. Why hadn't he called the police at the time? "I was tired," he said without emotion. "I went back to bed."

It was 4:25 A.M. when the ambulance arrived to take the body of Miss Genovese. It drove off. "Then," a solemn police detective said, "the people came out."

## STUDY QUESTIONS

1. Two professors at the Princeton Theological Seminary designed an experiment to find out why bystanders often ignore people in distress. They told several seminary students to report to the studio to record a Biblical text. The professors arranged that, on their way to the studio, the students would pass another student lying on the ground writhing and gasping. The researchers found that the only significant factor in determining who stopped was how much time students thought they had: Of those rushed for time, only 10 percent stopped; of those who had plenty of time, 63 percent. It seemed to make no statistical difference that half the students had been assigned to read the parable of the good Samaritan. Do these findings surprise you? Despite their poor showing, do you think the seminarians did better than a randomly selected group would have? Can we do anything as a society to increase the proportion of people who will stop?

2. Do you think more states should adopt a statute like the one in Vermont that legally requires bystanders to aid those in critical need when they can safely do so?
3. Do you agree with those who say that the thirty-eight witnesses to Kitty Genovese's death are accessories to murder?

# The Moral Insight

## JOSIAH ROYCE

Josiah Royce (1855–1916), a professor of philosophy at Harvard University, was a colleague of William James and a teacher of George Santayana during what are known as the "golden years" of Harvard philosophy. Royce wrote in almost every area of philosophy, but is principally known as a proponent of idealism. His best known work in ethics is *The Philosophy of Loyalty* (1908).

For Royce the key to moral understanding lies in the realization that our neighbor is a center of experience and desire just as we are. Royce asks that we look upon that neighbor in much the same way we look upon our *future* selves—as a distant and somewhat unreal center of experience, but nevertheless of great concern. Sympathy and pity for another are not enough: Fellow feeling must also bring us to the point of what Royce calls the moral insight: "Such as that is for me, so is it for him, nothing less."

. . . [The following] is our reflective account of the process that, in some form, must come to every one under the proper conditions. In this process we see the beginning of the real knowledge of duty to

THE MORAL INSIGHT From *The Religious Aspects of Philosophy* (Boston: Houghton Mifflin Co., 1885).

55

others. The process is one that any child can and does, under proper guidance, occasionally accomplish. It is the process by which we all are accustomed to try to teach humane behavior in concrete cases. We try to get people to realize what they are doing when they injure others. But to distinguish this process from the mere tender emotion of sympathy, with all its illusions, is what moralists have not carefully enough done. Our exposition [tries] to take this universally recognized process, to distinguish it from sympathy as such, and to set it up before the gates of ethical doctrine as the great producer of insight.

But when we say that to this insight common sense must come, under the given conditions, we do not mean to say: "So the man, once having attained insight, must act thenceforth." The realization of one's neighbor, in the full sense of the word realization, is indeed the resolution to treat him as if he were real, that is, to treat him unselfishly. But this resolution expresses and belongs to the moment of insight. Passion may cloud the insight in the very next moment. It always does cloud the insight after no very long time. It is as impossible for us to avoid the illusion of selfishness in our daily lives, as to escape seeing through the illusion at the moment of insight. We see the reality of our neighbor, that is, we determine to treat him as we do ourselves. But then we go back to daily action, and we feel the heat of hereditary passions, and we straightway forget what we have seen. Our neighbor becomes obscured. He is once more a foreign power. He is unreal. We are again deluded and selfish. This conflict goes on and will go on as long as we live after the manner of men. Moments of insight, with their accompanying resolutions; long stretches of delusion and selfishness: That is our life.

To bring home this view . . . to the reader, we ask him to consider carefully just what experience he has when he tries to realize his neighbor in the full sense that we have insisted upon. Not pity as such is what we desire him to feel. For whether or not pity happens to work in him as selfishly and blindly as we have found that it often does work, still not the emotion, but its consequences, must in the most favorable case give us what we seek. All the forms of sympathy are mere impulses. It is the insight to which they bring us that has moral value. And again, the realization of our neighbor's existence is not at all the discovery that he is more or less useful to us personally. All that would contribute to selfishness. In an entirely different way we must realize his existence, if we are to be really altruistic. What then is our neighbor?

56

We find that out by treating him in thought just as we do ourselves. What art thou? Thou art now just a present state, with its experiences, thoughts, and desires. But what is thy future Self? Simply future states, future experiences, future thoughts and desires, that, although not now existing for thee, are postulated by thee as certain to come, and as in some real relation to thy present Self. What then is thy neighbor? He too is a mass of states, of experiences, thoughts, and desires, just as real as thou art, no more but yet no less present to thy experience now than is thy future Self. He is not that face that frowns or smiles at thee, although often thou thinkest of him as only that. He is not the arm that strikes or defends thee, not the voice that speaks to thee, not that machine that gives thee what thou desirest when thou movest it with the offer of money. To be sure, thou dost often think of him as if he were that automaton yonder, that answers thee when thou speakest to it. But no, thy neighbor is as actual, as concrete, as thou art. Just as thy future is real, though not now thine, so thy neighbor is real, though his thoughts never are thy thoughts. Dost thou believe this? Art thou sure what it means? This is for thee the turning-point of thy whole conduct towards him. What we now ask of thee is no sentiment, no gush of pity, no tremulous weakness of sympathy, but a calm, clear insight. . . .

If he is real like thee, then is his life as bright a light, as warm a fire, to him, as thine to thee; his will is as full of struggling desires, of hard problems, of fateful decisions; his pains are as hateful, his joys as dear. Take whatever thou knowest of desire and of striving, of burning love and of fierce hatred, realize as fully as thou canst what that means, and then with clear certainty add: *Such as that is for me, so is it for him, nothing less.* If thou dost that, can he remain to thee what he has been, a picture, a plaything, a comedy, or a tragedy, in brief a mere Show? Behind all that show thou hast indeed dimly felt that there is something. Know that truth thoroughly. Thou hast regarded his thought, his feeling, as somehow different in sort from thine. Thou hast said: "A pain in him is not like a pain in me, but something far easier to bear." Thou hast made of him a ghost, as the imprudent man makes of his future self a ghost. Even when thou hast feared his scorn, his hate, his contempt, thou hast not fully made him for thee as real as thyself. His laughter at thee has made thy face feel hot, his frowns and clenched fists have cowed thee, his sneers have made thy throat feel choked. But that was only the social instinct in thee. It was not a full sense of his reality. Even so the little baby smiles back at one that smiles at it, but not because it realizes the approving joy of the other, only because it by instinct enjoys a smiling face; and even so the baby is frightened at harsh speech, but not because it realizes the other's anger. So, dimly and by instinct, thou hast lived with thy neighbor, and hast known him not, being blind. Thou hast even desired his pain, but thou hast not fully realized the pain that thou gavest. It has been to thee, not pain in itself, but the sight of his submission, of his tears, or of his pale terror. Of thy neighbor thou hast made a thing, no Self at all.

When thou hast loved, hast pitied, or hast reverenced thy neighbor, then thy feeling has possibly raised for a moment the veil of illusion. Then thou hast known what he truly is, a Self like thy present Self. But thy selfish feeling is too strong for thee. Thou hast forgotten soon again what thou hadst seen, and hast made even of thy beloved one only the instrument of thy own pleasure. Even out of thy power to pity thou hast made an object of thy vainglory. Thy reverence has turned again to pride. Thou hast accepted the illusion once more. No wonder that in his darkness thou findest selfishness the only rule of any meaning for thy conduct. Thou forgottest that without realization of thy future and as yet unreal self, even selfishness means nothing. Thou forgottest that if thou gavest thy present thought even so to the task of realizing thy neighbor's life, selfishness would seem no more plain to thee than the love of thy neighbor.

Have done then with this illusion that thy Self is all in all. Intuition tells thee no more about thy future Self than it tells thee about thy neighbors. Desire, bred in thee by generations of struggle for existence, emphasizes the expectation of thy own bodily future, the love for thy own bodily welfare, and makes thy body's life seem alone real. But simply try to know the truth. The truth is that all this world of life about thee is as real as thou art. All conscious life is conscious in its own measure. Pain is pain, joy is joy, everywhere even as in thee. The result of thy insight will be inevitable. The illusion vanishing, the glorious prospect opens before thy vision. Seeing the oneness of this life everywhere, the equal reality of all its moments, thou wilt be ready to treat it all with the reverence that prudence would have thee show to thy own little bit of future life. What prudence in its narrow respectability counseled, thou wilt be ready to do universally. As the prudent man, seeing the reality of his future self, inevitably works for it; so the enlightened man, seeing the reality of all conscious life, realizing that it is no shadow, but fact, at once and inevitably desires, if only for that one moment of insight, to enter into the service of the whole of it. . . . Lift up thy eyes, behold that life, and then turn away and forget it as thou canst; but if thou hast known that, thou hast begun to know thy duty.

## STUDY QUESTIONS

1. Some people call Royce's "Moral Insight" a description of the moral point of view. Do you agree?
2. Is Royce's Insight really another version of the Golden Rule?
3. Royce recommends that we look upon our neighbor in the same way we look upon our future selves. Are you morally considerate of your future self? Should this be a basic moral precept: Do unto others as you would do unto your future self?

# Billy Budd

HERMAN MELVILLE

Herman Melville (1819–1891) is considered one of the great American literary masters. *Billy Budd,* his last novel, was written the year of his death.

*Billy Budd* takes place in 1797 on the British naval ship *Bellipotent,* just following two notorious mutinies at Spithead and Nore. Billy Budd, a sailor on the *Bellipotent,* is gentle and trusting and well loved by the crew. He is also uneducated and has difficulty speaking when he is upset. John Claggart, Billy's superior officer, is a malicious and cruel man who deeply resents Billy's kindly nature and popularity among the men. Billy is unaware of Claggart's

BILLY BUDD From *Billy Budd: Sailor,* eds. Harrison Hayford and Merton M. Sealts, Jr. Reprinted by permission of The University of Chicago Press.

hatred until the moment he brings Billy before the ship's master, Captain Vere, and falsely accuses Billy of plotting a mutiny. Billy, stunned by Claggart's vicious lies and unable to speak, strikes out at him, accidentally killing him by the blow.

Everyone sympathizes with Billy. But Captain Vere (a good man who has been acting strange of late) sets up a military tribunal and, to everyone's surprise, testifies against Billy. In his testimony, Captain Vere acknowledges that Claggart was an evil man, but reminds the tribunal that they are a military court empowered only to judge Billy's deed—not his motives. According to military law, the punishment for striking a superior officer is death by hanging. Just as sailors must obey their superiors and not take the law into their own hands, so the tribunal has an absolute duty to obey the law. Moreover, because there had been several mutinies recently, it was all the more important that military law be enforced. Captain Vere says to the court: "Let not warm hearts betray heads that should be cool." Billy is convicted and hanged.

Critics disagree about the moral implications of Billy Budd. Some see Captain Vere as an evil man whose abstract notion of duty blinded him to true justice and compassion. For others, Vere is a moral hero who rises above sentiment to meet the need for order, authority, and law in human affairs.

Who in the rainbow can draw the line where the violet tint ends and the orange tint begins? Distinctly we see the difference of the colors, but where exactly does the one first blendingly enter into the other? So with sanity and insanity. In pronounced cases there is no question about them. But in some supposed cases, in various degrees supposedly less pronounced, to draw the exact line of demarcation few will undertake, though for a fee becoming considerate some professional experts will. There is nothing namable but that some men will, or undertake to, do it for pay.

Whether Captain Vere, as the surgeon professionally and privately surmised, was really the sudden victim of any degree of aberration, every one must determine for himself by such light as this narrative may afford.

That the unhappy event which has been narrated could not have happened at a worse juncture was but too true. For it was close on the heel of the suppressed insurrections, an aftertime very critical to naval authority, demanding from every English sea commander two qualities not readily interfusable—prudence and rigor. Moreover, there was something crucial in the case.

In the jugglery of circumstances preceding and attending the event on board the *Bellipotent,* and in the light of that martial code whereby it was formally to be judged, innocence and guilt personified in Claggart and Budd in effect changed places. In a legal view the apparent victim of the tragedy was he who had sought to victimize a man blameless; and the indisputable deed of the latter, navally regarded, constituted the most heinous of military crimes. Yet more. The essential right and wrong involved in the matter, the clearer that might be, so much the worse for the responsibility of a loyal sea commander, inasmuch as he was not authorized to determine the matter on that primitive basis.

Small wonder then that the *Bellipotent's* captain, though in general a man of rapid decision, felt that circumspectness not less than promptitude was necessary. Until he could decide upon his course, and in each detail; and not only so, but until the concluding measure was upon the point of being enacted, he deemed it advisable, in view of all the circumstances, to guard as much as possible against publicity. Here he may or may not have erred. Certain it is, however, that subsequently in the confidential talk of more than one or two gun rooms and cabins he was not a little criticized by some officers, a fact imputed by his friends and vehemently by his cousin Jack Denton to professional jealousy of Starry Vere. Some imaginative ground for invidious comment there was. The maintenance of secrecy in the matter, the confining all knowledge of it for a time to the place where the homicide occurred, the quarterdeck cabin; in these particulars lurked some resemblance to the policy adopted in those tragedies of the palace which have occurred more than once in the capital founded by Peter the Barbarian.

The case indeed was such that fain would the *Bellipotent's* captain have deferred taking any action whatever respecting it further than to keep the foretopman a close prisoner till the ship rejoined the squadron and then submitting the matter to the judgment of his admiral.

But a true military officer is in one particular like a true monk. Not with more of self-abnegation will the latter keep his vows of monastic obedience than the former his vows of allegiance to martial duty.

Feeling that unless quick action was taken on it, the deed of the foretopman, so soon as it should be known on the gun decks, would tend to awaken any slumbering embers of the Nore among the crew, a sense of the urgency of the case overruled in Captain Vere every other consideration. But though a conscientious disciplinarian, he was no lover of authority for mere authority's sake. Very far was he from embracing opportunities for monopolizing to himself the perils of moral responsibility, none at least that could properly be referred to an official superior or shared with him by his official equals or even subordinates. So thinking, he was glad it would not be at variance with usage to turn the matter over to a summary court of his own officers, reserving to himself, as the one on whom the ultimate accountability would rest, the right of maintaining a supervision of it, or formally or informally interposing at need. Accordingly a drumhead court was summarily convened, he electing the individuals composing it: the first lieutenant, the captain of marines, and the sailing master.

In associating an officer of marines with the sea lieutenant and the sailing master in a case having to do with a sailor, the commander perhaps deviated from general custom. He was prompted thereto by the circumstance that he took that soldier to be a judicious person, thoughtful, and not altogether incapable of grappling with a difficult case unprecedented in his prior experience. Yet even as to him he was not without some latent misgiving, for withal he was an extremely good-natured man, an enjoyer of his dinner, a sound sleeper, and inclined to obesity—a man who though he would always maintain his manhood in battle might not prove altogether reliable in a moral dilemma involving aught of the tragic. As to the first lieutenant and the sailing master, Captain Vere could not but be aware that though honest natures, of approved gallantry upon occasion, their intelligence was mostly confined to the matter of active seamanship and the fighting demands of their profession.

The court was held in the same cabin where the unfortunate affair had taken place. This cabin, the commander's, embraced the entire area under the poop deck. Aft, and on either side, was a small state-room, the one now temporarily a jail and the other a dead-house, and a yet smaller compartment, leaving a space between expanding forward into a goodly oblong of length coinciding with the ship's beam. A skylight of moderate dimension was overhead, and at each end of the oblong space were two sashed porthole windows easily convertible back into embrasures for short carronades.

All being quickly in readiness, Billy Budd was arraigned, Captain Vere necessarily appearing as the sole witness in the case, and as such temporarily sinking his rank, though singularly maintaining it in a matter apparently trivial, namely, that he testified from the ship's weather side, with that object having caused the court to sit on the lee side. Concisely he narrated all that had led up to the catastrophe, omitting nothing in Claggart's accusation and deposing as to the manner in which the prisoner had received it. At this testimony the three officers glanced with no little surprise at Billy Budd, the last man they would have suspected either of the mutinous design alleged by Claggart or the undeniable deed he himself had done. The first lieutenant, taking judicial primacy and turning toward the prisoner, said, "Captain Vere has spoken. Is it or is it not as Captain Vere says?"

In response came syllables not so much impeded in the utterance as might have been anticipated. They were these: "Captain Vere tells the truth. It is just as Captain Vere says, but it is not as the master-at-arms said. I have eaten the King's bread and I am true to the King."

"I believe you, my man," said the witness, his voice indicating a suppressed emotion not otherwise betrayed.

"God will bless you for that, your honor!" not without stammering said Billy, and all but broke down. But immediately he was recalled to self-control by another question, to which with the same emotional difficulty of utterance he said, "No, there was no malice between us. I never bore malice against the master-at-arms. I am sorry that he is dead. I did not mean to kill him. Could I have used my tongue I would not have struck him. But he foully lied to my face and in presence of my captain, and I had to say something, and I could only say it with a blow, God help me!"

In the impulsive aboveboard manner of the frank one the court saw confirmed all that was implied in words that just previously had perplexed them, coming as they did from the testifier to the tragedy and promptly following Billy's impassioned disclaimer of mutinous intent—Captain Vere's words, "I believe you, my man."

Next it was asked of him whether he knew of or suspected aught savoring of incipient trouble (meaning mutiny, though the explicit term was avoided) going on in any section of the ship's company.

The reply lingered. This was naturally imputed by the court to the same vocal embarrassment which had retarded or obstructed previous answers. But in main it was otherwise here, the question immediately recalling to Billy's mind the interview with the afterguardsman in the forechains. But an innate repugnance to playing a part at all approaching that of an informer against one's own shipmates—the same erring sense of uninstructed honor which had stood in the way of his reporting the matter at the time, though as a loyal man-of-war's man it was incumbent on him, and failure so to do, if charged against him and proven, would have subjected him to the heaviest of penalties; this, with the blind feeling now his that nothing really was being hatched, prevailed with him. When the answer came it was a negative.

"One question more," said the officer of marines, now first speaking and with a troubled earnestness. "You tell us that what the master-at-arms said against you was a lie. Now why should he have so lied, so maliciously lied, since you declare there was no malice between you?"

At that question, unintentionally touching on a spiritual sphere wholly obscure to Billy's thoughts, he was nonplused, evincing a confusion indeed that some observers, such as can readily be imagined, would have construed into involuntary evidence of hidden guilt. Nevertheless, he strove some way to answer, but all at once relinquished the vain endeavor, at the same time turning an appealing glance toward Captain Vere as deeming him his best helper and friend. Captain Vere, who had been seated for a time, rose to his feet, addressing the interrogator. "The question you put to him comes naturally enough. But how can he rightly answer it?—or anybody else, unless indeed it be he who lies within there," designating the compartment where lay the corpse. "But the prone one there will not rise to our summons. In effect, though, as it seems to me, the point you make is hardly material. Quite aside from any conceivable motive actuating the master-at-arms, and irrespective of the provocation to the blow, a martial court must needs in the present case confine its attention to the blow's consequence, which consequence justly is to be deemed not otherwise than as the striker's deed."

This utterance, the full significance of which it was not at all likely that Billy took in, nevertheless caused him to turn a wistful interrogative look toward the speaker, a look in its dumb expressiveness not unlike that which a dog of generous breed might turn upon his master, seeking in his face some elucidation of a previous gesture ambiguous to the canine intelligence. Nor was the same utterance without marked effect upon the three officers, more especially the soldier. Couched in it seemed to them a meaning unanticipated, involving a prejudgment on the speaker's part. It served to augment a mental disturbance previously evident enough.

The soldier once more spoke, in a tone of suggestive dubiety addressing at once his associates and Captain Vere: "Nobody is present—none of the ship's company, I mean—who might shed lateral light, if any is to be had, upon what remains mysterious in this matter."

"That is thoughtfully put," said Captain Vere; "I see your drift. Ay, there is a mystery; but, to use a scriptural phrase, it is a 'mystery of iniquity,' a matter for psychologic theologians to discuss. But what has a military court to do with it? Not to add that for us any possible investigation of it is cut off by the lasting tongue-tie of—him—in yonder," again designating the mortuary stateroom. "The prisoner's deed—with that alone we have to do."

To this, and particularly the closing reiteration, the marine soldier, knowing not how aptly to reply, sadly abstained from saying aught. The first lieutenant, who at the outset had not unnaturally assumed primacy in the court, now overrulingly instructed by a glance from Captain Vere, a glance more effective than words, resumed that primacy. Turning to the prisoner, "Budd," he said, and scarce in equable tones, "Budd, if you have aught further to say for yourself, say it now."

Upon this the young sailor turned another quick glance toward Captain Vere; then, as taking a hint from that aspect, a hint confirming his own instinct that silence was now best, replied to the lieutenant, "I have said all, sir."

The marine—the same who had been the sentinel without the cabin door at the time that the foretopman, followed by the master-at-arms, entered it—he, standing by the sailor throughout these judicial proceedings, was now directed to take him back to the after compartment originally assigned to the prisoner and his custodian. As the twain disappeared from view, the three officers, as partially liberated from some inward constraint associated with Billy's mere presence, simultaneously stirred in their seats. They exchanged looks of troubled indecision, yet feeling that decide they must and without long delay. For Captain Vere, he for the time stood—unconsciously with his back toward them, apparently in one of his absent fits— gazing out from a sashed porthole to windward upon the monotonous blank of the twilight sea. But the court's silence continuing, broken only at moments by brief consultations, in low earnest tones, this served to arouse him and energize him. Turning, he to-and-fro paced the cabin athwart; in the returning ascent to windward climbing the slant deck in the ship's lee roll, without knowing it symbolizing thus in his action a mind resolute to surmount difficulties even if against primitive instincts strong as the wind and the sea. Presently he came to a stand before the three. After scanning their faces he stood less as mustering his thoughts for expression than as one only deliberating how best to put them to well-meaning men not intellectually mature, men with whom it was necessary to demonstrate certain principles that were axioms to himself. Similar impatience as to talking is perhaps one reason that deters some minds from addressing any popular assemblies.

When speak he did, something, both in the substance of what he said and his manner of saying it, showed the influence of unshared studies modifying and tempering the practical training of an active career. This, along with his phraseology, now and then was suggestive of the grounds whereon rested that imputation of a certain pedantry socially alleged against him by certain naval men of wholly practical cast, captains who nevertheless would frankly concede that His Majesty's navy mustered no more efficient officer of their grade than Starry Vere.

What he said was to this effect: "Hitherto I have been but the witness, little more; and I should hardly think now to take another tone, that of your coadjutor for the time, did I not perceive in you— at the crisis too—a troubled hesitancy, proceeding, I doubt not, from the clash of military duty with moral scruple—scruple vitalized by compassion. For the compassion, how can I otherwise than share it? But, mindful of paramount obligations, I strive against scruples that may tend to enervate decision. Not, gentlemen, that I hide from myself that the case is an exceptional one. Speculatively regarded, it well might be referred to a jury of casuists. But for us here, acting not as casuists or moralists, it is a case practical, and under martial law practically to be dealt with.

"But your scruples: do they move as in a dusk? Challenge them. Make them advance and declare themselves. Come now; do they import something like this: If, mindless of palliating circumstances, we are bound to regard the death of the master-at-arms as the prisoner's deed, then does that deed constitute a capital crime whereof the penalty is a mortal one. But in natural justice is nothing but the prisoner's overt act to be considered? How can we adjudge to summary and shameful death a fellow creature innocent before God, and whom we feel to be so?—Does that state it aright? You sign sad assent. Well, I too feel that, the full force of that. It is Nature. But do these buttons that we wear attest that our allegiance is to Nature? No, to the King. Though the ocean, which is inviolate Nature primeval, though this be the element where we move and have our being as sailors, yet as the King's officers lies our duty in a sphere correspondingly natural? So little is that true, that in receiving our commissions we in the most important regards ceased to be natural free agents. When war is declared are we the commissioned fighters previously consulted? We fight at command. If our judgments approve the war, that is but coincidence. So in other particulars. So now. For suppose condemnation to follow these present proceedings. Would it be so much we ourselves that would condemn as it would be martial law operating through us? For that law and the rigor of it, we are not responsible. Our vowed responsibility is in this: That however pitilessly that law may operate in any instances, we nevertheless adhere to it and administer it.

"But the exceptional in the matter moves the hearts within you. Even so too is mine moved. But let not warm hearts betray heads that should be cool. Ashore in a criminal case, will an upright judge allow himself off the bench to be waylaid by some tender kinswoman of the accused seeking to touch him with her tearful plea? Well, the heart here, sometimes the feminine in man, is as that piteous woman, and hard though it be, she must here be ruled out."

He paused, earnestly studying them for a moment; then resumed.

"But something in your aspect seems to urge that it is not solely the heart that moves in you, but also the conscience, the private conscience. But tell me whether or not, occupying the position we

do, private conscience should not yield to that imperial one formulated in the mode under which alone we officially proceed?"

Here the three men moved in their seats, less convinced than agitated by the course of an argument troubling but the more the spon-
taneous conflict within.

Perceiving which, the speaker paused for a moment; then abruptly
changing his tone, went on.

"To steady us a bit, let us recur to the facts.—In wartime at sea a
man-of-war's man strikes his superior in grade, and the blow kills.
Apart from its effect the blow itself is, according to the Articles of
War, a capital crime, Furthermore————"

"Ay, sir," emotionally broke in the officer of marines, "in one sense
it was. But surely Budd purposed neither mutiny nor homicide."

"Surely not, my good man. And before a court less arbitrary and
more merciful than a martial one, that plea would largely extenuate.
At the Last Assizes it shall acquit. But how here? We proceed under
the law of the Mutiny Act. In feature no child can resemble his father
more than that Act resembles in spirit the thing from which it derives—War. In His Majesty's service—in this ship, indeed—there
are Englishmen forced to fight for the King against their will.
Against their conscience, for aught we know. Though as their fellow
creatures some of us may appreciate their position, yet as navy officers what reck we of it? Still less recks the enemy. Our impressed
men he would fain cut down in the same swath with our volunteers.
As regards the enemy's naval conscripts, some of whom may even
share our own abhorrence of the regicidal French Directory, it is the
same on our side. War looks but to the frontage, the appearance. And
the Mutiny Act, War's child, takes after the father. Budd's intent or
non-intent is nothing to the purpose.

"But while, put to it by those anxieties in you which I cannot but
respect, I only repeat myself—while thus strangely we prolong proceedings that should be summary—the enemy may be sighted and
an engagement result. We must do; and one of two things must we
do—condemn or let go."

"Can we not convict and yet mitigate the penalty?" asked the
sailing master, here speaking, and falteringly, for the first.

"Gentlemen, were that clearly lawful for us under the circumstances, consider the consequences of such clemency. The people"
(meaning the ship's company) "have native sense; most of them are

familiar with our naval usage and tradition; and how would they take it? Even could you explain to them—which our official position forbids—they, long molded by arbitrary discipline, have not that kind of intelligent responsiveness that might qualify them to comprehend and discriminate. No, to the people the foretopman's deed, however it be worded in the announcement, will be plain homicide committed in a flagrant act of mutiny. What penalty for that should follow, they know. But it does not follow. *Why?* they will ruminate. You know what sailors are. Will they not revert to the recent outbreak at the Nore? Ay. They know the well-founded alarm—the panic it struck throughout England. Your clement sentence they would account pusillanimous. They would think that we flinch, that we are afraid of them—afraid of practicing a lawful rigor singularly demanded at this juncture, lest it should provoke new troubles. What shame to us such a conjecture on their part, and how deadly to discipline. You see then, whither, prompted by duty and the law, I steadfastly drive. But I beseech you, my friends, do not take me amiss. I feel as you do for this unfortunate boy. But did he know our hearts, I take him to be of that generous nature that he would feel even for us on whom this military necessity so heavy a compulsion is laid."

With that, crossing the deck he resumed his place by the sashed porthole, tacitly leaving the three to come to a decision. On the cabin's opposite side the troubled court sat silent. Loyal lieges, plain and practical, though at bottom they dissented from some points Captain Vere had put to them, they were without the faculty, hardly had the inclination, to gainsay one whom they felt to be an earnest man, one too not less their superior in mind than in naval rank. But it is not improbable that even such of his words as were not without influence over them, less came home to them than his closing appeal to their instinct as sea officers: in the forethought he threw out as to the practical consequences to discipline, considering the unconfirmed tone of the fleet at the time, should a man-of-war's man's violent killing at sea of a superior in grade be allowed to pass for aught else than a capital crime demanding prompt infliction of the penalty.

Not unlikely they were brought to something more or less akin to that harassed frame of mind which in the year 1842 actuated the commander of the U.S. brig-of-war *Somers* to resolve, under the so-called Articles of War, Articles modeled upon the English Mutiny

Act, to resolve upon the execution at sea of a midshipman and two sailors as mutineers designing the seizure of the brig. Which resolution was carried out though in a time of peace and within not many days' sail of home. An act vindicated by a naval court of inquiry subsequently convened ashore. History, and here cited without comment. True, the circumstances on board the *Somers* were different from those on board the *Bellipotent*. But the urgency felt, well-warranted or otherwise, was much the same.

Says a writer whom few know, "Forty years after a battle it is easy for a noncombatant to reason about how it ought to have been fought. It is another thing personally and under fire to have to direct the fighting while involved in the obscuring smoke of it. Much so with respect to other emergencies involving considerations both practical and moral, and when it is imperative promptly to act. The greater the fog the more it imperils the steamer, and speed is put on though at the hazard of running somebody down. Little ween the snug card players in the cabin of the responsibilities of the sleepless man on the bridge."

In brief, Billy Budd was formally convicted and sentenced to be hung at the yardarm in the early morning watch, it being now night. Otherwise, as is customary in such cases, the sentence would forthwith have been carried out. In wartime on the field or in the fleet, a mortal punishment decreed by a drumhead court—on the field sometimes decreed by but a nod from the general—follows without delay on the heel of conviction, without appeal.

**STUDY QUESTIONS**

1. Billy never intended to kill Claggart. Is it fair to hold people responsible for the unforeseen consequences of their acts?

2. Write a defense of Captain Vere's decision to argue for Billy's conviction. Next write a critique of the decision. Which do you find more convincing?

3. Apply Jonathan Bennett's analysis of duty and sympathy (in "The Conscience of Huckleberry Finn") to *Billy Budd*. Do you agree with Bennett's analysis?

4. Do you agree with Captain Vere that news of Billy's acquittal really could undermine military discipline throughout the

British navy? Wouldn't other British sailors understand that
Billy Budd's was an exceptional case?
5.  Vere distinguishes between military duty and moral duty.
    Should the latter always take priority?

# Beyond Good and Evil

## FRIEDRICH NIETZSCHE

Friedrich Nietzsche (1844–1900) is considered the most
bizarre of the great philosophers. A small, sickly intellectual who lived with his mother, sister, and maiden aunts,
Nietzsche despised women and idolized classical warriors
and conquerors. He became insane just before his death.
Among his many works are *The Birth of Tragedy* (1872),
*Beyond Good and Evil* (1886), *Thus Spake Zarathustra*
(1891), and *The Gay Science* (1882).

Friedrich Nietzsche was contemptuous of the Judeo-
Christian ethic, an ethic he thought suitable for the low-
liest classes of mankind—"the cowardly, the timid and
the insignificant." Although in an aristocratic society
made up entirely of superior beings the ideal of equality
might work, in an ordinary world it bestowed power on
the weak and diminished the strong. A dynamic and
healthy society must allow its superior and noble individuals to prevail; it must give full expression to the "will to
power"—Nietzsche's famous phrase that describes an innate drive in all living things toward domination and
exploitation. Nietzsche deplores the "slave morality" that
defines good and evil in terms of what alleviates the misery of inferior beings—a morality that favors patience,

BEYOND GOOD AND EVIL Translated by Helen Zimmern. Reprinted by permission of George Allen
& Unwin (Publishers) Ltd.

humility, sympathy, and friendliness. Nietzsche defends
the "master morality" that honors pride, vanity, power,
and "dreadfulness."

To refrain mutually from injury, from violence, from exploitation,
and put one's will on a par with that of others: this may result in a
certain rough sense in good conduct among individuals when the
necessary conditions are given (namely, the actual similarity of the
individuals in amount of force and degree of worth, and their co-
relation within one organisation). As soon, however, as one wished
to take this principle more generally, and if possible even as *the fundamental principle of society,* it would immediately disclose what it
really is—namely, a Will to the *denial* of life, a principle of dissolution
and decay. Here one must think profoundly to the very basis and
resist all sentimental weakness: life itself is *essentially* appropriation,
injury, conquest of the strange and weak, suppression, severity, ob-
trusion of peculiar forms, incorporation, and at the least, putting it
mildest, exploitation;—but why should one for ever use precisely
these words on which for ages a disparaging purpose has been
stamped? Even the organisation within which, as was previously
supposed, the individuals treat each other as equal—it takes place in
every healthy aristocracy—must itself, if it be a living and not a
dying organisation, do all that towards other bodies, which the individuals within it refrain from doing to each other: it will have to
be the incarnated Will to Power, it will endeavour to grow, to gain
ground, attract to itself and acquire ascendency—not owing to any
morality or immorality, but because it *lives,* and because life *is* precisely Will to Power. On no point, however, is the ordinary consciousness of Europeans more unwilling to be corrected than on this
matter; people now rave everywhere, even under the guise of science,
about coming conditions of society in which "the exploiting character" is to be absent:—that sounds to my ears as if they promised to
invent a mode of life which should refrain from all organic functions.
"Exploitation" does not belong to a depraved, or imperfect and
primitive society: it belongs to the *nature* of the living being as a
primary organic function; it is a consequence of the intrinsic Will to
Power, which is precisely the Will to Life.—Granting that as a theory
this is a novelty—as a reality it is the *fundamental fact* of all history:
let us be so far honest towards ourselves!

72

In a tour through the many finer and coarser moralities which have hitherto prevailed or still prevail on the earth, I found certain traits recurring regularly together, and connected with one another, until finally two primary types revealed themselves to me, and a radical distinction was brought to light. There is *master-morality* and *slave-morality;*—I would at once add, however, that in all higher and mixed civilisations, there are also attempts at the reconciliation of the two moralities; but one finds still oftener the confusion and mutual misunderstanding of them, indeed, sometimes their close juxtaposition—even in the same man, within one soul. The distinctions of moral values have either originated in a ruling caste, pleasantly conscious of being different from the ruled—or among the ruled class, the slaves and dependents of all sorts. In the first case, when it is the rulers who determine the conception "good," it is the exalted, proud disposition which is regarded as the distinguishing feature, and that which determines the order of rank. The noble type of man separates from himself the beings in whom the opposite of this exalted, proud disposition displays itself: he despises them. Let it at once be noted that in this first kind of morality the antithesis "good" and "bad" means practically the same as "noble" and "despicable";—the antithesis "good" and "*evil*" is of a different origin. The cowardly, the timid, the insignificant, and those thinking merely of narrow utility are despised; moreover, also, the distrustful, with their constrained glances, the self-abasing, the dog-like kind of men who let themselves be abused, the mendicant flatterers and above all the liars:—it is a fundamental belief of all aristocrats that the common people are untruthful. "We truthful ones"—the nobility in ancient Greece called themselves. It is obvious that everywhere the designations of moral value were at first applied to *men,* and were only derivatively and at a later period applied to *actions;* it is a gross mistake, therefore, when historians of morals start with questions like, "Why have sympathetic actions been praised?" The noble type of man regards *himself* as a determiner of values; he does not require to be approved of; he passes the judgment: "What is injurious to me is injurious in itself"; he knows that it is he himself only who confers honour on things; he is a *creator of values.* He honours whatever he recognises in himself: such morality is self-glorification. In the foreground there is the feeling of plenitude, of power, which seeks to overflow, the happiness of high tension, the consciousness of a wealth which would fain give and bestow:—the noble man also helps the unfortunate, but not—or scarcely—out of pity, but rather from an impulse generated by the super-abundance of power. The noble man honours in himself the powerful one, him also who has power over himself, who knows how to speak and how to keep silence, who takes pleasure in subjecting himself to severity and hardness, and has reverence for all that is severe and hard. "Wotan placed a hard heart in my breast," says an old Scandinavian Saga: it is thus rightly expressed from the soul of a proud Viking. Such a type of man is even proud of *not* being made for sympathy; the hero of the Saga therefore adds warningly: "He who has not a hard heart when young, will never have one." The noble and brave who think thus are the furthest removed from the morality which sees precisely in sympathy, or in acting for the good of others, or in disinterestedness, the characteristic of the moral; faith in oneself, pride in oneself, a radical enmity and irony towards "self-lessness," belong as definitely to noble morality, as do a careless scorn and precaution in presence of sympathy and the "warm heart."—It is the powerful who *know* how to honour, it is their art, their domain for invention. The profound reverence for age and for tradition—all law rests on this double reverence,—the belief and prejudice in favour of ancestors and unfavourable to newcomers, is typical in the morality of the powerful; and if, reversely, men of "modern ideas" believe almost instinctively in "progress" and the "future," and are more and more lacking in respect for old age, the ignoble origin of these "ideas" has complacently betrayed itself thereby. A morality of the ruling class, however, is more especially foreign and irritating to present-day taste in the sternness of its principle that one has duties only to one's equals; that one may act towards beings of a lower rank, towards all that is foreign, just as seems good to one, or "as the heart desires," and in any case "beyond good and evil": it is here that sympathy and similar sentiments can have a place. The ability and obligation to exercise prolonged gratitude and prolonged revenge—both only within the circle of equals,—artfulness in retaliation, effete refinement of the idea in friendship, a certain necessity to have enemies (as outlets for the emotions of envy, quarrelsomeness, arrogance—in fact, in order to be a good *friend*): all these are typical characteristics of the noble morality, which, as has been pointed out, is not the morality of "modern ideas," and is therefore at present difficult to realise, and also to unearth and disclose.—It is otherwise with the second type of morality, *slave-morality*. Supposing that the abused, the oppressed, the suffering, the unemancipated, the weary, and those uncertain of themselves, should moralise, what will be the common element in their moral estimates? Probably a pessimistic suspicion with regard to the entire situation of man will find expression, perhaps a condemnation of man, together with his situation. The slave has an unfavourable eye for the virtues of the powerful; he has a scepticism and distrust, a *refinement* of distrust of everything "good" that is there honoured—he would fain persuade himself that the very happiness there is not genuine. On the other hand, *those* qualities which serve to alleviate the existence of sufferers are brought into prominence and flooded with light; it is here that sympathy, the kind, helping hand, the warm heart, patience, diligence, humility, and friendliness attain to honour; for here these are the most useful qualities, and almost the only means of supporting the burden of existence. Slave-morality is essentially the morality of utility. Here is the seat of the origin of the famous antithesis "good" and "evil":— power and dangerousness are assumed to reside in the evil, a certain dreadfulness, subtlety, and strength, which do not admit of being despised. According to slave-morality, therefore, the "evil" man arouses fear; according to master-morality, it is precisely the "good" man who arouses fear and seeks to arouse it, while the bad man is regarded as the despicable being. The contrast attains its maximum when, in accordance with the logical consequences of slave-morality, a shade of depreciation—it may be slight and well-intentioned—at last attaches itself to the "good" man of this morality; because, according to the servile mode of thought, the good man must in any case be the *safe* man: he is good-natured, easily deceived, perhaps a little stupid, *un bonhomme.*

. . .

I regard Christianity as the most fatal and seductive lie that has ever yet existed—as the greatest and most *impious lie:* I can discern the last sprouts and branches of its ideal beneath every form of disguise, I decline to enter into any compromise or false position in reference to it—I urge people to declare open war with it.

The *morality of paltry people* as the measure of all things: this is the most repugnant kind of degeneracy that civilisation has ever yet brought into existence. And this *kind of ideal* is hanging still, under the name of "God," over men's heads!!

However modest one's demands may be concerning intellectual cleanliness, when one touches the New Testament one cannot help experiencing a sort of inexpressible feeling of discomfort; for the unbounded cheek with which the least qualified people will have their say in its pages, in regard to the greatest problems of existence, and claim to sit in judgment on such matters, exceeds all limits. The impudent levity with which the most unwieldy problems are spoken of here (life, the world, God, the purpose of life), as if they were not problems at all, but the most simple things which these little bigots *know all about!!!* . . .

The *law,* which is the fundamentally realistic formula of certain self-preservative measures of a community, forbids certain actions that have a definite tendency to jeopardise the welfare of that community: it does *not* forbid the attitude of mind which gives rise to these actions—for in the pursuit of other ends the community requires these forbidden actions, namely, when it is a matter of opposing its *enemies*. The moral idealist now steps forward and says: "God sees into men's hearts: the action itself counts for nothing; the reprehensible attitude of mind from which it proceeds must be extirpated . . ." In normal conditions men laugh at such things; it is only in exceptional cases, when a community lives *quite* beyond the need of waging war in order to maintain itself, that an ear is lent to such things. Any attitude of mind is abandoned, the utility of which cannot be conceived.

This was the case, for example, when Buddha appeared among a people that was both peacable and afflicted with great intellectual weariness.

This was also the case in regard to the first Christian community (as also the Jewish), the primary condition of which was the absolutely *unpolitical* Jewish society. Christianity could grow only upon the soil of Judaism—that is to say, among a people that had already renounced the political life, and which led a sort of parasitic existence within the Roman sphere of government. Christianity goes a step *further:* it allows men to "emasculate" themselves even more; the circumstances actually favour their doing so.—*Nature* is *expelled* from morality when it is said, "Love ye your enemies": for *Nature's* injunction, "Ye shall *love* your neighbour and *hate* your enemy," has now become senseless in the law (in instinct); now, even *the love a man feels for his neighbour* must first be based upon something (*a sort of love of God*). *God* is introduced everywhere, and *utility* is withdrawn; the natural *origin* of morality is denied everywhere: the *veneration of Nature*, which lies in *acknowledging a natural morality*, is *destroyed* to the roots . . .

What is it I protest against? That people should regard this paltry and peaceful mediocrity, this spiritual equilibrium which knows nothing of the fine impulses of great accumulations of strength, as something high, or possibly as the standard of all things.

### STUDY QUESTIONS

1. In your own words characterize what Nietzsche calls the "slave morality" and the "master morality."
2. Nietzsche believes that exploitation and domination of the weak by the strong is a "fundamental fact of all history." Assuming this belief is true, would you consider this an argument for the validity of the master morality? Might one not argue instead that we should curb our aggressive impulses and protect the weak?
3. How much truth do you find in Nietzsche's characterization of the Judeo-Christian ethic as a slave morality? Is he right when he says that it is "the morality of paltry people"?
4. Organize a debate between Josiah Royce and Friedrich Nietzsche on the validity of the Golden Rule.
5. Nietzsche has sometimes been accused of inspiring Nazism. Does anything in the selection support such an accusation?
6. How would Nietzsche react to Hallie's account of what transpired in Le Chambon during World War II?

### SUGGESTED READINGS

Arendt, Hannah. *Eichmann in Jerusalem: A Report on the Banality of Evil*. New York: Viking Press, 1965.

Douglass, Frederick. *Life and Times of Frederick Douglass: Written by Himself*. New York: Collier Press, 1962.

Hallie, Philip. *Lest Innocent Blood Be Shed*. New York: Harper and Row, 1979.

Midgley, Mary. *Wickedness: A Philosophical Essay*. Boston: Routledge and Kegan Paul, 1984.

Milo, Richard D. *Immorality*. Princeton: Princeton University Press, 1984.

Nietzsche, Friedrich. *Beyond Good and Evil*. Chicago: Henry Regnery, 1965.

Rosenthal, Abigail. *A Good Look at Evil*. Philadelphia: Temple University Press, 1988.

Taylor, Richard. *Good and Evil*. Buffalo, NY: Prometheus Press, 1970.

Tiger, Lionel. *The Manufacture of Evil*. New York: Harper and Row, 1987.

*Chapter Two*

# MORAL DOCTRINES AND MORAL THEORIES

In this chapter we begin by presenting several sacred texts of the Judeo-Christian tradition that are central to the moral heritage of the Western world. The Ten Commandments, the Psalms, the Sermon on the Mount, and the Parable of the Good Samaritan have inspired and guided people for centuries. The view that our moral obligations come directly from God is known as the Divine Command theory of morality. A number of philosophers have sought alternative accounts of morality. Some are atheists and, of course, reject out of hand any theory that presupposes a deity; others, though believers, look for an account of right and wrong that does not rely on revelation. Plato, in his dialogue *The Euthyphro,* first asked a question that often arises in connection with the Divine Command theory: Are the actions that God decrees good only because God approves of them, or does He approve of them because they are good? Might God just as easily decree that we be cruel and refrain from kindness, or do the divine decrees conform to independently valid criteria of good and evil?

Perhaps the majority of moral philosophers believe that morality is independently valid. And some theologians move between the horns of the dilemma, maintaining that God's will and objective good are coincident. Much of moral philosophy since Plato consists of attempts to formulate objective criteria for what is right and good.

Two of the most influential alternatives to the Divine Command theory are utilitarianism and Kantianism. Utilitarianism was developed by British philosophers Jeremy Bentham (1748–1832) and John Stuart Mill (1806–1873). For the utilitarian, morally good actions are actions that increase the happiness of conscious beings. According to Mill's Greatest Happiness Principle, "Actions are right in proportion as they tend to promote happiness, wrong as they tend to produce the reverse of happiness." (And, says Mill, God's decrees are good precisely because obedience to them increases happiness; that is *why* God decreed them.) Mill and Bentham thought of the principle of utility as a moral yardstick. Just as two people who disagree over the height of a ceiling can settle the matter with a ruler, so two people who disagree over the rightness of an action need only subject it to the test of utility: Will it increase or diminish happiness?

Though many contemporary philosophers favor utilitarianism over other moral theories (indeed, one philosopher recently remarked that utilitarians constitute a silent majority among professional philosophers), they generally acknowledge it to be seriously flawed. Suppose we could greatly increase human happiness and diminish misery by occasionally, and perhaps secretly, abducting derelicts from city streets for use in fatal but urgent medical experiments. If utilitarian considerations were decisive, this practice might well be justifiable, even desirable. Yet it is surely wrong. Such a case suggests that we cannot always explain good and bad simply in terms of increasing or decreasing overall happiness.

Many philosophers reject utilitarianism in favor of Kantianism. Eighteenth-century philosopher Immanuel Kant (1724–1804) sought the foundations of morality in the human capacity to act rationally. A rational being is free to act out of principle and to refrain from acting from mere impulse or the desire for pleasure. According to Kant, the proper exercise of reason reveals to us our moral duties. It is not, he says, the *consequences* of an action (its "utility" as Bentham claims) that determine its moral character, but the principle on which the action is based. As rational creatures we must be consistent and objective. So, says Kant, we must always ask ourselves whether or not we base an action on a principle (Kant calls it a "maxim") that we consistently want to see adopted as a universal law governing the behavior of all rational beings. A utilitarian might justify an occasional lie that has pleasant consequences. For Kant this is unacceptable: Reason dictates honesty as a *universal* principle. Any deception, however one might try to justify it, is for Kant an affront to the dignity of the deceived. Principled behavior invariably respects oneself and others; it brooks no exceptions.

Kantianism is attractive for its emphasis on conscientiousness and human dignity, but, like utilitarianism, it faces difficulties. Acting on principle without regard for the consequences does not always seem right. According to Kant, if a murderer comes to your door demanding to know the whereabouts of an intended victim who is hiding in your house, you must not lie to him no matter what the consequences. Utilitarians criticize Kantians for their readiness to sacrifice human happiness for the sake of principles; on their side, Kantians object to utilitarians for failing to give moral principle a central place.

The Kantian willingness to sacrifice utility when a question of personal dignity is at stake shows up in Bernard Williams' criticism of J. J. C. Smart's contemporary version of utilitarianism. Williams is impatient with a doctrine that judges the moral worth of an action by referring to an impersonal calculus of pleasures and pains. On the other hand, others criticize Kant for dismissing consequences whenever a question of principle is at stake. James Rachels rejects Kant's view that one ought never to lie no matter how much misery telling the truth could cause. He recommends a modification of Kant's formulation of the categorical imperative that would avoid such implausible consequences.

Because Kant and Bentham differ in important ways, their fundamental similarities are easy to ignore. Both hold that morality is the same for everyone everywhere; thus both Bentham and Kant are prepared to judge exotic practices in other cultures by the same standards they judge practices of their own societies. In particular, both would condemn the practice that Mary Midgley cites in her essay "Trying Out One's New Sword," in which a Samurai warrior determines the effectiveness of his sword by seeing how cleanly it slices in two an unsuspecting passerby. And both theories are in keeping with the spirit of the sacred texts that begin this chapter. Indeed, both Kantians and utilitarians claim that their theories merely elaborate the Golden Rule.

Kantianism and Utilitarianism are mainstream ethical theories whose influence today is undiminished in the Anglo-Saxon world. A third ethical theory, more popular in the community at large than among moral theorists, is known as ethical relativism. The ethical relativist claims that there are no objective criteria or standards for determining right and wrong. Each society has its own ethic, just as it has its own rules of etiquette and style of dress. Ethical relativism became popular in the nineteenth century when social scientists traveled to exotic regions and discovered a wide variety of moral practices. According to the ethical relativist, the moral precepts found in the Bible are no more or less correct than the quite different moral precepts found in the sacred texts of other societies. Anthropologist Ruth Benedict (1887–1948) argues this position in "A Defense of Moral Relativism"; personal experiences as a field anthropologist convinced her that morals, like rules of etiquette, are just a matter of group practice. Thus, Benedict says, "Mankind has always preferred to say, 'It is morally good,' rather than 'It is habitual' . . . But historically the two phrases are synonymous."

Ethical relativism is a tempting doctrine because it appeals to our desire to be tolerant of other societies. But it has not found much favor among professional philosophers. John Hospers' article, "The Problem with Relativism," crisply presents many of the objections that can be raised against ethical relativism. Mary Midgley makes the interesting point in "Trying Out One's New Sword" that if each society is a distinct unit and not to be judged except on its own terms, then not only are we unable to criticize another society for practices we as outsiders find morally objectionable, but we are, by the same token, unable to praise that society for those things that we find admirable.

Several philosophers point out that those who adopt ethical relativism because they wish to be respectful of other cultures cannot be selective in what they choose to tolerate. For example, they must not only tolerate the Aztecs, who practiced human sacrifice in their religious service, but also the mercenaries and colonialists whose moral code permitted them to exterminate or enslave such "heathens." Tolerance of exotic practices is double-edged in another respect as well. On one hand, it is a manifestation of a sophisticated appreciation of difference; on the other hand, our tolerance of violence or cruelty in other cultures verges on callousness toward the sufferings of their unfortunate victims. And, generally, as long as the perpetrators of what we look upon as a crime can point out that their behavior is acceptable and customary on "their own island," we cannot say clearly that an honest and consistent ethical relativist has grounds to condemn them.

Finally, as the United Nations Declaration on Human Rights makes plain, ethical relativism is not a doctrine believed in by the majority of nations. The Declaration firmly asserts that all persons, regardless of cultural background or social status, have a number of the same rights. And while its provisions are not enforced, their acceptance by the United Nations General Assembly attests to the entrenched popularity of the belief that some fundamental ethical principles do apply universally.

# The Judeo-Christian Tradition

The Ten Commandments (Exodus 20:1–17) and the First, Fifteenth, and Twenty-third Psalms are from the Old Testament. The Sermon on the Mount (Luke 6:17–49) and the parable of the good Samaritan (Luke 10:25–37) are from the New Testament. The two testaments comprehend 1,000 years of Judeo-Christian history. They do not constitute a single ethical system. But they powerfully express moral ideals of incalculable authority and influence.

## The Ten Commandments

Then God delivered all these commandments:

"I, the LORD, am your God, who brought you out of the land of Egypt, that place of slavery. You shall not have other gods besides me. You shall not carve idols for yourselves in the shape of anything in the sky above or on the earth below or in the waters beneath the earth; you shall not bow down before them or worship them. For I, the LORD, your God, am a jealous God, inflicting punishment for their fathers' wickedness on the children of those who hate me, down to the third and fourth generation; but bestowing mercy down to the thousandth generation, on the children of those who love me and keep my commandments.

"You shall not take the name of the LORD, your God, in vain. For the LORD will not leave unpunished him who takes his name in vain.

"Remember to keep holy the sabbath day. Six days you may labor and do all your work, but the seventh day is the sabbath of the LORD, your God. No work may be done then either by you, or your son or daughter, or your male or female slave, or your beast, or by the alien who lives with you. In six days the LORD made the heavens and the earth, the sea and all that is in them; but on the seventh day he rested. That is why the LORD has blessed the sabbath day and made it holy.

"Honor your father and your mother, that you may have a long life in the land which the LORD, your God, is giving you.

"You shall not kill.

"You shall not commit adultery.

"You shall not steal.

"You shall not bear false witness against your neighbor.

"You shall not covet your neighbor's house. You shall not covet your neighbor's wife, nor his male or female slave, nor his ox or ass, nor anything else that belongs to him."

## Psalm 1

*True Happiness*

### I

Happy the man who follows not
  the counsel of the wicked
Nor walks in the way of sinners,
  nor sits in the company of the
    insolent,
But delights in the law of the LORD
  and meditates on his law day and
    night.
He is like a tree
  planted near running water,
That yields its fruit in due season,
  and whose leaves never fade.
  [Whatever he does, prospers.]

## II

Not so the wicked, not so;
　　they are like chaff which the wind
　　　drives away.
Therefore in judgment the wicked
　　　shall not stand,
　　nor shall sinners, in the assembly of
　　　the just.
For the LORD watches over the way
　　　of the just,
　　but the way of the wicked vanishes.

## Psalm 15

*The Guest of God*

A psalm of David.

## I

O LORD, who shall sojourn in your
　　　tent?
Who shall dwell on your holy
　　　mountain?

## II

He who walks blamelessly and does
　　　justice;
　　who thinks the truth in his heart
　　and slanders not with his tongue;
Who harms not his fellow man,
　　　nor takes up a reproach against his
　　　　neighbor;
By whom the reprobate is despised,
　　while he honors those who fear the
　　　LORD;
Who, though it be to his loss, changes
　　　not his pledged word;
　　who lends not his money at usury
　　and accepts not bribe against the
　　　innocent.

## Psalm 23

*The Lord, Shepherd and Host*

A psalm of David.

### I

The LORD is my shepherd; I shall not
    want
  In verdant pastures he gives me
    repose;
Beside restful waters he leads me;
  he refreshes my soul.
He guides me in right paths
  for his name's sake.
Even though I walk in the dark valley
  I fear no evil; for you are at my
    side
With your rod and your staff
  that give me courage.

### II

You spread the table before me
  in the sight of my foes;
You anoint my head with oil;
  my cup overflows.
Only goodness and kindness follow
    me
  all the days of my life;
And I shall dwell in the house of the
  LORD
  for years to come.

## The Sermon on the Mount

Coming down the mountain with them, he stopped at a level stretch
where there were many of his disciples; a large crowd of people was
with them from all Judea and Jerusalem and the coast of Tyre and
Sidon, people who came to hear him and be healed of their diseases.
Those who were troubled with unclean spirits were cured; indeed,

the whole crowd was trying to touch him because power went out from him which cured all.

Then, raising his eyes to his disciples, he said:

"Blest are you poor; the reign of God is yours.
Blest are you who hunger; you shall be filled.
Blest are you who are weeping; you shall laugh.

Blest shall you be when men hate you, when they ostracize you and insult you and proscribe your name as evil because of the Son of Man. On the day they do so, rejoice and exult, for your reward shall be great in heaven. Thus it was that their fathers treated the prophets.

"But woe to you rich, for your consolation is now.
Woe to you who are full; you shall go hungry.
Woe to you who laugh now; you shall weep in your grief.

"Woe to you when all speak well of you. Their fathers treated the false prophets in just this way.

*Love of One's Enemy*

"To you who hear me, I say: Love your enemies, do good to those who hate you; bless those who curse you and pray for those who maltreat you. When someone slaps you on one cheek, turn and give him the other; when someone takes your coat, let him have your shirt as well. Give to all who beg from you. When a man takes what is yours, do not demand it back. Do to others what you would have them do to you. If you love those who love you, what credit is that to you? Even sinners love those who love them. If you do good to those who do good to you, how can you claim any credit? Sinners do as much. If you lend to those from whom you expect repayment, what merit is there in it for you? Even sinners lend to sinners, expecting to be repaid in full.

"Love your enemy and do good; lend without expecting repayment. Then will your recompense be great. You will rightly be called sons of the Most High, since he himself is good to the ungrateful and the wicked.

"Be compassionate, as your Father is compassionate. Do not judge, and you will not be judged. Do not condemn, and you will not be condemned. Pardon, and you shall be pardoned. Give, and it shall be given to you. Good measure pressed down, shaken together, running over, will they pour into the fold of your garment. For the measure you measure with will be measured back to you."

He also used images in speaking to them: "Can a blind man act as guide to a blind man? Will they not both fall into a ditch? A student is not above his teacher; but every student when he has finished his studies will be on a par with his teacher.

"Why look at the speck in your brother's eye when you miss the plank in your own? How can you say to your brother, 'Brother, let me remove the speck from your eye,' yet fail yourself to see the plank lodged in your own? Hypocrite, remove the plank from your own eye first; then you will see clearly enough to remove the speck from your brother's eye.

"A good tree does not produce decayed fruit any more than a decayed tree produces good fruit. Each tree is known by its yield. Figs are not taken from thornbushes, nor grapes picked from brambles. A good man produces goodness from the good in his heart; an evil man produces evil out of his store of evil. Each man speaks from his heart's abundance. Why do you call me 'Lord, Lord,' and not put into practice what I teach you? Any man who desires to come to me will hear my words and put them into practice. I will show you with whom he is to be compared. He may be likened to the man who, in building a house, dug deeply and laid the foundation on a rock. When the floods came the torrent rushed in on that house, but failed to shake it because of its solid foundation. On the other hand, anyone who has heard my words but not put them into practice is like the man who built his house on the ground without any foundation. When the torrent rushed upon it, it immediately fell in and was completely destroyed."

## The Good Samaritan

On one occasion a lawyer stood up to pose him this problem: "Teacher, what must I do to inherit everlasting life?"

Jesus answered him: "What is written in the law? How do you read it?" He replied:

> "You shall love the Lord your God
> with all your heart,
> with all your soul,
> with all your strength,

and with all your mind;
and your neighbor as yourself."

Jesus said, "You have answered correctly. Do this and you shall live." But because he wished to justify himself he said to Jesus, "And who is my neighbor?" Jesus replied: "There was a man going down from Jerusalem to Jericho who fell prey to robbers. They stripped him, beat him, and then went off leaving him half-dead. A priest happened to be going down the same road; he saw him but continued on. Likewise there was a Levite who came the same way; he saw him and went on. But a Samaritan who was journeying along came on him and was moved to pity at the sight. He approached him and dressed his wounds, pouring in oil and wine. He then hoisted him on his own beast and brought him to an inn, where he cared for him. The next day he took out two silver pieces and gave them to the innkeeper with the request: 'Look after him, and if there is any further expense I will repay you on my way back.'

"Which of these three, in your opinion, was neighbor to the man who fell in with the robbers?" The answer came. "The one who treated him with compassion." Jesus said to him, "Then go and do the same."

**STUDY QUESTIONS**

1. Several of the Ten Commandments are theological. What, in your opinion, is the relationship between a belief in God and divine law and a belief in moral laws such as prohibition of theft and murder? What are the advantages or disadvantages of a moral theory not founded on religious beliefs?

2. Draw up and justify a list of commandments that have no theological content. Be succinct.

3. What moral ideals does Psalm 1 express? What rewards adhere to them? Do you believe that the descriptions of the contrasting lives of just and unjust individuals are substantially correct?

4. What principles of personal morality are prominent in the Fifteenth Psalm? Do you believe the principles are binding on yourself or would you wish to revise them? Explain and justify.

5. A sermon often contains hyperbole. Do you believe that the ideal of loving one's enemy and doing good to those who hate us is

seriously and literally intended? If it is not literal but rhetorical, what was the point of stating it?

6. The Sermon on the Mount exhorts us to be compassionate "as your Father is compassionate." We also find this theme of *imitatio dei* in the Old Testament. This suggests that one approach to the moral life is to conceive of ourselves as striving to imitate a perfect and divine being. Do you think that this is a helpful way of thinking about the moral life?

7. The moral teachings of Jesus are sometimes criticized for setting too high a standard for human behavior. Do you think the criticism is justified?

# The Principle of Utility

## JEREMY BENTHAM

Jeremy Bentham (1748–1832) is the father of modern Utilitarianism. He was one of the leading political philosophers of his time, and his book *The Principles of Morals and Legislation* is a classic of moral and political philosophy.

According to Bentham's "principle of utility," actions are right when they increase happiness and diminish misery, wrong when they have the opposite effect. By "utility" he means the property of producing pleasure or happiness in conscious beings. Thus we should always do those acts that tend to increase overall happiness. Bentham is known as a "hedonistic utilitarian": pleasure is to be pursued, pain to be avoided. A legislator, for example, should

THE PRINCIPLE OF UTILITY Excerpted from Jeremy Bentham, *The Principles of Morals and Legislation* (1789).

calculate the pleasure/pain ratio of each prospective law. Bentham proposes that we evaluate pleasures according to their intensity, duration, certainty, propinquity (nearness), fecundity (tendency to lead to other pleasures), purity (tendency *not* to be followed by pain), and, finally, extent (the number of persons to whom the pleasure extends). Bentham concedes that he cannot *prove* the truth of the principle of utility; but he claims that most of us implicitly accept it and act on it every day. And he suspects that any alternative principle will be "despotical, and hostile to all the rest of the human race."

The principle of utility is the foundation of the present work: it will be proper therefore at the outset to give an explicit and determinate account of what is meant by it. By the principle of utility is meant that principle which approves or disapproves of every action whatsoever, according to the tendency which it appears to have to augment or diminish the happiness of the party whose interest is in question: or, what is the same thing in other words, to promote or to oppose that happiness. I say of every action whatsoever; and therefore not only of every action of a private individual, but of every measure of government.

By utility is meant that property in any object, whereby it tends to produce benefit, advantage, pleasure, good, or happiness (all this in the present case comes to the same thing), or (what comes again to the same thing) to prevent the happening of mischief, pain, evil, or unhappiness to the party whose interest is considered: if that party be the community in general, then the happiness of the community: if a particular individual, then the happiness of that individual.

The interest of the community is one of the most general expressions that can occur in the phraseology of morals: no wonder that the meaning of it is often lost. When it has a meaning, it is this. The community is a fictitious *body*, composed of the individual persons who are considered as constituting as it were its *members*. The interest of the community then is, what?—the sum of the interests of the several members who compose it.

It is in vain to talk of the interests of the community, without understanding what is the interest of the individual. A thing is said to promote the interest, or to be *for* the interest, of an individual, when it tends to add to the sum total of his pleasures: or, what comes to the same thing, to diminish the sum total of his pains.

An action then may be said to be conformable to the principle of utility, or, for shortness sake, to utility (meaning with respect to the community at large), when the tendency it has to augment the happiness of the community is greater than any it has to diminish it.

A measure of government (which is but a particular kind of action, performed by a particular person or persons) may be said to be conformable to or dictated by the principle of utility, when in like manner the tendency which it has to augment the happiness of the community is greater than any which it has to diminish it.

When an action, or in particular a measure of government, is supposed by a man to be conformable to the principle of utility, it may be convenient, for the purposes of discourse, to imagine a kind of law or dictate, called a law or dictate of utility: and to speak of the action in question, as being conformable to such law or dictate.

A man may be said to be a partizan of the principle of utility, when the approbation or disapprobation he annexes to any action, or to any measure, is determined by and proportioned to the tendency which he conceives it to have to augment or to diminish the happiness of the community: or in other words, to its conformity or unconformity to the laws or dictates of utility.

Of an action that is conformable to the principle of utility one may always say either that it is one that ought to be done, or at least that it is not one that ought not to be done. One may say also, that it is right it should be done; at least that it is not wrong it should be done: that it is a right action; at least that it is not a wrong action. When thus interpreted, the words *ought,* and *right* and *wrong,* and others of that stamp, have a meaning: when otherwise, they have none.

Has the rectitude of this principle been ever formally contested? It should seem that it had, by those who have not known what they have been meaning. Is it susceptible of any direct proof? it should seem not: for that which is used to prove every thing else, cannot itself be proved: a chain of proofs must have their commencement somewhere. To give such proof is as impossible as it is needless.

Not that there is or ever has been that human creature breathing, however stupid or perverse, who has not on many, perhaps on most occasions of his life, deferred to it. By the natural constitution of the human frame, on most occasions of their lives men in general embrace this principle, without thinking of it: if not for the ordering of their own actions, yet for the trying of their own actions, as well as of those of other men. There have been, at the same time, not many, perhaps, even of the most intelligent, who have been disposed to embrace it purely and without reserve. There are even few who have not taken some occasion or other to quarrel with it, either on account of their not understanding always how to apply it, or on account of some prejudice or other which they were afraid to examine into, or could not bear to part with. For such is the stuff that man is made of: in principle and in practice, in a right track and in a wrong one, the rarest of all human qualities is consistency.

When a man attempts to combat the principle of utility, it is with reasons drawn, without his being aware of it, from that very principle itself. His arguments, if they prove any thing, prove not that the principle is *wrong,* but that, according to the applications he supposes to be made of it, it is *misapplied.* Is it possible for a man to move the earth? Yes; but he must first find out another earth to stand upon.

To disprove the propriety of it by arguments is impossible; but, from the causes that have been mentioned, or from some confused or partial view of it, a man may happen to be disposed not to relish it. Where this is the case, if he thinks the settling of his opinions on such a subject worth the trouble, let him take the following steps, and at length, perhaps, he may come to reconcile himself to it.

Let him settle with himself, whether he would wish to discard this principle altogether; if so, let him consider what it is that all his reasonings (in matters of politics especially) can amount to?

If he would, let him settle with himself, whether he would judge and act without any principle, or whether there is any other he would judge and act by?

If there be, let him examine and satisfy himself whether the principle he thinks he has found is really any separate intelligible principle; or whether it be not a mere principle in words, a kind of phrase, which at bottom expresses neither more nor less than the mere averment of his own unfounded sentiments; that is, what in another person he might be apt to call caprice?

If he is inclined to think that his own approbation or disapprobation, annexed to the idea of an act, without any regard to its consequences, is a sufficient foundation for him to judge and act upon, let him ask himself whether his sentiment is to be a standard of right and wrong, with respect to every other man, or whether every man's sentiment has the same privilege of being a standard to itself?

In the first case, let him ask himself whether his principle is not despotical, and hostile to all the rest of human race?

In the second case, whether it is not anarchial, and whether at this rate there are not as many different standards of right and wrong as there are men? and whether even to the same man, the same thing, which is right to-day, may not (without the least change in its nature) be wrong to-morrow? and whether the same thing is not right and wrong in the same place at the same time? and in either case, whether all argument is not at an end? and whether, when two men have said, "I like this," and "I don't like it," they can (upon such a principle) have any thing more to say?

If he should have said to himself, No: for that the sentiment which he proposes as a standard must be grounded on reflection, let him say on what particulars the reflection is to turn? if on particulars having relation to the utility of the act, then let him say whether this is not deserting his own principle and borrowing assistance from that very one in opposition to which he sets it up: or if not on those particulars, on what other particulars?

If he should be for compounding the matter, and adopting his own principle in part, and the principle of utility in part, let him say how far he will adopt it?

When he has settled with himself where he will stop, then let him ask himself how he justifies to himself the adopting it so far? and why he will not adopt it any farther?

Admitting any other principle than the principle of utility to be a right principle, a principle that it is right for a man to pursue; admitting (what is not true) that the word *right* can have a meaning without reference to utility, let him say whether there is any such thing as a *motive* that a man can have to pursue the dictates of it: if there is, let him say what that motive is, and how it is to be distinguished from those which enforce the dictates of utility: if not, then lastly let him say what it is this other principle can be good for?


Pleasures then, and the avoidance of pains, are the *ends* which the legislator has in view: it behoves him therefore to understand their *value*. Pleasures and pains are the *instruments* he has to work with: it behoves him therefore to understand their force, which is again, in other words, their value.

To a person considered *by himself,* the value of a pleasure or pain considered *by itself,* will be greater or less, according to the four following circumstances:

1. Its *intensity.*
2. Its *duration.*
3. Its *certainty* or *uncertainty.*
4. Its *propinquity* or *remoteness.*

These are the circumstances which are to be considered in estimating a pleasure or a pain considered each of them by itself. But when the value of any pleasure or pain is considered for the purpose of estimating the tendency of any *act* by which it is produced, there are two other circumstances to be taken into the account; these are,

5. Its *fecundity,* or the chance it has of being followed by sensations of the *same* kind: that is, pleasures, if it be a pleasure: pains, if it be a pain.
6. Its *purity,* or the chance it has of *not* being followed by sensations of the *opposite* kind: that is, pains, if it be a pleasure: pleasures, if it be a pain.

These two last, however, are in strictness scarcely to be deemed properties of the pleasure or the pain itself; they are not, therefore, in strictness to be taken into the account of the value of that pleasure or that pain. They are in strictness to be deemed properties only of the act, or other event, by which such pleasure or pain has been produced; and accordingly are only to be taken into the account of the tendency of such act or such event.

To a *number* of persons, with reference to each of whom the value of a pleasure or a pain is considered, it will be greater or less, according to seven circumstances: to wit, the six preceding ones; *viz.*

1. Its *intensity.*
2. Its *duration.*
3. Its *certainty* or *uncertainty.*
4. Its *propinquity* or *remoteness.*
5. Its *fecundity.*
6. Its *purity.*

And one other; to wit:

7. Its *extent;* that is, the number of persons to whom it *extends;* or (in other words) who are affected by it.

To take an exact account then of the general tendency of any act, by which the interests of a community are affected, proceed as follows. Begin with any one person of those whose interests seem most immediately to be affected by it: and take an account,

1. Of the value of each distinguishable *pleasure* which appears to be produced by it in the *first* instance.
2. Of the value of each *pain* which appears to be produced by it in the *first* instance.
3. Of the value of each pleasure which appears to be produced by it *after* the first. This constitutes the *fecundity* of the first *pleasure* and the *impunity* of the first *pain*.
4. Of the value of each *pain* which appears to be produced by it after the first. This constitutes the *fecundity* of the first *pain,* and the *impurity* of the first pleasure.
5. Sum up all the values of all the *pleasures* on the one side, and those of all the pains on the other. The balance, if it be on the side of pleasure, will give the *good* tendency of the act upon the whole, with respect to the interests of that *individual* person; if on the side of pain, the *bad* tendency of it upon the whole.
6. Take an account of the *number* of persons whose interests appear to be concerned; and repeat the above process with respect to each. *Sum* up the numbers expressive of the degrees of *good* tendency, which the act has, with respect to each individual, in regard to whom the tendency of it is *good* upon the whole: do this again with respect to each individual, in regard to whom the tendency of it is *bad* upon the whole. Take the *balance;* which, if on the side of *pleasure,* will give the general *good tendency* of the act, with respect to the total number or community of individuals concerned; if on the side of pain, the general *evil tendency,* with respect to the same community.

It is not to be expected that this process should be strictly pursued previously to every moral judgment, or to every legislative or judicial operation. It may, however, be always kept in view: and as near as the process actually pursued on these occasions approaches to it, so near will such process approach to the character of an exact one.

The same process is alike applicable to pleasure and pain, in whatever shape they appear: and by whatever denomination they are distinguished: to pleasure, whether it be called *good* (which is properly the cause or instrument of pleasure) or *profit* (which is distant pleasure, or the cause or instrument of distant pleasure), or *convenience*, or *advantage, benefit, emolument, happiness,* and so forth; to pain, whether it be called *evil* (which corresponds to *good*), or *mischief,* or *inconvenience,* or *disadvantage,* or *loss,* or *unhappiness,* and so forth.

Nor is this a novel and unwarranted, any more than it is a useless theory. In all this there is nothing but what the practice of mankind, whatsoever they have a clear view of their own interest, is perfectly conformable to. An article of property, an estate in land, for instance, is valuable, on what account? On account of the pleasures of all kinds which it enables a man to produce, and what comes to the same thing the pains of all kinds which it enables him to avert. But the value of such an article of property is universally understood to rise or fall according to the length or shortness of the time which a man has in it: the certainty or uncertainty of its coming into possession: and the nearness or remoteness of the time at which, if at all, it is to come into possession. As to the *intensity* of the pleasures which a man may derive from it, this is never thought of, because it depends upon the use which each particular person may come to make of it; which cannot be estimated till the particular pleasures he may come to derive from it, or the particular pains he may come to exclude by means of it, are brought to view. For the same reason, neither does he think of the *fecundity* or *purity* of those pleasures.

**STUDY QUESTIONS**

1. What does Bentham mean by the interest of the community? How does the interest of the community determine the rightness or wrongness of a proposed course of action?
2. What does Bentham think about the possibility of proving the principle of utility?
3. How does Bentham assess the value to be assigned to a given pleasure or pain when evaluating a course of action?

4.  How are the values of pleasures and pains related to the value of other things such as houses and symphonies?
5.  Debate the question:
    Bentham's moral philosophy is essentially at odds with the morality of the Judeo-Christian tradition.

# Utilitarianism

## J. J. C. SMART

J. J. C. Smart (b. 1920) is professor emeritus of the University of Adelaide and of the Australian National University. He is the author of several books, including *Philosophy and Scientific Realism* and *Ethics, Persuasion and Truth*.

Act utilitarians tell us to choose *actions* that increase happiness and diminish misery. Rule utilitarianism, on the other hand, tells us to act according to *rules* that tend to increase happiness and diminish misery. Thus an act utilitarian might break a promise whenever the principle of utility favored doing so; according to rule utilitarianism, it is better all around if everyone follows the rules ("Keep your promises"; "Tell the truth") even when, in a particular case, adherence to the rule does not increase utility. Smart is an act utilitarian, and he criticizes rule utilitarians for being "rule worshippers." Why, he asks, should someone follow a rule in cases in which there is greater utility in breaking it? Smart also considers the problem of the "higher" and "lower" pleasures. It may well be that a dog gets more pleasure chasing a rat than a philosopher does contemplating the mysteries of the universe.

UTILITARIANISM From "An Outline of a System of Utilitarian Ethics" in *Utilitarianism: For and Against*, edited by J. J. C. Smart and Bernard Williams. Reprinted by permission of Cambridge University Press.

Should we then try to reduce the number of discontented philosophers and fill the world with happy dogs? Smart answers that it is inaccurate to describe dogs as happy. To call human beings happy, however, is not merely to describe them as contented, but to express approval for their form of contentness. Developing an idea of Bentham, Smart argues that the higher pleasures of poetry, philosophy, and science tend to be more "fecund" (that is, conducive to other pleasures) than the lower pleasures, such as drunkeness, chasing rats, or playing bingo. Smart addresses a number of other problems facing Utilitarianism: Should we try to increase the *average* happiness of human beings or should we try to increase the *total* amount of happiness in the world? Must we consider the remote consequences of our actions? Is there a place for rules in act utilitarianism? Smart believes that act utilitarianism is a simple and natural doctrine that will eventually appeal to all who care about the happiness of humankind.

The system of normative ethics which I am here concerned to defend is . . . *act*-utilitarianism. Act-utilitarianism is to be contrasted with rule-utilitarianism. Act-utilitarianism is the view that the rightness or wrongness of an action is to be judged by the consequences, good or bad, of the action itself. Rule-utilitarianism is the view that the rightness or wrongness of an action is to be judged by the goodness and badness of the consequences of a rule that everyone should perform the action in like circumstances. . . .

I have argued elsewhere[1] the objections to rule-utilitarianism as compared with act-utilitarianism. Briefly they boil down to the accusation of rule worship: the rule-utilitarian presumably advocates

---

[1] In my article "Extreme and restricted utilitarianism," *Philosophical Quarterly* 6 (1956) 344–54. This contains bad errors and a better version of the article will be found in Philippa Foot (ed.), *Theories of Ethics* (London: Oxford University Press, 1967) or Michael D. Bayles (ed.) *Contemporary Utilitarianism* (New York: Doubleday, 1968). In this article I used the terms "extreme" and "restricted" instead of Brandt's more felicitous "act" and "rule" which I now prefer.

his principle because he is ultimately concerned with human happiness: why then should he advocate abiding by a rule when he knows that it will not in the present case be most beneficial to abide by it? The reply that in most cases it is most beneficial to abide by the rule seems irrelevant. And so is the reply that it would be better that everybody should abide by the rule than that nobody should. This is to suppose that the only alternative to "everybody does $A$" is "no one does $A$." But clearly we have the possibility "some people do $A$ and some don't." Hence to refuse to break a generally beneficial rule in those cases in which it is not most beneficial to obey it seems irrational and to be a case of rule worship.

The type of utilitarianism which I shall advocate will, then, be act-utilitarianism, not rule-utilitarianism. . . .

An act–utilitarian judges the rightness or wrongness of actions by the goodness and badness of their consequences. But is he to judge the goodness and badness of the consequences of an action solely by their pleasantness and unpleasantness? Bentham, who thought that quantity of pleasure being equal, the experience of playing pushpin was as good as that of reading poetry, could be classified as a hedonistic act-utilitarian. Moore, who believed that some states of mind, such as those of acquiring knowledge, had intrinsic value quite independent of their pleasantness, can be called an ideal utilitarian. Mill seemed to occupy an intermediate position. He held that there are higher and lower pleasures. This seems to imply that pleasure is a necessary condition for goodness but that goodness depends on other qualities of experience than pleasantness and unpleasantness. I propose to call Mill a quasi-ideal utilitarian. . . .

What Bentham, Mill and Moore are all agreed on is that the rightness of an action is to be judged solely by consequences, states of affairs brought about by the action. Of course we shall have to be careful here not to construe "state of affairs" so widely that any ethical doctrine becomes utilitarian. For if we did so we would not be saying anything at all in advocating utilitarianism. If, for example, we allowed "the state of having just kept a promise," then a deontologist who said we should keep promises simply because they are promises would be a utilitarian. And we do not wish to allow this. . . . Let us consider Mill's contention that it is "better to be Socrates dissatisfied than a fool satisfied." Mill holds that pleasure is not to be our sole criterion for evaluating consequences: the state of mind of Socrates might be less pleasurable than that of the fool, but, according to Mill, Socrates would be happier than the fool.

It is necessary to observe, first of all, that a purely hedonistic utilitarian, like Bentham, might agree with Mill in preferring the experiences of discontented philosophers to those of contented fools. His preference for the philosopher's state of mind, however, would not be an *intrinsic* one. He would say that the discontented philosopher is a useful agent in society and that the existence of Socrates is responsible for an improvement in the lot of humanity generally. Consider two brothers. One may be of a docile and easy temperament: he may lead a supremely contented and unambitious life, enjoying himself hugely. The other brother may be ambitious, may stretch his talents to the full, may strive for scientific success and academic honours, and may discover some invention or some remedy for disease or improvement in agriculture which will enable innumerable men of easy temperament to lead a contented life, whereas otherwise they would have been thwarted by poverty, disease or hunger. Or he may make some advance in pure science which will later have beneficial practical applications. Or, again, he may write poetry which will solace the leisure hours and stimulate the brains of practical men or scientists, thus indirectly leading to an improvement in society. That is, the pleasures of poetry or mathematics may be *extrinsically* valuable in a way in which those of pushpin or sunbathing may not be. Though the poet or mathematician may be discontented, society as a whole may be the more contented for his presence. . . .

Maybe we have gone wrong in talking of pleasure as though it were no more than contentment. Contentment consists roughly in relative absence of unsatisfied desires; pleasure is perhaps something more positive and consists in a balance between absence of unsatisfied desires and presence of satisfied desires. We might put the difference in this way: pure unconsciousness would be a limiting case of contentment, but not of pleasure. A stone has no unsatisfied desires, but then it just has no desires. Nevertheless, this consideration will not resolve the disagreement between Bentham and Mill. No doubt a dog has as intense a desire to discover rats as the philosopher has to discover the mysteries of the universe. Mill would wish to say that the pleasures of the philosopher were more valuable intrinsically than those of the dog, however intense these last might be. . . .

It is worth while enquiring how much practical ethics is likely to be affected by the possibility of disagreement over the question of Socrates dissatisfied versus the fool satisfied.

'Not very much,' one feels like saying at first. We noted that the most complex and intellectual pleasures are also the most fecund. Poetry elevates the mind, makes one more sensitive, and so harmonizes with various intellectual pursuits, some of which are of practical value. Delight in mathematics is even more obviously, on Benthamite views, a pleasure worth encouraging, for on the progress of mathematics depends the progress of mankind. Even the most hedonistic schoolmaster would prefer to see his boys enjoying poetry and mathematics rather than neglecting these arts for the pleasures of marbles or the tuckshop. Indeed many of the brutish pleasures not only lack fecundity but are actually the reverse of fecund. To enjoy food too much is to end up fat, unhealthy and without zest or vigour. To enjoy drink too much is even worse. In most circumstances of ordinary life the pure hedonist will agree in his practical recommendations with the quasi-ideal utilitarian.

This need not always be so. Some years ago two psychologists, Olds and Milner, carried out some experiments with rats. Through the skull of each rat they inserted an electrode. These electrodes penetrated to various regions of the brain. In the case of some of these regions the rat showed behaviour characteristics of pleasure when a current was passed from the electrode, in others they seemed to show pain, and in others the stimulus seemed neutral. That a stimulus was pleasure-giving was shown by the fact that the rat would learn to pass the current himself by pressing a lever. He would neglect food and make straight for this lever and start stimulating himself. In some cases he would sit there pressing the lever every few seconds for hours on end. This calls up a pleasant picture of the voluptuary of the future, a bald-headed man with a number of electrodes protruding from his skull, one to give the physical pleasure of sex, one for that of eating, one for that of drinking, and so on. Now is this the sort of life that all our ethical planning should culminate in? A few hours' work a week, automatic factories, comfort and security from disease, and hours spent at a switch, continually electrifying various regions of one's brain? Surely not. Men were made for higher things, one can't help wanting to say, even though one knows that men weren't made for anything, but are the product of evolution by natural selection.

103

It might be said that the objection to continual sensual stimulation of the above sort is that though it would be pleasant in itself it would be infecund of future pleasures. This is often so with the ordinary sensual pleasures. Excessive indulgence in the physical pleasures of sex may possibly have a debilitating effect and may perhaps interfere with the deeper feelings of romantic love. But whether stimulation by the electrode method would have this weakening effect and whether it would impair the possibility of future pleasures of the same sort is another matter. For example, there would be no excessive secretion of hormones. The whole biochemical mechanism would, almost literally, be short-circuited. Maybe, however, a person who stimulated himself by the electrode method would find it so enjoyable that he would neglect all other pursuits. Maybe if everyone became an electrode operator people would lose interest in everything else and the human race would die out.

Suppose, however, that the facts turned out otherwise: that a man could (and would) do his full share of work in the office or the factory and come back in the evening to a few hours contented electrode work, without bad after-effects. This would be his greatest pleasure, and the pleasure would be so great intrinsically and so easily repeatable that its lack of fecundity would not matter. Indeed perhaps by this time human arts, such as medicine, engineering, agriculture and architecture will have been brought to a pitch of perfection sufficient to enable most of the human race to spend most of its time electrode operating, without compensating pains of starvation, disease and squalor. Would this be a satisfactory state of society? Would this be the millennium towards which we have been striving? Surely the pure hedonist would have to say that it was.

It is time, therefore, that we had another look at the concept of happiness. Should we say that the electrode operator was really happy? This is a difficult question to be clear about, because the concept of happiness is a tricky one. But whether we should call the electrode operator 'happy' or not, there is no doubt (a) that he would be *contented* and (b) that he would be *enjoying himself.* . . .

. . . To call a person "happy" is to say more than that he is contented for most of the time, or even that he frequently enjoys himself and is rarely discontented or in pain. It is, I think, in part to express a favourable attitude to the idea of such a form of contentment and enjoyment. That is, for *A* to call *B* "happy," *A* must be contented at the prospect of B being in his present state of mind and at the prospect of A himself, should the opportunity arise, enjoying that sort of state of mind. That is, "happy" is a word which is mainly descriptive (tied to the concepts of contentment and enjoyment) but which is also partly evaluative. It is because Mill approves of the "higher" pleasures, e.g., intellectual pleasures, so much more than he approves of the more simple and brutish pleasures, that, quite apart from consequences and side effects, he can pronounce the man who enjoys the pleasures of philosophical discourse as "more happy" than the man who gets enjoyment from pushpin or beer drinking.

The word "happy" is not wholly evaluative, for there would be something absurd, as opposed to merely unusual, in calling a man who was in pain, or who was not enjoying himself, or who hardly ever enjoyed himself, or who was in a more or less permanent state of intense dissatisfaction, a "happy" man. For a man to be happy he must, as a minimal condition, be fairly contented and moderately enjoying himself for much of the time. Once this minimal condition is satisfied we can go on to evaluate various types of contentment and enjoyment and to grade them in terms of happiness. . . .

To sum up so far, happiness is partly an evaluative concept, and so the utilitarian maxim "You ought to maximize happiness" is doubly evaluative. There is the possibility of an ultimate disagreement between two utilitarians who differ over the question of pushpin versus poetry, or Socrates dissatisfied versus the fool satisfied. . . .

Leaving these more remote possibilities out of account, however, and considering the decisions we have to make at present, the question of whether the "higher" pleasures should be preferred to the "lower" ones does seem to be of slight practical importance. There are already perfectly good hedonistic arguments for poetry as against pushpin. As has been pointed out, the more complex pleasures are incomparably more fecund than the less complex ones: not only are they enjoyable in themselves but they are a means to further enjoyment. Still less, on the whole, do they lead to disillusionment, physical deterioration or social disharmony. The connoisseur of poetry may enjoy himself no more than the connoisseur of whisky, but he runs no danger of a headache on the following morning. Moreover the question of whether the general happiness would be increased by replacing most of the human population by a bigger population of contented sheep and pigs is not one which by any stretch of the imagination could become a live issue. Even if we thought, on abstract grounds, that such a replacement would be desirable, we should not have the slightest chance of having our ideas generally adopted. . . .

Another type of ultimate disagreement between utilitarians, whether hedonistic or ideal, can arise over whether we should try to maximize the *average* happiness of human beings (or the average goodness of their states of mind) or whether we should try to maximize the *total* happiness or goodness. . . . I have not yet elucidated the concept of total happiness, and you may regard it as a suspect notion. But for present purposes I shall put it in this way: Would you be quite indifferent between (a) a universe containing only one million happy sentient beings, all equally happy, and (b) a universe containing two million happy beings, each neither more nor less happy than any in the first universe? Or would you, as a humane and sympathetic person, give a preference to the second universe? I myself cannot help feeling a preference for the second universe. But if someone feels the other way I do not know how to argue with him. It looks as though we have yet another possibility of disagreement within a general utilitarian framework.

This type of disagreement might have practical relevance. It might be important in discussions of the ethics of birth control. This is not to say that the utilitarian who values total, rather than average, happiness may not have potent arguments in favour of birth control. But he will need more arguments to convince himself than will the other type of utilitarian.

In most cases the difference between the two types of utilitarianism will not lead to disagreement in practice. For in most cases the most effective way to increase the total happiness is to increase the average happiness, and vice versa. . . .

I shall now state the act–utilitarian doctrine. . . .

Let us say, then, that the only reason for performing an action $A$ rather than an alternative action $B$ is that doing $A$ will make mankind (or, perhaps, all sentient beings) happier than will doing $B$. . . . This is so simple and natural a doctrine that we can surely expect that many of my readers will have at least some propensity to agree. For I am talking . . . to sympathetic and benevolent men, that is, to men who desire the happiness of mankind. Since they have a favourable attitude to the general happiness, surely they will have a tendency to submit to an ultimate moral principle which does no more than express this attitude. It is true that these men, being human, will also have purely selfish attitudes. Either these attitudes will be in harmony with the general happiness (in cases where everyone's looking after his own interests promotes the maximum general happiness) or they will not be in harmony with the general happiness, in which case they will largely cancel one another out, and so could not be made the basis of an interpersonal discussion anyway. It is possible, then, that many sympathetic and benevolent people depart from or fail to attain a utilitarian ethical principle only under the stress of tradition, of superstition, or of unsound philosophical reasoning. If this hypothesis should turn out to be correct, at least as far as these readers are concerned, then the utilitarian may contend that there is no need for him to defend his position directly, save by stating it in a consistent manner, and by showing that common objections to it are unsound. After all, it expresses an ultimate attitude, not a liking for something merely as a means to something else. Save for attempting to remove confusions and discredit superstitions which may get in the way of clear moral thinking, he cannot, of course, appeal to argument and must rest his hopes on the good feeling of his readers. If any reader is not a sympathetic and benevolent man, then of course it cannot be expected that he will have an ultimate pro-attitude to human happiness in general. Also some good-hearted readers may reject the utilitarian position because of certain considerations relating to justice. . . .

The utilitarian's ultimate moral principle, let it be remembered, expresses the sentiment not of altruism but of benevolence, the agent counting himself neither more nor less than any other person. Pure altruism cannot be made the basis of a universal moral discussion in that it would lead different people to different and perhaps incompatible courses of action, even though the circumstances were identical. When two men each try to let the other through a door first a deadlock results. Altruism could hardly commend itself to those of a scientific, and hence universalistic, frame of mind. If you count in my calculations why should I not count in your calculations? And why should I pay more attention to my calculations than to yours? Of course we often tend to praise and honour altruism even more than generalized benevolence. This is because people too often err on the side of selfishness, and so altruism is a fault on the right side. If we can make a man try to be an altruist he may succeed as far as acquiring a generalized benevolence.

Suppose we could predict the future consequences of actions with certainty. Then it would be possible to say that the total future consequences of action *A* are such-and-such and that the total future consequences of action *B* are so-and-so. In order to help someone to decide whether to do *A* or to do *B* we could say to him: "Envisage the total consequences of *A*, and think them over carefully and imaginatively. Now envisage the total consequences of *B*, and think them over carefully. As a benevolent and humane man, and thinking of yourself just as one man among others, would you prefer the consequences of *A* or those of *B?*" That is, we are asking for a comparison of one (present and future) *total* situation with another (present and future) *total* situation. So far we are not asking for a *summation* or *calculation* of pleasures or happiness. We are asking only for a comparison of total situations. And it seems clear that we can frequently make such a comparison and say that one total situation is better than another. For example few people would not prefer a total situation in which a million people are well-fed, well-clothed, free of pain, doing interesting and enjoyable work, and enjoying the pleasures of conversation, study, business, art, humour, and so on, to a total situation where there are ten thousand such people only, or perhaps 999,999 such people plus one man with toothache, or neurotic, or shivering with cold. In general, we can sum things up by saying that if we are humane, kindly, benevolent people, we want as many people as possible now and in the future to be as happy as possible. Someone might object that we cannot envisage the total future situation, because this stretches into infinity. In reply to this we may say that it does not stretch into infinity, as all sentient life on earth will ultimately be extinguished, and furthermore we do not normally in practice need to consider very remote consequences, as these in the end approximate rapidly to zero like the furthermost ripples on a pond after a stone has been dropped into it.

But do the remote consequences of an action diminish to zero? Suppose that two people decide whether to have a child or remain childless. Let us suppose that they decide to have the child, and that they have a limitless succession of happy descendants. The remote consequences do not seem to get less. Not at any rate if these people are Adam and Eve. The difference would be between the end of the human race and a limitless accretion of human happiness, generation by generation. The Adam and Eve example shows that the "ripples on the pond" postulate is not needed in every case for a rational utilitarian decision. If we had some reason for thinking that every generation would be more happy than not we would not (in the Adam and Eve sort of case) need to be worried that the remote consequences of our action would be in detail unknown. The necessity for the "ripples in the pond" postulate comes from the fact that usually we do not know whether remote consequences will be good or bad. Therefore we cannot know what to do unless we can assume that remote consequences can be left out of account. This can often be done. Thus if we consider two actual parents, instead of Adam and Eve, then they need not worry about thousands of years hence. Not, at least, if we assume that there will be ecological forces determining the future population of the world. If these parents do not have remote descendants, then other people will presumably have more than they would otherwise. And there is no reason to suppose that my descendants would be more or less happy than yours. We must note, then, that unless we are dealing with "all or nothing" situations (such as the Adam and Eve one, or that of someone in a position to end human life altogether) we need some sort of "ripples in the pond" postulate to make utilitarianism workable in practice. I do not know how to prove such a postulate, though it seems plausible enough. If it is not accepted, not only utilitarianism, but also deontological systems like that of Sir David Ross, who at least admits beneficence as one *prima facie* duty among the others, will be fatally affected.

Sometimes, of course, more needs to be said. For example one course of action may make some people very happy and leave the rest as they are or perhaps slightly less happy. Another course of action may make all men rather more happy than before but no one very happy. Which course of action makes mankind happier on the whole? Again, one course of action may make it highly probable that everyone will be made a little happier whereas another course of action may give us a much smaller probability that everyone will be made very much happier. In the third place, one course of action may make everyone happy in a pig-like way, whereas another course of action may make a few people happy in a highly complex and intellectual way.

It seems therefore that we have to weigh the maximizing of happiness against equitable distribution, to weigh probabilities with happiness, and to weigh the intellectual and other qualities of states of mind with their pleasurableness. Are we not therefore driven back to the necessity of some calculus of happiness? Can we just say: "envisage two total situations and tell me which you prefer"? If this were possible, of course there would be no need to talk of summing happiness or of a calculus. All we should have to do would be to put total situations in an order of preference.

Let us now consider the question of equity. Suppose that we have the choice of sending four equally worthy and intelligent boys to a medium-grade public school or of leaving three in an adequate but uninspiring grammar school and sending one to Eton. (For sake of the example I am making the almost certainly incorrect assumption that Etonians are happier than other public-school boys and that these other public-school boys are happier than grammar-school boys.) Which course of action makes the most for the happiness of the four boys? Let us suppose that we can neglect complicating factors, such as that the superior Etonian education might lead one boy to develop his talents so much that he will have an extraordinary influence on the well-being of mankind, or that the unequal treatment of the boys might cause jealousy and rift in the family. Let us suppose that the Etonian will be as happy as (we may hope) Etonians usually are, and similarly for the other boys, and let us suppose that remote effects can be neglected. Should we prefer the greater happiness of one boy to the moderate happiness of all four? Clearly one parent may prefer one total situation (one boy at Eton and three at the grammar school) while another may prefer the other total situation (all four at the medium-grade public school). Surely both parents have an equal claim to being sympathetic and benevolent, and yet their difference of opinion here is not founded on an empirical disagreement about facts. I suggest, however, that there are not in fact many cases in which such a disagreement could arise. Probably the parent who wished to send one son to Eton would draw the line at sending one son to Eton plus giving him expensive private tuition during the holidays plus giving his other sons no secondary education at all. It is only within rather small limits that this sort of disagreement about equity can arise. Furthermore the cases in which we can make one person *very* much happier without increasing *general* happiness are rare ones. The law of diminishing returns comes in here. So, in most practical cases, a disagreement about what should be done will be an empirical disagreement about what total situation is likely to be brought about by an action, and will not be a disagreement about which total situation is preferable. For example the inequalitarian parent might get the other to agree with him if he could convince him that there was a much higher probability of an Etonian benefiting the human race, such as by inventing a valuable drug or opening up the mineral riches of Antarctica, than there is of a non-Etonian doing so. (Once more I should like to say that I do not myself take such a possibility very seriously!) I must again stress that since disagreement about what causes produce what effects is in practice so much the most important sort of disagreement, to have intelligent moral discussion with a person we do not in fact need complete agreement with him about ultimate ends: an approximate agreement is sufficient. . . .

According to the act-utilitarian, then, the rational way to decide what to do is to decide to perform that one of those alternative actions open to us (including the null-action, the doing of nothing) which is likely to maximize the probable happiness or well-being of humanity as a whole, or more accurately, of all sentient beings. The utilitarian position is here put forward as a criterion of rational choice. It is true that we may choose to habituate ourselves to behave in accordance with certain rules, such as to keep promises, in the belief that behaving in accordance with these rules is generally optimific, and in the knowledge that we most often just do not have time to work out individual pros and cons. When we act in such an habitual fashion we do not of course deliberate or make a choice. The act-utilitarian will, however, regard these rules as mere rules of thumb, and will use them only as rough guides. Normally he will act in accordance with them when he has no time for considering probable consequences or when the advantages of such a consideration of consequences are likely to be outweighed by the disadvantage of the waste of time involved. He acts in accordance with rules, in short, when there is no time to think, and since he does not think, the actions which he does habitually are not the outcome of moral thinking. When he has to think what to do, then there is a question of deliberation or choice, and it is precisely for such situations that the utilitarian criterion is intended.

It is, moreover, important to realize that there is no inconsistency whatever in an act-utilitarian's schooling himself to act, in normal circumstances, habitually and in accordance with stereotyped rules.

He knows that a man about to save a drowning person has no time to consider various possibilities, such as that the drowning person is a dangerous criminal who will cause death and destruction, or that he is suffering from a painful and incapacitating disease from which death would be a merciful release, or that various timid people, watching from the bank, will suffer a heart attack if they see anyone else in the water. No, he knows that it is almost always right to save a drowning man, and in he goes. Again, he knows that we would go mad if we went in detail into the probable consequences of keeping or not keeping every trivial promise: we will do most good and reserve our mental energies for more important matters if we simply habituate ourselves to keep promises in all normal situations. Moreover he may suspect that on some occasions personal bias may prevent him from reasoning in a correct utilitarian fashion. . . .

Though even the act–utilitarian may on occasion act habitually and in accordance with particular rules, his criterion is, as we have said, *applied* in cases in which he does not act habitually but in which he deliberates and chooses what to do.

**STUDY QUESTIONS**

1. Those who assess the moral value of an act in terms of its consequences must have ways to judge a consequence as good or bad. Discuss the views of Bentham, Mill, and G. E. Moore on evaluating consequences.
2. What do you think of Mill's famous remark: "Better to be Socrates dissatisfied than a fool satisfied"?
3. What is act utilitarianism? What is rule utilitarianism? Discuss Smart's objections to rule utilitarianism. Why do some utilitarians favor it?
4. What do utilitarians like Bentham and Smart mean by characterizing some pleasures as "fecund"? Why are the pleasures of poetry said to be more fecund than the pleasures of playing pushpin?
5. The utilitarian is sometimes accused of overlooking issues of equity. According to Smart, "The cases in which one can make one person very much happier without increasing the general

happiness are rare ones." Assuming that this is true, how does it bear on the question of equity. *Is* it true?
6. How does Smart deal with the objection that someone made euphorically happy through electronic means is a utilitarian success? Do you find Smart's answer plausible? Do you think his answer is true to the spirit of utilitarianism?

# A Critique of Utilitarianism

## BERNARD WILLIAMS

Bernard Williams (b. 1929) is Deutsch Professor of Philosophy at the University of California, Berkeley. His books include *Morality, Problems of the Self, Moral Luck,* and *Ethics and the Limits of Philosophy.*

Bernard William's critique of consequentialism takes off from Smart's version of act utilitarianism. If the consequences are decisive in determining the right/wrongness of an action, Williams says, then it will often be right to do what is *prima facie* wrong. He presents two cases in which, on utilitarian grounds, one would be forced to act in a way that violated one's intuitive moral feelings. In each case, "if the agent does not do a certain disagreeable thing, someone else will," and with much worse consequences. The utilitarian holds that the agent must then overcome his squeamishness and do the lesser evil. In one of Williams's examples, a soldier, Pedro, will shoot twenty innocent people unless a tourist, Jim, shoots one of them. If Jim agrees, the remaining nineteen will go free. So far as the utilitarian is concerned, for Jim to

A CRITIQUE OF UTILITARIANISM From "A Critique of Utilitarianism" in *Utilitarianism: For and Against,* edited by J. J. C. Smart and Bernard Williams. Reprinted by permission of Cambridge University Press.

refrain from the murder is consequentially as bad as the positive act of killing nineteen more people. This position, Williams argues, shows that utilitarianism has a confused notion of responsibility and a totally inadequate notion of personal integrity. Williams argues that our deepest convictions, projects, and attitudes "do not compute" in the utilitarian calculus.

It is perhaps worth mentioning that Bentham, at least, clearly separated the question of what action is objectively right in a given context from the quite different question of who, if anyone, should be held responsible.

. . . [L]et us look . . . at two examples to see what utilitarianism might say about them, what we might say about utilitarianism and, most importantly of all, what would be implied by certain ways of thinking about the situations. . . .

(1) George, who has just taken his Ph.D. in chemistry, finds it extremely difficult to get a job. He is not very robust in health, which cuts down the number of jobs he might be able to do satisfactorily. His wife has to go out to work to keep them, which itself causes a great deal of strain, since they have small children and there are severe problems about looking after them. The results of all this, especially on the children, are damaging. An older chemist, who knows about this situation, says that he can get George a decently paid job in a certain laboratory, which pursues research into chemical and biological warfare. George says that he cannot accept this, since he is opposed to chemical and biological warfare. The older man replies that he is not too keen on it himself, come to that, but after all George's refusal is not going to make the job or the laboratory go away; what is more, he happens to know that if George refuses the job, it will certainly go to a contemporary of George's who is not inhibited by any such scruples and is likely if appointed to push along the research with greater zeal than George would. Indeed, it is not merely concern for George and his family, but (to speak frankly and in confidence) some alarm about this other man's excess of zeal, which has led the older man to offer to use his influence to get George the job . . . George's wife, to whom he is deeply attached, has views (the details of which need not concern us) from which it follows that at least

there is nothing particularly wrong with research into CBW. What should he do?

(2) Jim finds himself in the central square of a small South American town. Tied up against the wall are a row of twenty Indians, most terrified, a few defiant, in front of them several armed men in uniform. A heavy man in a sweat-stained khaki shirt turns out to be the captain in charge and, after a good deal of questioning of Jim which establishes that he got there by accident while on a botanical expedition, explains that the Indians are a random group of the inhabitants who, after recent acts of protest against the government, are just about to be killed to remind other possible protestors of the advantages of not protesting. However, since Jim is an honoured visitor from another land, the captain is happy to offer him a guest's privilege of killing one of the Indians himself. If Jim accepts, then as a special mark of the occasion, the other Indians will be let off. Of course, if Jim refuses, then there is no special occasion, and Pedro here will do what he was about to do when Jim arrived, and kill them all. Jim, with some desperate recollection of schoolboy fiction, wonders whether if he got hold of a gun, he could hold the captain, Pedro and the rest of the soldiers to threat, but it is quite clear from the set-up that nothing of that kind is going to work: any attempt at that sort of thing will mean that all the Indians will be killed, and himself. The men against the wall, and the other villagers, understand the situation, and are obviously begging him to accept. What should he do?

To these dilemmas, it seems to me that utilitarianism replies, in the first case, that George should accept the job, and in the second, that Jim should kill the Indian. Not only does utilitarianism give these answers but, if the situations are essentially as described and there are no further special factors, it regards them, it seems to me, as *obviously* the right answers. But many of us would certainly wonder whether, in (1), that could possibly be the right answer at all; and in the case of (2), even one who came to think that perhaps that was the answer, might well wonder whether it was obviously the answer. Nor is it just a question of the rightness or obviousness of these answers. It is also a question of what sort of considerations come into finding the answer. A feature of utilitarianism is that it cuts out a kind of consideration which for some others makes a difference to what they feel about such cases: a consideration involving the idea, as we might first and very simply put it, that each of us is specially responsible for what *he* does, rather than for what other people do. This is an idea closely connected with the value of integrity. It is often suspected that utilitarianism, at least in its direct forms, makes integrity as a value more or less unintelligible. I shall try to show that this suspicion is correct. . . .

. . . I want to consider now two types of effect that are often invoked by utilitarians, and which might be invoked in connexion with these imaginary cases. The attitude or tone involved in invoking these effects may sometimes seem peculiar; but that sort of peculiarity soon becomes familiar in utilitarian discussions, and indeed it can be something of an achievement to retain a sense of it.

First, there is the psychological effect on the agent. Our descriptions of these situations have not so far taken account of how George or Jim will be after they have taken the one course or the other; and it might be said that if they take the course which seemed at first the utilitarian one, the effects on them will be in fact bad enough and extensive enough to cancel out the initial utilitarian advantages of that course. Now there is one version of this effect in which, for a utilitarian, some confusion must be involved, namely that in which the agent feels bad, his subsequent conduct and relations are crippled and so on, *because he thinks that he has done the wrong thing*—for if the balance of outcomes was as it appeared to be *before* invoking this effect, then he has not (from the utilitarian point of view) done the wrong thing. So that version of the effect, for a rational and utilitarian agent, could not possibly make any difference to the assessment of right and wrong. However, perhaps he is not a thoroughly rational agent, and is disposed to have bad feelings, whichever he decided to do. Now such feelings, which are from a strictly utilitarian point of view irrational—nothing, a utilitarian can point out, is advanced by having them—cannot, consistently, have any great weight in a utilitarian calculation. I shall consider in a moment an argument to suggest that they should have no weight at all in it. But short of that, the utilitarian could reasonably say that such feelings should not be encouraged, even if we accept their existence, and that to give them a lot of weight is to encourage them. Or, at the very best, even if they are straightforwardly and without any discount to be put into the calculation, their weight must be small: they are after all (and at best) one man's feelings.

That consideration might seem to have particular force in Jim's case. In George's case, his feelings represent a larger proportion of what is to be weighed, and are more commensurate in character with other items in the calculation. In Jim's case, however, his feelings might seem to be of very little weight compared with other things that are at stake. There is a powerful and recognizable appeal that can be made on this point: as that a refusal by Jim to do what he has been invited to do would be a kind of self-indulgent squeamishness. That is an appeal which can be made by other than utilitarians—indeed, there are some uses of it which cannot be consistently made by utilitarians, as when it essentially involves the idea that there is something dishonourable about such self-indulgence. But in some versions it is a familiar, and it must be said a powerful, weapon of utilitarianism. One must be clear, though, about what it can and cannot accomplish. The most it can do, so far as I can see, is to invite one to consider how seriously, and for what reasons, one feels that what one is invited to do is (in these circumstances) wrong, and in particular, to consider that question from the utilitarian point of view. When the agent is not seeing the situation from a utilitarian point of view, the appeal cannot force him to do so; and if he does come round to seeing it from a utilitarian point of view, there is virtually nothing left for the appeal to do. If he does not see it from a utilitarian point of view, he will not see his resistance to the invitation, and the unpleasant feelings he associates with accepting it, *just* as disagreeable experiences of his; they figure rather as emotional expressions of a thought that to accept would be wrong. He may be asked, as by the appeal, to consider whether he is right, and indeed whether he is fully serious, in thinking that. But the assertion of the appeal, that he is being self-indulgently squeamish, will not itself answer that question, or even help to answer it, since it essentially tells him to regard his feelings just as unpleasant experiences of his, and he cannot, by doing that, answer the question they pose when they are precisely not so regarded, but are regarded as indications of what he thinks is right and wrong. If he does come round fully to the utilitarian point of view then of course he will regard these feelings just as unpleasant experiences of his. And once Jim—at least—has come to see them in that light, there is nothing left for the appeal to do, since *of course* his feelings, so regarded, are of virtually no weight at all in relation to the other things at stake. The "squeamishness" appeal is not an argument which adds in a hitherto neglected consideration. Rather, it is an invitation to consider the situation, and one's own feelings, from a utilitarian point of view.

The reason why the squeamishness appeal can be very unsettling, and one can be unnerved by the suggestion of self-indulgence in going against utilitarian considerations, is not that we are utilitarians who are uncertain what utilitarian value to attach to our moral feelings, but that we are partially at least not utilitarians, and cannot regard our moral feelings merely as objects of utilitarian value. Because our moral relation to the world is partly given by such feelings, and by a sense of what we can or cannot "live with," to come to regard those feelings from a purely utilitarian point of view, that is to say, as happenings outside one's moral self, is to lose a sense of one's moral identity; to lose, in the most literal way, one's integrity. . . .

## Integrity

The [two] situations have in common that if the agent does not do a certain disagreeable thing, someone else will, and in Jim's situation at least the result, the state of affairs after the other man has acted, if he does, will be worse than after Jim has acted, if Jim does. The same, on a smaller scale, is true of George's case. I have already suggested that it is inherent in consequentialism that it offers a strong doctrine of negative responsibility: if I know that if I do $X$, $O_1$ will eventuate, and if I refrain from doing $X$, $O_2$ will, and that $O_2$ is worse than $O_1$, then I am responsible for $O_2$ if I refrain voluntarily from doing $X$. "You could have prevented it," as will be said, and truly, to Jim, if he refuses, by the relatives of the other Indians. . . . [But] what occurs if Jim refrains from action is not solely twenty Indians dead, but *Pedro's killing twenty Indians*. . . . That may be enough for us to speak, in some sense, of Jim's responsibility for that outcome, if it occurs; but it is certainly not enough, it is worth noticing, for us to speak of Jim's *making* those things happen. For granted this way of their coming about, he could have made them happen only by making Pedro shoot, and there is no acceptable sense in which his refusal makes Pedro shoot. If the captain had said on Jim's refusal, "you leave me with no alternative," he would have been lying, like most who use that phrase. While the deaths, and the killing, may be the outcome of Jim's refusal, it is misleading to think, in such a case, of Jim having an *effect* on the world through the medium (as it happens) of Pedro's acts; for this is to leave Pedro out of the picture in his essential role of one who has intentions and projects, projects for realizing which Jim's refusal would leave an opportunity. Instead of thinking in terms of supposed effects of Jim's projects on Pedro, it is more revealing to think in terms of the effects of Pedro's projects on Jim's decision. . . .

Utilitarianism would do well . . . to acknowledge the evident fact that among the things that make people happy is not only making other people happy, but being taken up or involved in any of a vast range of projects, or—if we waive the evangelical and moralizing associations of the word—commitments. One can be committed to such things as a person, a cause, an institution, a career, one's own genius, or the pursuit of danger.

Now none of these is itself the *pursuit of happiness:* by an exceedingly ancient platitude, it is not at all clear that there could be anything which was just that, or at least anything that had the slightest chance of being successful. Happiness, rather, requires being involved in, or at least content with, something else. It is not impossible for utilitarianism to accept that point: it does not have to be saddled with a naïve and absurd philosophy of mind about the relation between desire and happiness. What it does have to say is that if such commitments are worth while, then pursuing the projects that flow from them, and realizing some of those projects, will make the person for whom they are worth while, happy. It may be that to claim that is still wrong: it may well be that a commitment can make sense to a man (can make sense of his life) without his supposing that it will make him *happy.* But that is not the present point; let us grant to utilitarianism that all worthwhile human projects must conduce, one way or another, to happiness. The point is that even if that is true, it does not follow, nor could it possibly be true, that those projects are themselves projects of pursuing happiness. One has to believe in, or at least want, or quite minimally, be content with, other things, for there to be anywhere that happiness can come from.

Utilitarianism, then, should be willing to agree that its general aim of maximizing happiness does not imply that what everyone is doing is just pursuing happiness. On the contrary, people have to be pursuing other things. What those other things may be, utilitarianism, sticking to its professed empirical stance, should be prepared just to find out. No doubt some possible projects it will want to discourage, on the grounds that their being pursued involves a negative balance of happiness to others: though even there, the unblinking accountant's eye of the strict utilitarian will have something to put in the positive column, the satisfactions of the destructive agent. Beyond that, there will be a vast variety of generally beneficent or at least harmless projects; and some no doubt, will take the form not just of tastes or fancies, but of what I have called "commitments." It may even be that the utilitarian researcher will find that many of those with commitments, who have really identified themselves with objects outside themselves, who are thoroughly involved with other persons, or institutions, or activities or causes, are actually happier than those whose projects and wants are not like that. If so, that is an important piece of utilitarian empirical lore.

When I say "happier" here, I have in mind the sort of consideration which any utilitarian would be committed to accepting: as for instance that such people are less likely to have a break-down or commit suicide. Of course that is not all that is actually involved, but the point in this argument is to use to the maximum degree utilitarian notions, in order to locate a breaking point in utilitarian thought. In appealing to this strictly utilitarian notion, I am being more consistent with utilitarianism than Smart is. In his struggles with the problem of the brain-electrode man, Smart . . . commends the idea that "happy" is a partly evaluative term, in the sense that we call "happiness" those kinds of satisfaction which, as things are, we approve of. But *by what standard* is this surplus element of approval supposed, from a utilitarian point of view, to be allocated? There is no source for it, on a strictly utilitarian view, except further degrees of satisfaction, but there are none of those available, or the problem would not arise. Nor does it help to appeal to the fact that we dislike in prospect things which we like when we get there, for from a utilitarian point of view it would seem that the original dislike was merely irrational or based on an error. Smart's argument at this point seems to be embarrassed by a well-known utilitarian uneasiness, which comes from a feeling that it is not respectable to ignore the "deep," while not having anywhere left in human life to locate it.

On a utilitarian view . . . [t]he determination to an indefinite degree of my decisions by other people's projects is just another aspect of my unlimited responsibility to act for the best in a causal framework formed to a considerable extent by their projects.

The decision so determined is, for utilitarianism, the right decision. But what if it conflicts with some project of mine? This, the utilitarian will say, has already been dealt with: the satisfaction to you of fulfilling your project, and any satisfaction to others of your so doing, have already been through the calculating device and have been found inadequate. Now in the case of many sorts of projects, that is a perfectly reasonable sort of answer. But in the case of projects of the sort I have called "commitments," those with which one is more deeply and extensively involved and identified, this cannot just by itself be an adequate answer, and there may be no adequate answer at all. For, to take the extreme sort of case, how can a man, as a utilitarian agent, come to regard as one satisfaction among others, and a dispensable one, a project or attitude round which he has built his life, just because someone else's projects have so structured the causal scene that that is how the utilitarian sum comes out?

The point here is not, as utilitarians may hasten to say, that if the project or attitude is that central to his life, then to abandon it will be very disagreeable to him and great loss of utility will be involved. . . . On the contrary, once he is prepared to look at it like that, the argument in any serious case is over anyway. The point is that he is identified with his actions as flowing from projects and attitudes which in some cases he takes seriously at the deepest level, as what his life is about (or, in some cases, this section of his life—seriousness is not necessarily the same as persistence). It is absurd to demand of such a man, when the sums come in from the utility network which the projects of others have in part determined, that he should just step aside from his own project and decision and acknowledge the decision which utilitarian calculation requires. It is to alienate him in a real sense from his actions and the source of his action in his own convictions. It is to make him into a channel between the input of everyone's projects, including his own, and an output of optimific decision; but this is to neglect the extent to which *his* actions and *his* decisions have to be seen as the actions and decisions which flow from the projects and attitudes with which he is most closely identified. It is thus, in the most literal sense, an attack on his integrity.

[T]he immediate point of all this is to draw one particular contrast with utilitarianism: that to reach a grounded decision . . . should not be regarded as a matter of just discontinuing one's reactions, impulses and deeply held projects in the face of the pattern of utilities, nor yet merely adding them in—but in the first instance of trying to understand them.

Of course, time and circumstances are unlikely to make a grounded decision, in Jim's case at least, possible. Very often, we just act, as a possibly confused result of the situation in which we are engaged. That, I suspect, is very often an exceedingly good thing.

**STUDY QUESTIONS**

1. What are Williams' main objections to consequentialism? Do these objections apply more to act utilitarianism than to rule utilitarianism?

2. Williams brings two cases that pose difficulties for the consequentialists. Discuss both cases. Do you think George's refusal to take the job is right? Could it be construed as right on utilitarian grounds?

3. What does Williams mean by "deeply held projects"? Why should they count for more than utility?

4. What difference does Williams see between acting in ways that result in twenty people being killed and acting directly by killing one of them. Evidently the actual killing is worse. But why? Do his arguments persuade you? (What is so wonderful about having clean hands and avoiding direct responsibility for a death when they are gained at the expense of twenty lives?)

5. You are J. J. C. Smart and have just read Williams' essay. Write a short rejoinder to it.

# Good Will, Duty, and the Categorical Imperative

## IMMANUEL KANT

### TRANSLATED BY T. K. ABBOTT

Immanuel Kant (1724–1804) is considered to be one of the greatest philosophers of all time. He lived in Königsberg, in East Prussia, and was a professor at the University there. Kant made significant and highly original contributions to esthetics, jurisprudence, and the philosophy of religion as well as to ethics and epistemology. His best known works are the *Critique of Pure Reason* (1781) and the *Foundations of the Metaphysics of Morals* (1785).

Human beings have desires and appetites. They are also rational, capable of knowing what is right and capable of willing to do it. They can therefore exercise their wills in the rational control of desire for the purpose of right action. This is what persons of moral worth do. According to Kant, to possess moral worth is more important than to possess intelligence, humor, strength, or any other talent of the mind or body. These talents are valuable but moral worth has *absolute* value, commanding not mere admiration but reverence and respect. Human beings who do right merely because it pleases them are not yet intrinsically moral. For had it pleased them they would have done wrong. To act morally is to act from no other

GOOD WILL, DUTY, AND THE CATEGORICAL IMPERATIVE From *Fundamental Principles of the Metaphysics of Morals*, by Immanuel Kant. Translated by T. K. Abbott (1898).

motive than the motive of doing what is right. This kind of motive has nothing to do with anything as subjective as pleasure. To do right out of principle is to recognize an objective right that imposes an obligation on any rational being. Moral persons act in such a way that they could will that the principles of their actions should be universal laws for everyone else as well. This is one test of a moral act: Is it the kind of act that everyone should perform? Kant illustrates how this test can be applied to determine whether a given principle is moral and objective or merely subjective. For example, I may wish to break a promise, but that cannot be moral since I cannot will that promise-breaking be a universal practice.

Universal principles impose *categorical* imperatives. An imperative is a demand that I act in a certain fashion. For example, if I want to buy a house, it is imperative that I learn something about houses. But "Learn about houses!" is a *hypothetical* imperative since it is *conditional* on my wanting to buy a house. A *categorical* imperative is unconditional. An example is "Keep your promises." Thus an imperative is not preceded by any condition such as "if you want a good reputation." Hypothetical imperatives are "prudential": "If you want security, buy theft insurance." Categorical imperatives are moral: "Do not lie!" Kant argues that the categorical imperative presupposes the absolute worth of all rational beings as ends in themselves. Thus another formulation of the categorical imperative is, "So act as to treat humanity . . . as an end withal, never as a means only." Kant calls the domain of beings that are to be treated in this way the "kingdom of ends."

Nothing can possibly be conceived in the world, or even out of it, which can be called good, without qualification, except a Good Will. Intelligence, wit, judgment, and the other *talents* of the mind, however they may be named, or courage, resolution, perseverance, as qualities of temperament, are undoubtedly good and desirable in many respects; but these gifts of nature may also become extremely

124

bad and mischievous if the will which is to make use of them, and which, therefore, constitutes what is called *character,* is not good. It is the same with the *gifts of fortune.* Power, riches, honour, even health, and the general well-being and contentment with one's condition which is called *happiness,* inspire pride, and often presumption, if there is not a good will to correct the influence of these on the mind, and with this also to rectify the whole principle of acting, and adapt it to its end. The sight of a being who is not adorned with a single feature of a pure and good will, enjoying unbroken prosperity, can never give pleasure to an impartial rational spectator. Thus a good will appears to constitute the indispensable condition even of being worthy of happiness.

There are even some qualities which are of service to this good will itself, and may facilitate its action, yet which have no intrinsic unconditional value, but always presuppose a good will, and this qualifies the esteem that we justly have for them, and does not permit us to regard them as absolutely good. Moderation in the affections and passions, self-control, and calm deliberation are not only good in many respects, but even seem to constitute part of the intrinsic worth of the person; but they are far from deserving to be called good without qualification, although they have been so unconditionally praised by the ancients. For without the principles of a good will, they may become extremely bad; and the coolness of a villain not only makes him far more dangerous, but also directly makes him more abominable in our eyes than he would have been without it.

A good will is good not because of what it performs or effects, not by its aptness for the attainment of some proposed end, but simply by virtue of the volition, that is, it is good in itself, and considered by itself is to be esteemed much higher than all that can be brought about by it in favour of any inclination, nay, even of the sum-total of all inclinations. Even if it should happen that, owing to special disfavour of fortune, or the niggardly provision of a step-motherly nature, this will should wholly lack power to accomplish its purpose, if with its greatest efforts it should yet achieve nothing, and there should remain only the good will (not, to be sure, a mere wish, but the summoning of all means in our power), then, like a jewel, it would still shine by its own light, as a thing which has its whole value in itself. Its usefulness or fruitlessness can neither add to nor take away anything from this value.

Thus the moral worth of an action does not lie in the effect expected from it, nor in any principle of action which requires to borrow its motive from this expected effect. For all these effects—agreeableness of one's condition, and even the promotion of the happiness of others—could have been also brought about by other causes, so that for this there would have been no need of the will of a rational being; whereas it is in this alone that the supreme and unconditional good can be found. The pre-eminent good which we call moral can therefore consist in nothing else than *the conception of law* in itself, *which certainly is only possible in a rational being,* in so far as this conception, and not the expected effect, determines the will. This is a good which is already present in the person who acts accordingly, and we have not to wait for it to appear first in the result.

But what sort of law can that be, the conception of which must determine the will, even without paying any regard to the effect expected from it, in order that this will may be called good absolutely and without qualification? As I have deprived the will of every impulse which could arise to it from obedience to any law, there remains nothing but the universal conformity of its actions to law in general, which alone is to serve the will as a principle, *i.e.* I am never to act otherwise than *so that I could also will that my maxim should become a universal law.* Here, now, it is the simple conformity to law in general, without assuming any particular law applicable to certain actions, that serves the will as its principle, and must so serve it, if duty is not to be a vain delusion and a chimerical notion. The common reason of men in its practical judgments perfectly coincides with this and always has in view the principle here suggested. Let the question be, for example: May I when in distress make a promise with the intention not to keep it? I readily distinguish here between the two significations which the question may have: Whether it is prudent, or whether it is right, to make a false promise? The former may undoubtedly often be the case. I see clearly indeed that it is not enough to extricate myself from a present difficulty by means of this subterfuge, but it must be well considered whether there may not hereafter spring from this lie much greater inconveniene than that from which I now free myself, and as, with all my supposed *cunning,* the consequences cannot be so easily foreseen but that credit once lost may be much more injurious to me than any mischief which I seek to avoid at present, it should be considered whether it would not be more *prudent* to act herein according to a universal maxim, and to make it a habit to promise nothing except with the intention of keeping it. But it is soon clear to me that such a maxim will still only be based on the fear of consequences. Now it is a wholly different thing to be truthful from duty, and to be so from apprehension of injurious consequences. In the first case, the very notion of the action already implies a law for me; in the second case, I must first look about elsewhere to see what results may be combined with it which would affect myself. For to deviate from the principle of duty is beyond all doubt wicked; but to be unfaithful to my maxim of prudence may often be very advantageous to me, although to abide by it is certainly safer. The shortest way, however, and an unerring one, to discover the answer to this question whether a lying promise is consistent with duty, is to ask myself, Should I be content that my maxim (to extricate myself from difficulty by a false promise) should hold good as a universal law, for myself as well as for others? and should I be able to say to myself, "Every one may make a deceitful promise when he finds himself in a difficulty from which he cannot otherwise extricate himself"? Then I presently become aware that while I can will the lie, I can by no means will that lying should be a universal law. For with such a law there would be no promises at all, since it would be in vain to allege my intention in regard to my future actions to those who would not believe this allegation, or if they over-hastily did so, would pay me back in my own coin. Hence my maxim, as soon as it should be made a universal law, would necessarily destroy itself.

I do not, therefore, need any far-reaching penetration to discern what I have to do in order that my will be morally good. Inexperienced in the course of the world, incapable of being prepared for all its contingencies, I only ask myself: Canst thou also will that thy maxim should be a universal law? If not, then it must be rejected, and that not because of a disadvantage accruing from it to myself or even to others, but because it cannot enter as a principle into a possible universal legislation, and reason extorts from me immediate respect for such legislation. I do not indeed as yet *discern* on what this respect is based (this the philosopher may inquire), but at least I understand this, that it is an estimation of the worth which far outweighs all worth of what is recommended by inclination, and that the necessity of acting from *pure* respect for the practical law is what

constitutes duty, to which every other motive must give place, because it is the condition of a will being good *in itself,* and the worth
of such a will is above everything. . . .

. . . Everything in nature works according to laws. Rational
beings alone have the faculty of acting according *to the conception* of
laws, that is according to principles, *i.e.* have a *will.* Since the deduction of actions from principles requires *reason,* the will is nothing but
practical reason. If reason infallibly determines the will, then the
actions of such a being which are recognized as objectively necessary
are subjectively necessary also, *i.e.* the will is a faculty to choose *that
only* which reason independent on inclination recognizes as practically necessary, *i.e.* as good. But if reason of itself does not sufficiently determine the will, if the latter is subject also to subjective
conditions (particular impulses) which do not always coincide with
the objective conditions; in a word, if the will does not *in itself* completely accord with reason (which is actually the case with men), then
the actions which objectively are recognized as necessary are subjectively contingent, and the determination of such a will according to
objective laws is *obligation,* that is to say, the relation of the objective
laws to a will that is not thoroughly good is conceived as the determination of the will of a rational being by principles of reason, but
which the will from its nature does not of necessity follow.

The conception of an objective principle, in so far as it is obligatory
for a will, is called a command (of reason), and the formula of the
command is called an Imperative. . . .

Now all *imperatives* command either *hypothetically* or *categorically.*
The former represent the practical necessity of a possible action as
means to something else that is willed (or at least which one might
possibly will). The categorical imperative would be that which represented an action as necessary of itself without reference to another
end, *i.e.* as objectively necessary.

Since every practical law represents a possible action as good, and
on this account, for a subject who is practically determinable by
reason, necessary, all imperatives are formulae determining an action
which is necessary according to the principle of a will good in some
respects. If now the action is good only as a means *to something else,*
then the imperative is *hypothetical;* if it is conceived as good *in itself*
and consequently as being necessarily the principle of a will which of
itself conforms to reason, then it is *categorical.* . . .

When I conceive a hypothetical imperative, in general I do not know beforehand what it will contain until I am given the condition. But when I conceive a categorical imperative, I know at once what it contains. For as the imperative contains besides the law only the necessity that the maxims shall conform to this law, while the law contains no conditions restricting it, there remains nothing but the general statement that the maxim of the action should conform to a universal law, and it is this conformity alone that the imperative properly represents as necessary.

There is . . . but one categorical imperative, namely, this: *Act only on that maxim whereby thou canst at the same time will that it should become a universal law.*

Now if all imperatives of duty can be deduced from this one imperative as from their principle, then, although it should remain undecided whether what is called duty is not merely a vain notion, yet at least we shall be able to show what we understand by it and what this notion means.

Since the universality of the law according to which effects are produced constitutes what is properly called *nature* in the most general sense (as to form), that is the existence of things so far as it is determined by general laws, the imperative of duty may be expressed thus: *Act as if the maxim of thy action were to become by thy will a universal law of nature.*

We will now enumerate a few duties, adopting the usual division of them into duties to ourselves and to others, and into perfect and imperfect duties.

1. A man reduced to despair by a series of misfortunes feels wearied of life, but is still so far in possession of his reason that he can ask himself whether it would not be contrary to his duty to himself to take his own life. Now he inquires whether the maxim of his action could become a universal law of nature. His maxim is: From self-love I adopt it as a principle to shorten my life when its longer duration is likely to bring more evil than satisfaction. It is asked then simply whether this principle founded on self-love can become a universal law of nature. Now we see at once that a system of nature of which it should be a law to destroy life by means of the very feeling whose special nature it is to impel to the improvement of life would contradict itself, and therefore could not exist as a system of nature; hence that maxim cannot possibly exist as a universal law of

nature, and consequently would be wholly inconsistent with the supreme principle of all duty.

2. Another finds himself forced by necessity to borrow money. He knows that he will not be able to repay it, but sees also that nothing will be lent to him, unless he promises stoutly to repay it in a definite time. He desires to make this promise, but he has still so much conscience as to ask himself: Is it not unlawful and inconsistent with duty to get out of a difficulty in this way? Suppose, however, that he resolves to do so, then the maxim of his action would be expressed thus: When I think myself in want of money, I will borrow money and promise to repay it, although I know that I never can do so. Now this principle of self-love or of one's own advantage may perhaps be consistent with my whole future welfare; but the question now is, Is it right? I change then the suggestion of self-love into a universal law, and state the question thus: How would it be if my maxim were a universal law? Then I see at once that it could never hold as a universal law of nature, but would necessarily contradict itself. For supposing it to be a universal law that everyone when he thinks himself in a difficulty should be able to promise whatever he pleases, with the purpose of not keeping his promise, the promise itself would become impossible, as well as the end that one might have in view in it, since no one would consider that anything was promised to him, but would ridicule all such statements as vain pretences.

3. A third finds in himself a talent which with the help of some culture might make him a useful man in many respects. But he finds himself in comfortable circumstances, and prefers to indulge in pleasure rather than to take pains in enlarging and improving his happy natural capacities. He asks, however, whether his maxim of neglect of his natural gifts, besides agreeing with his inclination to indulgence, agrees also with what is called duty. He sees then that a system of nature could indeed subsist with such a universal law although men (like the South Sea islanders) should let their talents rest, and resolve to devote their lives merely to idleness, amusement, and propagation of their species—in a word, to enjoyment; but he cannot possibly *will* that this should be a universal law of nature, or be implanted in us as such by a natural instinct. For, as a rational being, he necessarily wills that his faculties be developed, since they serve him, and have been given him, for all sorts of possible purposes.

4. A fourth, who is in prosperity, while he sees that others have to contend with great wretchedness and that he could help them, thinks: What concern is it of mine? Let everyone be as happy as Heaven pleases, or as he can make himself; I will take nothing from him nor even envy him, only I do not wish to contribute anything to his welfare or to his assistance in distress! Now no doubt if such a mode of thinking were a universal law, the human race might very well subsist, and doubtless even better than in a state in which everyone talks of sympathy and good-will, or even takes care occasionally to put it into practice, but, on the other side, also cheats when he can, betrays the rights of men, or otherwise violates them. But although it is possible that a universal law of nature might exist in accordance with that maxim, it is impossible to *will* that such a principle should have the universal validity of a law of nature. For a will which resolved this would contradict itself, inasmuch as many cases might occur in which one would have need of the love and sympathy of others, and in which, by such a law of nature, sprung from his own will, he would deprive himself of all hope of the aid he desires. . . .

We have thus established at least this much, that if duty is a conception which is to have any import and real legislative authority for our actions, it can only be expressed in categorical, and not at all in hypothetical imperatives. We have also, which is of great importance, exhibited clearly and definitely for every practical application the content of the categorical imperative, which must contain the principle of all duty if there is such a thing at all. We have not yet, however, advanced so far as to prove *à priori* that there actually is such an imperative, that there is a practical law which commands absolutely of itself, and without any other impulse, and that the following of this law is duty. . . .

Now I say: man and generally any rational being *exists* as an end in himself, *not merely as a means* to be arbitrarily used by this or that will, but in all his actions, whether they concern himself or other rational beings, must be always regarded at the same time as an end. All objects of the inclinations have only a conditional worth; for if the inclinations and the wants founded on them did not exist, then their object would be without value. But the inclinations themselves being sources of want are so far from having an absolute worth for which they should be desired, that, on the contrary, it must be the universal wish of every rational being to be wholly free from them.

Thus the worth of any object which is *to be acquired* by our action is always conditional. Beings whose existence depends not on our will but on nature's, have nevertheless, if they are non-rational beings, only a relative value as means, and are therefore called *things;* rational beings, on the contrary, are called *persons,* because their very nature points them out as ends in themselves, that is as something which must not be used merely as means, and so far therefore restricts freedom of action (and is an object of respect). These, therefore, are not merely subjective ends whose existence has a worth *for us* as an effort of our action, but *objective ends,* that is things whose existence is an end in itself: an end moreover for which no other can be substituted, which they should subserve *merely* as means, for otherwise nothing whatever would possess *absolute worth;* but if all worth were conditioned and therefore contingent, then there would be no supreme practical principle of reason whatever.

If then there is a supreme practical principle or, in respect of the human will, a categorical imperative, it must be one which, being drawn from the conception of that which is necessarily an end for everyone because it is an *an end in itself,* constitutes an *objective* principle of will, and can therefore serve as a universal practical law. The foundation of this principle is: *rational nature exists as an end in itself.* Man necessarily conceives his own existence as being so: so far then this is a *subjective* principle of human actions. But every other rational being regards its existence similarly, just on the same rational principle, that holds for me: so that it is at the same time an objective principle, from which as a supreme practical law all laws of the will must be capable of being deduced. Accordingly the practical imperative will be as follows: *So act as to treat humanity, whether in thine own person or in that of any other, in every case as an end withal, never as means only. . . .*

The conception of every rational being as one which must consider itself as giving all the maxims of its will universal laws, so as to judge itself and its actions from this point of view—this conception leads to another which depends on it and is very fruitful, namely, that of a *kingdom of ends.*

By a *kingdom* I understand the union of different rational beings in a system by common laws. Now since it is by laws that ends are determined as regards their universal validity, hence, if we abstract from the personal differences of rational beings, and likewise from all the content of their private ends, we shall be able to conceive all ends combined in a systematic whole (including both rational beings as ends in themselves, and also the special ends which each may propose of himself), that is to say, we can conceive a kingdom of ends, which on the preceding principles is possible.

For all rational beings come under the *law* that each of them must treat itself and all others *never merely as means,* but in every case *at the same time as ends in themselves.* Hence results a systematic union of rational beings by common objective laws, *i.e.* a kingdom which may be called a kingdom of ends. . . .

**STUDY QUESTIONS**

1. Why does Kant say that the good will is good without qualification?
2. What relationship does duty have to appetite? Duty to reason?
3. What does Kant mean by saying that certain beings have intrinsic value as ends in themselves? What obligations do such beings impose on moral agents?
4. For Kant, animals are not ends in themselves because they cannot reason. So, says Kant, they have no moral rights. Does this seem right to you?
5. How does Kant distinguish between hypothetical and categorical imperatives? What kind of imperatives do "prudential" concerns enjoin?
6. In World War II, the British deciphered the German military intelligence code, thereby saving countless lives. Learning from messages that certain intelligence officers were going to be captured and tortured, they nevertheless sent them back to the Continent to preserve the secret that the code had been cracked. Evaluate this case from the standpoint of (a) a utilitarian, (b) a Kantian, (c) yourself.

# Kant and The Categorical Imperative

## JAMES RACHELS

James Rachels explains and criticizes Kant's categorical ties at the University of Alabama. He is the editor of several books, including *Moral Problems: A Collection of Philosophical Essays* (1979) and *Understanding Moral Philosophy* (1976), and the author of *The Elements of Moral Philosophy* (1986).

James Rachels explains and criticizes Kant's categorical imperative. Although his critical purpose is to examine what is wrong with it, his broad general purpose is to define what is basically right about it. An imperative tells us what we ought to do. A *hypothetical* imperative says: "You ought to do Y *if* you want to bring about a consequence X." A *categorical* imperative is unconditional. It says: "You ought to do Y *even if* the consequences are not what you want." Categorical oughts are binding on moral agents simply because any rational agent must accept them. To determine whether a contemplated action is categorical, we follow two steps:

1. First, formulate the rule under which the action is taking place.
2. Next, determine whether the rule is one to which you would want to see everyone adhere.

KANT AND THE CATEGORICAL IMPERATIVE From *Elements of Moral Philosophy* by James Rachels. Copyright © 1986 by Random House, Inc. Reprinted by permission of the publisher.

For example, if you are contemplating getting a loan by making a false promise to repay, you would formulate the rule as: "If one needs money and cannot get it honestly, one should use deceptive means to get it." Having determined that this is the rule of your proposed action, you next determine whether it is a rule that you would like to see applied universally. Clearly not. Such a rule is self-defeating; promises would be meaningless.

According to Kant, "Never lie" is a categorical imperative that, Rachels notes, leads Kant to the implausible view that one should tell the truth even if the consequences are monstrous. (Consider: suppose you are transporting Jewish children to Sweden and a Nazi naval patrol officer asks you what your cargo is, telling the truth would mean their deportation and death—and probably your own death as well.) Rachels points out that Kant's explanation of the categorical imperative is inadequate since he places no constraints on how to formulate the imperative. For example, "Should I tell the Nazi the truth?" Answer (1): Follow the maxim "Never lie." Answer (2): Follow the maxim "Always lie to save innocent lives." Both maxims suit the occasion, but only the second is plausibly "universalizable." Rachels also notes that Kant ignores the possibility that two maxims can conflict: "Never lie" and "Save lives." Thus, Kant's own formulation of the categorical imperative must be modified.

What is *right* about Kant's perspective on ethics is his insistence that ethical rules must be binding on all people at all times, and that ethical rules must be consistent with one another. Thus, there are rational constraints on what we may do. One cannot think consistently that one *may* act as others—in similar circumstances—*may not* act.

In spite of its horrifying title Kant's *Groundwork of the Metaphysics of Morals* is one of the small books which are truly great: it has exercised on human thought an influence almost ludicrously disproportionate to its size.

H. J. PATON, *THE MORAL LAW* (1948)

Imagine that someone is fleeing from a murderer and tells you he is going home to hide. Then the murderer comes along and asks where the first man went. You believe that if you tell the truth, the murderer will find his victim and kill him. What should you do—should you tell the truth or lie?

We might call this The Case of the Inquiring Murderer. In this case, most of us would think it is obvious what we should do: we should lie. Of course, we don't think we should go about lying as a general rule, but in these specific circumstances it seems the right thing to do. After all, we might say, which is more important, telling the truth or saving someone's life? Surely in a case such as *this* lying is justified.

There is one important philosopher, however, who thought we should *never* lie, even in a case such as this. Immanuel Kant (1724–1804) was one of the seminal figures in modern philosophy. Almost alone among the great thinkers, Kant believed that morality is a matter of following *absolute rules*—rules that admit no exceptions, that must be followed come what may. He believed, for example, that lying is never right, no matter what the circumstances. It is hard to see how such a radical view could be defended, unless, perhaps, one held that such rules are God's unconditional commands. But Kant did not appeal to theological considerations; he relied only on rational arguments, holding that *reason* requires that we never lie. Let us see how he reached this remarkable conclusion. First we will look briefly at his general theory of ethics.

Kant observed that the word "ought" is often used nonmorally. For example:

1. If you want to become a better chess player, you ought to study the games of Bobby Fischer.
2. If you want to go to law school, you ought to sign up to take the entrance examination.

Much of our conduct is governed by such "oughts." The pattern is: we have a certain wish (to become a better chess player, to go to law school); we recognize that a certain course of action would help us get what we want (studying Fischer's games, signing up for the entrance examination); and so we conclude that we should follow the indicated plan.

Kant called these "hypothetical imperatives" because they tell us what to do *provided that* we have the relevant desires. A person who did not want to improve his or her chess would have no reason to study Fischer's games; someone who did not want to go to law school would have no reason to take the entrance examination. Because the binding force of the "ought" depends on our having the relevant desire, we can *escape* its force simply by renouncing the desire. Thus by saying "I no longer want to go to law school," one can get out of the obligation to take the exam.

Moral obligations, by contrast, do not depend on our having particular desires. The form of a moral obligation is not "If you want so-and-so, then you ought to do such-and-such." Instead, moral requirements are *categorical:* they have the form, "You ought to do such-and-such, *period.*" The moral rule is not, for example, that you ought to help people *if* you care for them or *if* you have some other purpose that helping them might serve. Instead, the rule is that you should be helpful to people *regardless of* your particular wants and desires. That is why, unlike hypothetical "oughts," moral requirements cannot be escaped simply by saying "But I don't care about that."

Hypothetical "oughts" are easy to understand. They merely require us to adopt the means that are necessary to attain the ends we choose to seek. Categorical "oughts," on the other hand, are rather mysterious. How can we be obligated to behave in a certain way regardless of the ends we wish to achieve? Much of Kant's moral philosophy is an attempt to explain what categorical "oughts" are and how they are possible.

Kant holds that, just as hypothetical "oughts" are possible because we have desires, categorical "oughts" are possible because we have reason. Categorical "oughts" are binding on rational agents *simply because they are rational.* How can this be so? It is, Kant says, because categorical oughts are derived from a principle that every rational person must accept. He calls this principle *The Categorical Imperative.* In his *Groundwork of the Metaphysics of Morals* (1785), he expresses The Categorical Imperative like this:

> Act only according to that maxim by which you can at the same time will that it should become a universal law.

This principle summarizes a procedure for deciding whether an act is morally permissible. When you are contemplating doing a particular action, you are to ask what rule you would be following if you were to do that action. (This will be the "maxim" of the act.) Then you are to ask whether you would be willing for that rule to be followed by everyone all the time. (That would make it a "universal law" in the relevant sense.) If so, the rule may be followed, and the act is permissible. However, if you would *not* be willing for everyone to follow the rule, then you may not follow it, and the act is morally impermissible.

Kant gives several examples to explain how this works. Suppose, he says, a man needs to borrow money, and he knows that no one will lend it to him unless he promises to repay. But he also knows that he will be unable to repay. He therefore faces this question: Should he promise to repay the debt, knowing that he cannot do so, in order to persuade someone to make the loan? If he were to do that, the "maxim of the act" (the rule he would be following) would be: *Whenever you need a loan, promise to repay it, even though you know you cannot do so.* Now, could this rule become a universal law? Obviously not, because it would be self-defeating. Once this became a universal practice, no one would any longer believe such promises, and so no one would make loans because of them. As Kant himself puts it, "no one would believe what was promised to him but would only laugh at any such assertion as vain pretense."

Another of Kant's examples has to do with giving charity. Suppose, he says, someone refuses to help others in need, saying to himself "What concern of mine is it? Let each one be happy as heaven wills, or as he can make himself; I will not take anything from him or even envy him; but to his welfare or to his assistance in time of need I have no desire to contribute." This, again, is a rule that one cannot will to be a universal law. For at some time in the future this man might *himself* be in need of assistance from others, and he would not want others to be so indifferent to him.

### Absolute Rules and the Duty Not to Lie

Being a moral agent, then, means guiding one's conduct by "universal laws"—moral rules that hold, without exception, in all circumstances. Kant thought that the rule against lying was one such rule. Of course, this was not the *only* absolute rule Kant defended—he thought there are many others; morality is full of them. But it will be useful to focus on the rule against lying as a convenient example. Kant devoted considerable space to discussing this rule, and it is clear that he felt especially strong about it—he said that lying in any circumstances is "the obliteration of one's dignity as a human being."

Kant offered two main arguments for this view. Let us examine them one at a time.

1. His primary reason for thinking that lying is always wrong was that the prohibition of lying follows straightaway from The Categorical Imperative. We could not will that it be a universal law that we should lie, because it would be self-defeating; people would quickly learn that they could not rely on what other people said, and so the lies would not be believed. Surely there is something to this: in order for a lie to be successful, people must believe that others are telling the truth; so the success of a lie depends on there *not* being a "universal law" permitting it.

There is, however, an important problem with this argument, which will become clear if we spell out Kant's line of thought more fully. Let us return to The Case of the Inquiring Murderer. Should you tell him the truth? Kant would have you reason as follows:

1.  You should do only those actions that conform to rules that you could will to be adopted universally.
2.  If you were to lie, you would be following the rule "It is permissible to lie."
3.  This rule could not be adopted universally, because it would be self-defeating: people would stop believing one another, and then it would do no good to lie.
4.  Therefore, you should not lie.

The problem with this way of reasoning was nicely summarized by the British philosopher Elizabeth Anscombe when she wrote about Kant in the academic journal *Philosophy* in 1958:

> His own rigoristic convictions on the subject of lying were so intense that it never occurred to him that a lie could be relevantly described as anything but just a lie (e.g. as "a lie in such-and-such circumstances"). His rule about universalizable maxims is useless without stipulations as to what shall count as a relevant description of an action with a view to constructing a maxim about it.

The difficulty arises in step (2) of the argument. Exactly what rule would you be following if you lied? The crucial point is that there are many ways to formulate the rule; some of them might not be "universalizable" in Kant's sense, but some would be. Suppose we said you were following *this* rule (R): "It is permissible to lie when doing so would save someone's life." We *could* will that (R) be made a "universal law," and it would not be self-defeating.

It might be replied that the universal adoption of (R) *would* be self-defeating because potential murderers would cease to believe us. But they would believe us if they thought we did not know what they were up to; and if they thought we *did* know what they were up to, they would not bother to ask us in the first place. This is no different from the situation that exists now, in the real world: murderers know that people will not willingly aid them. Thus the adoption of (R) would help save lives, at little cost, and it would not undermine general confidence in what people say in ordinary circumstances.

The problem we have identified is a central difficulty for Kant's whole approach. It applies not only to the argument about lying but to any decision about what to do: for any action a person might contemplate, it is possible to specify more than one rule that he or she would be following; some of these rules will be "universalizable" and some will not; therefore, the test of "universalizability" cannot help us to establish which actions are permissible and which are not. This is equally a problem for any view that takes moral rules as absolute, regardless of whether the view takes its inspiration from Kant. For we can always get around any such rule by describing our action in such a way that it does not fall under that rule but instead comes under a different one.

2. The Case of the Inquiring Murderer is not simply an example I made up; it is Kant's own example. In an essay with the charmingly old-fashioned title "On a Supposed Right to Lie from Altruistic Motives," Kant discusses this case and gives a second argument for his view about it. He writes:

> After you have honestly answered the murderer's question as to whether his intended victim is at home, it may be that he has slipped out so that he does not come in the way of the murderer, and thus that the murder may not be committed. But if you had lied and said he was not at home when he had really gone out without your knowing it, and if the murderer had then met him as he went away and murdered him, you might justly be accused as the cause of his death. For if you had told the truth as far as you knew it, perhaps the murderer might have been apprehended by the neighbors while he searched the house and thus the deed might have been prevented. Therefore, whoever

tells a lie, however well intentioned he might be, must answer for the consequences, however unforeseeable they were, and pay the penalty for them. . . .

To be truthful (honest) in all deliberations, therefore, is a sacred and absolutely commanding decree of reason, limited by no expediency.

This argument may be stated in a more general form: We are tempted to make exceptions to the rule against lying because in some cases we think the consequences of truthfulness would be bad and the consequences of lying good. However, we can never be certain about what the consequences of our actions will be; we cannot *know* that good results will follow. The results of lying *might* be unexpectedly bad. Therefore, the best policy is always to avoid the known evil—lying— and let the consequences come as they will. Even if the consequences are bad, they will not be our fault, for we will have done our duty.

The problems with this argument are obvious enough—so obvious, in fact, that it is surprising a philosopher of Kant's stature was not more sensitive to them. In the first place, the argument depends on an unreasonably pessimistic view of what we can know. Sometimes we can be quite confident of what the consequences of our actions will be, and justifiably so; in which case we need not hesitate because of uncertainty. Moreover—and this is a more interesting matter, from a philosophical point of view—Kant seems to assume that although we would be morally responsible for any bad consequences of lying, we would *not* be similarly responsible for any bad consequences of telling the truth. Suppose, as a result of our telling the truth, the murderer found his victim and killed him. Kant seems to assume that we would be blameless. But can we escape responsibility so easily? After all, we aided the murderer. This argument, then, like the first one, is not very convincing.

## Conflicts Between Rules

The idea that moral rules are absolute, allowing no exceptions, is implausible in light of such cases as The Case of the Inquiring Murderer, and Kant's arguments for it are unsatisfactory. But are there any convincing arguments against the idea, apart from its being implausible?

The principal argument against absolute moral rules has to do with the possibility of conflict cases. Suppose it is held to be absolutely wrong to do A in any circumstances and also wrong to do B in any circumstances. Then what about the case in which a person is faced with the choice between doing A and doing B—when he must do something and there are no other alternatives available? This kind of conflict case seems to show that it is *logically* untenable to hold that moral rules are absolute.

Is there any way that this objection can be met? One way would be for the absolutist to deny that such cases ever actually occur. The British philosopher P. T. Geach takes just this view. Like Kant, Geach argues that moral rules are absolute; but his reasons are very different from Kant's. Geach holds that moral rules must be understood as absolute divine commands, and so he says simply that God will not allow conflict situations to arise. We can describe fictitious cases in which there is no way to avoid violating one of the absolute rules, but, he says, God will not permit such circumstances to exist in the real world. In his book *God and the Soul* (1969) Geach writes:

> "But suppose circumstances are such that observance of one Divine law, say the law against lying, involves breach of some other absolute Divine prohibition?"—If God is rational, he does not command the impossible; if God governs all events by his providence, he can see to it that circumstances in which a man is inculpably faced by a choice between forbidden acts do not occur. Of course such circumstances (with the clause "and there is no way out" written into their description) are consistently describable; but God's providence could ensure that they do not in fact arise. Contrary to what nonbelievers often say, belief in the existence of God does make a difference to what one expects to happen.

Do such circumstances ever actually arise? The Case of the Inquiring Murderer is, of course, a fictitious example; but it is not difficult to find real-life examples that make the same point. During the Second World War, Dutch fishermen regularly smuggled Jewish refugees to England in their boats, and the following sort of thing sometimes happened. A Dutch boat, with refugees in the hold, would be stopped by a Nazi patrol boat. The Nazi captain would call out and ask the Dutch captain where he was bound, who was on board, and so forth. The fishermen would lie and be allowed to pass. Now it is clear that the fishermen had only two alternatives, to lie or to allow their passengers (and themselves) to be taken and shot. No third alternative was available; they could not, for example, remain silent and outrun the Nazis.

Now suppose the two rules "It is wrong to lie" and "It is wrong to permit the murder of innocent people" are both taken to be absolute. The Dutch fishermen would have to do one of these things; therefore a moral view that absolutely prohibits both is incoherent. Of course this difficulty could be avoided if one held that only *one* of these rules is absolute; that would apparently be Kant's way out. But this dodge cannot work in every such case; so long as there are at least two "absolute rules," whatever they might be, the possibility will always exist that they might come into conflict. And that makes the view of those rules as absolute impossible to maintain.

## Another Look at Kant's Basic Idea

Few philosophers would dispute Paton's statement that Kant's *Groundwork* "has exercised on human thought an influence almost ludicrously disproportionate to its size." Yet at the same time, few would defend The Categorical Imperative as Kant formulated it—as we have seen, it is beset by serious, perhaps insurmountable, problems. What, then, accounts for Kant's influence? Is there some basic idea underlying The Categorical Imperative that we might accept, even if we do not accept Kant's particular way of expressing it? I believe that there is, and that the power of this idea accounts, at least in part, for Kant's vast influence.

Remember that Kant thinks The Categorical Imperative is binding on rational agents simply because they are rational—in other words, a person who did not accept this principle would be guilty not merely of being immoral but of being *irrational*. This is a fascinating idea—that there are rational as well as moral constraints on what a good person may believe and do. But what exactly does this mean? In what sense would it be irrational to reject The Categorical Imperative?

The basic idea seems to be this: A moral judgment must be backed by good reasons—if it is true that you ought (or ought not) to do such-and-such, then there must be a *reason why* you should (or should not) do it. For example, you may think that you ought not to set forest fires because property would be destroyed and people would be killed. But if you accept those as reasons in *one* case, you must also accept them as reasons in *other* cases. It is no good saying that you accept those reasons some of the time, but not all the time; or that other people must respect them, but not you. Moral reasons, if they are valid at all, are binding on all people at all times. This is a requirement of consistency; and Kant was right to think that no rational person could deny it.

This is the Kantian idea—or, I should say, one of the Kantian ideas—that has been so influential. It has a number of important implications. It implies that a person cannot regard himself as special, from a moral point of view: he cannot consistently think that *he* is permitted to act in ways that are forbidden to others, or that *his* interests are more important than other people's interests. As one commentator remarked, I cannot say that it is all right for me to drink your beer and then complain when you drink mine. Moreover, it implies that there are *rational constraints* on what we may do: we may want to do something—say, drink someone else's beer—but recognize that we cannot *consistently* do it, because we cannot at the same time accept its implications. If Kant was not the first to recognize this, he was the first to make it the cornerstone of a fully worked-out system of morals. That was his great contribution.

But Kant went one step further and concluded that consistency requires rules that have no exceptions. It is not hard to see how his basic idea pushed him in that direction; but the extra step was not necessary, and it has caused trouble for his theory ever since. Rules, even within a Kantian framework, *need not* be regarded as absolute. All that is required by Kant's basic idea is that when we violate a rule, we do so for a reason that we would be willing for anyone to accept, were they in our position. In The Case of the Inquiring Murderer, this means that we may violate the rule against lying only if we would be willing for anyone to do so were they faced with the same situation. And *that* proposition causes little trouble.

### The Idea of "Human Dignity"

The great German philosopher Immanuel Kant thought that human beings occupy a special place in creation. Of course he was not alone in thinking this. It is an old idea: from ancient times, humans have considered themselves to be essentially different from all other creatures—and not just different but *better*. In fact, humans have traditionally thought themselves to be quite fabulous. Kant certainly did. On his view, human beings have "an intrinsic worth, i.e., *dignity,*" which makes them valuable "above all price." Other animals, by contrast, have value only insofar as they serve human purposes. In his *Lectures on Ethics* (1779), Kant said:

> But so far as animals are concerned, we have no direct duties. Animals . . . are there merely as means to an end. That end is man.

We can, therefore, use animals in any way we please. We do not even have a "direct duty" to refrain from torturing them. Kant admits that it probably is wrong to torture them, but the reason is not that *they* would be hurt; the reason is only that *we* might suffer indirectly as a result of it, because "he who is cruel to animals becomes hard also in his dealings with men." Thus on Kant's view, mere animals have no moral importance at all. Human beings are, however, another story entirely. According to Kant, humans may never be "used" as means to an end. He even went so far as to suggest that this is the ultimate law of morality.

Like many other philosophers, Kant believed that morality can be summed up in one ultimate principle, from which all our duties and obligations are derived. He called this principle *The Categorical Imperative*. In the *Groundwork of the Metaphysics of Morals* (1785) he expressed it like this:

> Act only according to that maxim by which you can at the same time will that it should become a universal law.

However, Kant also gave *another* formulation of The Categorical Imperative. Later in the same book, he said that the ultimate moral principle may be understood as saying:

> Act so that you treat humanity, whether in your own person or in that of another, always as an end and never as a means only.

Scholars have wondered ever since why Kant thought these two rules were equivalent. They *seem* to express very different moral conceptions. Are they, as he apparently believed, two versions of the same basic idea, or are they really different ideas? We will not pause over this question. Instead we will concentrate here on Kant's belief that morality requires us to treat persons "always as an end and never as a means only." What exactly does this mean, and why did he think it true?

When Kant said that the value of human beings "is above all price," he did not intend this as mere rhetoric but as an objective judgment about the place of human beings in the scheme of things. There are two important facts about people that, in his view, support this judgment.

First, because people have desires and goals, other things have value *for them,* in relation to *their* projects. Mere "things" (and this includes nonhuman animals, whom Kant considered unable to have self-conscious desires and goals) have value only as means to ends, and it is human ends that *give* them value. Thus if you want to become a better chess player, a book of chess instruction will have value for you; but apart from such ends the book has no value. Or if you want to travel about, a car will have value for you; but apart from this desire the car will have no value.

Second, and even more important, humans have "an intrinsic worth, i.e., *dignity,*" because they are *rational agents*—that is, free agents capable of making their own decisions, setting their own goals, and guiding their conduct by reason. Because the moral law is the law of reason, rational beings are the embodiment of the moral law itself. The only way that moral goodness can exist at all in the world is for rational creatures to apprehend what they should do and, acting from a sense of duty, do it. This, Kant thought, is the *only* thing that has "moral worth." Thus if there were no rational beings, the moral dimension of the world would simply disappear.

It makes no sense, therefore, to regard rational beings merely as one kind of valuable thing among others. They are the beings *for whom* mere "things" have value, and they are the beings whose conscientious actions have moral worth. So Kant concludes that their value must be absolute, and not comparable to the value of anything else.

If their value is "beyond all price," it follows that rational beings must be treated "always as an end, and never as a means only." This means, on the most superficial level, that we have a strict duty of beneficence toward other persons: we must strive to promote their welfare; we must respect their rights, avoid harming them, and generally "endeavor, so far as we can, to further the ends of others."

But Kant's idea also has a somewhat deeper implication. The

beings we are talking about are *rational* beings, and "treating them as ends-in-themselves" means *respecting their rationality*. Thus we may never *manipulate* people, or *use* people, to achieve our purposes, no matter how good those purposes may be. Kant gives this example, which is similar to an example he uses to illustrate the first version of his categorical imperative: Suppose you need money, and so you want a "loan," but you know you will not be able to repay it. In desperation, you consider making a false promise (to repay) in order to trick a friend into giving you the money. May you do this? Perhaps you need the money for a good purpose—so good, in fact, that you might convince yourself the lie would be justified. Nevertheless, if you lied to your friend, you would merely be manipulating him and using him "as a means."

On the other hand, what would it be like to treat your friend "as an end"? Suppose you told the truth, that you need the money for a certain purpose but will not be able to repay it. Then your friend could make up his own mind about whether to let you have it. He could exercise his own powers of reason, consulting his own values and wishes, and make a free, autonomous choice. If he did decide to give the money for this purpose, he would be choosing to make that purpose *his own*. Thus you would not merely be using him as a means to achieving *your* goal. This is what Kant meant when he said, "Rational beings . . . must always be esteemed at the same time as ends, i.e., only as beings who must be able to contain in themselves the end of the very same action."

**STUDY QUESTIONS**

1. How does Rachels explain Kant's enormous influence on human thought in the area of moral theory?
2. What does Rachels think is wrong with Kant's formulation of the categorical imperative? How does Rachels use the "never lie" example to expose what is wrong?
3. Rachels argues that Kant's contribution is his view of the moral agent as essentially rational. In what sense is Kant's morality centered on "rationality"?
4. How does conflict between rules prove embarrassing to Kant's

theory? Does Rachels' modified form of Kantianism escape this embarrassment?

5.  Kant's stress on rationality leads him to a conception of human dignity that excludes animals from the domain of beings who are morally "considerable." Examine this facet of Kant's theory. Do you agree with it? If you do not, how would you modify Kant to retain what you deem valuable in his conception of dignity?

# A Defense of Moral Relativism

## RUTH BENEDICT

Ruth Benedict (1887–1948) was one of America's foremost anthropologists. Her *Patterns of Culture* (1935) is considered a classic of comparative anthropology.

Morality, says Benedict, is a convenient term for socially approved customs (mores). What one society approves may be disgraceful and unacceptable to another. Moral rules, like rules of etiquette or styles of dress, vary from society to society. Morality is culturally relative. Values are shaped by culture. As Benedict points out, trances are highly regarded in India, so in India many people have trances. Some ancient societies praised homosexual love, so there homosexuality was a norm. Where material possessions are highly valued, people amass property. "Most individuals are plastic to the moulding force of the society into which they are born."

A DEFENSE OF MORAL RELATIVISM From "Anthropology and the Abnormal," by Ruth Benedict, in *The Journal of General Psychology* 10 (1934): 59–82. Reprinted by permission of Clark University Press.

Modern social anthropology has become more and more a study of the varieties and common elements of cultural environment and the consequences of these in human behavior. For such a study of diverse social orders primitive peoples fortunately provide a laboratory not yet entirely vitiated by the spread of a standardized worldwide civilization. Dyaks and Hopis, Fijians and Yakuts are significant for psychological and sociological study because only among these simpler peoples has there been sufficient isolation to give opportunity for the development of localized social forms. In the higher cultures the standardization of custom and belief over a couple of continents has given a false sense of the inevitability of the particular forms that have gained currency, and we need to turn to a wider survey in order to check the conclusions we hastily base upon this near-universality of familiar customs. Most of the simpler cultures did not gain the wide currency of the one which, out of our experience, we identify with human nature, but this was for various historical reasons, and certainly not for any that gives us as its carriers a monopoly of social good or of social sanity. Modern civilization, from this point of view, becomes not a necessary pinnacle of human achievement but one entry in a long series of possible adjustments.

These adjustments, whether they are in mannerisms like the ways of showing anger, or joy, or grief in any society, or in major human drives like those of sex, prove to be far more variable than experience in any one culture would suggest. In certain fields, such as that of religion or of formal marriage arrangements, these wide limits of variability are well known and can be fairly described. In others it is not yet possible to give a generalized account, but that does not absolve us of the task of indicating the significance of the work that has been done and of the problems that have arisen.

One of these problems relates to the customary modern normal-abnormal categories and our conclusions regarding them. In how far are such categories culturally determined, or in how far can we with assurance regard them as absolute? In how far can we regard inability to function socially as diagnostic of abnormality, or in how far is it necessary to regard this as a function of the culture?

As a matter of fact, one of the most striking facts that emerge from a study of widely varying cultures is the ease with which our abnormals function in other cultures. It does not matter what kind of "abnormality" we choose for illustration, those which indicate extreme instability, or those which are more in the nature of character

149

traits like sadism or delusions of grandeur or of persecution, there are well-described cultures in which these abnormals function at ease and with honor, and apparently without danger or difficulty to the society.

The most notorious of these is trance and catalepsy. Even a very mild mystic is aberrant in our culture. But most peoples have regarded even extreme psychic manifestations not only as normal and desirable, but even as characteristic of highly valued and gifted individuals. This was true even in our own cultural background in that period when Catholicism made the ecstatic experience the mark of sainthood. It is hard for us, born and brought up in a culture that makes no use of the experience, to realize how important a role it may play and how many individuals are capable of it, once it has been given an honorable place in any society. . . .

Cataleptic and trance phenomena are, of course, only one illustration of the fact that those whom we regard as abnormals may function adequately in other cultures. Many of our culturally discarded traits are selected for elaboration in different societies. Homosexuality is an excellent example, for in this case our attention is not constantly diverted, as in the consideration of trance, to the interruption of routine activity which it implies. Homosexuality poses the problem very simply. A tendency toward this trait in our culture exposes an individual to all the conflicts to which all aberrants are always exposed, and we tend to identify the consequences of this conflict with homosexuality. But these consequences are obviously local and cultural. Homosexuals in many societies are not incompetent, but they may be such if the culture asks adjustments of them that would strain any man's vitality. Wherever homosexuality has been given an honorable place in any society, those to whom it is congenial have filled adequately the honorable roles society assigns to them. Plato's *Republic* is, of course, the most convincing statement of such a reading of homosexuality. It is presented as one of the major means to the good life, and it was generally so regarded in Greece at that time.

The cultural attitude toward homosexuals has not always been on such a high ethical plane, but it has been very varied. Among many American Indian tribes there exists the institution of the berdache, as the French called them. These men-women were men who at puberty or thereafter took the dress and the occupations of women. Sometimes they married other men and lived with them. Sometimes they were men with no inversion, persons of weak sexual endowment who chose this rôle to avoid the jeers of the women. The berdaches were never regarded as of first-rate super-natural power, as similar men-women were in Siberia, but rather as leaders in women's occupations, good healers in certain diseases, or, among certain tribes, as the genial organizers of social affairs. In any case, they were socially placed. They were not left exposed to the conflicts that visit the deviant who is excluded from participation in the recognized patterns of his society.

The most spectacular illustrations of the extent to which normality may be culturally defined are those cultures where an abnormality of our culture is the cornerstone of their social structure. It is not possible to do justice to these possibilities in a short discussion. A recent study of an island of northwest Melanesia by Fortune describes a society built upon traits which we regard as beyond the border of paranoia. In this tribe the exogamic groups look upon each other as prime manipulators of black magic, so that one marries always into an enemy group which remains for life one's deadly and unappeasable foes. They look upon a good garden crop as a confession of theft, for everyone is engaged in making magic to induce into his garden the productiveness of his neighbors'; therefore no secrecy in the island is so rigidly insisted upon as the secrecy of a man's harvesting of his yams. Their polite phrase at the acceptance of a gift is, "And if you now poison me, how shall I repay you this present?" Their preoccupation with poisoning is constant; no woman ever leaves her cooking pot for a moment untended. Even the great affinal economic exchanges that are characteristic of this Melanesian culture area are quite altered in Dobu since they are incompatible with this fear and distrust that pervades the culture. They go farther and people the whole world outside their own quarters with such malignant spirits that all-night feasts and ceremonials simply do not occur here. They have even rigorous religiously enforced customs that forbid the sharing of seed even in one family group. Anyone else's food is deadly poison to you, so that communality of stores is out of the question. For some months before harvest the whole society is on the verge of starvation, but if one falls to the temptation and eats up one's seed yams, one is an outcast and a beachcomber for life. There is no coming back. It involves, as a matter of course, divorce and the breaking of all social ties.

Now in this society where no one may work with another and no one may share with another, Fortune describes the individual who was regarded by all his fellows as crazy. He was not one of those who periodically ran amok and, beside himself and frothing at the mouth, fell with a knife upon anyone he could reach. Such behavior they did not regard as putting anyone outside the pale. They did not even put the individuals who were known to be liable to these attacks under any kind of control. They merely fled when they saw the attack coming on and kept out of the way. "He would be all right tomorrow." But there was one man of sunny, kindly disposition who liked work and liked to be helpful. The compulsion was too strong for him to repress it in favor of the opposite tendencies of his culture. Men and women never spoke of him without laughing; he was silly and simple and definitely crazy. Nevertheless, to the ethnologist used to a culture that has, in Christianity, made his type the model of all virtue, he seemed a pleasant fellow. . . .

. . . Among the Kwakiutl it did not matter whether a relative had died in bed of disease, or by the hand of an enemy, in either case death was an affront to be wiped out by the death of another person. The fact that one had been caused to mourn was proof that one had been put upon. A chief's sister and her daughter had gone up to Victoria, and either because they drank bad whiskey or because their boat capsized they never came back. The chief called together his warriors. "Now I ask you, tribes, who shall wail? Shall I do it or shall another?" The spokesman answered, of course, "Not you, Chief. Let some other of the tribes." Immediately they set up the war pole to announce their intention of wiping out the injury, and gathered a war party. They set out, and found seven men and two children asleep and killed them. "Then they felt good when they arrived at Sebaa in the evening."

The point which is of interest to us is that in our society those who on that occasion would feel good when they arrived at Sebaa that evening would be the definitely abnormal. There would be some, even in our society, but it is not a recognized and approved mood under the circumstances. On the Northwest Coast those are favored and fortunate to whom that mood under those circumstances is congenial, and those to whom it is repugnant are unlucky. This latter minority can register in their own culture only by doing violence to their congenial responses and acquiring others that are difficult for them. The person, for instance, who, like a Plains Indian whose wife has been taken from him, is too proud to fight, can deal with the Northwest Coast civilization only by ignoring its strongest bents. If he cannot achieve it, he is the deviant in that culture, their instance of abnormality.

This head-hunting that takes place on the Northwest Coast after a death is no matter of blood revenge or of organized vengeance. There is no effort to tie up the subsequent killing with any responsibility on the part of the victim for the death of the person who is being mourned. A chief whose son has died goes visiting wherever his fancy dictates, and he says to his host, "My prince has died today, and you go with him." Then he kills him. In this, according to their interpretation, he acts nobly because he has not been downed. He has thrust back in return. The whole procedure is meaningless without the fundamental paranoid reading of bereavement. Death, like all the other untoward accidents of existence, confounds man's pride and can only be handled in the category of insults.

Behavior honored upon the Northwest Coast is one which is recognized as abnormal in our civilization, and yet it is sufficiently close to the attitudes of our own culure to be intelligible to us and to have a definite vocabulary with which we may discuss it. The megalomaniac paranoid trend is a definite danger in our society. It is encouraged by some of our major preoccupations, and it confronts us with a choice of two possible attitudes. One is to brand it as abnormal and reprehensible, and is the attitude we have chosen in our civilization. The other is to make it an essential attribute we have chosen in our civilization. The other is to make it an essential attribute of ideal man, and this is the solution in the culture of the Northwest Coast.

These illustrations, which it has been possible to indicate only in the briefest manner, force upon us the fact that normality is culturally defined. An adult shaped to the drives and standards of either of these cultures, if he were transported into our civilization, would fall into our categories of abnormality. He would be faced with the psychic dilemmas of the socially unavailable. In his own culture, however, he is the pillar of society, the end result of socially inculcated mores, and the problem of personal instability in his case simply does not arise.

No one civilization can possibly utilize in its mores the whole potential range of human behavior. Just as there are great numbers of possible phonetic articulations, and the possibility of language depends on a selection and standardization of a few of these in order that speech communication may be possible at all, so the possibility of organized behavior of every sort, from the fashions of local dress and houses to the dicta of a people's ethics and religion, depends upon a similar selection among the possible behavior traits. In the field of recognized economic obligations or sex tabus this selection is as non-rational and subconscious a process as it is in the field of phonetics. It is a process which goes on in the group for long periods of time and is historically conditioned by innumerable accidents of isolation or of contact of peoples. In any comprehensive study of psychology, the selection that different cultures have made in the course of history within the great circumference of potential behavior is of great significance.

Every society, beginning with some slight inclination in one direction or another, carries its preference farther and farther, integrating itself more and more completely upon its chosen basis, and discarding those types of behavior that are uncongenial. Most of those organizations of personality that seem to us most uncontrovertibly abnormal have been used by different civilizations in the very foundations of their institutional life. Conversely the most valued traits of normal individuals have been looked on in differently organized cultures as aberrant. Normality, in short, within a very wide range, is culturally defined. It is primarily a term for the socially elaborated segment of human behavior in any culture; and abnormality, a term for the segment that that particular civilization does not use. The very eyes with which we see the problem are conditioned by the long traditional habits of our own society.

It is a point that has been made more often in relation to ethics than in relation to psychiatry. We do not any longer make the mistake of deriving the morality of our locality and decade directly from the inevitable constitution of human nature. We do not elevate it to the dignity of a first principle. We recognize that morality differs in every society, and is a convenient term for socially approved habits. Mankind has always preferred to say, "It is morally good," rather than "It is habitual," and the fact of this preference is matter enough for a critical science of ethics. But historically the two phrases are synonymous.

The concept of the normal is properly a variant of the concept of the good. It is that which society has approved. A normal action is one which falls well within the limits of expected behavior for a particular society. Its variability among different peoples is essentially a function of the variability of the behavior patterns that different societies have created for themselves, and can never be wholly divorced from a consideration of culturally institutionalized types of behavior.

Each culture is a more or less elaborate working-out of the potentialities of the segment it has chosen. In so far as a civilization is well integrated and consistent within itself, it will tend to carry farther and farther, according to its nature, its initial impulse toward a particular type of action, and from the point of view of any other culture those elaborations will include more and more extreme and aberrant traits.

Each of these traits, in proportion as it reinforces the chosen behavior patterns of that culture, is for that culture normal. Those individuals to whom it is congenial either congenitally, or as the result of childhood sets, are accorded prestige in that culture, and are not visited with the social contempt or disapproval which their traits would call down upon them in a society that was differently organized. On the other hand, those individuals whose characteristics are not congenial to the selected type of human behavior in that community are the deviants, no matter how valued their personality traits may be in a contrasted civilization.

The Dobuan who is not easily susceptible to fear of treachery, who enjoys work and likes to be helpful, is their neurotic and regarded as silly. On the Northwest Coast the person who finds it difficult to read life in terms of an insult contest will be the person upon whom fall all the difficulties of the culturally unprovided for. The person who does not find it easy to humiliate a neighbor, nor to see humiliation in his own experience, who is genial and loving, may, of course, find some unstandardized way of achieving satisfactions in his society, but not in the major patterned responses that his culture requires of him. If he is born to play an important rôle in a family with many hereditary privileges, he can succeed only by doing violence to his whole personality. If he does not succeed, he has betrayed his culture; that is, he is abnormal.

I have spoken of individuals as having sets toward certain types of behavior, and of these sets as running sometimes counter to the types of behavior which are institutionalized in the culture to which they belong. From all that we know of contrasting cultures it seems clear that differences of temperament occur in every society. The matter has never been made the subject of investigation, but from the available material it would appear that these temperament types are very likely of universal recurrence. That is, there is an ascertainable range of human behavior that is found wherever a sufficiently large series of individuals is observed. But the proportion in which behavior types stand to one another in different societies is not universal. The vast majority of the individuals in any group are shaped to the fashion of that culture. In other words, most individuals are plastic to the moulding force of the society into which they are born. In a society that values trance, as in India, they will have supernormal experience. In a society that institutionalizes homosexuality, they will be homosexual. In a society that sets the gathering of possessions as the chief human objective, they will amass property. The deviants, whatever the type of behavior the culture has institutionalized, will remain few in number, and there seems no more difficulty in moulding that vast malleable majority to the "normality" of what we consider an aberrant trait, such as delusions of reference, than to the normality of such accepted behavior patterns as acquisitiveness. The small proportion of the number of the deviants in any culture is not a function of the sure instinct with which that society has built itself upon the fundamental sanities, but of the universal fact that, happily, the majority of mankind quite readily take any shape that is presented to them. . . .

**STUDY QUESTIONS**

1. Do you think that the fact of cultural diversity is itself an argument for ethical relativism?

2. If Benedict's defense of ethical relativism is correct, then the correct way to resolve a personal dilemma might be to take a survey or poll to see what the majority in your society thinks is right. If the majority favors capital punishment and opposes abortion, for example, then capital punishment is right and abortion is wrong. Can you defend Benedict against this odd consequence?

3. Do you think that certain types of behavior (for example, executing children or beating animals to death) are wrong wherever they occur, despite attitudes prevailing in the societies that practice them? What makes these acts wrong?

4. How could Benedict account for notions of moral enlightenment and moral progress?

156

# The Problem with Relativism

## JOHN HOSPERS

John Hospers (b. 1918) is director of the School of Philosophy at the University of Southern California. He is the author of several books, including *Libertarianism: A Political Philosophy for Tomorrow* (1971) and *Understanding the Arts* (1982).

John Hospers distinguishes between two kinds of relativism. *Sociological Relativism* makes the empirical claim that many acts considered wrong in some societies are considered right in others. Although surely correct, this empirical claim carries no ethical implications.

*Ethical Relativism* (focusing on the diversity of ethical beliefs in different groups) asserts that "right" and "wrong" are defined sociologically. X is "right" means that X is right in group G. The same act or practice (X) may be wrong in another group.

Hospers gives several reasons for rejecting ethical relativism, among which are:

1. "What's right in one group is wrong in another." But no one belongs to one group only. [So] which group counts? My family? My country? Suppose my family believes one thing and my country enjoins another?

2. How many of the groups should count? A majority? Is there any reason to hold that what the majority of one group wants should be morally decisive?

3. Ethical error would be impossible if ethical relativism were true. By definition the (majority of the) group cannot be wrong. That is implausible.

Hospers holds the view that most people who think of themselves as ethical relativists simply are unaware of the unacceptable implications of this doctrine.


Relativism, when analyzed, breaks down into several different views.

1. *Sociological relativism* is simply the view that different groups of people—different tribes, different cultures, different civilizations—have different moral standards for evaluating acts as right or wrong. For example, in our society we believe that it is better to be caught for stealing than to escape capture; but the Spartan youth who allowed the fox to gnaw at his vital organs rather than be caught for stealing . . . reflected a popular belief that being caught was bad but stealing was not. The Dobu tribesmen of New Guinea believe that growing your own vegetables is honorable but stealing your neighbor's vegetables is still more honorable. The ancient Romans, unlike the Christians, had more respect for honor than for pity. They could be forgiving if they could gain some advantage from being so; otherwise they had virtually no feeling for victims, such as prisoners of war. Courage was prized; mercy and humility were not. Some desert tribes think it a sacred obligation, when one of their number has been killed or captured by an opposing tribe, to capture and kill (by slow torture) a member of that tribe, even if he is not the same man who committed the offense—a perfectly innocent man will do just as well. The Eskimos think it right to kill their parents after the parents have reached a certain age—indeed, the parents expect this—rather than take them along on their hazardous journeys. . . .

No one is likely to deny relativism in this sense. It would ill become the moral philosopher to say, "You sociologists and anthropologists are all wrong in the alleged facts which you report. It is all a tissue of lies!" Those who are best qualified to know what the Dobu tribesmen believe are those who have lived among the Dobu and seen for themselves.

Even so, the term "sociological relativism" is ambiguous. If the term merely means that there are moral beliefs held by one group which are not held by another, this is obviously true—an empirical fact. But if the term means that different groups have different *basic* moral principles, the statement is not obviously true and may even be false. Different groups *may* be using the same basic moral principles but applying them in different ways to different situations. Imagine two tribes, each believing that they should do what is most conducive to the survival of as many people as possible within the tribe. One of the tribes lives in the desert, and the other where there is plenty of water. In the first tribe wasting even a small amount of water is considered a grave moral offense, perhaps even a capital offense; in the second tribe there are no rules at all about wasting water. This is an example of sociological relativism in the first sense; the one believes that wasting water is wrong and the other does not. But it is not an example of sociological relativism in the second sense, for both moral rules equally illustrate one basic moral principle, that what is right is what promotes survival. On this assumption they do not differ at all; what differs is the application of this one principle to different circumstances.

2. Sociological relativism is not an ethical doctrine at all; it tries to describe what people's moral beliefs *are;* it says nothing about whether any of them are preferable to others. *Ethical relativism,* however, goes further; it has a definite view about right and wrong, and thus it enters the domain of ethics. According to ethical relativism, if there are two tribes or societies, and in one of them it is believed that acts of a certain kind are wrong while in the other it is believed that acts of that same kind are right, *both beliefs* are true: in the first society acts of that kind *are* wrong and in the other society they *are* right. Polygamy is right in polygamous societies but not in monogamous societies. Thus there is no overall standard of right and wrong—what is right and what is wrong depends on the society of which you are a member.

Here at once we have an ambiguity. Let us suppose, for the moment, that slavery is right in one society and wrong in another—not just that it is thought to be so, which would be sociological relativism, but that it really is so, as ethical relativism says. But a person

159

who holds this belief need not be a relativist at all. He may believe in some one over-all standard of right, such as the maximum happiness of the people concerned. . . . And if so, since he has one standard of rightness, he is no relativist. A certain practice might make for the happiness of one society but not of another, and in that event it would be right in the one society but not in the other; only the application of the moral principle differs from one society to another, not the principle itself. Probably most people who call themselves ethical relativists are not so at all, for they believe in one moral standard which applies in different ways to different societies because of the various conditions in which they live. One might as well talk about gravitational relativism because a stone falls and a balloon rises; yet both events are equally instances of one law of universal gravitation.

But suppose that the person believes that there *is* no one over-all standard and that what is right and what is wrong varies from one society to another without reference to any one overall moral principle. A person might believe that what is right for one group may be wrong for another and what is right for one individual may be wrong for another, though *not* because there is one over-all moral principle of which these are different applications. The relativist will be hard put to it to give any reason *why* he believes this to be so, but he may state the position without any attempt to give reasons. In that event he can truly be called a relativist. But now he must face certain problems:

a. If we ask him *why* a practice that is right in one society is wrong in another, he will have no reason to present. There seems to be no general principle from which his position follows. This weakness, to put it mildly, will leave many people dissatisfied.

b. "What is right in one group is wrong in another," he says. But what exactly is a group? and which group is one to select? Every person is a member of many different groups—his nation, his state, his city, his club, his school, church, fraternity, or athletic association. Suppose that most of the people in his club think that a certain kind of act is wrong and that most of the people in his nation think it is right; what then?

c. How many of the group—whatever group it turns out to be— must think it is wrong before it really is wrong? The usual answer is, "The majority." Presumably this means anything over 50 per cent. If 51 per cent of his countrymen think adultery is wrong, then it is wrong for the people in that country; but if only 49 per cent of them think it wrong, then it isn't. This conclusion is strange, to say the least. Can't a majority be mistaken? A minority view may sometimes spread and become a majority view later; in that event, was the act wrong before and right now? It is very easy to say, "Head hunting is right in a headhunting society, and if most of the people in the United States became headhunters, then headhunting would be right for us," and the same with such practices as polygamy, witchburning, conviction without a trial, cannibalism. But is there any reason why what most people believe should be true?

d. If what the majority of a society or group approves is *ipso facto* right in that society, how can there be any such thing as moral improvement? If someone in a headhunting society were convinced that headhunting was cruel, barbarous, and wrong and proceeded to share these sentiments with his chieftain, the relativistic chieftain would reply, "But the majority in our tribe considers it right, so it *is* right." In a society in which most people cheated the government on their income tax, it would be right to do so, though it would no longer be right once the percentage of cheaters dropped below 50. If ethical relativism is correct, it is clearly impossible for the moral beliefs of a society to be mistaken because the certainty of the majority that its beliefs were right would prove that those beliefs *were* right for that society at that time. The minority view would therefore be mistaken, no matter what it was. Needless to say, most people who state that "in morals everything is relative" and who proceed to call themselves ethical relativists are unaware of these implications of their theory.

**STUDY QUESTIONS**

1. Discuss the distinction between sociological relativism and ethical relativism. In what sense is the former not an ethical doctrine?
2. According to Hospers, one could believe that slavery is right in some societies and yet not be an ethical relativist. What *would* make one an ethical relativist?
3. Discuss two of Hospers' objections to ethical relativism that seem especially convincing to you. Do the objections persuade you to reject the doctrine?

4.   Hospers says that most people who call themselves ethical relativists are not aware of the objections to it. Do you think they
are aware but discount the objections? What, if anything, would
it take to dislodge hard-line relativists from their position?

# Trying Out One's New Sword

MARY MIDGLEY

Mary Midgley is a senior Lecturer at the University of
Newcastle-upon-Tyne, England. She is the author of
several books, including *Beast and Man* (1978) and *Heart
and Mind* (1981).

Midgley criticizes "moral isolationalists" who disapprove of those who morally judge other cultures. She
notes that moral isolationists disapprove less when someone from another culture passes moral judgment on *our*
culture. Also, moral isolationists are inconsistent: They
do not oppose *praising* an exotic culture. Moral judgment, says Midgley, is a human necessity: Why ban it
interculturally? She points out that such a ban would not
permit us to express disapproval of the Samurai custom
of trying out a new sword by cleanly slicing an innocent
passerby in two.

All of us are, more or less, in trouble today about trying to understand cultures strange to us. We hear constantly of alien customs. We
see changes in our lifetime which would have astonished our parents.
I want to discuss here one very short way of dealing with this difficulty, a drastic way which many people now theoretically favour. It

TRYING OUT ONE'S NEW SWORD From *Heart and Mind* by Mary Midgley. © by M. Midgley, to be
used with permission from St. Martin's Press, Inc.

consists in simply denying that we can ever understand any culture except our own well enough to make judgments about it. Those who recommend this hold that the world is sharply divided into separate societies, sealed units, each with its own system of thought. They feel that the respect and tolerance due from one system to another forbids us ever to take up a critical position to any other culture. Moral judgment, they suggest, is a kind of coinage valid only in its country of origin.

I shall call this position "moral isolationism." I shall suggest that it is certainly not forced upon us, and indeed that it makes no sense at all. People usually take it up because they think it is a respectful attitude to other cultures. In fact, however, it is not respectful. Nobody can respect what is entirely unintelligible to them. To respect someone, we have to know enough about him to make a *favorable* judgment, however general and tentative. And we do understand people in other cultures to this extent. Otherwise a great mass of our most valuable thinking would be paralysed.

To show this, I shall take a remote example, because we shall probably find it easier to think calmly about it than we should with a contemporary one, such as female circumcision in Africa or the Chinese Cultural Revolution. The principles involved will still be the same. My example is this. There is, it seems, a verb in classical Japanese which means "to try out one's new sword on a chance wayfarer." (The world is *tsujigiri,* literally "crossroads-cut.") A samurai sword had to be tried out because, if it was to work properly, it had to slice through someone at a single blow, from the shoulder to the opposite flank. Otherwise, the warrior bungled his stroke. This could injure his honour, offend his ancestors, and even let down his emperor. So tests were needed, and wayfarers had to be expended. Any wayfarer would do—provided, of course, that he was not another Samurai. Scientists will recognize a familiar problem about the rights of experimental subjects.

Now when we hear of a custom like this, we may well reflect that we simply do not understand it; and therefore are not qualified to criticize it at all, because we are not members of that culture. But we are not members of any other culture either, except our own. So we extend the principle to cover all extraneous cultures, and we seem therefore to be moral isolationists. But this is, as we shall see, an impossible position. Let us ask what it would involve.

We must ask first: Does the isolating barrier work both ways? Are people in other cultures equally unable to criticize *us?* This question struck me sharply when I read a remark in *The Guardian* by an anthropologist about a South American Indian who had been taken into a Brazilian town for an operation, which saved his life. When he came back to his village, he made several highly critical remarks about the white Brazilians' way of life. They may very well have been justified. But the interesting point was that the anthropologist called these remarks "a damning indictment of Western civilization." Now the Indian had been in that town about two weeks. Was he in a position to deliver a damning indictment? Would we ourselves be qualified to deliver such an indictment on the Samurai, provided we could spend two weeks in ancient Japan? What do we really think about this?

My own impression is that we believe that outsiders can, in principle, deliver perfectly good indictments—only, it usually takes more than two weeks to make them damning. Understanding has degrees. It is not a slapdash yes–or–no matter. Intelligent outsiders can progress in it, and in some ways will be at an advantage over the locals. But if this is so, it must clearly apply to ourselves as much as anybody else.

Our next question is this: Does the isolating barrier between cultures block praise as well as blame? If I want to say that the Samurai culture has many virtues, or to praise the South American Indians, am I prevented from doing *that* by my outside status? Now, we certainly do need to praise other societies in this way. But it is hardly possible that we could praise them effectively if we could not, in principle, criticize them. Our praise would be worthless if it rested on definite grounds, if it did not flow from some understanding. Certainly we may need to praise things which we do not *fully* understand. We say "there's something very good here, but I can't quite make out what it is yet." This happens when we want to learn from strangers. And we can learn from strangers. But to do this we have to distinguish between those strangers who are worth learning from and those who are not. Can we then judge which is which?

This brings us to our third question: What is involved in judging? Now plainly there is no question here of sitting on a bench in a red robe and sentencing people. Judging simply means forming an opinion, and expressing it if it is called for. Is there anything wrong about this? Naturally, we ought to avoid forming—and expressing—*crude* opinions, like that of a simple-minded missionary, who might dismiss the whole Samurai culture as entirely bad, because non-Christian. But this is a different objection. The trouble with crude opinions is that they are crude, whoever forms them, not that they are formed by the wrong people. Anthropologists, after all, are outsiders quite as much as missionaries. Moral isolationism forbids us to form *any* opinions on these matters. Its ground for doing so is that we don't understand them. But there is much that we don't understand in our own culture too. This brings us to our last question: If we can't judge other cultures, can we really judge our own? Our efforts to do so will be much damaged if we are really deprived of our opinions about other societies, because these provide the range of comparison, the spectrum of alternatives against which we set what we want to understand. We would have to stop using the mirror which anthropology so helpfully holds up to us.

In short, moral isolationism would lay down a general ban on moral reasoning. Essentially, this is the programme of immoralism, and it carries a distressing logical difficulty. Immoralists like Nietzsche are actually just a rather specialized sect of moralists. They can no more afford to put moralizing out of business than smugglers can afford to abolish customs regulations. The power of moral judgment is, in fact, not a luxury, not a perverse indulgence of the self-righteous. It is a necessity. When we judge something to be bad or good, better or worse than something else, we are taking it as an example to aim at or avoid. Without opinions of this sort, we would have no framework of comparison for our own policy, no chance of profiting by other people's insights or mistakes. In this vacuum, we could form no judgments on our own actions.

Now it would be odd if Homo sapiens had really got himself into a position as bad as this—a position where his main evolutionary asset, his brain, was so little use to him. None of us is going to accept this sceptical diagnosis. We cannot do so, because our involvement in moral isolationism does not flow from apathy, but from a rather acute concern about human hypocrisy and other forms of wickedness. But we polarize that concern around a few selected moral truths. We are rightly angry with those who despise, oppress or steamroll other cultures. We think that doing these things is actually *wrong*. But this is itself a moral judgment. We could not condemn oppression and insolence if we thought that all our condemnations were just a trivial local quirk of our own culture. We could still less do it if we tried to stop judging altogether.

Real moral scepticism, in fact, could lead only to inaction, to our losing all interest in moral questions, most of all in those which concern other societies. When we discuss these things, it becomes instantly clear how far we are from doing this. Suppose, for instance, that I criticize the bisecting Samurai, that I say his behavior is brutal. What will usually happen next is that someone will protest, will say that I have no right to make criticisms like that of another culture. But it is most unlikely that he will use this move to end the discussion of the subject. Instead, he will justify the Samurai. He will try to fill in the background, to make me understand the custom, by explaining the exalted ideals of discipline and devotion which produced it. He will probably talk of the lower value which the ancient Japanese placed on individual life generally. He may well suggest that this is a healthier attitude than our own obsession with security. He may add, too, that the wayfarers did not seriously mind being bisected, that in principle they accepted the whole arrangement.

Now an objector who talks like this is implying that it *is* possible to understand alien customs. That is just what he is trying to make me do. And he implies, too, that if I do succeed in understanding them, I shall do something better than giving up judging them. He expects me to change my present judgment to a truer one—namely, one that is favourable. And the standards I must use to do this cannot just be Samurai standards. They have to be ones current in my own culture. Ideals like discipline and devotion will not move anybody unless he himself accepts them. As it happens, neither discipline nor devotion is very popular in the West at present. Anyone who appeals to them may well have to do some more arguing to make *them* acceptable, before he can use them to explain the Samurai. But if he does succeed here, he will have persuaded us, not just that there was something to be said for them in ancient Japan, but that there would be here as well.

Isolating barriers simply cannot arise here. If we accept something as a serious moral truth about one culture, we can't refuse to apply it—in however different an outward form—to other cultures as well, wherever circumstance admit it. If we refuse to do this, we just are not taking the other culture seriously. This becomes clear if we look at the last argument used by my objector—that of justification by consent of the victim. It is suggested that sudden bisection is quite in order, *provided* that it takes place between consenting adults. I cannot now discuss how conclusive this justification is. What I am pointing out is simply that it can only work if we believe tht *consent* can make such a transaction respectable—and this is a thoroughly modern and Western idea. It would probably never occur to a Samurai; if it did, it would surprise him very much. It is *our* standard. In applying it, too, we are likely to make another typically Western demand. We shall ask for good factual evidence that the wayfarers actually do have this rather surprising taste—that they are really willing to be bisected. In applying Western standards in this way, we are not being confused or irrelevant. We are asking the questions which arise *from where we stand,* questions which we can see the sense of. We do this because asking questions which you can't see the sense of is humbug. Certainly we can extend our questioning by imaginative effort. We can come to understand other societies better. By doing so, we may make their questions our own, or we may see that they are really forms of the questions which we are asking already. This is not impossible. It is just very hard work. The obstacles which often prevent it are simply those of ordinary ignorance, laziness and prejudice.

If there were really an isolating barrier, of course, our own culture could never have been formed. It is no sealed box, but a fertile jungle of different influences—Greek, Jewish, Roman, Norse, Celtic and so forth, into which further influences are still pouring—American, Indian, Japanese, Jamaican, you name it. The moral isolationist's picture of separate, unmixable cultures is quite unreal. People who talk about British history usually stress the value of this fertilizing mix, no doubt rightly. But this is not just an odd fact about Britain. Except for the very smallest and most remote, all cultures are formed out of many streams. All have the problem of digesting and assimilating things which, at the start, they do not understand. All have the choice of learning something from this challenge, or, alternatively, of refusing to learn, and fighting it mindlessly instead.

This universal predicament has been obscured by the fact that anthropologists used to concentrate largely on very small and remote cultures, which did not seem to have this problem. These tiny societies, which had often forgotten their own history, made neat, self-contained subjects for study. No doubt it was valuable to emphasize their remoteness, their extreme strangeness, their independence of our cultural tradition. This emphasis was, I think, the root of moral isolationism. But, as the tribal studies themselves showed, even there the anthropologists were able to interpret what they saw and make

167

judgments—often favourable—about the tribesmen. And the tribes-men, too, were quite equal to making judgments about the anthro-pologists—and about the tourists and Coca-Cola salesmen who followed them. Both sets of judgments, no doubt, were somewhat hasty, both have been refined in the light of further experience. A similar transaction between us and the Samurai might take even longer. But that is no reason at all for deeming it impossible. Morally as well as physically, there is only one world, and we all have to live in it.

**STUDY QUESTIONS**

1. How would a philosophical Samurai defend the practice of trying out a new sword? Does this defense have any merit? Explain your answer.
2. The word "mores" usually connotes a variety of social practices. Yet Midgley says, "Morally as well as physically, there is only one world." If you believe she is right about this, then defend her view that we can judge the social practices and traditions of exotic cultures. If you disagree, show where she goes wrong.
3. Someone else might call Midgley's "moral isolationism" a "sophisticated tolerance of cultural difference." Argue the case against Midgley and for "tolerance" to see whether you end up convincing yourself that she is wrong.

# The United Nations Charter: The Universal Declaration of Human Rights

The Universal Declaration of Human Rights was adopted by the United Nations General Assembly on December 10, 1948. The Declaration was characterized as "a common standard of achievement for all peoples and all nations." The first twenty-one articles of the Declaration of Human Rights are similar to the first ten amendments of the U.S. Constitution, the Bill of Rights. Articles twenty-two through twenty-seven, which assert rights to economic and social benefits, reflect specific articles in the Soviet constitution.

The Declaration was condemned by the American Association of Anthropology as "a statement of rights conceived only in terms of the values prevalent in Western Europe and America." Calling it "ethnocentric," the association suggested that the Declaration betrayed a lack of respect for cultural differences.

The articles of the Universal Declaration of Human Rights declare that all human beings have the right to a dignified and secure existence. They prohibit torture and slavery. They enjoin equality before the law and prohibit

169

arbitrary arrest in any country. They prohibit limitations of movement within national borders.

The Articles assert the right of political asylum; the right to citizenship in some country; the right of adults to marry and have families; the right to one's property; the right to freedom of thought, conscience, and religion; the right to social security; the right to belong to unions; the right to a decent standard of living and access to health; the right to an education. The Articles assert the principle of freedom of assembly—the freedom to take part in the government of one's country.

Finally, the Articles assure that no state may engage in any activity aimed at the restriction of any of the rights and liberties set forth in the declaration.

It should be noted that the members of the United Nations General Assembly, in thus proclaiming universal standards of social ethics for all societies, are not ethical relativists.

## Preamble

Whereas recognition of the inherent dignity and of the equal and inalienable rights of all members of the human family is the foundation of freedom, justice and peace in the world,

Whereas disregard and contempt for human rights have resulted in barbarous acts which have outraged the conscience of mankind, and the advent of a world in which human beings shall enjoy freedom of speech and belief and freedom from fear and want has been proclaimed as the highest aspiration of the common people,

Whereas it is essential, if man is not to be compelled to have recourse, as a last resort, to rebellion against tyranny and oppression, that human rights should be protected by the rule of law,

Whereas it is essential to promote the development of friendly relations between nations,

Whereas the people of the United Nations have in the Charter reaffirmed their faith in fundamental human rights, in the dignity and worth of the human person and in the equal rights of men and women and have determined to promote social progress and better standards of life in larger freedom,

Whereas Member States have pledged themselves to achieve, in cooperation with the United Nations, the promotion of universal respect for and observance of human rights and fundamental freedoms,

Whereas a common understanding of these rights and freedoms is of the greatest importance for the full realization of this pledge,

Now, Therefore,

## The General Assembly Proclaims

This Universal Declaration of Human Rights as a common standard of achievement for all peoples and all nations, to the end that every individual and every organ of society, keeping this Declaration constantly in mind, shall strive by teaching and education to promote respect for these rights and freedoms and by progressive measures, national and international, to secure their universal and effective recognition and observance, both among the peoples of Member States themselves and among the peoples of territories under their jurisdiction.

*Article 1*    All human beings are born free and equal in dignity and rights. They are endowed with reason and conscience and should act towards one another in a spirit of brotherhood.

*Article 2*    Everyone is entitled to all the rights and freedoms set forth in this Declaration, without distinction of any kind, such as race, colour, sex, language, religion, political or other opinion, national or social origin, property, birth or other status.

Furthermore, no distinction shall be made on the basis of the political, jurisdictional or international status of the country or territory to which a person belongs, whether it be independent, trust, non-self-governing or under any other limitation of sovereignty.

*Article 3*    Everyone has the right to life, liberty and security of person.

*Article 4*    No one shall be held in slavery or servitude; slavery and the slave trade shall be prohibited in all their forms.

*Article 5*    No one shall be subjected to torture or to cruel, inhuman or degrading treatment or punishment.

171

*Article 6*    Everyone has the right to recognition everywhere as a person before the law.

*Article 7*    All are equal before the law and are entitled without any discrimination to equal protection of the law. All are entitled to equal protection against any discrimination in violation of this Declaration and against any incitement to such discrimination.

*Article 8*    Everyone has the right to an effective remedy by the competent national tribunals for acts violating the fundamental rights granted him by the constitution or by law.

*Article 9*    No one shall be subjected to arbitrary arrest, detention or exile.

*Article 10*    Everyone is entitled in full equality to a fair and public hearing by an independent and impartial tribunal, in the determination of his rights and obligations and of any criminal charge against him.

*Article 11*    (1) Everyone charged with a penal offence has the right to be presumed innocent until proved guilty according to law in a public trial at which he has had all the guarantees necessary for his defence.

(2) No one shall be held guilty of any penal offence on account of any act or omission which did not constitute a penal offence, under national or international law, at the time when it was committed. Nor shall a heavier penalty be imposed than the one that was applicable at the time the penal offence was committed.

*Article 12*    No one shall be subjected to arbitrary interference with his privacy, family, home or correspondence, nor to attacks upon his honour and reputation. Everyone has the right to the protection of the law against such interference or attacks.

*Article 13*    (1) Everyone has the right to freedom of movement and residence within the borders of each state.

(2) Everyone has the right to leave any country, including his own, and to return to his country.

*Article 14*    (1) Everyone has the right to seek and to enjoy in other countries asylum from persecution.

(2) This right may not be invoked in the case of prosecutions

genuinely arising from non-political crimes or from acts contrary to the purposes and principles of the United Nations.

*Article 15*    (1) Everyone has the right to a nationality.

(2) No one shall be arbitrarily deprived of his nationality nor denied the right to change his nationality.

*Article 16*    (1) Men and women of full age, without any limitation due to race, nationality or religion, have the right to marry and to found a family. They are entitled to equal rights as to marriage, during marriage and at its dissolution.

(2) Marriage shall be entered into only with the free and full consent of the intending spouses.

(3) The family is the natural and fundamental group unity of society and is entitled to protection by society and the State.

*Article 17*    (1) Everyone has the right to own property alone as well as in association with others.

(2) No one shall be arbitrarily deprived of his property.

*Article 18*    Everyone has the right to freedom of thought, conscience and religion; this right includes freedom to change his religion or belief, and freedom, either alone or in community with others and in public or private, to manifest his religion or belief in teaching, practice, worship and observance.

*Article 19*    Everyone has the right to freedom of opinion and expression; this right includes freedom to hold opinions without interference and to seek, receive and impart information and ideas through any media and regardless of frontiers.

*Article 20*    (1) Everyone has the right to freedom of peaceful assembly and association.

(2) No one may be compelled to belong to an association.

*Article 21*    (1) Everyone has the right to take part in the government of his country, directly or through freely chosen representatives.

(2) Everyone has the right of equal access to public service in his country.

(3) The will of the people shall be the basis of the authority of government; this will shall be expressed in periodic and genuine

elections which shall be by universal and equal suffrage and shall be held by secret vote or by equivalent free voting procedures.

*Article 22*   Everyone, as a member of society, has the right to social security and is entitled to realization, through national effort and international co-operation and in accordance with the organization and resources of each State, of the economic, social and cultural rights indispensable for his dignity and the free development of his personality.

*Article 23*   (1) Everyone has the right to work, to free choice of employment, to just and favourable conditions of work and to protection against unemployment.

(2) Everyone, without any discrimination, has the right to equal pay for equal work.

(3) Everyone who works has the right to just and favourable remuneration ensuring for himself and his family an existence worthy of human dignity, and supplemented, if necessary, by other means of social protection.

(4) Everyone has the right to form and to join trade unions for the protection of his interests.

*Article 24*   Everyone has the right to rest and leisure, including reasonable limitation of working hours and periodic holidays with pay.

*Article 25*   (1) Everyone has the right to a standard of living adequate for the health and well-being of himself and of his family, including food, clothing, housing and medical care and necessary social services, and the right to security in the event of unemployment, sickness, disability, widowhood, old age or other lack of livelihood in circumstances beyond his control.

(2) Motherhood and childhood are entitled to special care and assistance. All children, whether born in or out of wedlock, shall enjoy the same social protection.

*Article 26*   (1) Everyone has the right to education. Education shall be free, at least in the elementary and fundamental stages. Elementary education shall be compulsory. Technical and professional education shall be made generally available and higher education shall be equally accessible to all on the basis of merit.

(2) Education shall be directed to the full development of the

human personality and to the strengthening of respect for human rights and fundamental freedoms. It shall promote understanding, tolerance and friendship among all nations, racial or religious groups, and shall further the activities of the United Nations for the maintenance of peace.

(3) Parents have a prior right to choose the kind of education that shall be given to their children.

*Article 27* (1) Everyone has the right freely to participate in the cultural life of the community, to enjoy the arts and to share in scientific advancement and its benefits.

(2) Everyone has the right to the protection of the moral and material interests resulting from any scientific, literary or artistic production of which he is the author.

*Article 28* Everyone is entitled to a social and international order in which the rights and freedoms set forth in this Declaration can be fully realized.

*Article 29* (1) Everyone has duties to the community in which alone the free and full development of his personality is possible.

(2) In the exercise of his rights and freedoms, everyone shall be subject only to such limitations as are determined by law solely for the purpose of securing due recognition and respect for the rights and freedoms of others and of meeting the just requirements of morality, public order and the general welfare in a democratic society.

(3) These rights and freedoms may in no case be exercised contrary to the purposes and principles of the United Nations.

*Article 30* Nothing in this Declaration may be interpreted as implying for any State, group or person any right to engage in any activity or to perform any act aimed at the destruction of any of the rights and freedoms set forth herein.

## STUDY QUESTIONS

1. The Declaration contains thirty articles. Discuss three that you consider very important and defend their fundamental character.
2. Obviously the Declaration has not been enforced. What then is its value, if any? Discuss.

3. Do you agree that all human beings throughout the world have the rights and liberties outlined in the articles? How would you argue in their defense if someone challenged some or all of the articles?

4. The first twenty-one articles assert *negative* rights of freedom from governmental interference. Later articles (21–28) assert positive rights that require a government to ensure such basic benefits as work, housing, and medical care. Many conservatives object to the inclusion of positive rights as endorsing socialism. On the other hand, many socialists maintain that exclusive rights of liberty merely give everyone the right to starve. Critically discuss this issue.

5. The American Anthropological Association objected to the Universal Declaration of Human Rights being "ethnocentric." Critically discuss. Do you agree with the Association that the lack of moral consensus in the world "validates" ethical relativism?

## SUGGESTED READINGS

Baier, Kurt. *The Moral Point of View*. Ithaca, NY: Cornell University Press, 1958.

Benedict, Ruth. *Patterns of Culture*. Boston: Houghton Mifflin Company, 1934.

Blum, Lawrence C. *Friendship, Altruism and Morality*. Boston: Routledge and Kegan Paul, 1980.

Butler, Joseph. *Fifteen Sermons Upon Human Nature*. 1726.

Frankena, William. *Ethics*. Englewood Cliffs, NJ: Prentice-Hall, 1973.

Gert, Bernard. *The Moral Rules: A New Rational Foundation for Morality*. New York: Harper and Row, 1970.

Harman, Gilbert. *The Nature of Morality: An Introduction to Ethics*. New York: Oxford University Press, 1977.

Hospers, John. *Human Conduct*. New York: Harcourt, Brace and World, 1961.

Kittay, Eva Feder, and Diana T. Meyers, eds. *Women and Moral Theory*. Totowa, NJ: Littlefield, Adams and Company, 1987.

Ladd, John, ed. *Ethical Relativism*. Belmont, CA: Wadsworth Books, 1973.

Mackie, J. L. *Ethics: Inventing Right and Wrong*. New York: Penguin Books, 1977.

Midgley, Mary. *Heart and Mind*. New York: St. Martin's Press, 1981.

Singer, Marcus. *Generalization in Ethics*. New York: Alfred A. Knopf, 1961.

Smart, J. J. C., and Bernard Williams. *Utilitarianism: For and Against*. Cambridge: Cambridge University Press, 1973.

Sumner, W. G. *Folkways*. Boston: Ginn Press, 1907.

Warnock, G. J. *The Object of Morality*. London: Methuen and Company, 1971.

Williams, Bernard. *Ethics and the Limits of Philosophy*. Cambridge: Harvard University Press, 1985.

Wong, David. *Moral Relativity*. Los Angeles: University of California Press, 1984.

## Chapter Three

# VIRTUE

Several acorns fall from a tree. One is eaten by a squirrel. Another decays on the ground. A third grows into an oak tree. We say that the third acorn's fate is appropriate to it, that it succeeds where the other two fail. In our view, the acorn's goal or purpose is to become an oak tree, as if its self-fulfillment depends on achieving this goal. Yet we are aware that to speak of a goal here is grossly anthropomorphic. The acorn is not a conscious being trying to achieve the happy outcome of development. Nor do we feel that this happy outcome is really more natural than the outcome of rotting or being eaten. Indeed, since only a tiny minority of acorns become oak trees, the unhappy outcomes are more natural than the happy one.

All the same, our intuition that becoming an oak tree is the appropriate career for an acorn is sound. Any organic matter, a leaf, for example, can rot on the ground; any nut can serve as squirrel fodder. But only the acorn can grow into an oak tree. The Greeks defined the function or natural purpose of a thing as an activity that is specific to it—an activity that it alone performs or one that it performs better than anything else can. In this sense we think that the third acorn's career is the "happy" or proper one. The metaphor of a happy outcome for the acorn leans heavily on the Greek meaning of happiness (*eudaimonia*) as well-functioning, self-fulfilling activity.

A biologist could tell us quite a bit about the special characteristics that enable the acorn to perform its function. The Greeks called such characteristics "excellences" or "virtues." In the broad sense a virtue is any trait or capacity that enables an object to perform its appropriate function. More commonly, "virtue" refers to a special kind of excellence that only human beings possess or lack. In this narrow sense the virtues are *moral* excellences that contribute to a life of human fulfillment. And in this sense we speak of the virtues in contrast to vices. A question now arises: What goal is appropriate for human beings? There are in fact rival conceptions of human fulfillment; some of them are represented by the selections in this chapter.

The Greeks confronted this question with their characteristic simplicity and boldness. Human beings, says Aristotle, are rational animals. They are also social animals. They naturally fulfill themselves in functioning as rational and social beings. Given such conceptions of human purpose, such virtues as temperance, magnanimity, and courage come to the fore as traits that allow people to lead graceful lives in a political community.

Saint Augustine conceives of the life appropriate to a human being rather differently. Human beings are rational and social beings, but that they are creatures of God is even more important: Human purpose and happiness are found in following God. While the Greeks— with their secular conception of the good life—primarily emphasize such "cardinal virtues" as wisdom, courage, and temperance, Augustine—with his Christian conception of the good life—gives priority to such other virtues as charity, humility, and faith. The modern philosopher is less ready to state a conception of the good life for all human beings at all times. Alasdair MacIntyre's conception of human fulfillment is historical. He argues that social context and tradition are always crucial in defining moral obligations: "There is no way to possess the virtues except as part of a tradition in which we inherit them. . . ."

Several articles presented in Chapter Three give a good idea of the sort of investigation into particular virtues the contemporary philosopher pursues. In his article on generosity, James D. Wallace distinguishes economic generosity from generous-mindedness. Wallace formulates characteristics of generosity, one of which is that the generous person gives more than duty requires. Here we touch on an important difference between a morality of duty and a morality of virtue. Godlovitch's topic is wisdom, which he finds less well understood than other virtues, despite its status as a cardinal virtue. Taylor flouts the tradition that pride is a vice. Distinguishing pride from conceit, Taylor argues it is a virtuous trait, necessary for self-respect and a sense of moral worth.

Most modern philosophers believe that no one universally accept-able conception of human fulfillment exists, and largely have dropped the effort to formulate one. They do not do so because they generally disagree with Aristotle's conception of humans as rational and social beings. That conception is, after all, a truism. But philos-ophers by now recognize it as a very general truism from which they cannot deduce an interesting set of particular virtues. In fact, some argue that Aristotle himself does not proceed in a teleological way when he specifies the particular virtues. In any case, most current philosophers of virtue proceed without conceiving of human hap-piness as neatly tied to certain moral traits that contribute to the good life. Reading Philippa Foot or Robert C. Roberts, we see a careful attempt to clarify the virtues by isolating the features that distinguish them from other excellences. They do not justify the virtues by some teleogical deduction, although in a general way we are brought to recognize that the virtues are beneficial to their possessor. The con-temporary philosopher's hardest work comes in understanding the virtues not through the contribution they make to human happiness, but as qualities, in themselves, of a good and decent person. In effect, the virtues themselves define the good life.

# The Moral Virtues

## ARISTOTLE

**TRANSLATED BY J. A. K. THOMSON**

Aristotle (384–322 B.C.) is one of the greatest philosophers of all time. He was the son of a Macedonian physician, the personal tutor of Alexander the Great, and a student of Plato. He wrote on a wide range of subjects, including logic (which he founded as a science), metaphysics, biology, ethics, politics, and literature. During the Middle Ages, the authority of his teachings in all matters of secular philosophy was undisputed. It would be difficult to exaggerate his influence on the development of Western culture.

Aristotle defines happiness as functioning well. The function of a thing is its special kind of activity, what it can do better than anything else. Thus, the function of human beings is the exercise of their capacity to reason. A capacity that enables a thing or a being to function well is a virtue. Aristotle defines happiness (well-functioning) as an activity in accordance with virtue. Reason plays a part in all of the specified human virtues. Courageous persons, for example, use reason to control fear; temperate persons use it to control their appetites. Properly employed, reason directs us to a course of moderation between extremes (for example, between the excesses of fear and folly, or gluttony and abstemiousness). Aristotle gives some general rules for pursuing the course of virtuous

THE MORAL VIRTUES From The *Ethics of Aristotle*. Translated by J. A. K. Thomson. Reprinted with permission of George Allen & Unwin (Publishers) Ltd.

moderation: (i) avoid the extreme that more strongly opposes the virtue, (ii) guard against excessive hedonism, and (iii) attend to your characteristic faults. These are not hard and fast rules, but rough and ready guides.

Aristotle worked out in detail the means, excesses, and deficiencies for all the moral virtues that he recognized. W. T. Jones, a historian of philosophy, conveniently summarizes Aristotle's views in the following table:

| Activity | Vice (excess) | Virtue (mean) | Vice (deficit) |
|---|---|---|---|
| Facing death | Too much fear (i.e., cowardice) | Right amount of fear (i.e., courage) | Too little fear (i.e., foolhardiness) |
| Bodily actions (eating, drinking, sex, etc.) | Profligacy | Temperance | No name for this state, but it may be called "insensitivity" |
| Giving money | Prodigality | Liberality | Illiberality |
| Large-scale giving | Vulgarity | Magnificence | Meanness |
| Claiming honors | Vanity | Pride | Humility |
| Social intercourse | Obsequiousness | Friendliness | Sulkiness |
| According honors | Injustice | Justice | Injustice |
| Retribution for wrongdoing | Injustice | Justice | Injustice |

*Source:* W. T. Jones, *The Classical Mind* (New York: Harcourt, Brace, & World, 1952, 1969), p. 268.

No doubt people will say, "To call happiness the highest good is a truism. We want a more distinct account of what it is." We might arrive at this if we could grasp what is meant by the "function" of a human being. If we take a flautist or a sculptor or any craftsman—in fact any class of men at all who have some special job or profession—we find that his special talent and excellence comes out in that job, and this is his function. The same thing will be true of man simply as man—that is of course if "man" does have a function. But is it likely that joiners and shoemakers have certain functions or specialized activities, while man as such has none but has been left by Nature a functionless being? Seeing that eye and hand and foot and every one of our members has some obvious function, must we not believe that in like manner a human being has a function over and above these particular functions? Then what exactly is it? The mere act of living is not peculiar to man—we find it even in the vegetable kingdom—and what we are looking for is something peculiar to him. We must therefore exclude from our definition the life that manifests itself in mere nurture and growth. A step higher should come the life that is confined to experiencing sensations. But that we see is shared by horses, cows, and the brute creation as a whole. We are left, then, with a life concerning which we can make two statements. First, it belongs to the rational part of man. Secondly, it finds expression in actions. The rational part may be either active or passive: passive in so far as it follows the dictates of reason, active in so far as it possesses and exercises the power of reasoning. A similar distinction can be drawn within the rational life; that is to say, the reasonable element in it may be active or passive. Let us take it that what we are concerned with here is the reasoning power in action, for it will be generally allowed that when we speak of "reasoning" we really mean *exercising* our reasoning faculties. (This seems the more correct use of the word). Now let us assume for the moment the truth of the following propositions. (a) The function of a man is the exercise of his non-corporeal faculties or "soul" in accordance with, or at least not divorced from, a rational principle. (b) The function of an individual and of a *good* individual in the same class— a harp player, for example, and a good harp player, and so through the classes—is generically the same, except that we must add superiority in accomplishment to the function, the function of the harp player being merely to play on the harp, while the function of the good harp player is to play on it well. (c) The function of man is a certain form of life, namely an activity of the soul exercised in combination with a rational principle or reasonable ground of action. (d) The function of a good man is to exert such activity well. (e) A function is performed well when performed in accordance with the excellence proper to it.—If these assumptions are granted, we conclude that the good for man is "an activity of soul in accordance with goodness" or (on the supposition that there may be more than one form of goodness) "in accordance with the best and most complete form of goodness."

. . . Let us begin, then, with this proposition. Excellence of whatever kind affects that of which it is the excellence in two ways. (1) It produces a good state in it. (2) It enables it to perform its function well. Take eyesight. The goodness of your eye is not only that which makes your eye good, it is also that which makes it function well. Or take the case of a horse. The goodness of a horse makes him a good horse, but it also makes him good at running, carrying a rider, and facing the enemy. Our proposition, then, seems to be true, and it enables us to say that virtue in a man will be the disposition which (a) makes him a good man, (b) enables him to perform his function well. We have already touched on this point, but more light will be thrown upon it if we consider what is the specific nature of virtue.

Every form, then, of applied knowledge, when it performs its function well, looks to the mean and works to the standard set by that. It is because people feel this that they apply the *cliché*, "You couldn't add anything to it or take anything from it" to an artistic masterpiece, the implication being that too much and too little alike destroy perfection, while the mean preserves it. Now if this be so, and if it be true, as we say, that good craftsmen work to the standard of the mean, then, since goodness like Nature is more exact and of a higher character than any art, it follows that goodness is the quality that hits the mean. By "goodness" I mean goodness of moral character, since it is moral goodness that deals with feelings and actions, and it is in them that we find excess, deficiency, and a mean. It is possible, for example, to experience fear, boldness, desire, anger, pity, and pleasures and pains generally, too much or too little or to the right amount. If we feel them too much or too little, we are wrong. But to have these feelings at the right times on the right occasions towards the right people for the right motive and in the right way is to have them in the right measure, that is, somewhere between the extremes; and this is what characterizes goodness. The same may be said of the mean and extremes in actions. Now it is in the field of actions and feelings that goodness operates; in them we find excess, deficiency, and, between them, the mean, the first two being wrong, the mean right and praised as such. Goodness, then, is a mean condition in the sense that it aims at hits the mean.

Consider, too, that it is possible to go wrong in more ways than one. (In Pythagorean terminology evil is a form of the Unlimited, good of the Limited.) But there is only one way of being right. That is why going wrong is easy, and going right is difficult; it is easy to miss the bull's-eye and difficult to hit it. Here, then, is another explanation of why the too much and the too little are connected with evil and the mean with good. As the poet says,

> Goodness is one, evil is multiform.

We may now define virtue as a disposition of the soul in which, when it has to choose among actions and feelings, it observes the mean relative to us, this being determined by such a rule or principle as would take shape in the mind of a man of sense or practical wisdom. We call it a mean condition as lying between two forms of badness, one being excess and the other deficiency; and also for this reason, that, whereas badness either falls short of or exceeds the right measure in feelings and actions, virtue discovers the mean and deliberately chooses it. Thus, looked at from the point of view of its essence as embodied in its definition, virtue no doubt is a mean; judged by the standard of what is right and best, it is an extreme.

*Aristotle enters a caution. Though we have said that virtue observes the mean in actions and passions, we do not say this of all acts and all feelings. Some are essentially evil and, when these are involved, our rule of applying the mean cannot be brought into operation.*[1]

But choice of a mean is not possible in every action or every feeling. The very names of some have an immediate connotation of evil. Such are malice, shamelessness, envy among feelings, and among actions adultery, theft, murder. All these and more like them have a ban name as being evil in themselves; it is not merely the excess or deficiency of them that we censure. In their case, then, it is impossible to act rightly; whatever we do is wrong. Nor do circumstances make any difference in the rightness or wrongness of them. When a man commits adultery there is no point in asking whether it is with the right woman or at the right time or in the right way, for to do anything like that is simply wrong. It would amount to claiming that there is a mean and excess and defect in unjust or cowardly or intemperate actions. If such a thing were possible, we should find ourselves with a mean quantity of excess, a mean of deficiency, an excess of excess and a deficiency of deficiency. But just as in temperance and justice there can be no mean or excess or deficiency, because the mean

---

[1]The italicized interpolations in this selection are the translator's.

in a sense *is* an extreme, so there can be no mean or excess or deficiency in those vicious actions—however done, they are wrong. Putting the matter into general language, we may say that there is no
mean in the extremes, and no extreme in the mean, to be observed
by anybody.

*After the definition comes its application to the particular virtues. In these
it is always possible to discover a mean—at which the virtue aims—between
an excess and a deficiency. Here Aristotle found that a table or diagram of
the virtues between their corresponding vices would be useful, and we are to
imagine him referring to this in the course of his lectures.*

But a generalization of this kind is not enough; we must show that
our definition fits particular cases. When we are discussing actions
particular statements come nearer the heart of the matter, though
general statements cover a wider field. The reason is that human
behaviour consists in the performance of particular acts, and our
theories must be brought into harmony with them.

You see here a diagram of the virtues. Let us take our particular
instances from that. In the section confined to the feelings inspired
by danger you will observe that the mean state is "courage." Of
those who go to extremes in one direction or the other the man who
shows an excess of fearlessness has no name to describe him, the man
who exceeds in confidence or daring is called "rash" or "foolhardy,"
the man who shows an excess of fear and a deficiency of confidence
is called a "coward." In the pleasures and pains—though not all
pleasures and pains, especially pains—the virtue which observes the
mean is "temperance," the excess is the vice of "intemperance." Persons defective in the power to enjoy pleasures are a somewhat rare
class, and so have not had a name assigned to them: suppose we call
them "unimpressionable." Coming to the giving and acquiring of
money, we find that the mean is "liberality," the excess "prodigality,"
the deficiency "meanness." But here we meet a complication. The
prodigal man and the mean man exceed and fall short in opposite
ways. The prodigal exceeds in giving and falls short in getting
money, whereas the mean man exceeds in getting and falls short in
giving it away. Of course this is but a summary account of the
matter—a bare outline. But it meets our immediate requirements.
Later on these types of character will be more accurately delineated.

But there are other dispositions which declare themselves in the way they deal with money. One is "lordliness" or "magnificence," which differs from liberality in that the lordly man deals in large sums, the liberal man is small. Magnificence is the mean state here, the excess is "bad taste" or "vulgarity," the defect is "shabbiness." These are not the same as the excess and defect on either side of liberality. How they differ is a point which will be discussed later. In the matter of honour the mean is "proper pride," the excess "vanity," the defect "poor-spiritedness." And just as liberality differs, as I said, from magnificence in being concerned with small sums of money, so there is a state related to proper pride in the same way, being concerned with small honours, while pride is concerned with great. For it is possible to aspire to small honours in the right way, or to a greater or less extent than is right. The man who has this aspiration to excess is called "ambitious;" if he does not cherish it enough, he is "unambitious;" but the man who has it to the right extent—that is, strikes the mean—has no special designation. This is true also of corresponding dispositions with one exception, that of the ambitious man, which is called "ambitiousness." This will explain why each of the extreme characters stakes out a claim in the middle region. Indeed we ourselves call the character between the extremes sometimes "ambitious" and sometimes "unambitious." That is proved by our sometimes praising a man for being ambitious and sometimes for being unambitious. The reason will appear later. In the meantime let us continue our discussion of the remaining virtues and vices, following the method already laid down.

Let us next take anger. Here too we find excess, deficiency, and the mean. Hardly one of the states of mind involved has a special name; but, since we call the man who attains the mean in this sphere "gentle," we may call his disposition "gentleness." Of the extremes the man who is angry over-much may be called "irascible," and his vice "irascibility;" while the man who reacts too feebly to anger may be called "poor-spirited" and his disposition "poor-spiritedness."

. . . As regards veracity, the character who aims at the mean may be called "truthful" and what he aims at "truthfulness." Pretending, when it goes too far, is "boastfulness" and the man who shows it is a "boaster" or "braggart." If it takes the form of understatement, the pretence is called "irony" and the man who shows it "ironical." In agreeableness in social amusement the man who hits the mean is "witty" and what characterizes him is "wittiness." The excess is "buffoonery" and the man who exhibits that is a "buffoon." The opposite of the buffoon is the "boor" and his characteristic is "boor-ishness." In the other sphere of the agreeable—the general business of life—the person who is agreeable in the right way is "friendly" and his disposition "friendliness." The man who makes himself too agreeable, supposing him to have no ulterior object, is "obsequious;" if he has such an object, he is a "flatterer." The man who is deficient in this quality and takes every opportunity of making himself disagreeable may be called "peevish" or "sulky" or "surly."

*But it is not only in settled dispositions that a mean may be observed in passing states of emotion.*

Even when feelings and emotional states are involved one notes that mean conditions exist. And here also, it would be agreed, we may find one man observing the mean and another going beyond it, for instance, the "shamefaced" man, who is put out of countenance by anything. Or a man may fall short here of the due mean. Thus any one who is deficient in a sense of shame, or has none at all, is called "shameless." The man who avoids both extremes is "modest," and him we praise. For, while modesty is not a form of goodness, it is praised; it and the modest man. Then there is "righteous indignation." This is felt by any one who strikes the mean between "envy" and "malice," by which last word I mean a pleased feeling at the misfortunes of other people. These are emotions concerned with the pains and pleasures we feel at the fortunes of our neighbours. The man who feels righteous indignation is pained by undeserved good fortune; but the envious man goes beyond that and is pained at anybody's success. The malicious man, on the other hand, is so far from being pained by the misfortunes of another that he is actually tickled by them.

However, a fitting opportunity of discussing these matters will present itself in another place. And after that we shall treat of justice. In that connexion we shall have to distinguish between the various kinds of justice—for the word is used in more senses than one—and show in what way each of them is a mean.

*But after all, proceeds Aristotle, the true determinant of the mean is not the geometer's rod but the guiding principle in the good man's soul. The diagram of the virtues and vices, then, is just an arrangement and, as Aristotle goes on to show, an unimportant one at that.*

Thus there are three dispositions, two of them taking a vicious form (one in the direction of excess, the other of defect) and one a good form, namely, the observance of the mean. They are all opposed to one another, though not all in the same way. The extreme states are opposed both to the mean and one another, and the mean is opposed to both extremes. For just as the equal is greater compared with the less, and less compared with the greater, so the mean states (whether in feelings or actions) are in excess if compared with the deficient, and deficient if compared with the excessive, states. Thus a brave man appears rash when set beside a coward, and cowardly when set beside a rash man; a temperate man appears intemperate beside a man of dull sensibilities, and dull if contrasted with an intemperate man. This is the reason why each extreme character tries to push the mean nearer the other. The coward calls the brave man rash, the rash man calls him a coward. And so in the other cases. But, while all the dispositions are opposed to one another in this way, the greatest degree of opposition is that which is found between the two extremes. For they are separated by a greater interval from one another than from the mean, as the great is more widely removed from the small, and the small from the great, than either from the equal. It may be added that sometimes an extreme bears a certain resemblance to a mean. For example, rashness resembles courage, and prodigality resembles liberality. But between the extremes there is always the maximum dissimilarity. Now opposites are by definition things as far removed as possible from one another. Hence the farther apart things are, the more opposite they will be. Sometimes it is the deficiency, in other instances it is the excess, that is more directly opposed to the mean. Thus cowardice, a deficiency, is more opposed to courage than is rashness, an excess. And it is not insensibility, the deficiency, that is more opposed to temperance but intemperance, the excess. This arises from one or other of two causes. One lies in the nature of the thing itself and may be explained as follows. When one extreme is nearer to the mean and resembles it more, it is not that extreme but the other which we tend to oppose to the mean. For instance, since rashness is held to be nearer and liker to courage than is cowardice, it is cowardice which we tend to oppose to courage on the principle that the extremes which are remoter from the mean strike us as more opposite to it. The other cause lies in ourselves. It is the things to which we are naturally inclined that appear to us more opposed to the mean. For example, we have a natural inclination to pleasure, which makes us prone to fall into intemperance. Accordingly we tend to describe as opposite to the mean those things towards which we have an instinctive inclination. For this reason intemperance, the excess, is more opposed to temperance than is insensibility to pleasure, the deficiency.

I have said enough to show that moral excellence is a mean, and I have shown in what sense it is so. It is, namely, a mean between two forms of badness, one of excess and the other of defect, and is so described because it aims at hitting the mean point in feelings and in actions. This makes virtue hard of achievement, because finding the middle point is never easy. It is not everybody, for instance, who can find the centre of a circle—that calls for a geometrician. Thus, too, it is easy to fly into a passion—anybody can do that—but to be angry with the right person and to the right extent and at the right time and with the right object and in the right way—that is not easy, and it is not everyone who can do it. This is equally true of giving or spending money. Hence we infer that to do these things properly is rare, laudable and fine.

*Aristotle now suggests some rules for our guidance.*

In view of this we shall find it useful when aiming at the mean to observe these rules. (1) *Keep away from that extreme which is the more opposed to the mean.* It is Calypso's advice:

> Swing around the ship clear of this surf and surge.

For one of the extremes is always a more dangerous error than the other; and—since it is hard to hit the bull's-eye—we must take the next best course and choose the least of the evils. And it will be easiest for us to do this if we follow the rule I have suggested. (2) *Note the errors into which we personally are most liable to fall.* (Each of us has his natural bias in one direction or another.) We shall find out what ours are by noting what gives us pleasure and pain. After that we must drag ourselves in the opposite direction. For our best way of reaching the middle is by giving a wide berth to our darling sin. It is the method used by a carpenter when he is straightening a warped board. (3) *Always be particularly on your guard against pleasure and pleasant things.* When Pleasure is at the bar the jury is not impartial. So it will be best for us if we feel towards her as the Trojan elders felt towards Helen, and regularly apply their words to her. If we are for packing her off, as they were with Helen, we shall be the less likely to go wrong.

To sum up. These are the rules by observation of which we have the best chance of hitting the mean. But of course difficulties spring up, especially when we are confronted with an exceptional case. For example, it is not easy to say precisely what is the right way to be angry and with whom and on what grounds and for how long. In fact, we are inconsistent on this point, sometimes praising people who are deficient in the capacity for anger and calling them "gentle," sometimes praising the choleric and calling them "stout fellows." To be sure we are not hard on a man who goes off the straight path in the direction of too much or too little, if he goes off only a little way. We reserve our censure for the man who swerves widely from the course, because then we are bound to notice it. Yet it is not easy to find a formula by which we may determine how far and up to what point a man may go wrong before he incurs blame. But this difficulty of definition is inherent in every object of perception; such questions of degree are bound up with the circumstances of the individual case, where our only criterion *is* the perception.

So much, then, has become clear. In all our conduct it is the mean state that is to be praised. But one should lean sometimes in the direction of the more, sometimes in that of the less, because that is the readiest way of attaining to goodness and the mean.

## STUDY QUESTIONS

1.  How, according to Aristotle, does reason determine right action? How does this connect with the general principle that virtuous action is a mean between extremes?

2.  In Aristotle's view, what is happiness and how does it relate to virtue?

3.  Of two extremes, one is usually worse, being "more opposed to the mean." Aristotle proposes that we take special care to avoid that extreme. Give an example (not found in Aristotle) of a person in a situation that falls under Aristotle's rule. Be concrete in showing how to apply the rule.

4.  In the typical situation where we must choose an action guided by Aristotle's principles, do we have several choices, all falling within the range of the mean between two extremes, or does the

principle of the mean uniquely determine a particular course of action? Answer this question, supplying a concrete example of your own.

# Of the Morals of the Catholic Church

## SAINT AUGUSTINE

Saint Augustine (A.D. 354–420) born in North Africa, is recognized as one of the very greatest Christian philosophers. His best known works are his *Confessions* (A.D. 400) and *The City of God* (A.D. 427).

Augustine defines happiness as the enjoyment of the highest good. The highest good is not something that can be lost by accident or misfortune, for then we cannot enjoy it confidently. Such a good must therefore be of the soul and not the body. Augustine concludes that the chief good is the possession of virtue. The virtuous Christian follows God, avoiding sin and obeying His will.

**Happiness is in the enjoyment of man's chief good. Two conditions of the chief good: 1st, Nothing is better than it; 2d, it cannot be lost against the will.**

How then, according to reason, ought man to live? We all certainly desire to live happily; and there is no human being but assents to this statement almost before it is made. But the title happy cannot, in my

OF THE MORALS OF THE CATHOLIC CHURCH From *The Works of Aurelius Augustine.* Edited by M. Dods (T. & T. Clark, Edinburgh, 1892). Reprinted with permission from T. & T. Clark Ltd., Edinburgh, Scotland.

opinion, belong either to him who has not what he loves, whatever it may be, or to him who has what he loves if it is hurtful, or to him who does not love what he has, although it is good in perfection. For one who seeks what he cannot obtain suffers torture, and one who has got what is not desirable is cheated, and one who does not seek for what is worth seeking for is diseased. Now in all these cases the mind cannot but be unhappy, and happiness and unhappiness cannot reside at the same time in one man; so in none of these cases can the man be happy. I find, then, a fourth case, where the happy life exists,—when that which is man's chief good is both loved and possessed. For what do we call enjoyment but having at hand the object of love? And no one can be happy who does not enjoy what is man's chief good, nor is there any one who enjoys this who is not happy. We must then have at hand our chief good, if we think of living happily.

We must now inquire what is man's chief good, which of course cannot be anything inferior to man himself. For whoever follows after what is inferior to himself, becomes himself inferior. But every man is bound to follow what is best. Wherefore man's chief good is not inferior to man. Is it then something similar to man himself? It must be so, if there is nothing above man which he is capable of enjoying. But if we find something which is both superior to man, and can be possessed by the man who loves it, who can doubt that in seeking for happiness man should endeavour to reach that which is more excellent than the being who makes the endeavour? For if happiness consists in the enjoyment of a good than which there is nothing better, which we call the chief good, how can a man be properly called happy who has not yet attained to his chief good? or how can that be the chief good beyond which something better remains for us to arrive at? Such, then, being the chief good, it must be something which cannot be lost against the will. For no one can feel confident regarding a good which he knows can be taken from him, although he wishes to keep and cherish it. But if a man feels no confidence regarding the good which he enjoys, how can he be happy while in such fear of losing it?

## Man—what?

Let us then see what is better than man. This must necessarily be hard to find, unless we first ask and examine what man is. I am not now called upon to give a definition of man. The question here seems to me to be,—since almost all agree, or at least, which is enough, those I have now to do with are of the same opinion with me, that we are made up of soul and body,—What is man? Is he both of these? or is he the body only, or the soul only? For although the things are two, soul and body, and although neither without the other could be called man (for the body would not be man without the soul, nor again would the soul be man if there were not a body animated by it), still it is possible that one of these may be held to be man, and may be called so. What then do we call man? Is he soul and body, as in a double harness, or like a centaur? Or do we mean the body only, as being in the service of the soul which rules it, as the word lamp denotes not the light and the case together, but only the case, though on account of the light? Or do we mean only mind, and that on account of the body which it rules, as horseman means not the man and the horse, but the man only, and that as employed in ruling the horse? This dispute is not easy to settle; or, if the proof is plain, the statement requires time. This is an expenditure of time and strength which we need not incur. For whether the name man belongs to both, or only to the soul, the chief good of man is not the chief good of the body; but what is the chief good either of both soul and body, or of the soul only, that is man's chief good.

## Man's chief good is not the chief good of the body only, but the chief good of the soul.

Now if we ask what is the chief good of the body, reason obliges us to admit that it is that by means of which the body comes to be in its best state. But of all the things which invigorate the body, there is nothing better or greater than the soul. The chief good of the body, then, is not bodily pleasure, not absence of pain, not strength, not beauty, not swiftness, or whatever else is usually reckoned among the goods of the body, but simply the soul. For all the things mentioned the soul supplies to the body by its presence, and, what is above them all, life. Hence I conclude that the soul is not the chief good of man, whether we give the name of man to soul and body together, or to the soul alone. For as, according to reason, the chief good of the body is that which is better than the body, and from which the body receives vigour and life, so whether the soul itself is man, or soul and body both, we must discover whether there is anything which goes before the soul itself, in following which the soul comes to the perfection of good of which it is capable in its own kind. If such a thing can be found, all uncertainty must be at an end, and we must pronounce this to be really and truly the chief good of man.

If, again, the body is man, it must be admitted that the soul is the chief good of man. But clearly, when we treat of morals,—when we inquire what manner of life must be held in order to obtain happiness,—it is not the body to which the precepts are addressed, it is not bodily discipline which we discuss. In short, the observance of good customs belongs to that part of us which inquires and learns, which are the prerogatives of the soul; so, when we speak of attaining to virtue, the question does not regard the body. But if it follows, as it does, that the body which is ruled over by a soul possessed of virtue is ruled both better and more honourably, and is in its greatest perfection in consequence of the perfection of the soul which rightfully governs it, that which gives perfection to the soul will be man's chief good, though we call the body man. For if my coachman, in obedience to me, feeds and drives the horses he has charge of in the most satisfactory manner, himself enjoying the more of my bounty in proportion to his good conduct, can any one deny that the good condition of the horses, as well as that of the coachman, is due to me? So the question seems to me to be not, whether soul and body is man, or the soul only, or body only, but what gives perfection to the soul; for when this is obtained, a man cannot but be either perfect, or at least much better than in the absence of this one thing.

### Virtue gives perfection to the soul; the soul obtains virtue by following God; following God is the happy life.

No one will question that virtue gives perfection to the soul. But it is a very proper subject of inquiry whether this virtue can exist by itself or only in the soul. Here again arises a profound discussion, needing lengthy treatment; but perhaps my summary will serve the purpose. God will, I trust, assist me, so that, notwithstanding our feebleness, we may give instruction on these great matters briefly as well as intelligibly. In either case, whether virtue can exist by itself without the soul, or can exist only in the soul, undoubtedly in the pursuit of virtue the soul follows after something, and this must be either the soul itself, or virtue, or something else. But if the soul follows after itself in the pursuit of virtue, it follows after a foolish thing; for before obtaining virtue it is foolish. Now the height of a follower's desire is to reach that which he follows after. So the soul must either not wish to reach what it follows after, which is utterly absurd and unreasonable, or, in following after itself while foolish, it reaches the folly which it flees from. But if it follows after virtue in the desire to reach it, how can it follow what does not exist? or how can it desire to reach what it already possesses? Either, therefore, virtue exists beyond the soul, or if we are not allowed to give the name of virtue except to the habit and disposition of the wise soul, which can exist only in the soul, we must allow that the soul follows after something else in order that virtue may be produced in itself; for neither by following after nothing, nor by following after folly, can the soul, according to my reasoning, attain to wisdom.

This something else, then, by following after which the soul becomes possessed of virtue and wisdom, is either a wise man or God. But we have said already that it must be something that we cannot lose against our will. No one can think it necessary to ask whether a wise man, supposing we are content to follow after him, can be taken from us in spite of our unwillingness or our persistence. God then remains, in following after whom we live well, and in reaching whom we life both well and happily.

**STUDY QUESTIONS**

1. What does Augustine mean by happiness? How does this conception of happiness differ from others with which you are acquainted?
2. What does Augustine mean by "following God"? How does he argue that happiness consists in following God?
3. What does the idea of virtue as primarily theological imply for morality in general?

# Virtue or Duty?

## BERNARD MAYO

Bernard Mayo (b. 1920) is an English philosopher. He is the author of *Ethics and the Modern Life* (1958).

Mayo points out that the classical philosophers did not lay down principles of moral behavior but concentrated instead on the character of the moral person. He claims that classical moral theory is superior to a modern (Kantian) ethics of duty. "The basic moral question, for Aristotle, is not, What shall I do? but, What shall I be?" The morality of "doing" is logically simple: We determine what we ought to do by seeing whether it maximizes happiness (utilitarianism) or is universalizable (Kantianism). The morality of "being" has another kind of simplicity, which Mayo calls the unity of character. Persons of character, heroes or saints, do not merely give us principles to follow; more importantly, they provide an example for us to follow. An ethics of character is more flexible than an ethics of rules. We can find more than one good way to follow a good personal example.

The philosophy of moral principles, which is characteristic of Kant and the post-Kantian era, is something of which hardly a trace exists in Plato. . . . Plato says nothing about rules or principles or laws, except when he is talking politics. Instead he talks about virtues and vices, and about certain types of human character. The key word in

VIRTUE OR DUTY? From *Ethics and the Moral Life* by Bernard Mayo. Reprinted by permission of Macmillan Accounts and Administration Ltd., London and Basingstoke.

Platonic ethics is Virtue; the key word in Kantian ethics is Duty. And modern ethics is a set of footnotes, not to Plato, but to Kant. . . .

Attention to the novelists can be a welcome correction to a tendency of philosophical ethics of the last generation or two to lose contact with the ordinary life of man which is just what the novelists, in their own way, are concerned with. Of course there are writers who can be called in to illustrate problems about Duty (Graham Greene is a good example). But there are more who perhaps never mention the words duty, obligation or principle. Yet they are all concerned—Jane Austen, for instance, entirely and absolutely—with the moral qualities or defects of their heroes and heroines and other characters. This points to a radical one-sidedness in the philosophers' account of morality in terms of principles: it takes little or no account of qualities, of what people *are*. It is just here that the old-fashioned word Virtue used to have a place; and it is just here that the work of Plato and Aristotle can be instructive. Justice, for Plato, though it is closely connected with acting according to law, does not *mean* acting according to law: it is a quality of character, and a just action is one such as a just man would do. Telling the truth, for Aristotle, is not, as it was for Kant, fulfilling an obligation; again it is a quality of character, or, rather, a whole range of qualities of character, some of which may actually be defects, such as tactlessness, boastfulness, and so on—a point which can be brought out, in terms of principles, only with the greatest complexity and artificiality, but quite simply and naturally in terms of character.

If we wish to enquire about Aristotle's moral views, it is no use looking for a set of principles. Of course we can find *some* principles to which he must have subscribed—for instance, that one ought not to commit adultery. But what we find much more prominently is a set of character-traits, a list of certain types of person—the courageous man, and the niggardly man, the boaster, the lavish spender and so on. The basic moral question, for Aristotle, is not, What shall I do? but, What shall I be?

These contrasts between doing and being, negative and positive, and modern as against Greek morality were noted by John Stuart Mill; I quote from the *Essay on Liberty:*

> Christian morality (so-called) has all the characters of a reaction; it is, in great part, a protest against Paganism. Its ideal is negative rather

than positive, passive rather than active; Innocence rather than Nobleness; Abstinence from Evil, rather than energetic Pursuit of the Good; in its precepts (as has been well said) "Thou shalt not" predominates unduly over "Thou shalt . . ." Whatever exists of magnanimity, high-mindedness, personal dignity, even the sense of honour, is derived from the purely human, not the religious part of our education, and never could have grown out of a standard of ethics in which the only worth, professedly recognised, is that of obedience.

Of course, there are connections between being and doing. It is obvious that a man cannot just *be;* he can only be what he is by doing what he does; his moral qualities are ascribed to him because of his actions, which are said to manifest those qualities. But the point is that an ethics of Being must include this obvious fact, that Being involves Doing; whereas an ethics of Doing, such as I have been examining, may easily overlook it. As I have suggested, a morality of principles is concerned only with what people do or fail to do, since that is what rules are for. And as far as this sort of ethics goes, people might well have no moral qualities at all except the possession of principles and the will (and capacity) to act accordingly.

When we speak of a moral quality such as courage, and say that a certain action was courageous, we are not merely saying something about the action. We are referring, not so much to what is done, as to the kind of person by whom we take it to have been done. We connect, by means of imputed motives and intentions, with the character of the agent as courageous. This explains, incidentally, why both Kantians and Utilitarians encounter, in their different ways, such difficulties in dealing with motives, which their principles, on the face of it, have no room for. A Utilitarian, for example, can only praise a courageous action in some such way as this: the action is of a sort such as a person of courage is likely to perform, and courage is a quality of character the cultivation of which is likely to increase rather than diminish the sum total of human happiness. But Aristotelians have no need of such circumlocution. For them a courageous action just is one which proceeds from and manifests a certain type of character, and is praised because such a character trait is good, or better than others, or is a virtue. An evaluative criterion is sufficient: there is no need to look for an imperative criterion as well, or rather instead, according to which it is not the character which is good, but the cultivation of the character which is right. . . .

199

No doubt the fundamental moral question is just "What ought I to do?" And according to the philosophy of moral principles, the answer (which must be an imperative "Do this") must be derived from a conjunction of premises consisting (in the simplest case) firstly of a rule, or universal imperative, enjoining (or forbidding) all actions of a certain type in situations of a certain type, and, secondly, a statement to the effect that this is a situation of that type, falling under that rule. In practice the emphasis may be on supplying only one of these premises, the other being assumed or taken for granted: one may answer the question "What ought I to do?" either by quoting a rule which I am to adopt, or by showing that my case is legislated for by a rule which I do adopt. To take a previous example of moral perplexity, if I am in doubt whether to tell the truth about his condition to a dying man, my doubt may be resolved by showing that the case comes under a rule about the avoidance of unnecessary suffering, which I am assumed to accept. But if the case is without precedent in my moral career, my problem may be soluble only by adopting a new principle about what I am to do now and in the future about cases of this kind.

This second possibility offers a connection with moral ideas. Suppose my perplexity is not merely an unprecedented situation which I could cope with by adopting a new rule. Suppose the new rule is thoroughly inconsistent with my existing moral code. This may happen, for instance, if the moral code is one to which I only pay lip-service; if . . . its authority is not yet internalised, or if it has ceased to be so; it is ready for rejection, but its final rejection awaits a moral crisis such as we are assuming to occur. What I now need is not a rule for deciding how to act in this situation and others of its kind. I need a whole set of rules, a complete morality, new principles to live by.

Now according to the philosophy of moral character, there is another way of answering the fundamental question "What ought I to do?" Instead of quoting a rule, we quote a quality of character, a virtue: we say "Be brave," or "Be patient" or "Be lenient." We may even say "Be a man": if I am in doubt, say, whether to take a risk, and someone says "Be a man," meaning a morally sound man, in this case a man of sufficient courage. (Compare the very different ideal invoked in "Be a gentleman." I shall not discuss whether this is a *moral* ideal.) Here, too, we have the extreme cases, where a man's moral perplexity extends not merely to a particular situation but to his whole way of living. And now the question "What ought I to do?" turns into the question "What ought I to be?"—as, indeed, it was treated in the first place. ("Be brave.") It is answered, not by quoting a rule or a set of rules, but by describing a quality of character or a type of person. And here the ethics of character gains a practical simplicity which offsets the greater logical simplicity of the ethics of principles. We do not have to give a list of characteristics or virtues, as we might list a set of principles. We can give a unity to our answer.

Of course we can in theory give a unity to our principles: this is implied by speaking of a *set* of principles. But if such a set is to be a system and not merely aggregate, the unity we are looking for is a logical one, namely the possibility that some principles are deductible from others, and ultimately from one. But the attempt to construct a deductive moral system is notoriously difficult, and in any case ill-founded. Why should we expect that all rules of conduct should be ultimately reducible to a few?

## Saints and Heroes

But when we are asked "What shall I be?" we can readily give a unity to our answer, though not a logical unity. It is the unity of character. A person's character is not merely a list of dispositions; it has the organic unity of something that is more than the sum of its parts. And we can say, in answer to our morally perplexed questioner, not only "Be this" and "Be that," but also "Be like So-and-So"—where So-and-So is either an ideal type of character, or else an actual person taken as representative of the ideal, an exemplar. Examples of the first are Plato's "just man" in the Republic; Aristotle's man of practical wisdom, in the Nicomachean Ethics; Augustine's citizen of the City of God; the good Communist; the American way of life (which is a collective expression for a type of character). Examples of the second kind, the exemplar, are Socrates, Christ, Buddha, St. Francis, the heroes of epic writers and of novelists. Indeed the idea of the Hero, as well as the idea of the Saint, are very much the expression of this attitude to morality. Heroes and saints are not merely people who did things. They are people whom we are expected, and expect ourselves, to imitate. And imitating them means not merely doing what they did; it means being like them. Their status is not in the least like that of legislators whose laws we admire; for the character of a legislator is irrelevant to our judgment about his legislation. The heroes and saints did not merely give us principles to live by (though some of them did that as well): they gave us examples to follow.

Kant, as we should expect, emphatically rejects this attitude as "fatal to morality." According to him, examples serve only to render *visible* an instance of the moral principle, and thereby to demonstrate its practical feasibility. But every exemplar, such as Christ himself, must be judged by the independent criterion of the moral law, before we are entitled to recognize him as worthy of imitation. I am not suggesting that the subordination of exemplars to principles is incorrect, but that it is one-sided and fails to do justice to a large area of moral experience.

Imitation can be more or less successful. And this suggests another defect of the ethics of principles. It has no room for ideals, except the ideal of a perfect set of principles (which, as a matter of fact, is intelligible only in terms of an ideal character or way of life), and the ideal of perfect conscientiousness (which is itself a character-trait). This results, of course, from the "black-or-white" nature of moral verdicts based on rules. There are no degrees by which we approach or recede from the attainment of a certain quality or virtue; if there were not, the word "ideal" would have no meaning. Heroes and saints are not people whom we try to be *just* like, since we know that is impossible. It is precisely because it is impossible for ordinary human beings to achieve the same qualities as the saints, and in the same degree, that we do set them apart from the rest of humanity. It is enough if we try to be a little like them. . . .

**STUDY QUESTIONS**

1. Morality, says Mayo, involves "being" as well as "doing." What does he mean by "being" and "doing" in this context? What sort of moral theory concentrates on doing? On being?

2. Philosophers of virtue or moral character tell us how to develop ourselves as moral persons. They answer the question "What ought I to do?" by telling us what to be. How does that work?

3. Mayo says that the moral content of literature emphasizes character and virtue more than duty and obligation. Is he right about this? If he is, then is a moral philosophy of duty necessarily inadequate?

# Tradition and the Virtues

## ALASDAIR MACINTYRE

Alasdair MacIntyre (b. 1929) is professor of philosophy at Vanderbilt University. He has authored many books, including *After Virtue* (1981) and *Whose Justice? Which Rationality?* (1988).

Alasdair MacIntyre's perspective on virtue is historical and "particularist." "[We] all approach our own circumstances as bearers of a particular social identity." Each of us "inhabits a role" in our social environment. (We are citizens of a country; a son, daughter, parent, aunt, and so forth, in a family.) Such roles provide our "moral starting points." What is good for a person also must be good for one who inhabits the particular role. "As such I inherit from the past of my family, my city, my tribe, my nation, a variety of debts, inheritances, rightful expectations and obligations."

Ideally, each human life is a unity. The meaning and ethical worth of any person's act can be understood only as a part of the life story of that person. But a person's history only makes sense in terms of the social and historical contexts that define his or her roles, expectations, and obligations.

Because virtue is best understood in terms of the way one lives one's roles in a narrative the background of

TRADITION AND THE VIRTUES Excerpted from "The Virtues, The Unity of a Human Life and the Concept of Tradition," in *After Virtue* by Alasdair MacIntyre. Copyright © 1981 by Notre Dame University Press. Reprinted by permission of the publisher.

which is richly historical and traditional, the *teaching* of virtue is best accomplished through stories. "Man is essentially a story telling animal," and moral education is realized primarily through narrative means. "Deprive children of stories and you leave them unscripted, anxious stutterers in their actions as in their words."

MacIntyre criticizes most modern approaches to ethics for neglecting history and tradition by attending exclusively to principles that apply universally to all individuals regardless of social role. He warns that the insistence on evaluating all acts and projects in terms of abstract universal principles is dangerous. On the other hand, a virtuous respect for particular traditions is conducive to a decent and balanced life. MacIntyre therefore urges that we should recognize and promote a special virtue: "the virtue of having an adequate sense of the traditions to which one belongs or which confront one."

Any contemporary attempt to envisage each human life as a whole, as a unity, whose character provides the virtues with an adequate *telos* encounters two different kinds of obstacle, one social and one philosophical. The social obstacles derive from the way in which modernity partitions each human life into a variety of segments, each with its own norms and modes of behavior. So work is divided from leisure, private life from public, the corporate from the personal. So both childhood and old age have been wrenched away from the rest of human life and made over into distinct realms. And all these separations have been achieved so that it is the distinctiveness of each and not the unity of the life of the individual who passes through those parts in terms of which we are taught to think and to feel.

The philosophical obstacles derive from two distinct tendencies, one chiefly, though not only, domesticated in analytical philosophy and one at home in both sociological theory and in existentialism. The former is the tendency to think atomistically about human action and to analyze complex actions and transactions in terms of simple components. Hence the recurrence in more than one context of the notion of a "basic action." That particular actions derive their character as parts of larger wholes is a point of view alien to our dominant ways of thinking and yet one which it is necessary at least to consider if we are to begin to understand how a life may be more than a sequence of individual actions and episodes.

Equally the unity of a human life becomes invisible to us when a sharp separation is made either between the individual and the roles he or she plays . . . or between the different role . . . enactments of an individual life so that the life comes to appear as nothing but a series of unconnected episodes—a liquidation of the self. . . .

[T]he liquidation of the self into a set of demarcated areas of role-playing allows no scope for the exercise of dispositions which could genuinely be accounted virtues in any sense remotely Aristotelian. For a virtue is not a disposition that makes for success only in some one particular type of situation. What are spoken of as the virtues of a good committee man or of a good administrator or of a gambler or a pool hustler are professional skills professionally deployed in those situations where they can be effective, not virtues. Someone who genuinely possesses a virtue can be expected to manifest it in very different types of situation, many of them situations where the practice of a virtue cannot be expected to be effective in the way that we expect a professional skill to be. Hector exhibited one and the same courage in his parting from Andromache and on the battlefield with Achilles; Eleanor Marx exhibited one and the same compassion in her relationship with her father, in her work with trade unionists and in her entanglement with Aveling. And the unity of a virtue in someone's life is intelligible only as a characteristic of a unitary life, a life that can be conceived and evaluated as a whole. Hence just as in the discussion of the changes in and fragmentation of morality which accompanied the rise of modernity in the earlier parts of this book, each stage in the emergence of the characteristically modern views of the moral judgment was accompanied by a corresponding stage in the emergence of the characteristically modern conceptions of self-hood; so now, in defining the particular pre-modern concept of the virtues with which I have been preoccupied, it has become necessary to say something of the concomitant concept of selfhood, a concept of a self whose unity resides in the unity of a narrative which links birth to life to death as narrative beginning to middle to end.

Such a conception of the self is perhaps less unfamiliar than it may appear at first sight. Just because it has played a key part in the cultures which are historically predecessors of our own, it would not be surprising if it turned out to be still an unacknowledged presence in many of our ways of thinking and acting. Hence it is not inappropriate to begin by scrutinizing some of our most taken-for-granted, but clearly correct conceptual insights about human actions and selfhood in order to show how natural it is to think of the self in a narrative mode.

It is a conceptual commonplace, both for philosophers and for ordinary agents, that one and the same segment of human behavior may be correctly characterized in a number of different ways. To the question "What is he doing?" the answers may with equal truth and appropriateness be "Digging," "Gardening," "Taking exercise," "Preparing for winter" or "Pleasing his wife." Some of these answers will characterize the agent's intentions, other unintended consequences of his actions, and of these unintended consequences some may be such that the agent is aware of them and others not. What is important to notice immediately is that any answer to the questions of how we are to understand or to explain a given segment of behavior will presuppose some prior answer to the question of how these different correct answers to the question "What is he doing?" are related to each other. For if someone's primary intention is to put the garden in order before the winter and it is only incidentally the case that in so doing he is taking exercise and pleasing his wife, we have one type of behavior to be explained; but if the agent's primary intention is to please his wife by taking exercise, we have quite another type of behavior to be explained and we will have to look in a different direction for understanding and explanation.

In the first place the episode has been situated in an annual cycle of domestic activity, and the behavior embodies an intention which presupposes a particular type of household-cum-garden setting with the peculiar narrative history of that setting in which this segment of behavior now becomes an episode. In the second instance the episode has been situated in the narrative history of a marriage, a very different, even if related, social setting. We cannot, that is to say, characterize behavior independently of intentions, and we cannot characterize intentions independently of the settings which make those intentions intelligible both to agents themselves and to others.

I use the word "setting" here as a relatively inclusive term. A social setting may be an institution, it may be what I have called a practice, or it may be a milieu of some other human kind. But it is central to the notion of a setting as I am going to understand it that a setting has a history, a history within which the histories of individual agents not only are, but have to be, situated, just because without the setting and its changes through time the history of the individual agent and his changes through time will be unintelligible. Of course one and the same piece of behavior may belong to more than one setting. There are at least two different ways in which this may be so.

In my earlier example the agent's activity may be part of the history both of the cycle of household activity and of his marriage, two histories which have happened to intersect. The household may have its own history stretching back through hundreds of years, as do the histories of some European farms, where the farm has had a life of its own, even though different families have in different periods inhabited it; and the marriage will certainly have its own history, a history which itself presupposes that a particular point has been reached in the history of the institution of marriage. If we are to relate some particular segment of behavior in any precise way to an agent's intentions and thus to the settings which that agent inhabits, we shall have to understand in a precise way how the variety of correct characterizations of the agent's behavior relate to each other first by identifying which characteristics refer us to an intention and which do not and then by classifying further the items in both categories.

Where intentions are concerned, we need to know which intention or intentions were primary, that is to say, of which it is the case that, had the agent intended otherwise, he would not have performed that action. Thus if we know that a man is gardening with the self-avowed purposes of healthful exercise and of pleasing his wife, we do not yet know how to understand what he is doing until we know the answer to such questions as whether he would continue gardening if he continued to believe that gardening was healthful exercise, but discovered that his gardening no longer pleased his wife, *and* whether he would continue gardening, if he ceased to believe that gardening was healthful exercise, but continued to believe that it pleased his wife, *and* whether he would continue gardening if he changed his beliefs on both points. That is to say, we need to know both what certain of his beliefs are and which of them are causally effective; and, that is to say, we need to know whether certain contrary-to-fact hypothetical statements are true or false. And until we know this, we shall not know how to characterize correctly what the agent is doing. . . .

Consider what the argument so far implies about the interrelationships of the intentional, the social and the historical. We identify a particular action only by invoking two kinds of context, implicitly if not explicitly. We place the agent's intentions, I have suggested, in causal and temporal order with reference to their role in his or her history; and we also place them with reference to their role in the history of the setting or settings to which they belong. In doing this, in determining what causal efficacy the agent's intentions had in one or more directions, and how his short-term intentions succeeded or failed to be constitutive of long-term intentions, we ourselves write a further part of these histories. Narrative history of a certain kind turns out to be the basic and essential genre for the characterization of human action. . . .

At the beginning of this chapter I argued that in successfully identifying and understanding what someone else is doing we always move towards having a particular episode in the context of a set of narrative histories, histories both of the individuals concerned and of the settings in which they act and suffer. It is now becoming clear that we render the actions of others intelligible in this way because action itself has a basically historical character. It is because we all live out narratives in our lives and because we understand our own lives in terms of the narratives that we live out that the form of narrative is appropriate for understanding the actions of others. Stories are lived before they are told—except in the case of fiction. . . .

A central thesis then begins to emerge: man is in his actions and practice, as well as in his fictions, essentially a story-telling animal. He is not essentially, but becomes through his history, a teller of stories that aspire to truth. But the key question for men is not about their own authorship; I can only answer the question "What am I to do?" if I can answer the prior question "Of what story or stories do I find myself a part?" We enter human society, that is, with one or more imputed characters—roles into which we have been drafted— and we have to learn what they are in order to be able to understand how others respond to us and how our responses to them are apt to be construed. It is through hearing stories about wicked stepmothers, lost children, good but misguided kings, wolves that suckle twin boys, youngest sons who receive no inheritance but must make their own way in the world and eldest sons who waste their inheritance on riotous living and go into exile to live with the swine, that children learn or mislearn both what a child and what a parent is, what the cast of characters may be in the drama into which they have been born and what the ways of the world are. Deprive children of stories and you leave them unscripted, anxious stutterers in their actions as in their words. Hence there is no way to give us an understanding of any society, including our own, except through the stock of stories which constitute its initial dramatic resources. Mythology, in its original sense, is at the heart of things. Vico was right and so was Joyce. And so too of course is that moral tradition from heroic society to its medieval heirs according to which the telling of stories has a key part in educating us into the virtues.

To be the subject of a narrative that runs from one's birth to one's death is, I remarked earlier, to be accountable for the actions and experiences which compose a narratable life. It is, that is, to be open to being asked to give a certain kind of account of what one did or what happened to one or what one witnessed at any earlier point in one's life than the time at which the question is posed. Of course someone may have forgotten or suffered brain damage or simply not attended sufficiently at the relevant time to be able to give the relevant account. But to say of someone under some one description ("The prisoner of the Chateau d'If") that he is the same person as someone characterized quite differently ("The Count of Monte Cristo") is precisely to say that it makes sense to ask him to give an intelligible narrative account enabling us to understand how he could at different times and different places be one and the same person and yet be so differently characterized. Thus personal identity is just that identity presupposed by the unity of the character which the unity of a narrative requires. Without such unity there would not be subjects of whom stories could be told.

The other aspect of narrative selfhood is correlative: I am not only accountable, I am one who can always ask others for an account, who can put others to the question. I am part of their story, as they are part of mine. The narrative of any one life is part of an interlocking set of narratives. Moreover this asking for and giving of accounts itself plays an important part in constituting narratives. Asking you what you did and why, saying what I did and why, pondering the differences between your account of what I did and my account of what I did, and *vice versa,* these are essential constituents of all but the very simplest and barest of narratives. Thus without the account-ability of the self those trains of events that constitute all but the simplest and barest of narratives could not occur; and without that same accountability narratives would lack that continuity required to make both them and the actions that constitute them intelligible. . . .

It is now possible to return to the question from which this enquiry into the nature of human action and identity started: In what does the unity of an individual life consist? The answer is that its unity is the unity of a narrative embodied in a single life. To ask "What is the good for me?" is to ask how best I might live out that unity and bring it to completion. To ask "What is the good for man?" is to ask what all answers to the former question must have in common. But now it is important to emphasize that it is the systematic asking of these two questions and the attempt to answer them in deed as well as in word which provide the moral life with its unity. The unity of a human life is the unity of a narrative quest. Quests sometimes fail, are frustrated, abandoned or dissipated into distractions; and human lives may in all these ways also fail. But the only criteria for success or failure in a human life as a whole are the criteria of success or failure in a narrated or to-be-narrated quest. A quest for what?

Two key features of the medieval conception of a quest need to be recalled. The first is that without some at least partly determinate conception of the final *telos* there could not be any beginning to a quest. Some conception of the good for man is required. Whence is such a conception to be drawn? Precisely from those questions which led us to attempt to transcend that limited conception of the virtues which is available in and through practices. It is in looking for a conception of *the* good which will enable us to order other goods, for a conception of *the* good which will enable us to extend our understanding of the purpose and content of the virtues, for a conception of *the* good which will enable us to understand the place of integrity and constancy in life, that we initially define the kind of life which is a quest for the good. But secondly it is clear the medieval conception of a quest is not at all that of a search for something already adequately characterized, as miners search for gold or geologists for oil. It is in the course of the quest and only through encountering and coping with the various particular harms, dangers, temptations and distractions which provide any quest with its episodes and incidents that the goal of the quest is finally to be understood. A quest is always an education both as to the character of that which is sought and in self-knowledge.

The virtues therefore are to be understood as those dispositions which will not only sustain practices and enable us to achieve the goods internal to practices, but which will also sustain us in the relevant kind of quest for the good, by enabling us to overcome the harms, dangers, temptations and distractions which we encounter, and which will furnish us with increasing self-knowledge and increasing knowledge of the good. The catalogue of the virtues will therefore include the virtues required to sustain the kind of households and the kind of political communities in which men and women can seek for the good together and the virtues necessary for philosophical enquiry about the character of the good. We have then arrived at a provisional conclusion about the good life for man: the good life for man is the life spent in seeking for the good life for man, and the virtues necessary for the seeking are those which will enable us to understand what more and what else the good life for man is. We have also completed the second stage in our account of the virtues, by situating them in relation to the good life for man and not only in relation to practices. But our enquiry requires a third stage.

For I am never able to seek for the good or exercise the virtues only *qua* individual. This is partly because what it is to live the good life concretely varies from circumstance to circumstance even when it is one and the same conception of the good life and one and the same set of virtues which are being embodied in a human life. What the good life is for a fifth-century Athenian general will not be the same as what it was for a medieval nun or a seventeenth-century farmer. But it is not just that different individuals live in different social circumstances; it is also that we all approach our own circumstances as bearers of a particular social identity. I am someone's son or daughter, someone else's cousin or uncle; I am a citizen of this or that city, a member of this or that guild or profession; I belong to this clan, that tribe, this nation. Hence what is good for me has to be the good for one who inhabits these roles. As such, I inherit from the past of my family, my city, my tribe, my nation, a variety of debts, inheritances, rightful expectations and obligations. These constitute the given of my life, my moral starting point. This is in part what gives my life its own moral particularity.

This thought is likely to appear alien and even surprising from the standpoint of modern individualism. From the standpoint of individualism I am what I myself choose to be. I can always, if I wish to, put in question what are taken to be the merely contingent social features of my existence. I may biologically be my father's son; but I cannot be held responsible for what he did unless I choose implicitly or explicitly to assume such responsibility. I may legally be a citizen of a certain country; but I cannot be held responsible for what my country does or has done unless I choose implicitly or explicitly to assume such responsibility. Such individualism is expressed by those modern Americans who deny any responsibility for the effects of slavery upon black Americans, saying "I never owned any slaves." It is more subtly the standpoint of those other modern Americans who accept a nicely calculated responsibility for such effects measured precisely by the benefits they themselves as individuals have indirectly received from slavery. In both cases "being an American" is not in itself taken to be part of the moral identity of the individual. And of course there is nothing peculiar to modern Americans in this attitude: the Englishman who says, "*I* never did any wrong to Ireland; why bring up that old history as though it had something to do with *me?*" or the young German who believes that being born after 1945 means that what Nazis did to Jews has no moral relevance to his relationship to his Jewish contemporaries, exhibit the same attitude, that according to which the self is detachable from its social and historical roles and statuses. And the self so detached is of course a self very much at home in either Sartre's or Goffman's perspective, a self that can have no history. The contrast with the narrative view of the self is clear. For the story of my life is always embedded in the story of those communities from which I derive my identity. I am born with a past; and to try to cut myself off from that past, in the individualist mode, is to deform my present relationships. The possession of an historical identity and the possession of a social identity coincide. Notice that rebellion against my identity is always one possible mode of expressing it.

Notice also that the fact that the self has to find its moral identity in and through its membership in communities such as those of the family, the neighborhood, the city and the tribe does not entail that the self has to accept the moral *limitations* of the particularity of those forms of community. Without those moral particularities to begin from there would never be anywhere to begin; but it is in moving forward from such particularity that the search for the good, for the universal, consists. Yet particularity can never be simply left behind or obliterated. The notion of escaping from it into a realm of entirely universal maxims which belong to man as such, whether in its eighteenth-century Kantian form or in the presentation of some modern analytical moral philosophies, is an illusion and an illusion with painful consequences. When men and women identify what are in fact their partial and particular causes too easily and too completely with the cause of some universal principle, they usually behave worse than they would otherwise do.

What I am, therefore, is in key part what I inherit, a specific past that is present to some degree in my present. I find myself part of a history and that is generally to say, whether I like it or not, whether I recognize it or not, one of the bearers of a tradition. It was important when I characterized the concept of a practice to notice that practices always have histories and that at any given moment what a practice is depends on a mode of understanding it which has been transmitted often through many generations. And thus; insofar as the virtues sustain the relationships required for practices, they have to sustain relationships to the past—and to the future—as well as in the present. But the traditions through which particular practices are transmitted and reshaped never exist in isolation for larger social traditions. What constitutes such traditions?

We are apt to be misled here by the ideological uses to which the concept of a tradition has been put by conservative political theorists. Characteristically such theorists have followed Burke in contrasting tradition with reason and the stability of tradition with conflict. Both contrasts obfuscate. For all reasoning takes place within the context of some traditional mode of thought, transcending through criticism and invention the limitations of what had hitherto been reasoned in that tradition; this is as true of modern physics as of medieval logic. Moreover when a tradition is in good order it is always partially constituted by an argument about the goods the pursuit of which gives to that tradition its particular point and purpose.

So when an institution—a university, say, or a farm, or a hospital—is the bearer of a tradition of practice or practices, its common life will be partly, but in a centrally important way, constituted by a continuous argument as to what a university is and ought to be or

213

what good farming is or what good medicine is. Traditions, when vital, embody continuities of conflict. Indeed when a tradition becomes Burkean, it is always dying or dead. . . .

A living tradition then is an historically extended, socially embodied argument, and an argument precisely in part about the goods which constitute that tradition. Within a tradition the pursuit of goods extends through generations, sometimes through many generations. Hence the individual's search for his or her good is generally and characteristically conducted within a context defined by those traditions of which the individual's life is a part, and this is true both of those goods which are internal to practices and of the goods of a single life. Once again the narrative phenomenon of embedding is crucial: the history of a practice in our time is generally and characteristically embedded in and made intelligible in terms of the larger and longer history of the tradition through which the practice in its present form was conveyed to us; the history of each of our own lives is generally and characteristically embedded in and made intelligible in terms of the larger and longer histories of a number of traditions. I have to say "generally and characteristically" rather than "always," for traditions decay, disintegrate and disappear. What then sustains and strengthens traditions? What weakens and destroys them?

The answer in key part is: the exercise or the lack of exercise of the relevant virtues. The virtues find their point and purpose not only in sustaining those relationships necessary if the variety of goods internal to practices are to be achieved and not only in sustaining the form of an individual life in which that individual may seek out his or her good as the good of his or her whole life, but also in sustaining those traditions which provide both practices and individual lives with their necessary historical context. Lack of justice, lack of truthfulness, lack of courage, lack of the relevant intellectual virtues—these corrupt traditions, just as they do those institutions and practices which derive their life from the traditions of which they are the contemporary embodiments. To recognize this is of course also to recognize the existence of an additional virtue, one whose importance is perhaps most obvious when it is least present, the virtue of having an adequate sense of the traditions to which one belongs or which confront one. . . .

214

**STUDY QUESTIONS**

1. What roles do history and tradition play in MacIntyre's moral philosophy? Choose a specific moral question and describe how MacIntyre approaches it. Then choose another moral philosopher whom you have studied and illustrate the difference in approach.

2. Discuss and explain: "I can only answer the question 'What am I to do?' if I can answer the question 'Of what story or stories am I a part?'"

3. "I am someone's son or daughter . . . I belong to this clan, that tribe, this nation. Hence, what is good for me must be good for one who inhabits these roles." Critically discuss the concept of the virtues implied by the way in which they are related to one's role and to one's place in the community.

4. What does MacIntyre find wrong with "modern individualism"? How is individualism at odds with a life of virtue? How does it conflict with tradition? In what ways is individualism morally irresponsible?

5. What does MacIntyre mean by a "living tradition"? How do the virtues sustain traditions? How do traditions and practices help give content to the virtues?

# Virtues and Vices

### PHILIPPA FOOT

Philippa Foot (b. 1920) is a Senior Research Fellow of Somerville College, Oxford. She also teaches at the University of California at Los Angeles. She is the author of *Theories of Ethics* (1967) and *Virtues and Vices* (1978).

Foot distinguishes the virtues from other beneficial human traits such as health or good memory. These latter are not virtues since they do not engage a person's will and character. A generous or courageous person is virtuous in wanting the good fortune or safety of others and in having the strength of character to act. Wisdom presents a difficulty: How can knowledge or wisdom be a matter of intention or desire? Foot replies that a wise person values (wants) the proper ends; such valuation engages the will. The virtues are also "corrective" in inhibiting the tendency to yield to temptation. Foot addresses a special problem: Can anyone with evil purpose exercise a virtue, for example, show courage in murdering someone? Her answer is no.

## I

. . . It seems clear that virtues are, in some general way, beneficial. Human beings do not get on well without them. Nobody can get on well if he lacks courage, and does not have some measure of temperance and wisdom, while communities where justice and charity are lacking are apt to be wretched places to live, as Russia was under the

VIRTUES AND VICES From *Virtues and Vices* by Philippa Foot. Reprinted by permission of the publisher, University of California Press.

Stalinist terror, or Sicily under the Mafia. But now we must ask to whom the benefit goes, whether to the man who has the virtue or rather to those who have to do with him? In the case of some of the virtues the answer seems clear. Courage, temperance and wisdom benefit both the man who has these dispositions and other people as well; and moral failings such as pride, vanity, worldliness, and avarice harm both their possessor and others, though chiefly perhaps the former. But what about the virtues of charity and justice? These are directly concerned with the welfare of others, and with what is owed to them; and since each may require sacrifice of interest on the part of the virtuous man both may seem to be deleterious to their possessor and beneficial to others. Whether in fact it is so has, of course, been a matter of controversy since Plato's time or earlier. It is a reasonable opinion that on the whole man is better off for being charitable and just, but this is not to say that circumstances may not arise in which he will have to sacrifice everything for charity or justice.

Nor is this the only problem about the relation between virtue and human good. For one very difficult question concerns the relation between justice and the common good. Justice, in the wide sense in which it is understood in discussions of the cardinal virtues, and in this paper, has to do with that to which someone has a right—that which he is owed in respect of non-interference and positive service—and rights may stand in the way of the pursuit of the common good. Or so at least it seems to those who reject utilitarian doctrines. This dispute cannot be settled here, but I shall treat justice as a virtue independent of charity, and standing as a possible limit on the scope of that virtue.

Let us say then, leaving unsolved problems behind us, that virtues are in general beneficial characteristics, and indeed ones that a human being needs to have, for his own sake and that of his fellows. This will not, however, take us far towards a definition of a virtue, since there are many other qualities of a man that may be similarly beneficial, as for instance bodily characteristics such as health and physical strength, and mental powers such as those of memory and concentration. What is it, we must ask, that differentiates virtues from such things?

As a first approximation to an answer we might say that while health and strength are excellences of the body, and memory and concentration of the mind, it is the will that is good in a man of virtue. But this suggestion is worth only as much as the explanation that follows it. What might we mean by saying that virtue belongs to the will?

In the first place we observe that it is primarily by his intentions that a man's moral dispositions are judged. If he does something unintentionally this is usually irrelevant to our estimate of his virtue. But of course this thesis must be qualified, because failures in performance rather than intention may show a lack of virtue. This will be so when, for instance, one man brings harm to another without realising he is doing it, but where his ignorance is itself culpable. Sometimes in such cases there will be a previous act or omission to which we can point as the source of the ignorance. Charity requires that we take care to find out how to render assistance where we are likely to be called on to do so, and thus, for example, it is contrary to charity to fail to find out about elementary first aid. But in an interesting class of cases in which it seems again to be performance rather than intention that counts in judging a man's virtue there is no possibility of shifting the judgment to previous intentions. For sometimes one man succeeds where another fails not because there is some specific difference in their previous conduct but rather because his heart lies in a different place; and the disposition of the heart is part of virtue.

Thus it seems right to attribute a kind of moral failing to some deeply discouraging and debilitating people who say, without lying, that they mean to be helpful; and on the other side to see virtue *par excellence* in one who is prompt and resourceful in doing good. In his novel *A Single Pebble* John Hersey describes such a man, speaking of a rescue in a swift flowing river.

> It was the head tracker's marvellous swift response that captured my admiration at first, his split second solicitousness when he heard a cry of pain, his finding in mid-air, as it were, the only way to save the injured boy. But there was more to it than that. His action, which could not have been mulled over in his mind, showed a deep, instinctive love of life, a compassion, an optimism, which made me feel very good . . .

What this suggests is that a man's virtue may be judged by his innermost desires as well as by his intentions and this fits with our idea that a virtue such as generosity lies as much in someone's attitudes as in his actions. Pleasure in the good fortune of others is, one thinks, the sign of a generous spirit; and small reactions of pleasure and displeasure often the surest signs of a man's moral disposition.

None of this shows that it is wrong to think of virtues as belonging to the will; what it does show is that "will" must here be understood in its widest sense, to cover what is wished for as well as what is sought.

A different set of considerations will, however, force us to give up any simple statement about the relation between virtue and will, and these considerations have to do with the virtue of wisdom. Practical wisdom, we said, was counted by Aristotle among the intellectual virtues, and while our *wisdom* is not quite the same as *phronēsis* or *prudentia* it too might seem to belong to the intellect rather than the will. Is not wisdom a matter of knowledge, and how can knowledge be a matter of intention or desire? The answer is that it isn't, so that there is good reason for thinking of wisdom as an intellectual virtue. But on the other hand wisdom has special connexions with the will, meeting it at more than one point.

In order to get this rather complex picture in focus we must pause for a little and ask what it is that we ourselves understand by wisdom: what the wise man knows and what he does. Wisdom, as I see it, has two parts. In the first place the wise man knows the means to certain good ends; and secondly he knows how much particular ends are worth. Wisdom in its first part is relatively easy to understand. It seems that there are some ends belonging to human life in general rather than to particular skills such as medicine or boatbuilding, ends having to do with such matters as friendship, marriage, the bringing up of children, or the choice of ways of life; and it seems that knowledge of how to act well in these matters belongs to some people but not to others. We call those who have this knowledge wise, while those who do not have it are seen as lacking wisdom. So, as both Aristotle and Aquinas insisted, wisdom is to be contrasted with cleverness because cleverness is the ability to take the right steps to any end, whereas wisdom is related only to good ends, and to human life in general rather than to the ends of particular arts.

Moreover, we should add, there belongs to wisdom only that part of knowledge which is within the reach of any ordinary adult human being: knowledge that can be acquired only by someone who is clever or who has access to special training is not counted as part of wisdom, and would not be so counted even if it could serve the ends that wisdom serves. It is therefore quite wrong to suggest that wisdom cannot be a moral virtue because virtue must be within the reach of anyone who really wants it and some people are too stupid to be anything but ignorant even about the most fundamental matters of human life. Some people are wise without being at all clever or well informed: they make good decisions and they know, as we say, "what's what."

In short wisdom, in what we called its first part, is connected with the will in the following ways. To begin with it presupposes good ends: the man who is wise does not merely know *how* to do good things such as looking after his children well, or strengthening someone in trouble, but must also want to do them. And then wisdom, in so far as it consists of knowledge which anyone can gain in the course of an ordinary life, is available to anyone who really wants it. As Aquinas put it, it belongs "to a power under the direction of the will."[1]

The second part of wisdom, which has to do with values, is much harder to describe, because here we meet ideas which are curiously elusive, such as the thought that some pursuits are more worthwhile than others, and some matters trivial and some important in human life. Since it makes good sense to say that most men waste a lot of their lives in ardent pursuit of what is trivial and unimportant it is not possible to explain the important and the trivial in terms of the amount of attention given to different subjects by the average man. But I have never seen, or been able to think out, a true account of this matter, and I believe that a complete account of wisdom, and of certain other virtues and vices must wait until this gap can be filled. What we can see is that one of the things a wise man knows and a foolish man does not is that such things as social position, and wealth, and the good opinion of the world, are too dearly bought at the cost of health or friendship or family ties. So we may say that a man who lacks wisdom "has false values," and that vices such as vanity and worldliness and avarice are contrary to wisdom in a special way. There is always an element of false judgment about these vices, since the man who is vain for instance sees admiration as more important than it is, while the worldly man is apt to see the good life as one of wealth and power. Adapting Aristotle's distinction between the weak-willed man (the akratēs) who follows pleasure though he

---

[1]Aquinas, *Summa Theologica*, 1a2ae Q.56 a.3.

knows, in some sense, that he should not, and the licentious man (the akolastos) who sees the life of pleasure as the good life,[2] we may say that moral failings such as these are never purely "akratic." It is true that a man may criticise himself or his worldliness or vanity or love of money, but then it is his values that are the subject of his criticism.

Wisdom in this second part is, therefore, partly to be described in terms of apprehension, and even judgment, but since it has to do with a man's attachments it also characterises his will.

The idea that virtues belong to the will, and that this helps to distinguish them from such things as bodily strength or intellectual ability has, then, survived the consideration of the virtue of wisdom, albeit in a fairly complex and slightly attenuated form. And we shall find this idea useful again if we turn to another important distinction that must be made, namely that between virtues and other practical excellences such as arts and skills.

Aristotle has sometimes been accused, for instance by von Wright, of failing to see how different virtues are from arts or skills,[3] but in fact one finds, among the many things that Aristotle and Aquinas say about this difference, the observation that seems to go the heart of the matter. In the matter of arts and skills, they say, voluntary error is preferable to involuntary error, while in the matter of virtues (what we call virtues) it is the reverse.[4] The last part of the thesis is actually rather hard to interpret, because it is not clear what is meant by the idea of involuntary viciousness. But we can leave this aside and still have all we need in order to distinguish arts or skills from virtues. If we think, for instance, of someone who deliberately makes a spelling mistake (perhaps when writing on the blackboard in order to explain this particular point) we see that this does not in any way count against his skill as a speller: "I did it deliberately" rebuts an accusation of this kind. And what we can say without running into any difficulties is that there is no comparable rebuttal in the case of an accusation relating to lack of virtue. If a man acts unjustly or uncharitably, or in a cowardly or intemperate manner, "I did it deliberately" cannot on any interpretation lead to exculpation. So, we may say, a virtue is not, like a skill or an art, a mere capacity: it must actually engage the will.

---

[2] Aristotle, *Nicomachean Ethics*, especially bk. VII.

[3] G. H. von Wright, *The Varieties of Goodness* (London, 1963), chapter VIII.

[4] Aristotle op. cit. 1140 b. 22–25. Aquinas op. cit. 1a2ae Q.57 a.4.

# II

I shall now turn to another thesis about the virtues, which I might express by saying that they are *corrective,* each one standing at a point at which there is some temptation to be resisted or deficiency of motivation to be made good. As Aristotle put it, virtues are about what is difficult for men, and I want to see in what sense this is true, and then to consider a problem in Kant's moral philosophy in the light of what has been said.

Let us first think about coverage and temperance. Aristotle and Aquinas contrasted these vitues with justice in the following respect. Justice was concerned with operations and courage and temperance with passions.[5] What they meant by this seems to have been, primarily, that the man of courage does not fear immoderately nor the man of temperance have immoderate desires for pleasure, and that there was no corresponding moderation of a passion implied in the idea of justice. This particular account of courage and temperance might be disputed on the ground that a man's courage is measured by his action and not by anything as uncontrollable as fear; and similarly that the temperate man who must on occasion refuse pleasures need not *desire* them any less than the intemperate man. Be that as it may (and something will be said about it later) it is obviously true that courage and temperance have to do with particular springs of action as justice does not. Almost any desire can lead a man to act unjustly, not even excluding the desire to help a friend or to save a life, whereas a cowardly act must be motivated by fear or a desire for safety, and an act of intemperance by a desire for pleasure, perhaps even for a particular range of pleasures such as those of eating or drinking or sex. And now, going back to the idea of virtues as correctives one may say that it is only because fear and the desire for pleasure often operate as temptations that courage and temperance exist as virtues at all. As things are we often want to run away not only where that is the right thing to do but also where we should stand firm; and we want pleasure not only where we should seek pleasure but also where we should not. If human nature had been different there would have been no need of a corrective disposition in either place, as fear and pleasure would have been good guides to conduct throughout life. So Aquinas says, about the passions,

---

[5] Aristotle op. cit. 1106 b. 15 and 1129 a.4 have this implication; but Aquinas is more explicit in op. cit. 1a2ae Q.60 a.2.

They may incite us to something against reason, and so we need a curb, which we name *temperance*. Or they may make us shirk a course of action dictated by reason, through fear of dangers or hardships. Then a person needs to be steadfast and not run away from what is right; and for this *courage* is named.[6]

As with courage and temperance so with many other virtues: there is, for instance, a virtue of industriousness only because idleness is a temptation; and of humility only because men tend to think too well of themselves. Hope is a virtue because despair too is a temptation; it might have been that no one cried that all was lost except where he could really see it to be so, and in this case there would have been no virtue of hope.

With virtues such as justice and charity it is a little different, because they correspond not to any particular desire or tendency that has to be kept in check but rather to a deficiency of motivation; and it is this that they must make good. If people were as much attached to the good of others as they are to their own good there would no more be a general virtue of benevolence than there is a general virtue of self-love. And if people cared about the rights of others as they care about their own rights no virtue of justice would be needed to look after the matter, and rules about such things as contracts and promises would only need to be made public, like the rules of a game that everyone was eager to play.

On this view of the virtues and vices everything is seen to depend on what human nature is like, and the traditional catalogue of the two kinds of dispositions is not hard to understand. Nevertheless it may be defective, and anyone who accepts the thesis that I am putting forward will feel free to ask himself where the temptations and deficiencies that need correcting are really to be found. It is possible, for example, that the theory of human nature lying behind the traditional list of virtues and vices puts too much emphasis on hedonistic and sensual impulses, and does not sufficiently take account of less straightforward inclinations such as the desire to be put upon and dissatisfied, or the unwillingness to accept good things as they come along.

It should now be clear why I said that virtues should be seen as

---

[6]Aquinas op. cit. 1a2ae Q.61 a.3.

correctives; and part of what is meant by saying that virtue is about things that are difficult for men should also have appeared. The further application of this idea is, however, controversial, and the following difficulty presents itself: that we both are and are not inclined to think that the harder a man finds it to act virtuously the more virtue is needed where it is particularly hard to act virtuously; yet on the other it could be argued that difficulty in acting virtuously shows that the agent is imperfect in virtue: according to Aristotle, to take pleasure in virtuous action is the mark of true virtue, with the self-mastery of the one who finds virtue difficult only a second best. How then is this conflict to be decided? Who shows most courage, the one who wants to run away but does not, or the one who does not even want to run away? Who shows most charity, the one who finds it easy to make the good of others his object, or the one who finds it hard?

What is certain is that the thought that virtues are corrective does not constrain us to relate virtue to difficulty in each individual man. Since men in general find it hard to face great dangers or evils, and even small ones, we may count as courageous those few who without blindness or indifference are nevertheless fearless even in terrible circumstances. And when someone has a natural charity or generosity it is, at least part of the virtue that he has; if natural virtue cannot be the whole of virtue this is because a kindly or fearless disposition could be disastrous without justice and wisdom, and these virtues have to be learned, not because natural virtue is too easily acquired. I have argued that the virtues can be seen as correctives in relation to human nature in general but not that each virtue must present a difficulty to each and every man.

Nevertheless many people feel strongly inclined to say that it is for moral effort that moral praise is to be bestowed, and that in proportion as a man finds it easy to be virtuous so much the less is he to be morally admired for his good actions. The dilemma can be resolved only when we stop talking about difficulties standing in the way of virtuous action as if they were of only one kind. The fact is that some kinds of difficulties do indeed provide an occasion for much virtue, but that others rather show that virtue is incomplete.

To illustrate this point I shall first consider an example of honest action. We may suppose for instance that a man has an opportunity to steal, in circumstances where stealing is not morally permissible, but that he refrains. And now let us ask our old question. For one man it is hard to refrain from stealing and for another man it is not: which shows the greater virtue in acting as he should? It is not difficult to see in this case that it makes all the difference whether the difficulty comes from circumstances, as that a man is poor, or that his theft is unlikely to be detected, or whether it comes from something that belongs to his own character. The fact that a man is *tempted* to steal is something about him that shows a certain lack of honesty: of the thoroughly honest man we say that it "never entered his head," meaning that it was never a real possibility for him. But the fact that he is poor is something that makes the occasion more *tempting,* and difficulties of this kind make honest action all the more virtuous.

A similar distinction can be made between different obstacles standing in the way of charitable action. Some circumstances, as that great sacrifice is needed, or that the one to be helped is a rival, give an occasion on which a man's charity is severely tested. Yet in given circumstances of this kind it is the man who acts easily rather than the one who finds it hard who shows the most charity. Charity is a virtue of attachment, and that sympathy for others which makes it easier to help them is part of the virtue itself.

These are fairly simple cases, but I am not supposing that it is always easy to say where the relevant distinction is to be drawn. What, for instance, should we say about the emotion of fear as an obstacle to action? Is a man more courageous if he fears much and nevertheless acts, or if he is relatively fearless? Several things must be said about this. In the first place it seems that the emotion of fear is not a necessary condition for the display of courage; in face of a great evil such as death or injury a man may show courage even if he does not tremble. On the other hand even irrational fears may give an occasion for courage: if someone suffers from claustrophobia or a dread of heights he may require courage to do that which would not be a courageous action for others. But not all fears belong from this point of view to the circumstances rather than to a man's character. For while we do not think of claustrophobia or a dread of heights as features of character, a general timorousness may be. Thus, although pathological fears are not the result of a man's choices and values some fears may be. The fears that count against a man's courage are those that we think he could overcome, and among them, in a special class, those that reflect the fact that he values safety too much.

In spite of problems such as these, which have certainly not all been solved, both the distinction between different kinds of obstacles to virtuous action, and the general idea that virtues are correctives, will be useful in resolving a difficulty in Kant's moral philosophy closely related to the issues discussed in the preceding paragraphs. In a passage in the first section of the *Groundwork of the Metaphysics of Morals* Kant notoriously tied himself into a knot in trying to give an account of those actions which have as he put it "positive moral worth." Arguing that only actions done out of a sense of duty have this worth he contrasts a philanthropist who "takes pleasure in spreading happiness around him" with one who acts out of respect for duty, saying that the actions of the latter but not the former have moral worth. Much scorn has been poured on Kant for this curious doctrine, and indeed it does seem that something has gone wrong, but perhaps we are not in a position to scoff unless we can give our own account of the idea on which Kant is working. After all it does seem that he is right in saying that some actions are in accordance with duty, and even required by duty, without being the subjects of moral praise, like those of the honest trader who deals honestly in a situation in which it is in his interest to do so.

It was this kind of example that drove Kant to his strange conclusion. He added another example, however, in discussing acts of self-preservation; these he said, while they normally have no positive moral worth, have it when a man preserves his life not from inclination but without inclination and from a sense of duty. Is he not right in saying that acts of self-preservation normally have no moral significance but that they may have it, and how do we ourselves explain this fact?

To anyone who approaches this topic from a consideration of the virtues the solution readily suggests itself. Some actions are in accordance with virtue without requiring virtue for their performance, whereas others are both in accordance with virtue and such as to show possession of a virtue. So Kant's trader was dealing honestly in a situation in which the virtue of honesty is not required for honest dealing, and it is for this reason that his action did not have "positive moral worth." Similarly, the care that one ordinarily takes for one's life, as for instance on some ordinary morning in eating one's breakfast and keeping out of the way of a car on the road, is something for which no virtue is required. As we said earlier there is no general virtue of self-love as there is a virtue of benevolence or charity, because men are generally attached sufficiently to their own good. Nevertheless in special circumstances virtues such as temperance, courage, fortitude, and hope may be needed if someone is to preserve his life. Are these circumstances in which the preservation of one's own life is a duty? Sometimes it is so, for sometimes it is what is owed to others that should keep a man from destroying himself, and then he may act out of a sense of duty. But not all cases in which acts of self-preservation show virtue are like this. For a man may display each of the virtues just listed even where he does not do any harm to others if he kills himself or fails to preserve his life. And it is this that explains why there may be a moral aspect to suicide which does not depend on possible injury to other people. It is not that suicide is "always wrong," whatever that would mean, but that suicide is *sometimes* contrary to virtues such as courage and hope.

Let us now return to Kant's philanthropists, with the thought that it is action that is in accordance with virtue and also displays a virtue that has moral worth. We see at once that Kant's difficulties are avoided, and the happy philanthropist reinstated in the position which belongs to him. For charity is, as we said, a virtue of attachment as well as action, and the sympathy that makes it easier to act with charity is part of the virtue. The man who acts charitably out of a sense of duty is not to be undervalued, but it is the other who most shows virtue and therefore to the other that most moral worth is attributed. Only a detail of Kant's presentation of the case of the dutiful philanthropist tells on the other side. For what he actually said was that this man felt no sympathy and took no pleasure in the good of others because "his mind was clouded by some sorrow of his own," and this is the kind of circumstance that increases the virtue that is needed if a man is to act well.

### III

It was suggested above that an action with "positive moral worth," or as we might say a positively good action, was to be seen as one which was in accordance with virtue, by which I mean contrary to no virtue, and moreover one for which a virtue was required. Nothing has so far been said about another case, excluded by the formula, in which it might seem that an act displaying one virtue was nevertheless contrary to another. In giving this last description I am thinking not of two virtues with competing claims, as if what were required by justice could nevertheless be demanded by charity, or something of that kind, but rather of the possibility that a virtue such as courage or temperance or industry which overcomes a special temptation, might be displayed in an act of folly or villainy. Is this something that we must allow for, or is it only good or innocent actions which can be acts of these virtues? Aquinas, in his definition of virtue, said that virtues can produce only good actions, and that they are dispositions "of which no one can make bad use,"[7] except when they are treated as objects, as in being the subject of hatred or pride. The common opinion nowadays is, however, quite different. With the notable exception of Peter Geach hardly anyone sees any difficulty in the thought that virtues may sometimes be displayed in bad actions. Von Wright, for instance, speaks of the courage of the villain as if this were a quite unproblematic idea, and most people take it for granted that the virtues of courage and temperance may aid a bad man in his evil work. It is also supposed that charity may lead a man to act badly, as when someone does what he has no right to do, but does it for the sake of a friend.

There are, however, reasons for thinking that the matter is not as simple as this. If a man who is willing to do an act of injustice to help a friend, or for the common good, is supposed to act out of charity, and he so acts where a just man will not, it should be said that the unjust man has more charity than the just man. But do we not think that someone not ready to act unjustly may yet be perfect in charity, the virtue having done its whole work in prompting a man to do the acts that are permissible? And is there not more difficulty than might appear in the idea of an act of injustice which is nevertheless an act of courage? Suppose for instance that a sordid murder were in question, say a murder done for gain or to get an inconvenient person out of the way, but that this murder had to be done in alarming circumstances or in the face of real danger; should we be happy to say that such an action was an act of courage or a courageous act? Did the murderer, who certainly acted boldly, or with intrepidity, if he did the murder, also act courageously? Some people insist that they are ready to say this, but I have noticed that they like to move over to a murder for the sake of conscience, or to some other act done in the course of a villainous enterprise but whose immediate end is innocent or positively good. On their hypothesis, which is that bad acts can

---

[7]Aquinas op. cit. 1a2ae Q.56 a.5.

easily be seen as courageous acts or acts of courage, my original example should be just as good.

What are we to say about this difficult matter? There is no doubt that the murderer who murdered for gain was *not a coward:* he did not have a second moral defect which another villain might have had. There is no difficulty about this because it is clear that one defect may neutralise another. As Aquinas remarked, it is better for a blind horse if it is slow.[8] It does not follow, however, that an act of villainy can be courageous; we are inclined to say that it "took courage," and yet it seems wrong to think of courage as equally connected with good actions and bad.

One way out of this difficulty might be to say that the man who is ready to pursue bad ends does indeed have courage, and shows courage in his action, but that in him courage is not a virtue. Later I shall consider some cases in which this might be the right thing to say, but in this instance it does not seem to be. For unless the murderer consistently pursues bad ends his courage will often result in good; it may enable him to do many innocent or positively good things for himself or for his family and friends. On the strength of an individual bad action we can hardly say that in him courage is not a virtue. Nevertheless there is something to be said even about the individual action to distinguish it from one that would readily be called an act of courage or a courageous act. Perhaps the following analogy may help us to see what it is. We might think of words such as "courage" as naming characteristics of human beings in respect of a certain power, as words such as "poison" and "solvent" and "corrosive" so name the properties of physical things. The power to which virtue-words are so related is the power of producing good action, and good desires. But just as poisons, solvents and corrosives do not always operate characteristically, so it could be with virtues. If P (say arsenic) is a poison it does not follow that P acts as a poison wherever it is found. It is quite natural to say on occasion "P does not act as a poison here" though P is a poison and it is P that is acting here. Similarly courage is not operating as a virtue when the murderer turns his courage, which is a virtue to bad ends. Not surprisingly the resistance that some of us registered was not to the expression "the courage of the murderer" or to the assertion that what he did "took courage" but rather to the description of that action as an

---

[8]Aquinas op. cit. 1a2ae Q.58 a.4.

act of courage or a courageous act. It is not that the action *could* not be so described, but that the fact that courage does not here have its characteristic operation is a reason for finding the description strange.

In this example we were considering an action in which courage was not operating as a virtue, without suggesting that in that agent it generally failed to do so. But the latter is also a possibility. If someone is both wicked and foolhardy this may be the case with courage, and it is even easier to find examples of a general connexion with evil rather than good in the case of some other virtues. Suppose, for instance, that we think of someone who is overindustrious, or too ready to refuse pleasure, and this is characteristic of him rather than something we find on one particular occasion. In this case the virtue of industry, or the virtue of temperance, has a systematic connexion with defective action rather than good action; and it might be said in either case that the virtue did not operate as a virtue in this man. Just as we might say in a certain setting "P is not a poison here" though P is a poison and P is here, so we might say that industriousness, or temperance, is not a virtue in some. Similarly in a man habitually given to wishful thinking, who clings to false hopes, hope does not operate as a virtue and we may say that it is not a virtue in him.

The thought developed in the last paragraph, to the effect that not every may who has a virtue has something that is a virtue in him, may help to explain a certain discomfort that one may feel when discussing the virtues. It is not easy to put one's finger on what is wrong, but it has something to do with a disparity between the moral ideas that may seem to be implied in our talk about the virtues, and the moral judgments that we actually make. Someone reading the foregoing pages might, for instance, think that the author of this paper always admired most those people who had all the virtues, being wise and temperate as well as courageous, charitable, and just. And indeed it is sometimes so. There are some people who do possess all these virtues and who are loved and admired by all the world, as Pope John XXIII was loved and admired. Yet the fact is that many of us look up to some people whose chaotic lives contain rather little of wisdom or temperance, rather than to some others who possess these virtues. And while it may be that this is just romantic nonsense I suspect that it is not. For while wisdom always operates as a virtue, its close relation prudence does not, and it is prudence rather than wisdom that inspires many a careful life. Prudence is not a virtue in everyone, any more than industriousness is, for in some it is rather an overanxious concern for safety and propriety, and a determination to keep away from people or situations which are apt to bring trouble with them; and by such defensiveness much good is lost. It is the same with temperance. Intemperance can be an appalling thing, as it was with Henry VIII of whom Wolsey remarked that

> rather than he will either miss or want any part of his will or appetite, he will put the loss of one half of his realm in danger.

Nevertheless in some people temperance is not a virtue, but is rather connected with timidity or with a grudging attitude to the acceptance of good things. Of course what is best is to live boldly yet without imprudence or intemperance, but the fact is that rather few can manage that.

**STUDY QUESTIONS**

1. What does Foot mean by saying "Virtue belongs to the will?"
2. How do the virtues benefit their possessors? What special features must a beneficial trait possess to be counted as a virtue?
3. What is wisdom's relation to the will? To all of the other virtues?
4. Foot argues that what appears to be courage in a murder really is not. Do you agree with her?
5. Do you agree with Foot that wise persons know the means to good ends *and* want those ends? Can wise persons not desire the ends they judge to be worthwhile?
6. In what sense are the virtues "corrective"? What significance does Foot give to this feature of virtue?

# Will Power and the Virtues

### ROBERT C. ROBERTS

Robert C. Roberts (b. 1942) is professor of philosophy and psychological studies at Wheaton College. He has written numerous articles on psychology, theology, and ethics.

Robert C. Roberts distinguishes between motivated virtues and virtues of the will, the former characterized by some desire or motive to behave in a morally correct manner. Here the presence of the right desire (e.g., to tell the truth, to help the needy) is a condition for possessing the virtue (e.g., of honesty, of compassion). Virtues of the will are not grounded in desire, but grounded in the capacity to *resist* desire (e.g., courage resists the desire to flee; self-control and perseverence resist the desire to relax and enjoy oneself).

The two kinds of virtues complement each other. One who possesses only the virtues of the will could be a moral monster (having great powers of self-control and patience in the service of evil). On the other hand, a weak-willed person who possesses the passionate virtues will be at the mercy of nonmoral passions. Such a person will be unable to resist temptation.

The second half of Roberts' paper is devoted to arguments for the thesis that virtues of the will have the char-

FROM WILL POWER AND THE VIRTUES First appeared in *Philosophical Review* (April 1984), pp. 227–247. Extensively revised by author for this edition. Revision reprinted by permission of the author.

acter of personal skills or techniques. The person who can control his impulses possesses certain skills of self-mastery. Although such skills are in part innate, they are learnable, and a weak-willed person can learn techniques for strengthening will. "The virtue of will power is the athletic side of the moral life."

# I

Since Elizabeth Anscombe's challenge to modern moral philosophy in 1958[1], a number of authors have tried to answer the general question "What is a virtue?" or as G. H. von Wright says, to "shape a concept of a virtue." This project has thrown light on the nature of the virtues, but has sometimes raised the expectation that they must all be the same kind of trait.[2] One broad consensus has been that virtues are not skill-like dispositions or powers. I shall argue here that one group of virtues, which I call the moral strengths or virtues of will power, are largely skill-like.

Some theorists have proposed that moral virtues are all determinations of the good will, but a broad-ranging list of traits having moral relevance will probably include some that are not easily corralled into this pen. For example, foresight and psychological insight are characteristics of an ideally moral person, yet it seems wrong to call them determinations of the will. Gentleness, politeness, and friendliness, in some people at least, are styles of behavioral demeanor that may be neither characteristics of the will nor willed into being by their possessors. So probably not all morally relevant traits are matters of the will. Yet it is clear why philosophers might make this mistake, for many of the virtues most central to the moral life, such as truthfulness, courage, justice, compassion, and self-control, *are* determinations of the will.

---

[1]"Modern Moral Philosophy," *Philosophy*, vol. 33 (1958), pp. 1–19.

[2]Important essays in which the tendency is evident are chapter 7 of von Wright's *The Varieties of Goodness* (London: Routledge, 1963); R. B. Brandt's "Traits of Character: A Conceptual Analysis," *American Philosophical Quarterly*, vol. 7 (1970), pp. 23–37; Philippa Foot's "Virtues and Vices" in *Virtues and Vices* (Berkeley: University of California Press, 1978); and John McDowell's "Virtue and Reason," *Monist*, vol. 62 (1979), pp. 331–50.

But this observation won't get us very far unless we know what will is. Broadly, we employ "will" and its cognates in two ways. In the first kind of case we designate inclinations and disinclinations, desires and aversions, motivations. If I go willingly to a horse race, I go gladly or at least with minimal distaste. A willful person does just whatever he wants to, without regard for the rights or concerns of others. To lose the will to live is no longer to care much about living. In the second kind of case "will" designates not motivations, but a family of capacities for resisting adverse inclinations. When we say someone has a "strong will" we are often referring to the presence in her of such virtues as perseverance, resoluteness, courage, patience, and self-control. When we speak of "efforts of will," we refer to the acts or activities corresponding to such virtues: fighting boredom, controlling one's emotions, resisting temptation, persevering in the face of discouragement, overcoming the impulse to flee, fighting anxiety, forcing oneself to the magnanimous gesture, and the like.[3] That this use of "will" is distinct from its use to designate motivation is suggested by the oddity of the expression "an effort of wanting."

Where people make efforts, there exist human capacities. A person can make a muscular effort because in general he has muscular powers, and an effort to pay attention because he can pay attention. (Obviously, it doesn't follow that he has the power to do the particular act he tries to do; efforts can fail in many ways, and some of these involve a failure to possess, or to possess enough of, the relevant capacity.) So if people do make efforts of will—that is, efforts to resist adverse inclinations—then there exist human capacities by which to resist adverse inclinations. I contend in this paper that the virtues of will power are indeed largely capacities, and that these are best thought of as skills. But first I want to discuss the relation between the virtues of will power and some other virtues.

---

[3]When I call a virtue a "virtue of will power," I do not suggest that every action exemplifying it is an exercise of will power. There are acts of courage and patience and perseverance (I do not say this about self-control) that do not require will power, much less an effort of will. I use this name to indicate a salient, but not necessary, feature of these virtues. Also, will power is probably, as a matter of psychological fact, always needed in the *acquisition* of these virtues.

234

## II

Virtues can be classified in different ways for different purposes. A broad division that throws light on the psychology of the moral life is the distinction between the virtues of will power and those that are substantive and motivational. I call virtues like truthfulness, compassion, justice, generosity, promise-keeping, and gratitude "substantive" because they are the psychological embodiment of ethical rules—the substance of the ethical patterns of behavior and judgment and emotion. To be truthful is to be disposed to tell the truth in appropriate situations, to judge well which situations demand telling the truth, to be "alive" to dishonesty in oneself and others, and to feel uneasiness, guilt, indignation, sadness, and other emotions upon encountering dishonesty in oneself and others. Compassion is the disposition to help others who are suffering, to notice and recognize sufferers as sufferers, to see them as in some fundamental way similar to oneself, and to be sad to see suffering and glad to see it relieved.

By contrast, patience does not imply any characteristically ethical patterns of behavior, judgment, or emotion. Racists, cheats, sadists, and thieves may well be persevering, resolute, and self-controlled; and indeed will be more likely to succeed in their several callings if they are. Whether courage is equally lacking in moral substance has been questioned.[4] Philippa Foot has noted that we are disinclined to call particularly heinous acts, such as "a murder done for gain or to get an inconvenient person out of the way"[5] courageous, even if they are done in circumstances which would require courage. But our disinclination here can be accounted for by the *associations* that "courage" has for us: we do associate courage with the substantive moral virtues, and there are important ethical and anthropological reasons

---

[4]Lester Hunt has argued that all virtues are dispositions to act on principles. See his "Character and Thought," *American Philosophical Quarterly*, vol. 15 (1978), pp. 177–86 and his "Generosity and the Diversity of the Virtues," in R. B. Kruschwitz and R. C. Roberts (eds.) *The Virtues* (Belmont, CA: Wadsworth, 1986). He has thus sought the principle on which courage is the disposition to act. He comes up with the following: courageous acts "are the ones which are done from the principle that one's own safety, in general, has no more than a certain measure of importance." "Courage and Principle," *Canadian Journal of Philosophy*, vol. 10 (1980) p. 289. But this principle does not seem to me a moral one; to act morally one needs to know *what* is worth risking one's safety for, and it is the principles embodied in the substantive virtues that tell one that.

[5]Foot, "Virtues and Vices," p. 15.

for this association, which in turn give courage its moral importance. And Foot admits that it is only the attribution of courage to the *act* that troubles us; we find no difficulty in calling a murderer courageous, nor in saying that his act "took courage."

By saying the substantive virtues are "motivational," I mean what I think Aristotle is talking about when he says

> We may even go so far as to state that the man who does not enjoy performing noble actions is not a good man at all. Nobody would call a man just who does not enjoy acting justly, nor generous who does not enjoy generous actions, and so on (*Nicomachean Ethics* 1099a).

To be just is to want just states of affairs to prevail and consequently, in the appropriate circumstances, to want to do what will bring about such states of affairs. Thus the just person takes satisfaction ("pleasure") in the performance and beholding of such actions, and feels frustration ("pain") at failure in them. But Aristotle seems to be less than lucid about the distinction between kinds of virtues that I am pointing out. For he says that "A man who endures danger with joy, or at least without pain, is courageous; if he endures it with pain, he is a coward (*Nicomachean Ethics* 1104b)."[6] But enjoying facing dangers is surely not a criterion of courage. There may be a psychological connection between a person's achieving self-mastery and his taking pleasure either in some aspects of the activity itself or in the fruits of it. But the quality of a person's self-mastery cannot be called into question on the account of his failing to enjoy it. Whereas the idea of a just person who nevertheless hates doing just actions, or is indifferent to their fruits, is a contradiction.

A person who enjoys enduring dangers is better called daredevilish than brave. A particularly bizarre illustration of one way for courage to be a motivational virtue has been collected by William James.[7]

---

[6]But compare 1117b.

[7]*The Varieties of Religious Experience* (Garden City, NY: Doubleday, 1978), pp. 266–67, note. H. A. Prichard finds another way of making courage a passional virtue: for him it is not an enjoyment of dangers, but "the desire to conquer one's feelings of terror arising from the sense of shame which they arouse." *Moral Obligation* (New York: Oxford University Press, 1950), p. 13. Although some courageous actions are motivated by shame of fear, the most typical moral examples are motivated in other ways (see[8]). I hold that there is *no* motive characteristic of courageous actions as a class.

> I believe, says General Skobeleff, that my bravery is simply the passion for and at the same time the contempt of danger. The risk of life fills me with an exaggerated rapture. The fewer there are to share it, the more I like it . . . a meeting of man to man, a duel, a danger into which I can throw myself head-foremost, attracts me, moves me, intoxicates me. I am crazy for it, I love it, I adore it. I run after danger as one runs after women . . . my entire nature runs to meet the peril with an impetus that my will would in vain try to resist.

If joy in enduring danger were a mark of courage, General Skobeleff would appear to be an exceptually courageous man. And no doubt a casual observer of his exploits might call him courageous. But this peek at the General's interiority shows that his disposition is not courage. For whatever else courage may be, it is a virtue; but the disposition he describes is a vice. Even the courage of the thief elicits our admiration; for though his disregard for property rights is despicable, still he possesses a capacity without which one leads a crippled life. But there is nothing admirable about the General's lust for dangers; and we can guess that people who possess it tend to be a menace both to society and to themselves. For positions of leadership we want courageous persons, but not daredevils. We do not want our generals to be enthusiasts for military exploits.

Unlike justice, compassion, generosity, and friendship, courage and self-control do not in themselves supply motives. A person can feed the poor out of compassion, struggle on behalf of the oppressed out of concern for justice (i.e., out of concern for people who are being treated unjustly), and perform sacrifices out of friendship. But actions exhibiting courage and self-control are not done *out of* courage and self-control.[8] Actions done out of moral motives may, however, be done *in virtue of* courage and self-control and patience, if

---

[8] Though they are sometimes done for the sake of courage and self-control, as when you "do every day or two something for no other reason than that you would rather not do it, so that when the hour of dire need draws nigh, it may find you not unnerved and untrained to stand the test." William James, *Principles of Psychology*, vol. 1 (Cambridge, MA: Harvard University Press, 1981), p. 126. Or as when, like G. Gordon Liddy, you eat a rat as an exercise in mastering your fear of rats. *Will: The Autobiography of G. Gordon Liddy* (New York: St. Martin's Press, 1981), p. 24. But this kind of case is untypical, the typical case being that of acting courageously or self-controlledly for the sake of some other end. If someone always acted courageously only to exhibit courage or train herself in it, and never out of friendship, justice, compassion, and so forth, her action would not be moral. And to the extent that acting courageously out of the desire to be courageous is morally praiseworthy, this is because courage is in aid of the actions characteristic of the substantive and motivational virtues.

the circumstances, psychological and environmental, demand such virtues.[9]

I think Plato is on the right track when he calls courage a "preservative."[10] A preservative is in the service of something other than itself that is cherished, and needed because this cherished thing is in some way threatened. Courage, self-control and patience are in the service of the moral and prudential life, and needed because this life is beset with trials. These trials, which are part of the everyday context in which we exercise the virtues, are functions of our desires and aversions. The virtues of will power are the capacities by which a person copes with these trials in the interests of the moral and prudential life.

Philippa Foot has noticed this "corrective" character of the virtues of will power:[11]

> As things are we often want to run away not only where that is the right thing to do but also where we should stand firm; and we want pleasure not only where we should seek pleasure but also where we should not. If human nature had been different there would have been no need of a corrective disposition in either place. . . .

But she mistakenly generalizes this characteristic to all the virtues:

> There is . . . a virtue of industriousness only because idleness is a temptation; and of humility only because men tend to think too well of themselves. Hope is a virtue because despair is a temptation. . . .

Her mistake is that of confusing the existence of something with the existence of its name or concept. If people were never led astray by

---

[9]Aquinas seems to be aware of the distinction to which I point when he says, "By its nature virtue is concerned with the good rather than the difficult" and "A man exposes himself to mortal danger only to preserve justice. Therefore the praise accorded to courage derives in a sense from justice" (*Summa Theologiae* 2a2ae 123.12). But Aquinas is not consistent in this observation that courage and similar virtues do not supply a motive, for he assimilates courage and charity by saying, "Charity does prompt the act of martyrdom as its first and most important moving force by being the virtue commanding it, but courage does so as the directly engaged moving force, being the virtue which brings out the act" (2a2ae 124.2). But unless the martyr is acting not just courageously but for the sake of courage (which is not the typical case and certainly not necessary for martyrdom), it seems wrong to say that courage "prompts" the act in any sense. Courage *facilitates* the act, but only motives *prompt* it.

[10]*Republic* 429c–e.

[11]"Virtues and Vices," p. 9.

fears and pleasures, it is plausible that courage and self-control them-selves would not arise. For courage and self-control are the capacities to manage our inclinations, when they are wayward, to flee dangers and seek pleasures. But industriousness is needed not basically be-cause people are prone to laziness, but because work is a good thing. Industriousness could exist in a world in which no one suffered from laziness, and hope in a world where no one ever despaired, and hon-esty in a world where no one lied—though it is likely that in such a world these virtues would not be named or much noticed. The sub-stantive virtues are "corrective" in the trivial sense that there are vices which correspond to them; the virtues of will power are correc-tive in the significant sense that, in our present psychological condi-tion but not in every imaginable one, they are needed to keep us on the path of virtue and our higher self-interest.

## III

But this is not the whole story. In assessing the degree to which an action reflects moral credit on its agent, we often feel two contrary tendencies. On the one side, like Kant, we are inclined to give greater credit for actions (or character traits) that result from moral struggle. We might call this the hero assessment: just as running a mile in under four minutes is praised not as a speedy mode of transportation, but as an extraordinary feat for legs and lungs and spirit, so some acts are morally praised not just because they are good, but also because they are difficult. Why do we tend to think a moral achieve-ment greater if more difficult? Not, I think, just because we have confused morality with athletics. One obvious reason is that morally difficult actions display some virtues—namely the virtues of will power. But I think a deeper basis for our feeling here is that the greater the moral obstacles a person has overcome in doing some-thing the more her action seems to be her own *achievement*, her own *choice*, and thus to reflect credit on her as an *agent*. It seems to show that her action is *hers* in a special way.

But the moment we make the hero assessment we may have some doubts and think: The very fact that somebody *has* those fears and lusts and countermoral impulses which make right action difficult for him reflects discredit on him; an action is the more praiseworthy the more it is done purely out of moral inclinations and in the absence of contrary inclinations—that is, the more it is done *without* moral

239

struggle. This we might call the purity of heart assessment. Here the emphasis is not on the agent as an achiever, but rather, I should almost say, as a personal *artifact*. Here we assess the individual not with respect to how he brought off the act or how he got to be the kind of person he is, but just with respect to what he *is* in the sense of the configuration of his cares and uncares. The ideally moral person is one who is concerned about important things and relatively unconcerned about relatively unimportant things, and so he does not have to struggle with himself to do what is right.

These kinds of assessments correspond to the kinds of virtues I have distinguished. When we make the hero assessment, we are asking of an action or trait that its accomplishment require one or more of the virtues of will power. If we make the purity of heart assessment, we are laying emphasis on the motivational virtues. The virtues of will power are needed on the road to purity of heart because in most of us the moral inclinations are so weak and the road so strewn with psychological obstacles. But unlike the motivational virtues, these are not the substance of the moral life, and their "corrective" function is no longer needed when full sainthood has been attained.

As I have suggested, however, the virtues of will power are needed not only for their "corrective" function, but also because they are essential to the development of the agent's agenthood. Struggles are an important part of the way we become centers of initiation of actions and passions. They are the contexts in which the shape of our personality takes on that toughness and independence that we call "autonomy," and that seems to be a basic feature of mature personhood. Could a person gain autonomy without struggle, and thus without the capacities necessary to win in struggles? In a famous letter John Keats wrote,[12]

> The common cognomen of this world among the misguided and superstitious is "a vale of tears" from which we are to be redeemed by a certain arbitrary interposition of God and taken to Heaven—What a little circumscribe [d] straightened notion! Call the world if you Please "The vale of Soul-making." Then you will find out the use of the world . . . I say "Soul making." Soul as distinguished from an Intel-

---

[12]*The Letters of Keats*, vol. 2 (Cambridge, MA: Harvard University Press, 1958) pp. 101 *f.*

ligence—There may be intelligences or sparks of the divinity in millions—but they are not Souls . . . till they acquire identities, till each
one is personally itself . . . Do you not see how necessary a World of
Pains and troubles is to school an intelligence and make it a soul?

We might generalize Keats' "World of Pains and troubles" to "a
World of temptations" (psychological adversities). We can guess that
it will never be possible to give a person a moral "identity"—a tough
and abiding passion for justice or a stable and focused desire to relieve
suffering—by injecting him with a drug or giving him a brain operation or fiddling with his genes. But the impossibility of giving
somebody moral character in this way seems to be more than psychological. For even if we could in this way produce a being who
was indistinguishable, in terms of his present dispositions, from a
saint, still I think we would have no inclination whatsoever to can-
onize him. For the praise for his saintliness, and thus for his deeds,
would not be due *him*. If it were due anyone, the pharmacologist or
brain surgeon would seem more likely candidates. So the idea of
somebody acquiring moral character without struggle seems not
only psychologically, but logically amiss. Such a person does not
have an appropriate moral history. Thus, if powers of will are those
powers by which moral struggles are prosecuted, they are more than
just "corrective." They are a logically and psychologically necessary
part of our development as persons.

The relation, then, between the virtues of will power and the
substantive virtues is mutual need: neither kind can exist as moral
virtues without the other kind. Without the virtues of will power,
the moral motives would too often be sabotaged by counter-moral
impulses and the relative weakness of the substantive virtues; nor
would these latter be gained in a morally appropriate way. On the
other hand, the character of a person who had only the virtues of
will power would be empty of moral content.

## IV

I want now to consider the view of the virtues of will power that I
take to be the strongest alternative to my suggestion that they are
capacities. Richard Brandt has argued[13] that moral character traits

---

[13]"Traits of Character: A Conceptual Analysis," *American Philosophical Quarterly*,
vol. 7 (1970), pp. 23–37.

are "the kind of dispositions that wants and aversions are." They are inclinations that can be called into activity by features of a subject's environment or thoughts and which, when they have become active, issue in behavior of a type corresponding to the inclination. Thus a person with the trait of sympathy, if he sees a child in distress from falling off his bicycle, will go to the child and help or comfort him, if some other, competing and stronger, inclination is not presently active in him. For example, if what knocked the child from his bike is a bag of $100 bills falling off a truck, which are now floating up the street in the wind, the active trait of sympathy may start to be challenged by that of avarice. Assuming the sympathetic and avaricious individual judges the wind strong enough to render the fulfillment of the one desire incompatible with that of the other, then his behavior at that moment will be determined by the relative strength of these two inclinations. Brandt generalizes:

> The motivation theory of character traits holds that, under conditions not fully understood, they become active and generate "force vectors" in the psychological field of the person, their direction and degree depending partly on the person's beliefs; what the person actually does is a function of the force vectors in his psychological field at the moment of action.

This account, like Aristotle's, begins to fidget when virtues of will power are mentioned. Unlike Aristotle and Prichard, Brandt does not treat courage as though it is a motivational virtue; but he does treat it as nothing but a function of motivations, among which are to be found some moral ones. Such virtues, though not themselves tendencies of the desire/aversion sort, must be understood as the relative weakness of desires/aversions that stand in opposition to virtuous behavior. Thus the courage of the rat-phobic who crawls under the house after a child is simply the weakness, relative to his desire to free the child, of his desire to avoid the company of rats. On this analysis a generally courageous or self-controlled person is just one who has sufficiently intense moral and prudential desires and aversions that they override, usually, his morally and prudentially aversive motivations.

Some cases of courage, and the like, fit Brandt's analysis. We do sometimes ascribe courage to a person whose impulse to act virtuously is strong enough, by itself, to override his impulse to flee. Maybe this is typical of the courage of the saints: in them the motivational virtues are so strong that in a sense they do not need courage. That is, in them courage is not a function of will power. But most of us would not have much courage or patience if we didn't have will power, so we are led, like James D. Wallace, to feel that Brandt's analysis has neglected something. These virtues are not just "privative states," but some kind of "positive capacity."[14]

## V

If desires and aversions (duly shaped by our beliefs) were the only kind of element contributing to our psychological "force vectors," the virtues of will power would not be capacities or powers, but only patterns of relative strength among our desires and aversions. However, our desires and aversions are not the only psychological factors contributing to our actions and the course of our lives; for there is also such a thing as our *management* of our desires and aversions. People are capacitated in numerous ways. We have bodily powers like food and oxygen assimilation, physical strengths (muscles and bones), faculties (sight, hearing, smell), and aptitudes (mathematics, music, linguistics). The capacities to resist adverse inclinations seem to be learned. Since learned capacities are called skills, I propose that powers of will are skills of self-management.

Skills may be more or less completely mental, like the ability to focus attention at will, or motor, like riding a bicycle. But most skills have both motor and mental aspects. Riding a bike in traffic requires a combination of motor skill and knowledge of rules of the road, attentiveness to events occurring in the traffic, judgment about the speed of cars relative to their distance from oneself and one another and one's own speed or potential for speed, and so forth. It is characteristic of skills in both their mental and motor aspects that they become in large part "automatic" and unnoticed by their practitioners. Many skills combine procedures governed by rules which can be

---

[14] *Virtues and Vices* (Ithaca, NY: Cornell University Press, 1978), p. 61. Wallace suggests that the "positiveness" of virtues like courage is their capacity to preserve us in the course of practical reason. But as Amélie Rorty has pointed out, the *akrates* need not consider the course which he fails to take to be the more rational of the choices which conflict in him. "Where Does the Akratic Break Take Place?" *Australasian Journal of Philosophy*, vol. 58 (1980), pp. 336f. Just as *akrasia* cannot be defined as a form of irrationality, so courage and other virtues that are the opposites of *akrasia* cannot be defined as capacities to preserve rationality. Their "positiveness" lies not here, but in their being capacities.

(though by no means always are) formulated, patterns of such "automatic" physical and mental behavior, and a certain element of creativity in the application of the rules and the "automatic" behaviors to new challenges. Most sports and games, and activities such as weaving, portrait photography, algebra, speaking a language, cooking, getting dressed, and cabinet building would be skills falling under this last description.

People can be more or less skilled in the management of their own inclinations, and these skills are an important part of the virtues of will power. We can be more or less good at breaking bad habits and forming new ones, at deferring gratification, at resisting cravings and impulses; we can be trained and/or train ourselves in the control of emotions like anxiety, fear, disappointment, anger, and hatred. I want to illustrate and partially analyze these truths in a moment. But before I do, let me consider four *a priori* objections to the proposal that virtues can be skills.

Three such arguments are found in James D. Wallace's book *Virtues and Vices*, pp. 44–47. The first argument is this:

1. Courage and patience are capacities to overcome difficulties arising from inclinations contrary to right action.
2. Inclinations contrary to right action are not technical difficulties, but skills are always capacities to overcome technical difficulties.

So courage and patience are not skills.

The crux of the argument is the word "technical." It sounds right to say that of the various kinds of difficulties standing in the way of acting compassionately toward a rebellious and abusive teenage son, the difficulty of overcoming one's feelings of resentment toward him (which might be met by possessing patience) is not a *technical* one. (We might say, "Not technical, but *moral!*") "Technical" difficulties in this situation might be questions of psychological strategy: What is in the son's best interest? Confront him and have it out? Assert some authority over him? Use benign neglect? Shower him with affection? Or some combination of these? To answer a "technical" question like this, one might consult a professional, thus perhaps increasing one's skill in handling rebellious sons. But one would not (so suggests Wallace's argument) seek such "technical" guidance as to, or training in, how to handle one's *own* feelings of resentment toward the son. *That* is a matter not of "technique," but of morality.

But why not seek such "technical" help in handling one's own emotions? One reason we are inclined to accept the "not technical, but moral" disjunction is a failure to distinguish virtues like courage and patience from the substantive moral virtues like caring for one's children. But if somebody already has a moral motive, and then finds that bad habits and adverse emotions are getting in the way of acting lovingly, the psychologist has a potential role. And though we would not normally call this role "technical," what she may supply here is precisely information and training of a "how to" sort. I suggest that when this "how to" knowledge has become assimilated, the person will have gained in the virtue of patience.

Here is Wallace's second argument:

1. If any trait is a skill, then it can be inculcated through instruction in techniques and by practice that leads to proficiency.
2. But no virtue can be so inculcated.

So no virtue is a skill.

But the second premise is false. As Aristotle points out,

> By being habituated to despise things that are terrible and to stand our ground against them we become brave, and it is when we have become so that we shall be most able to stand our ground against them (1104b).

In the next section I shall illustrate how the virtues of will power can be inculcated through instruction and practice.

Wallace next adapts an insight from Gilbert Ryle, namely that it is logically amiss to say someone has forgotten the difference between right and wrong. Wallace's third argument is this:

1. If any trait is a skill, it can be forgotten
2. But courage, self-control, and patience cannot be forgotten.

So these traits are not skills.

Both premisses are questionable. In general it is only more complicated skills that are forgettable, and even here it is unlikely that a skill, well-learned, will be completely forgotten. Someone who has played the piano well, and then lets twenty years elapse without practicing, will get rusty indeed. But that she has not lost all her skill

245

will be evident from how quickly the skill returns with practice. A total loss of the skill would require more than forgetting; it would take some kind of injury or illness or aging process resulting in neurological or muscular deterioration. But simple skills are virtually unforgettable: one does not forget how to swim, or ride a bike, or walk. It is possible that courage and self-control are simple enough to be as unforgettable as bike riding. (Though perhaps like bike riding they are susceptible of considerable development and sophistication.)

It seems to me that courage, and the like, cannot be flat forgotten; but if we allow that getting "rusty" is a sort of forgetting or partial forgetting, it is not so obvious that one cannot forget courage. Consider the autobiography of Gordon Liddy, who in prison felt it necessary to exercise himself in withstanding pain, to make sure that he hadn't gone soft.

Unlike Wallace, Ryle nowhere claims it is logically amiss to say someone has forgotten a virtue, but only to say that someone has forgotten the difference between right and wrong.[15] Ryle explains this impossibility by the fact that to know the difference between right and wrong is a matter of caring about right and wrong, and ceasing to care is not a sort of forgetting. In my terms, Ryle is only claiming the impossibility of forgetting the motivational virtues— because only these "tell us" the difference between right and wrong.

Wallace is clear enough about the difference between the substantive virtues and the virtues of will power not to explain the supposed unforgettability of self-control and patience by the supposition that they are modes of caring.

> The reason is not that there is a motivational component to these things that cannot be lost by forgetting. The reason why one cannot forget how to be brave or honest is like the reason why one cannot forget how to see or how to be strong: there is no "how to" to these things.

But as we shall see in the next section, this supposition too is false.

A fourth argument that no virtue is a skill has been presented by Philippa Foot. Following Aristotle and Aquinas she notes that when a person's action bespeaks a lack of a skill (let us say he misspells a word), he can defend himself against the implication by saying "I did it intentionally." But when his action bespeaks a lack of virtue (let us

---

[15]Gilbert Ryle, *Collected Papers*, vol. 2 (London: Hutchinson, 1971), pp. 381*ff.*

say he tells a lie), he does not exculpate himself by saying "I did it intentionally." Thus no virtue is a skill.[16]

Foot's argument overlooks that virtues relate in more than one way to morality. It is of course true that an action does not become any the less immoral by being intentional; and so when doing the moral thing (say, being compassionate) requires the exercise of a skill virtue (say, patience), the fact that one's failure of patience was intentional is no *moral* exculpation. But claiming that the failure to exercise patience was intentional *would* defend against the accusation of lacking patience. If patience is a virtue, then one can defend against the implication of failure to possess a virtue by claiming that failure to exercise it was intentional.

## VI

I shall now indicate sketchily some ways people manage their adverse inclinations, and draw attention to the skill-likeness of these ways. Like other skills, some of these ways are strategic, like the duck hunter's knowledge of the precise moment to rise in the blind, while others are more basic, like his ability to squeeze the trigger without disrupting his aim. My argument is not that because there are strategies for developing courage, courage must be a skill. One might develop compassion by the strategy of meditating on the lives of compassionate people. It is rather that being courageous is *in itself* (often subtly and subconsciously) in part strategic, and so is formally like those many skills that have strategic dimensions. Nor is my argument that merely because the exercise of these virtues can develop them, they must be skills. Performing compassionate actions can perhaps cause a person to become more compassionate. Instead, I shall try to describe the specific similarities between these exercises and ones which issue in skills. I shall speak first of the management of cravings and impulses, then of emotions.

*Cravings and Impulses* Søren Kierkegaard depicts a gambler struggling against his compulsion:[17]

> Imagine that he . . . said to himself in the morning, "So I solemnly vow by all that is holy that I shall nevermore have anything to do with

---

[16]See Foot, "Virtues and Vices," pp. 7*f.*

[17]*For Self-Examination and Judge For Yourselves!* trans. Walter Lowrie (Princeton, NJ: Princeton University Press, 1968), p. 69.

gambling, nevermore—tonight shall be the last time." Ah, my friend, he is lost! Strange as it may seem I should venture to bet rather on the opposite, supposing that there was a gambler who at such a moment said to himself, "Very well, thou shalt be allowed to gamble all the rest of thy life, every blessed day—but tonight thou shalt let it alone," and so he did . . . For the resolution of the first man was a knavish trick of lust, but that of the other is a way of hoaxing lust . . . Lust is strong merely in the instant. . . .

The more normal development of this aspect of self-control might occur as follows: parents teaching their children to defer gratification would begin with small stretches of time. They would say not, "Here is your Easter basket, and you may eat your chocolate bunny the day after tomorrow," but instead, "After dinner, you may bite off his ear." (And, by the way, they will not set the temptation out of the child's reach until the appointed time, nor keep a nervous eagle eye out so as to slap the hand that reaches for the bunny, but will let the child develop her own ability to resist the impulses she may feel.) If the parents are wise in engineering settings for gratification-deferment that are manageable for the child, she may, with some trial-and-error of her own, grow up with a nearly unreflective tendency to pick for herself deferment goals that are realistic given her own powers of resistance, and thus put herself in for a minimum of discouragement. It is imaginable that this skill of self-management might develop without any explicit discussion of its rules or reflection on them, and might be as natural as speaking one's native language. This is not to say that the tougher cases of urge-control would be without struggle.

A cabinet builder follows a dictum that might be expressed, "He who starts a project square and level has less need of compensating exercises in ensuing stages." When he was a novice his teacher perhaps had to voice the dictum a few times, but after he had built some cabinets himself the dictum became integrated into the practice, sinking to the status of a mentally unrehearsed policy or rule of skill founded on the ineluctable geometric properties of cabinets, floors, and walls. The remark that "Lust is strong merely in the instant" is an easily accessible piece of psychological wisdom, one that can become as integral a part of a person's dealings with himself as the carpenter's dictum is of his dealings with boards and nails. The more self-mastering person knows, either intuitively or perhaps expressly, such things as that committing oneself to long-term abstention from the fulfilment of a strong impulse is probably either self-deceptive or likely to overwhelm and discourage. (I am told that "one day at a time" is one of the basic tenets of Alcoholics Anonymous.) Skill at the management of impulses and cravings must take this fact of human nature into consideration, just as carpentry must take geometric truths into consideration.

We can imagine that at first, upon hearing or formulating for himself this dictum, the weak-willed gambler might succeed in "hoaxing his lust" by explicitly telling himself that he is not promising to abstain for life, after all, but only for the next twenty-four hours. Then when the next day comes he renews his commitment, assuring himself that it is only for the day, and so on. But after the rule has been applied successfully a few times, the "hoaxing" may change gradually to a habit, a subconscious policy of choosing manageable time-parameters for one's choices of self-denial. When this happens, the individual is beginning to gain a stronger will.

The way of mastering impulses that I have just discussed is strategic: In its more self-conscious (though not in its deeper and more usual) forms it involves considering what one is up against and then, in the light of this, figuring out a way to meet the challenge. But there may also be an aspect of impulse-mastery that is more basic. Boyd Barrett[18] proposes a number of exercises by which a person can increase his ability to resist impulses. These involve doing such "useless" things as standing on a chair for ten consecutive minutes and trying to do so contentedly; listening to the ticking of a clock and making some definite movements at every fifth tick; and replacing in a box, slowly and deliberately, one hundred matches. In all such activities one is almost certain to get impulses to quit: boredom, physical discomfort, thoughts of things one would rather be doing. We might speculate that here one does not necessarily resist the impulse by some "method" such as hoaxing the lust or reconstruing the impulse. Maybe one resists the impulse to discontinue the activity by simply continuing the activity. If this interpretation is correct,

---

[18]In a book called *Strength of Will and How to Develop It*, discussed in Robert Assagioli, *The Act of Will* (New York: Viking Press, 1973), pp. 39 *ff.*

then there would seem to be a power to resist impulses that is a basic ability—basic not in the sense that it is unlearned, but in the sense that one does not exercise it by exercising some other ability. It would be like some people's ability to look cross-eyed or wiggle their ears.

*Emotions*  Some impulses are emotions, as when fear is the impulse to flee or boredom the impulse to quit an activity. But other impulses are not emotions: for example, physical pain, and lusts for sex, money, gambling, and philosophical discussion. Conversely, not all adverse emotions are impulses. An impulse, it seems, must be directed at *doing* something, and when I experience an adverse emotion such as malicious joy, I may not be inclined to do anything at all except continue dwelling on whatever it is I am maliciously joyful about. In such cases the emotion is adverse not because of what it may lead to but because it is itself unfitting, morally or from the point of view of psychological health or happiness.

There are two senses in which we may control an emotion. If it is an impulse to some undesirable behavior such as fleeing a situation that should be faced or emitting some angry behavior that will have untoward consequences, then controlling it may just mean resisting the act to which it is an impulse. But it may also mean the reshaping of the emotion itself: mitigating the anger or fear, or eliminating them altogether, or mutating them into some less offensive cousin. For the sake of brevity I shall focus here on the control of emotions in the second sense.

Any of the virtues of will power may be directed upon emotions. Self-control can be, among other things, a mastery of anger, resentment, malicious joy, envy, contempt, and boredom. Where patience is directed to a task, emotions with which it typically must deal are boredom and frustration. (A related virtue is tenaciousness or perseverance, whose primary emotional adversary seems to be discouragement or some degree of hopelessness.) Where patience is used in dealing with people, typically mastered emotions are anger and resentment and boredom. The emotions to which courage relates are fear and anxiety.

In some cases anger diminishes with oblique behavioral "expression." Thus a worker may diminish anger at an oppressive superior by kicking pasteboard boxes around in the privacy of a garage and cursing loudly. It may help to imagine the superior's face or backside in the boxes and to go through the procedure in a somewhat ritualisic

250

and comical[19] manner. Similar activities may have the effect of increasing one's anger at the superior, so knowing when this sort of thing will work and prescribing to oneself and carrying out appropriate rituals is clearly a skill-like ability, a kind of self-directed practical wisdom.

One can often alter an emotion by behaving in a way that conflicts with it. Thus if I am afraid of someone, one way to handle the fear is to stand up straight, look him in the eye, and speak clearly in a strong and even voice. Although the fear may not disappear entirely, it will certainly be less than if I shrink back, speak in a weak mumble, and generally present myself to myself as one who is in an oppressive situation.[20] I think that courageous people typically are aware, intuitively, of the influence that their bodily dispositions and voice and speech have on their anxiety and fear, and practice this kind of self-management. It is far from obvious that courageous people typically feel fears and anxieties less intensely than cowardly people. But through practice in facing up to threatening situations, they have learned how to manage and mitigate their fears.

Skillful self-talk is another way of controlling emotion. I am becoming impatient with my four-year-old's bedtime delaying tactics, and verging on anger; so I talk to myself: "I did the same when I was four," or "Notice how ingenious her tactics are—bright little gal, huh?" or "Just relax and bear with it a moment longer; it *will* soon be over." Such self-talk often mitigates or even dispels the welling anger, along with the urges to be abrupt, to behave punishingly, and generally to lose my cool. Perseverance may also involve self-talk, making use of "the power of positive thinking," as well as the tactics of reading encouraging literature (e.g., to help one persevere in a diet or a language-learning program) and associating with encouraging people. But self-talk and these more external self-management tactics are crude forms of this aspect of self-control: the experienced self-controller just flashes the strategic thoughts across her mind at the appropriate moments, the way a basketball player moves intelligently but without deliberation in the split-second of court action.

---

[19]For an account of how comical representations, and the capacity to appreciate them, can be connected with moral virtues, see my essay "Humor and the Virtues," *Inquiry*, vol. 31 (1988), p. 2.

[20]For an explanation of why techniques like this work, see my "Solomon on the Control of Emotions," *Philosophy and Phenomenological Research* (March 1984) and "What An Emotion Is: A Sketch," *Philosophical Review* (April 1988).

## VII

Before I end, I must put the thesis of this paper in perspective.[21] I have argued that the virtues of will power are in an important aspect skills or skill-like powers. But I have nowhere claimed that this is the whole story of these virtues.

There may be saints whose patience and courage do not involve any exercise of will power, in the form either of efforts of will or of an effortless mastery of adverse impulses and emotions. The reason their goodness involves no exercise of will power is what makes them saints: they don't have any adverse impulses or emotions to which will power might be applied. Whether there are any saints in this sense I don't know; but there are certainly particular acts of courage and perseverence that involve no exercise of will power. Some acts of heroic courage are performed so spontaneously that there can be no question of the individual overcoming his fears; he just doesn't have any fears at the moment.

But even when skills of self-mastery are still needed, there are two other features typical of people with the virtues of will power. First, they *care* intensely about something. I have argued that the virtues of will power, when they are moral, derive their moral import from the concerns in the interest of which they are exercised. But the virtues of will power are never exercised apart from any motivation whatsoever; and generally speaking, the more intense the concerns, the more likely that the skills of self-mastery will be exercised and their power increased. So where courage does have moral import, it generally will be true that the deeper the courage the more powerful the

---

[21]Another kind of perspective is the diversity of the moralities in which virtues of will power appear. In this paper I have tried to characterize these virtues in a generic way. But within a given moral tradition they will also have nongeneric features. Stoic courage and Christian courage, though both capacities for managing fear and anxiety, are different enough to be considered different virtues. The traditions provide distinctive resources for dealing with these adverse emotions, and the resources get incorporated in the skills. Thus a major resource in the stoic repertoire is the characteristically stoic thought that "harms" are unavoidable anyway; resignation, then, becomes part of the strategy for reducing fear. Christian courage, by contrast, trades heavily on the thought of the presence and trustworthiness of God, and it is these that the developed Christian brings to bear on fearsome situations. In both traditions something like meditation on the respective resources is essential to the cultivation of the virtue.

For an elaboration of three virtues of will power (self-control, patience, and perseverance) in a distinctively Christian form, see my *The Strengths of a Christian* (Philadelphia: Westminster Press, 1984).

moral concerns of the individual. Not all morally passionate people are courageous, but it is typical of courageous people that they are passionate.

The second feature typical of people with the virtues of will power is self-confidence. There is a correlation between people's ability to handle their adverse inclinations and their confidence in their ability to determine their own destiny. Of course, it is generally typical of skilled people that they are confident of themselves respecting the skill in question. And so, since self-mastery is so fundamental to the successful conduct of a human life, it might seem that self-confidence is a by-product of the virtues of will power rather than an element of them. But while self-mastering skills clearly cause self-confidence, it is equally true that self-confidence grounds the exercise of self-mastery skills. When an athlete loses her self-confidence, she loses some of her ability to exercise her skill, even though her skill *per se* is not at all diminished. Similarly, in a situation of testing the individual who has ceased to believe that she can persevere will show herself as weak even though she possesses all the necessary skills to see her through her difficulty. An athlete needs three things for success: the requisite skills, an enthusiasm for the game, and a belief in her own powers. And the virtues of will power are the athletic side of the moral life.

**STUDY QUESTIONS**

1. Courage, says Roberts, is not a motivational virtue—so no courageous act is "done out of courage." What does Roberts mean by a "motivational virtue"? List some examples.
2. What is a substantive virtue? Why does Roberts think that someone who exercises a substantive virtue must enjoy exercising it?
3. What are "virtues of will-power," and how do these virtues perform "corrective functions"? How do they help us develop our "moral agency"?
4. According to Roberts, the application of the will in managing our inclination to do wrong requires skill. Give an example of the skill required to master anger, temptation, or envy. How does "practice" in such self-mastery help make us more proficient?

5.  Roberts notes that some people are so good by nature as not to be tempted to do wrong. Such people have no need of the virtues of will power. Roberts suggests that such people may be the true moral saints. Do you think this is true of some ordinary people with respect to particular virtues? For example, some people seem not to "know the meaning of fear"; these are naturally courageous people. Others are never tempted to sexual sin or excess; these are naturally chaste people. And so forth. Are people more virtuous when they have to overcome temptations to do wrong? Or does the very temptation to do wrong detract somewhat from the goodness of that person? Is someone who "wouldn't hurt a fly" more virtuous than another who successfully curbs a violent temper? (Here the medieval moralists are helpful; the student may, for example, wish to look again at Abelard's essay.)

# *Generosity*

## JAMES D. WALLACE

James D. Wallace (b. 1937) is a professor of philosophy at the University of Illinois in Urbana. He is the author of *Virtues and Vices* (1978).

Generosity is a virtue concerned with giving. Wallace distinguishes between economic generosity, where the object one gives has a market value, and generosity of the heart or mind, where one gives intangible things such as kindness or encouragement. In primary generosity, agents directly concern themselves with the good of others rather than being inadvertently helpful. Normally, generosity exceeds what is expected or required by cus-

GENEROSITY From *Virtues and Vices* by James D. Wallace. Reprinted by permission of the author and Cornell University Press.

tom. The distinguishing features of economic generosity are (1) giving with the intention to benefit, (2) giving what has market value, and (3) giving more than is normally required. In the case of generous-mindedness, what one gives has no market value but the other criteria apply. The virtue of generosity illustrates that morality is sometimes a matter of acting beyond the call of duty.

## Economic Generosity

Generosity is concerned with giving, and different kinds of generosity can be distinguished according to the kind of things given. Aristotle said that generosity (*eleutheriotēs*) has to do with giving and taking of things whose value is measured in money.[1] There is a virtue called generosity, the actions fully characteristic of which are meritorious, which has to do with freely giving things that have a *market value*—freely giving goods and services of a type that normally are exchanged on the open market. This sort of generosity I call "economic generosity" to distinguish it from other varieties. One can be generous in the judgments one makes about the merits and demerits of others, and one can be generous in forgiving those who trespass against one. "Generous-mindedness" and "generous-heartedness," as these other kinds of generosity might be called, do not involve being generous with things whose value is measured in money. These are like economic generosity in certain ways, but they also differ in important respects, as I shall try subsequently to show. Unless otherwise indicated, however, by generosity I mean economic generosity.

A generous person is one who has a certain attitude toward his own things, the value of which is measured in money, and who also has a certain attitude toward other people. Generosity, like other forms of benevolence, in its primary occurrence, involves as one of its constitutents a concern for the happiness and well-being of others. The actions fully characteristic of generosity have as their goal promoting someone else's well-being, comfort, happiness, or pleasure—someone else's good. In *primary generosity,* the agent is concerned

---

[1]*Nicomachean Ethics*, IV, 1, 1119b21–27.

directly about the good of another. Thus, an action fully character-istic of generosity might be done to please someone or to help some-one, with no further end in view beyond pleasing or helping. "I just wanted to do something nice for them" or "I just wanted her to have it" are typical explanations of generous acts.

That an act fully characteristic of *the virtue,* generosity, is moti-vated in this way by a direct concern for the good of another is not immediately obvious, because we sometimes call giving "generous" and mean only that the giver is giving more than someone in his situation normally gives. Thus, the host is being generous with the mashed potatoes when he unthinkingly heaps unusually large por-tions on the plates. Or perhaps he does not do it unthinkingly. It might be that he is giving such generous portions because he wants to use up all the potatoes to prevent them from spoiling. Being generous in this way—giving a lot for reasons such as these—would not tend to show that the host is a *generous person,* even if he did so frequently. If we restrict ourselves to the kind of generous action that is fully characteristic of a generous person, then in every case, the agent's giving will be motivated by a direct concern for the good (in the broad sense) of another. I shall say in such cases that the agent intends to *benefit* the recipient.

There is a further complication. The virtue generosity, in its *pri-mary occurrence,* I have said, involves a sort of direct concern for the good of others, as do other forms of benevolence. Someone who is deficient in such concern or who lacks it altogether might admire generous people for their generosity and want as far as he can to be like them. He might then want to do in certain situations what a generous person would do. Acting as a generous person would act because one regards generosity as a virtue, and wants, therefore, to emulate the generous person is meritorious, and it reflects credit upon the agent. It is, however, a secondary sort of generosity. It depends, for its merit, upon the fact that primary generosity *is* a virtue and is thus a worthy ideal at which to aim. I will concentrate, therefore, upon primary generosity, which does involve a direct concern for the good of another. An account of why this is a virtue is easily extended to explain why a generous person is worthy of emulation.

A certain sort of attitude on the part of the agent toward what he gives is also a feature of actions fully characteristic of the virtue generosity. In acting generously, one must give something that one values—something that one, therefore, has some reason to keep rather than discard or abandon. If, for example, one is about to throw away an article of clothing, and on the way to the trash barrel one meets someone who would like to have it, it would not be *generous* of one to give it to him. What disqualifies such giving from being generous is neither the giver's motive nor the nature of what is given but rather the fact that the giver himself does not value the object enough. Similarly, when we do favors for one another, giving matches or coins for parking meters, often what is given is too insignificant for the giving of it to be generous. One may be being kind in giving things that one does not particularly value, but for the giving to be generous, one must value the thing given for some reason. I may have acquired a particularly repulsive piece of primitive art that I have no desire to keep. Still, I might generously give it to a museum if it were a valuable piece—one I could sell or exchange for something I really want. How *generous* one is being in giving something generally depends upon how much one values the thing given, how much one is giving up.

Usually, the giver must give in excess of what he is required to give by morality or custom, if his giving is to be generous. Where there exists a generally recognized moral obligation to give, or where giving is customary, then normally one's giving is not generous even though it is prompted by a direct concern for the good of the recipient. If one were certain of a more than ample and continuing supply of food, so that it would clearly be wrong not to give some food to a neighbor who would otherwise go hungry, giving the neighbor a portion of food would not be generous. Similarly, to give a person a gift when one is expected to do so, because it is customary to exchange gifts (for example birthdays, Christmas, weddings, etc.), is normally not a matter of generosity, even though one aims to please the recipient. If one gives *more* than what is expected in such cases, then the giving might be generous. A generous person is one who exceeds normal expectations in giving, and one who gives no more than what is generally expected in the circumstances is not apt to be cited for generosity.

A special problem arises in cases of the following sort. Although it would clearly be wrong for a certain person *not* to give, he does not see this. Nevertheless, he does give on a generous impulse. Suppose, for example, that a certain person is a social Darwinist, convinced that it is wrong to give the necessities of life to people in need, because this enables the weak to survive, thus weakening the species.

She encounters a starving family, and touched by their plight, she provides food for them, though not without a twinge of social Darwinist guilt. Assuming that what she gives is not insignificant to her, but that it is no more than what the family needs to keep them alive, is her giving generous? On the one hand, she is really doing no more than the minimum required of her by the duty to help people in distress, and this makes one hesitate to say that she is being generous. On the other hand, *she* does not recognize any moral obligation here, and it is the kind and generous side of her nature that overcomes her cruel principles and leads her to give. This seems to support the view that she is being generous.

An act fully characteristic of generosity will normally have the following features.

1. The agent, because of his direct concern for the good of the recipient, gives something with the intention of benefiting the recipient.
2. The agent gives up something of his that has a market value and that he has some reason to value and, therefore, to keep.
3. The agent gives more than one is generally expected, because of moral requirements or custom, to give in such circumstances.

In normal cases, an act that meets these three conditions will be a generous act, and a generous act will have these three features. There are, however, abnormal cases—cases in which the agent has, concerning the circumstances mentioned in the three conditions, a false belief or an unusual or eccentric attitude. The case of the social Darwinist is such a case. She thinks she is morally required *not* to give, when in fact she is required to give. If one accepts *her* view of the situation, her act is generous. In fact, however, the third condition is not satisfied. In another sort of abnormal case, the agent values what he gives, but in fact the gift is utterly worthless—it is literally trash. Here it is not clear that the second condition is fulfilled, but from the agent's odd point of view, the act is generous. The very rich often give to charity sums of money that are large in comparison with what others give, and their gifts seem generous. These sums, however, which are substantial, may be relatively insignificant to the donors, and one may wonder whether condition (2) is satisfied in such a case. Does the donor, who has so much, in fact have reason to value and keep what he gives, or is his "gift" analogous to an ordinary person's giving away a book of matches? In a rather different sort of case, someone might be convinced that he is morally required to give away nearly all he has to the poor. For this reason, he divests himself of a substantial fortune. In such cases, it may be that condition (1) is not satisfied. The agent believes, in effect, that condition (3) is not satisfied, since he believes that he is required to do this. These circumstances will make one hesitate to call his giving generous, although other features of the case incline one toward the view that he is being generous.

In these cases involving unusual beliefs or attitudes, one is pulled simultaneously in two different directions. The way the agent sees the situation and the way one expects him to see the situation diverge. Crucial conditions are satisfied from one way of regarding the case and unsatisfied from the other. It is not surprising that one is reluctant to say simply that the act is (or is not) fully characteristic of the virtue generosity. Any such statement must be qualified, and the actual consequences of the qualification may or may not be important, depending upon the case. Normally, of course, the agent's beliefs about the features in (1)–(3) will not be grossly mistaken nor will his attitudes toward those things be unusual or eccentric. In such cases, if the three conditions are satisfied, the act is unqualifiedly generous, and vice versa.

A generous person is one who has a tendency to perform actions that meet these conditions. The stronger the tendency, the more generous the person.

## Generous-Mindedness

The conditions in the preceding section are meant as an account of actions that are fully characteristic of *economic generosity*—generosity that involves giving things whose value is measured in money. Another kind of generosity, however, has to do with making judgments about the merits and failings of other people. This too is a virtue, which sometimes is called *generous-mindedness*.[2] I will try briefly to

---

[2] I am indebted to David Shwayder for bringing this topic to my attention.

indicate some similarities and differences between this virtue and economic generosity.

Generous-mindedness is shown by seeing someone else's merit (technical, moral, etc.) in cases where it is difficult to see because the facts of the case admit of other, not unreasonable interpretations, or because the situation is complex and the merit is not immediately apparent. Generous-mindedness is also shown by seeing that a derogatory judgment is not called for in cases where the facts might not unreasonably be taken to indicate a derogatory judgment. Many of us actually dislike to find that others are as good or better than we are, so that we have some desire to find grounds for derogatory judgments. It is plausible to think that people of othewise fair judgment are sometimes led to think less of others than they should because they do not want to think well of them or because they want to think ill of them. They do not purposely close their eyes to merit; rather because they do not wish to find it, they do not try hard enough to find it. This may involve a certain amount of self-deception, but I suspect that in many cases the matter is more straightforward. If someone wants to find another inferior to himself in some respect, then where he sees some (prima facie) grounds for such a judgment, he is apt to be quick to seize upon it and regard the matter as settled. A generous-minded person is one who wants to think well of other people, so that in such cases he will look and find the merit that might otherwise go overlooked. Of course, it is possible to be too generous-minded—to overlook demerit because one does not want to find it.

If someone exhibits generous-mindedness in his judgment on a particular occasion, his act of judgment will not fulfill the conditions for an act of economic generosity. It will have features, however, that can be seen as analogous to the features characteristics of economic generosity. If an individual is well-disposed toward other people, then besides wanting to benefit them by giving them things, he will wish them well. He will tend to want their undertakings to succeed and to reflect well on them. If he wants to think well of others, he will be apt to look harder for merit, and he will, therefore, be more likely to find it. Generous-mindedness seems properly regarded as a manifestation of good will toward others that shows a direct concern for the well-being of others.

Economic generosity generally involves giving more than is

required or customary, and there is a counterpart to this in generous-mindedness. The generous-minded person sees merit where a competent evaluator might miss it, where it would be reasonable (though incorrect) to find that there is no such merit. In this way, one might say that generous-mindedness leads a person to go beyond what is required of an evaluator. . . .

For generous-mindedness not to distort one's judgment—for it not to lead one to incorrect evaluations—an individual must be a competent evaluator and be conscientious about reaching a correct judgment. Also, it does seem that if one has sufficiently good judgment and is sufficiently concerned to make the right judgment, then this by itself should lead one to see merit when it is present just as well as would the desire to *find merit*. The strong desire to make favorable judgments, moreover, *may* distort one's judgment. It may lead one to overlook defects and to find merit where it is not. A strong desire to make *the correct evaluation* cannot distort one's judgment in this way. Generous-mindedness should not be regarded as a primary virtue of evaluators. It can counteract an inclination to build oneself up by tearing others down, but so too can a strong desire to evaluate correctly. Generous-mindedness is a manifestation of the sort of concern for others that is characteristic of all forms of benevolence. It derives the greatest part of its merit from this concern. . . .

**STUDY QUESTIONS**

1. How would you measure the extent of generosity when (a) the person is mean-spirited but forces himself to give out of a sense of moral obligation; or (b) the person is innately kind and gives effortlessly?

2. What does Wallace mean by generous-mindedness? Do you believe that a stingy person who lacks economic generosity can be generous-minded? Conversely, can a mean-spirited person be economically generous?

3. Do we have a duty to be generous? Would not that be like having a duty to do more than our duty?

# On Wisdom

### STANLEY GODLOVITCH

Stanley Godlovitch (b. 1947) teaches at Mount Royal College in Calgary, Canada. He is a frequent writer of articles on ethics.

Stanley Godlovitch says that philosophers, despite all their protestations about its importance and all their praise of it, show little interest in wisdom. He tries to give an account of wisdom that will explain why wisdom is so neglected, why it is so difficult to understand, and why, as a virtue, wisdom is so rare.

Godlovitch considers and rejects several popular conceptions of wisdom that identify wisdom with age or experience, or with prudential competence. He then turns to Socrates' definition of wisdom as knowledge and critical understanding. However, using Socrates as the paradigm of a wise person creates puzzles. For one of Socrates' themes is that most people do not know what they think they know: Socratic wisdom consists in knowing that we do not know. Yet, this is not the entire story. For Socrates also points to a stage in human understanding when a person comes into "contact with the unchanging . . . and this state of the soul is called wisdom." Among the unchanging truths whose grasp makes us wise are that we shall all die and that immediate triumphs are evanescent. Such truisms enable us to assess our experience by giving it its true worth, and one reason we associate wisdom with age is that older persons are in a

ON WISDOM First appeared in *Canadian Journal of Philosophy* (March 1981). Reprinted by permission of the author.

better position psychologically to appreciate the significance of the eternal verities and to apply them in evaluating the significance of a particular act or event. Wisdom is a virtue of perspective. Unlike courage, it is not episodic. Godlovitch puts wisdom alongside such nonutilitarian personal characteristics as dignity, self-respect, and decency.

Wisdom is so rare precisely because it demands of us a perspective that is psychologically difficult to achieve and live by. In many ways wisdom is an unpopular and embarrassing virtue, quite at odds with the lives that most of us choose to lead. The wise person—by his or her life or his or her teaching—tends to expose us, debunking our lives as somewhat pointless. This is not easy to accept, and so we may react to this perspective with hostility. Socrates' fate stands as a warning to those who too zealously advertise the value of wisdom.

When I first began to study philosophy I was introduced to the discipline in that magically traditional way by being assured that what lay before me was the love of wisdom. Why this had any adolescent appeal still puzzles me, but, like many others, I joined in as spectator to and occasionally as a removed participant in all the rough and tumble of a Socratic sparring match in the Athenian marketplace. There was some talk of wisdom, to be sure, which seemed to link it with a humble admission of ignorance or a pitch against yielding to temptation, but neither was ever deeply revealing. I waited for more. My next encounter a few years later turned up little more than the surname of an English disciple of Wittgenstein. Somehow the trail had gone to brush, despite the apparent health and energy of philosophy.

I'm not sure whether or not philosophy has anything to do with wisdom. If it does, then it seems to pursue it with no more success than any of a number of other branches of learning. Tradition, however, and sentiment prod me to try to understand a little better what wisdom is and what it's not if only to discover why philosophers are so disinterested in it.

The idea of wisdom certainly invades much of the folklore of our own and of other cultures. Wise men, literally so called, appear in much religious literature. We live with the wisdom of the ancients, the wisdom of the elderly, and even transplant this quality metaphorically to time or nature or the body. And philosophy, of course, began putatively as a method for seeking it out.

We appear to see wisdom as a human feature associated with age and experience. It carries much positive moral force in being regarded as a rare and noble virtue, one which we would all wish to have. It has an epistemic quality, and is linked with some special variety of knowledge the acquisition of which is reserved for the privileged. There are, further, connections it has with behaviour, with the way things are done and with the nature of decisions and choices. This is no transient visitor to our discourse, nor has it gone so dated as to rank with such relics as chivalry and gallantry. The more we extend the catalogue of its appearances, the more apparent it becomes that we are dealing with a wide range of notions, some of which lack the dignity we give to whatever wisdom the Wise have. Moreover, as will become apparent, that mystical variety of wisdom, the one mention of which is the most familiar of all, seems less clear than many of the others.

Consider, for example, the most humdrum of cases. A man is seized with a powerful temptation to hop a plane to Bermuda. He books his seat and makes a reservation at a hotel. A few days before departure he begins to regard his plans as silly and recognizes that there are quite a few things he really should see to at home. So he cancels the trip. A day after his would-be departure he learns that the hotel he was to have been in has been struck by a tidal wave with great loss of life. His relief, needless to say, is immense. A friend, having heard the story, drops by and compliments him on the wisdom of his having stayed at home. Here, the decision to refrain from a holiday is wise only because it is lucky. True, in the light of undesirable consequences, the man has certainly avoided what he would have shunned had he known in advance. But his choice was deprived of that information, and so its so-called wisdom is not his as such. This is a very minimal sense of wisdom, perhaps one common to all other senses. We can formulate it as follows: a given choice or decision or action is a wise one provided that our making it avoids the undesirable consequences that would have arisen had we chosen some other considered alternative. The paradigm of the wise choice (though shot through with irony) is the beloved gun-to-the-head offer-he-couldn't-refuse case.

There are two disappointing features about this species of wisdom. It certainly doesn't make wise men of us, and it doesn't even seem to rise above sheer coincidence. Surely, wisdom ought to draw more out of us than a sigh of relief. So, let us strengthen the brew. Another man is offered a job at a very attractive salary by a competitor of the firm he works for. He is, naturally, flattered and very gripped with the prospect. However, before betraying his parent firm, he undertakes a little research and discovers that the firm about to snatch him up has a rather shaky financial record, that it has undergone an epidemic of high-level resignations, that its sales forecasts are not healthy, and so on. He weighs up the risks, and declines the offer. Sure enough, within a year the company has gone into receivership and many of its executives are out looking for employment. Our man does not sigh and thankfully mop his brow. He knew this would happen. He confides the tale to a colleague who replies robustly: "Good thinking. Wise decision. Stick with Acme and you'll never want."

We have here the minimal element but we have something else as well. The factors that go into making the decision reflect directly upon the likelihood of certain consequences. The decision itself is one which is unequivocally grounded in a careful prediction about its beneficial outcome. This takes in a concern for foresight, and has the smell of plans, and plots and calculation about it. The mere desire for monetary gain has been but one considered feature, and has been shelved in the light of overriding discoveries. This type of case gets quite close to Plato's view of wisdom as the supremacy of reason over the passions. Because the choice is guided by a learned appraisal of its consequences, the choice is a rational one. From that it inherits its wisdom. We rise to the next level. A given choice is a wise one provided that the choice calculatedly avoids the undesirable consequences that would otherwise have arisen.

The disappointments do not vanish. No one will deny that our executive is cautious and clever. His good fortune is very much due to his own effort. But the wisdom of his ways comes a little too cheaply. Though we have rid ourselves of accident and luck, we've got little more than prudence and craft as replacements. Insofar as any of us chooses carefully, the prize for which is the maximal satisfaction of our desires, we become wise in this sense. Merely being self-interestedly sensible, however, does not usher us into the elite class of the Wise. There are besides, the usual worries about the extent to which we wish to press the notion. A man who calculatedly and successfully commits mass murder and escapes punishment may indeed be cunning and, as it happens, act in his own best interest but I, for one, would gag a little on the words: "There is wisdom in what he has done." Not all prudent choices display wisdom; though, in this slightly supra-minimal sense, all may be wise. The trouble is that we expect something special in the epistemic content of wisdom, something out of the ordinary; and we also expect some presence of value beyond the mean triviality of self-interest. We need not fare any better if we conceive of cases where the calculated decision relates to actions which are designed to benefit others. In the first place, such benefit need not rank particularly high on a moral scale even if the act is in some way altruistic. If I plan, by weighing strategies, to secure for my family a monopoly on the North American heroin traffic, and succeed, my moves may well be considered as having been wise ones by my successors, but the context somehow forbids my entry to sainthood. Secondly, even if my intentions are of supreme worthiness, my wisdom will certainly be in doubt (if considered at all) should my calculations backfire.

Whatever the wisdom philosophers used to seek is, it does not shine forth in these considerations of the "the wise thing to do." In this regard, the strictures on any lofty variety of wisdom are more stringent than they are on moral goodness. Good men and good deeds seem to travel together. Though choices, when praised for their goodness might still smack of prudence and self-interest (the virtues of the sensible man), the goodness of an action hangs heavy with the moral stature of the agent. Very few individuals who manage usually to do the wise thing make the grade of the wise man.

The reason for this impasse is that the special and important notion of wisdom we admire has very little, if anything, to do with practical action and its antecedents. We should, then, turn to more profitable ground wherein the more refined epistemic and moral connotations may be located.

One starting point might be the emphasis we place on the connection between wisdom and age. It is not uncommon for us to deny the possibility of wisdom to a young, though mature, person. Again, following Plato's lead in the *Republic,* Socrates first seeks out revelation not from the sharp-witted ambitious youngsters on the make, but from the retired and successful business man, Cephalus. For Plato and his mentor, it is painfully obvious that, though wisdom may come with age, it need not. Cephalus is superficial, uncritical, a little bored by this line of inquiry, and probably quite absorbed by clipping stock coupons. However biting this portrayal might be, Plato himself does not forsake the line between wisdom and age when he gives us his hero on trial. So, we may ask, what is the attraction?

It may just contingently happen that all those who have been deemed to have been wise have been old at the time. This, though possible, is not convincing. The number of societies that have reserved an honoured place for their councils of elders is too large. In our own society, the wisdom of a politician or statesman seems to be correlated with age. From the young we're supposed to reap dynamism, daring, and efficiency; from the old, judiciousness, selflessness, and wisdom. Empirically we discover these connections to be shattered hourly. It's the expectation, however, which survives disconfirmation.

Though few would say that age as such imparts wisdom without accepting liberal exceptions—for age also may bring senility or dogmatism—some see it as necessary. Why? The aged have lived longer and so have more experience of life, may be one reply. This might be a pattern of thought which claims that, given hindsight and retrospect, we are better equipped to judge ourselves after the fact. This view is, of course, best captured by Shaw's lament that youth is wasted on the young.

The link between wisdom and age must be grounded not in the number of years as such but the quantity and quality of experience long life has provided. Simple quantity will not suffice because a lifetime of unending repetition of experience could hardly be said to contribute to a stockpile of wisdom. I suppose that many societies, some of the lifestyles of which are very elemental, will nevertheless attribute wisdom to their elders. If we consider a simple agrarian society, the vast extent of all expected experiential variety may well be had before a life is half over. What might count in such cases is not the assortment of experiences had by any individual, but some presumption about changes in the assessment of that experience. These changes are themselves part of experience and so provide the life with reflective if not physical variety.

This approach sounds persuasive but for a few awkward comparisons. Let us say I faithfully attend a showing of *Citizen Kane* every year for years. Further, suppose that each time I see the film differently so that the differences in my viewing history go well beyond the ritual repetition of the same visual input. This might stand as a stripped-down model of the wisdom of the elders. Although it may be true that each experience is distinct and distinctly revealing, it may nevertheless be pressing matters to say that, in some sense, each viewing is more perceptive or profoundly comprehended than its predecessor. Difference of experience in no way assures superiority of experience. Furthermore, any given later collection of such experiences is not guaranteed superiority of insight (or whatever is valuable about them) over any one earlier experience. At least, I see no special reason for saying they are. After all, it is certainly possible that any one viewing should be seen as the best one. Merely re-considering the sameness of experience over time from slightly different perspectives each time does not give the quantity of such reviews or the latest of them special significance.

It would seem most sensible to say that the attribute of wisdom lies in the nature of the assessment of experience rather than in the stage of life at which such assessment is made. But this does damage to the link between age and wisdom. If such an alliance exists, it must be founded on stronger stuff. There must in other words, be something about the experience and assessment of experience of the old that gives it majesty. What may it be?

There is a frequent temptation to say that the acquisition of wisdom may be complete as is humanly possible near the end of life but that, nevertheless, the very process of living is one accompanied by greater and greater wisdom. If it's true that 'as one gets older, one gets wiser' we must be able to say that at any one point in our lives we possess more wisdom than we had at any earlier point. The only factor that distinguishes the elderly is that they've acquired as much as can be acquired given our mortality. I think it would be very hard to make this guarantee stick. My attitudes about and evaluations of life may remain substantially unchanged despite the growing conflagration on my birthday cake. Many people just happen to be conservative in this way. If we persist in loyalty to our motto, then we seem to have made it a matter of definition and not one subject to meaningful confirmation or disconfirmation in any given case. I hope there is more to it than this because, otherwise, it is just reminiscent of the fake profundity playfully satirized by Henry Reed in "Chard Whitlow":

> As we get older we do not get any younger.
> Seasons return, and to-day I am fifty-five
> And this time last year I was fifty-four,
> And this time next year I shall be sixty-two.

So, we might admit, though hesitantly, that as one gets older, sometimes all that happens is that one gets older. Wisdom oughtn't to come quite so effortlessly.

Let's grant the existence of a case where wisdom has increased with age. (Perhaps we should also grant that it can decrease as well if we insist upon the empirical way). How can we characterize greater wisdom? We know that something must have changed with time, something in the perspective of the aging individual. For this perspective to be a wiser one it must also be an improvement of some sort. The later experience must be superior in quality. What would count in its favour? It cannot merely be the evaluation of the person himself. We may chronically fancy our latest insights to be our best ones, but that just shows that human vanity is always freshest in its most recent phase. Nor can we trust entirely the judgment of others about this individual because they may merely be paying tribute to something they've not yet thought of. We have to have a conception of greater wisdom which, in the weak sense, couldn't have been had by this person at any earlier stage in his life, and more strongly, perhaps, in the light of the greatest wisdom being the prize of the elderly, couldn't have been had by anyone else who happened to be younger.

We must avoid the triviality of the definitional sense of 'greater age, greater wisdom' as well. In a sublimely unimportant sense, given the life I have led, the uniqueness of perspective I now have couldn't have been mine earlier if I never had it before. There seems, however, nothing to dissuade me from saying that I could possibly have led a different life such that what I now know about experience I could have known while twenty years younger. Indeed, if the elderly can impart wisdom, if wisdom is a variety of knowledge or perspective, then the very young have the opportunity to short-cut the cost of aging in order to get where the aged are.

This hits a few snags. Providing we persist in attributing greater wisdom to the old, either wisdom cannot be imparted, or the young cannot understand what is imparted. If the former is the case, then we certainly have no grounds for calling the wisdom of the aged greater because, we the younger, have not, *ex hypothesi,* been given anything with which to compare it. Should the latter be advocated, it seems the wise can only communicate with the wise in which case, given that final wisdom comes complete and consistent, they'd have rather little to say to one another, and certainly no cause for chatting with youngsters. Neither is satisfactory because wisdom is characteristically sought out and appreciated by those who think they've less of it than others. Many great wise men of our culture are revered as teachers. Who has ever thought much of a circumstance where the teacher couldn't teach or the student couldn't hack the course?

What this amounts to is, I think, a serious erosion of the age-wisdom axis. If it makes any sense at all to say that wisdom can be imparted then no particular supremacy can conceivably go to the wisdom of the elders other than that they may be the first ones to spread it round. But once it is in circulation, age, the deposit of experience, will not matter very much. It all becomes very like the syndrome which has it, with great truth, that any decent freshman in physics knows far more about matter in motion than did Galileo.

This last adage may, however, provide a reprieve. What the freshman cannot be said to have under his belt are more discoveries about mechanics than the son of the famous Florentine lute composer. Learning about experience and acquiring that experience through living are powerfully distinct. Just as the freshman's impressive knowledge of physics does not make him a genius, so the young Plato is not made wise by taking to heart the message of his teacher. So it goes for the individual case. The greater wisdom I may now feel I have is derived not only from the conclusions of experience but from the struggle through it. Though this last route seems hopeful, the issue is not at all settled. It's unavoidably true that the older I become the more experience I will have had. It's quite another thing to say that the mere having of it need do anything to boost my sagacity. Further experience can just as easily dull my perception of life as it can improve it. Nor is there anything to dismiss my saying that my later experience was in large part moulded by my earlier contact with someone who had wisdom.

We like to believe that, having lived through some momentous experience, the insight we have about it is greater, more intense, or clearer than that of those we may have imparted it to. We may fancy that our contacts with love or sorrow, fame or failure, have given us something which of necessity just cannot be had by those who learn by our stories without having played the parts. Academics, for example, are not commonly attributed with more than infancy in the down-in-the-gutter disquisitions on "the real world out there" generously supplied by their mercantile brethren. It must be something like this which we generalize about when we twist together age and wisdom.

I'm uneasy about all of this. What we take to be greater clarity and so greater wisdom may be somewhat exaggerated. Such experiences are certainly more personal and strikingly so. They are also more memorable. But these of themselves do not reward the conclusions we draw with any greater virtue they have on their own. That someone may have lived through insightful experience is often a matter of chance unless one sought it out in the first place. We would be oddly beneficent to credit anyone for simply having had certain experiences which, contingently, led to those insights we call wise. For those reasons, the argument "I've lived longer, so I know more about life" does not shed any blinding light on wisdom. If wisdom lies anywhere, it must rest at least with the ability to draw certain types of conclusion from experience, and not from mere persistence through life. Having that ability cannot merely rest with a high score in years.

Age as such then is not a sure guide to wisdom nor is wisdom something we can all look forward to in our later years as we might our pensions or retirement. The Shavian retort that we can when older more fully appreciate what we couldn't have appreciated when younger fails at least on two counts to gain much ground. If the quantity of experience is necessary for the appreciation of experience, then a young man with an older man's appreciation of his youth is an impossibility. Knowing Shaw, this might indeed have been precisely what he meant. Secondly, if appreciation is not so dependent, then there is nothing in the reflections of maturity as such that give them superiority over the reflections of youth no matter how mistaken, rash, and unreflective they may seem in retrospect. Remarks like Shaw's are akin to regrets at not having done earlier what one cannot do now. Regrets may be frequent episodes in later life and they may command our fullest sympathy, but the most regretful of men cannot as such compel us to venerate his wisdom.

One last comment on the theme of age. Though now considered a little old-fashioned, there have been common references to the wisdom of the ancients or the wisdom of the fathers or some such reference to folkloric heroes of the past. These seem extensions of the links between wisdom and old age except they are spread over entire cultural histories. The frailty of such views is readily visible. The culture of the present is necessarily older than the culture of the past. Its accumulated experience and opportunity for hindsight are therefore greater. Greater wisdom attributed to members of younger and probably more primitive societies seems more nostalgic than consistent. Perhaps the confusion lies in a temptation to think of "the good old days" as historically older rather than historically former. When I reflect on my own past I remember the activities of a younger man. Odd, isn't it, that we conceive our cultural present as youthful in relation to the earlier stages it has passed through. However we take birthdays, Beethoven is not two hundred and ten years old. He died at fifty-seven in a society with a musically youthful culture that had not yet amassed enough knowledge and experience to fit him up with a passable hearing aid.

Perhaps the ideas we have considered have been incidental. It certainly does not seem as though too much store is to be placed in the relationship between wisdom and action, and that between wisdom and old age. Though both are decidedly part of our framework of thought, the former deals with little more than enlightened egoism and the latter with peculiar analogies we draw between increasing wealth as a result of continual savings and growing wisdom ensured by continual experience. What positive gains we have made have been slight; namely, that wisdom is somehow linked to the avoidance of the undesirable and that it has something to do with the assessment of and the capacity to reflect upon experience.

Another Platonic theme, the relation between wisdom and knowledge, might prove more helpful. The Wise are customarily taken to be endowed with a variety of knowledge and understanding quite out of the ordinary. If anything shows up the inadequacy of the avenues we have already travelled on, this does. The wise thing to do does not constitute wisdom if it's simply a sensible and well-planned course of action. No saying of an elder counts as wise if it's just platitudinous.

The account Plato gives of Socrates' finest hour is fraught with irony, replete with the paradoxical ways of the world's greatest sophist:

> And I am called wise for my hearers always imagine that I myself possess the wisdom which I find wanting in others: but the truth is, O men of Athens, that God only is wise; and by his answer he intends to show that the wisdom of men is worth little or nothing: he is not speaking of Socrates, he is only using my name by way of illustration, as if he said, He, O men, is the wisest who, like Socrates, knows that his wisdom is in truth worth nothing.[1]

We can take this in at least two ways. The first is that there is no body of knowledge which can go by the name of wisdom, but only specific bodies of knowledge pertinent only to very particular matters. This is a favourite Socratic strategy, the moral of which is; do not seek wisdom because all you're ever going to find is musicianship, or salesmanship, or statesmanship, and so on. The second is the ploy of the collapsing ladder which once climbed, deposits you where you started. Wisdom is the knowledge that one knows nothing, a revelation with a built-in-self-destruct device. Either way there is no human wisdom.

Though the message here seems unrepentently pessimistic, I think we can soften it somewhat and give it some hope. If taken at his word, Socrates would have to be denying the possibility of his own chosen vocation. At the very least he would have to be admitting that the journey has no destination. Besides, the perennial recognition of wisdom cannot be so easily dismissed. Let us suppose this milder message; namely, that whatever knowledge the wise have it is not the sort of knowledge bound by the particularities of expertise. No matter how thorough a knowledge of a craft, trade, or profession a man might have, none of this counts one whit towards his pretension to wisdom. Needless to say, this does away with virtually all varieties of knowledge. It certainly rids us of role-related knowledge, i.e., the knowledge that comes with being a chemist or violin maker or historian and so on. When we seek clarification of what remains we are left, whatever the case, with knowledge at a level of generality which seems to be neutral with respect to whatever other knowledge of the world we happen to have via other domains of learning.

---

[1]Plato, *Apology* (trans. B. Jowett), 23a–b.

One typical Socratic candidate emerges from the *Phaedo:*

> But when returning into herself (the soul) reflects, then she passes into
> the other world, the region of purity, and eternity, and immortality,
> and unchangeableness . . . then she ceases from her wandering, and
> being in contact with things unchanging is unchanging in relation to
> them. And this state of the soul is called wisdom?[2]

If we can make any contemporary mileage out of this lyricism, the
most we can say is that wisdom consists of knowledge of necessary
truth, truth no matter what. There is no doubt that this has a warming effect if only because a recognition of wisdom carries with it a
variety of complete faith in the soundness of the judgment no matter
what culture or time we happen to inhabit. This is to say, the knowledge of the wise is knowledge which fits whatever world it happens
to emerge in.

Not every candidate fulfilling the formal requirement is going to
do. All those necessary truths we see in tautologies will scarcely
impress, nor will we be moved by Pythagorean excesses about number and shapes. Logic and mathematics have no claim to wisdom, no
more than do the quasi-Aristotelian appeals to natural essences and
necessary *a posteriori* truth. What we want are claims blazened with
undying truth about human life and experience which stand outside
the incidental changes in the range of that experience and the culturally tied attitudes about it.

Suddenly we appear to have some prospect for success, but the
optimism is perhaps premature. There are numerous claims which
fit as well as do any the restrictions we have placed on wise sayings,
yet which somehow lack the grandeur and mystery they ought to
have. If we require such unhesitating truths, we seem free to consult
the class of judgments about the necessities of existence. Judgments
like "All men must die" or "All men must eat and sleep," no matter
how ponderously and pontifically uttered, are scarcely gems of wisdom. They're true to be sure, and possibly even true of all of us no
matter when and where we live, but they fall flat, and that is because
they're so obvious and trivial we would scarcely appreciate let alone
revere their utterance. Furthermore, they fail to secure uncompromising conviction because we can easily anticipate their being falsi-
fied by some future innovation in bio-medical research.

---

[2]Plato, *Phaedo* (trans B. Jowett), 79d.

Even if we search in other directions such as the Socratic discovery that we are all inevitably and hopelessly ignorant in that grand sense which prods us to recognize our unavoidable limitations, we may still question why that revelation deserves the title of wisdom. The reason for this is simply that no one would deny such claims. They are so broad as to be platitudinous, at least as truths about the human condition. After all, how seriously could a man resist the imputation that he will never know everything, and why indeed should he? Such claims which dodge the fallibility of the empirical, claims about the limitations of the individual or those vast hazy truths like 'this too will pass,' are not in themselves deeply profound because they fail almost stunningly to tell us anything about ourselves which we might possibly have missed. Their cosmic generality is won only through their seemingly banal immunity from question. Though they are not formally empty as are tautologies, they are, as truths, just as hollow. The flight to the pure, eternal, and unchangeable seems scheduled to land at the mundane and mouldy. Wisdom still awaits clearance.

There is always room at this juncture for a return match. I have suggested that although we may understand wisdom as a unique variety of knowledge, that very uniqueness is suspect. The necessity and generality it must carry merely disguise its actual poverty of content. What seems to be missed is any sense of revelation or profundity which, surely, must be the gift of the wise. However, it is not clear whether these supposed truisms are quite as uninteresting as they appear.

Those who see in wisdom a variety of knowledge may quite pertinently say that the general truisms of the wise take on an entirely different tinge when cast in the perspective of the ways men are prone to regard their own experience. It may just be a fact of our existence that we live and think of our lives as though such universal truths had no substance. We may indeed bathe in the illusions of arrogant omniscience, or immortality, and fashion our activities as though these were genuinely to be counted on. The wisdom of the Stoic, for example, cuts deeply into our expectations and deceptions, and persists in the reminder that our individual affairs are not quite nearly so magnificent in their triumph or grief as we care to imagine them. What the wise have is not a secret repository of knowledge unavailable to the masses, but rather the good sense to take seriously the unquestionable truth of the truism.

Wisdom becomes then a variety of knowledge not by virtue of its inscrutable depth, but rather by virtue of a suspicion that such knowledge should have priority in our assessment of experience. This, however, changes the picture considerably. For the advice of the wise becomes, on this interpretation, more like a reminder and perhaps even an admonition rather than the transmission of exotic information. The previous attempts at linking wisdom with action and with age take on a new perspective. If we couple consistently the necessary truth of the wise with our behavior we move considerably farther than the achievement of good solid sense. That calculating aspect must be ruled out because it is simply too particular, too specific, to yield anything more than expertise. The reliance upon age gains importance not because of the years of experience the aged have, but because there is a sense in which the aged no longer care about the plans and prospects they once had and so are psychologically in the best position to be freed of the forgetfulness of unchanging truths, a forgetfulness which helps feed the fires of those whose future is still largely a product of hopeful imagination.

What now emerges is not a vital link between wisdom and knowledge, because I think it fair to insist that the actual content of that knowledge is not special and mysterious in the way, say, that a layman may find the latest esoteric discoveries of physics. It certainly is not knowledge requiring expertise of any kind, nor need we prepare in any way to be privy to it. The knowledge involved is, however, universal, unchanging, and whatever else one may need to characterize its necessity. Where the wise emerge amidst this apparent banality of content is in their taking such knowledge seriously, recognizing how very stably true it is in the midst of passing deception so easily winning its victims.

The emphasis alters because it is not the knowledge of the wise we acknowledge to be special but the value they place and invite us to place on it. In some sense, the recognition of wisdom is the recognition of that which we, the unwise, not only have known but should have known all along. This last feature draws closer the connection between wisdom and virtue, perhaps the most recurrent bond to be established between the two.

In this regard, a number of matters come to light. The truisms of the wise gain respect not only because we are prone to accept their truth, but because the nature of that truth renders insignificant whatever screen of revealed illusions we have used to shield ourselves from it. The sayings of the wise are thus subtle provocations directed at our tendency to illusion. Were this tendency absent, were we naturally inclined to gauge our experience in the light of those features which, in the end, we cannot deny, there would be no virtue of wisdom in our conception of things. That there is, and that it is one we value without hesitation can only point to the confession that we see ourselves as unmindful at heart.

What are we doing when we call a given human feature a virtue? Amongst other things, we draw attention to a quality which would, if found in all men, improve life. We also point to something which is, under the title of virtue, in fact not very common amongst men nor on the whole eagerly accepted by them. Wisdom appears to be a virtue we give an honoured place. However, unlike other more modest virtues like honesty or courage, loyalty or charitableness, wisdom is not generally regarded as something which manifests itself episodically. The others attach to persons because they distinguish the behavior of such persons. We know quite well enough what brave or loyal people do to earn their stripes. As we discovered, however, 'the wise thing to do' does not in any way confer wisdom upon an agent the way doing the courageous thing might encourage the attribute of bravery. Wisdom is not that tidily dispositional, nor do the wise perform as identifiable a service to their fellows as do the honest.

This raises an interesting peculiarity about wisdom. It is as if it is deliberately hidden from view quite in contrast to the public advertisement of numerous other virtues. A man may spend his entire life tending a flower garden and yet be wise nonetheless. Wisdom is not a virtue revealed by display, and seems, indeed, to grow more gracious with retirement.

This might easily cause us to ask wherein the virtue of wisdom lies. It is not as if our history were punctuated by the actions of the wise which have demonstrably made matters better than they might otherwise have been. We do not stand on firm ground if we try to exhort others to wisdom in the way we might encourage generosity or patience. We need not even feel comfortable with the thought of modelling our lives after those of the wise, and so their existence cannot be counted on as an example for all of us to follow.

What has this virtue of wisdom to offer? Why should we applaud it and wish it one of our features. Here the history of philosophy can provide a few tentative answers. The repository of wisdom has been rooted in a conception of human nature which is other-worldly. If we consider Plato and Aristotle's philosopher, Spinoza's free man, or Kant's moral agent much becomes clear, for in all cases do we have ideals of character severed utterly from the continual impact of all those events and states of mind which draw us toward that very special status we seek for ourselves. Whereas the brave man is attended to for his personal accomplishment, the wise man may boast no such individuating traits. What on the contrary is in common amongst the models of wisdom given to us through Greek and European philosophy is an image lacking all personality. Plato and Aristotle sought their release from the individual through conceptions of serenity detached from concern for all those items like possessions or social station which carve boundaries around individuals. Spinoza yielded himself up to a universal determinism so fierce as to leave freedom little more extravagance than the recognition by an atom of consciousness of determinisms's ubiquity. Kant submerged all particularity into the anonymity of reason alone. There is no question that, for these philosophers, the state of wisdom lay locked in these conceptions. It is no wonder then that the wise, though thought so grand, should appear at the vanishing point of human business. It is also no surprise that we seem unable to locate any cultural display of public commendation for wisdom. In the end this can only be because this puzzling virtue is antagonistic to all that is public.

The prize of wisdom, its unlikely appeal, must lie in a recognition that, relative to the truisms about life, it is the only rational response possible. Its rarity as a virtue is, in a way, a tribute to the value we place on such rationality and also a helpless realization that the type of life it demands is not psychologically compatible with the lives we generally choose to lead.

The consideration of typical virtues throws wisdom into a class of its own. This is because a typical virtue is merely one the possession of which is typically achievable without overstepping the bounds of psychological plausibility. There are whole hosts of virtues which are simply not all that difficult to acquire. One need only consider the characteristic lists so beloved by the civilized gentlemen of the eighteenth century. Hume, for example, is no exception when he wishes us to be openly warm to the following constituents of the good man: justice, fidelity, honour, allegiance, chastity, humanity, generosity, charity, affability, lenity, mercy, moderation, public spirit, discretion, caution, enterprise, industry, assiduity, frugality, economy, good-sense, prudence, discernment, temperance, sobriety, patience, constancy, perseverance, forethought, considerateness, secrecy, order, insinuation, address, presence of mind, quickness of conception, facility of expression. "These and a thousand more of the same kind, no man will ever deny to be excellencies and perfections."[3] Nor must we forget Wit and Manners. These are all distinguished by at least two features. We can, all of us, aspire (without condemnation to sainthood) to develop these characteristics in ourselves without too much fuss; and, all of these virtues reflect directly upon our successful dealings with others. The common virtue is notably a social feature and is directed largely to smoothing out the rougher edges of human association. Further, such virtues can be deliberately acquired. They can be groomed and cultivated and, in the end, made to work for us.

Wisdom sits alone. We cannot rehearse or practice it. We cannot be prompted to assume it—whether for our sake or for the sake of others. We cannot expect, should we be in possession of it, to win friends and influence people. Wisdom calls into prominence a state of mind rather than a readiness to act in specified ways. As such, its status as a virtue must remain rather aloof.

I asked at the outset why it was that modern philosophers appear so uninterested in wisdom and think, now, I might be able to provide some answer. If wisdom deserves any mention at all, it seems to fit naturally, though superficially, into talk about morality. Indeed, there appears to be no other role it is fit to play in a philosophical environment which no longer accepts that the function of philosophy is to furnish a guide for the perplexed. But the study of morality, if it is at all an investigation into virtue, must centre round the complex of issues that deal with our public lives, our responses and reactions to others. Needless to say, the grip of utilitarianism holds such concerns strongly. In such a light, whatever wisdom is, it scarcely is fashionable as a *moral* virtue because those are seen of necessity to be social. Wisdom cannot even be made to look like those darlings of Hume's, i.e. 'qualities useful to ourselves' or 'qualities immediately agreeable to others,' simply because in our tradition the release sought by Plato as the ultimate moral end is considered best buried in the ascetic fanaticism of the past. Hume again:

---

[3]David Hume, *Inquiry Concerning the Principles of Morals*, Section VI, part I.

> Celibacy, fasting, penance, mortification, self-denial, humility, silence, solitude, and the whole train of monkish virtues; for what reason are they everywhere rejected by men of sense, but because they serve no manner of purpose; neither qualify him for the entertainment of company, nor increase his power of self-enjoyment?[4]

Whether or not this represents a mindless castigation of the virtue of wisdom I am not in a position to say. What does seem unavoidable is that the absence of talk about wisdom seems linked to a belief that it is associated with the 'monkish virtues' and so has no power of benefit in discussions of morality. This surely derives from the inherent privacy of wisdom and its abrasive separation from the demands of a gregarious species. It also stems from a split between the attainment of wisdom and the value placed on self-love. A tradition of struggle to liberate and justify self-concern as morally acceptable cannot do much business with a conception of virtue which presses to blast "the dear self" out of existence. The history of the search for wisdom reveals attitudes which confess that, as a whole, we're not quite as important as we think we are, and that, as individuals, we're not really important at all. If morality is seen as one sphere in which the conflict and cooperation between me and others is manifested, the grand and possibly ineffable vanishing act of the Wise is not likely to be asked in for a guest appearance.

What this means, of course, is that wisdom cannot comfortably assume a role within moral philosophy. It cannot even be used as a target in attacks on such awkward remainders as supererogation because, though other virtues may be seen as casting obligations on us, no one has ever suggested that we have a duty to be wise. Indeed, within the entire sphere of what is now taken to be moral concern, the moral field populated by rights, duties, the valuation of acts and men, intentions, motives, and consequences there is no cause to speak of wisdom at all. It might even be unintelligible to conceive it as a moral virtue lacking as it does all pretence to refashion human affairs in the name of universal benefit.

Though this might explain the neglect of the concept of wisdom, it certainly fails to warrant it. Thought about wisdom calls to mind many thematically related notions few of which have themselves seen

---

[4] David Hume, *op. cit.*, Section IX, part 1.

extensive contemporary treatment. For, if we look at wisdom as it was looked at we detect a concern with a conception of human virtue which, though only marginally geared toward happiness or well-being, seems nevertheless to survive in the darker corners of morality. I refer with a deliberate sense of the old-fashioned to the notion of human excellence, that itself reflecting on certain exceptional qualities of members of our species which are distinct in force from the social utility of altruism. Examples would be notions like dignity, integrity, decency, self-respect, rationality, serenity, or wisdom. Some of these are occasionally used to counter the supposed evils within moral theories—notably utilitarianism—and that can only be because some of those theories are clearly felt to belittle or, worse, manipulate aspects of life which cannot be sacrificed at any costs. But these reminders about human excellence do not themselves constitute an alternative moral picture; not, that is, one dedicated to the guidance of decision. This is because we do not really know what it is if anything these peculiar virtues do for human life, nor do we know what precisely would count as restoring them should they be abused. Perhaps some understanding of these universally respected features might account for the growing frustration with ethical theory, and also prepare the way for its future development. Whatever the case, some room need be made for these, even if it means recasting our current rather mercantile models of moral behavior.

I have throughout this paper attempted to clarify some features of wisdom against a backdrop of general philosophical neglect. What has emerged is by no means an uninteresting concept, but one which, for some of the reasons outlined, falls outside contemporary philosophical concern. In examining wisdom in its epistemic and moral dimensions I have tried to show that it fails to rouse any special puzzles about some inscrutable sense of profundity as far as content is concerned, and also that it gains its title to virtue only at the expense of moving clear of our conception of typical virtues. I have, despite this, urged that a notion like wisdom points relevantly beyond our customary views about moral thought in much the same way as do attributes like dignity or self-respect. That is to say that such qualities belong to our moral schemes even though they slip past the usual emphasis upon the interaction of humans and the moral mechanisms of rights, obligations, moral strategies, and the like, which govern such interaction. Because of this I would argue that modern moral philosophy cannot afford to dismiss an approach to morality in the spirit of the Athenians or the rationalists of the enlightenment as dated.

Before closing, there is another small matter that need be discussed; namely, the features supposed to contrast with wisdom. These will illuminate, I think, some of the less accessible characteristics of wisdom. I have, so far, hedged round the question of the nature of the other-than-wise. At times I have allowed the young to fill the role, at others the unmindful, and sometimes have merely smeared the class round with the epithet 'unwise.' The traditional account is not nearly so courteous, for it is here that the fool rises to prominence. Just as wisdom is held to ride higher than the wise thing to do, so the fool is not merely one who happens unwittingly to do foolish deeds. The fault of the fool is far more brutally base than that.

What is interesting is that there is hardly a denunciation of a person so cutting and dismissive as that of calling someone a fool. What is even more fascinating is that we tend not to invoke moral derision in the customary sense when branding someone as a fool. There is, though, a strange uneasiness about such attributions, one which leaves them not quite as contrary to wisdom as might first appear. People are called fools when, for example, they stubbornly and almost naively act against their own best interest. Some are seen to be fools in contrast to pragmatic and 'realistic' agents. Here there is no question that the fool is a character somehow devoid of expertise, perhaps hopelessly so. Such fools, to our disgrace, might nevertheless have wisdom. There is another species of fool closely related to the first. Those are people whose manner and demeanour fail grotesquely to meet accepted standards. Such fools are born at formal dinner parties and august gatherings. These fools, too, are not antithetical to the wise. Where all fools join ranks, however, is in lacking something like an appropriate and expected level of intelligent perspective. The fool cast apart from wisdom must be as empty of the recognition of necessity as the wise are deeply involved with it. The fool, then, is not merely one lacking manipulative skill or elegant poise. His defects are far less redeemable because unlike his colleagues, he cannot be cured by any training program. Unfortunately, the fool turns out to be one whose entire life is misconceived. Further, and more damaging, the wise give us to understand that the fool is no passing stranger to the world. Indeed, he is present in all of us lacking wisdom. Here perhaps is the least acceptable aspect of those virtue theories in which wisdom is given extreme importance. Whatever wisdom is, it is very rare. If it is necessary as a component of the properly moral man, then it must be that the vast majority of us cannot make the grade. The numerous charges of elitism brought against Plato or of iciness lodged against Kant are the reactions of moral democrats all of whom fashion morality as a system acessible to everyone. In these liberal conceptions, the only requirement (and even this is not very pressing) is that one learn to temper one's unfortunate but forgiveable selfishness on those occasions when others might happen to be affected by one's actions. The achievement of wisdom has clearly never been viewed as so relatively minor an effort. This too might explain the neglect and also account for reactions such as Hume's which would brand such conceptions of human ineptitude as pointlessly negative and hardly worth the anguish. The wise, then, are tarred with the same brush used to silence the chronic tradition of fanatical harangue directed at the sorry state of our souls.

Of course, this assimilation is unfair because it has never been the tradition of the wise to pummel us with our limitations, let alone threaten us with their mortal danger. The aftershock is rather more subtly damaging. By contrast to the wise, we are enjoined in the end to see ourselves as pathetic. This is far harder to swallow and yet is gracefully easy to ignore. The one philosopher who bothered passionately about this matter got himself into a great deal of trouble. Perhaps we've learned a professional lesson. One is always wise to avoid litigation.

**STUDY QUESTIONS**

1. Why does the popular identification of wisdom with age and experience give an inadequate concept of wisdom?
2. Why is the identification of wisdom with prudential understanding and skill inadequate?
3. In what sense is wisdom a knowledge of truisms? How does wisdom enable us to remove the illusion and deceptions that hide the truisms from us?
4. Discuss the relation of wisdom to serenity.
5. Godlovitch suggests that, unlike the other virtues, wisdom cannot be cultivated deliberately. For this reason, no one has a duty

283

to be wise. Also, wisdom is rare. Is there anything paradoxical about a virtue that is not enjoined on us as a duty and that is inaccessible to all but a few?

6. Everyone thinks well of wisdom, yet wise people are often scorned. What is there about wisdom that renders it unpopular and suspect?

# The Virtue of Pride

### RICHARD TAYLOR

Richard Taylor (b. 1919) is the Leavitt-Spencer Professor of Philosophy at Union College. Previously he taught at the University of Rochester. Among Taylor's many books are *Good and Evil* (1971), *With Heart and Mind* (1973), and *Ethics, Faith and Reason* (1985).

Richard Taylor defines "pride" as *justified* love of oneself, as distinguished from conceit, vanity, and egoism. Proud persons may be unjustified in feeling proud; if so, they are merely "conceited." The vain person delights in the admiration of others, regardless of the qualities in themselves that arouse the admiration. Egoism is characterized by excessive absorption in oneself. Conceit, vanity, and egoism usually are not compatible with the virtue of pride. For Taylor, pride is a general virtue that presupposes other virtues such as courage, honor, and discipline.

## The Nature of Pride

Pride is not a matter of manners or demeanor. One does not become proud simply by affecting certain behavior or projecting an impression that has been formed in the mind. It is a personal excellence

THE VIRTUE OF PRIDE From *Ethics, Faith and Reason* by Richard Taylor. Copyright © 1985 by Prentice-Hall. Reprinted by permission of the publisher.

much deeper than this. In fact, it is the summation of most of the other virtues, since it presupposes them.

Pride is the justified love for oneself. The qualification "justified" is crucial. Simpletons can love themselves and are, in fact, very apt to do so; but they are not proud, for there are no qualities of excellence to justify that love. They have not pride but mere conceit, which is something different altogether. Conceit is the simpleton's unwarranted sense of self-importance. Conceited persons thus imagine themselves as possessed of great worth, when in fact they have little or none; and that is why they are simple, as well as being very tiresome to others and of little worth in the eyes of those who are genuinely proud.

Genuinely proud people perceive themselves as better than others, and their pride is justified because their perception is correct. Thus they love themselves, not as children and ordinary people do, for these do not possess the kind of worth that justifies such self-esteem, but because they really are, in the classical sense of the term, good. Their virtues are not assimilated ones, nor do they consist merely in the kind of innocence that wins the approbation of others. Instead, they are their own in the truest sense: that they come from within themselves and win the approbation of the only judge who counts—oneself.

## Arrogance, Vanity, and Egoism

Pride is not arrogance, and a proud person would never be overbearing towards others. While conceit is an attitude towards oneself, which in that respect resembles pride, arrogance is a way of behaving, a mannerism, and one that is profoundly offensive. One is arrogant only towards other persons. Arrogance cannot be exhibited in solitude, although conceit can—in vainglorious fantasy, for example, or at the other extreme, in solitary weeping.

Arrogance implies a belittling of the opinions, conduct, or personal qualities of another person in an effort to draw attention to one's own presumed superiority. It is, therefore, most easily exhibited towards persons who stand in an inferior position, such as waiters or other servants, employees, clerks, and so on. Police officers, particularly those who are vulgar or otherwise lacking in personal excellence, are very prone to arrogance, for one's inferior position cannot be more manifest than in the presence of a police officer's

gun. It is for this same reason that cowards, given suitable circumstances, are likely to be arrogant. Since the fault that cancels their
personal worth, namely cowardice, is so grave and ineradicable, they
attempt to compensate with arrogance and browbeating or, given
the opportunity, outright cruelty.

Vanity and egoism, too, must be distinguished from pride, for
they have little in common with it. Vanity is the delight people derive
from praise or flattering allusions to themselves, from whatever
source, and with respect to whatever things are alluded to, whether
significant or not. Thus vain people delight in flattering comment
from inferior persons, such as from children, or even from total
strangers, whereas a truly proud person would be quite oblivious to
this. Vain people can even be seen trying to elicit attention and admiring comment in public places, and from persons entirely unknown to them, by their loud and excessive laughter, for example,
or their swaggering gait, or by their attire, or by the importance or
beauty of their companions. Thus a man sometimes enjoys entering
a restaurant with a beautiful companion on his arm, even though he
may never have been there before and may know no one in the room.
Similarly, a woman is sometimes pleased to draw looks, even from
strangers, to her tasteful clothing. Such are familiar examples of
vanity, and they could be multiplied at length. It is something to
which every normal person is prone, for who can fail to be pleasantly
aware of the admiring attention of others? A vain person, however,
seeks that attention, sometimes going to great length to get it, while
a proud person tries to ignore it, and would be ashamed to actually
set about trying to elicit it. This would be especially true with respect
to such things as clothing, or the influence one has over other people
or external things, in other words, things having no connection with
one's true nature or excellence.

Egoism is similar to vanity, though perhaps some distinctions
between the two are useful. Egoism is a certain cast of mind, characterized by excessive absorption in oneself, to the extent that one's
awareness of others is clouded. Vanity, as noted, is the delight evoked
by the favorable attention of others, quite regardless of what qualities
elicit such attention. Thus egoism may be more characteristic of
men, and vanity of women, though of course such broad generalizations are not without many exceptions. Men do often tend to be
absorbed in themselves to the detriment of their awareness of others,

seeing these others as instruments to the pursuit of their own goals. This is perhaps an expression of the male concern for power and influence. Women, on the other hand, are sometimes more concerned to be "attractive," something which has very much to do with appearance. And the lesser self-absorption on the part of women may explain, to some extent at least, their sometimes greater awareness of the feelings of others; these others might include children and animals, and this awareness sometimes rises to genuine compassion. To be sure, men are also capable of this, but there seem to be differences of degree.

Neither vanity nor egoism is very compatible with genuine pride, even though no one can hope or pretend to be entirely without them. While vain people delight in others' admiration for things they *have*—possessions, for instance—proud people have little interest in the admiration of others except for what they *are;* and even that admiration must come only from such persons, always relatively few, who are themselves proud people, in the truest sense, and hence better. Thus, while no one would want to be poor, a proud person does not mind being erroneously thought to be poor. A person of excessive vanity or egoism, on the other hand, tries very hard to create the impression of affluence even when that is a false impression, something a proud person would not think of doing. Vain or self-centered persons live beyond their means, or spend what limited resources they have on things that will be seen by others—cars, house furnishings, clothing, and so on. Such persons thus try to compensate for their limitations as persons by augmenting those things that are external to themselves and their characters. One who is quite stupid, for example, tries to compensate with a showy car or house; or one who fears danger or dreads death tries to compensate with excessive but insincere affability. They try, in other words, to be *thought* good, in the original, nonmoral sense of that term, when in fact they are not.

## Pride and Self-Approbation

Proud people are not much concerned with what others think of them and care nothing at all for the opinions of insignificant persons, but are instead concerned with what they think of themselves. Others know you for what you appear to be, which can be misleading, but you know yourself for what you are—at least, you are in a privileged position to. If it is you who are ignorant, or silly, or weak-willed, or fearful, or vain, then, however well you may succeed in concealing these faults from others, you cannot entirely conceal them from yourself unless you are very stupid. And for this reason proud people would not try to conceal themselves from themselves nor have any reason to, regardless of how little they care about the opinions of others. For proud people, as noted, are those who *justifiably* love themselves, that is, who have a high *and correct* opinion of their real worth. They therefore do not compare themselves with others with respect to things that are extraneous to themselves. For example, they do not compare their possessions with those of their neighbors or associates, or if they happen to be aware that what they own far exceeds what their neighbors own, they do not let on to this. Instead, they compare themselves only with the best. They are properly ashamed if others are wiser than they, or if others conduct their lives with better order and rationality, or if others have greater courage and self-discipline. Similarly, their envy is reserved, not for those who are praised by the multitude, for whatever reason, but for those whose honor is deserved and is bestowed only by the best.

Proud people do not bow to any others, except in such purely ceremonious ways as tipping their hats; nor are they deferential to persons of special status or rank, such as those holding high offices, or persons who are wealthy, or persons of a special and conspicuous class, such as priests—with the exception, once again, of purely ceremonious gestures of deference, such as the use of "sir" and "ma'm" in addressing them. The most conspicuous exception to these generalizations is old people who have grown wise with their years. Such persons are truly venerable, and pride is never compromised by treating them as such. The experience of years, quite by itself, may confer wisdom, and nothing is more deserving of honor than this; so it is not inappropriate that others, aspiring to wisdom, should bow to those who have won it.

## The Marks of Pride

Pride is seen in things both great and small. One of the great tests, for example, is the individual's response to acute danger, or his or her reaction to a life-threatening disease or to humiliation at the hands of enemies. One type of person bears these things with a natural, unpracticed fortitude and nobility while, at the other extreme, some collapse into whimpering and self-pity. With respect to death, a proud person knows that even his or her own life is not worth clinging to at the cost of pride or honor; would never want it prolonged beyond the point where the virtues upon which pride rests have become debilitated; and would, for this reason, prefer to die ten years too soon than ten days too late.

And there are other great tests, such as one's reaction to the death of a son or daughter who was intelligent, and strong, and filled with promise of great achievement.

But such things as these are negative, being tests of strength in adversity. There are great positive tests as well; the power one displays in writing and speech, sensitivity to music and other things of great beauty, and perhaps above all else, one's own creative power. Whether you follow experience and reason to form your beliefs on either great or petty matters, or whether, on the other hand, you simply embrace whatever opinions answer to your fondest desires, this, as well as any other test, distinguishes a wise and proud person from a vain and foolish one. Thus people who are given to ideologies and faiths, that is, to large and untested claims that they find satisfying and reassuring, are not wise and cannot therefore be proud; for whatever love they may have for themselves can hardly be justified. On the other hand, those who accept even unpleasant facts because they are facts, or do not shrink from drawing appropriate inferences from what they observe, even when these facts or observations may run counter to everything they have been taught and everything they desperately hope is true, such persons are wise, whether learned or not, and have at least that one correct basis for self-approbation. If, in addition, they are learned, then they have still another. And if, in addition to those qualities, they are creative, self-disciplined, and courageous, then they have still others; and there comes a point where external things which contribute nothing to those qualities are clearly seen by them to be worth very little, however much they may delight simple people.

But there are also, as noted, lesser marks of pride, easily recognized by other proud persons, though not understood by the meek and the foolish. A proud person is, for example, serious, but not solemn, whereas a meek person's effort to be serious results only in a laughable solemnity. Such a person puts on a grave face and a reserved manner and imagines that he or she has become serious. Hearty laughter and the enjoyment of life are compatible with seriousness, which is positive and affirmative, but not with mere solemnity, which is negative and withdrawn. Again, a proud person is not garrulous and does not speak merely for the sake of "making conversation" or of hearing words flow. On matters not worthy of comment—such as weather, minor political issues, or things in the immediate surroundings—proud people normally say nothing at all. They do not mind long periods of dead silence, feel no embarrassment or anxiety at this, nor any need to break such silence with idle observations except when silence would be interpreted as rudeness. Proud people delight in the company of other proud and worthwhile persons, and seek above all to discover and appreciate their strengths and virtues. Their awareness of these is not clouded by self-absorption, nor by any desire to project a good impression of themselves; for they know that their own excellences will be recognized by others of similar excellence and do not care if they are not seen by those who lack this.

One category of behavior which is sometimes erroneously associated with pride is the fastidious observance of what is called etiquette. Etiquette comprises the many rules of social intercourse, often petty in nature, which enable people to associate comfortably in special circumstances such as social gatherings. These rules are often important in preventing embarrassment and awkwardness, but they have almost nothing to do with pride and can sometimes even work against it. Thus, proud people are not ashamed to whistle in public places where such behavior is harmless though uncommon, nor do they mind wearing old or baggy clothing, for example, if that is their taste. Etiquette, by its very nature, encourages a kind of mindless conformity, whereas those who are proud conform their behavior to standards which are their own.

A proud person does not pretend to an insincere equality with others who are inferior, that is, who are meek, foolish, or silly. A person is not worthy of esteem just by the fact of being a person but, rather, by the fact of being a person of outstanding worth, which is something quite rare.

### The Place of Externals

Among the lesser marks of pride are also those things that moralists once referred to as "externals," meaning by this all those things that are extraneous to what a person inherently is. Dress, for instance, is an external thing, as are one's reputation and standing in the popular mind, the praise or honors one receives from small-minded people, and so on.

Thus, with respect to dress, proud people do not ask what others expect of them, or how they wish them to look, and the least consideration in their minds is how *others* dress. They ask instead what will please themselves. It is compatible with perfect and beautiful pride never to wear a suit or necktie, to dress in baggy trousers and sweat shirt and cheap shoes. This description fits the appearance of one of the proudest persons of our century, Albert Einstein, whose almost superhuman virtues were combined with a boundless compassion and sweetness. But let it be added that affectation in dress, or the deliberate attempt to be outlandish and garish and to attract the attention of others, is not pride but, as noted before, vanity. For again, the good opinion that one should seek is one's own, not others', and certainly not that of strangers.

## Pride and Morality

With respect to what is popularly called "morality," a proud person is in the best sense the creator of his or her own. Nothing is done *merely* because it is recommended and done by others. Rather, something is done because *he* or *she* sees it as worthy of being done, and especially because it is worthy of himself or herself. Thus a proud person would not injure or betray a friend, not because it would be "wrong," or would violate vulgar morality, but because it would be shameful. Nor would a proud person cheat or take dishonest advantage of anyone, again, not because it would be wrong, but because it would be incompatible with his or her own worth. To act otherwise would imply that there are external things that are of greater importance than one's own excellence, which would be totally inconsistent with pride. But perhaps the clearest indication of the ethics of pride is found in those situations for which popular morality has no clear rules. Consider, for example, the finding of things whose ownership is uncertain, or for which no owner can be determined at all. Thus, for example, if money or other valuables are found on the ground, a proud person does not hesitate to take them; but such a person could not be imagined seeing someone drop these things and then picking them up unless, of course, to restore them to the person who dropped them. The reason for such behavior does not rest upon any common notion of theft but on one's own clear notion of honor. But perhaps the best illustration of all is found in the opportunity to take money or other valuables from a corpse. These things, in the nature of the case, do not belong to anyone (assuming no surviving kin) and are thus, for all practical purposes, simply found. There is no clear rule of popular morality covering such a situation, for it is of rare occurrence, never occurring at all in the lives of most people. Yet a proud person would not have the slightest inclination to do such a thing, and for a reason that is overwhelming and conclusive, namely that such an act would be shameful. It is not shameful in the sense that we have been taught to regard it as such, for little has ever been said on such infrequent things. Rather, it is shameful in the true sense of the word, as being incompatible with one's own worth as a person, a worth that is possessed only by the proud. To be sure, this does leave humble persons with little incentive for personal honor, but that is not an ontoward consequence, for such persons have little of this incentive anyway. They can be cajoled to decency by others, or compelled by laws and morality, but a genuinely proud person is cajoled to nothing at all by others, and is law-abiding and moral only as a condition of civilized life. Someone possessed of personal excellence requires more than morality for a life that is, in its true and original sense, good.

Such (in outline and with much omitted) is the virtue of pride. It is not the only virtue, nor even the highest, that being, without doubt, wisdom; but it is nevertheless, in the sense that was explained, a kind of summation of the virtues.

It is also a specimen of aspiration, which cannot be proved to be worth having. But in this area little can be proved anyway. We are dealing not with things that are true, in the usual sense, but with things that are good, in the philosophical sense. And as to the question whether this or any other virtue is worth having and worth giving a great deal to have, one has, of course, to find the answer within oneself. Conduct can sometimes be forced upon one, but virtue can only be discovered.

**STUDY QUESTIONS**

1. Taylor says that genuinely proud people perceive themselves as better than others and that their pride is justified because their perception is correct. Do you agree?

2. Does Taylor's justifiably proud individual appear to be a likable person? A moral person?
3. Taylor says that egoism may be more characteristic of men and vanity of women. Do you think he is right?
4. What does Taylor mean when he says pride is "justified" self-love? How does one know when one's self-love is justified?
5. Is Taylor a Nietzschean?

# Ideals of Human Excellence and Preserving Natural Environments

## THOMAS E. HILL, JR.

Thomas E. Hill, (b. 1937) is professor of philosophy at the University of North Carolina, Chapel Hill. He has published numerous articles on contemporary moral issues.

Thomas Hill's essay investigates the relationship between a regard for the environment and a regard for persons. He seeks to articulate the grounds for the widespread feeling that, utility aside, there is something very wrong with the person who treats nonsentient nature as a mere resource to be exploited. Some environmentalists have argued that plants and trees have rights of their own. Hill rejects this as too controversial.

Other philosophers argue that a world in which trees and plants exist is a better world than one that lacks such

IDEALS OF HUMAN EXCELLENCE AND PRESERVING NATURAL ENVIRONMENTS Excerpted from an article of the same name that first appeared in *Environmental Ethics*, vol. 5, 1983. Reprinted by permission of The University of Georgia and the author.

things. But the idea of the intrinsic goodness of nature abstracted from all human preferences is also dismissed by Hill as too controversial. For similar reasons, Hill finds religious answers inadequate.

Hill then suggests that we turn away from attempts to characterize nature itself as having rights or being intrinsically good to look at what may be morally wrong with the person who looks upon nature as a mere resource. What sort of person can be indifferent to the destruction of a forest? According to Hill, the destroyer of a forest tends to value all things instrumentally and narrowly; the attitude of such a person betrays a lack of humility. "If a person views all nonsentient nature merely as a resource, then it seems unlikely that he has developed the capacity needed to overcome self-importance."

Hill holds that those who tend to be ungrateful and insensitive to what nature gives us tend to be ungrateful and insensitive to their fellow human beings. Conversely, those who value such traits as humility, gratitude, and sensitivity have reason to promote the love of nature.

# I

A wealthy eccentric bought a house in a neighborhood I know. The house was surrounded by a beautiful display of grass, plants, and flowers, and it was shaded by a huge old avocado tree. But the grass required cutting, the flowers needed tending, and the man wanted more sun. So he cut the whole lot down and covered the yard with asphalt. After all it was his property and he was not fond of plants.

It was a small operation, but it reminded me of the strip mining of large sections of the Appalachians. In both cases, of course, there were reasons for the destruction, and property rights could be cited as justification. But I could not help but wonder, "What sort of person would do a thing like that?"

Many Californians had a similar reaction when a recent governor defended the leveling of ancient redwood groves, reportedly saying, "If you have seen one redwood, you have seen them all."

Incidents like these arouse the indignation of ardent environmentalists and leave even apolitical observers with some degree of moral discomfort. The reasons for these reactions are mostly obvious. Uprooting the natural environment robs both present and future generations of much potential use and enjoyment. Animals too depend on the environment; and even if one does not value animals for their own sakes, their potential utility for us is incalculable. Plants are needed, of course, to replenish the atmosphere quite aside from their aesthetic value. These reasons for hesitating to destroy forests and gardens are not only the most obvious ones, but also the most persuasive for practical purposes. But, one wonders, is there nothing more behind our discomfort? Are we concerned solely about the potential use and enjoyment of the forests, etc., for ourselves, later generations, and perhaps animals? Is there not something else which disturbs us when we witness the destruction or even listen to those who would defend it in terms of cost/benefit analysis?

Imagine that in each of our examples those who would destroy the environment argue elaborately that, even considering future generations of human beings and animals, there are benefits in "replacing" the natural environment which outweigh the negative utilities which environmentalists cite.[1] No doubt we could press the argument on the facts, trying to show that the destruction is shortsighted and that its defenders have underestimated its potential harm or ignored some pertinent rights or interests. But is this all we could say? Suppose we grant, for a moment, that the utility of destroying the redwoods, forests, and gardens is equal to their potential for use and enjoyment by nature lovers and animals. Suppose, further, that we even grant that the pertinent human rights and animal rights, if any, are evenly divided for and against destruction. Imagine that we also concede, for argument's sake, that the forests contain no potentially useful endangered species of animals and plants. Must we then conclude that there is no further cause for moral concern? Should we then feel morally indifferent when we see the natural environment uprooted?

---

[1]When I use the expression "the natural environment," I have in mind the sort of examples with which I began. For some purposes it is important to distinguish cultivated gardens from forests, virgin forests from replenished ones, irreplaceable natural phenomena from the replaceable, and so on; but these distinctions, I think, do not affect my main points here. There is also a broad sense, as Hume and Mill noted, in which all that occurs, miracles aside, is "natural." In this sense, of course, strip mining is as natural as a beaver cutting trees for his dam, and, as parts of nature, we cannot destroy the "natural" environment but only alter it. As will be evident, I shall use *natural* in a narrower, more familiar sense.

## II

Suppose we feel that the answer to these questions should be negative. Suppose, in other words, we feel that our moral discomfort when we confront the destroyers of nature is not fully explained by our belief that they have miscalculated the best use of natural resources or violated rights in exploiting them. Suppose, in particular, we sense that part of the problem is that the natural environment is being viewed exclusively as a natural *resource*. What could be the ground of such a feeling? That is, what is there in our system of normative principles and values that could account for our remaining moral dissatisfaction?[2]

Some may be tempted to seek an explanation by appeal to the interests, or even the rights, of plants. After all, they may argue, we only gradually came to acknowledge the moral importance of all human beings, and it is even more recently that consciences have been aroused to give full weight to the welfare (and rights?) of animals. The next logical step, it may be argued, is to acknowledge a moral requirement to take into account the interests (and rights?) of plants. The problem with the strip miners, redwood cutters, and the like, on this view, is not just that they ignore the welfare and rights of people and animals; they also fail to give due weight to the survival and health of the plants themselves.

The temptation to make such a reply is understandable if one assumes that all moral questions are exclusively concerned with whether *acts* are right or wrong, and that this, in turn, is determined entirely by how the acts impinge on the rights and interests of those directly affected. On this assumption, if there is cause for moral concern, some right or interest has been neglected; and if the rights and interests of human beings and animals have already been taken into account, then there must be some other pertinent interests, for example those of plants. A little reflection will show that the assumption is mistaken; but, in any case, the conclusion that plants have

---

[2]This paper is intended as a preliminary discussion in *normative* ethical theory (as opposed to *metaethics*). The task, accordingly, is the limited, though still difficult, one of articulating the possible basis in our beliefs and values for certain particular moral judgments. Questions of ultimate justification are set aside. What makes the task difficult and challenging is not that conclusive proofs from the foundation of morality are attempted; it is rather that the particular judgments to be explained seem at first not to fall under the most familiar moral principles (e.g., utilitarianism, respect for rights).

rights or morally relevant interests is surely untenable. We do speak of what is "good for" plants, and they can "thrive" and also be "killed." But this does not imply that they have "interests" in any morally relevant sense. Some people apparently believe that plants grow better if we talk to them, but the idea that the plants suffer and enjoy, desire and dislike, etc., is clearly outside the range of both common sense and scientific belief. The notion that the forests should be preserved to avoid *hurting* the trees or because they have a *right* to life is not part of a widely shared moral consciousness, and for good reason.[3]

Another way of trying to explain our moral discomfort is to appeal to certain religious beliefs. If one believes that all living things were created by a God who cares for them and entrusted us with the use of plants and animals only for limited purposes, then one has a reason to avoid careless destruction of the forests, etc., quite aside from their future utility. Again, if one believes that a divine force is immanent in all nature, then too one might have reason to care for more than sentient things. But such arguments require strong and controversial premises, and, I suspect, they will always have a restricted audience.

Early in this century, due largely to the influence of G. E. Moore, another point of view developed which some may find promising.[4] Moore introduced, or at least made popular, the idea that certain states of affairs are intrinsically valuable—not just valued, but valuable, and not necessarily because of their effects on sentient beings. Admittedly Moore came to believe that in fact the only intrinsically valuable things were conscious experiences of various sorts,[5] but this

---

[3] I assume here that having a right presupposes having interests in a sense which in turn presupposes a capacity to desire, suffer, etc. Since my main concern lies in another direction, I do not argue the point, but merely note that some regard it as debatable. See, for example, W. Murray Hunt, "Are *Mere Things* Morally Considerable?" *Environmental Ethics* 2 (1980): 59–65; Kenneth E. Goodpaster, "On Stopping at Everything," *Environmental Ethics* 2 (1980): 288–94; Joel Feinberg, "the Rights of Animals and Unborn Generations," in William Blackstone, ed., *Philosophy and Environmental Crisis* (Athens: University of Georgia Press, 1974), pp. 43–68; Tom Regan, "Feinberg on What Sorts of Beings Can Have Rights," *Southern Journal of Philosophy* (1976): 485–98; Robert Elliot, "Regan on the Sort of Beings that Can Have Rights," *Southern Journal of Philosophy* (1978): 701–05; Scott Lehmann, "Do Wildernesses Have Rights?" *Environmental Ethics* 2 (1981): 129–46.

[4] G. E. Moore, *Principia Ethica* (Cambridge: Cambridge University Press, 1903); *Ethics* (London: H. Holt, 1912).

[5] G. E. Moore, "Is Goodness a Quality?" *Philosophical Papers* (London: George Allen and Unwin, 1959), pp. 95–97.

restriction was not inherent in the idea of intrinsic value. The intrinsic goodness of something, he thought, was an objective, nonrelational property of the thing, like its texture or color, but not a property perceivable by sense perception or detectable by scientific instruments. In theory at least, a single tree thriving alone in a universe without sentient beings, and even without God, could be intrinsically valuable. Since, according to Moore, our duty is to maximize intrinsic value, his theory could obviously be used to argue that we have reason not to destroy natural environments independently of how they affect human beings and animals. The survival of a forest might have worth beyond its worth *to* sentient beings.

This approach, like the religious one, may appeal to some but is infested with problems. There are, first, the familiar objections to intuitionism, on which the theory depends. Metaphysical and epistemological doubts about nonnatural, intuited properties are hard to suppress, and many have argued that the theory rests on a misunderstanding of the words *good, valuable,* and the like.[6] Second, even if we try to set aside these objections and think in Moore's terms, it is far from obvious that everyone would agree that the existence of forests, etc., is intrinsically valuable. The test, says Moore, is what we would say when we imagine a universe with just the thing in question, without any effects or accompaniments, and then we ask, "Would its existence be better than its nonexistence?" Be careful, Moore would remind us, not to construe this question as, "Would you *prefer* the existence of that universe to its nonexistence?" The question is, "Would its existence have the objective, nonrelational property, intrinsic goodness?"

Now even among those who have no worries about whether this really makes sense, we might well get a diversity of answers. Those prone to destroy natural environments will doubtless give one answer, and nature lovers will likely give another. When an issue is as controversial as the one at hand, intuition is a poor arbiter.

The problem, then, is this. We want to understand what underlies our moral uneasiness at the destruction of the redwoods, forests, etc., even apart from the loss of these as resources for human beings and animals. But I find no adequate answer by pursuing the questions, "Are rights or interests of plants neglected?" "What is God's will on the matter?" and "What is the intrinsic value of the existence of a tree

[6]See, for example, P. H. Nowell-Smith, *Ethics* (New York: Penguin Books, 1954).

or forest?" My suggestion, which is in fact the main point of this paper, is that we look at the problem from a different perspective. That is, let us turn for a while from the effort to find reasons why certain *acts* destructive of natural environments are morally wrong to the ancient task of articulating our ideals of human excellence. Rather than argue directly with destroyers of the environment who say, "Show me why what I am doing is *immoral*," I want to ask, "what sort of person would want to do what they propose?" The point is not to skirt the issue with an *ad hominem,* but to raise a different moral question, for even if there is no convincing way to show that the destructive acts are wrong (independently of human and animal use and enjoyment), we may find that the willingness to indulge in them reflects the absence of human traits that we admire and regard morally important.

This strategy of shifting questions may seem more promising if one reflects on certain analogous situations. Consider, for example, the Nazi who asks, in all seriousness, "Why is it wrong for me to make lampshades out of human skin—provided, of course, I did not myself kill the victims to get the skins?" We would react more with shock and disgust than with indignation, I suspect, because it is even more evident that the question reveals a defect in the questioner than that the proposed act is itself immoral. Sometimes we may not regard an act wrong at all though we see it as reflecting something objectionable about the person who does it. Imagine, for example, one who laughs spontaneously to himself when he reads a newspaper account of a plane crash that kills hundreds. Or, again, consider an obsequious grandson who, having waited for his grandmother's inheritance with mock devotion, then secretly spits on her grave when at last she dies. Spitting on the grave may have no adverse consequences and perhaps it violates no rights. The moral uneasiness which it arouses is explained more by our view of the agent than by any conviction that what he did was immoral. Had he hesitated and asked, "Why shouldn't I spit on her grave?" it seems more fitting to ask him to reflect on the sort of person he is than to try to offer reasons why he should refrain from spitting.

### III

What sort of person, then, would cover his garden with asphalt, strip mine a wooded mountain, or level an irreplaceable redwood grove? Two sorts of answers, though initially appealing, must be ruled out. The first is that persons who would destroy the environment in these ways are either shortsighted, underestimating the harm they do, or else are too little concerned for the well-being of other people. Perhaps too they have insufficient regard for animal life. But these considerations have been set aside in order to refine the controversy. Another tempting response might be that we count it a moral virtue, or at least a human ideal, to love nature. Those who value the environment only for its utility must not really love nature and so in this way fall short of an ideal. But such an answer is hardly satisfying in the present context, for what is at issue is *why* we feel moral discomfort at the activities of those who admittedly value nature only for its utility. That it is ideal to care for nonsentient nature beyond its possible use is really just another way of expressing the general point which is under controversy.

What is needed is some way of showing that this ideal is connected with other virtues, or human excellences, not in question. To do so is difficult and my suggestions, accordingly, will be tentative and subject to qualification. The main idea is that, though indifference to nonsentient nature does not *necessarily* reflect the absence of virtues, it often signals the absence of certain traits which we want to encourage because they are, in most cases, a natural basis for the development of certain virtues. It is often thought, for example, that those who would destroy the natural environment must lack a proper appreciation of their place in the natural order, and so must either be ignorant or have too little humility. Though I would argue that this is not necessarily so, I suggest that, given certain plausible empirical assumptions, their attitude may well be rooted in ignorance, a narrow perspective, inability to see things as important apart from themselves and the limited groups they associate with, or reluctance to accept themselves as natural beings. Overcoming these deficiencies will not guarantee a proper moral humility, but for most of us it is probably an important psychological preliminary. Later I suggest, more briefly, that indifference to nonsentient nature typically reveals absence of either aesthetic sensibility or a disposition to cherish what has enriched one's life and that these, though not themselves moral virtues, are a natural basis for appreciation of the good in others and gratitude.[7]

---

[7]The issues I raise here, though perhaps not the details of my remarks, are in line with Aristotle's view of moral philosophy, a view revitalized recently by Philippa Foot's

Consider first the suggestion that destroyers of the environment lack an appreciation of their place in the universe.[8] Their attention, it seems, must be focused on parochial matters, on what is, relatively speaking, close in space and time. They seem not to understand that we are a speck on the cosmic scene, a brief stage in the evolutionary process, only one among millions of species on Earth, and an episode in the course of human history. Of course, they know that there are stars, fossils, insects, and ancient ruins; but do they have any idea of the complexity of the processes that led to the natural world as we find it? Are they aware how much the forces at work within their own bodies are like those which govern all living things and even how much they have in common with inanimate bodies? Admittedly scientific knowledge is limited and no one can master it all; but could one who had a broad and deep understanding of his place in nature really be indifferent to the destruction of the natural environment?

This first suggestion, however, may well provoke a protest from a sophisticated anti-environmentalist.[9] "Perhaps *some* may be indifferent to nature from ignorance," the critic may object, "but *I* have studied astronomy, geology, biology, and biochemistry, and I still unashamedly regard the nonsentient environment as simply a resource for our use. It should not be wasted, of course, but what should be preserved is decidable by weighing longterm costs and benefits." "Besides," our critic may continue, "as philosophers you

---

*Virtue and Vice* (Berkeley: University of California Press, 1979), Alasdair McIntyre's *After Virtue* (Notre Dame: Notre Dame Press, 1981), and James Wallace's *Virtues and Vices* (Ithaca and London: Cornell University Press, 1978), and other works. For other reflections on relationships between character and natural environments, see John Rodman, "The Liberation of Nature," *Inquiry* (1976):83–131 and L. Reinhardt, "Some Gaps in Moral Space: Reflections on Forests and Feelings," in Mannison, McRobbie, and Routley, eds., *Environmental Philosophy* (Canberra: Australian National University Research School of Social Sciences, 1980).

[8]Though for simplicity I focus upon those who do strip mining, etc., the argument is also applicable to those whose utilitarian calculations lead them to preserve the redwoods, mountains, etc., but who care for only sentient nature for its own sake. Similarly the phrase "indifferent to nature" is meant to encompass those who are indifferent *except* when considering its benefits to people and animals.

[9]For convenience I use the labels *environmentalist* and *anti-environmentalist* (or *critic*) for the opposing sides in the rather special controversy I have raised. Thus, for example, my "environmentalist" not only favors conserving the forests, etc., but finds something objectionable in wanting to destroy them even aside from the costs to human beings and animals. My "anti-environmentalist" is not simply one who wants to destroy the environment; he is a person who has no qualms about doing so independent of the adverse effects on human beings and animals.

should know the old Humean formula, 'You cannot derive an *ought* from an *is*.' All the facts of biology, biochemistry, etc., do not entail that I ought to love nature or want to preserve it. What one understands is one thing; what one values is something else. Just as nature lovers are not necessarily scientists, those indifferent to nature are not necessarily ignorant."

Although the environmentalist may concede the critic's logical point, he may well argue that, as a matter of fact, increased understanding of nature tends to heighten people's concern for its preservation. If so, despite the objection, the suspicion that the destroyers of the environment lack deep understanding of nature is not, in most cases, unwarranted, but the argument need not rest here.

The environmentalist might amplify his original idea as follows: "When I said that the destroyers of nature do not appreciate their place in the universe, I was not speaking of intellectual understanding alone, for, after all, a person can *know* a catalog of facts without ever putting them together and seeing vividly the whole picture which they form. To see oneself as just one part of nature is to look at oneself and the world from a certain perspective which is quite different from being able to recite detailed information from the natural sciences. What the destroyers of nature lack is this perspective, not particular information."

Again our critic may object, though only after making some concessions: "All right," he may say, "*some* who are indifferent to nature may lack the cosmic perspective of which you speak, but again there is no *necessary* connection between this failing, if it is one, and any particular evaluative attitude toward nature. In fact, different people respond quite differently when they move to a wider perspective. When *I* try to picture myself vividly as a brief, transitory episode in the course of nature, I simply get depressed. Far from inspiring me with a love of nature, the exercise makes me sad and hostile. You romantics think only of poets like Wordsworth and artists like Turner, but you should consider how differently Omar Khayyam responded when he took your wider perspective. His reaction, when looking at his life from a cosmic viewpoint, was 'Drink up, for tomorrow we die.' Others respond in an almost opposite manner with a joyless Stoic resignation, exemplified by the poet who pictures the wise man, at the height of personal triumph, being served a magnificent banquet, and then consummating his marriage to his beloved, all the while reminding himself, 'Even this shall pass away.' "[10] In sum, the critic may object, "Even if one should try to see oneself as one small transitory part of nature, doing so does not dictate any particular normative attitude. Some may come to love nature, but others are moved to live for the moment; some sink into sad resignation; others get depressed or angry. So indifference to nature is not necessarily a sign that a person fails to look at himself from the larger perspective."

The environmentalist might respond to this objection in several ways. He might, for example, argue that even though some people who see themselves as part of the natural order remain indifferent to nonsentient nature, this is not a common reaction. Typically, it may be argued, as we become more and more aware that we are parts of the larger whole we come to value the whole independently of its effect on ourselves. Thus, despite the possibilities the critic raises, indifference to nonsentient nature is still in most cases a sign that a person fails to see himself as part of the natural order.

If someone challenges the empirical assumption here, the environmentalist might develop the argument along a quite different line. The initial idea, he may remind us, was that those who would destroy the natural environment fail to *appreciate* their place in the natural order. "Appreciating one's place" is not simply an intellectual appreciation. It is also an attitude, reflecting what one values as well as what one knows. When we say, for example, that both the servile and the arrogant person fail to *appreciate* their place in a society of equals, we do not mean simply that they are ignorant of certain empirical facts, but rather that they have certain objectionable attitudes about their importance relative to other people. Similarly, to fail to appreciate one's place in nature is not merely to lack knowledge or breadth of perspective, but to take a certain attitude about what matters. A person who *understands* his place in nature but still views nonsentient nature merely as a resource takes the attitude that nothing is *important* but human beings and animals. Despite first appearances, he is not so much like the pre-Copernican astronomers who made the intellectual error of treating the Earth as the "center of the universe" when they made their calculations. He is more like the

---

[10] "Even this shall pass away," by Theodore Tildon, in *The Best Loved Poems of the American People*, ed. Hazel Felleman (Garden City, N.Y.: Doubleday & Co., 1936).

racist who, though well aware of other races, treats all races but his own as insignificant.

So construed, the argument appeals to the common idea that awareness of nature typically has, and should have, a humbling effect. The Alps, a storm at sea, the Grand Canyon, towering redwoods, and "the starry heavens above" move many a person to remark on the comparative insignificance of our daily concerns and even of our species, and this is generally taken to be a quite fitting response.[11] What seems to be missing, then, in those who understand nature but remain unmoved is a proper humility.[12] Absence of proper humility is not the same as selfishness or egoism, for one can be devoted to self-interest while still viewing one's own pleasures and projects as trivial and unimportant.[13] And one can have an exaggerated view of one's own importance while grandly sacrificing for those one views as inferior. Nor is the lack of humility identical with belief that one has power and influence, for a person can be quite puffed up about himself while believing that the foolish world will never acknowledge him. The humility we miss seems not so much a belief about one's relative effectiveness and recognition as an attitude which measures the importance of things independently of their relation to oneself or to some narrow group with which one identifies. A paradigm of a person who lacks humility is the self-important emperor who grants status to his family because it is *his*, to his subordinates because *he* appointed them, and to his country because *he* chooses to glorify it. Less extreme but still lacking proper humility is the elitist who counts events significant solely in proportion to how they affect his class. The suspicion about those who would destroy the environment, then, is that what they count important is too narrowly confined insofar as it encompasses only what affects beings who, like us, are capable of feeling.

This idea that proper humility requires recognition of the importance of nonsentient nature is similar to the thought of those who

---

[11]An exception, apparently, was Kant, who thought "the starry heavens" sublime and compared them with "the moral law within," but did not for all that see our species as comparatively insignificant.

[12]By "*proper* humility" I mean that sort and degree of humility that is a morally admirable character trait. How precisely to define this is, of course, a controversial matter; but the point for present purposes is just to set aside obsequiousness, false modesty, underestimation of one's abilities, and the like.

[13]I take this point from some of Philippa Foot's remarks.

charge meat eaters with "species-ism." In both cases it is felt that people too narrowly confine their concerns to the sorts of beings that are most like them. But, however intuitively appealing, the idea will surely arouse objections from our nonenvironmentalist critic. "Why," he will ask, "do you suppose that the sort of humility I *should* have requires me to acknowledge the importance of nonsentient nature aside from its utility? You cannot, by your own admission, argue that nonsentient nature *is* important, appealing to religious or intuitionist grounds. And simply to assert, without further argument, that an ideal humility requires us to view nonsentient nature as important for its own sake begs the question at issue. If proper humility is acknowledging the relative importance of things as one should, then to show that I must lack this you must first establish that one *should* acknowledge the importance of nonsentient nature."

Though some may wish to accept this challenge, there are other ways to pursue the connection between humility and response to nonsentient nature. For example, suppose we grant that proper humility requires only acknowledging a due status to sentient beings. We must admit, then, that it is logically possible for a person to be properly humble even though he viewed all nonsentient nature simply as a resource. But this logical possibility may be a psychological rarity. It may be that, given the sort of beings we are, we would never learn humility before persons without developing the general capacity to cherish, and regard important, many things for their own sakes. The major obstacle to humility before persons is self-importance, a tendency to measure the significance of everything by its relation to oneself and those with whom one identifies. The processes by which we overcome self-importance are doubtless many and complex, but it seems unlikely that they are exclusively concerned with how we relate to other people and animals. Learning humility requires learning to feel that something matters besides what will affect oneself and one's circle of associates. What leads a child to care about what happens to a lost hamster or a stray dog he will not see again is likely also to generate concern for a lost toy or a favorite tree where he used to live.[14] Learning to value things for their own sake, and to count

---

[14]The causal history of this concern may well depend upon the object (tree, toy) having given the child pleasure, but this does not mean that the object is then valued only for further pleasure it may bring.

what affects them important aside from their utility, is not the same as judging them to have some intuited objective property, but it is necessary to the development of humility and it seems likely to take place in experiences with nonsentient nature as well as with people and animals. If a person views all nonsentient nature merely as a resource, then it seems unlikely that he has developed the capacity needed to overcome self-importance.

## IV

This last argument, unfortunately, has its limits. It presupposes an empirical connection between experiencing nature and overcoming self-importance, and this may be challenged. Even if experiencing nature promotes humility before others, there may be other ways people can develop such humility in a world of concrete, glass, and plastic. If not, perhaps all that is needed is limited experience of nature in one's early, developing years; mature adults, having overcome youthful self-importance, may lie well enough in artificial surroundings. More importantly, the argument does not fully capture the spirit of the intuition that an ideal person stands humbly before nature. That idea is not simply that experiencing nature tends to foster proper humility before other people; it is, in part, that natural surroundings encourage and are appropriate to an ideal sense of oneself as part of the natural world. Standing alone in the forest, after months in the city, is not merely good as a means of curbing one's arrogance before others; it reinforces and fittingly expresses one's acceptance of oneself as a natural being.

Previously we considered only one aspect of proper humility, namely, a sense of one's relative importance with respect to other human beings. Another aspect, I think, is a kind of *self-acceptance*. This involves acknowledging, in more than a merely intellectual way, that we are the sort of creatures that we are. Whether one is self-accepting is not so much a matter of how one attributes *importance* comparatively to oneself, other people, animals, plants, and other things as it is a matter of understanding, facing squarely, and responding appropriately to who and what one is, e.g., one's powers and limits, one's affinities with other beings and differences from them, one's unalterable nature and one's freedom to change. Self-acceptance is not merely intellectual awareness, for one can be intellectually aware that one is growing old and will eventually die while nevertheless behaving in a thousand foolish ways that reflect a refusal to acknowledge these facts. On the other hand, self-acceptance is not passive resignation, for refusal to pursue what one truly wants within one's limits is a failure to accept the freedom and power one has. Particular behaviors, like dying one's gray hair and dressing like those twenty years younger, do not *necessarily* imply lack of self-acceptance, for there could be reasons for acting in these ways other than the wish to hide from oneself what one really is. One fails to accept oneself when the patterns of behavior and emotion are rooted in a desire to disown and deny features of oneself, to pretend to oneself that they are not there. This is not to say that a self-accepting person makes no value judgments about himself, that he likes all facts about himself, wants equally to develop and display them; he can, and should feel remorse for his past misdeeds and strive to change his current vices. The point is that he does not disown them, pretend that they do not exist or are facts about something other than himself. Such pretense is incompatible with proper humility because it is seeing oneself as better than one is.

Self-acceptance of this sort has long been considered a human excellence, under various names, but what has it to do with preserving nature? There is, I think, the following connection. As human beings we are part of nature, living, growing, declining, and dying by natural laws similar to those governing other living beings; despite our awesomely distinctive human powers, we share many of the needs, limits, and liabilities of animals and plants. These facts are neither good nor bad in themselves, aside from personal preference and varying conventional values. To say this is to utter a truism which few will deny, but to accept these facts, as facts about oneself, is not so easy—or so common. Much of what naturalists deplore about our increasingly artificial world reflects, and encourages, a denial of these facts, an unwillingness to avow them with equanimity.

Like the Victorian lady who refuses to look at her own nude body, some would like to create a world of less transitory stuff, reminding us only of our intellectual and social nature, never calling to mind our affinities with "lower" living creatures. The "denial of death," to which psychiatrists call attention,[15] reveals an attitude incompatible with the sort of self-acceptance which philosophers, from the

---

[15]See, for example, Ernest Becker, *The Denial of Death* (New York: Free Press, 1973).

ancients to Spinoza and on, have admired as a human excellence. My suggestion is not merely that experiencing nature causally promotes such self-acceptance, but also that those who fully accept themselves as part of the natural world lack the common drive to disassociate themselves from nature by replacing natural environments with artificial ones. A storm in the wilds helps us to appreciate our animal vulnerability, but, equally important, the reluctance to experience it may *reflect* an unwillingness to accept this aspect of ourselves. The person who is too ready to destroy the ancient redwoods may lack humility, not so much in the sense that he exaggerates his importance relative to others, but rather in the sense that he tries to avoid seeing himself as one among many natural creatures.

## V

My suggestion so far has been that, though indifference to nonsentient nature is not itself a moral vice, it is likely to reflect either ignorance, a self-importance, or a lack of self-acceptance which we must overcome to have proper humility. A similar idea might be developed connecting attitudes toward nonsentient nature with other human excellences. For example, one might argue that indifference to nature reveals a lack of either an aesthetic sense or some of the natural roots of gratitude.

When we see a hillside that has been gutted by strip miners or the garden replaced by asphalt, our first reaction is probably, "How ugly!" The scenes assault our aesthetic sensibilities. We suspect that no one with a keen sense of beauty could have left such a sight. Admittedly not everything in nature strikes us as beautiful, or even aesthetically interesting, and sometimes a natural scene is replaced with a more impressive architectural masterpiece. But this is not usually the situation in the problem cases which environmentalists are most concerned about. More often beauty is replaced with ugliness.

At this point our critic may well object that, even if he does lack a sense of beauty, this is no moral vice. His cost/benefit calculations take into account the pleasure others may derive from seeing the forests, etc., and so why should he be faulted?

Some might reply that, despite contrary philosophical traditions, aesthetics and morality are not so distinct as commonly supposed. Appreciation of beauty, they may argue, is a human excellence which morally ideal persons should try to develop. But, setting aside this controversial position, there still may be cause for moral concern about those who have no aesthetic response to nature. Even if aesthetic sensibility is not itself a moral virtue, many of the capacities of mind and heart which it presupposes may be ones which are also needed for an appreciation of other people. Consider, for example, curiosity, a mind open to novelty, the ability to look at things from unfamiliar perspectives, empathetic imagination, interest in details, variety, and order, and emotional freedom from the immediate and the practical. All these, and more, seem necessary to aesthetic sensibility, but they are also traits which a person needs to be fully sensitive to people of all sorts. The point is not that a moral person must be able to distinguish beautiful from ugly people; the point is rather that unresponsiveness to what is beautiful, awesome, dainty, dumpy, and otherwise aesthetically interesting in nature probably reflects a lack of the openness of mind and spirit necessary to appreciate the best in human beings.

The anti-environmentalist, however, may refuse to accept the charge that he lacks aesthetic sensibility. If he claims to appreciate seventeenth-century miniature portraits, but to abhor natural wildernesses, he will hardly be convincing. Tastes vary, but aesthetic sense is not *that* selective. He may, instead, insist that he *does* appreciate natural beauty. He spends his vacations, let us suppose, hiking in the Sierras, photographing wildflowers, and so on. He might press his argument as follows: "I enjoy natural beauty as much as anyone, but I fail to see what this has to do with preserving the environment independently of human enjoyment and use. Nonsentient nature is a resource, but one of its best uses is to give us pleasure. I take this into account when I calculate the costs and benefits of preserving a park, planting a garden, and so on. But the problem you raised explicitly set aside the desire to preserve nature as a means to enjoyment. I say, let us enjoy nature fully while we can, but if all sentient beings were to die tomorrow, we might as well blow up all plant life as well. A redwood grove that no one can use or enjoy is utterly worthless."

The attitude expressed here, I suspect, is not a common one, but it represents a philosophical challenge. The beginnings of a reply may be found in the following. When a person takes joy in something, it is a common (and perhaps natural) response to come to cherish it. To cherish something is not simply to be happy with it at the moment, but to care for it for its own sake. This is not to say that one necessarily sees it as having feelings and so wants it to feel good; nor does it imply that one judges the thing to have Moore's intrinsic value. One simply wants the thing to survive and (when appropriate) to thrive, and not simply for its utility. We see this attitude repeatedly regarding mementos. They are not simply valued as a means to remind us of happy occasions; they come to be valued for their own sake. Thus, if someone really took joy in the natural environment, but was prepared to blow it up as soon as sentient life ended, he would lack this common human tendency to cherish what enriches our lives. While this response is not itself a moral virtue, it may be a natural basis of the virtue we call "gratitude." People who have no tendency to cherish things that give them pleasure may be poorly disposed to respond gratefully to persons who are good to them. Again the connection is not one of logical necessity, but it may nevertheless be important. A nonreligious person unable to "thank" anyone for the beauties of nature may nevertheless feel "grateful" in a sense; and I suspect that the person who feels no such "gratitude" toward nature is unlikely to show proper gratitude toward people.

Suppose these conjectures prove to be true. One may wonder what is the point of considering them. Is it to disparage all those who view nature merely as a resource? To do so, it seems, would be unfair, for, even if this attitude typically stems from deficiencies which affect one's attitudes toward sentient beings, there may be exceptions and we have not shown that their view of nonsentient nature is itself blameworthy. But when we set aside questions of blame and inquire what sorts of human traits we want to encourage, our reflections become relevant in a more positive way. The point is not to insinuate that all anti-environmentalists are defective, but to see that those who value such traits as humility, gratitude, and sensitivity to others have reason to promote the love of nature.

## STUDY QUESTIONS

1. Hill is looking for moral reasons to be respectful of nature. Can

one reasonably maintain that nonsentient nature is, in no sense, something that one must "respect"?

2. Why, in Hill's view, are utilitarian considerations inadequate as grounds for an environmental ethic?

3. Discuss the attempts to ground environmental ethics in a religious belief or attitude. Discuss G. E. Moore's idea of "intrinsically valuable states of affairs."

4. What do you think of Hill's contention that treating nature as a mere resource is morally insensitive?

5. Kant maintained that animals and nonsentient beings are outside the moral domain. Nevertheless, he held that people should not be cruel to animals because of the effect on their own characters. Is Hill's position somewhat similar to Kant's?

**SUGGESTED READINGS**

Aristotle. *Nichomachean Ethics.*

Aquinas, Saint Thomas. *Treatise on the Virtues*, Translated and edited by John Oesterle. Englewood Cliffs, NJ: Prentice-Hall, 1966.

Cooper, John M. *Reason and the Human Good in Aristotle.* Cambridge, MA: Harvard University Press, 1975.

Dent, N. J. H. *The Moral Psychology of the Virtues.* Cambridge, England: Cambridge University Press, 1984.

Feinberg, Joel. *Moral Concepts.* Oxford University Press, 1969.

Fried, Charles. *Right and Wrong.* Cambridge, MA: Harvard University Press, 1978.

Geach, Peter. *The Virtues.* Cambridge, MA: Cambridge University Press, 1977.

Hauerwas, Stanley. *A Community of Character.* Notre Dame, IN: University of Notre Dame Press, 1981.

MacIntyre, Alasdair. *After Virtue.* Notre Dame, IN: University of Notre Dame Press, 1981.

Mayo, Bernard. *Ethics and the Moral Life.* New York: Saint Martin's Press, 1958.

Murdoch, Iris. *The Sovereignty of the Good.* New York: Schocken Books, 1971.

Pieper, Joseph. *The Four Cardinal Virtues.* Notre Dame, IN: University of Notre Dame Press, 1966.

Plato, *The Republic.*

Rescher, Nicholas. *Unselfishness.* Pittsburgh: University of Pittsburgh Press, 1975.

Slote, Michael. *Goods and Virtues.* Oxford University Press, 1983.

Von Wright, G. H. *The Varieties of Goodness.* London: Humanities' Press, 1963.

Wallace, J. D. *Virtues and Vices.* Ithaca, NY: Cornell University Press, 1978.

Warnock, G. J. *The Object of Morality.* Princeton, NJ: Princeton University Press, 1969.

# Chapter Four

# VICE

What is vice? The question has both Christian and pagan answers. The philosophers of antiquity, from Plato to Plutarch, saw vice as a defect that we may overcome by education and discipline, including self-discipline. Virtuous persons are free of vice; their lives are ordered and rational. Plutarch's analysis of vice and virtue is fairly representative of the views of most educated thinkers in the pre-Christian era. Base persons are not controlled by reason; they are prone to impulse, discontented, ridden with anxiety. Plutarch was influenced as much by the Stoic and Epicurean philosophers as he was by Plato and Aristotle. The popular connotations of the word "epicurean" distort the doctrine; the Epicureans were far more concerned with the problem of avoiding pain and frustration than with the pursuit of pleasure and satisfaction. For both Stoics and Epicureans, contentment and inner tranquility, not pleasure, is the essence of the good life. Conversely, a vice is a character defect that promotes inner tensions and chaos as well as outer deeds that are base or ignoble.

Why are some people so susceptible to vice? The pagans attribute vice to improper development. Aristotle and Plato, in somewhat different ways, stress the *learned* character of the virtues. Virtue is a product of an education that includes self-discipline as well as discipline by parents and teachers. Persons of vice, then, have failed to shape a better character for themselves and are responsible for what they are.

The great pagan philosophers thought of virtue as the disposition to do what is right and the developed disinclination to do what is wrong. The Christian philosophers did not disagree with this, but their conception of vice is more highly seasoned. For Augustine and Abelard, to do wrong is to *sin,* to rebel against God: The sinner defies God by transgressing His law. Augustine argues that the impulse to sin is not simply a drive to satisfy desires. As he sees it, sin needs no motive beyond the perverse desire to sin. The desire to do evil is an endowment of Adam and Eve, the original sinners: Since the Fall, man has loved sin for its own sake; sin is, as it were, its own reward. According to Augustine, the pagan view that humans are fully able to control vice and develop the virtues by education and self-discipline is unduly optimistic. He maintains that we cannot achieve salvation or happiness without God's grace.

The question of human perfectability is important whether or not one views it in theological terms. Is it altogether utopian to hope for a day when cruelty and gratuitous malice are things of the past? If Augustine is right, this change will take a miracle.

Sin construed as defiance and rebellion against the powers of good is a more dramatic affair than character defect due to improper education. Augustine and Abelard locate the moment of sin at the moment one consents to do wrong. The act itself is anticlimactic. If, for example, I decide to murder someone, then the moment I *intend* to do this is the moment of sin. Even if I subsequently fail to carry out my intention, my sin is already complete. Kant's deontological ethic of the good will ("nothing is absolutely good except the good will") is a later variant of the Christian doctrine that locates the moment of doing right or wrong in the consent rather than in the act itself.

We should note that Abelard's view of sin is somewhat more complimentary to humanity than Augustine's. Abelard does not emphasize perversity, stressing instead the natural pleasure we achieve by sinning. The inclination to sin is natural and not blameworthy, but we are obligated to resist temptation; in failing to resist we "consent" to wrong and sin. Thus Christian philosophers differ on the nature of vice: Are we vicious because we succumb to natural desire (Abelard), or are we somewhat diabolical (Augustine)?

Recognizing a strong tendency to evil in humans, the Christian philosophers consider persons who have base desires to be virtuous provided they do not "consent" to those desires. The pagan philosophers would have found this odd. Philippa Foot echoes their view (see her "Virtues and Vices" in Chapter 3) when she points out that we feel something is not quite right about the idea of a virtuous person beset by base desires and constantly overcoming them. Both viewpoints have strengths. Surely the pagans were not realistic in thinking of virtue as freedom from even the temptation to do wrong. And surely, as Abelard says, the very merit of doing what is right is due at least in part to the existence of a temptation to do what is wrong, a temptation we resist. If the temptation to vice is absent altogether, we are less praiseworthy for remaining virtuous. On the other hand, we do think of people as virtuous if they are not even tempted to do what is base. The two intuitions conflict, yet each is persuasive. This usually shows that more analysis is needed. The interested reader may wish to go back to Foot's article and proceed from there.

Modern philosophers tend to reject the Augustinian thesis that something in man is ineradicably corrupt. Kant and Butler do so explicitly. Butler argues that all vice is due to self-deception stemming from a false regard for oneself. He denies that anyone loves sin.

> Vice in general consists in having an unreasonable and too great regard for ourselves, in comparison of others. Robbery and murder is never from the love of injustice or cruelty, but to gratify some other passion, to gain some supposed advantage: and it is false selfishness alone, whether cool or passionate, which makes a man resolutely pursue that end, be it ever so much to the injury of another.

Kant, too, denies the existence of any impulse to evil that is not connected with a desire to satisfy oneself in some way. "We have . . . no direct inclination towards evil as evil, but only an indirect one." If Kant and Butler are right, the evil we do is always inadvertent: It is not what we are after.

Most traditional philosophers agree that we need a uniform account of vice and virtue. We have already seen that Augustine and Abelard find the common denominator of the vices in the consent to wrongdoing in defiance of God. Butler finds it in the element of self-deception that permits people to do what they want without admitting to themselves that an action is wrong and self-debasing. Kant, we saw, finds the unity of virtue in the will. The very first philosopher to propose a unified theory of the virtues and vices was Plato, who identified virtue with knowledge and vice with ignorance. Ever since then, philosophers have been hard at work trying to give meaningful substance to what seems right about these identifications.

Several of the selections represented here belong to the kind of writing called "phenomenological description." The philosopher takes a particular vice and carefully describes it and its effects on the person who possesses it. Pure phenomenological description is free of theory or the attempt to explain what is being described. In that respect, all of the selections fall short of being purely phenomenological. But some, such as Dante's "Hypocrites," Samuel Johnson's "On Self-Deception," and Theroux's "Revenge," are pretty nearly that. And Kant's description of jealousy, envy, and spite is very straightforward with many acute insights into these vices.

Though contemporary philosophers (and some novelists) are still in the business of praising virtue and condemning vice, the atmosphere in which this is done has changed. Nowadays writers on virtue will take pains to show that what they are praising really is a virtue and beneficial, or, if they are condemning a particular vice, will be at some pains to show that it really is a vice and harmful. For example, in "The Evil of Lying," Charles Fried argues that the liar is indeed a bad character. And Alexander Theroux seeks to persuade us that revenge harms the person who seeks it. And where the Christian philosopher confidently assumed that greed or promiscuity are vices, the contemporary philosopher is more hesitant.

# *Vice*

## PLUTARCH

### TRANSLATED BY FRANK COLE BABBITT

Plutarch (A.D. 46–120) was a Greek moralist and biographer. His *Lives* is a classic in the genre of short biography. Plutarch's philosophy was neo-Platonic and he was a sharp critic of Epicureanism.

Plutarch contrasts persons of virtue with persons of vice, claiming that the former can achieve equanimity even in poverty. He depicts the latter as ill and peevish, incapable of truly enjoying even the external things they covet. Plutarch points out that we cannot rid ourselves of vice the way we rid ourselves of bad company. Vicious persons must live in constant proximity to their unpleasant selves.

1. Clothes are supposed to make a man warm, not of course by warming him themselves in the sense of adding their warmth to him, because each garment by itself is cold, and for this reason very often persons who feel hot and feverish keep changing from one set of clothes to another; but the warmth which a man gives off from his own person the clothing, closely applied to the body, confines and enwraps, and does not allow it, when thus imprisoned in the body, to be dissipated again. Now the same condition existing in human affairs deceives most people, who think that, if they surround themselves with vast houses, and get together a mass of slaves and money, they shall live pleasantly. But a pleasant and happy life comes not

VICE Reprinted by permission of the publishers and the Loeb Classical Library from Plutarch's *Moralia*, trans. by Frank Cole Babbitt (Cambridge, MA: Harvard University Press, 1928, 1956, 1962).

from external things, but, on the contrary, man draws on his own character as a source from which to add the element of pleasure and joy to the things which surround him.

> Bright with a blazing fire a house looks far more cheerful,

and wealth is pleasanter, and repute and power more resplendent, if with them goes the gladness which springs from the heart; and so too men bear poverty, exile, and old age lightly and gently in proportion to the serenity and mildness of their character.

2. As perfumes make coarse and ragged garments fragrant, but the body of Anchises gave off a noisome exudation,

> Damping the linen robe adown his back,

so every occupation and manner of life, if attended by virtue, is untroubled and delightful, while, on the other hand, any admixture of vice renders those things which to others seem splendid, precious, and imposing, only troublesome, sickening, and unwelcome to their possessors.

> This man is happy deemed 'mid public throng,
> But when he opens his door he's thrice a wretch;
> His wife controls, commands, and always fights.

Yet it is not difficult for any man to get rid of a bad wife if he be a real man and not a slave; but against his own vice it is not possible to draw up a writing of divorcement and forthwith to be rid of troubles and to be at peace, having arranged to be by himself. No, his vice, a settled tenant of his very vitals always, both at night and by day,

> Burns, but without e'er a brand, and consigns to an eld all untimely.

For in travelling vice is a troublesome companion because of arrogance, at dinner an expensive companion owing to gluttony, and a distressing bedfellow, since by anxieties, cares and jealousies it drives out and destroys sleep. For what slumber there may be is a sleep and repose for the body only, but for the soul terrors, dreams, and agitations, because of superstition.

> When grief o'ertakes me as I close my eyes,
> I'm murdered by my dreams.

says one man. In such a state do envy, fear, temper, and licentiousness put a man. For by day vice, looking outside of itself and conforming

318

its attitude to others, is abashed and veils its emotions, and does not give itself up completely to its impulses, but oftentimes resists them and struggles against them; but in the hours of slumber, when it has escaped from opinion and law, and got away as far as possible from feeling fear or shame, it sets every desire stirring, and awakens its depravity and licentiousness. It "attempts incest," as Plato says, partakes of forbidden meats, abstains from nothing which it wishes to do, but revels in lawlessness so far as it can, with images and visions which end in no pleasure or accomplishment of desire, but have only the power to stir to fierce activity the emotional and morbid propensities.

3. Where, then, is the pleasure in vice, if in no part of it is to be found freedom from care and grief, or contentment or tranquillity or calm? For a well-balanced and healthy condition of the body gives room for engendering the pleasures of the flesh; but in the soul lasting joy and gladness cannot possibly be engendered, unless it provide itself first with cheerfulness, fearlessness, and courageousness as a basis to rest upon, or as a calm tranquillity that no billows disturb; otherwise, even though some hope or delectation lure us with a smile, anxiety suddenly breaks forth, like a hidden rock appearing in fair weather, and the soul is overwhelmed and confounded.

4. Heap up gold, amass silver, build stately promenades, fill your house with slaves and the city with your debtors; unless you lay level the emotions of your soul, put a stop to your insatiate desires, and quit yourself of fears and anxieties, you are but decanting wine for a man in a fever, offering honey to a bilious man, and preparing tidbits and dainties for sufferers from colic or dysentery, who cannot retain them or be strengthened by them, but are only brought nearer to death thereby. Does not your observation of sick persons teach you that they dislike and reject and decline the finest and costliest viands which their attendants offer and try to force upon them; and then later, when their whole condition has changed, and good breathing, wholesome blood, and normal temperature have returned to their bodies, they get up and have joy and satisfaction in eating plain bread with cheese and cress? It is such a condition that reason creates in the soul. You will be contented with your lot if you learn what the honourable and good is. You will be luxurious in poverty, and live like a king, and you will find no less satisfaction in the care-free life of a private citizen than in the life connected with high military or civic office. If you become a philosopher, you will live not unplea-

santly, but you will learn to subsist pleasantly anywhere and with any resources. Wealth will give your gladness for the good you will do to many, poverty for your freedom from many cares, repute for the honours you will enjoy, and obscurity for the certainty that you shall not be envied.

**STUDY QUESTIONS**

1. Plutarch seems to deny that vice contains any real pleasure or satisfaction. Do you agree?
2. Do you agree with his claim that persons given over to vice are "poor company" for everyone, including themselves?
3. Plutarch associates vice with a troubled nature, and virtue with a contented, serene nature. Are these correlations realistic?
4. Plutarch claims that the person of vice is subject to the ills of poverty, while the person of virtue transcends them. Does this claim have merit? In your opinion, what effect does economic circumstance have on a virtuous or a vicious nature?

# The Depths of Vice

### SAINT AUGUSTINE

TRANSLATED BY JOHN K. RYAN

A biographical sketch of Saint Augustine is found on page 159.

Augustine, writing about his sixteenth year, describes the time he and his friends stole some pears for which they had no use. He ponders the motive and concludes that the perverse desire to defy God's will, an expression of man's corrupted nature, was itself the motive. Augustine is now

THE DEPTHS OF VICE From *The Confessions of St. Augustine*. Translated by John K. Ryan. Copyright © 1960 by Doubleday and Company, Inc. Reprinted by permission of the publisher.

> disgusted with his past self, but confesses that he was
> once ready to sin whenever someone urged, "Let's go!
> Let's do it!"

I wish to bring back to mind my past foulness and the carnal corruptions of my soul. This is not because I love them, but that I may love you, my God. Out of love for your love I do this. In the bitterness of my remembrance, I tread again my most evil ways, so that you may grow sweet to me, O sweetness that never fails, O sweetness happy and enduring, which gathers me together again from that disordered state in which I lay in shattered pieces, wherein, turned away from you, the one, I spent myself upon the many. For in my youth, I burned to get my fill of hellish things. I dared to run wild in different darksome ways of love. My comeliness wasted away. I stank in your eyes, but I was pleasing to myself and I desired to be pleasing to the eyes of men. . . .

## The Stolen Fruit

Surely, Lord, your law punishes theft, as does that law written on the hearts of men, which not even iniquity itself blots out. What thief puts up with another thief with a calm mind? Not even a rich thief will pardon one who steals from him because of want. But I willed to commit theft, and I did so, not because I was driven to it by any need, unless it were by poverty of justice, and dislike of it, and by a glut of evildoing. For I stole a thing of which I had plenty of my own and of much better quality. Nor did I wish to enjoy that thing which I desired to gain by theft, but rather to enjoy the actual theft and the sin of theft.

In a garden nearby to our vineyard there was a pear tree, loaded with fruit that was desirable neither in appearance nor in taste. Late one night—to which hour, according to our pestilential custom, we had kept our street games—a group of very bad youngsters set out to shake down and rob this tree. We took great loads of fruit from it, not for our own eating, but rather to throw it to the pigs; even if we did eat a little of it, we did this to do what pleased us for the reason that it was forbidden. . . .

When there is discussion concerning a crime and why it was committed, it is usually held that there appeared possibility that the appetites would obtain some of these goods, which we have termed lower, or there was fear of losing them. These things are beautiful and fitting, but in comparison with the higher goods, which bring happiness, they are mean and base. A man commits murder: why did he do so? He coveted his victim's wife or his property; or he wanted to rob him to get money to live on; or he feared to be deprived of some such thing by the other; or he had been injured, and burned for revenge. Would anyone commit murder without reason and out of delight in murder itself? Who can believe such a thing? Of a certain senseless and utterly cruel man it was said that he was evil and cruel without reason. Nevertheless, a reason has been given, for he himself said, "I don't want to let my hand or will get out of practice through disuse." Why did he want that? Why so? It was to the end that after he had seized the city by the practice of crime, he would attain to honors, power, and wealth, and be free from fear of the law and from trouble due to lack of wealth or from a guilty conscience. Therefore, not even Catiline himself loved his crimes, but something else, for sake of which he committed them.

## The Anatomy of Evil

What was it that I, a wretch, loved in you, my act of theft, my deed of crime done by night, done in the sixteenth year of my age? You were not beautiful, for you were but an act of thievery. In truth, are you anything at all, that I may speak to you? The fruit we stole was beautiful, for it was your creation, O most beautiful of all beings, creator of all things, God the good, God the supreme good and my true good. Beautiful was the fruit, but it was not what my unhappy soul desired. I had an abundance of better pears, but those pears I gathered solely that I might steal. The fruit I gathered I threw away, devouring in it only iniquity, and that I rejoiced to enjoy. For if I put any of that fruit into my mouth, my sin was its seasoning. But now, O Lord my God, I seek out what was in that theft to give me delight, and lo, there is no loveliness in it. I do not say such loveliness as there is in justice and prudence, or in man's mind, and memory, and senses, and vigorous life, nor that with which the stars are beautiful and glorious in their courses, or the land and the sea filled with their living kinds, which by new births replace those that die, nor even that flawed and shadowy beauty found in the vices that deceive us.

For pride imitates loftiness of mind, while you are the one God, highest above all things. What does ambition seek, except honor and glory, while you alone are to be honored above all else and are glorious forever? The cruelty of the mighty desires to be feared: but who is to be feared except the one God, and from his power what can be seized and stolen away, and when, or where, or how, or by whom? The caresses of the wanton call for love; but there is naught more caressing than your charity, nor is anything to be loved more wholesomely than your truth, which is beautiful and bright above all things. Curiosity pretends to be a desire for knowledge, while you know all things in the highest degree. Ignorance itself and folly are cloaked over the names of simplicity and innocence, because nothing more simple than you can be found. What is more innocent than you, whereas to evil men their own works are hostile? Sloth seeks rest as it were, but what sure rest is there apart from the Lord? Luxury of life desires to be called plenty and abundance; you are the fullness and the unfailing plenty of incorruptible pleasure. Prodigality casts but the shadow of liberality, while you are the most affluent giver of all good things. Avarice desires to possess many things, and you possess all things. Envy contends for excellence: what is more excellent than you? Anger seeks vengeance: who takes vengeance with more justice than you? Fear shrinks back at sudden and unusual things threatening what it loves, and is on watch for its own safety. But for you what is unusual or what is sudden? Or who can separate you from what you love? Where, except with you, is there firm security? Sadness wastes away over things now lost in which desire once took delight. It did not want this to happen, whereas from you nothing can be taken away.

Thus the soul commits fornication when it is turned away from you and, apart from you, seeks such pure, clean things as it does not find except when it returns to you. In a perverse way, all men imitate you who put themselves far from you, and rise up in rebellion against you. Even by such imitation of you they prove that you are the creator of all nature, and that therefore there is no place where they can depart entirely from you.

What, therefore did I love in that theft of mine, in what manner did I perversely or viciously imitate my Lord? Did it please me to go against your law, at least by trickery, for I could not do so with might? Did it please me that as a captive I should imitate a deformed liberty, by doing with impunity things illicit bearing a shadowy likeness of your omnipotence? Behold, your servant flees from his Lord and follows after a shadow! O rottenness! O monstrous life and deepest death! Could a thing give pleasure which could not be done lawfully, and which was done for no other reason but because it was unlawful? . . .

## Evil Communications

What was my state of mind? Truly and clearly, it was most base, and woe was it to me who had it. Yet, what was it? Who understands his sins? It was like a thing of laughter, which reached down as it were into our hearts, that we were tricking those who did not know what we were doing and would most strenuously resent it. Why, then, did even the fact that I did not do it alone give me pleasure? Is it because no one can laugh readily when he is alone? No one indeed does laugh readily when alone. However, individual men, when alone and when no one else is about, are sometimes overcome by laughter if something very funny affects their senses or strikes their mind. But that deed I would not have done alone; alone I would never have done it.

Behold, the living record of my soul lies before you, my God. By myself I would not have committed that theft in which what pleased me was not what I stole but the fact that I stole. This would have pleased me not at all if I had done it alone; nor by myself would I have done it at all. O friendship too unfriendly! Unfathomable seducer of the mind, greed to do harm for fun and sport, desire for another's injury, arising not from desire for my own gain or for vengeance, but merely when someone says, "Let's go! Let's do it!" and it is shameful not to be shameless!

## A Soul in Waste

Who can untie this most twisted and intricate mass of knots? It is a filthy thing: I do not wish to think about it; I do not wish to look upon it. I desire you, O justice and innocence, beautiful and comely to all virtuous eyes, and I desire this unto a satiety that can never be satiated. With you there is true rest and life untroubled. He who enters into you enters into the joy of his Lord, and he shall have no fear, and he shall possess his soul most happily in him who is the supreme good. I fell away from you, my God, and I went astray, too far astray from you, the support of my youth, and I became to myself a land of want.

**STUDY QUESTIONS**

1.  Do you agree with Augustine that we often pursue vice for its own sake?
2.  Explain what Augustine means when he says that, "in a perverse way, all men imitate [God] who put themselves far from [Him], and rise up in rebellion against [Him]."
3.  Do you agree with Augustine's implicit claim that a crime such as theft is worse when committed for the thrill of it rather than for personal material gain?
4.  People sometimes say that evil will be greatly mitigated when human nature changes for the better. Do you believe that human beings have evolved morally? Can we reasonably expect that they may become significantly more moral than they now are? What would Augustine say?

# *Desire and Sin*

## PETER ABELARD

TRANSLATED BY R. MCCALLUM

Peter Abelard (1079–1142) was the foremost logician of his age and one of the greatest philosophers of the Middle Ages. He is best known, however, for his tragic love affair with Heloise. He wrote influential treatises on theology, metaphysics, logic, and ethics.

Abelard distinguishes moral defects from other "defects of the mind" such as poor memory or dullwittedness. Moral defects dispose us to bad actions; morally defective individuals have characters that lead them or allow them to do the evil they want to do. In actually sinning they consent to an evil impulse: Instead of resisting it, they

DESIRE AND SIN From *Abelard's Ethics*. Translated by R. McCallum. Reprinted by permission of the publisher, Basil Blackwell Publisher Limited.

325

will it and act on it. Abelard denies that the truly virtuous person is free of evil impulses. To be virtuous is precisely to have the capacity or disposition to control the evil impulses that even the good person possesses, by not consenting to act on those impulses. By emphasizing the active will to do right in the face of a natural desire to do wrong, Abelard is a forerunner of Kant.

## Prologue

In the study of morals we deal with the defects or qualities of the mind which dispose us to bad or good actions. Defects and qualities are not only mental, but also physical. There is bodily weakness; there is also the endurance which we call strength. There is sluggishness or speed; blindness or sight. When we now speak of defects, therefore, we pre-suppose defects of the mind, so as to distinguish them from the physical ones. The defects of the mind are opposed to the qualities; injustice to justice; cowardice to constancy; intemperance to temperance.

## Chapter I. The Defect of Mind Bearing upon Conduct

Certain defects or merits of mind have no connection with morals. They do not make human life a matter of praise or blame. Such are dull wits or quick insight; a good or a bad memory; ignorance or knowledge. Each of these features is found in good and bad alike. They have nothing to do with the system of morals, nor with making life base or honourable. To exclude these we safeguarded above the phrase "defects of mind" by adding "which dispose to bad actions," that is, those defects which incline the will to what least of all either should be done or should be left undone.

## Chapter II. How Does Sin Differ from a Disposition to Evil?

Defect of this mental kind is not the same thing as sin. Sin, too, is not the same as a bad action. For example, to be irascible, that is, prone or easily roused to the agitation of anger is a defect and moves the mind to unpleasantly impetuous and irrational action. This defect, however, is in the mind so that the mind is liable to wrath, even when it is not actually roused to it. Similarly, lameness, by reason of which a man is said to be lame, is in the man himself even when he does not walk and reveal his lameness. For the defect is there though action be lacking. So, also, nature or constitution renders many liable to luxury. Yet they do not sin because they are like this, but from this very fact they have the material of a struggle whereby they may, in the virtue of temperance, triumph over themselves and win the crown. As Solomon says: "Better a patient than a strong man; and the Lord of his soul than he that taketh a city." (Prov. xvi, 32.) For religion does not think it degrading to be beaten by man; but it is degrading to be beaten by one's lower self. The former defeat has been the fate of good men. But, in the latter, we fall below ourselves. The Apostle commends victory of this sort; "No one shall be crowned who has not truly striven." (2 Tim. ii, 5.) This striving, I repeat, means standing less against men than against myself, so that defects may not lure me into base consent. Though men cease to oppose us, our defects do not cease. The fight with them is the more dangerous because of its repetition. And as it is the more difficult, so victory is the more glorious. Men, however much they prevail over us, do not force baseness upon us, unless by their practice of vice they turn us also to it and overcome us through our own wretched consent. They may dominate our body; but while our mind is free, there is no danger to true freedom. We run no risk of base servitude. Subservience to vice, not to man, is degradation. It is the overlordship of defects and not physical serfdom which debases the soul.

## Chapter III. Definition of 'Defect' and of Sin

Defect, then, is that whereby we are disposed to sin. We are, that is, inclined to consent to what we ought not to do, or to leave undone what we ought to do. Consent of this kind we rightly call sin. Here is the reproach of the soul meriting damnation or being declared guilty by God. What is that consent but to despise God and to violate His laws? God cannot be set at enmity by injury, but by contempt. He is the highest power, and is not diminished by any injury, but He avenges contempt of Himself. Our sin, therefore, is contempt of the Creator. To sin is to despise the Creator; that is, not to do for Him what we believe we should do for Him, or, not to renounce what we think should be renounced on His behalf. We have defined sin negatively by saying that it means not doing or not renouncing what we ought to do or renounce. Clearly, then, we have shown that sin has no reality. It exists rather in *not being* than in *being*. Similarly we could define shadows by saying: The absence of light where light usually is.

Perhaps you object that sin is the desire or will to do an evil deed, and that this will or desire condemns us before God in the same way as the will to do a good deed justifies us. There is as much quality, you suggest, in the good will as there is sin in the evil will; and it is no less "in being" in the latter than in the former. By willing to do what we believe to be pleasing to God we please Him. Equally, by willing to do what we believe to be displeasing to God, we displease Him and seem either to violate or despise His nature.

But diligent attention will show that we must think far otherwise of this point. We frequently err, and from no evil will at all. Indeed, the evil will itself, when restrained, though it may not be quenched, procures the palm-wreath for those who resist it. It provides, not merely the materials for combat, but also the crown of glory. It should be spoken of rather as a certain inevitable weakness than as sin. Take, for example, the case of an innocent servant whose harsh master is moved with fury against him. He pursues the servant, drawing his sword with intent to kill him. For a while the servant flies and avoids death as best he can. At last, forced all unwillingly to it, he kills his master so as not to be killed by him. Let anyone say what sort of evil will there was in this deed. His will was only to flee from death and preserve his own life. Was this an evil will? You reply: "I do not think this was an evil will. But the will that he had to kill the master who was pursuing him was evil." Your answer would be admirable and acute if you could show that the servant really willed what you say that he did. But, as I insisted, he was unwillingly forced to his deed. He protracted his master's life as long as he could, knowing that danger also threatened his own life from such a crime. How, then was a deed done voluntarily by which he incurred danger to his own life? . . .

Sin, therefore, is sometimes committed without an evil will. Thus sin cannot be defined as "will." True, you will say, when we sin under constraint, but not when we sin willingly, for instance, when we will to do something which we know ought not to be done by us. There the evil will and sin seem to be the same thing. For example a man sees a woman; his concupiscence is aroused; his mind is enticed by fleshly lust and stirred to base desire. This wish, this lascivious longing, what else can it be, you say, than sin?

I reply: What if that wish may be bridled by the power of temperance? What if its nature is never to be entirely extinguished but to persist in struggle and not fully fail even in defeat? For where is the battle if the antagonist is away? Whence the great reward without grave endurance? When the fight is over nothing remains but to reap the reward. Here we strive in contest in order elsewhere to obtain as victors a crown. Now, for a contest, an opponent is needed who will resist, not one who simply submits. This opponent is our evil will over which we triumph when we subjugate it to the divine will. But we do not entirely destroy it. For we needs must ever expect to encounter our enemy. What achievement before God is it if we undergo nothing contrary to our own will, but merely practice what we please? Who will be grateful to us if in what we say we do for him we merely satisfy our own fancy?

You will say, what merit have we with God in acting willingly or unwillingly? Certainly none: I reply. He weighs the intention rather than the deed in his recompense. Nor does the deed, whether it proceed from a good or an evil will, add anything to the merit, as we shall show shortly. But when we set His will before our own so as to follow His and not ours, our merit with God is magnified, in accordance with that perfect word of Truth: "I came not to do mine own will, but the will of Him that sent me." (John vi, 38.) To this end He exhorts us: "If anyone comes to me, and does not hate father, and mother . . . yea his own soul also, he is not worthy of me." (Luke xiv, 26.) That is to say, "unless a man renounces his parents' influence and his own will and submits himself to my teaching, he is not worthy of me." Thus we are bidden to hate our father, not to destroy him. Similarly with our own will. We must not be led by it; at the same time, we are not asked to root it out altogether.

When the Scripture says: "Go not after your own desires" (Eccles. xviii, 30) . . . I think that it is plain that no natural physical delight can be set down as sin, nor can it be called guilt for men to delight in what, when it is done, must involve the feeling of delight.

For example, if anyone obliged a monk, bound in chains, to lie among women, and the monk by the softness of the couch and by contact with his fair flatterers is allured into delight, though not into consent, who shall presume to designate guilt the delight which is naturally awakened?

You may urge, with some thinkers, that the carnal pleasure, even in lawful intercourse, involves sin. Thus David says: "Behold in sin was I conceived." (Ps. 1, 7.) And the Apostle, when he had said: "Ye return to it again" (I Cor. vii, 5), adds nevertheless, "This I say by way of concession, not of command." (ibid., v, 6.) Yet authority rather than reason, seems to dictate the view that we should allow simple physical delight to be sin. For, assuredly, David was conceived not in fornication, but in matrimony: and concession, that is forgiveness, does not, as this standpoint avers, condone when there is no guilt to forgive. As for what David meant when he says that he had been conceived "in iniquity" or "in sin" and does not say "whose" sin, he referred to the general curse of original sin, wherein from the guilt of our first parents each is subject to damnation, as it is elsewhere stated: "None are pure of stain, not the infant a day old, if he has life on this earth." As the blessed Jerome reminds us and as manifest reason teaches, the soul of a young child is without sin. If, then, it is pure of sin, how is it also impure by sinful corruption? We must understand the infant's purity from sin in reference to its personal guilt. But its contact with sinful corruption, its "stain," is in reference to penalty owed by mankind because of Adam's sin. He who has not yet perceived by reason what he ought to do cannot be guilty of contempt of God. Yet he is not free from the contamination of the sin of his first parents, from which he contracts the penalty, though not the guilt, and bears in penalty what they committed in guilt. When, therefore, David says that he was conceived in iniquity or sin, he sees himself subject to the general sentence of damnation from the guilt of his racial parents, and he assigns the sins, not to his father and mother but to his first parents. . . .

We come, then, to this conclusion, that no one who sets out to assert that all fleshly desire is sin may say that the sin itself is increased by the doing of it. For this would mean extending the consent of the soul into the exercise of the action. In short, one would be stained not only by consent to baseness, but also by the mire of the deed, as if what happens externally in the body could possibly soil the soul. Sin is not, therefore, increased by the doing of an action: and nothing mars the soul except what is of its own nature, namely consent. This we affirmed was alone sin, preceding action in will, or subsequent to the performance of action. Although we wish for, or do, what is unseemly, we do not therefore sin. For such deeds not uncommonly occur without there being any sin. On the other hand, there may be consent without the external effects, as we have indicated. There was wish without consent in the case of the man who was attracted by a woman whom he caught sight of, or who was tempted by his neighbour's fruit, but who was not enticed into consent. There was evil consent without evil desire in the servant who unwillingly killed his master.

Certain acts which ought not to be done often are done, and without any sin, when, for instance, they are commited under force or ignorance. No one, I think, ignores this fact. A woman under constraint of violence, lies with another's husband. A man, taken by some trick, sleeps with one whom he supposed to be his wife, or kills a man, in the belief that he himself has the right to be both judge and executioner. Thus to desire the wife of another or actually lie with her is not sin. But to consent to that desire or to that action is sin. This consent to covetousness the law calls covetousness in saying: "Thou shalt not covet." (Deut. v, 21.) Yet that which we cannot avoid ought not to be forbidden, nor that wherein, as we said, we do not sin. But we should be cautioned about the consent to covetousness. So, too, the saying of the Lord must be understood: "Whosoever shall look upon a woman to desire her." (Matt. v, 28.) That is, whosoever shall so look upon her as a slip into consent to covetousness, "has already committed adultery with her in his heart" (Matt. v, 28), even though he may not have committed adultery in deed. He is guilty of sin, though there be no sequel to his intention. . . .

Blessed Augustine, in his careful view of this question, reduces every sin or command to terms of charity and covetousness, and not to works. "The law," he says, "inculcates nothing but charity, and forbids nothing but covetousness." The Apostle, also, asserts: "All the law is contained in one word: thou shalt love thy neighbour as thyself," (Rom. xiii, 8, 10), and again, "Love is the fulfilling of the law." (ibid.)

Whether you actually give alms to a needy person, or charity makes you ready to give, makes no difference to the merit of the deed. The will may be there when the opportunity is not. Nor does it rest entirely with you to deal with every case of need which you encounter. Actions which are right and actions which are far from right are done by good and bad men alike. The intention alone separates the two classes of men. . . .

Briefly to summarize the above argument: Four things were postulated which might be carefully distinguished from one another.

1. Imperfection of soul, making us liable to sin.
2. Sin itself, which we decided is consent to evil or contempt of God.
3. The will or desire of evil.
4. The evil deed.

To wish is not the same thing as to fulfil a wish. Equally, to sin is not the same as to carry out a sin. In the first case, we sin by consent of the soul: the second is a matter of the external effect of an action, namely, when we fulfil in deed that whereunto we have previously consented. When, therefore, temptation is said to proceed through three stages, suggestion, delight, consent, it must be understood that, like our first parents, we are frequently led along these three paths to the commission of sin. The devil's persuasion comes *first* promising from the taste of the forbidden fruit immortality. Delight follows. When the woman sees the beautiful tree, and perceives that the fruit is good, her appetite is whetted by the anticipated pleasure of tasting. This desire she ought to have repressed, so as to obey God's command. But in consenting to it, she was drawn *secondly* into sin. By penitence she should have put right this fault, and obtained pardon. Instead, she *thirdly* consummated the sin by the deed. Eve thus passed through the three stages to the commission of sin.

By the same avenues we also arrive not at sin, but at the action of sin, namely, the doing of an unseemly deed through the suggestion or prompting of something within us. If we already know that such a deed will be pleasant, our imagination is held by anticipatory delight and we are tempted thereby in thought. So long as we give consent to such delight, we sin. Lastly, we pass to the third stage, and actually commit the sin.

It is agreed by some thinkers that carnal suggestion, even though the person causing the suggestion be not present, should be included under sinful suggestion. For example, a man having seen a woman falls into a sensual desire for her. But it seems that this kind of suggestion should simply be called delight. This delight, and other delights of the like kind, arise naturally and, as we said above, they are not sinful. The Apostle calls them "human temptations." No temptation has taken you yet which was not common to men. God is faithful, and will not suffer you to be tempted above what you are able; but will, with the temptation make a way of escape, that you may be able to bear it. By temptation is meant, in general, any movement of the soul to do something unseemly, whether in wish or consent. We speak of human temptation without which it is hardly or never possible for human weakness to exist. Such are sexual desire, or the pleasures of the table. From these the Psalmist asks to be delivered when he says: "Deliver me from my wants, O Lord" (Ps. xxiv, 17); that is, from the temptations of natural and necessary appetites that they may not influence him into sinful consent. Or, he may mean: "When this life is over, grant me to be without those temptations of which life has been full."

When the Apostle says: "No temptation has taken you but what is human," his statement amounts to this: Even if the soul be stirred by that delight which is, as we said, human temptation, yet God would not lead the soul into that consent wherein sin consists. Someone may object: But by what power of our own are we able to resist those desires? We may reply: "God is faithful, who will not allow you to resist those desires?" We may reply: "God is faithful, who will not allow you to be tempted," as the Scripture says. In other words: We should rather trust him than rely upon ourselves. He promises help, and is true to his promises. He is faithful, so that we should have complete faith in him. Out of pity God diminishes the degree of human temptation, does not suffer us to be tempted above what we are able, in order that it may not drive us to sin at a pace we cannot endure, when, that is, we strive to resist it. Then, too, God turns the temptation to our advantage: for He trains us thereby so that the recurrence of temptation causes us less care, and we fear less the onset of a foe over whom we have already triumphed, and whom we know how to meet. . . .

**STUDY QUESTIONS**

1. Abelard maintains that persons who will to murder others but are externally prevented from carrying out their purpose have sinned as completely as those who actually murder. Do you agree? What are the implications of this for moral philosophy?

333

2. The moral report card has one grade for accomplishment and another for effort. Which grade counts more for Abelard? How does he argue for giving it more weight?
3. What does Abelard mean by "consent to baseness"? How does "consent" differ from "desire"? Can consent to baseness occur without base desire?
4. How does Abelard's Christian conception of vice differ from one that is not grounded in a religious doctrine? Is the difference significant?

# The Hypocrites

## DANTE ALIGHIERI

**TRANSLATED BY JOHN CIARDI**

Dante Alighieri (1265–1321) is the Floretine author of the *Divine Comedy,* which is regarded as one of the supreme literary works of all time. It recounts the poet's journey through Hell (the *Inferno*), Purgatory (the *Purgatorio*), and finally Heaven (the *Paradiso*), and describes the fate of human souls after death.

Dante intended the *Divine Comedy* as an allegory. In a letter to his patron he wrote, "[I]ts subject is: 'Man, as by good or ill deserts, in the exercise of his free choice, becomes liable to rewarding or punishing justice.'" The *Inferno* is also meant as an allegorical description of the state of sinners' souls while they are still alive. Thus, hypocrites, even while alive, may appear to be "all dazzle, golden and fair," but on the inside they are heavy, leaden, and tormented. For Dante, the internal effects of sin are as punishing as the torments of Hell.

THE HYPOCRITES From the *Inferno* by Dante Alighieri. Translated by John Ciardi. Copyright 1954, 1982 by John Ciardi. Reprinted by arrangement with the New American Library.

About us now in the depth of the pit we found
a painted people, weary and defeated.
Slowly, in pain, they paced it round and round.

All wore great cloaks cut to as ample a size
as those worn by the Benedictines of Cluny.[1]
The enormous hoods were drawn over their eyes.

The outside is all dazzle, golden and fair;
the inside, lead, so heavy that Frederick's capes,[2]
compared to these, would seem as light as air.

O weary mantle for eternity!
We turned to the left again along their course,
listening to their moans of misery,

but they moved so slowly down that barren strip,
tired by their burden, that our company
was changed at every movement of the hip.[3]

And walking thus, I said: "As we go on,
may it please you to look about among these people
for any whose name or history may be known."

And one who understood Tuscan cried to us there
as we hurried past: "I pray you check your speed,
you who run so fast through the sick air:

it may be I am one who will fit your case."
And at his words my Master turned and said:
"Wait now, then go with him at his own pace."

I waited there, and saw along that track
two souls who seemed in haste to be with me;
but the narrow way and their burden held them back.

---

[1] *the Benedictines of Cluny:* The habit of these monks was especially ample and elegant. St. Bernard once wrote ironically to a nephew who had entered this monastery: "If length of sleeves and amplitude of hood made for holiness, what could hold me back from following [your lead]."

[2] *Frederick's capes:* Frederick II executed persons found guilty of treason by fastening them into a sort of leaden shell. The doomed man was then placed in a cauldron over a fire and the lead was melted around him.

[3] *our company was changed, etc.:* Another tremendous Dantean figure. Sense: "They moved so slowly that at every step (movement of the hip) we found ourselves beside new sinners."

When they had reached me down that narrow way
  they stared at me in silence and amazement,
  then turned to one another. I heard one say:

"This one seems, by the motion of his throat,
  to be alive; and if they are dead, how is it
  they are allowed to shed the leaden coat?"

And then to me "O Tuscan, come so far
  to the college of the sorry hypocrites,
  do not disdain to tell us who you are."

And I: "I was born and raised a Florentine
  on the green and lovely banks of Arno's waters,
  I go with the body that was always mine.

But who are *you,* who sighing as you go
  distill in floods of tears that drown your cheeks?
  What punishment is this that glitters so?"

"These burnished robes are of thick lead," said one,
  "and are hung on us like counterweights, so heavy
  that we, their weary fulcrums, creak and groan.

Jovial Friars and Bolognese were we.[4]
  We were chosen jointly by your Florentines[5]
  to keep the peace, an office usually

held by a single man; near the Gardingo[6]
  one still may see the sort of peace we kept.
  I was called Catalono, he, Loderingo."

---

[4]*Jovial Friars:* A nickname given to the military monks of the order of the Glorious
Virgin Mary founded at Bologna in 1261. Their original aim was to serve as peace-
makers, enforcers of order, and protectors of the weak, but their observance of their
rules became so scandalously lax, and their management of worldly affairs so self-
seeking, that the order was disbanded by Papal decree.

[5]*We were chosen jointly . . . to keep the peace:* Catalano del Malavolti (c. 1210–1285), a
Guelph, and Loderingo degli Andolo (c. 1210–1293), a Ghibelline, were both Bolognese and, as brothers of the Jovial Friars, both had served as *podestà* (the chief officer
charged with keeping the peace) of many cities for varying terms. In 1266 they were
jointly appointed to the office of *podestà* of Florence on the theory that a bipartisan
administration by men of God would bring peace to the city. Their tenure of office
was marked by great violence, however; and they were forced to leave in a matter of
months. Modern scholarship has established the fact that they served as instruments
of Clement IV's policy in Florence, working at his orders to overthrow the Ghibellines
under the guise of an impartial administration.

I began: "O Friars, your evil . . ."—and then I saw
   a figure crucified upon the ground[7]
   by three great stakes, and I fell still in awe.

When he saw me there, he began to puff great sighs
   into his beard, convulsing all his body;
   and Friar Catalano, following my eyes,

said to me: "That one nailed across the road
   counselled the Pharisees that it was fitting
   one man be tortured for the public good.

Naked he lies fixed there, as you see,
   in the path of all who pass; there he must feel
   the weight of all through all eternity.

His father-in-law and the others of the Council[8]
   which was a seed of wrath to all the Jews,
   are similarly staked for the same evil."

Then I saw Virgil marvel for a while[9]
   over that soul so ignominiously
   stretched on the cross in Hell's eternal exile.

Then, turning, he asked the Friar: "If your law permit,
   can you tell us if somewhere along the right
   there is some gap in the stone wall of the pit

through which we two may climb to the next brink
   without the need of summoning the Black Angels
   and forcing them to raise us from this sink?"

He: "Nearer than you hope, there is a bridge
   that runs from the great circle of the scarp
   and crosses every ditch from ridge to ridge,

---

[6]*Gardingo:* The site of the palace of the Ghibelline family degli Uberti. In the riots resulting from the maladministration of the two Jovial Friars, the Ghibellines were forced out of the city and the Uberti palace was razed.

[7]*a figure crucifed upon the ground:* Caiaphas. His words were: "It is expedient that one man shall die for the people and that the whole nation perish not." (*John* xi, 50).

[8]*his father-in-law and the others:* Annas, father-in-law of Caiaphas, was the first before whom Jesus was led upon his arrest. (*John* xviii, 13). He had Jesus bound and delivered to Caiaphas.

[9]*I saw Virgil marvel:* Caiaphas had not been there on Virgil's first descent into Hell.

except that in this it is broken; but with care
    you can mount the ruins which lie along the slope
    and make a heap on the bottom." My Guide stood
                                          there

motionless for a while with a dark look.
    At last he said: "He lied about this business,
    who spears the sinners yonder with his hook."[10]

And the Friar: "Once at Bologna I heard the wise
    discussing the Devil's sins; among them I heard
    that he is a liar and the father of lies."

When the sinner had finished speaking, I saw the face
    of my sweet Master darken a bit with anger:[11]
    he set off at a great stride from that place,

and I turned from that weighted hypocrite
    to follow in the prints of his dear feet.

### STUDY QUESTIONS

1. Why is hypocrisy a vice?
2. What forms of hypocrisy are most damaging?
3. Do hypocrites deceive themselves as well as others?
4. Is Dante right about the psychological and spiritual effects of hypocrisy? Does hypocrisy weigh people down and make them "weary and defeated"?
5. Can a hypocrite be happy?

---

[10]*he lied . . . who spears the sinners yonder:* Malacoda.

[11]*darken a bit:* The original is *turbato un poco d'ira.* A bit of anger befits the righteous indignation of Human Reason, but immoderate anger would be out of character. One of the sublimities of Dante's writing is the way in which even the smallest details reinforce the great concepts.

# Self-deception

~~~

## SAMUEL JOHNSON

Samuel Johnson (1709–1784), immortalized by his famous biographer, Boswell, was one of the most prominent figures of eighteenth-century English intellectual
life. He wrote essays, novels, biographies, political tracts,
a dictionary, and poetry, all in a scintillating style.

Johnson examines the devices of self-deceivers. One device they use is to congratulate themselves on a single act
of generosity, thereby conferring on themselves the attribute "compassionate" or "generous," even though the
vast majority of their actions are mean and self-serving.
Or they may praise goodness verbally, and thereby deceive themselves into thinking they are good. Still another device is to appear virtuous by dwelling on the evils
of others. Self-deceivers will try to keep their distance
from people who truly know what they are like, preferring the company of those who won't expose them to
themselves. And they avoid "self-communion."

One sophism by which men persuade themselves that they have those
virtues which they really want, is formed by the substitution of single
acts for habits. A miser who once relieved a friend from the danger
of a prison, suffers his imagination to dwell for ever upon his own
heroick generosity; he yields his heart up to indignation at those who
are blind to merit, or insensible to misery, and who can please themselves with the enjoyment of that wealth, which they never permit
others to partake. From any censures of the world, or reproaches of

his conscience, he has an appeal to action and to knowledge; and though his whole life is a course of rapacity and avarice, he concludes himself to be tender and liberal, because he has once performed an act of liberality and tenderness.

As a glass which magnifies objects by the approach of one end to the eye, lessens them by the application of the other, so vices are extenuated by the inversion of that fallacy, by which virtues are augmented. Those faults which we cannot conceal from our own notice, are considered, however frequent, not as habitual corruptions, or settled practices, but as casual failures, and single lapses. A man who has, from year to year, set his country to sale, either for the gratification of his ambition or resentment, confesses that the heat of party now and then betrays the severest virtue to measures that cannot be seriously defended. He that spends his days and nights in riot and debauchery, owns that his passions oftentimes overpower his resolution. But each comforts himself that his faults are not without precedent, for the best and the wisest men have given way to the violence of sudden temptations.

There are men who always confound the praise of goodness with the practice, and who believe themselves mild and moderate, charitable and faithful, because they have exerted their eloquence in commendation of mildness, fidelity, and other virtues. This is an error almost universal among those that converse much with dependents, with such whose fear or interest disposes them to a seeming reverence for any declamation, however enthusiastick, and submission to any boast, however arrogant. Having none to recall their attention to their lives, they rate themselves by the goodness of their opinions, and forget how much more easily men may shew their virtue in their talk than in their actions.

The tribe is likewise very numerous of those who regulate their lives, not by the standard of religion, but the measure of other men's virtue; who lull their own remorse with the remembrance of crimes more atrocious than their own, and seem to believe that they are not bad while another can be found worse.

For escaping these and a thousand other deceits, many expedients have been proposed. Some have recommended the frequent consultation of a wise friend, admitted to intimacy, and encouraged to sincerity. But this appears a remedy by no means adapted to general use: for in order to secure the virtue of one, it presupposes more virtue in two than will generally be found. In the first, such a desire of rectitude and amendment, as may incline him to hear his own accusation from the mouth of him whom he esteems, and by whom, therefore, he will always hope that his faults are not discovered; and in the second such zeal and honesty, as will make him content for his friend's advantage to lose his kindness.

A long life may be passed without finding a friend in whose understanding and virtue we can equally confide, and whose opinion we can value at once for its justness and sincerity. A weak man, however honest, is not qualified to judge. A man of the world, however penetrating, is not fit to counsel. Friends are often chosen for similitude of manners, and therefore each palliates the other's failings, because they are his own. Friends are tender and unwilling to give pain, or they are interested, and fearful to offend.

These objections have inclined others to advise, that he who would know himself, should consult his enemies, remember the reproaches that are vented to his face, and listen for the censures that are uttered in private. For his great business is to know his faults, and those malignity will discover, and resentment will reveal. But this precept may be often frustrated; for it seldom happens that rivals or opponents are suffered to come near enough to know our conduct with so much exactness as that conscience should allow and reflect the accusation. The charge of an enemy is often totally false, and commonly so mingled with falsehood, that the mind takes advantage from the failure of one part to discredit the rest, and never suffers any disturbance afterward from such partial reports.

Yet it seems that enemies have been always found by experience the most faithful monitors; for adversity has ever been considered as the state in which a man most easily becomes acquainted with himself, and this effect it must produce by withdrawing flatterers, whose business it is to hide our weaknesses from us, or by giving loose to malice, and licence to reproach; or at least by cutting of those pleasures which called us away from meditation on our conduct, and repressing that pride which too easily persuades us, that we merit whatever we enjoy.

Part of these benefits it is in every man's power to procure himself, by assigning proper portions of his life to the examination of the rest, and by putting himself frequently in such a situation by retirement and abstraction, as may weaken the influence of external objects. By this practice he may obtain the solitude of adversity without its melancholy, its instructions without its censures, and its sensibility without its perturbations.

The necessity of setting the world at a distance from us, when we are to take a survey of ourselves, has sent many from high stations to the severities of a monastick life; and indeed, every man deeply engaged in business, if all regard to another state be not extinguished, must have the conviction, tho', perhaps, not the resolution of Valdesso, who, when he solicited Charles the Fifth to dismiss him, being asked, whether he retired upon disgust, answered that he laid down his commission, for no other reason but because "there ought to be some time for sober reflection between the life of a soldier and his death."

There are few conditions which do not entangle us with sublunary hopes and fears, from which it is necessary to be at intervals disencumbered, that we may place ourselves in his presence who views effects in their causes, and actions in their motives; that we may, as Chillingworth expresses it, consider things as if there were no other beings in the world but God and ourselves; or, to use language yet more awful, "may commune with our own hearts, and be still."

### STUDY QUESTIONS

1. Self-deceivers are sometimes virtuous. How, in Johnson's opinion, does this aid in self-deception?
2. What part does self-deception play in our choice of friends?
3. Why does Johnson say that we should consult not our friends but our enemies if we want to learn about ourselves? Do you think he is right?
4. What techniques of self-deception does Johnson mention? Can you think of others?

# Upon Self-deceit

## BISHOP BUTLER

Joseph Butler (1692–1752) was an English moral philosopher and theologian. In 1738, he was made a bishop of
the Church of England. Butler's *Fifteen Sermons*, from
which the present selection is taken, are still admired for
their style, acumen, and good sense.

Butler cites the example of King David to show how
easily even good persons can deceive themselves. King
David commited an injustice without condemning himself, but was morally outraged on hearing that someone
else had done a similar thing. Butler points out the difficulty of living by the ancient dictum "Know thyself."
Self-deception often works in the service of self-regard.
We want something and make ourselves believe we do
right in acquiring it when, in fact, we do wrong. Moreover, we retain a good opinion of ourselves by avoiding
the company of those who would condemn us. Self-deceit
is especially prevalent in the undefined areas of moral
behavior where moral duties are not *explicit*. There self-
deceivers can be ungenerous and spiteful, and still remain
within the letter of the law, comfortably at peace with
their conscience. Butler argues that self-deception is a
very grave moral defect because it enables us to do evil in
a self-righteous manner. Self-deception "undermines the
whole principle of good" and so is worse than open,
unhypocritical wickedness.

UPON SELF–DECEIT From *Fifteen Sermons upon Human Nature* by Joseph Butler (1726).

And Nathan said to David, Thou art the man. *2 Samuel 12.7*

These words are the application of Nathan's parable to David, upon occasion of his adultery with Bathsheba, and the murder of Uriah her husband. The parable, which is related in the most beautiful simplicity, is this: *There were two men in one city; the one rich, and the other poor. The rich man had exceeding many flocks and herds: but the poor man had nothing, save one little ewe lamb, which he had bought and nourished up: and it grew up together with him, and with his children: it did eat of his own meat, and drank of his own cup, and lay in his bosom, and was unto him as a daughter. And there came a traveller unto the rich man, and he spared to take of his own flock and of his own herd, to dress for the wayfaring man that was come unto him; but took the poor man's lamb, and dressed it for the man that was come to him. And David's anger was greatly kindled against the man; and he said to Nathan, As the Lord liveth, the man that hath done this thing shall surely die: and he shall restore the lamb fourfold, because he did this thing, and because he had not pity.* David passes sentence, not only that there should be a fourfold restitution made; but he proceeds to the rigour of justice, *the man that hath done this thing shall die:* and this judgment is pronounced with the utmost indignation against such an act of inhumanity; *As the Lord liveth, he shall surely die: and his anger was greatly kindled against the man.* And the Prophet answered, *Thou art the man.* He had been guilty of much greater inhumanity, with the utmost deliberation, thought, and contrivance. Near a year must have passed, between the time of the commission of his crimes, and the time of the Prophet's coming to him; and it does not appear from the story, that he had in all this while the least remorse or contrition.

## Nothing is more strange than our self-partiality.

There is not any thing, relating to men and characters, more surprising and unaccountable, than this partiality to themselves, which is observable in many; as there is nothing of more melancholy reflection, respecting morality, virtue, and religion. Hence it is that many men seem perfect strangers to their own characters. They think, and reason, and judge quite differently upon any matter relating to themselves, from what they do in cases of others where they are not interested. Hence it is one hears people exposing follies, which they themselves are eminent for; and talking with great severity against particular vices, which, if all the world be not mistaken, they themselves are notoriously guilty of. This self-ignorance and self-partiality may be in all different degrees. It is a lower degree of it which David himself refers to in these words, *Who can tell how oft he offendeth? O cleanse thou me from my secret faults.* This is the ground of that advice of Elihu to Job: *Surely it is meet to be said unto God,—That which I see not, teach thou me; if I have done iniquity, I will do no more.* And Solomon saw this thing in a very strong light, when he said, *He that trusteth his own heart is a fool.*

### Hence the 'Know thyself' of the ancients.

This likewise was the reason why that precept, *Know thyself,* was so frequently inculcated by the philosophers of old. For if it were not for that partial and fond regard to ourselves, it would certainly be no great difficulty to know our own character, what passes within, the bent and bias of our mind; much less would there be any difficulty in judging rightly of our own actions. But from this partiality it frequently comes to pass, that the observation of many men's being themselves last of all acquainted with what falls out in their own families, may be applied to a nearer home, to what passes within their own breasts.

### Usual temper: (a) absence of mistrust: (b) assumption that all is right: (c) disregard of precept, when against ourselves.

There is plainly, in the generality of mankind, an absence of doubt or distrust, in a very great measure, as to their moral character and behaviour; and likewise a disposition to take for granted, that all is right and well with them in these respects. The former is owing to their not reflecting, not exercising their judgment upon themselves; the latter, to self-love. I am not speaking of that extravagance, which is sometimes to be met with; instances of persons declaring in words at length, that they never were in the wrong, nor had ever any diffidence to the justness of their conduct, in their whole lives. No, these people are too far gone to have anything said to them. The thing before us is indeed of this kind, but in a lower degree, and confined to the moral character; somewhat of which we almost all of us have, without reflecting upon it. Now consider how long, and how grossly, a person of the best understanding might be imposed upon by one of whom he had not any suspicion, and in whom he placed an entire confidence; especially if there were friendship and real kindness in the case: surely this holds even stronger with respect to that self we are all so fond of. Hence arises in men a disregard of reproof and instruction, rules of conduct and moral discipline, which occasionally come in their way: a disregard, I say, of these; not in every respect, but in this single one, namely, as what may be of service to them in particular towards mending their own hearts and tempers, and making them better men. It never in earnest comes into their thoughts, whether such admonitions may not relate, and be of service to themselves; and this quite distinct from a positive persuasion to the contrary, a persuasion from reflection that they are innocent and blameless in those respects. Thus we may invert the observation which is somewhere made upon Brutus, that he never read, but in order to make himself a better man. It scarce comes into the thoughts of the generality of mankind, that this use is to be made of moral reflections which they meet with; that this use, I say, is to be made of them by themselves, for every body observes and wonders that it is not done by others.

## Also exclusive self-interest.

Further, there are instances of persons having so fixed and steady an eye upon their own interest, whatever they place it in, and the interest of those whom they consider as themselves, as in a manner to regard nothing else; their views are almost confined to this alone. Now we cannot be acquainted with, or in any propriety of speech be said to know any thing, but what we attend to. If therefore they attend only to one side, they really will not, cannot see or know what is to be alleged on the other. Though a man hath the best eyes in the world, he cannot see any way but that which he turns them. Thus these persons, without passing over the least, the most minute thing, which can possibly be urged in favour of themselves, shall overlook entirely the plainest and most obvious things on the other side.

## They inquire only to justify.

And whilst they are under the power of this temper, thought and consideration upon the matter before them has scarce any tendency to set them right: because they are engaged; and their deliberation concerning an action to be done, or reflection upon it afterwards, is not to see whether it be right, but to find out reasons to justify or palliate it; palliate it, not to others, but to themselves.

## With self-ignorance, perhaps, only in the favourite propensity.

In some there is to be observed a general ignorance of themselves, and wrong way of thinking and judging in every thing relating to themselves; their fortune, reputation, every thing in which self can come in: and this perhaps attended with the rightest judgment in all other matters. In others this partiality is not so general, has not taken hold of the whole man, but is confined to some particular favourite passion, interest, or pursuit; suppose ambition, covetousness, or any other. And these persons may probably judge and determine what is perfectly just and proper, even in things in which they themselves are concerned, if these things have no relation to their particular favourite passion or pursuit. Hence arises that amazing incongruity, and seeming inconsistency of character, from whence slight observers take it for granted, that the whole is hypocritical and false; not being able otherwise to reconcile the several parts: whereas in truth there is real honesty, so far as it goes. There is such a thing as men's being honest to such a degree, and in such respects, but no further. And this, as it is true, so it is absolutely necessary to be taken notice of, and allowed them; such general and undistinguishing censure of their whole character, as designing and false, being one main thing which confirms them in their self-deceit. They know that the whole censure is not true; and so take for granted that no part of it is.

## The judgment is perverted through the passions.

But to go on with the explanation of the thing itself: Vice in general consists in having an unreasonable and too great regard to ourselves, in comparison of others. Robbery and murder is never from the love of injustice or cruelty, but to gratify some other passion, to gain some supposed advantage: and it is false selfishness alone, whether cool or passionate, which makes a man resolutely pursue that end, be it ever so much to the injury of another. But whereas, in common and ordinary wickedness, this unreasonableness, this partiality and selfishness, relates only, or chiefly, to the temper and passions in the characters we are now considering, it reaches to the understanding, and influences the very judgment. And, besides that general want of

347

distrust and diffidence concerning our own character, there are, you see, two things, which may thus prejudice and darken the understanding itself: that overfondness for ourselves, which we are all so liable to; and also being under the power of any particular passion or appetite, or engaged in any particular pursuit. And these, especially the last of the two, may be in so great a degree, as to influence our judgment, even of other persons and their behavior. Thus a man, whose temper is former to ambition or covetousness, shall even approve of them sometimes in others. . . .

## Frequent difficulty of defining: enhanced by vice.

It is to be observed then, that as there are express determinate acts of wickedness, such as murder, adultery, theft: so, on the other hand, there are numberless cases in which the vice and wickedness cannot be exactly defined; but consists in a certain general temper and course of action, or in the neglect of some duty, suppose charity or any other, whose bounds and degrees are not fixed. This is the very province of self-deceit and self-partiality: here it governs without check or control. "For what commandment is there broken? Is there a transgression where there is no law? a vice which cannot be defined?"

Whoever will consider the whole commerce of human life, will see that a great part, perhaps the greatest part, of the intercourse amongst mankind, cannot be reduced to fixed determinate rules. Yet in these cases there is a right and a wrong: a merciful, a liberal, a kind and compassionate behaviour, which surely is our duty; and an unmerciful contracted spirit, an hard and oppressive course of behaviour, which is most certainly immoral and vicious. But who can define precisely, wherein that contracted spirit and hard usage of others consist, as murder and theft may be defined? There is not a word in our language, which expresses more detestable wickedness than *oppression:* yet the nature of this vice cannot be so exactly stated, nor the bounds of it so determinately marked, as that we shall be able to say in all instances, where rigid right and justice ends, and oppression begins. In these cases there is great latitude left, for every one to determine for, and consequently to deceive himself. It is chiefly in these cases that self-deceit comes in; as every one must see that there is much larger scope for it here, than in express, single, determinate acts of wickedness. . . .

**It is safer to be wicked in the ordinary way, than from this corruption lying at the root.**

Upon the whole it is manifest, that there is such a thing as this self-partiality and self-deceit: that in some persons it is to a degree which would be thought incredible, were not the instances before our eyes; of which the behaviour of David is perhaps the highest possible one, in a single particular case; for there is not the least appearance, that it reached his general character: that we are almost all of us influenced by it in some degree, and in some respects: that therefore every one ought to have an eye to and beware of it. And all that I have further to add upon this subject is, that either there is a difference between right and wrong, or there is not: religion is true, or it is not. If it be not, there is no reason for any concern about it: but if it be true, it requires real fairness of mind and honesty of heart. And, if people will be wicked, they had better of the two be so from the common vicious passions without such refinements, than from this deep and calm source of delusion; which undermines the whole principle of good; darkens that light, that *candle of the Lord within,* which is to direct our steps; and corrupts conscience, which is the guide of life.

**STUDY QUESTIONS**

1. What does Butler mean when he says that many people are strangers to their own character? How far is he right in believing that we succeed in deceiving ourselves? Is there not a part of us that knows the truth?
2. Do you agree that the injunction "Know thyself" should be a fundamental moral rule?
3. According to Butler, vice results from having an unreasonably high regard for ourselves in comparison with others. Do you think he is right?
4. What does Butler mean when he tells us that being wicked in "ordinary ways" is safer than being deeply self-deluded?
5. Why is self-deception most prevalent where the vice is undefined?

# *Jealousy, Envy, and Spite*

## IMMANUEL KANT

### TRANSLATED BY LOUIS ENFIELD

A biographical sketch of Immanuel Kant is found on page 86.

In this selection, excerpted from his lectures on ethics, Kant gives readers an account of the vices of jealousy, envy, spite, ingratitude, and malice. When we compare ourselves with others who are morally or materially better than us, we may become jealous of what they possess; then we may either attempt to depreciate that possession or try to emulate them by acquiring those same moral qualities or material objects. *Grudge* is the displeasure we feel when someone else has what we lack. Grudge becomes *envy* when we begrudge others their happiness. If we possess a good we do not need, but take pleasure in refusing to give it to someone who needs it, then we are *spiteful.* Another vice, *ingratitude,* has its origin in the resentment of another's superiority. In the extreme, ungrateful persons hate their benefactors. Kant calls the extremes of envy and ingratitude "devilish vices." A third devilish vice is *malice*—the gratuitous desire to see others fail. Malicious persons enjoy the misery of others. Kant denies that people are directly inclined to be "devilish." In this respect he differs from Augustine.

JEALOUSY, ENVY, AND SPITE From "Jealousy, Envy, and Grudge" from *Lectures on Ethics* by Immanuel Kant. Translated by Louis Enfield (Harper & Row, 1963). Reprinted by permission of Methuen and Company Ltd.

There are two methods by which men arrive at an opinion of their worth: by comparing themselves with the idea of perfection and by comparing themselves with others. The first of these methods is sound; the second is not, and it frequently even leads to a result diametrically opposed to the first. The Idea of perfection is a proper standard, and if we measure our worth by it, we find that we fall short of it and feel that we must exert ourselves to come nearer to it; but if we compare ourselves with others, much depends upon who those others are and how they are constituted, and we can easily believe ourselves to be of great worth if those with whom we set up comparison are rogues. Men love to compare themselves with others, for by that method they can always arrive at a result favourable to themselves. They choose as a rule the worst and not the best of the class with which they set up comparison; in this way their own excellence shines out. If they choose those of greater worth the result of the comparison is, of course, unfavourable to them.

When I compare myself with another who is better than I, there are but two ways by which I can bridge the gap between us. I can either do my best to attain to his perfections, or else I can seek to depreciate his good qualities. I either increase my own worth, or else I diminish his so that I can always regard myself as superior to him. It is easier to depreciate another than to emulate him, and men prefer the easier course. They adopt it, and this is the origin of jealousy. When a man compares himself with another and finds that the other has many more good points, he becomes jealous of each and every good point he discovers in the other, and tries to depreciate it so that his own good points may stand out. This kind of jealousy may be called grudging. The other species of the genus jealousy, which makes us try to add to our good points so as to compare well with another, may be called emulating jealousy. The jealousy of emulation is, as we have stated, more difficult than the jealousy of grudge and so is much the less frequent of the two.

Parents ought not, therefore, when teaching their children to be good, to urge them to model themselves on other children and try to emulate them, for by so doing they simply make them jealous. If I tell my son, "Look, how good and industrious John is," the result will be that my son will bear John a grudge. He will think to himself that, but for John, he himself would be the best, because there would be no comparison. By setting up John as a pattern for imitation I anger my son, make him feel a grudge against this so-called paragon,

351

and I instil jealousy in him. My son might, of course, try to emulate John, but not finding it easy, he will bear John ill-will. Besides, just as I can say to my son, "Look, how good John is," so can he reply: "Yes, he is better than I, but are there not many who are far worse? Why do you compare me with those who are better? Why not with those who are worse than I?" Goodness must, therefore, be commended to children in and for itself. Whether other children are better or worse has no bearing on the point. If the comparison were in the child's favour, he would lose all ground of impulse to improve his own conduct. To ask our children to model themselves on others is to adopt a faulty method of upbringing, and as time goes on the fault will strike its roots deep. It is jealousy that parents are training and presupposing in their children when they set other children before them as patterns. Otherwise, the children would be quite indifferent to the qualities of others. They will find it easier to belittle the good qualities of their patterns than to emulate them, so they will choose the easier path and learn to show a grudging disposition. It is true that jealousy is natural, but that is no excuse for cultivating it. It is only a motive, a reserve in case of need. While the maxims of reason are still undeveloped in us, the proper course is to use reason to keep it within bounds. For jealousy is only one of the many motives, such as ambition, which are implanted in us because we are designed for a life of activity. But so soon as reason is enthroned, we must cease to seek perfection in emulation of others and must covet it in and for itself. Motives must abdicate and let reason bear rule in their place.

Persons of the same station and occupation in life are particularly prone to be jealous of each other. Many business-men are jealous of each other; so are many scholars, particularly in the same line of scholarship; and women are liable to be jealous of each other regarding men.

Grudge is the displeasure we feel when another has an advantage; his advantage makes us feel unduly small and we grudge it him. But to grudge a man his share of happiness is envy. To be envious is to desire the failure and unhappiness of another not for the purpose of advancing our own success and happiness but because we might then ourselves be perfect and happy as we are. An envious man is not happy unless all around him are unhappy; his aim is to stand alone in the enjoyment of his happiness. Such is envy, and we shall learn below that it is satanic. Grudge, although it too should not be countenanced, is natural. Even a good-natured person may at times be grudging. Such a one may, for instance, begrudge those around him their jollity when he himself happens to be sorrowful; for it is hard to bear one's sorrow when all around are joyful. When I see everybody enjoying a good meal and I alone must content myself with inferior fare, it upsets me and I feel a grudge; but if we are all in the same boat I am content. We find the thought of death bearable, because we know that all must die; but if everybody were immortal and I alone had to die, I should feel aggrieved. It is not things themselves that affect us, but things in their relation to ourselves. We are grudging because others are happier than we. But when a goodnatured man feels happy and cheerful, he wishes that every one else in the world were as happy as he and shared his joy; he begrudges no one his happiness.

When a man would not grant to another even that for which he himself has no need, he is spiteful. Spite is a maliciousness of spirit which is not the same thing as envy. I may not feel inclined to give to another something which belongs to me, even though I myself have no use for it, but it does not follow that I grudge him his own possessions, that I want to be the only one who has anything and wish him to have nothing at all. There is a deal of grudge in human nature which could develop into envy but which is not itself envy. We feel pleasure in gossiping about the minor misadventures of other people; we are not averse, although we may express no pleasure thereat, to hearing of the fall of some rich man; we may enjoy in stormy weather, when comfortably seated in our warm, cosy parlour, speaking of those at sea, for it heightens our own feeling of comfort and happiness; there is grudge in all this, but it is not envy.

The three vices which are the essence of vileness and wickedness are ingratitude, envy, and malice. When these reach their full degree they are devilish.

Men are shamed by favours. If I receive a favour, I am placed under an obligation to the giver; he has a call upon me because I am indebted to him. We all blush to be obliged. Noble-minded men accordingly refuse to accept favours in order not to put themselves under an obligation. But this attitude predisposes the mind to ingratitude. If the man who adopts it is noble-minded, well and good; but if he be proud and selfish and has perchance received a favour, the feeling that he is beholden to his benefactor hurts his pride and, being selfish, he cannot accommodate himself to the idea that he owes his benefactor anything. He becomes defiant and ungrateful. His ingratitude

353

might even conceivably assume such dimensions that he cannot bear his benefactor and becomes his enemy. Such ingratitude is of the devil; it is out of all keeping with human nature. It is inhuman to hate and persecute one from whom we have reaped a benefit, and if such conduct were the rule it would cause untold harm. Men would then be afraid to do good to anyone lest they should receive evil in return for their good. They would become misanthropic.

The second devilish vice is envy. Envy is in the highest degree detestable. The envious man does not merely want to be happy; he wants to be the only happy person in the world; he is really contented only when he sees nothing but misery around him. Such an intolerable creature would gladly destroy every source of joy and happiness in the world.

Malice is the third kind of viciousness which is of the devil. It consists in taking a direct pleasure in the misfortunes of others. Men prone to this vice will seek, for instance, to make mischief between husband and wife, or between friends, and then enjoy the misery they have produced. In these matters we should make it a rule never to repeat to a person anything that we may have heard to his disadvantage from another, unless our silence would injure him. Otherwise we start an enmity and disturb his peace of mind, which our silence would have avoided, and in addition we break faith with our informant. The defence against such mischief-makers is upright conduct. Not by words but by our lives we should confute them. As Socrates said: We ought so to conduct ourselves that people will not credit anything spoken in disparagement of us.

These three vices—ingratitude (*ingratitudo qualificata*), envy, and malice—are devilish because they imply a direct inclination to evil. There are in man certain indirect tendencies to wickedness which are human and not unnatural. The miser wants everything for himself, but it is no satisfaction to him to see that his neighbour is destitute. The evilness of a vice may thus be either direct or indirect. In these three vices it is direct.

We may ask whether there is in the human mind an immediate inclination to wickedness, an inclination to the devilish vices. Heaven stands for the acme of happiness, hell for all that is bad, and the earth stands midway between these two extremes; and just as goodness which transcends anything which might be expected of a human being is spoken of as being angelic, so also do we speak of devilish

wickedness when the wickedness oversteps the limits of human nature and becomes inhuman. We may take it for granted that the
human mind has no immediate inclination to wickedness, but is only
indirectly wicked. Man cannot be so ungrateful that he simply must
hate his neighbour; he may be too proud to show his gratitude and
so avoid him, but he wishes him well. Again, our pleasure in the
misfortune of another is not direct. We may rejoice, for example, in
a man's misfortunes, because he was haughty, rich and selfish; for
man loves to preserve equality. We have thus no direct inclination
towards evil as evil, but only an indirect one. But how are we to
explain the fact that even young children have the spirit of mischief
strongly developed? For a joke, a boy will stick a pin in an unsuspecting playmate, but it is only for fun. He has no thought of the
pain the other must feel on all such occasions. In the same spirit he
will torture animals; twisting the cat's tail or the dog's. Such tendencies must be nipped in the bud, for it is easy to see where they
will lead. They are, in fact, something animal, something of the beast
of prey which is in us all, which we cannot overcome, and the source
of which we cannot explain. There certainly are in human nature
characteristics for which we can assign no reason. There are animals
too who steal anything that comes their way, though it is quite useless
to them; and it seems as if man had retained this animal tendency in
his nature.

Ingratitude calls for some further observations here. To help a man
in distress is charity; to help him in less urgent needs is benevolence;
to help him in the amenities of life is courtesy. We may be the recipi-
ents of a charity which has not cost the giver much and our gratitude
is commensurate with the degree of good-will which moved him to
the action. We are grateful not only for what we have received but
also for the good intention which prompted it, and the greater the
effort it has cost our benefactor, the greater our gratitude.

Gratitude may be either from duty or from inclination. If an act of
kindness does not greatly move us, but if we nevertheless feel that it
is right and proper that we should show gratitude, our gratitude is
merely prompted by a sense of duty. Our heart is not grateful, but
we have principles of gratitude. If however, our heart goes out to our
benefactor, we are grateful from inclination. There is a weakness of
the understanding which we often have cause to recognize. It consists
in taking the conditions of our understanding as conditions of the

355

thing understood. We can estimate force only in terms of the obstacles it overcomes. Similarly, we can only estimate the degree of goodwill in terms of the obstacles it has to surmount. In consequence we cannot comprehend the love and goodwill of a being for whom there are no obstacles. If God has been good to me, I am liable to think that after all it has cost God no trouble, and that gratitude to God would be mere fawning on my part. Such thoughts are not at all unnatural. It is easy to fear God, but not nearly so easy to love God from inclination because of our consciousness that God is a being whose goodness is unbounded but to whom it is no trouble to shower kindness upon us. This is not to say that such should be our mental attitude; merely that when we examine our hearts, we find that this is how we actually think. It also explains why to many races God appeared to be a jealous God, seeing that it cost Him nothing to be more bountiful with His goodness; it explains why many nations thought that their gods were sparing of their benefits and that they required propitiating with prayers and sacrifices. This is the attitude of man's heart; but when we call reason to our aid we see that God's goodness must be of a high order if He is to be good to a being so unworthy of His goodness. This solves our difficulty. The gratitude we owe to God is not gratitude from inclination, but from duty, for God is not a creature like ourselves, and can be no object of our inclinations.

We ought not to accept favours unless we are either forced to do so by dire necessity or have implicit confidence in our benefactor (for he ceases to be our friend and becomes our benefactor) that he will not regard it as placing us under an obligation to him. To accept favours indiscriminately and to be constantly seeking them is ignoble and the sign of a mean soul which does not mind placing itself under obligations. Unless we are driven by such dire necessity that it compels us to sacrifice our own worth, or unless we are convinced that our benefactor will not account it to us as a debt, we ought rather to suffer deprivation than accept favours, for a favour is a debt which can never be extinguished. For even if I repay my benefactor tenfold, I am still not even with him, because he has done me a kindness which he did not owe. He was the first in the field, and even if I return his gift tenfold I do so only as repayment. He will always be the one who was the first to show kindness and I can never be beforehand with him.

The man who bestows favours can do so either in order to make the recipient indebted to him or as an expression of his duty. If he makes the recipient feel a sense of indebtedness, he wounds his pride and diminishes his sense of gratitude. If he wishes to avoid this he must regard the favours he bestows as the discharge of a duty he owes to mankind, and he must not give the recipient the impression that it is a debt to be repaid. On the other hand, the recipient of the favour must still consider himself under an obligation to his benefactor and must be grateful to him. Under these conditions there can be benefactors and beneficiaries. A right-thinking man will not accept kindnesses, let alone favours. A grateful disposition is a touching thing and brings tears to our eyes on the stage, but a generous disposition is lovelier still. Ingratitude we detest to a surprising degree; even though we are not ourselves the victims of it, it angers us to such an extent that we feel inclined to intervene. But this is due to the fact that ingratitude decreases generosity.

Envy does not consist in wishing to be more happy than others—that is grudge—but in wishing to be the only one to be happy. It is this feeling which makes envy so evil. Why should not others be happy along with me? Envy shows itself also in relation to things which are scarce. Thus the Dutch, who as a nation are rather envious, once valued tulips at several hundreds of florins apiece. A rich merchant, who had one of the finest and rarest specimens, heard that another had a similar specimen. He thereupon bought it from him for 2,000 florins and trampled it underfoot, saying that he had no use for it, as he already possessed a specimen, and that he only wished that no one else should share that distinction with him. So it is also in the matter of happiness.

Malice is different. A malicious man is pleased when others suffer, he can laugh when others weep. An act which wilfully brings unhappiness is cruel; when it produces physical pain it is bloodthirsty. Inhumanity is all these together, just as humanity consists in sympathy and pity, since these differentiate man from the beasts. It is difficult to explain what gives rise to a cruel disposition. It may arise when a man considers another so evilly disposed that he hates him. A man who believes himself hated by another, hates him in return, although the former may have good reason to hate him. For if a man is hated because he is selfish and has other vices, and he knows that he is hated for these reasons, he hates those who hate him although

357

these latter do him no injustice. Thus kings who know that they are hated by their subjects become even more cruel. Equally, when a man has done a good deed to another, he knows that the other loves him, and so he loves him in return, knowing that he himself is loved. Just as love is reciprocated, so also is hate. We must for our own sakes guard against being hated by others lest we be affected by that hatred and reciprocate it. The hater is more disturbed by his hatred than is the hated.

### STUDY QUESTIONS

1. How does Kant distinguish spite from envy? Why is the extreme of envy "devilish"?
2. We sometimes say to a friend, "I envy you." Can we envy people without begrudging their happiness? How does Kant view this?
3. Why does Kant advise us to compare ourselves with the ideal of perfection? What vices are associated with comparing ourselves with others?
4. What are the three devilish vices and what is devilish about them? Does Kant believe that the devilish vices are natural? What is their origin in people?
5. What does Kant think is wrong about accepting favors? Do you think Kant demands too much of the average person? Is his doctrine too austere?

# *Revenge*

## ALEXANDER THEROUX

Alexander Theroux is a novelist. His most recent work is *Darconville's Cat* (1981).

Theroux describes the effects that desire for revenge has on those who seek it; it transfigures them, poisons their lives, and turns them into monsters. Persons who give themselves over to revenge consent to their own destruction. Theroux recommends foregiveness, the contrary of revenge.

I remember—forgive the paradox—an unmemorable girlfriend of mine who in leaving me for someone else left me as well with a previously unfelt and inadmissible emotion, it being for a moment impossible to face the truth, never mind tell it; but as surprise ebbed another urge flowed. My immediate thought was a simple and un-complicated one: I wanted to kill her.

Revenge, exactly what I felt, is forgiveness's other face. It is an emotion, discounting mercy, neat to the taste and born of a desperate need to rectify a wrong by inflicting harm in return for an injury, a slight, or an insult and to exact satisfaction for that which, at least in the sufferer's eye, blind and stupid fate (never, of course, without its specific agent) not only has allowed but in a way has cruelly fostered. The sole desire in retribution is to equalize: "I'll get even with you!" To revenge is, in fact, to avenge. Simply put, it seeks—it demands—justice.

A popular legend has it that the Italian composer Antonio Salieri, overshadowed by his rival Mozart's glory but, worse, nursing a deep wound at the cosmic inequality of things-as-distributed, at the first-night performance of *Don Giovanni,* alone of all the others, hissed and stormed out of the theater—and then when opportunity arose poisoned his enemy. Caesar was stabbed by senators, Socrates was murdered by judges, and Christ was slapped by lackeys. So envy is always involved in revenge, but that is only the beginning, for the overwhelming and monomaniacal conviction superseding it is the thought on the revenger's part that without his personal intervention, correcting happenstance, the galling want of fairness will forever prevail and the suddenly—and often reasonlessly—despised will go scot-free. It will be remembered that while Salieri toiled desperately over his own mediocre compositions, feeling ever unrewarded, Mozart's work reputedly came easy and fame followed. Salieri couldn't abide this. In *Mozart and Salieri* (1830), Pushkin gives us his complaint:

> Where, where is justice, when the sacred gift,
> When deathless genius comes not to reward
> Perfervid love and utter self-denial,
> And toils and strivings and beseeching prayers,
> But puts her halo round a lack-wit's skull,
> A frivolous idler's brow? . . . O Mozart, Mozart!

Revenge transfigures you. It boils and concocts into poisonous nourishment all the facts and fictions it compounds from the lives of its enemies, and fuels the delight it abhors, for your grief has found the one thing in this life that *causes* it. Alive, it is your plague, instigates against you, throttles all you are. The vigorous if irrational idea is that you alone of all others on earth are left to correct what otherwise must go forever uncorrected. And in spite of the fact that in the process you become a cauldron of pure pain—owned, in fact, by that which you would sell, and are diminished by ("The murderer," writes Nabokov, "is always the victim's inferior")—there is often a crazy comfort in the obsession with whatever must be vindicated by whomever must be abused or punished or killed.

Revenge, like hemorrhoids, seems to have been created to locate in one particular place one particular pain to absolve the body in all other places of all other pains.

Do we fear the Gorgon or simply create it to locate our fears? The retributive aspect of revenge, in any case, whether logical or not—to put things right—is nevertheless its primal scream, what indeed gives it its most commonly applied epithet: "sweet."

Revenge! Where hasn't this shadow reached? It is a poem by Tennyson, the name of Sir Richard Grenville's famous ship, and a tragedy by Edward Young. There is an Iranian drink so named. Fairy tales virtually have no other plot. It is as old as the first murder ("And Cain was very wroth and his countenance fell") and as recent as the summer of 1982, when the Israelis invaded Lebanon and announced that this was in retaliation for the shooting of a diplomat in London. It is the central theme of Elizabethan and Jacobean tragedy, animates every discussion of capital punishment, and is even implied in the Virginia state motto: *Sic semper tyrannis*—Booth, avenging the lost Civil War, shot Lincoln howling those very words. I'd suggest that along with love and war, with which themes, let us say, it has more than passing acquaintance, revenge is the single most informing element of great world literature. And George Orwell, in his essay "Why I Write" (1947), cites it as the first motive for many taking up the profession ("the desire . . . to get your own back on grownups who snubbed you in childhood, etc."). The revengeful personality— it is more often than not an intellectual's, of which Hamlet, a thinker, not a "rash and splenetic" type, is only one example—very often has the power, in fact, to give a significant penetrating quality to literary expression; one thinks of Juvenal on Roman decadence, Luther on papistical excesses, Milton on Charles I, and Hitler on the Treaty of Versailles. But for the pure, unadulterated masterpiece of contumely very little surpasses Alexander Pope's almost gibbering attack, in his "Epistle to Dr. Arbuthnot" (1735), on the effeminate Lord Hervey ("Sporus"), who had been collaborating with Lady Mary Wortley Montagu on scurrilities against him and so met with this response:

> Let Sporus tremble—"What? that Thing of silk,
> Sporus, that mere white Curd of Ass's milk?
> Satire or sense alas! Can Sporus feel?
> Who breaks a Butterfly upon a Wheel?"
> Yet let me flap this Bug with gilded wings,
> This painted Child of Dirt that stinks and stings . . .
> Whether in florid Impotence he speaks

And, as the Prompter breathes, the Puppet squeaks;
Or at the Ear of Eve, familiar Toad,
Half Froth, half Venom, spits himself abroad . . .

While black, there is something splendid, almost mythological, in such ramping revenge, the wicked ebullience, the *folie de grandeur* mounted to frame a prose so determined to collaborate with anger, disappointment, and fury. The beating heart of revenge is its excessiveness, and its excesses—the pathological lengths to which it will go—are astonishing. The misandrous Delia Bacon, part critic, part crank, spent her entire life trying to besmirch William Shakespeare. Rufus W. Griswolda, who secretly hated Poe but was made his literary executor by wheedling it out of Mrs. Clemm, maliciously proceeded upon Poe's death to blacken his reputation through hundreds of lies and falsifications. Revenge is a feral branch of hatred. The anticlerical historian of philosophy Will Durant (educated by the Jesuits) dismisses all of medieval philosophy in one sentence: "A baffling circuit from faith to reason and back to faith again."

There is something intriguing here worth another word. Another sort of pathos seems involved. There is a certain hopeless kind of revenge, never far from insanity, that insists on mounting itself against the abstract, the too vast, the uncircumscribable, a few examples of which might be Nietzsche's opposition to Christianity, Frederick Rolfe's position against the Anglicans, Hitler's vindictiveness toward the Jews. Otto Weininger, riding his hobbyhorse, wrote the dense neo-Kantian *Sex and Character* to prove women had no souls! Such mountainous fury can only consume, wear away, and rot the antagonist, but it is a type on intransigence, even if in a negative way, that in its uncompromising madness approaches genius. The person given over to revenge is never an ordinary man. The New York Yankees played so poorly in a doubleheader against Chicago on the night of August 3, 1982, dropping both games, that owner George Steinbrenner, rancid with fury, publicly declared as a humiliation to his team—"they weren't worth even watching"—that all 34,000 fans attending that night could attend another game free!

It is the lot of such people, if to be opposed, then also to be invigorated by opposition, beholding their enemies in an eternal vigil, like the lifeless cobra in whose eye the murderer's image is forever embedded, and they actually crave to hate that constant hallucination of face—whether smirking through the attack it signals or the absolution it seeks—which becomes, in fact, almost a badge of those enemies, for one attributes to them not that state of normal human happiness, shot through with the common moods of mankind, that should move us to entertain for them a feeling of kindly sympathy, but a species of arrogant delight that merely pours oil on the furnace of our rage. One thinks of Richard Nixon and the press, imagined leaks, the enemies list.

In its usual form, revenge is the change in behavior that is classic reaction—a response to a stimulus. For instance, Mr. Ahme Tariki, the radical Saudi Arabian founder of OPEC (currently living in exile), organized the oil-exporting states specifically to strike a blow at the United States, where, because of the treatment he received during six years' engineering study in Texas in the late 1950s—the "Jim Crow" years, when he was considered black and treated vilely—he became embittered for life. The not-to-be-disowned John Hinckley was shown in his trial for shooting President Reagan to be nursing a deep grudge against authority figures (his wealthy father, advised by a psychiatrist, had sent him packing with only $100), who in his confused mind seemed fully unimpressed with his young, impossibly high, certainly megalomaniacal ambitions to be a successful rock star and boyfriend of a famous movie star. And then Peter Sutcliffe, the "Yorkshire Ripper," was a pathetic and cowardly little boy who, bullied at school, grew to take up body-building and was soon snarling at the weak himself. He adored his mother, who, however, had an affair that desolated him, and within months of his marriage (he both hated and feared his wife, Sonia) he began attacking and killing women—prostitutes—who, queerly, were an essential part of both his despair and his marriage. There is something in the dark soul of the mass murderer—J. B. Troppmann, who did away with a woman and her five children, Henri Desiré Landru, the French Bluebeard, and Theodore Bundy come immediately to mind—that is never far from revenge, its weird little posture giving destruction added motive in early failure, grievous disappointment, remembered scorn.

The revenger is, by definition, a victim. He is solitary, often in exile, forgoing communion with the society he terrifies. "What dog," asks George Eliot in *Silas Marner,* "likes a figure bent under a heavy bag?" The world has done badly by him. A formula of rupture has taken place; suddenly his consciousness is heightened, for he has

spied (a word he'd favor) what he immediately can neither countenance nor forgive, and he fixes upon that one thing that the reduc-
tionist mind madly isolates as the only solution to the world's woes.
Every former excellence of his enemy becomes every conceivable
fault, every promise—expected, if not actually made—an imperves-
tigable lie, and every memory a viper eating through the bowels of
his benefits, all to set in motion such a fell and deadly hate that
through a sea of sins he'd wade to his revenge. Human feeling cur-
dles. Lenin, visiting Maxim Gorky, once demanded that he shut off
a phonograph playing Beethoven's "Appassionata" lest it weaken his
anticzarist resolve with feelings of sentiment. Oliver Cromwell sent
his soldiers back to Drogheda to slaughter the Irish children they
thought to spare, with the remark "Nits will be lice." There are many
passions that we are condemned to feel only in reduced form: never
revenge. With it you have come under the shadow. You would countenance black magic. And yet how little is achieved, though other
problems be solved! How *mistakenly* can a person have wanted what,
taken away, repudiates the meaning of life itself?

Revenge is a restless desire precisely for the *ideal*. The tormented
soul, hobbled by denial, by prohibition, sees himself betrayed and
so, paradoxically, tries to recover by an act of supreme alienation and
anger that which has been taken from him and which, constantly
fleering at and ridiculing him by the very nature of its existence,
mocks the mind to murder. "I want satisfaction!" cried the duelist in
his humiliation. And yet what most generates, most often animates,
revenge? Disappointed love, perfidy, dissolved friendship. And why
so? The revenger is a person, usually, who has expected eternal un-
flinching fidelity from family and from friendship, and often in a
quite ungainsayable way, but having lost it—he literally suffers a
reverse—then employs the most effective and rigorous means of
correction and so goes through life fixed on delirious hope in order
to pledge allegiance to an inverted form of the same ideal. "Oh,"
cries Ahab, "now I feel my topmost greatness lies in my topmost
grief."

The smoldering aspect of revenge is often in direct proportion to
the degree in which the person's right to exist as a human being has
been taken away. In his illness—he is literally infected—he has been
handed, so to speak, a writ of non exeat. He must be cured. The cure
is freedom. Whoever will set the revenger free—and the cry for
release is the sine qua non of his gnawing vindictiveness—can be the

only one, in fact, able to do so, and so ironically remains, as the singular agent of deliverance, also the sole abettor of his own destruction. It is a marriage, pledged until death do them part. A man in the grip of revenge has not so much lost the ideal as he has transferred the whole concept of one ideal to the furthest extreme of another, and challenging in the process the necessity of injustice that exists—often as the emanation of a punitive or arbitrary God—he writes in his own bitter soul not just a complaint but an entire destructive theology.

Revenge, indeed, has curiously theological implications. The law of talion—an eye for an eye, a tooth for a tooth—cries out to its cognate, "Retaliate!" Blood revenge is actually sanctioned in the Old Testament, the returning of evil for evil, blood for blood, a "justifying"—in the printer's phrase—of an unbalanced line. In Melville's *Moby Dick*, the rankling Captain Ahab, named after the Old Testament ruler who "did more to provoke the Lord God of Israel to anger than all the Kings of Israel that were before him," becomes the embodiment of revenge itself. He has been wounded ("unmanned") by the whale, inexplicably, and the dismemberment has driven him to such a pitch of anguish—homicidal, suicidal, and deicidal, all at once—that in maniacal pursuit of his nemesis ("the incarnation of all those malicious agencies which some deep men feel eating in them . . .") he has to be confined at times to a straitjacket in which, mad, he "swung to the rockings of the gales."

Ahab's intellect is enslaved but yet also concentrated by his madness, and, as happens in the matter of revenge, he has lost his humanity in the very act of vindicating it—the essential paradox of revenge—and has become the very image of the thing he hates, a statue of penalty cast in a single mold, a fireman of punishment and egotism. "I'd strike the sun if it insulted me!" he shrieks. Every dilemma has two horns. For Ahab has made himself not just a proud, self-appointed judge like Prometheus, Faust, Manfred, and Lucifer but also, like them, revenge's plaintiff, a tragic scapegoat. He is both victim and executioner—revenge always involves both—who in his compulsion for seeking equality has also elected to accept vengeance as the sole law of existence (the opposite was his intention), and so transmogrifies virtue into vice.

The greater the punishment each revenger feels merited by his action, the greater the value the agent of revenge attributes to the burden of his having to do so. Each constructs his revenge more or

365

less according to the only logic available to him in a world that, however, illogically presents itself, for since he is forced to accept the fact that a positive, lost, is evil, the alternative of a negative, found, must perforce be the only good at hand to address it—and so the breach actually becomes the observance in a desperate attempt to settle a matter of contradiction by means of conflicting evidence. There is no better poacher than an ex-gamekeeper. We have here inversion, a topsyturvification of moral values that in revenge becomes its canon law. The condition is found in, among others, the autobiographer as avenger, the rejected lover, the disaffiliated child who grows up to settle the score.

Shakespeare's *Hamlet*, which takes its cue from Kyd's *The Spanish Tragedy* (1587), the father of all revenge plays, simply cannot be understood except in its theological context. It is, characteristically, not just the case of an eye for an eye, for the jaw must be taken, along with the tongue and ears—and the victim must, after exquisite torments of both body and mind, go straight to hell. Revenge, to the Elizabethans and Jacobeans, demanded hellfire and everlasting torment.

Excess is all. Extremism in the pursuit of justice—the revenger's conundrum—is no vice. And it's to be taken as a matter of breviary, this supernatural backdrop before which revenge is enacted—heaven, hell, and purgatory—that only with so much at stake can this terrible emotion be comprehended or, in fact, taken to have in it something akin to the slow grinding of the mills of divine vengeance—slow, yes, for often extreme patience is required.

Revenge is not always blister upon heat. It loiters, it bides its time, it grows. It perhaps alone gives full *meaning* to the full measure of the injury suffered. Months, years, decades may wear away, but not the corrosive and intolerable recollection of an injustice burning a hole in your sleep, if ever sleep there is. The nightmare that prevents, however, eventually *corrects* sleep. The wheel of fortune turns. It is the gift opportunity hands to adversity, a reward crowning pursuit and throwing up the exact set of circumstances that only time can give when, for the victim, it is most inopportune—he has moved away, say, remarried, grown older, changed his name, and, perhaps best of all, *forgotten*—but when, for the executioner, irony is made iron in the delirious turnabout that literally defines serendipity and without which, it may be argued, revenge can never be sufficiently *raffiné.* The revenger is a sinner with patience, a saint without forbearance, a master of what Borges calls the art of the *cachada* (to grab, to take somebody unawares). Delay is in fact only a kind of subtlety. The infernal deity Nemesis, goddess of vengeance—her statue in Rome was in the Capitol—is the daughter of Nox, and under the carapace of night one waits, waits, until all is ready. Revenge a hundred years old still has milk teeth.

Edmond Dantès, left to rot for fourteen years as a prisoner in the gloomy Château d'If in Dumas's *The Count of Monte Cristo,* finally escapes ("Enough of this prison, let me now seek the antidote . . .") masterfully—and premeditatively—to wreak vengeance on each of his persecutors. "They'll remember my carbuncles," said Karl Marx from obscurity, writing *Das Kapital* in ill health, poverty, and the exile forced on him, as on others, by a corrupt economic system.

This is what's called "revenge in lavender"—revenge reserved—hanging fire, truly, as the years lope over the hill. But the cancer has metastasized. And that's just when the fun begins. "I'm back!" cries the revenger, demanding remembrance. "Look at me! Pay attention!" I read in the papers a few years ago of a man whose son had been hazed to death during an initiation by several fraternity boys, and the aggrieved father chose to take his revenge only after ten long years had passed when, *pro re nata,* he methodically hunted down each of their sons and killed them in kind. "Thus," says Shakespeare in *Twelfth Night,* "the whirligig of time brings in his revenges." Revenge, as the proverb says, is a dish best served up cold.

There is finally—and importantly—a penalty in revenge that can never be disregarded, the calm willingness to slay the self in the attempt to free it by those who, in daring personally to mete out justice, even if as only they see it, must also take the medicine they dispense. There was, for example, an uprising in the Sixties on Pulau Senang Prison Island, off the coast of Singapore. The prisoners could have fled. But they lingered to mutilate their guards—they castrated them, put out their eyes, etc.—and because the revenge was such time-consuming cruelty they were quickly caught and hanged, sixty-six of them, six at a time, on the Singapore gallows.

It is a sensibility, the revenger's, that, if open to the asperity of insult and keen to redress it, is also one equally arranged to feel all the while the criminal denial of true justice his very act contravenes. The tragedy is that he can't do otherwise. Forgiveness to him is the absence of justice, and so he "commits" justice, so to speak, in order to abolish crime—even as he perpetuates it. The crime is the punishment. It's as if he reasons: I am pleased with defeat in what I do because secretly for what I do I know I am guilty and only punishment can redeem me. Revenge has something about it oddly propitiative, an act often spitefully but inexorably united to contrition. Let heaven exist, he seems to say, even though my dwelling place is hell.

Of penalties there are many. There's often an unconscious wish for revenge in alcoholism, an indirect aggression born of anger and resentment against either oneself or others, and the same might be said of impotence and frigidity—a disposition, often, involving a subconscious impulse to thwart—and I have no doubt that this might also apply to failure in school or gluttony or bedwetting.

There's suicide. The Chinese and Chuvashes often hanged themselves on the doors of their enemies. In Hugo's *Les Misérables,* the crafty, inexorable, and ubiquitous Inspector Javert dogs Jean Valjean for forty years (for stealing a loaf of bread to feed his sister's starving children) and then, robbed of his chance for retribution, commits suicide. His absolute fixation on revenge—*and in the name of law*—alone has given meaning to his sterile life. He has known only one emotion. Crazed with that detail, he cannot understand the whole. Or can he? Perversely, dreadfully, he comes to win *admiration* for the thief he's so long hated and pursued—a galley slave, a convict, who illogically, cruelly, returns pardon for hatred, good for evil! His nemesis in his forgiveness becomes his benefactor. An entire order of unexpected facts, fragmenting all certainty, arises to subjugate him, a moral sun rising only to blind him like an owl. All the axioms that had been the supports of his existence suddenly crumble:

> He saw before him two roads, both equally straight; but he saw two; and that terrified him—him who had never in his life known but one straight line. And, bitter anguish, these two roads were contradictory. One of these two straight lines excluded the other. Which of the two was the true one? His condition was inexpressible . . . what should he do? Give up Jean Valjean, that was wrong; leave Jean Valjean, that was wrong . . . what then! Such enormities should happen and nobody should be punished?

But someone must be punished. That is just the *point* of revenge, that which for so long has given to it the battle cry "Somebody's going to pay for this!"

But who? Compelled to recognize all of a sudden the existence of forgiveness, Javert can only conclude—a horror of himself almost as if he had lost his faith (which, in fact, he has)—that *he* has become depraved, and so what should he then do? Call for Pontius Pilate's basin and wash his claws? That is ontologically impossible for him, precisely what the revengeful man is unable to do, for, as we've seen, this emotion—"so durable and obstinate," according to La Bruyère, "that reconciliation on a sickbed is the greatest sign of death"—is fed by the law of balance, equality, and a mania for justice that, even if it turns on itself, must be satisfied. And so, like the pygmy rattlesnake that bites and poisons itself in the convulsions of its fury, the empty Javert—"getting even"—revenges himself on himself and plunges headlong in suicidal despair from a parapet into the murky Seine. This is not victory, but if it is not victory it is yet revenge, and that is perhaps its most terrifying side, that, meeting nothing else, it becomes an end in itself. Who fights with monsters may thereby become one. Let Ahab beware Ahab. It is always ourselves we must fear first.

**STUDY QUESTIONS**

1. Do you agree with Theroux that the vengeful person is always envious?
2. If Theroux is right, why is revenge said to be sweet?
3. In *The Brothers Karamazov,* Fyodor Dostoyevski describes how a nobleman punishes a child who has thrown a stone at the paw of one of the man's favorite hounds. The child is forced to run naked through the woods and, before his mother's eyes, is torn apart by hounds. Ivan Karamazov asks his saintly brother Alyosha what he would do with the nobleman. Alyosha replies, "Shoot him." Could Theroux agree with Alyosha here? If so, how could he explain this in light of his condemnation of revenge?
4. Is vengefulness a vice? Is revenge always wrong?
5. Do you believe that the evil of revenge is the same for society as it is for individuals? Does society have the right to avenge itself by punishing criminals? Or is punishment more a matter of reform or constraint against further criminal action?

# The Evil of Lying

## CHARLES FRIED

Charles Fried (b. 1935) is a professor of law at the Harvard University School of Law. He has written several books and articles in the area of ethics; his most recent books are *Right and Wrong* (1978) and *Contract as Promise: A Theory of Contractual Obligation* (1981).

Fried distinguishes between acts that are merely bad and acts that are wrong. He cites Bentham's belief that lying is not wrong and not always bad. He discusses the views of Kant and Augustine, who hold that lying is wrong even when the effects are good. We lie, says Fried, when we intentionally induce a false belief. He asks, If that effect is not bad, how can lying be wrong? He answers that lying is wrong because the effect of lying is *always* bad; lies tamper with the judgment of the persons lied to, thereby interfering with them in a fundamentally disrespectful way. If you could intentionally induce a false belief in yourself, that too would be wrong.

Lying is wrong because it violates the integrity of another's mind, and because it violates trust. In breaking that trust—here Fried quotes Kant—one does wrong to men in general, not only to the gullible victims. Fried compares lying to passing a counterfeit bill.

The evil of lying is as hard to pin down as it is strongly felt. Is lying wrong or is it merely something bad? If it is bad, why is it bad—is it

THE EVIL OF LYING Reprinted by permission of the author and publisher from *Right and Wrong* by Charles Fried (Cambridge, MA) Harvard University Press. Copyright © 1978 by the President and Fellows of Harvard College.

bad in itself or because of some tendency associated with it? Compare lying to physical harm. Harm is a state of the world and so it can only be classified as bad; the wrong I argued for was the *intentional doing* of harm. Lying, on the other hand, can be wrong, since it is an action. But the fact that lying is an action does not mean that it *must* be wrong rather than bad. It might be that the action of lying should be judged as just another state of the world—a time-extended state, to be sure, but there is no problem about that—and as such it would count as a negative element in any set of circumstances in which it occurred. Furthermore, if lying is judged to be bad it can be bad in itself, like something ugly or painful, or it can be bad only because of its tendency to produce results that are bad in themselves.

If lying were bad, not wrong, this would mean only that, other things being equal, we should avoid lies. And if lying were bad not in itself but merely because of its tendencies, we would have to avoid lies only when those tendencies were in fact likely to be realized. In either case lying would be permissible to produce a net benefit, including the prevention of more or worse lies. By contrast the categorical norm "Do not lie" does not evaluate states of affairs but is addressed to moral agents, forbidding lies. Now if lying is wrong it is also bad in itself, for the category of the intrinsically bad is weaker and more inclusive than the category of the wrong. And accordingly, many states of the world are intrinsically bad (such as destruction of valuable property) but intentional acts bringing them about are not necessarily wrong.

Bentham plainly believed that lying is neither wrong nor even intrinsically bad: "Falsehood, take it by itself, consider it as not being accompanied by any other material circumstances, nor therefore productive of any material effects, can never, upon the principle of utility, constitute any offense at all" (*An Introduction to the Principles of Morals and Legislation,* ch. 16, sec. 24). By contrast, Kant and Augustine argued at length that lying is wrong. Indeed, they held that lying is not only wrong *unless* excused or justified in defined ways (which is my view) but that lying is always wrong. Augustine sees lying as a kind of defilement, the liar being tainted by the lie, quite apart from any consequences of the lie. Kant's views are more complex. He argues at one point that lying undermines confidence and trust among men generally: "Although by making a false statement I do no wrong to him who unjustly compels me to speak, yet I do wrong to men in general . . . I cause that declarations in general find no credit, and hence all rights founded on contract should lose their force; and this is a wrong to mankind" ("On a Supposed Right to Tell Lies from Benevolent Motives," in *Kant's Critique of Practical Reason and Other Works,* translated by T. K. Abbott [London: Longmans, Green, 1973]). This would seem to be a consequentialist argument, according to which lying is bad only insofar as it produces these bad results. But elsewhere he makes plain that he believes these bad consequences to be necessarily, perhaps even conceptually linked to lying. In this more rigoristic vein, he asserts that lying is a perversion of one's uniquely human capacities irrespective of any consequences of the lie, and thus lying is not only intrinsically bad but wrong.[1]

Finally, a number of writers have taken what looks like an intermediate position: the evil of lying is indeed identified with its consequences, but the connection between lying and those consequences, while not a necessary connection, is close and persistent, and the consequences themselves are pervasive and profound. Consider this passage from a recent work by G. F. Warnock:

> I do not necessarily do you any harm at all by deed or word if I induce you to believe what is not in fact the case; I may even do you good, possibly by way, for example, of consolation or flattery. Never-

---

[1] "The greatest violation of man's duty to himself merely as a moral being (to humanity in his own person) is . . . the lie. In the doctrine of Law an intentional wrong is called a lie only if it infringes on another's right. But . . . in ethics . . . every deliberate untruth deserves this harsh name. By a lie a man makes himself contemptible . . . and violates the dignity of humanity in his own person. And so, since the harm that can come to others from it is not the characteristic property of this vice (for if it were, the vice would consist only in violating one's duty to others), we do not take this harm into account here . . . By a lie man throws away and, as it were, annihilates his dignity as a man. A man [who lies] . . . has even less worth than if he were a mere thing. For a thing, as something real and given, has the property of being serviceable . . . But the man who communicates his thoughts to someone in words which yet (intentionally) contain the contrary of what he thinks on the subject has a purpose directly opposed to the natural purposiveness of the power of communicating one's thoughts and therefore renounces his personality and makes himself a mere deceptive appearance of man, not man himself.

"A lie (in the ethical sense of the term), as an intentional untruth as such, need not be harmful to others in order to be pronounced reprehensible; for then it would be a violation of the rights of others . . . A lie requires a second person whom one intends to deceive, and intentionally to deceive oneself seems to contain a contradiction.

"Man as a moral being (*homo noumenon*), cannot use his natural being (*homo phaenomenon*) as a mere means (a speaking machine), as if it were not bound to its intrinsic end (the communication of thought)." (*Tugendlehre* [428–430], translated by Mary J. Gregor, *The Doctrine of Virtue,* Philadelphia: University of Pennsylvania Press, 1964.)

theless, though deception is not thus necessarily directly damaging it is easy to see how crucially important it is that the natural inclination to have recourse to it should be counteracted. It is, one might say, not the implanting of false beliefs that is damaging, but rather the generation of the suspicion that they may be being implanted. For this undermines trust; and, to the extent that trust is undermined, all cooperative undertakings, in which what one person can do or has reason to do is dependent on what others have done, are doing, or are going to do, must tend to break down. . . . There is no sense in my asking you for your opinion on some point, if I do not suppose that your answer will actually express your opinion (verbal communication is doubtless the most important of all our co-operative undertakings). (*The Object of Morality* [London: Methuen, 1971], p. 84.)

Warnock does not quite say that truth-telling is good in itself or that lying is wrong, yet the moral quality of truth-telling and lying is not so simply instrumental as it is, for instance, for Bentham. Rather, truth-telling seems to bear a fundamental, pervasive relation to the human enterprise, just as lying appears to be fundamentally subversive of that enterprise. What exactly is the nature of this relation? How does truth-telling bear to human goods a relation which is more than instrumental but less than necessary?

The very definition of lying makes plain that consequences are crucial, for lying is intentional and the intent is an intent to produce a consequence: false belief. But how can I then resist the consequentialist analysis of lying? Lying is an attempt to produce a certain effect on another, and if that effect (consequence) is not bad, now can lying be wrong? I shall have to argue, therefore, that to lie is to intend to produce an effect which always has something bad about it, an effect moreover of the special sort that it is wrong to produce it intentionally. To lay that groundwork for my argument about lying, I must consider first the moral value of truth.

## Truth and Rationality

A statement is true when the world is the way the statement says it is.[2] Utilitarians insist (as in the quotation from Bentham above) that

---

[2]This definition is derived from Alfred Tarski via Donald Davidson, "Meaning and Truth," in Jay F. Rosenberg and Charles Travis, eds., *Reading in the Philosophy of Language* (Englewood Cliffs, N.J.: Prentice-Hall, 1971). See also Gottlob Frege,

truth, like everything else, has value just exactly as it produces value—pleasure, pain, the satisfaction or frustration of desire. And of course it is easy to show that truth (like keeping faith, not harming the innocent, respecting rights) does not always lead to the net satisfactions of desire, to the production of utility. It may *tend* to do so, but that tendency explains only why we should discriminate between occasions when truth does and when it does not have value—an old story. It is an old story, for truth—like justice, respect, and self-respect—has a value which consequentialist analyses (utilitarian or any other) do not capture. Truth, like respect, is a foundational value.

The morality of right and wrong does not count the satisfaction of desire as the overriding value. Rather, the integrity of persons, as agents and as the objects of the intentional agency of others, has priority over the attainment of the goals which agents choose to attain. I have sought to show how respect for physical integrity is related to respect for the person. The person, I argued, is not just a locus of potential pleasure and pain but an entity with determinate characteristics. The person is, among other things, necessarily an incorporated, a physical, not an abstract entity. In relation to truth we touch another necessary aspect of moral personality: the capacity for judgment, and thus for choice. It is that aspect which Kant used to ground his moral theory, arguing that freedom and rationality are the basis for moral personality. John Rawls makes the same point, arguing that "moral personality and not the capacity for pleasure and pain . . . [is] the fundamental aspect of the self . . . The essential unity of the self is . . . provided by the concept of right" (*A Theory of Justice* [Cambridge, Mass.: Harvard University Press, 1971], p. 563). The concept of the self is prior to the goods which the self chooses, and these goods gather their moral significance from the fact that they have been chosen by moral beings—beings capable of understanding and acting on moral principles.

In this view freedom and rationality are complementary capacities, or aspects of the same capacity, which is moral capacity. A man is free insofar as he is able to act on a judgment because he perceives it

---

"The Thought: A Logical Inquiry," and Michael Dummett, "Truth," both in Peter Strawson, ed., *Philosophical Logic* (Oxford: Oxford University Press, 1967). The difficulties in arriving at a satisfactory conception of truth do not touch the moral issues that I discuss in this chapter. Indeed, I suppose that any of a large class of definitions might be substituted for the one I used in the text and my substantive argument would go through without a hitch.

to be correct; he is free insofar as he may be moved to action by the judgments his reason offers to him. This is the very opposite of the Humean conception of reason as the slave of the passions. There is no slavery here. The man who follows the steps of a mathematical argument to its conclusion because he judges them to be correct is free indeed. To the extent that we choose our ends we are free; and as to objectively valuable ends which we choose because we see their value, we are still free.

Now, rational judgment is true judgment, and so the moral capacity for rational choice implies the capacity to recognize the matter on which choice is to act and to recognize the kind of result our choices will produce. This applies to judgments about other selves and to judgments in which one locates himself as a person among persons, a self among selves. These judgments are not just arbitrary suppositions: *they are judged to be true of the world.* For consider what the self would be like if these judgments were not supposed to be true. Maybe one might be content to be happy in the manner of the fool of Athens who believed all the ships in the harbor to be his. But what of our perceptions of other people? Would we be content to have those whom we love and trust the mere figments of our imaginations? The foundational values of freedom and rationality imply the foundational value of truth, for the rational man is the one who judges aright, that is, truly. Truth is not the same as judgment, as rationality; it is rather the proper subject of judgment. If we did not seek to judge truly, and if we did not believe we could judge truly, the act of judgment would not be what we know it to be at all.

Judgment and thus truth are *part* of a structure which as a whole makes up the concept of self. A person's relation to his body and the fact of being an incorporated self are another part of that structure. These two parts are related. The bodily senses provide matter for judgments of truth, and the body includes the physical organs of judgment.

## The Wrong of Lying

So our capacity for judgment is foundational and truth is the proper object of that capacity, but how do we get to the badness of lying, much less its categorical wrongness? The crucial step to be supplied has to do not with the value of truth but with the evil of lying. We must show that to lie to someone is to injure him in a way that

375

particularly touches his moral personality. From that, the passage is indeed easy to the conclusion that to inflict such injury intentionally (remember that all lying is by hypothesis intentional) is not only bad but wrong. It is this first, crucial step which is difficult. After all, a person's capacity for true judgment is not necessarily impaired by inducing in him a particular false belief. Nor would it seem that a person suffers a greater injury in respect to that capacity when he is induced to believe a falsity than when we intentionally prevent him from discovering the truth, yet only in the first case do we lie. Do we really do injury to a person's moral personality when we persuade him falsely that it rained yesterday in Bangkok—a fact in which he has no interest? And do we do him more injury than when we fail to answer his request for yesterday's football scores, in which he is mildly interested? Must we not calculate the injury by the *other* harm it does: disappointed expectations, lost property, missed opportunities, physical harm? In this view, lying would be a way of injuring a person in his various substantive interests—a way of stealing from him, hurting his feelings, perhaps poisoning him—but then the evil of lying would be purely instrumental, not wrong at all.

All truth, however irrelevant or trivial, has value, even though we may cheerfully ignore most truths, forget them, erase them as encumbrances from our memories. The value of every truth is shown just in the judgment that the only thing we must not do is falsify truth. Truths are like other people's property, which we can care nothing about but may not use for our own purposes. It is as if the truth were not ours (even truth we have discovered and which is known only to us), and so we may not exercise an unlimited dominion over it. Our relations to other people have a similar structure: we may perhaps have no duty to them, we may be free to put them out of our minds to make room for others whom we care about more, but we may not harm them. And so we may not falsify truth. But enough of metaphors—what does it mean to say that the truth is not ours?

The capacity for true judgment is the capacity to arrive at judgments which are in fact true of the world as it exists apart from our desires, our choices, our values. It is the world presented to us by true judgments—including true judgments about ourselves—which we then make the subject of our choices, our valuation. Now, if we treat the truth as our own, it must be according to desire or valuation. But for rational beings these activities are supposed to depend on truth; we are supposed to desire and choose according to the world as it is. To choose that something not be the case when it is in fact the case is very nearly self-contradictory—for choice is not *of* truth but *on the basis of* truth. To deliberate about whether to believe a truth (not whether it is indeed true—another story altogether) is like deciding whether to cheat at solitaire. All this is obvious. In fact I suppose one cannot even coherently talk about choosing to believe something one believes to be false. And this holds equally for all truths—big and little, useful, useless, and downright inconvenient. But we do and must calculate *about* (and not just *with*) truths all the time as we decide what truths to acquire, what to forget. We decide all the time not to pursue some inquiry because it is not worth it. Such calculations surely must go forward on the basis of what truths are useful, given one's plans and desires. Even when we pursue truth for its own sake, we distinguish between interesting and boring truths.

Considering what truth to acquire or retain differs, however, from deliberately acquiring false beliefs. All truths are acquired as propositions correctly (truly) corresponding to the world, and in this respect, all truths are equal. A lie, however, has the form and occupies the role of truth in that it too purports to be a proposition about the world; only the world does not correspond to it. So the choice of a lie is not like a choice among truths, for the choice of a lie is a choice to affirm as the basis for judgment a proposition which does not correspond to the world. So, when I say that truth is foundational, that truth precedes choice, what I mean is *not* that this or that truth is foundational but that judging according to the facts is foundational to judging at all. A scientist may deliberate about which subject to study and, having chosen his subject, about the data worth acquiring, but he cannot even deliberate as a scientist about whether to acquire false data. Clearly, then, there is something funny (wrong?) about lying to oneself, but how do we go from there to the proposition that it is wrong to lie to someone else? After all, much of the peculiarity about lying to oneself consists in the fact that it seems not so much bad as downright self-contradictory, logically impossible, but that does not support the judgment that it is wrong to lie to another. I cannot marry myself, but that hardly makes it wrong to marry someone else.

Let us imagine a case in which you come as close as you can to lying to yourself: You arrange some operation, some fiddling with your brain that has no effect other than to cause you to believe a proposition you know to be false and also to forget entirely the prior history of how you came to believe that proposition. It seems to me that you do indeed harm yourself in such an operation. This is because a free and rational person wishes to have a certain relation to reality: as nearly perfect as possible. He wishes to build his conception of himself and the world and his conception of the good on the basis of truth. Now if he affirms that the truth is available for fiddling in order to accommodate either his picture of the world or his conception of the good, then this affirms that reality is dependent on what one wants, rather than what one wants being fundamentally constrained by what there is. Rationality is the respect for this fundamental constraint of truth. This is just another way of saying that the truth is prior to our plans and prospects and must be respected whatever our plans might be. What if the truth we "destroy" by this operation is a very trivial and irrelevant truth—the state of the weather in Bangkok on some particular day? There is still an injury to self, because the fiddler must have some purpose in his fiddling. If it is a substantive purpose, then the truth is in fact relevant to that purpose, and my argument holds. If it is just to show it can be done, then he is only trying to show he can do violence to his rationality—a kind of moral blasphemy. Well, what if it is a very *little* truth? Why, then, it is a very little injury he does himself—but that does not undermine my point.[3]

Now, when I lie to you, I do to you what you cannot actually do to yourself—brain-fiddling being only an approximation. The nature of the injury I would do to myself, if I could, explains why lying to you is to do you harm, indeed why it is wrong. The lie is an injury because it produces an effect (or seeks to) which a person as a moral agent should not wish to have produced in him, and thus it is as much an injury as any other effect which a moral agent would not wish to have produced upon his person. To be sure, some people may want to be lied to. That is a special problem; they are like people who want to suffer (not just are willing to risk) physical injury. In

---

[3]Distinguish from this the frequent and important instances where one refuses to receive certain truths: the man of honor who will not read scandalous accusations about another's private life, the judge who will not receive unauthorized information about a matter before him. These do not involve deliberate espousals of falsity. There is, after all, a proper domain of secret, private truths and of things which are none of our business.

general, then, I do not want you to lie to me in the same way that as a rational man I would not lie to myself if I could. But why does this make lying wrong and not merely bad?[4]

Lying is wrong because when I lie I set up a relation which is essentially exploitative. It violates the principle of respect, for I must affirm that the mind of another person is available to me in a way in which I cannot agree my mind would be available to him—for if I do so agree, then I would not expect my lie to be believed. When I lie, I am like a counterfeiter: I do not want the market flooded with counterfeit currency; I do not want to get back my own counterfeit bill. Moreover, in lying to you, I affirm such an unfairly unilateral principle in respect to an interest and capacity which is crucial, as crucial as physical integrity: your freedom and your rationality. When I do intentional physical harm, I say that your body, your person, is available for my purposes. When I lie, I lay claim to your mind.

Lying violates respect and is wrong, as is any breach of trust. Every lie is a broken promise, and the only reason this seems strained is that in lying the promise is made and broken at the same moment. Every lie necessarily implies—as does every assertion—an assurance, a warranty of its truth. The fact that the breach accompanies the making should, however, only strengthen the conclusion that this is wrong. If promise-breaking is wrong, then a lie must be wrong, since there cannot be the supervening factor of changed circumstances which may excuse breaches of promises to perform in the future.

The final one of the convergent strands that make up the wrong of lying is the shared, communal nature of language. This is what I think Kant had in mind when he argued that a lie does wrong "to men in general." If whether people stood behind their statements depended wholly on the particular circumstances of the utterance, then the whole point of communication would be undermined. For every utterance would simply be the occasion for an analysis of the total circumstances (speaker's and hearer's) in order to determine what, if anything, to make of the utterance. And though we do often

---

[4]It may be the case that every instance of any intentional injury to another person constitutes a wrongful relation (is wrong), but I am not prepared to argue that. I would rather examine the circumstances of this one kind of injury, lying, and show how that is wrong.

wonder and calculate whether a person is telling the truth, we do so from a baseline, a presumption that people do stand behind their statements. After all, the speaker surely depends on such a baseline. He wants us to think that he is telling the truth. Speech is a paradigm of communication, and all human relations are based on some form of communication. Our very ability to think, to conceptualize, is related to speech. Speech allows the social to penetrate the intimately personal. Perhaps that is why Kant's dicta seem to vacillate between two positions: lying as a social offense, and lying as an offense against oneself; the requirement of an intent to deceive another, and the insistence that the essence of the wrong is not injury to another but to humanity. Every lie violates the basic commitment to truth which stands behind the social fact of language.

I have already argued that bodily integrity bears a necessary relation to moral integrity, so that an attack upon bodily integrity is wrong, not just bad. The intimate *and* social nature of truth make the argument about lying stronger. For not only is the target aspect of the victim crucial to him as a moral agent but, by lying, we attack that target by a means which itself offends his moral nature; the means of attack are social means which can be said to belong as much to the victim as to his assailant. There is not only the attack at his moral vitals, but an attack with a weapon which belongs to him. Lying is, thus, a kind of treachery. (*Kind of* treachery? Why not treachery pure and simple?) It is as if we not only robbed a man of his treasure but in doing so used his own servants or family as our agents. That speech is our *common* property, that it belongs to the liar, his victim and all of us makes the matter if anything far worse.

So this is why lying is not only bad (a hurt), but wrong, why lying is wrong apart from or in addition to any other injury it does, and why lying seems at once an offense against the victim and against mankind in general, an offense against the liar himself, and against the abstract entity, truth. Whom do you injure when you pass a counterfeit bill?

What about little pointless lies? Do I really mean they are wrong? Well, yes, even a little lie is wrong, *if* it is a true piece of communication, an assertion of its own truth and not just a conventional way of asserting nothing at all or something else (as in the case of polite or diplomatic formulas). A little lie is a little wrong, but it is still something you must not do.

380

**STUDY QUESTIONS**

1. Why does Fried think that lying is both wrong and bad?
2. What does Fried mean when he says, "Truth, like respect, is a foundational value." What does this imply for the nature of lying?
3. Lying must be deliberate. Can you lie to yourself? Could that be wrong? What is Fried's view?
4. What, precisely, is the effect of a lie on the person lied to? What is wrong with this effect? Give your own arguments in defense of the view that a serious lie is sometimes (never) justified.

**SUGGESTED READINGS**

Alighieri, Dante. *Inferno*.

Bloomfield, Morton. *The Seven Deadly Sins*. East Lansing, MI: Michigan State University Press, 1967.

Burton, Robert. *The Anatomy of Melancholy* (originally published 1621). New York: Vintage Press, 1977.

Freud, Sigmund. *Civilization and Its Discontents*. Edited and translated by James Strachey. New York: Norton, 1962.

Jacoby, Susan. *Wild Justice: The Evolution of Revenge*. New York: Harper and Row, 1983.

Ross, Edward Alsworth. *Sin and Society: An Analysis of Latter Day Iniquity*. (originally published 1907). New York: Harper Torchbooks, 1973.

# *Chapter Five*

# WHY BE MORAL?

Philosophers have long affirmed the need for moral rules. But it is one thing to recognize the value of living in a community that acknowledges and enforces some rules of conduct, and quite another to answer the question, "Why should I be moral?" Here the stress is on *I*. Why should *I* not take advantage of the fact that most people respect the rules. One answer is that crime is risky, that it does not pay. But that is a dubious proposition. And what if I can disobey the moral law with impunity? Why should I not then selfishly ignore the moral rules that most people obey?

One doctrine recognizes the force of this question by affirming that there is indeed nothing wrong in being selfish and egoistic. The *locus classicus* for ethical egoism (as this doctrine is called) is the story, told by Plato, of Gyges, the shepherd who finds a ring that can render him invisible. Gyges uses the ring to murder the King and take over the government. The ethical egoist might well approve of Gyges' behavior. But Plato is sharply opposed to this doctrine; Plato believes he has refuted it in *The Republic* by showing that the selfish and unjust human being is flawed and unhappy.

A contemporary version of ethical egoism is here represented by Harry Browne's essay. Unsurprisingly, most moral philosophers reject ethical egoism. James Rachels argues that it is a morally perverse theory and seeks to expose its logical errors. Once the constraints of morality are thrown off, there seem to be no limits to what egoists may do, short of harming themselves in some way. As Rachels puts it, the ethical egoist who enjoys watching fires could consistently hold that burning down department stores full of people is "right for him."

Peter Singer tackles the question by arguing, as Plato did, that being moral is essential to happiness. Plato sought to persuade his readers that human well-functioning included moral behavior: To live immorally is to live an inferior existence that shuts out all light and health. Singer argues that amoral people (such as psychopaths) and selfish people (prudent egoists) lead dreary, boring, and meaningless lives.

The amoralist is a negative ideal type. The opposed ideal is the supermoralist or *Moral Saint*. The life of the moral saint is, in Susan Wolf's words, "dominated by the commitment to improving the welfare of others or of society as a whole." Wolf rejects the ideal of moral sainthood; the supermoralist has no time for art, amusements, and other "frivolities." Such people may be worthy, but they are undeveloped in important ways, and may well be dull and boring companions. Robert Adams sees them differently: Moral saints are fascinating, exciting people of great religious passion. He denies that they are totally committed to good works; on the contrary, the moral saint overflows with goodness and does not begrudge time spent on fun. A more concrete picture of moral sainthood is given by George Orwell's description of Mahatma Gandhi. Orwell's portrait is more closely in accord with Adams. But Orwell too has reservations about the ideal of moral sainthood—at least as Gandhi embodied it. Unquestionably, Gandhi was an extraordinary human being; he was inspirational and original. (Gandhi was the first to appreciate the political force of nonviolent resistance.) Yet, says Orwell, there was something inhuman and unattractive about Gandhi's sainthood.

Both the amoralist and the supermoralist are looked upon with suspicion by the majority of moral philosophers concerned with the bread-and-butter questions of what it means to live morally and decently. Such suspicion is perhaps a tribute to the powerful influence of Aristotle on moral philosophy. Aristotle thought of the ideally moral person as one who avoids extremes: the ideal is a moderate mode of behavior available to all well-meaning persons of good sense. That perspective on morality occupies the moral center; it is not easily put aside for long.

# The Ring of Gyges

## PLATO

Plato [*ca* 428–348 (or 347) B.C.], considered by many to be the greatest philosopher who ever lived, is the author of *The Republic* and other great dialogues. Plato's influence on Western culture is incalculable.

In *The Republic,* Plato describes the ideal society where justice reigns supreme. It opens with a scene in which Socrates confronts powerful arguments that disparage justice. We find Glaucon summarizing the views of those who think that justice is merely a compromise between the freedom to do wrong with impunity and to suffer wrong without redress. Because we would risk punitive action by doing wrong, we accept a limitation on our freedom. So justice is a kind of arrangement (like a system of traffic lights) that is not in itself valuable or desirable, but is put in place (to prevent accidents) to prevent our suffering wrong from others.

The Ring of Gyges rendered the wearer invisible, enabling the shepherd Gyges to do as he pleased without fear of reprisal—and he used it to murder the King of Lydia. But did Gyges behave unnaturally? Glaucon argues that anyone in Gyges' situation would be a fool not to take full advantage of the power to do wrong with impunity. This suggests that justice is nothing more than a preventive device—only we lack the power that Gyges possessed.

THE RING OF GYGES From *The Republic* by Plato. Translated by G. M. A. Grube (Indianapolis, IN: Hackett, 1974), pp. 31–33. Reprinted by permission of the publisher.

385

In the remainder of *The Republic,* Socrates argues that the citizens of an ideal society would be just because they loved justice and not (merely) because they feared the consequences of suffering injustice.

GLAUCON (TO SOCRATES): I have never heard from anyone the sort of defence of justice that I want to hear, proving that it is better than injustice. I want to hear it praised for itself, and I think I am most likely to hear this from you. Therefore I am going to speak at length in praise of the unjust life and in doing so I will show you the way I want to hear you denouncing injustice and praising justice. See whether you want to hear what I suggest.

SOCRATES: I want it more than anything else. Indeed, what subject would a man of sense talk and hear about more often with enjoyment?

GLAUCON: Splendid, then listen while I deal with the first subject I mentioned: the nature and origin of justice.

They say that to do wrong is naturally good, to be wronged is bad, but the suffering of injury so far exceeds in badness the good of inflicting it that when men have done wrong to each other and suffered it, and have had a taste of both, those who are unable to avoid the latter and practise the former decide that it is profitable to come to an agreement with each other neither to inflict injury nor to suffer it. As a result they begin to make laws and covenants, and the law's command they call lawful and just. This, they say, is the origin and essence of justice; it stands between the best and the worst, the best being to do wrong without paying the penalty and the worst to be wronged without the power of revenge. The just then is a mean between two extremes; it is welcomed and honoured because of men's lack of the power to do wrong. The man who has that power, the real man, would not make a compact with anyone not to inflict injury or suffer it. For him that would be madness. This then,

Socrates, is, according to their argument, the nature and origin of justice.

Even those who practise justice do so against their will because they lack the power to do wrong. This we could realize very clearly if we imagined ourselves granting to both the just and the unjust the freedom to do whatever they liked. We could then follow both of them and observe where their desires led them, and we would catch the just man redhanded travelling the same road as the unjust. The reason is the desire for undue gain which every organism by nature pursues as a good, but the law forcibly sidetracks him to honour equality. The freedom I just mentioned would most easily occur if these men had the power which they say the ancestor of the Lydian Gyges possessed. The story is that he was a shepherd in the service of the ruler of Lydia. There was a violent rainstorm and an earthquake which broke open the ground and created a chasm at the place where he was tending sheep. Seeing this and marvelling, he went down into it. He saw, besides many other wonders of which we are told, a hollow bronze horse. There were window-like openings in it; he climbed through them and caught sight of a corpse which seemed of more than human stature, wearing nothing but a ring of gold on its finger. This ring the shepherd put on and came out. He arrived at the usual monthly meeting which reported to the king on the state of the flocks, wearing the ring. As he was sitting among the others he happened to twist the hoop of the ring towards himself, to the inside of his hand, and as he did this he became invisible to those sitting near him and they went on talking as if he had gone. He marvelled at this and, fingering the ring, he turned the hoop outward again and became visible. Perceiving this he tested whether the ring had this power and so it happened: if he turned the hoop inwards he became invisible, but was visible when he turned it outwards. When he realized this, he at once arranged to become one of the messengers to the king. He went, committed adultery with the king's wife, attacked the king with her help, killed him, and took over the kingdom.

Now if there were two such rings, one worn by the just man, the other by the unjust, no one, as these people think, would be so incorruptible that he would stay on the path of justice or bring himself to keep away from other people's property and not touch it, when he could with impunity take whatever he wanted from the market, go into houses and have sexual relations with anyone he wanted, kill anyone, free all those he wished from prison, and do the other things which would make him like a god among men. His actions would be in no way different from those of the other and they would both follow the same path. This, some would say, is a great proof that no one is just willingly[1] but under compulsion, so that justice is not one's private good, since wherever either thought he could do wrong with impunity he would do so. Every man believes that injustice is much more profitable to himself than justice, and any exponent of this argument will say that he is right. The man who did not wish to do wrong with that opportunity, and did not touch other people's property, would be thought by those who knew it to be very foolish and miserable. They would praise him in public, thus deceiving one another, for fear of being wronged. So much for my second topic.

As for the choice between the lives we are discussing, we shall be able to make a correct judgment about it only if we put the most just man and

---

[1]This of course directly contradicts the famous Socratic paradox that no one is willingly bad and that people do wrong because they have not the knowledge to do right, which is virtue.

the most unjust man face to face; otherwise we cannot do so. By face to face I mean this: let us grant to the unjust the fullest degree of injustice and to the just the fullest justice, each being perfect in his own pursuit. First, the unjust man will act as clever craftsmen do—a top navigator for example or physician distinguishes what his craft can do and what it cannot; the former he will undertake, the latter he will pass by, and when he slips he can put things right. So the unjust man's correct attempts at wrongdoing must remain secret; the one who is caught must be considered a poor performer, for the extreme of injustice is to have a reputation for justice, and our perfectly unjust man must be granted perfection in injustice. We must not take this from him, but we must allow that, while committing the greatest crimes, he has provided himself with the greatest reputation for justice; if he makes a slip he must be able to put it right; he must be a sufficiently persuasive speaker if some wrongdoing of his is made public; he must be able to use force, where force is needed, with the help of his courage, his strength, and the friends and wealth with which he has provided himself.

Having described such a man, let us now in our argument put beside him the just man, simple as he is and noble, who, as Aeschylus put it, does not wish to appear just but to be so. We must take away his reputation, for a reputation for justice would bring him honour and rewards, and it would then not be clear whether he is what he is for justice's sake or for the sake of rewards and honour. We must strip him of everything except justice and make him the complete opposite of the other. Though he does no wrong, he must have the greatest reputation for wrongdoing so that he may be tested for justice by not weakening under ill repute and its consequences. Let him go his incorruptible way until death with a reputation for injustice throughout his life, just though he is, so that our two men may reach the extremes, one of justice, the other of injustice, and let them be judged as to which of the two is the happier.

SOCRATES:    Whew! My dear Glaucon, what a mighty scouring you have given those two characters, as if they were statues in a competition.

### STUDY QUESTIONS

1. Glaucon presents a popular conception of the origin of justice as an agreement by each individual to refrain from doing wrong on condition that one is protected from wrongdoing by others. What does this "social contract theory" imply about the nature of justice?

2. Glaucon notes that the person who appears just to others but who is not just seems happier than one who appears unjust to others but who in fact is just. What challenge does this present to Socrates?

3. Gyges can do wrong with impunity. But we cannot. We are told that crime does not pay. But is this true? Suppose it is false. Can we still make out a case for being just and refraining from crime?

4. Glaucon's arguments seem to present Socrates with an insuperable problem since justice seems to be for "losers." How would you set about resolving the problem?

# The Unselfishness Trap

### HARRY BROWNE

Harry Browne is a journalist and lives in New York City. He is the author of *How I Found Freedom in an Unfree World* (1973).

Harry Browne objects to the view of many moralists that we should put others' happiness ahead of our own. If we were all to sacrifice our own happiness for the sake of others, eventually no one would be happy. "The unselfishness concept is a merry-go-round that has no ultimate purpose." Gift-givers and favor-doers presuppose that they know what will make others happy. Spending money on yourself is much more efficient (you know what makes you happy) and creates more happiness all around. Browne recommends "prudential generosity": Be sensitive to the needs and desires of those who might in turn benefit you. He grounds his views on psychological egoism, the doctrine that human beings act from a single motive—self-love. "Why should you feel guilty for seeking your own happiness when that's what everyone else is doing too?"

The Unselfishness Trap is the belief that you must put the happiness of others ahead of your own.

Unselfishness is a very popular ideal, one that's been honored

THE UNSELFISHNESS TRAP From *How I Found Freedom in an Unfree World* by Harry Browne. Reprinted by permission of Macmillan Publishing Company. Copyright © 1973 by Harry Browne.

throughout recorded history. Wherever you turn, you find encouragement to put the happiness of others ahead of your own—to do what's best for the world, not for yourself.

If the ideal is sound, there must be something unworthy in seeking to live your life as you want to live it.

So perhaps we should look more closely at the subject—to see if the ideal *is* sound. For if you attempt to be free, we can assume that someone's going to consider that to be selfish.

We saw in Chapter 2 that each person always acts in ways he believes will make him feel good or will remove discomfort from his life. Because everyone is different from everyone else, each individual goes about it in his own way.

One man devotes his life to helping the poor. Another one lies and steals. Still another person tries to create better products and services for which he hopes to be paid handsomely. One woman devotes herself to her husband and children. Another one seeks a career as a singer.

In every case, the ultimate motivation has been the same. Each person is doing what *he* believes will assure his happiness. What varies between them is the *means* each has chosen to gain his happiness.

We could divide them into two groups labeled "selfish" and "unselfish," but I don't think that would prove anything. For the thief and the humanitarian each have the same motive—to do what he believes will make him feel good.

In fact, we can't avoid a very significant conclusion: *Everyone is selfish.* Selfishness isn't really an issue, because everyone selfishly seeks his own happiness.

What we need to examine, however, are the means various people choose to achieve their happiness. Unfortunately, some people oversimplify the matter by assuming that there are only two basic means: sacrifice yourself for others or make them sacrifice for you. Happily, there's a third way that can produce better consequences than either of those two.

## A Better World?

Let's look first at the ideal of living for the benefit of others. It's often said that it would be a better world if everyone were unselfish. But would it be?

392

If it were somehow possible for everyone to give up his own happiness, what would be the result? Let's carry it to its logical conclusion and see what we find.

To visualize it, let's imagine that happiness is symbolized by a big red rubber ball. I have the ball in my hands—meaning that I hold the ability to be happy. But since I'm not going to be selfish, I quickly pass the ball to you. I've given up my happiness for you.

What will you do? Since you're not selfish either, you won't keep the ball; you'll quickly pass it on to your next-door neighbor. But he doesn't want to be selfish either, so he passes it to his wife, who likewise gives it to her children.

The children have been taught the virtue of unselfishness, so they pass it to playmates, who pass it to parents, who pass it to neighbors, and on and on and on.

I think we can stop the analogy at this point and ask what's been accomplished by all this effort. Who's better off for these demonstrations of pure unselfishness?

*How* would it be a better world if everyone acted that way? Whom would we be unselfish for? There would have to be a selfish person who would receive, accept, and enjoy the benefits of our unselfishness for there to be any purpose to it. But that selfish person (the object of our generosity) would be living by lower standards than we do.

For a more practical example, what is achieved by the parent who "sacrifices" himself for his children, who in turn are expected to sacrifice themselves for *their* children, etc.? The unselfishness concept is a merry-go-round that has no ultimate purpose. No one's self-interest is enhanced by the continual relaying of gifts from one person to another to another.

Perhaps most people have never carried the concept of unselfishness to this logical conclusion. If they did, they might reconsider their pleas for an unselfish world.

## Negative Choices

But, unfortunately, the pleas continue, and they're a very real part of your life. In seeking your own freedom and happiness, you have to deal with those who tell you that you shouldn't put yourself first. That creates a situation in which you're pressured to act negatively—

to put aside your plans and desires in order to avoid the condemnation of others.

As I've said before, one of the characteristics of a free man is that he's usually choosing positively—deciding which of several alternatives would make him the happiest; while the average person, most of the time, is choosing which of two or three alternatives will cause him the least discomfort.

When the reason for your actions is to avoid being called "selfish" you're making a negative decision and thereby restricting the possibilities for your own happiness.

You're in the Unselfishness Trap if you regretfully pay for your aunt's surgery with the money you'd saved for a new car, or if you sadly give up the vacation you'd looked forward to in order to help a sick neighbor.

You're in the trap if you feel you're *required* to give part of your income to the poor, or if you think that your country, community, or family has first claim on your time, energy, or money.

You're in the Unselfishness Trap any time you make negative choices that are designed to avoid being called "selfish."

It isn't that no one else is important. You might have a self-interest in someone's well-being, and giving a gift can be a gratifying expression of the affection you feel for him. But you're in the trap if you do such things in order to appear unselfish.

## Helping Others

There *is* an understandable urge to give to those who are important and close to you. However, that leads many people to think that indiscriminate giving is the key to one's own happiness. They say that the way to be happy is to make others happy; get your glow by basking in the glow you've created for someone else.

It's important to identify that as a personal opinion. If someone says that giving is the key to happiness, isn't he saying that's the key to *his* happiness?

I think we can carry the question further, however, and determine how efficient such a policy might be. The suggestion to be a giver presupposes that you're able to judge what will make someone else happy. And experience has taught me to be a bit humble about assuming what makes others happy.

My landlady once brought me a piece of her freshly baked cake because she wanted to do me a favor. Unfortunately, it happened to be a kind of cake that was distasteful to me. I won't try to describe the various ways I tried to get the cake plate back to her without being confronted with a request for my judgment of her cake. It's sufficient to say that her well-intentioned favor interfered with my own plans.

And now, whenever I'm sure I know what someone else "needs," I remember that incident and back off a little. There's no way that one person can read the mind of another to know all his plans, goals, and tastes.

You may know a great deal about the desires of your intimate friends. But *indiscriminate* gift-giving and favor-doing is usually a waste of resources—or, worse, it can upset the well-laid plans of the receiver.

When you give to someone else, you might provide something he values—but probably not the thing he considers most important. If you expend those resources for *yourself*, you automatically devote them to what you consider to be most important. The time or money you've spent will most likely create more happiness that way.

If your purpose is to make someone happy, you're most apt to succeed if you make yourself the object. You'll never know another person more than a fraction as well as you can know yourself.

Do you want to make someone happy? Go to it—use your talents and your insight and benevolence to bestow riches of happiness upon the one person you understand well enough to do it efficiently—yourself. I guarantee that you'll get more genuine appreciation from yourself than from anyone else.

Give to you.

Support your local self.

## Alternatives

As I indicated earlier in this chapter, it's too often assumed that there are only two alternatives: (1) sacrifice your interests for the benefit of others; or (2) make others sacrifice their interests for you. If nothing else were possible, it would indeed be a grim world.

Fortunately, there's more to the world than that. Because desires vary from person to person, it's possible to create exchanges between individuals in which both parties benefit.

For example, if you buy a house, you do so because you'd rather have the house than the money involved. But the seller's desire is different—he'd rather have the money than the house. When the sale is completed, each of you has received something of greater value than what you gave up—otherwise you wouldn't have entered the exchange. Who, then, has had to sacrifice for the other?

In the same way, your daily life is made up of dozens of such exchanges—small and large transactions in which each party gets something he values more than what he gives up. The exchange doesn't have to involve money; you may be spending time, attention, or effort in exchange for something you value.

Mutually beneficial relationships are possible when desires are compatible. Sometimes the desires are the same—like going to a movie together. Sometimes the desires are different—like trading your money for someone's house. In either case, it's the *compatibility* of the desires that makes the exchange possible.

No sacrifice is necessary when desires are compatible. So it makes sense to seek out people with whom you can have mutually beneficial relationships.

Often the "unselfishness" issue arises only because two people with nothing in common are trying to get along together—such as a man who likes bowling and hates opera married to a woman whose tastes are the opposite. If they're to do things together, one must "sacrifice" his pleasure for the other. So each might try to encourage the other to be "unselfish."

If they were compatible, the issue wouldn't arise because each would be pleasing the other by doing what was in his own self-interest.

An efficiently selfish person *is* sensitive to the needs and desires of others. But he doesn't consider those desires to be demands upon him. Rather, he sees them as *opportunities*—potential exchanges that might be beneficial to him. He identifies desires in others so that he can decide if exchanges with them will help him get what he wants.

He doesn't sacrifice himself for others, nor does he expect others to be sacrificed for him. He takes the third alternative—he finds relationships that are mutually beneficial so that no sacrifice is required.

## Please Yourself

Everyone is selfish; everyone is doing what he believes will make himself happier. The recognition of that can take most of the sting out of accusations that you're being "selfish." Why should you feel guilty for seeking your own happiness when that's what everyone else is doing, too?

The demand that you be unselfish can be motivated by any number of reasons: that you'd help create a better world, that you have a moral obligation to be unselfish, that you give up your happiness to the selfishness of someone else, or that the person demanding it has just never thought it out.

Whatever the reason, you're not likely to convince such a person to stop his demands. But it will create much less pressure on you if you realize that its *his* selfish reason. And you can eliminate the problem entirely by looking for more compatible companions.

To find constant, profound happiness requires that you be free to seek the gratification of your own desires. It means making positive choices.

If you slip into the Unselfishness Trap, you'll spend a good part of your time making negative choices—trying to avoid the censure of those who tell you not to think of yourself. You won't have time to be free.

If someone finds happiness by doing "good works" for others, let him. That doesn't mean that's the best way for you to find happiness.

And when someone accuses you of being selfish, just remember that he's only upset because you aren't doing what *he* selfishly wants you to do.

**STUDY QUESTIONS**

1. Browne claims that when we behave unselfishly we, more often than not, sacrifice our own happiness. Do you agree?
2. Browne says that everyone is selfish because we all do what we believe will make us feel good. Critics of egoism such as James Rachels claim that what makes an act selfish or unselfish is its *object*, not simply that it makes you feel good. If you are the sort of person who feels good *when you help others*, then you are unselfish. If you feel good only *when helping yourself*, then you are selfish. Critically discuss the issue that divides Rachels and Browne and assess their respective positions.
3. Medical researchers appear to have discovered some astonishing correlations between behaving unselfishly and a higher

resistance to some major diseases. What implications might such a finding have for ethical egoism?

# Egoism and Moral Skepticism

## JAMES RACHELS

James Rachels (1941) is Dean of the School of Humanities at the University of Alabama. He is editor of several books, including *Moral Problems: A Collection of Philosophical Essays* (1979) and *Understanding Moral Philosophy* (1976).

Psychological egoism is the view that human beings always act from a single motive: self-love. Ethical egoism is the moral theory that says we *ought* to act only from self-love. Rachels tries to expose the logical and moral weaknesses of both theories. For example, he challenges the view often proffered by defenders of psychological egoism: We are selfish because we *always do what we want to do*. One person *wants* to visit and cheer up a lonely elderly neighbor; another wants to rob and terrorize his neighbor. Both do what they want; both are selfish. Rachels points out that what makes an act selfish is its *object,* not that you want to do it. If the object of most of your actions is to please yourself, then you are selfish; if you often want to please your neighbors, you are kind. If you want to harm them, you are malicious. Rachels also argues that both psychological and ethical egoisms rest upon a distorted view of human nature. Most of us are

EGOISM AND MORAL SKEPTICISM From *A New Introduction to Philosophy* by James Rachels. Edited by Steven M. Cahn. Copyright © 1971 by Steven M. Cahn. Reprinted by permission of Steven M. Cahn.

sympathetic and care about the well-being of others. The reason we do not burn down a department store is not because it might not be in our long-range best interest to do so, but because "people might be burned to death."

# I

Our ordinary thinking about morality is full of assumptions that we almost never question. We assume, for example, that we have an obligation to consider the welfare of other people when we decide what actions to perform or what rules to obey; we think that we must refrain from acting in ways harmful to others, and that we must respect their rights and interests as well as our own. We also assume that people are in fact capable of being motivated by such considerations, that is, that people are not wholly selfish and that they do sometimes act in the interests of others.

Both of these assumptions have come under attack by moral skeptics, as long ago as by Glaucon in Book II of Plato's *Republic*. Glaucon recalls the legend of Gyges, a shepherd who was said to have found a magic ring in a fissure opened by an earthquake. The ring would make its wearer invisible and thus would enable him to go anywhere and do anything undetected. Gyges used the power of the ring to gain entry to the Royal Palace where he seduced the Queen, murdered the King, and subsequently seized the throne. Now Glaucon asks us to determine that there are two such rings, one given to a man of virtue and one given to a rogue. The rogue, of course, will use his ring unscrupulously and do anything necessary to increase his own wealth and power. He will recognize no moral constraints on his conduct, and, since the cloak of invisibility will protect him from discovery, he can do anything he pleases without fear of reprisal. So there will be no end to the mischief he will do. But how will the so-called virtuous man behave? Glaucon suggests that he will behave no better than the rogue: "No one, it is commonly believed, would have such iron strength of mind as to stand fast in doing right or keep his hands off other men's goods, when he could go to the market-place and fearlessly help himself to anything he wanted, enter houses and sleep with any woman he chose, set prisoners free and kill men at his pleasure, and in a word go about among men with the powers of a god. He would behave no better than the other; both would take the same course."[1] Moreover, why shouldn't he? Once he is freed from the fear of reprisal, why shouldn't a man simply do what he pleases, or what he thinks is best for himself? What reason is there for him to continue being "moral" when it is clearly not to his own advantage to do so?

These skeptical views suggested by Glaucon have come to be known as *psychological egoism* and *ethical egoism* respectively. Psychological egoism is the view that all men are selfish in everything that they do, that is, that the only motive from which anyone ever acts is self-interest. On this view, even when men are acting in ways apparently calculated to benefit others, they are actually motivated by the belief that acting in this way is to their own advantage, and if they did not believe this, they would not be doing that action. Ethical egoism is, by contrast, a normative view about how men *ought* to act. It is the view that, regardless of how men do in fact behave, they have no obligation to do anything except what is in their own interests. According to the ethical egoist, a person is always justified in doing whatever is in his own interest, regardless of the effect on others.

Clearly, if either of these views is correct, then "the moral institution of life" (to use Butler's well-turned phrase) is very different than what we normally think. The majority of mankind is grossly deceived about what is, or ought to be, the case, where morals are concerned.

## II

Psychological egoism seems to fly in the face of the facts. We are tempted to say, "Of course people act unselfishly all the time. For example, Smith gives up a trip to the country, which he would have enjoyed very much, in order to stay behind and help a friend with his studies, which is a miserable way to pass the time. This is a perfectly clear case of unselfish behavior, and if the psychological egoist thinks that such cases do not occur, then he is just mistaken." Given such obvious instances of "unselfish behavior," what reply can the egoist make? There are two general arguments by which he might try to show that all actions, including those such as the one just outlined, are in fact motivated by self-interest. Let us examine these in turn:

---

[1] *The Republic of Plato,* trans. F. M. Cornford (Oxford, 1941), p. 45.

A. The first argument goes as follows. If we describe one person's action as selfish, and another person's action as unselfish, we are overlooking the crucial fact that in both cases, assuming that the action is done voluntarily, *the agent is merely doing what he most wants to do.* If Smith stays behind to help his friend, that only shows that he wanted to help his friend more than he wanted to go to the country. And why should he be praised for his "unselfishness" when he is only doing what he wants to do, he cannot be said to be acting unselfishly.

This argument is so bad that it would not deserve to be taken seriously except for the fact that so many otherwise intelligent people have been taken in by it. First, the argument rests on the premise that people never voluntarily do anything except what they want to do. But this is patently false; there are at least two classes of actions that are exceptions to this generalization. One is the set of actions which we may not want to do, but which we do anyway as a means to an end which we want to achieve; for example, going to the dentist in order to stop a toothache, or going to work every day in order to be able to draw our pay at the end of the month. These cases may be regarded as consistent with the spirit of the egoist argument, however, since the ends mentioned are wanted by the agent. But the other set of actions are those which we do, not because we want to, nor even because there is an end which we want to achieve, but because we feel ourselves *under an obligation* to do them. For example, someone may do something because he has promised to do it, and thus feels obligated, even though he does not want to do it. It is sometimes suggested that in such cases we do the action, because, after all, we want to keep our promises; so, even here, we are doing what we want. However, this dodge will not work: If I have promised to do something, and if I do not want to do it, then it is simply false to say that I want to keep my promise. In such cases we feel a conflict precisely because we do not want to do what we feel obligated to do. It is reasonable to think that Smith's action falls roughly into this second category: He might stay behind, not because he wants to, but because he feels that his friend needs help.

But suppose we were to concede, for the sake of the argument, that all voluntary action is motivated by the agent's wants, or at least that Smith is so motivated. Even if these were granted, it would not follow that Smith is acting selfishly or from self-interest. For if Smith wants to do something that will help his friend, even when it means forgoing his own enjoyments, that is precisely what makes him *un-selfish*. What else could unselfishness be, if not wanting to help others? Another way to put the same point is to say that it is the *object* of a want that determines whether it is selfish or not. The mere fact that I am acting on *my* wants does not mean that I am acting selfishly; that depends on *what it is* that I want. If I want only my own good, and care nothing for others, then I am selfish; but if I also want other people to be well-off and happy, and if I act on *that* desire, then my action is not selfish. So much for this argument.

B. The second argument for psychological egoism is this. Since so-called unselfish actions always produce a sense of self-satisfaction in the agent,[2] and since this sense of satisfaction is a pleasant state of consciousness, it follows that the point of the action is really to achieve a pleasant state of consciousness, rather than bring about any good for others. Therefore, the action is "unselfish" only at a superficial level of analysis. Smith will feel much better with himself for having stayed to help his friend—if he had gone to the country, he would have felt terrible about it—and that is the real point of the action. According to a well-known story, this argument was once expressed by Abraham Lincoln:

> Mr. Lincoln once remarked to a fellow-passenger on an old-time mud-coach that all men were prompted by selfishness in doing good. His fellow-passenger was antagonizing this position when they were passing over a corduroy bridge that spanned a slough. As they crossed this bridge they espied an old razor-backed sow on the bank making a terrible noise because her pigs had got into the slough and were in danger of drowning. As the old coach began to climb the hill, Mr. Lincoln called out, "Driver, can't you stop just a moment?" Then Mr. Lincoln jumped out, ran back, and lifted the little pigs out of the mud and water and placed them on the bank. When he returned, his companion remarked: "Now, Abe, where does selfishness come in on this little episode?" "Why, bless your soul, Ed, that was the very essence of selfishness. I should have had no peace of mind all day had I gone on and left that suffering old sow worrying over those pigs. I did it to get peace of mind, don't you see?"[3]

---

[2]Or, as it is sometimes said, "It gives him a clear conscience," or "He couldn't sleep at night if he had done otherwise," or "He would have been ashamed of himself for not doing it," and so on.

This argument suffers from defects similar to the previous one. Why should we think that merely because someone derives satisfaction from helping others this makes him selfish? Isn't the unselfish man precisely the one who *does* derive satisfaction from helping others, while the selfish man does not? If Lincoln "got peace of mind" from rescuing the piglets, does this show him to be selfish, or, on the contrary, doesn't it show him to be compassionate and good-hearted? (If a man were truly selfish, why should it bother his conscience that *others* suffer—much less pigs?) Similarly, it is nothing more than shabby sophistry to say, because Smith takes satisfaction in helping his friend, that he is behaving selfishly. If we say this rapidly, while thinking about something else, perhaps it will sound all right; but if we speak slowly, and pay attention to what we are saying, it sounds plain silly.

Moreover, suppose we ask *why* Smith derives satisfaction from helping his friend. The answer will be, it is because Smith cares for him and wants him to succeed. If Smith did not have these concerns, then he would take no pleasure in assisting him; and these concerns, as we have already seen, are the marks of unselfishness, not selfishness. To put the point more generally: If we have a positive attitude toward the attainment of some goal, then we may derive satisfaction from attaining that goal. But the *object* of our attitude is *the attainment of that goal;* and we must want to attain the goal *before* we can find any satisfaction in it. We do not, in other words, desire some sort of "pleasurable consciousness" and then try to figure out how to achieve it; rather, we desire all sorts of different things—money, a new fishing-boat, to be a better chessplayer, to get a promotion in our work, etc.—and because we desire these things, we derive satisfaction from attaining them. And so, if someone desires the welfare and happiness of another person, he will derive satisfaction from that; but this does not mean that this satisfaction is the object of his desire, or that he is in any way selfish on account of it.

It is a measure of the weakness of psychological egoism that these insupportable arguments are the ones most often advanced in its favor. Why, then, should anyone ever have thought it a true view? Perhaps because of a desire for theoretical simplicity: In thinking

---

[3]Frank C. Sharp, *Ethics* (New York, 1928), pp. 74–75. Quoted from the Springfield (Ill.) *Monitor* in the *Outlook*, vol. 56, p. 1059.

about human conduct, it would be nice if there were some simple formula that would unite the diverse phenomena of human behavior under a single explanatory principle, just as simple formulae in physics bring together a great many apparently different phenomena. And since it is obvious that self-regard is an overwhelmingly important factor in motivation, it is only natural to wonder whether all motivation might not be explained in these terms. But the answer is clearly No; while a great many human actions are motivated entirely or in part by self-interest, only by a deliberate distortion of the facts can we say that all conduct is so motivated. This will be clear, I think, if we correct three confusions which are commonplace. The exposure of these confusions will remove the last traces of plausibility from the psychological egoist thesis.

The first is the confusion of selfishness with self-interest. The two are clearly not the same. If I see a physician when I am feeling poorly, I am acting in my own interest but no one would think of calling me "selfish" on account of it. Similarly, brushing my teeth, working hard at my job, and obeying the law are all in my self-interest but none of these are examples of selfish conduct. This is because selfish behavior is behavior that ignores the interests of others, in circumstances in which their interests ought not to be ignored. This concept has a definite evaluative flavor; to call someone "selfish" is not just to describe his action but to condemn it. Thus, you would not call me selfish for eating a normal meal in normal circumstances (although it may surely be in my self-interest); but you would call me selfish for hoarding food while others about are starving.

The second confusion is the assumption that every action is done *either* from self-interest or from other-regarding motives. Thus, the egoist concludes that if there is no such thing as genuine altruism then all actions must be done from self-interest. But this is certainly a false dichotomy. The man who continues to smoke cigarettes, even after learning about the connection between smoking and cancer, is surely not acting from self-interest, not even by his own standards—self-interest would dictate that he quit smoking at once—and he is not acting altruistically either. He *is*, no doubt, smoking for the pleasure of it, but all that this shows is that undisciplined pleasure-seeking and acting from self-interest are very different. This is what led Butler to remark that "The thing to be lamented is, not that men have so great regard to their own good or interest in the present world, for they have not enough."[4]

The last two paragraphs show (*a*) that it is false that all actions are selfish, and (*b*) that it is false that all actions are done out of self-interest. And it should be noted that these two points can be made, and were, without any appeal to putative examples of altruism.

The third confusion is the common but false assumption that a concern for one's own welfare is incompatible with any genuine concern for the welfare of others. Thus, since it is obvious that everyone (or very nearly everyone) does desire his own well-being, it might be thought that no one can really be concerned with others. But again, this is false. There is no inconsistency in desiring that everyone, including oneself *and* others, be well-off and happy. To be sure, it may happen on occasion that our own interests conflict with the interests of others, and in these cases we will have to make hard choices. But even in these cases we might sometimes opt for the interests of others, especially when the others involved are our family or friends. But more importantly, not all cases are like this: Sometimes we are able to promote the welfare of others when our own interests are not involved at all. In these cases not even the strongest self-regard need prevent us from acting considerately toward others.

Once these confusions are cleared away, it seems to me obvious enough that there is no reason whatever to accept psychological egoism. On the contrary, if we simply observe people's behavior with an open mind, we may find that a great deal of it is motivated by self-regard, but by no means all of it; and that there is no reason to deny that "the moral institution of life" can include a place for the virtue of beneficence.[5]

## III

The ethical egoist would say at this point, "Of course it is possible for people to act altruistically, and perhaps many people do act that way—but there is no reason why they *should* do so. A person is under no obligation to do anything except what is in his own interests."[6]

---

[4]*The Works of Joseph Butler*, ed. W. E. Gladstone (Oxford, 1896), vol. 2, p. 26.

[5]The capacity for altruistic behavior is not unique to human beings. Some interesting experiments with rhesus monkeys have shown that these animals will refrain from operating a device for securing food if this causes other animals to suffer pain. See Masserman, Wechkin, and Terris, "'Altruistic Behavior in Rhesus Monkeys," *The American Journal of Psychiatry*, vol. 121 (1964), 584–585.

[6]I take this to be the view of Ayn Rand, insofar as I understand her confusing doctrine.

This is really quite a radical doctrine. Suppose I have an urge to set fire to some public building (say, a department store) just for the fascination of watching the spectacular blaze: According to this view, the fact that several people might be burned to death provides no reason whatever why I should not do it. After all, this only concerns *their* welfare, not my own, and according to the ethical egoist the only person I need think of is myself.

Some might deny that ethical egoism has any such monstrous consequences. They would point out that it is really to my own advantage not to set the fire—for, if I do that I may be caught and put into prison (unlike Gyges, I have no magic ring for protection). Moreover, even if I could avoid being caught it is still to my advantage to respect the rights and interests of others, for it is to my advantage to live in a society in which people's rights and interests are respected. Only in such a society can I live a happy and secure life; so, in acting kindly toward others, I would merely be doing my part to create and maintain the sort of society which it is to my advantage to have.[7] Therefore, it is said, the egoist would not be such a bad man; he would be as kindly and considerate as anyone else, because he would see that it is to his own advantage to be kindly and considerate.

This is a seductive line of thought, but it seems to me mistaken. Certainly it is to everyone's advantage (including the egoist's) to preserve a stable society where people's interests are generally protected. But there is no reason for the egoist to think that merely because *he* will not honor the rules of the social game, decent society will collapse. For the vast majority of people are not egoists, and there is no reason to think that they will be converted by his example—especially if he is discreet and does not unduly flaunt his style of life. What this line of reasoning shows is not that the egoist himself must act benevolently, but that he must encourage *others* to do so. He must take care to conceal from public view his own self-centered method of decision-making, and urge others to act on precepts very different from those on which he is willing to act.

The rational egoist, then, cannot advocate that egoism be universally adopted by everyone. For he wants a world in which his own interests are maximized; and if other people adopted the egoistic

---

[7] *Cf.* Thomas Hobbes, *Leviathan* (London, 1651), chap. 17.

policy of pursuing their own interests to the exclusion of his interest, as he pursues his interest to the exclusion of theirs, then such a world would be impossible. So he himself will be egoist, but he will want others to be altruists.

This brings us to what is perhaps the most popular "refutation" of ethical egoism current among philosophical writers—the argument that ethical egoism is at bottom inconsistent because it cannot be universalized.[8] The argument goes like this:

To say that any action or policy of action is *right* (or that it *ought* to be adopted) entails that it is right for *anyone* in the same sort of circumstances. I cannot, for example, say that it is right for me to lie to you, and yet object when you lie to me (provided, of course, that the circumstances are the same). I cannot hold that it is all right for me to drink your beer and then complain when you drink mine. This is just the requirement that we be consistent in our evaluations; it is a requirement of logic. Now it is said that ethical egoism cannot meet this requirement because, as we have already seen, the egoist would not want others to act in the same way that he acts. Moreover, suppose he *did* advocate the universal adoption of egoistic policies: he would be saying to Peter, "You ought to pursue your own interests even if it means destroying Paul"; and he would be saying to Paul, "You ought to pursue your own interests even if it means destroying Peter." The attitudes expressed in these two recommendations seem clearly inconsistent—he is urging the advancement of Peter's interest at one moment, and countenancing their defeat at the next. Therefore, the argument goes, there is no way to maintain the doctrine of ethical egoism as a consistent view about how we ought to act. We will fall into inconsistency whenever we try.

What are we to make of this argument? Are we to conclude that ethical egoism has been refuted? Such a conclusion, I think, would be unwarranted; for I think that we can show, contrary to this argument, how ethical egoism can be maintained consistently. We need only to interpret the egoist's position in a sympathetic way: We should say that he has in mind a certain kind of world which he would prefer over all others; it would be a world in which his own interests were maximized, regardless of the effects on other people.

---

[8]See, for example, Brian Medlin, "Ultimate Principles and Ethical Egoism," *Australasian Journal of Philosophy,* vol. 35 (1957), 111–118; and D. H. Monro, *Empiricism and Ethics* (Cambridge, 1967), chap. 16.

The egoist's primary policy of action, then, would be to act in such a way as to bring about, as nearly as possible, this sort of world. Regardless of however morally reprehensible we might find it, there is nothing *inconsistent* in someone's adopting this as his ideal and acting in a way calculated to bring it about. And if someone did adopt this as his ideal, then he would advocate universal altruism; as we have already seen, he would want other people to be altruists. So if he advocates any principles of conduct for the general public, they will be altruistic principles. This would not be inconsistent; on the contrary, it would be perfectly consistent with his goal of creating a world in which his own interests are maximized. To be sure, he would have to be deceitful; in order to secure the good will of others, and a favorable hearing for his exhortations to altruism, he would have to pretend that he was himself prepared to accept altruistic principles. But again, that would be all right; from the egoist's point of view, this would merely be a matter of adopting the necessary means to the achievement of his goal—and while we might not approve of this, there is nothing inconsistent about it. Again, it might be said, "He advocates one thing, but does another. Surely *that's* inconsistent." But it is not; for what he advocates and what he does are both calculated as means to an end (the *same* end, we might note); and as such, he is doing what is rationally required in each case. Therefore, contrary to the previous argument, there is nothing inconsistent in the ethical egoist's view. He cannot be refuted by the claim that he contradicts himself.

Is there, then, no way to refute the ethical egoist? If by "refute" we mean show that he has made some *logical* error, the answer is that there is not. However, there is something more that can be said. The egoist challenge to our ordinary moral convictions amounts to a demand for an explanation of why we should adopt certain policies of action, namely policies in which the good of others is given importance. We can give an answer to this demand, albeit an indirect one. The reason one ought not to do actions that would hurt other people is: Other people would be hurt. The reason one ought to do actions that would benefit other people is: Other people would be benefited. This may at first seem like a piece of philosophical sleight-of-hand, but it is not. The point is that the welfare of human beings is something that most of us value *for its own sake,* and not merely for the sake of something else. Therefore, when *further* reasons are demanded for valuing the welfare of human beings, we cannot point to anything further to satisfy this demand. It is not that we have no reason for pursuing these policies, but that our reason *is* that these policies are for the good of human beings.

So if we are asked, "Why shouldn't I set fire to this department store?" one answer would be, "Because if you do, people may be burned to death." This is a complete, sufficient reason which does not require qualification or supplementation of any sort. If someone seriously wants to know why this action shouldn't be done, that's the reason. If we are pressed further and asked the skeptical question, "But why shouldn't I do actions that will harm others?" we may not know what to say—but this is because the questioner has included in his question the very answer we would like to give: "Why shouldn't you do actions that will harm others? Because doing those actions would harm others." The egoist, no doubt, will not be happy with this. He will protest that *we* may accept this as a reason, but *he* does not. And here the argument stops: There are limits to what can be accomplished by argument, and if the egoist really doesn't care about other people—if he honestly doesn't care whether they are helped or hurt by his actions—then we have reached those limits. If we want to persuade him to act decently toward his fellow humans, we will have to make our appeal to such other attitudes as he does possess, by threats, bribes, or other cajolery. That is all that we can do.

Though some may find this situation distressing (we would like to be able to show that the egoist is just *wrong*), it holds no embarrassment for common morality. What we have come up against is simply a fundamental requirement of rational action, namely, that the existence of reasons for action always depends on the prior existence of certain attitudes in the agent. For example, the fact that a certain course of action would make the agent a lot of money is a reason for doing it only if the agent wants to make money; the fact that practicing at chess makes one a better player is a reason for practicing only if one wants to be a better player; and so on. Similarly, the fact that a certain action would help the agent is a reason for doing the action only if the agent cares about his own welfare, and the fact that an action would help others is a reason for doing it only if the agent cares about others. In this respect ethical egoism and what we might call ethical altruism are in exactly the same fix: Both require that the agent *care* about himself, or other people, before they can get started.

So a nonegoist will accept "It would harm another person" as a reason not to do an action simply because he cares about what happens to that other person. When the egoist says that he does *not* accept that as a reason, he is saying something quite extraordinary. He is saying that he has no affection for friends or family, that he never feels pity or compassion, that he is the sort of person who can look on scenes of human misery with complete indifference, so long as he is not the one suffering. Genuine egoists, people who really don't care at all about anyone than themselves, are rare. It is important to keep this in mind when thinking about ethical egoism; it is easy to forget just how fundamental to human psychological makeup the feeling of sympathy is. Indeed, a man without any sympathy at all would scarcely be recognizable as a man; and that is what makes ethical egoism such a disturbing doctrine in the first place.

## IV

There are, of course, many different ways in which the skeptic might challenge the assumptions underlying our moral practice. In this essay I have discussed only two of them, the two put forward by Glaucon in the passage that I cited from Plato's *Republic*. It is important that the assumptions underlying our moral practice should not be confused with particular judgments made within that practice. To defend one is not to defend the other. We may assume—quite properly, if my analysis has been correct—that the virtue of beneficence does, and indeed should, occupy an important place in "the moral institution of life"; and yet we may make constant and miserable errors when it comes to judging when and in what ways this virtue is to be exercised. Even worse, we may often be able to make accurate moral judgments, and know what we ought to do, but not do it. For these ills, philosophy alone is not the cure.

### STUDY QUESTIONS

1. The great Renaissance philosopher Thomas Hobbes was a proponent of psychological egoism. Someone once saw him giving money to a beggar and asked if this kindly gesture did not prove that psychological egoism was wrong. Hobbes replied that his

action was indeed self-interested because helping beggars made him feel good. Evaluate Hobbes's riposte in light of Rachel's discussion.

2.  If you found the Ring of Gyges and no longer needed to appear to abide by moral rules, do you think you would behave as Gyges did? Do you think that other controls would prevent you from becoming amoral?

3.  What is Rachel's strongest argument against psychological egoism? Against ethical egoism? Are Rachel's arguments persuasive?

4.  The psychological egoist says that self-love motivates all human action. A number of philosophers have argued that self-hate, altruism, and malice also motivate human beings. Who do you think is right?

# *Why Not Murder?*

## FYODOR DOSTOYEVSKI

Fyodor Dostoyevski (1821–1881) was one of the greatest Russian novelists. His stories are both dramatic and philosophical. Among his most famous works are *The House of the Dead* (1860), *Crime and Punishment* (1866), *The Idiot* (1867), and *The Brothers Karamazov* (1879).

The "criminal mind" fascinated Fyodor Dostoyevski. The crime in *Crime and Punishment* is murder. The victim is a wealthy and heartless old woman who "deserves to die." Raskolnikov is not so much interested in getting her money as he is in righting the injustice of the fact that she possesses it while so many other people suffer want. Dostoyevski suggests that Raskolnikov may even distribute the money once he gets it. Of course murder is a

WHY NOT MURDER? From *Crime and Punishment* by Fyodor Dostoyevski. Translated by Jessie Coulson (Oxford University Press, 1953). Reprinted by permission of the publisher.

crime, but is it *morally* wrong to rid the world of this woman? Raskolnikov convinces himself that this evil woman does not deserve the protection of the law. She is "not human." Why not murder her and put her money to good use? Raskolnikov decides to kill her after he overhears others arguing that killing this evil and miserly old woman would be right. Raskolnikov believes there would be general agreement that the world would be better without her. In any case, she would hardly be an "innocent victim." Yet in the course of the crime, Raskolnikov finds himself killing a second victim, one who is altogether innocent. Now Raskolnikov sees himself to be morally as well as legally culpable. Dostoyevski's novel is an implicit argument against putting oneself above the moral law.

Later Raskolnikov learnt, by some chance, why the dealer and his wife had asked Lizaveta to come and see them. It was a perfectly usual transaction, with nothing out of the ordinary about it. An impoverished family, lately come to St. Petersburg, wished to dispose of some articles of women's clothing and similar things. It would not have paid them to sell in the market and so they were looking for a dealer. Lizaveta undertook such transactions, selling on commission, and going round arranging business deals, and she had a large clientele because she was honest and never haggled, but named her price and stuck to it. She did not talk much and, as we have said, was timid and meek . . .

Raskolnikov had recently become superstitious. Traces of this superstition remained in him long afterwards, almost ineradicable. And in after years he was always inclined to see something strange and mysterious in all the happenings of this time, as if special coincidences and influences were at work. As long before as the previous winter a fellow student, Pokorev, who was leaving for Kharkov, had mentioned Alëna Ivanovna's address to him in conversation, in case he ever needed to pawn anything. For a long time he did not go near her, since he had his lessons and was managing to get along somehow, but six weeks earlier he had remembered the address. He had two things suitable for pawning: his father's old silver watch and a gold ring set with three little red stones, given to him as a keepsake by his sister when they parted. He decided to take the ring, and sought out the old woman; at first sight, before he knew anything about her, he felt an irresistible dislike of her. He took her two rouble notes and on his way home stopped at a miserable little tavern and asked for tea. He sat down, deep in thought; a strange idea seemed to be pecking away in his head, like a chicken emerging from the shell, and all his attention was fixed on it.

At another table near by, a student, who was unknown to him and whom he did not remember ever seeing, was sitting with a young officer. They had been playing billiards and were drinking tea. Suddenly he heard the student talking about the moneylender Alëna Ivanovna, giving the officer her address. This struck Raskolnikov as rather odd: he had just left her, and here they were talking about her. Of course, it was the merest chance, but exactly when he was finding it impossible to rid himself of an extraordinary impression, here was somebody reinforcing it, for the student was beginning to tell his friend some details about this Alëna Ivanovna.

"She's quite famous," he said; "she always has money to lay out. She's as rich as a Jew, she can put her hands on five thousand roubles at once, and yet she doesn't turn up her nose at the interest on a rouble. A lot of our fellows have been to her. But she's an old bitch . . ."

And he began to recount how spiteful and cranky she was, and how, if payment was only one day overdue, the pledge would be lost. She would lend only a quarter as much as things were worth, she would demand five or even seven per cent a month, and so on. The student's tongue had run away with him, and, among other things, he informed his hearer that the old woman had a sister, Lizaveta, whom the vicious little thing was always beating and whom she kept in complete subjection and treated as if she were a child, although Lizaveta stood at least five foot ten . . .

"She's another extraordinary creature, you know!" cried the student, and burst out laughing.

They began to talk about Lizaveta. The student seemed greatly to enjoy this and kept on laughing, and the officer listened with great interest and asked the student to send this Lizaveta to do his mending. Raskolnikov also learned all about her, not missing one word. Lizaveta was the old woman's younger step-sister (they had different mothers) and was about thirty-five. She worked for her sister day in and day out, did all the cooking and washing in the house, and in addition took in sewing and even went out scrubbing floors, and everything she earned she handed over to her sister. She dared not accept any orders or undertake any work without the old woman's permission. As Lizaveta knew, the old woman had already made her will, leaving to the younger sister only furniture and other chattels, while all the money went to a monastery in N—— Province for masses for the eternal repose of her soul. Lizaveta was a woman of the working-class, not educated, and unmarried; she was remarkably tall and extremely ungainly, with big, long, splay feet, shod with down-at-heel goat-skin shoes, and she always kept herself very clean. But what the student found the most surprising and amusing was that Lizaveta was pregnant . . .

"But I thought you said she was monstrously ugly," remarked the officer.

"Well, she's very dark-skinned, and looks like a guardsman in disguise, but, you know, she's no monster. She has a nice kind face and eyes—she's even very attractive. The proof is, a lot of people like her. She is so quiet and gentle and mild, and will consent to anything. And she's really got a very nice smile."

"You like her yourself, don't you?" laughed the officer.

"Because she's an oddity. But I'll tell you what: I swear I could kill that damned old woman and rob her, without a single twinge of conscience," exclaimed the student hotly.

The officer laughed again, but Raskolnikov found this so strange that he shuddered.

"Let me ask you a serious question," went on the student, even more heatedly. "I was joking just now, of course, but look here: on the one hand you have a stupid, silly, utterly unimportant, vicious, sickly old woman, no good to anybody, but in fact quite the opposite, who doesn't know herself why she goes on living, and will probably die tomorrow without any assistance. Do you understand what I am saying?"

"Oh, I follow you," answered the officer, earnestly studying his companion's vehemence.

"Listen, then. On the other hand you have new, young forces running to waste for want of backing, and there are thousands of them, all over the place. A hundred, a thousand, good actions and promising beginnings might be forwarded and directed aright by the money that old woman destines for a monastery; hundreds, perhaps thousands, of existences might be set on the right path, scores of families saved from beggary, from decay, from ruin and corruption, from the lock hospitals—and all with her money! Kill her, take her money, on condition that you dedicate yourself with its help to the service of humanity and the common good: don't you think that thousands of good deeds will wipe out one little, insignificant transgression? For one life taken, thousands saved from corruption and decay! One death, and a hundred lives in exchange—why, it's simple arithmetic! What is the life of that stupid, spiteful, consumptive old woman weighed against the common good? No more than the life of a louse or a cockroach—less, indeed, because she is actively harmful. She battens on other people's lives, she is evil; not long since she bit Lizaveta's finger, out of sheer malice, and it almost had to be amputated!"

"She doesn't deserve to live, certainly," remarked the officer, "but there you are, that's nature."

"But don't you see, man, nature must be guided and corrected, or else we should all be swamped with prejudices. Otherwise there could never be one great man. They talk of 'duty, conscience'—I've got nothing to say against duty and conscience—but what are we to understand by them? Stop, I will put another question to you. Listen!"

"No, you stop; I will ask you a question. Listen!"

"Well?"

"Here you've been holding forth and making a regular speech, but tell me this: would you kill the old woman with your own hands, or not?"

"Of course not! For the sake of justice, I . . . This is not a question of me at all!"

"Well, if you ask me, so long as you won't, justice doesn't come into it. Let's have another game!"

Raskolnikov was deeply disturbed. No doubt there was nothing in all this but the most usual and ordinary youthful talk and ideas, such as he had heard often enough in other forms and about other subjects. But why must he listen at this particular moment to that particular talk and those particular ideas when there had just been born in his own brain *exactly the same ideas*? And why, at the very moment when he was carrying away from the old woman's flat the germ of his idea, should he chance upon a conversation about that same old woman? . . . This always seemed to him a strange coincidence. This casual public-house conversation had an extraordinary influence on the subsequent development of the matter, as if there were indeed something fateful and fore-ordained about it.

When he returned home from the Haymarket he threw himself on the sofa and sat there without moving for an hour. It grew dark, and he had no candles, not that it would have entered his head to light one if he had. Afterwards he was never able to remember whether he had been thinking of anything definite during that hour. At length he felt his recent chills and fever return, and realized with pleasure that he could lie down where he was. Soon a heavy leaden sleep weighed him down.

He slept unusually long and dreamlessly. Nastasya, coming into his room next morning at ten o'clock, could hardly shake him awake. She had brought him some tea and bread. The tea was once again what remained in her own teapot.

"Goodness, he's still asleep!" she exclaimed indignantly, "he's always asleep!"

He raised himself with an effort. His head ached; he stood up, took a few steps, and fell back on the sofa again.

"Are you going to sleep again?" exclaimed Nastasya. "Are you ill, or what?"

He did not answer.

"Do you want any tea?"

"Afterwards," he said with an effort, closing his eyes again and turning to the wall. Nastasya stood over him.

"Perhaps he really *is* ill," she said, turned on her heel and went out.

She came back at two o'clock with some soup. He was lying there as before. The tea was untouched. Nastasya was quite offended and began to shake him roughly.

"Whyever do you still go on sleeping?" she exclaimed, looking at him with positive dislike. He sat up and remained gazing at the floor without a word to her.

"Are you ill or aren't you?" asked Nastasya, and again received no answer.

"You want to go out for a bit," she said, after a short silence, "and get a bit of a blow. Are you going to have anything to eat, eh?"

"Later," he said feebly. "Clear out!" He waved her away.

She stood there a little longer, looking at him pityingly, and then went out.

After a few minutes he raised his eyes and stared at the tea and soup. Then he took up some bread and a spoon and began to eat.

He ate a little—two or three spoonfuls—but without appetite, and quite mechanically. His head no longer ached so much. When he had eaten, he stretched out once more on the sofa, but he could not go to sleep again and lay without stirring, face downwards, with his head buried in the pillow. He lost himself in a maze of waking dreams, and very strange ones they were; in the one that recurred most often he was in Africa, in Egypt, at some oasis. A caravan was resting, the camels lying peacefully and the men eating their evening meal; all around, the palms stood in a great circle. He was drinking the water from a stream which flowed babbling beside him, clear and cool, running marvellously bright and blue over the coloured stones and the clean sand with its gleams of gold . . . All at once he distinctly heard a clock strike. He roused himself with a start, raised his head and looked at the window, trying to estimate the time, and then, suddenly wide awake, sprang up as if he had been catapulted from the sofa. He crept to the door on tiptoe, quietly eased it open, and stood listening for sounds from the staircase. His heart was beating wildly. But the staircase was quiet, as though everyone were asleep . . . It seemed to him incredibly strange that he could have gone on sleeping in such utter forgetfulness ever since the previous night, without having made the least preparation . . . And it might have been six o'clock that struck just now . . . An extraordinarily confused and feverish bustle had now replaced his sleepy torpor. He had not many preparations to make. He was straining every nerve to take everything into consideration and let nothing slip his memory, and his heart thumped so heavily that he could scarcely breathe. First of all he must make a loop and sew it into his overcoat, the work of a moment. He groped under his pillow and drew out from among the linen stuffed under it an old unwashed shirt that was falling to pieces. From among its tatters he ripped out a strip about an inch and a half wide and twelve long. He folded this strip in two, took off his only outer garment, a loose summer overcoat of thick stout cotton material, and sewed the two ends of the strip together to the inside, under the left armhole. His hands shook as he sewed, but he controlled them, and when he put the coat on again nothing showed from the outside. He had got the needle and thread ready long before, and had kept them on the little table, pinned into a piece of paper. As for the loop, that was an ingenious device of his own; it was meant to hold the axe. He could hardly carry an axe in his hands through the streets. And even if he had hidden it under his coat, he would still have had to support it with his hand, which would be noticeable. But now he need only lay the axe-head in the loop and it would hang peacefully under his arm all the way. With his hand in his pocket he could support the end of the shaft so that it would not swing; and as the coat was very wide and hung like a sack, nobody could possibly notice that he was holding something through the pocket. He had thought of this loop at least two weeks before.

Having finished this task, he thrust his fingers into the narrow crevice between the bottom of his "Turkish" divan and the floor, groping under the left-hand corner for the *pledge* he had prepared and hidden there. It was not really a pledge at all, however, but simply a piece of smoothly-planed board, about the size and thickness of a silver cigarette-case. He had found it by chance, on one of his walks, in a yard where there was some sort of workshop in an out-building. On the same occasion he picked up in the street, a little later, a smooth thin iron plate, rather smaller than the wood, apparently broken off something. Laying the two together, he had tied them securely with thread and then wrapped them neatly and carefully in clean white paper and made them into a parcel with thin string tied in a complicated knot that would need a great deal of skill to undo. This was done in order to distract the old woman's attention for a time while she dealt with the knot, and thus enable him to choose his moment. The iron plate had been added to increase the weight, so that she should not immediately recognize that the "pledge" was made of wood. He had hidden the whole thing under the sofa until he needed it. He had just got it out when he heard someone shouting in the courtyard.

"It went six ages ago."

"Ages ago! Oh God!"

He flung himself towards the door, listened, seized his hat, and crept as stealthily as a cat down his thirteen stairs. The most important step still lay before him—stealing an axe from the kitchen. He had long since come to the conclusion that he needed an axe to accomplish his purpose. He did possess a folding garden-knife, but he could not rely on a knife, or on his own strength in wielding it, and therefore finally settled on an axe. One noticeable peculiarity

418

characterized all the final decisions he arrived at in this affair: the more settled they were, the more hideous and absurd they appeared in his eyes. In spite of his agonizing internal struggles he could never throughout the whole time believe for one instant in the practicability of his schemes.

If it had somehow come about that the whole project had been analysed and finally decided down to the last detail, and no further doubts remained, he would very likely have renounced the whole idea for its absurdity, enormity, and impossibility. But there were in fact innumerable doubts and unsettled details. As for where he would obtain the axe, this trifle did not disturb him in the slightest, for nothing could be easier. The fact was that Nastasya was often out of the house, especially in the evening; she was always calling on the neighbours or running out to the shops, and the door was always left wide open; this was the landlady's only quarrel with her. Thus it would only be necessary to slip quietly into the kitchen, when the time came, take the axe, and then an hour later (when *it* was all over), put it back again. One doubt still remained, however: suppose he came back after an hour to return the axe, and found Nastasya back at home? It would, of course, be necessary to go straight past and wait until she went out again, but what if meanwhile she remembered the axe and looked for it, and raised an outcry? That would create suspicion, or at least give grounds for it.

But all these were trifles, about which he had not even begun to think, and there was no time for them now. He had thought about the main point, but he had put the details aside until *he had convinced himself.* This last, however, appeared definitely unrealizable. So at least it seemed to him. He could not, for example, picture himself ceasing at a given moment to think about it, getting up and—simply going there . . . Even his recent *rehearsal* (that is, his visit for a final survey of the scene) had been no more than a *test,* and far from a serious one, as though he had said to himself: "Very well, let us go and try whether it's just an idle fancy!"—and then immediately failed in the test, spat, and run away, exasperated with himself. And yet it would seem that his analysis, in the sense of a moral solution of the question, was concluded; his casuistry had the cutting edge of a razor, and he could no longer find any conscious objections in his own mind. But in the last resort he simply did not believe himself and obstinately, slavishly groped for objections on all sides, as if he were driven by some compulsion. His reactions during this last day, which had come upon him so unexpectedly and settled everything at one stroke, were almost completely mechanical, as though someone had taken his hand and pulled him along irresistibly, blindly, with super-natural strength and without objection. It was as if a part of his clothing had been caught in the wheel of a machine and he was being dragged into it.

The first question he had been concerned with—a long time ago now—was why most crimes were so easily discovered and solved, and why nearly every criminal left so clear a trail. He arrived by degrees at a variety of curious conclusions, and, in his opinion, the chief cause lay not so much in the material impossibility of conceal-ing the crime as in the criminal himself; nearly every criminal, at the moment of the crime, was subject to a collapse of will-power and reason, exchanging them for an extraordinarily childish heedless-ness, and that just at the moment when judgement and caution were most indispensable. He was convinced that this eclipse of reason and failure of will attacked a man like an illness, developed gradually and reached their height shortly before the commission of the crime, continuing unchanged at the moment of commission and for some time, varying with the individual, afterwards; their subsequent course was that of any other disease. The further question whether the disease engenders the crime, or whether the nature of crime some-how results in its always being accompanied by some manifestation of disease, he did not feel competent to answer.

Having arrived at this conclusion, he decided that he personally would not be subject to any such morbid subversion, that his judge-ment and will would remain steadfast throughout the fulfilment of his plans, for the simple reason that what he contemplated was "no crime" . . . We omit the course of reasoning by which he arrived at this latter verdict, since we have already run too far ahead . . . We shall add only that the practical, material difficulties played only a very secondary role in his thinking. "It will suffice to concentrate my will and my judgement on them, and they will all be overcome, when the time comes, when I have to come to grips with all the details of the affair, down to the most minute . . ." But he made no progress towards action. He continued to have less and less faith in his final decisions, and when the hour struck, everything seemed to go awry, in a haphazard and almost completely unexpected way.

One small circumstance nonplussed him even before he reached the foot of the stairs. As he drew level with his landlady's kitchen door, which stood open as usual, he peered carefully round it to make sure beforehand that the landlady herself was not there in Nastasya's absence, and if she was not, that her door was firmly closed so that she would not happen to look out and see him when he went in for the axe. But what was his consternation at seeing that Nastasya was at home in her kitchen on this occasion, and busy taking linen from a basket and hanging it on a line. When she caught sight of him she ceased her occupation and turned towards him, watching him as he went past. He turned his eyes away and walked on as if he had not noticed her. But it was all over: he had no axe! It was a terrible blow.

"Where did I get the idea," he thought, going out through the gate, "where did I get the idea that she was certain to be out now? Why, why, why, was I so convinced of it?" He felt crushed, even humiliated, and ready to laugh spitefully at himself . . . He was seething with dull, brutal rage.

He had stopped uncertainly in the gateway. To go out now and walk about the steets for form's sake, and to return to his room, were both equally repugnant to him. "What an opportunity is lost for ever!" he muttered, standing aimlessly in the gateway, just opposite the porter's dark little room, which also stood open. Suddenly he started. Inside the little room, not two paces away, under a bench on the right-hand side, something shining caught his eye . . . He looked all round—nobody! On tiptoe he approached the porter's lodge, went down the two steps, and called the porter in a feeble voice. "Yes, he's out! but he must be somewhere near, in the courtyard, since the door is open." He threw himself headlong on the axe (it was an axe), drew it out from where it lay between two logs under the bench, hung it in the loop on the spot, thrust both hands into his pockets and went out. He had not been seen. "It was not my planning, but the devil, that accomplished that!" he thought, and laughed strangely, extraordinarily heartened by this stroke of luck.

He walked quietly and sedately, without hurrying, so as not to arouse suspicion. He paid little attention to the passers-by, and carefully avoided looking at their faces, trying to be unnoticed himself. Suddenly he remembered his hat. "My God! I had the money two days ago, and hadn't the sense to spend it on a cap!" and he cursed himself from the bottom of his heart.

Glancing casually into a shop, he saw from the clock that hung on the wall that it was already ten minutes past seven. He would have to hurry; he wanted to go round about, so as to approach the house from the other side.

Earlier, when he had tried to imagine what all this would be like, he had thought he would be very frightened. But he was not; indeed he was not frightened at all. His mind was even occupied, though not for long together, with irrelevant thoughts.

Passing the Yusupov Gardens, he began to consider the construction of tall fountains in all the squares, and how they would freshen the air. Following this train of thought he came to the conclusion that if the Summer Gardens could be extended right across the Champ de Mars and joined to those of the Mikhaylovsky Palace, it would add greatly to the beauty and amenities of the city. Then he suddenly began to wonder why, in big towns, people chose of their own free will to live where there were neither parks nor gardens, but only filth and squalor and evil smells. This reminded him of his own walks in the neighbourhood of the Haymarket, and brought him back to himself. "What rubbish!" he thought. "It would be better not to think at all!"

"So it is true that men going to execution are passionately interested in any object they chance to see on the way." The thought passed through his mind as briefly as a flash of lightning, for he suppressed it at once . . . But he had arrived; here was the house and the gate. Somewhere a clock struck, once. "What, can it possibly be half-past seven? Surely not; time is really flying!"

Luck was again with him as he turned in at the gate. At that very moment, as if by design, a huge load of hay also turned in, just in front of him, and completely screened him while he was passing through the archway. As soon as it had cleared the gateway and was in the courtyard, he slipped past it to the right. On the other side of the cart he could hear several voices shouting and quarrelling, but nobody noticed him and nobody passed him. Many of the windows opening on to the great courtyard stood open, but he could not find the strength to raise his head. The old woman's staircase was near, immediately to the right of the gate. Already he was on the stairs.

Drawing a deep breath and pressing his hand above his wildly beating heart, he once more felt for the axe and settled it in its loop, then began to mount the stairs carefully and quietly, listening at every step. But the staircase was empty at this hour; all the doors were closed and nobody was to be seen. On the second floor, it is true, the door of an empty flat was open, and painters were at work inside, but they did not even look up. He stopped for a moment, considering, and then went on. "Of course, it would be better if they were not there, but . . . there are two floors above them."

But here was the fourth floor, here was the door, here was the empty flat opposite. On the third floor the flat immediately below the old woman's also showed every sign of being empty: the visiting-card tacked to the door had been removed—they had left . . . He was out of breath. For a moment the thought stirred in his mind: "There is still time to go away." But he ignored it and began to listen at the old woman's door—dead silence! Then once more he listened down the stairs, long and attentively . . . Then he looked round for the last time, crept close to the door, straightened his clothes, and once again tried the axe in its loop. "I wonder if I look too pale," he thought, "and too agitated. She is mistrustful . . . Wouldn't it be better if I waited a little longer . . . until my heart stops thumping so? . . ."

But his heart did not stop. On the contrary, its throbbing grew more and more violent . . . He could stand it no longer, but stretched his hand slowly towards the bell, and rang it. After a few moments he rang again, louder.

There was no answer. There was no point in going on ringing in vain, and he was not in the mood to do so. The old woman was certainly at home, but she was suspicious and she was alone. He knew something of her habits . . . and he applied his ear to the door again. Either his hearing had grown strangely acute (which did not seem likely) or the sound was really distinctly audible, but at any rate he suddenly heard the careful placing of a hand on the handle of a lock and the rustle of clothing close to the door. Someone was standing silently just inside the door and listening, just as he was doing outside it, holding her breath and probably also with her ear to the door . . .

He purposely shifted his position and audibly muttered something, so as not to give the impression that he was being furtive; then he rang a third time, but quietly and firmly, without betraying any impatience. When he was afterwards able to recall everything clearly and plainly, that minute seemed stamped into his memory for ever; he could not understand whence he had acquired so much cunning, especially as his mind seemed momentarily to cloud over, and he lost all consciousness of his own body . . . A moment later, he heard the bolt being lifted.

As before, the door opened the merest crack, and again two sharp and mistrustful eyes peered at him from the darkness. Then Raskolnikov lost his head and made what might have been a serious mistake.

Apprehensive that the old woman might be alarmed at their being alone, and without any hope that his appearance would reassure her, he took hold of the door and pulled it towards him, so that she should not be tempted to lock herself in again. Although she did not pull the door shut again at this, she did not relinquish the handle, so that he almost pulled her out on the stairs. When he saw that she was standing across the doorway in such a way that he could not pass, he advanced straight upon her, and she stood aside startled. She seemed to be trying to say something but finding it impossible, and she kept her eyes fixed on him.

"Good evening, Alëna Ivanovna," he began, as easily as possible, but his voice refused to obey him, and was broken and trembling, "I have . . . brought you . . . something . . . but hadn't we better come in here . . . to the light? . . ." And without waiting for an invitation, he passed her and went into the room. The old woman hastened after him; her tongue seemed to have been loosened.

"God Lord! What are you doing? . . . Who are you? What do you want?"

"Excuse me, Alëna Ivanovna . . . You know me . . . Raskolnikov . . . See, I have brought the pledge I promised the other day," and he held it out to her.

The old woman threw a glance at it, but then immediately fixed her eyes on those of her uninvited guest. She looked at him attentively, ill-naturedly, and mistrustfully. A minute or so went by; he even thought he could see a glint of derision in her eyes, as if she had guessed everything. He felt that he was losing his nerve and was frightened, so frightened that he thought if she went on looking at him like that, without a word, for even half a minute longer, he would turn tail and run away.

"Why are you looking at me like that, as though you didn't recognize me?" he burst out angrily. "Do you want it, or don't you? I can take it somewhere else; it makes no difference to me."

He had not intended to say this, but it seemed to come of its own accord.

The old woman collected herself, and her visitor's resolute tone seemed to lull her mistrust.

"Why be so hasty, my friend? . . . What is it?" she asked, looking at the packet.

"A silver cigarette case; surely I told you that last time?"

She stretched out her hand.

"But what makes you so pale? And your hands are trembling. Are you ill or something?"

"Fever," he answered abruptly. "You can't help being pale . . . when you haven't anything to eat," he added, hardly able to articulate his words. His strength was failing again. But apparently the answer was plausible enough; the old woman took the packet.

"What is it?" she asked, weighing it in her hand and once again fixing her eyes on Raskolnikov.

"A thing . . . a cigarette-case . . . silver . . . look at it."

"It doesn't feel like silver. Lord, what a knot!" Trying to undo the string she turned for light towards the window (all her windows were closed, in spite of the oppressive heat), moved away from him and stood with her back to him. He unbuttoned his coat and freed the axe from the loop, but still kept it concealed, supporting it with his right hand under the garment. His arms seemed to have no strength in them; he felt them growing more and more numb and stiff with every moment. He was afraid of letting the axe slip and fall . . . His head was whirling.

"Why is it all wrapped up like this?" exclaimed the woman sharply, and turned towards him.

There was not a moment to lose. He pulled the axe out, swung it up with both hands, hardly conscious of what he was doing, and almost mechanically, without putting any force behind it, let the butt-end fall on her head. His strength seemed to have deserted him, but as soon as the axe descended it all returned to him.

The old woman was, as usual, bare-headed. Her thin fair hair, just turning grey, and thick with grease, was plaited into a rat's tail and fastened into a knot above her nape with a fragment of horn comb. Because she was so short the axe struck her full on the crown of the head. She cried out, but very feebly, and sank in a heap to the floor, still with enough strength left to raise both hands to her head. One of them still held the "pledge." Then he struck her again and yet again, with all his strength, always with the blunt side of the axe, and always on the crown of the head. Blood poured out as if from an overturned glass and the body toppled over on its back. He stepped away as it fell, and then stooped to see the face: she was dead. Her wide-open eyes looked ready to start out of their sockets, her forehead was wrinkled and her whole face convulsively distorted.

He laid the axe on the floor near the body and, taking care not to smear himself with the blood, felt in her pocket, the right-hand pocket, from which she had taken her keys last time. He was quite collected, his faculties were no longer clouded nor his head swimming, but his hands still shook. Later he remembered that he had been very painstakingly careful not to get bedaubed . . . He pulled out the keys; they were all together, as he remembered them, on a steel ring. He hurried straight into the bedroom with them. It was a very small room; on one wall was an enormous case of icons, and another was occupied by the big bed, very clean, covered with a silk patchwork quilt. The chest of drawers stood against the third wall. It was strange, but as soon as he began to try the keys in it, and heard their jingling, a convulsive shudder shook him; he longed suddenly to abandon the whole affair and go away. But this lasted only for a moment; it was too late now to retreat. He was even laughing at himself when another, most alarming, idea flashed into his mind, the idea that perhaps the old woman was still alive and might yet recover consciousness. He left the keys and the chest and ran back to the body, seized the axe and brandished it over the old woman again, but did not bring it down. There could be no doubt that she was dead. Stooping down again to examine the body more closely, he saw clearly that the skull was shattered. He stretched out his hand to touch her, but drew it back again; he could see plainly enough without that. By this time the blood had formed a pool on the floor. Then he noticed a cord round the old woman's neck and tugged at it, but it was too strong to snap, and besides, it was slippery with blood. He tried to draw it out from the bosom of her dress, but it seemed to be caught on something and would not come. Impatiently he raised the axe again, to sever the cord with a blow as it lay on the body, but he could not bring himself to do this, and finally, after struggling with it for two minutes, and getting the axe and his hands smeared with blood, he managed with some difficulty to cut the cord without touching the body with the axe; he took it off, and found, as he expected, a purse hanging there. There were two crosses on the cord, one of cypress-wood and the other of brass, as well as an enamelled religious medal, and beside them hung a small, soiled, chamois-leather purse, with a steel frame and clasp. It was crammed full;

Raskolnikov thrust it into his pocket without examining it and threw the crosses down on the old woman's breast; then, this time taking the axe with him, he hurried back into the bedroom.

With dreadful urgency he seized the keys and began to struggle with them once more. But all his efforts failed to force them into the locks, not so much because his hands were trembling as because his energy was misdirected; he would see, for example, that a key was the wrong one and would not fit, and yet go on thrusting at the lock with it. He pulled himself together and remembered that the big key with toothed wards, hanging with the other smaller ones, could not possibly belong to the chest of drawers, but must be for some trunk or other (as he had thought on the previous occasion), and that perhaps it was there that everything was hidden. He left the chest and looked first of all under the bed, knowing that old women usually keep their trunks there. He was right; there stood an important-looking steel-studded trunk of red leather, about thirty inches long, with a rounded lid. The toothed key fitted the lock and opened the trunk. On top, under a white sheet, lay a hare-skin coat with a red lining; under this were a silk dress, then a shawl, and then, at the bottom, what looked like a heap of rags. His first impulse was to wipe his bloody hands on the red lining of the fur coat. "It is red, so blood will not show on it," he reasoned, and then suddenly realized what he was doing and thought, with fear in his heart, "Good God, am I going out of my mind?"

But no sooner had he disturbed the rags than a gold watch slid out from under the coat. Hastily he began turning everything over, and found a number of gold articles thrust in among the rags, bracelets, chains, earrings, pins, and so forth, probably pledges, some of them perhaps unredeemed. Some were in cases, some simply wrapped in newspaper, but neatly and carefully, with the paper tidily folded and the packets tied with tape. He began to cram them hastily into the pockets of his overcoat and trousers, without opening the cases or undoing the parcels, but he did not manage to collect very many . . .

A footstep sounded in the room where the old woman lay. He stopped and remained motionless as the dead. But all was still; he must have imagined it. Then he distinctly heard a faint cry, or perhaps rather a feeble interrupted groaning, then dead silence again for a minute or two. He waited, crouching by the trunk, hardly daring to breathe; then he sprang up, seized the axe, and ran out of the room.

427

There in the middle of the floor, with a big bundle in her arms, stood Lizaveta, as white as a sheet, gazing in frozen horror at her murdered sister and apparently without the strength to cry out. When she saw him run in, she trembled like a leaf and her face twitched spasmodically; she raised her hand as if to cover her mouth, but no scream came and she backed slowly away from him towards the corner, with her eyes on him in a fixed stare, but still without a sound, as though she had no breath left to cry out. He flung himself forward with the axe; her lips writhed pitifully, like those of a young child when it is just beginning to be frightened and stands ready to scream, with its eyes fixed on the object of its fear. The wretched Lizaveta was so simple, brow-beaten, and utterly terrified that she did not even put up her arms to protect her face, natural and almost inevitable as the gesture would have been at this moment when the axe was brandished immediately above it. She only raised her free left hand a little and slowly stretched it out towards him as though she were trying to push him away. The blow fell on her skull, splitting it open from the top of the forehead almost to the crown of the head, and felling her instantly. Raskolnikov, completely beside himself, snatched up her bundle, threw it down again, and ran to the entrance.

The terror that possessed him had been growing greater and greater, especially after this second, unpremeditated murder. He wanted to get away as quickly as possible. If he had been in a condition to exercise a soberer judgement and see things more clearly, if he could only have recognized all the difficulty of his position and how desperate, hideous, and absurd it was, if he could have understood how many obstacles to surmount, perhaps even crimes to commit, still lay before him, before he could escape from the house and reach home—very probably he would have abandoned everything and given himself up, not out of fear for himself so much as from horror and repulsion for what he had done. Repulsion, indeed, was growing in his heart with every moment. Not for anything in the world would he have returned to the trunk, or even to the room.

But a growing distraction, that almost amounted to absentmindedness, had taken possession of him; at times he seemed to forget what he was doing, or rather to forget the important things and cling to trivialities. However, when he glanced into the kitchen and saw a pail half full of water on a bench, it gave him the idea of washing his hands and the axe. His hands were sticky with blood. He put the head of the axe in the water, then took a piece of soap that lay in a broken saucer on the window-sill, and began to wash his hands in the pail. When he had washed them he drew out the axe and washed the blade and then spent some three minutes trying to clean the part of the handle that was blood-stained, using soap to get the blood out. After this he wiped it with a cloth which was drying on a line stretched across the kitchen, and then spent a long time examining it carefully at the window. There were no stains left, but the handle was still damp. With great care he laid the axe in the loop under his coat. Then, as well as the dim light in the kitchen allowed, he examined his overcoat, trousers, and boots. At first glance there was nothing to give him away, except for some stains on his boots. He wiped them with a damp rag. He knew, however, that he had not been able to see very well, and might have failed to notice something quite conspicuous. He stood hesitating in the middle of the room. A dark and tormenting idea was beginning to rear its head, the idea that he was going out of his mind and that he was not capable of reasoning or of protecting himself. Perhaps what he was doing was not at all what ought to be done . . . "My God, I must run, I must run!" he muttered and hurried back to the entrance. Here there awaited him a more extreme terror than any he had yet experienced.

He stood still, staring, unable to believe his eyes; the door, the outer door leading to the staircase, the door at which he had rung a short time ago, and by which he had entered, was at least a hand's-breadth open; all this time it had been like that, neither locked nor bolted, all the time! The old woman had not locked it behind him, perhaps by way of precaution. But, good God, he had seen Lizaveta after that! And how could he have failed to realize that she had come from outside, and could certainly not have come through the wall?

He flung himself at the door and put up the bolt.

"But no, that's not right either! I must go, I must go . . ."

He lifted the bolt clear, opened the door, and stood listening on the landing.

He stood there a long time. Somewhere far below, probably under the gateway, two voices were raised loudly and shrilly in argument. "What are they doing?" He waited patiently. At last the voices fell silent, as though they had been cut off; "they" had gone away. He was preparing to descend when suddenly a door on the floor below opened noisily and somebody started down the stairs, humming a tune. "Why are they making so much noise?" he wondered for a moment. He closed the door again behind him and waited. At last all was quiet; there was not a sound. He was already setting his foot on the stairs when once more he heard footsteps.

When he first heard them, the steps were far away, at the very bottom of the staircase, but he afterwards remembered clearly and distinctly that from the very first sound he guessed that they were certainly coming *here,* to the fourth floor, to the old woman's flat. Why? Was there something special, something significant, about them? The steps were heavy, regular, unhurrying. Already they had reached the first floor, they were coming on, their sound was clearer and clearer. He could hear the newcomer's heavy breathing. Already the steps had passed the second floor . . . They were coming here! Suddenly he felt as if he had turned to stone, like a sleeper who dreams that he is being hotly pursued and threatened with death, and finds himself rooted to the spot, unable to stir a finger.

At length, when the footsteps had begun the last flight, he started to life, and just managed to slip swiftly and dextrously back from the landing into the flat and close the door behind him. Then he grasped the bolt and slid it gently, without a sound, into its socket. Instinct had come to his aid. When he had done, he stayed quiet, holding his breath, close to the door. The unknown visitor was also at the door. They were standing now, opposite one another, as he and the old woman had stood, with the door dividing them, when he had listened there a short time ago.

The visitor drew several heavy breaths. "He must be a big stout man," thought Raskolnikov, grasping the axe tightly. Everything seemed to be happening in a dream. The visitor seized the bell and rang it loudly.

As soon as its tinny sound had died, Raskolnikov imagined he heard movement inside the room, and for some seconds he listened as seriously as though it were possible. The unknown rang again, waited a little longer and then suddenly began to tug impatiently at the door-handle with all his might. Terrified, Raskolnikov watched the bolt rattling in its socket and waited in numb fear for it to jump clean out. This seemed likely to happen at any moment, so violently was the door shaken. He would have held the bar with his hand, except that *he* might discern it. His head was beginning to spin again. "I am going to faint!" he thought, but the unknown began to speak and he recovered himself immediately.

"Are they fast asleep in there, or dead, or what, confound them?"

the visitor boomed in a resounding voice. "Hey! Alëna Ivanovna, you old witch! Lizaveta Ivanovna, my peerless beauty! Open the door! Oh, confound it all, they must be asleep or something!"

Thoroughly annoyed, he tugged at the bell again with all his might, a dozen times in succession. He was plainly a person of imperious temper and familiar with the place.

At this moment light, hurrying footsteps sounded not very far down the stairs. Somebody else was approaching, whom Raskolnikov had not heard at first.

"Isn't anybody in?" cried the new arrival in loud and cheerful tones to the first visitor, who was still tugging at the bell. "How are you, Koch?"

"Judging by his voice, he must be very young," thought Raskolnikov.

"God only knows! I've nearly broken the door down," answered Koch. "But how is it that you know me?"

"Surely you remember? The day before yesterday, at Gambrinus's, I beat you three times running at billiards."

"O-o-oh . . ."

"Aren't they here then? That's strange. In fact, it's quite absurd. The old woman's got nowhere to go to. And I am here on business."

"So am I, old man."

"Well, what are we to do? Go back, I suppose. And I was expecting to get some money!" exclaimed the young man.

"Of course we must go back, but why make an appointment? The old witch fixed a time with me herself. It's a long way for me to come here, too. And where the devil she can have got to, I don't know. She sits here, day in and day out, the old witch, with her bad legs, and never lifts a finger, and now all at once she goes gallivanting off!"

"Hadn't we better ask the porter?"

"Ask him what?"

"Where she's gone and when she's coming back."

"Hm . . . the devil! . . . ask him . . . But she never goes anywhere . . ." and he pulled at the handle again. "The devil! There's nothing for it; we must go."

"Stop!" exclaimed the young man. "Look! Do you see how the door resists when you pull it?"

"Well?"

"That means it's bolted, not locked! Can you hear the bar rattling?"

"Well?"

"Don't you understand? That means one of them is at home. If everybody were out, they would have locked the door from outside, not bolted it from inside. But now—do you hear the bolt rattle? But to bolt the door from inside, somebody must be at home. Do you understand? They must be in, but they aren't opening the door."

"Tck! That's quite right!" exclaimed Koch, surprised. "Then what on earth are they doing?" And he shook the door again, in a rage.

"Stop!" cried the young man again, "leave the door alone! There's something very wrong here . . . After all, you rang, and shook the door, and they haven't opened it; so either they've both fainted, or . . ."

"What?"

"I'll tell you what; let's go to the porter and get him to rouse them."

"Done!" Both started downstairs.

"Stop! Why don't you stay here while I run down for the porter?"

"Why?"

"Well, one never knows!"

"All right . . ."

"You see, I am studying to be an examining magistrate. There is plainly, plai-ainly something wrong here!" cried the young man excitedly, as he ran down the stairs.

Koch, left alone, touched the bell again, so softly that it made only one tinkle; then, as though he were considering the matter and making tests to convince himself once more that the door was held only by the bolt, he began to move the handle, pulling it towards him and letting it go again. Then he stooped down, puffing, and looked through the keyhole, but the key was in it on the inside and consequently nothing could be seen.

Raskolnikov stood clutching his axe, in a sort of delirium. He was even prepared to fight them when they came in. While they were knocking at the door and arranging what they would do, he was more than once tempted to put an end to it all at once by calling out to them from behind the door. Several times he felt like railing and jeering at them, while the door remained closed. "If only they would be quick!" he thought.

"What the devil? . . ."

The time was passing—one minute, two minutes, and nobody came. Koch was getting restless.

"Oh, the devil! . . ." he exclaimed impatiently, abandoning his watch and starting to hurry downstairs, with his boots clattering on the steps. The sounds died away.

"Oh, God, what am I to do?"

Raskolnikov took off the bolt and opened the door a little. Since he could hear nothing, he walked out without stopping to consider, closed the door behind him as well as he could, and went downstairs.

He had gone down three flights when a great commotion broke out below him. Where could he go? There was nowhere to hide. He was on the point of running back to the flat.

"Hi, stop! You devil! Just wait!"

Down below someone tore out of a flat shouting and did not so much run as tumble down the stairs, yelling at the top of his voice:

"Mitka! Mitka! Mitka! Mitka! Blast your eyes!"

The shout rose to a shriek; its last echoes resounded from the courtyard; it died away. At the same instant several persons talking loudly and rapidly started noisily up the stairs. There were three or four of them. He could distinguish the young man's voice. "It's them!"

In complete desperation he went straight towards them: let come what might! If they stopped him, all was lost; if they let him pass, all was still lost: they would remember him. They were already close; only one flight still lay between them—and suddenly, salvation! A few steps below him on the right, the door of an empty flat was wide open; it was the second-floor flat in which painters had been working, but now, most opportunely, they had gone. Probably it was they who had run out so noisily a few minutes before. The floors had just been painted, and in the middle of the room stood a tub and an earthenware crock of paint with a brush in it. In a trice he had slipped through the open door and hidden himself against the wall. It was none too soon; *they* had already reached the landing. They turned up the stairs and went on to the fourth floor, talking loudly. He waited a little, tiptoed out and ran downstairs.

There was nobody on the stairs, nobody in the gateway. He walked through quickly and turned to the left along the street.

He knew very well, he was terribly aware, that at this moment they were inside the flat, that they had been astonished to find the door unfastened when it had been closed against them so recently, that they had already seen the bodies and that no more than a minute would pass before they would begin to suspect, and then realize fully, that the murderer had only just left, and had managed to conceal himself somewhere, slip past them, and make his escape; perhaps they would even guess that he had been in the empty flat when they passed it on their way upstairs. All the same, he simply dared not increase his pace, even though it was still nearly a hundred yards to the first turning. "Hadn't I better slip into some gateway and wait on a staircase? No, that would be disastrous! Oughtn't I to get rid of the axe? What about taking a cab? . . . A fatal blunder!"

At last he reached a side-street and, half dead, turned into it; now he knew that he was already half-way to safety; his presence here was less suspicious, and besides there were very many people about and he could lose himself among them like one grain of sand on the seashore. But his racking anxieties had taken so much out of him that he could hardly move. Sweat poured out of him; his neck was quite wet. "You've had a drop too much!" someone called after him as he came out on the canal.

He no longer knew quite what he was doing, and the farther he went the worse his condition became. Afterwards he remembered, however, that he had been afraid, coming to the canal bank, because there were fewer people about, which made him more conspicuous, and he nearly turned back into the street he had just left. Although he could hardly stand he took a roundabout way and arrived home from an entirely different direction.

Even when he entered his own gateway he had hardly recovered control of himself; at least, he was already on the stairs before he remembered the axe. Now he had to face a very important task— returning it without being seen. He was certainly in no condition to realize that perhaps it would be much better if he did not restore the axe to its former place but threw it away, perhaps later, in some other courtyard.

Everything, however, went without a hitch. The porter's door was closed but not locked, which meant that he was probably at home. But Raskolnikov had so completely lost his powers of reasoning that he went straight to the door of the lodge and opened it. If the porter had asked him what he wanted, he might quite possibly have simply handed him the axe. But the porter was again out and he put the axe in its former place under the bench; he even partly covered it with logs as before. Afterwards, on his way to his room, he met no one, not a soul; even the landlady's door was closed. He went in and flung himself down on the sofa just as he was. He did not sleep, but lay there in a stupor. If anybody had entered the room he would have sprung up at once with a cry. Disjointed scraps and fragments of ideas floated through his mind, but he could not seize one of them, or dwell upon any, in spite of all his efforts . . .

**STUDY QUESTIONS**

1. Raskolnikov thinks that those who spread misery do not deserve the protection of the law. Discuss this proposition.
2. Raskolnikov's act defies conventional morality. Does it do so in the name of some higher morality? Is Raskolnikov a kind of Nietzschean who cannot make the grade?
3. What, in your view, is Dostoyevski's moral position? How does *he* see Raskolnikov?
4. There is the hint that Raskolnikov might have had in mind distributing the money to others far more worthy than the evil old moneylender. Discuss the morality of robbing the rich to give to the poor. Can such conduct be justified on utilitarian grounds? (In this connection look again at the distinction between "act utilitarianism" and "rule utilitarianism" in the J. J. C. Smart selection.)

# Why Act Morally?

## PETER SINGER

Peter Singer (b. 1946) teaches philosophy at La Trobe
University in Victoria, Australia. His books include *Animal Liberation* (1975), *Practical Ethics* (1979), and *The Expanding Circle* (1981).

Singer examines the link between vice and unhappiness
from a utilitarian standpoint. Psychopaths have a character type that enables them to pursue pleasure with indifference to the suffering they cause others. The existence
of psychopaths untroubled by conscience and apparently
enjoying themselves seems to count against the thesis that
immorality leads to unhappiness. Singer counters this by
arguing that psychopaths and others who completely lack
such virtues as benevolence and compassion are unable to
do more than pursue short-range objectives. All they can
do is continue their selfish pursuit of more pleasure. But
their satisfactions are short lived and their capacity for
enjoyment soon becomes jaded. Even prudent egoists
whose selfish goals are long range end up desperately
bored and without the resources to relieve that boredom.
If Singer is right, the utilitarian, too, can consistently
maintain that a virtuous character is needed for an interesting and meaningful life.

It might be said that since philosophers are not empirical scientists,

WITHOUT VIRTUE From *Practical Ethics* by Peter Singer. Reprinted by permission of the publisher,
Cambridge University Press.

discussion of the connection between acting ethically and living a fulfilled and happy life should be left to psychologists, sociologists and other appropriate experts. The question is not, however, dealt with by any other single discipline and its relevance to practical ethics is reason enough for our looking into it.

What facts about human nature could show that ethics and self-interest coincide? One theory is that we all have benevolent or sympathetic inclinations which make us concerned about the welfare of others. Another relies on a natural conscience which gives rise to guilt feelings when we do what we know to be wrong. But how strong are these benevolent desires or feelings of guilt? Is it possible to suppress them? If so, isn't it possible that in a world in which humans and other animals are suffering in great numbers, suppressing one's conscience and sympathy for others is the surest way to happiness?

To meet this objection those who would link ethics and happiness must assert that we cannot be happy if these elements of our nature are suppressed. Benevolence and sympathy, they might argue, are tied up with the capacity to take part in friendly or loving relations with others, and there can be no real happiness without such relationships. For the same reason it is necessary to take at least some ethical standards seriously, and to be open and honest in living by them— for a life of deception and dishonesty is a furtive life, in which the possibility of discovery always clouds the horizon. Genuine acceptance of ethical standards is likely to mean that we feel some guilt— or at least that we are less pleased with ourselves than we otherwise would be—when we do not live up to them.

These claims about the connection between our character and our prospects of happiness are no more than hypotheses. Attempts to confirm them by detailed research are sparse and inadequate. A. H. Maslow, an American psychologist, asserts that human beings have a need for self-actualization, which involves growing towards courage, kindness, knowledge, love, honesty, and unselfishness. When we fulfil this need we feel serene, joyful, filled with zest, sometimes euphoric, and generally happy. When we act contrary to our need for self-actualization we experience anxiety, despair, boredom, shame, emptiness and are generally unable to enjoy ourselves. It would be nice if Maslow should turn out to be right; unfortunately the data Maslow produces in support of his theory consist of very limited studies of selected people. The theory must await confirmation or falsification from larger, more rigorous and more representative studies.

Human nature is so diverse that one may doubt if any generalization about the kind of character that leads to happiness could hold for all human beings. What, for instance, of those we call "psychopaths"? Psychiatrists use this term as a label for a person who is asocial, impulsive, egocentric, unemotional, lacking in feelings of remorse, shame or guilt, and apparently unable to form deep and enduring personal relationships. Psychopaths are certainly abnormal, but whether it is proper to say that they are mentally ill is another matter. At least on the surface, they do not *suffer* from their condition, and it is not obvious that it is in their interest to be "cured." Hervey Cleckley, the author of a classic study of psychopathy entitled *The Mask of Sanity,* notes that since his book was first published he has received countless letters from people desperate for help—but they are from the parents, spouses and other relatives of psychopaths, almost never from the psychopaths themselves. This is not surprising, for while psychopaths are asocial and indifferent to the welfare of others, they seem to enjoy life. Psychopaths often appear to be charming, intelligent people, with no delusions or other signs of irrational thinking. When interviewed they say things like:

> A lot has happened to me, a lot more will happen. But I enjoy living and I am always looking forward to each day. I like laughing and I've done a lot. I am essentially a clown at heart—but a happy one. I always take the bad with the good.

There is no effective therapy for psychopathy, which may be explained by the fact that psychopaths see nothing wrong with their behaviour and often find it extremely rewarding, at least in the short term. Of course their impulsive nature and lack of a sense of shame or guilt means that some psychopaths end up in prison, though it is hard to tell how many do not, since those who avoid prison are also more likely to avoid contact with psychiatrists. Studies have shown that a surprisingly large number of psychopaths are able to avoid prison despite grossly antisocial behaviour, probably because of their well-known ability to convince others that they are truly repentant, that it will never happen again, that they deserve another chance, etc., etc.

The existence of psychopathic people counts against the contention that benevolence, sympathy and feelings of guilt are present in everyone. It also appears to count against attempts to link happiness with the possession of these inclinations. But let us pause before we accept this latter conclusion. Must we accept psychopaths' own evaluations of their happiness? They are, after all, notoriously persuasive liars. Moreover, even if they are telling the truth as they see it, are they qualified to say that they are really happy, when they seem unable to experience the emotional states that play such a large part in the happiness and fulfilment of more normal people? Admittedly, a psychopath could use the same argument against us: how can we say that we are truly happy when we have not experienced the excitement and freedom that comes from complete irresponsibility? Since we cannot enter into the subjective states of psychopathic people, nor they into ours, the dispute is not easy to resolve.

Cleckley suggests that the psychopaths' behaviour can be explained as a response to the meaninglessness of their lives. It is characteristic of psychopaths to work for a while at a job and then just when their ability and charm have taken them to the crest of success, commit some petty and easily detectable crime. A similar pattern occurs in their personal relationships. (There is support to be found here for Thomas Nagel's account of imprudence as rational only if one fails to see oneself as a person existing over time, with the present merely one among other times one will live through. Certainly psychopathic people live largely in the present and lack any coherent life plan.)

Cleckley explains this erratic and to us inadequately motivated behaviour by likening the psychopath's life to that of children forced to sit through a performance of *King Lear*. Children are restless and misbehave under these conditions because they cannot enjoy the play as adults do. They act to relieve boredom. Similarly, Cleckley says, psychopaths are bored because their emotional poverty means that they cannot take interest in, or gain satisfaction from, what for others are the most important things in life: love, family, success in business or professional life, etc. These things simply do not matter to them. Their unpredictable and anti-social behaviour is an attempt to relieve what would otherwise be a tedious existence.

These claims are speculative and Cleckley admits that they may not be possible to establish scientifically. They do suggest, however, an aspect of the psychopath's life that undermines the otherwise attractive nature of the psychopath's free-wheeling life. Most reflective people, at some time or other, want their life to have some kind of meaning. Few of us could deliberately choose a way of life which we regarded as utterly meaningless. For this reason most of us would not choose to live a psychopathic life, however enjoyable it might be.

Yet there is something paradoxical about criticizing the psychopath's life for its meaninglessness. Don't we have to accept, in the absence of religious belief, that life really is meaningless, not just for the psychopath but for all of us? And if this is so, why should we not choose—if it were in our powers to choose our personality—the life of a psychopath? But is it true that, religion aside, life is meaningless? Now our pursuit of reasons for acting morally has led us to what is often regarded as the ultimate philosophical question.

### Has Life a Meaning?

In what sense does rejection of belief in a god imply rejection of the view that life has any meaning? If this world had been created by some divine being with a particular goal in mind, it could be said to have a meaning, at least for that divine being. If we could know what the divine being's purpose in creating us was, we could then know what the meaning of our life was for our creator. If we accepted our creator's purpose (though why we should do that would need to be explained) we could claim to know the meaning of life.

When we reject belief in a god we must give up the idea that life on this planet has some preordained meaning. Life *as a whole* has no meaning. Life began, as the best available theories tell us, in a chance combination of gases; it then evolved through random mutations and natural selection. All this just happened; it did not happen for any overall purpose. Now that it has resulted in the existence of beings who prefer some states of affairs to others, however, it may be possible for particular lives to be meaningful. In this sense atheists can find meaning in life.

Let us return to the comparison between the life of a psychopath and that of a more normal person. Why should the psychopath's life not be meaningful? We have seen that psychopaths are egocentric to an extreme: neither other people, nor worldly success, nor anything else really matters to them. But why is their own enjoyment of life not sufficient to give meaning to their lives?

Most of us would not be able to find happiness by deliberately setting out to enjoy ourselves without caring about anyone or anything else. The pleasures we obtained in that way would seem empty, and soon pall. We seek a meaning for our lives beyond our own pleasures, and find fulfilment and happiness in doing what we see to be meaningful. If our life has no meaning other than our own happiness, we are likely to find that when we have obtained what we think we need to be happy, happiness itself still eludes us.

That those who aim at happiness for happiness's sake often fail to find it, while others find happiness in pursuing altogether different goals, has been called "the paradox of hedonism." It is not, of course, a logical paradox but a claim about the way in which we come to be happy. Like other generalizations on this subject it lacks empirical confirmation. Yet it matches our everyday observations, and is consistent with our nature as evolved, purposive beings. Human beings survive and reproduce themselves through purposive action. We obtain happiness and fulfilment by working towards and achieving our goals. In evolutionary terms we could say that happiness functions as an internal reward for our achievements. Subjectively, we regard achieving the goal (or progressing towards it) as a reason for happiness. Our own happiness, therefore, is a by-product of aiming at something else, and not to be obtained by setting our sights on happiness alone.

The psychopath's life can now be seen to be meaningless in a way that a normal life is not. It is meaningless because it looks inward to the pleasures of the present moment and not outward to anything more long-term or far-reaching. More normal lives have meaning because they are lived to some larger purpose.

All this is speculative. You may accept or reject it to the extent that it agrees with your own observation and introspection. My next—and final—suggestion is more speculative still. It is that to find an enduring meaning in our lives it is not enough to go beyond psychopaths who have no long-term commitments or life-plans; we must also go beyond more prudent egoists who have long-term plans concerned only with their own interests. The prudent egoists may find meaning in their lives for a time, for they have the purpose of furthering their own interests; but what, in the end, does that amount to? When everything in our interests has been achieved, do we just sit back and be happy? Could we be happy in this way? Or would we decide that we had still not quite reached our target, that there was something else we needed before we could sit back and enjoy it all? Most materially successful egoists take the latter route, thus escaping the necessity of admitting that they cannot find happiness in permanent holidaying. People who slaved to establish small businesses, telling themselves they would do it only until they had made enough to live comfortably, keep working long after they have passed their original target. Their material "needs" expand just fast enough to keep ahead of their income. Retirement is a problem for many because they cannot enjoy themselves without a purpose in life. The recommended solution is, of course, to find a new purpose, whether it be stamp collecting or voluntary work for a charity.

Now we begin to see where ethics comes into the problem of living a meaningful life. If we are looking for a purpose broader than our own interests, something which will allow us to see our lives as possessing significance beyond the narrow confines of our own conscious states, one obvious solution is to take up the ethical point of view. The ethical point of view does, as we have seen, require us to go beyond a personal point of view to the standpoint of an impartial spectator. Thus looking at things ethically is a way of transcending our inward-looking concerns and identifying ourselves with the most objective point of view possible—with, as Sidgwick put it, "the point of view of the universe."

The point of view of the universe is a lofty standpoint. In the rarefied air that surrounds it we may get carried away into talking, as Kant does, of the moral point of view "inevitably" humbling all who compare their own limited nature with it. I do not want to suggest anything as sweeping as this. Earlier in this chapter, in rejecting Thomas Nagel's argument for the rationality of altruism, I said that there is nothing irrational about being concerned with the quality of one's own existence in a way that one is not concerned with the quality of existence of other individuals. Without going back on this, I am now suggesting that rationality, in the broad sense which includes self-awareness and reflection on the nature and point of our own existence, may push us towards concerns broader than the quality of our own existence; but the process is not a necessary one and those who do not take part in it—or, in taking part, do not follow it all the way to the ethical point of view—are not irrational or in error. Psychopaths, for all I know, may simply be unable to obtain as much happiness through caring about others as they obtain by antisocial acts. Other people find collecting stamps an entirely adequate way of giving purpose to their lives. There is nothing irrational about that; but others again grow out of stamp collecting as they become more aware of their situation in the world and more reflective about their purposes. To this third group the ethical point of view offers a meaning and purpose in life that one does not grow out of.

(At least, one cannot grow out of the ethical point of view until all ethical tasks have been accomplished. If that utopia were ever achieved, our purposive nature might well leave us dissatisfied, much as the egoist is dissatisfied when he has everything he needs to be happy. There is nothing paradoxical about this, for we should not expect evolution to have equipped us, in advance, with the ability to enjoy a situation that has never previously occurred. Nor is this going to be a practical problem in the near future.)

"Why act morally?" cannot be given an answer that will provide everyone with overwhelming reasons for acting morally. Ethically indefensible behaviour is not always irrational. We will probably always need the sanctions of the law and social pressure to provide additional reasons against serious violations of ethical standards. On the other hand, those reflective enough to ask the question we have been discussing in this chapter are also those most likely to appreciate the reasons that can be offered for taking the ethical point of view.

**STUDY QUESTIONS**

1.  Do you think ethics and self-interest coincide? Compare Singer's defense of this general proposition with that of some classical philosophers who also believe that the virtuous person is happy.
2.  Should we accept the psychopaths' claim that they are actually happy when they appear to be enjoying themselves?
3.  Singer believes that the lives of psychopaths and rational egoists are meaningless and boring, perhaps even despairingly so. Has he made a persuasive case for this conclusion?
4.  What does Singer mean by the ethical point of view and why does he recommend it to us?

# *Moral Saints*

## SUSAN WOLF

Susan Wolf (b. 1952) is an associate professor of philosophy at the University of Maryland. She has published numerous essays in ethics and metaphysics.

Susan Wolf critically examines the assumption that we ought to be as morally good as possible, i.e., that we ought to strive to be moral saints. She finds the idea of moral sainthood to be wanting because it discourages the development of desirable personal traits and styles that are at odds with "a life dominated by a commitment to improving the welfare of others or society as a whole." Two kinds of moral saints are distinguished. The Loving Saint enjoys total commitment: "His happiness lies in the happiness of others." The Rational Saint is dominated by duty: "This person sacrifices his own interest to others and feels the sacrifice as such."

The Moral Saint abjures such morally profitless activities as playing games or reading novels. Moreover, it goes against the grain for him to enjoy cynical wit. "[He] might well enjoy a good episode of *Father Knows Best* [but] he may not in good conscience be able to laugh at a Marx Brothers movie . . ." In short, the Moral Saint is dull. The idea of moral sainthood disturbs us because it demands that we sacrifice many things we rightly hold dear or amusing.

MORAL SAINTS By Susan Wolf. Reprinted from *The Journal of Philosophy*, August 1982, pp. 419–439. By permission of the publisher and author.

Wolf roughly correlates the two ideas of moral saint-hood with the two mainstream moral theories of Utilitarianism (the Loving Saint) and Kantianism (the Rational Saint). She considers other approaches that seem to place a limit on moral extremism (Aristotle's idea of moderation). But Wolf concludes that no moral theory that takes morality itself to be the overriding guide to human conduct can be satisfactory. Some persons may choose to be moral saints, and that is legitimate. But it is wrong to treat moral perfection as something that all should strive for. "[A] person may be perfectly wonderful without being perfectly moral."

I don't know whether there are any moral saints. But if there are, I am glad that neither I nor those about whom I care most are among them. By *moral saint* I mean a person whose every action is as morally good as possible, a person, that is, who is as morally worthy as can be. Though I shall in a moment acknowledge the variety of types of person that might be thought to satisfy this description, it seems to me that none of these types serve as unequivocally compelling personal ideals. In other words, I believe that moral perfection, in the sense of moral saintliness, does not constitute a model of personal well-being toward which it would be particularly rational or good or desirable for a human being to strive.

Outside the context of moral discussion, this will strike many as an obvious point. But, within that context, the point, if it be granted, will be granted with some discomfort. For within that context it is generally assumed that one ought to be as morally good as possible and that what limits there are to morality's hold on us are set by features of human nature of which we ought not to be proud. If, as I believe, the ideals that are derivable from common sense and philosophically popular moral theories do not support these assumptions, then something has to change. Either we must change our moral theories in ways that will make them yield more palatable ideals, or, as I shall argue, we must change our conception of what is involved in affirming a moral theory.

In this paper, I wish to examine the notion of a moral saint, first, to understand what a moral saint would be like and why such a being would be unattractive, and, second, to raise some questions about the significance of this paradoxical figure for moral philosophy. I shall look first at the model(s) of moral sainthood that might be extrapolated from the morality or moralities of common sense. Then I shall consider what relations these have to conclusions that can be drawn from utilitarian and Kantian moral theories. Finally, I shall speculate on the implications of these considerations for moral philosophy.

## Moral Saints and Common Sense

Consider first what, pretheoretically, would count for us—contemporary members of Western culture—as a moral saint. A necessary condition of moral sainthood would be that one's life be dominated by a commitment to improving the welfare of others or of society as a whole. As to what role this commitment must play in the individual's motivational system, two contrasting accounts suggest themselves to me which might equally be thought to qualify a person for moral sainthood.

First, a moral saint might be someone whose concern for others plays the role that is played in most of our lives by more selfish, or, at any rate, less morally worthy concerns. For the moral saint, the promotion of the welfare of others might play the role that is played for most of us by the enjoyment of material comforts, the opportunity to engage in the intellectual and physical activities of our choice, and the love, respect, and companionship of people whom we love, respect, and enjoy. The happiness of the moral saint, then, would truly lie in the happiness of others, and so he would devote himself to others gladly, and with a whole and open heart.

On the other hand, a moral saint might be someone for whom the basic ingredients of happiness are not unlike those of most of the rest of us. What makes him a moral saint is rather that he pays little or no attention to his own happiness in light of the overriding importance he gives to the wider concerns of morality. In other words, this person sacrifices his own interests to the interests of others, and feels the sacrifice as such.

Roughly, these two models may be distinguished according to whether one thinks of the moral saint as being a saint out of love or one thinks of the moral saint as being a saint out of duty (or some other intellectual appreciation and recognition of moral principles). We may refer to the first model as the model of the Loving Saint; to the second, as the model of the Rational Saint.

[A]bove all, a moral saint must have and cultivate those qualities which are apt to allow him to treat others as justly and kindly as possible. He will have the standard moral virtues to a nonstandard degree. He will be patient, considerate, even–tempered, hospitable, charitable in thought as well as in deed. He will be very reluctant to make negative judgments of other people. He will be careful not to favor some people over others on the basis of properties they could not help but have.

Perhaps what I have already said is enough to make some people begin to regard the absence of moral saints in their lives as a blessing. For there comes a point in the listing of virtues that a moral saint is likely to have where one might naturally begin to wonder whether the moral saint isn't, after all, too good—if not too good for his own good, at least too good for his own well-being. For the moral virtues, given that they are, by hypothesis, *all* present in the same individual, and to an extreme degree, are apt to crowd out the nonmoral virtues, as well as many of the interests and personal characteristics that we generally think contribute to a healthy, well-rounded, richly developed character.

In other words, if the moral saint is devoting all his time to feeding the hungry or healing the sick or raising money for Oxfam, then necessarily he is not reading Victorian novels, playing the oboe, or improving his backhand. Although no one of the interests or tastes in the category containing these latter activities could be claimed to be a necessary element in a life well lived, a life in which *none* of these possible aspects of character are developed may seem to be a life strangely barren.

The reasons why a moral saint cannot, in general, encourage the discovery and development of significant nonmoral interests and skills are not logical but practical reasons. There are, in addition, a class of nonmoral characteristics that a moral saint cannot encourage in himself for reasons that are not just practical. There is a more substantial tension between having any of these qualities unashamedly and being a moral saint. These qualities might be described as going against the moral grain. For example, a cynical or sarcastic wit, or a sense of humor that appreciates this kind of wit in

447

others, requires that one take an attitude of resignation and pessimism toward the flaws and vices to be found in the world. A moral saint, on the other hand, has reason to take an attitude in opposition to this—he should try to look for the best in people, give them the benefit of the doubt as long as possible, try to improve regrettable situations as long as there is any hope of success. This suggests that, although a moral saint might well enjoy a good episode of *Father Knows Best,* he may not in good conscience be able to laugh at a Marx Brothers movie or enjoy a play by George Bernard Shaw.

An interest in something like gourmet cooking will be, for different reasons, difficult for a moral saint to rest easy with. For it seems to me that no plausible argument can justify the use of human resources involved in producing a *paté de canard en croute* against possible alternative beneficent ends to which these resources might be put. If there is a justification for the institution of haute cuisine, it is one which rests on the decision *not* to justify every activity against morally beneficial alternatives, and this is a decision a moral saint will never make. Presumably, an interest in high fashion or interior design will fare much the same, as will, very possibly, a cultivation of the finer arts as well.

A moral saint will have to be very, very nice. It is important that he not be offensive. The worry is that, as a result, he will have to be dull-witted or humorless or bland.

This worry is confirmed when we consider what sorts of characters, taken and refined both from life and from fiction, typically form our ideals. One would hope they would be figures who are morally good—and by this I mean more than just not morally bad—but one would hope, too, that they are not just morally good, but talented or accomplished or attractive in nonmoral ways as well. We may make ideals out of athletes, scholars, artists—more frivolously, out of cowboys, private eyes, and rock stars. We may strive for Katherine Hepburn's grace, Paul Newman's "cool"; we are attracted to the high-spirited passionate nature of Natasha Rostov; we admire the keen perceptiveness of Lambert Strether. Though there is certainly nothing immoral about the ideal characters or traits I have in mind, they cannot be superimposed upon the ideal of a moral saint. For although it is a part of many of these ideals that the characters set high, and not merely acceptable, moral standards for themselves, it is also essential to their power and attractiveness that the moral strengths go, so to speak, alongside of specific, independently admirable, nonmoral ground projects and dominant personal traits.

When one does finally turn one's eyes toward lives that are dominated by explicitly moral commitments, moreover, one finds oneself relieved at the discovery of idiosyncrasies or eccentricities not quite in line with the picture of moral perfection. One prefers the blunt, tactless, and opinionated Betsy Trotwood to the unfailingly kind and patient Agnes Copperfield; one prefers the mischievousness and the sense of irony in Chesterton's Father Brown to the innocence and undiscriminating love of St. Francis.

It seems that, as we look in our ideals for people who achieve nonmoral varieties of personal excellence in conjunction with or colored by some version of high moral tone, we look in our paragons of moral excellence for people whose moral achievements occur in conjunction with or colored by some interests or traits that have low moral tone. In other words, there seems to be a limit to how much morality we can stand. . . .

Moreover, there is something odd about the idea of morality itself, or moral goodness, serving as the object of a dominant passion in the way that a more concrete and specific vision of a goal (even a concrete *moral* goal) might be imagined to serve. Morality itself does not seem to be a suitable object of passion. Thus, when one reflects, for example, on the Loving Saint easily and gladly giving up his fishing trip or his stereo or his hot fudge sundae at the drop of the moral hat, one is apt to wonder not at how much he loves morality, but at how little he loves these other things. One thinks that, if he can give these up so easily, he does not know what it *is* to truly love them. There seems, in other words, to be a kind of joy which the Loving Saint, either by nature or by practice, is incapable of experiencing. The Rational Saint, on the other hand, might retain strong nonmoral and concrete desires—he simply denies himself the opportunity to act on them. But this is no less troubling. The Loving Saint one might suspect of missing a piece of perceptual machinery, of being blind to some of what the world has to offer. The Rational Saint, who sees it but foregoes it, one suspects of having a different problem—a pathological fear of damnation, perhaps, or an extreme form of self-hatred that interferes with his ability to enjoy the enjoyable in life.

In other words, the ideal of a life of moral sainthood disturbs not simply because it is an ideal of a life in which morality unduly dominates. The normal person's direct and specific desires for objects, activities, and events that conflict with the attainment of moral perfection are not simply sacrificed but removed, suppressed, or subsumed. The way in which morality, unlike other possible goals, is apt to dominate is particularly disturbing, for it seems to require either the lack or the denial of the existence of an identifiable, personal self.

This distinctively troubling feature is not, I think, absolutely unique to the ideal of the moral saint, as I have been using that phrase. It is shared by the conception of the pure aesthete, by a certain kind of religious ideal, and, somewhat paradoxically, by the model of the thorough-going, self-conscious egoist. It is not a coincidence that the ways of comprehending the world of which these ideals are the extreme embodiments are sometimes described as "moralities" themselves. At any rate, they compete with what we ordinarily mean by "morality." Nor is it a coincidence that these ideals are naturally described as fanatical. But it is easy to see that these other types of perfection cannot serve as satisfactory personal ideals; for the realization of these ideals would be straightforwardly immoral. It may come as a surprise to some that there may in addition be such a thing as a *moral* fanatic.

Some will object that I am being unfair to "common-sense morality"—that it does not really require a moral saint to be either a disgusting goody-goody or an obsessive ascetic. Admittedly, there is no logical inconsistency between having any of the personal characteristics I have mentioned and being a moral saint. It is not morally wrong to notice the faults and shortcomings of others or to recognize and appreciate nonmoral talents and skills. Nor is it immoral to be an avid Celtics fan or to have a passion for caviar or to be an excellent cellist. With enough imagination, we can always contrive a suitable history and set of circumstances that will embrace such characteristics in one or another specific fictional story of a perfect moral saint.

If one turned onto the path of moral sainthood relatively late in life, one may have already developed interests that can be turned to moral purposes. It may be that a good golf game is just what is needed to secure that big donation to Oxfam. Perhaps the cultivation of one's exceptional artistic talent will turn out to be the way one can make one's greatest contribution to society. Furthermore, one might stumble upon joys and skills in the very service of morality. If, because the children are short a ninth player for the team, one's generous offer to serve reveals a natural fielding arm or if one's part in the campaign against nuclear power requires accepting a lobbyist's invitation to lunch at Le Lion d'Or, there is no moral gain in denying the satisfaction one gets from these activities. The moral saint, then, may, by happy accident, find himself with nonmoral virtues on which he can capitalize morally or which make psychological demands to which he has no choice but to attend. The point is that, for a moral saint, the existence of these interests and skills can be given at best the status of happy accidents—they cannot be encouraged for their own sakes as distinct, independent aspects of the realization of human good.

It must be remembered that from the fact that there is a tension between having any of these qualities and being a moral saint it does not follow that having any of these qualities is immoral. For it is not part of common-sense morality that one ought to be a moral saint. Still, if someone just happened to want to be a moral saint, he or she would not have or encourage these qualities, and, on the basis of our common-sense values, this counts as a reason not to want to be a moral saint. . . .

The fact that the moral saint would be without qualities which we have and which, indeed, we like to have, does not in itself provide reason to condemn the ideal of the moral saint. The fact that some of these qualities are good qualities, however, and that they are qualities we *ought* to like, does provide reason to discourage this ideal and to offer other ideals in its place. In other words, some of the qualities the moral saint necessarily lacks are virtues, albeit nonmoral virtues, in the unsaintly characters who have them. The feats of Groucho Marx, Reggie Jackson, and the head chef at Lutèce are impressive accomplishments that it is not only permissible but positively appropriate to recognize as such. In general, the admiration of and striving toward achieving any of a great variety of forms of personal excellence are character traits it is valuable and desirable for people to have. In advocating the development of these varieties of excellence, we advocate nonmoral reasons for acting, and in thinking that it is good for a person to strive for an ideal that gives a substantial role to the interests and values that correspond to these virtues, we implicitly acknowledge the goodness of ideals incompatible with that of the moral saint. Finally, if we think that it is *as* good, or even better for a person to strive for one of these ideals than it is for him or her to strive for and realize the ideal of the moral saint, we express a conviction that it is good not to be a moral saint.

## Moral Saints and Moral Theories

I have tried so far to paint a picture—or, rather, two pictures—of what a moral saint might be like, drawing on what I take to be the attitudes and beliefs about morality prevalent in contemporary, common-sense thought. To my suggestion that common-sense morality generates conceptions of moral saints that are unattractive or otherwise unacceptable, it is open to someone to reply, "so much the worse for common-sense morality." After all, it is often claimed that the goal of moral philosophy is to correct and improve upon common-sense morality, and I have as yet given no attention to the question of what conceptions of moral sainthood, if any, are generated from the leading moral theories of our time.

A quick, breezy reading of utilitarian and Kantian writings will suggest the images, respectively, of the Loving Saint and the Rational Saint. A utilitarian, with his emphasis on happiness, will certainly prefer the Loving Saint to the Rational one, since the Loving Saint will himself be a happier person than the Rational Saint. A Kantian, with his emphasis on reason, on the other hand, will find at least as much to praise in the latter as in the former. Still, both models, drawn as they are from common sense, appeal to an impure mixture of utilitarian and Kantian intuitions. A more careful examination of these moral theories raises questions about whether either model of moral sainthood would really be advocated by a believer in the explicit doctrines associated with either of these views.

Certainly, the utilitarian in no way denies the value of self-realization. He in no way disparages the development of interests, talents, and other personally attractive traits that I have claimed the moral saint would be without. Indeed, since just these features enhance the happiness both of the individuals who possess them and of those with whom they associate, the ability to promote these features both in oneself and in others will have considerable positive weight in utilitarian calculations.

This implies that the utilitarian would not support moral

sainthood as a universal ideal. A world in which everyone, or even a large number of people, achieved moral sainthood—even a world in which they *strove* to achieve it—would probably contain less happiness than a world in which people realized a diversity of ideals involving a variety of personal and perfectionist values. More pragmatic considerations also suggest that, if the utilitarian wants to influence more people to achieve more good, then he would do better to encourage them to pursue happiness-producing goals that are more attractive and more within a normal person's reach.

These considerations still leave open, however, the question of what kind of an ideal the committed utilitarian should privately aspire to himself. Utilitarianism requires him to want to achieve the greatest general happiness, and this would seem to commit him to the ideal of the moral saint.

One might try to use the claims I made earlier as a basis for an argument that a utilitarian should choose to give up utilitarianism. If, as I have said, a moral saint would be a less happy person both to be and to be around than many other possible ideals, perhaps one could create more total happiness by not trying too hard to promote the total happiness. But this argument is simply unconvincing in light of the empirical circumstances of our world. The gain in happiness that would accrue to oneself and one's neighbors by a more well-rounded, richer life than that of the moral saint would be pathetically small in comparison to the amount by which one could increase the general happiness if one devoted oneself explicitly to the care of the sick, the downtrodden, the starving, and the homeless. Of course, there may be psychological limits to the extent to which a person can devote himself to such things without going crazy. But the utilitarian's individual limitations would not thereby become a positive feature of his personal ideals.

The unattractiveness of the moral saint, then, ought not rationally convince the utilitarian to abandon his utilitarianism. It may, however, convince him to take efforts not to wear his saintly moral aspirations on his sleeve. If it is not too difficult, the utilitarian will try not to make those around him uncomfortable. He will not want to appear "holier than thou"; he will not want to inhibit others' ability to enjoy themselves. In practice, this might make the perfect utilitarian a less nauseating companion than the moral saint I earlier portrayed. But insofar as this kind of reasoning produces a more bearable public personality, it is at the cost of giving him a personality that must be evaluated as hypocritical and condescending when his private thoughts and attitudes are taken into account.

Still, the criticisms I have raised against the saint of common-sense morality should make some difference to the utilitarian's conception of an ideal which neither requires him to abandon his utilitarian principles nor forces him to fake an interest he does not have or a judgment he does not make. For it may be that a limited and carefully monitored allotment of time and energy to be devoted to the pursuit of some nonmoral interests or to the development of some nonmoral talents would make a person a better contributor to the general welfare than he would be if he allowed himself no indulgences of this sort. The enjoyment of such activities in no way compromises a commitment to utilitarian principles as long as the involvement with these activities is conditioned by a willingness to give them up whenever it is recognized that they cease to be in the general interest.

This will go some way in mitigating the picture of the loving saint that an understanding of utilitarianism will on first impression suggest. But I think it will not go very far. For the limitations on time and energy will have to be rather severe, and the need to monitor will restrict not only the extent but also the quality of one's attachment to these interests and traits. They are only weak and somewhat peculiar sorts of passions to which one can consciously remain so conditionally committed. Moreover, the way in which the utilitarian can enjoy these "extra-curricular" aspects of his life is simply not the way in which these aspects are to be enjoyed insofar as they figure into our less saintly ideals.

The problem is not exactly that the utilitarian values these aspects of his life only as a means to an end, for the enjoyment he and others get from these aspects are not a means to, but a part of, the general happiness. Nonetheless, he values these things only because of and insofar as they *are* a part of the general happiness. He values them, as it were, under the description "a contribution to the general happiness." This is to be contrasted with the various ways in which these aspects of life may be valued by nonutilitarians. A person might love literature because of the insights into human nature literature affords. Another might love the cultivation of roses because roses are things of great beauty and delicacy. It may be true that these features of the respective activities also explain why these activities are happiness-producing. But, to the nonutilitarian, this may not be to the point.

For if one values these activities in these more direct ways, one may not be willing to exchange them for others that produce an equal, or even a greater amount of happiness. From that point of view, it is not because they produce happiness that these activities are valuable; it is because these activities are valuable in more direct and specific ways that they produce happiness.

To adopt a phrase of Bernard Williams', the utilitarian's manner of valuing the not explicitly moral aspects of his life "provides (him) with one thought too many."[1] The requirement that the utilitarian have this thought—periodically, at least—is indicative of not only a weakness but a shallowness in his appreciation of the aspects in question. Thus, the ideals toward which a utilitarian could acceptably strive would remain too close to the model of the common-sense moral saint to escape the criticisms of that model which I earlier suggested. Whether a Kantian would be similarly committed to so restrictive and unattractive a range of possible ideals is a somewhat more difficult question.

The Kantian believes that being morally worthy consists in always acting from maxims that one could will to be universal law, and doing this not out of any pathological desire but out of reverence for the moral law as such. Or, to take a different formulation of the categorical imperative, the Kantian believes that moral action consists in treating other persons always as ends and never as means only. Presumably, and according to Kant himself, the Kantian thereby commits himself to some degree of benevolence as well as to the rules of fair play. But we surely would not will that *every* person become a moral saint, and treating others as ends hardly requires bending over backwards to protect and promote their interests. On one interpretation of Kantian doctrine, then, moral perfection would be achieved simply by unerring obedience to a limited set of side-constraints. On this interpretation, Kantian theory simply does not yield an ideal conception of a person of any fullness comparable to that of the moral saints I have so far been portraying.

On the other hand, Kant does say explicitly that we have a duty of benevolence, a duty not only to allow others to pursue their ends, but to take up their ends as our own. In addition, we have positive duties to ourselves, duties to increase our natural as well as our moral

---

[1]"Persons, Character and Morality" in Amelie Rorty, ed., *The Identities of Persons* (Berkeley: University of California Press, 1976), 214.

perfection. These duties are unlimited in the degree to which they *may* dominate a life. If action in accordance with and motivated by the thought of these duties is considered virtuous, it is natural to assume that the more one performs such actions, the more virtuous one is. Moreover, of virtue in general Kant says, "it is an ideal which is unattainable while yet our duty is constantly to approximate to it."[2] On this interpretation, then, the Kantian moral saint, like the other moral saints I have been considering, is dominated by the motivation to be moral.

Which of these interpretations of Kant one prefers will depend on the interpretation and the importance one gives to the role of the imperfect duties in Kant's over-all system. Rather than choose between them here, I shall consider each briefly in turn.

On the second interpretation of Kant, the Kantian moral saint is, not surprisingly, subject to many of the same objections I have been raising against other versions of moral sainthood. Though the Kantian saint may differ from the utilitarian saint as to *which* actions he is bound to perform and which he is bound to refrain from performing, I suspect that the range of activities acceptable to the Kantian saint will remain objectionably restrictive. Moreover, the manner in which the Kantian saint must think about and justify the activities he pursues and the character traits he develops will strike us, as it did with the utilitarian saint, as containing "one thought too many." As the utilitarian could value his activities and character traits only insofar as they fell under the description of "contributions to the general happiness," the Kantian would have to value his activities and character traits insofar as they were manifestations of respect for the moral law. If the development of our powers to achieve physical, intellectual, or artistic excellence, or the activities directed toward making others happy are to have any moral worth, they must arise from a reverence for the dignity that members of our species have as a result of being endowed with pure practical reason. This is a good and noble motivation, to be sure. But it is hardly what one expects to be dominantly behind a person's aspirations to dance as well as Fred Astaire, to paint as well as Picasso, or to solve some outstanding

---

[2]Immanuel Kant, *The Doctrine of Virtue*, trans. Mary J. Gregor (New York: Harper and Row, 1964), 71.

problem in abstract algebra, and it is hardly what one hopes to find lying dominantly behind a father's action on behalf of his son or a lover's on behalf of her beloved.

Since the basic problem with any of the models of moral sainthood we have been considering is that they are dominated by a single, all-important value under which all other possible values must be subsumed, it may seem that the alternative interpretation of Kant, as providing a stringent but finite set of obligations and constraints, might provide a more acceptable morality. According to this interpretation of Kant, one is as morally good as can be so long as one devotes some limited portion of one's energies toward altruism and the maintenance of one's physical and spiritual health, and otherwise pursues one's independently motivated interests and values in such a way as to avoid overstepping certain bounds. Certainly, if it be a requirement of an acceptable moral theory that perfect obedience to its laws and maximal devotion to its interests and concerns be something we can wholeheartedly strive for in ourselves and wish for in those around us, it will count in favor of this brand of Kantianism that its commands can be fulfilled without swallowing up the perfect moral agent's entire personality.

Even this more limited understanding of morality, if its connection to Kant's views is to be taken at all seriously, is not likely to give an unqualified seal of approval to the nonmorally directed ideals I have been advocating. For Kant is explicit about what he calls "duties of apathy and self-mastery"—duties to ensure that our passions are never so strong as to interfere with calm, practical deliberation, or so deep as to wrest control from the more disinterested, rational part of ourselves. The tight and self-conscious rein we are thus obliged to keep on our commitments to specific individuals and causes will doubtless restrict our value in these things, assigning them a necessarily attenuated place.

A more interesting objection to this brand of Kantianism, however, comes when we consider the implications of placing the kind of upper bound on moral worthiness which seemed to count in favor of this conception of morality. For to put such a limit on one's capacity to be moral is effectively to deny, not just the moral necessity, but the moral goodness of a devotion to benevolence and the maintenance of justice that passes beyond a certain, required point. It is to deny the possibility of going morally above and beyond the call of a restricted

457

set of duties. Despite my claim that all-consuming moral saintliness is not a particularly healthy and desirable ideal, it seems perverse to insist that, were moral saints to exist, they would not, in their way, be remarkably noble and admirable figures. Despite my conviction that it is as rational and as good for a person to take Katharine Hepburn or Jane Austen as her role model instead of Mother Teresa, it would be absurd to deny that Mother Teresa is a morally better person.

I can think of two ways of viewing morality as having an upper bound. First, we can think that altruism and impartiality are indeed positive moral interests, but that they are moral only if the degree to which these interests are actively pursued remains within certain fixed limits. Second, we can think that these positive interests are only incidentally related to morality and that the essence of morality lies elsewhere, in, say, an implicit social contract or in the recognition of our own dignified rationality. According to the first conception of morality, there is a cut-off line to the amount of altruism or to the extent of devotion to justice and fairness that is worthy of moral praise. But to draw this line earlier than the line that brings the altruist in question into a worse-off position than all those to whom he devotes himself seems unacceptably artificial and gratuitous. According to the second conception, these positive interests are not essentially related to morality at all. But then we are unable to regard a more affectionate and generous expression of good will toward others as a natural and reasonable extension of morality, and we encourage a cold and unduly self-centered approach to the development and evaluation of our motivations and concerns.

A moral theory that does not contain the seeds of an all-consuming ideal of moral sainthood thus seems to place false and unnatural limits on our opportunity to do moral good and our potential to deserve moral praise. Yet the main thrust of the arguments of this paper has been leading to the conclusion that, when such ideals are present, they are not ideals to which it is particularly reasonable or healthy or desirable for human beings to aspire. These claims, taken together, have the appearance of a dilemma from which there is no obvious escape. In a moment, I shall argue that, despite appearances, these claims should not be understood as constituting a dilemma. But, before I do, let me briefly describe another path which those who are convinced by my above remarks may feel inclined to take.

458

If the above remarks are understood to be implicitly critical of the views on the content of morality which seem most popular today, an alternative that naturally suggests itself is that we revise our views about the content of morality. More specifically, my remarks may be taken to support a more Aristotelian, or even a more Nietzschean, approach to moral philosophy. Such a change in approach involves substantially broadening or replacing our contemporary intuitions about which character traits constitute moral virtues and vices and which interests constitute moral interests. If, for example, we include personal bearing, or creativity, or sense of style, as features that contribute to one's *moral* personality, then we can create moral ideals which are incompatible with and probably more attractive than the Kantian and utilitarian ideals I have discussed. Given such an alteration of our conception of morality, the figures with which I have been concerned above might, far from being considered to be moral saints, be seen as morally inferior to other more appealing or more interesting models of individuals.

This approach seems unlikely to succeed, if for no other reason, because it is doubtful that any single, or even any reasonably small number of substantial personal ideals could capture the full range of possible ways of realizing human potential or achieving human good which deserve encouragement and praise. Even if we could provide a sufficiently broad characterization of the range of positive ways for human beings to live, however, I think there are strong reasons not to want to incorporate such a characterization more centrally into the framework of morality itself. For, in claiming that a character trait or activity is morally good, one claims that there is a certain kind of reason for developing that trait or engaging in that activity. Yet, lying behind our criticism of more conventional conceptions of moral sainthood, there seems to be a recognition that among the immensely valuable traits and activities that a human life might positively embrace are some of which we hope that, if a person does embrace them, he does so *not* for moral reasons. In other words, no matter how flexible we make the guide to conduct which we choose to label "morality," no matter how rich we make the life in which perfect obedience to this guide would result, we will have reason to hope that a person does not wholly rule and direct his life by the abstract and impersonal consideration that such a life would be morally good.

Once it is recognized that morality itself should not serve as a comprehensive guide to conduct, moreover, we can see reasons to retain the admittedly vague contemporary intuitions about what the classification of moral and nonmoral virtues, interests, and the like should be. That is, there seem to be important differences between the aspects of a person's life which are currently considered appropriate objects of moral evaluation and the aspects that might be included under the altered conception of morality we are now considering, which the latter approach would tend wrongly to blur or to neglect. Moral evaluation now is focused primarily on features of a person's life over which that person has control; it is largely restricted to aspects of his life which are likely to have considerable effect on other people. These restrictions seem as they should be. Even if responsible people could reach agreement as to what constituted good taste or a healthy degree of well-roundedness, for example, it seems wrong to insist that everyone try to achieve these things or to blame someone who fails or refuses to conform.

If we are not to respond to the unattractiveness of the moral ideals that contemporary theories yield either by offering alternative theories with more palatable ideals or by understanding these theories in such a way as to prevent them from yielding ideals at all, how, then, are we to respond? Simply, I think, by admitting that moral ideals do not, and need not, make the best personal ideals. Earlier, I mentioned one of the consequences of regarding as a test of an adequate moral theory that perfect obedience to its laws and maximal devotion to its interests be something we can wholeheartedly strive for in ourselves and wish for in those around us. Drawing out the consequences somewhat further should, I think, make us more doubtful of the proposed test than of the theories which, on this test, would fail. Given the empirical circumstances of our world, it seems to be an ethical fact that we have unlimited potential to be morally good, and endless opportunity to promote moral interests. But this is not incompatible with the not-so-ethical fact that we have sound, compelling, and not particularly selfish reasons to choose not to devote ourselves univocally to realizing this potential or to taking up this opportunity.

Thus, in one sense at least, I am not really criticizing either Kantianism or utilitarianism. Insofar as the point of view I am offering bears directly on recent work in moral philosophy, in fact, it bears on critics of these theories who, in a spirit not unlike the spirit of most of this paper, point out that the perfect utilitarian would be

460

flawed in this way or the perfect Kantian flawed in that.[3] The assumption lying behind these claims, implicitly or explicitly, has been that the recognition of these flaws shows us something wrong with utilitarianism as opposed to Kantianism, or something wrong with Kantianism as opposed to utilitarianism, or something wrong with both of these theories as opposed to some nameless third alternative. The claims of this paper suggest, however, that this assumption is unwarranted. The flaws of a perfect master of a moral theory need not reflect flaws in the intramoral content of the theory itself.

## Moral Saints and Moral Philosophy

In pointing out the regrettable features and the necessary absence of some desirable features in a moral saint, I have not meant to condemn the moral saint or the person who aspires to become one. Rather, I have meant to insist that the ideal of moral sainthood should not be held as a standard against which any other ideal must be judged or justified, and that the posture we take in response to the recognition that our lives are not as morally good as they might be need not be defensive.[4] It is misleading to insist that one is *permitted* to live a life in which the goals, relationships, activities, and interests that one pursues are not maximally morally good. For our lives are not so comprehensively subject to the requirement that we apply for permission, and our nonmoral reasons for the goals we set ourselves are not excuses, but may rather be positive, good reasons which do not exist *despite* any reasons that might threaten to outweigh them. In other words, a person may be *perfectly wonderful* without being *perfectly moral*.[5]

---

[3]See, e.g., Williams, "Persons, Character," and J. J. C. Smart and Bernard Williams, *Utilitarianism: For and Against* (New York: Cambridge, 1973). Also, Michael Stocker, "The Schizophrenia of Modern Ethical Theories," *Journal of Philosophy* 63, 14 (August 12, 1976): 453–66. See reprint of Stocker's article in this volume, pp. 36–45.

[4]George Orwell makes a similar point in "Reflections on Gandhi," in *A Collection of Essays by George Orwell* (New York: Harcourt Brace Jovanovich, 1945), 176: "sainthood is . . . a thing that human beings must avoid. . . . It is too readily assumed that . . . the ordinary man only rejects it because it is too difficult; in other words, that the average human being is a failed saint. It is doubtful whether this is true. Many people genuinely do not wish to be saints, and it is probable that some who achieve or aspire to sainthood have never felt much temptation to be human beings."

[5]I have benefited from the comments of many people who have heard or read an earlier draft of this paper. I wish particularly to thank Douglas MacLean, Robert Nozick, Martha Nussbaum, and the Society for Ethics and Legal Philosophy.

1. Discuss Wolf's thematic remark that morality does not seem to be a suitable object of passion. Is this why she sees the moral saint as a dull personality? What is wrong with being worthy and right without being very interesting? (Is it necessary to be "interesting"?)

2. Wolf distinguishes between the Loving Saint and the Rational Saint. The former emphasizes benevolence, the latter emphasizes duty—thereby reflecting the two mainstream ethical theories of Utilitarianism and Kantianism. Elaborate on the different ways of being perfectly moral and how such differences correspond to the moral philosophies of Bentham and Kant.

3. What specifically does Wolf find unattractive about the Loving Saint? The Rational Saint? Do you share her reactions?

4. Morality seems by its very nature to invite a total dedication, one that has no upper limit. It would seem that there is nothing wrong with those who exclusively dedicate themselves to being moral, even at the expense of other ways of living. Yet Wolf finds that the ideal of total dedication is unattractive and not universally worthy of pursuit. How does Wolf deal with the fact that morality seems to call for extreme dedication?

# Saints

━━━━━━━━━━━━━━━━━━━━━━━━━━━━━━━━━━━━━━━ ♪♪▬

## ROBERT M. ADAMS

Robert M. Adams (b. 1937) is professor of philosophy at
the University of California at Los Angeles. He has published articles on topics in ethics, metaphysics, and the
history of modern philosophy. Oxford University Press
has recently published a collection of Adams' papers entitled *The Virtue of Faith and Other Essays in Philosophical
Theology*.

Robert Adams defends sainthood from the charge of
dullness. He first points out that Wolf's unattractive picture of the moral saint as "so very, very nice" and as
lacking the "ability to enjoy the enjoyable in life" is not
true to life. Real saints are not bland. Adams argues that
Wolf arrived at her unsympathetic picture by adopting a
conception of saints as persons who maximize moral
value in every one of their actions. According to Adams,
Wolf errs in seeing value only in those actions that improve the lot of others. While real saints certainly have
been devoted to others, such devotion has not been exclusive. Saints perceive their goodness as overflowing from
a boundless divine source. They are not obsessed with
being perfect; nor do we think any the less of them for
this. In characterizing the saint as a moral perfectionist,
Wolf gets it wrong.

SAINTS By Robert M. Adams. Reprinted from *The Journal of Philosophy*, July 1984, pp. 392–401.
By permission of the publisher and author.

Adams agrees with Wolf that maximal devotion to morality is not the sole ideal of perfection. But because Adams' conception of sainthood differs from Wolf's, Adams does not accept Wolf's view that not everyone should aspire to sainthood. For Adams sees nothing wrong in the attempt to tap the source of divine inspiration in the pursuit of perfection in art or philosophy, or in any of the fields that take time away from a life exclusively devoted to good moral works. Adams agrees with Wolf that morality can be exaggerated when he says, "we ought not to make a religion of morality." Indeed, from a religious point of view, the kind of narrow and exclusive preoccupation with morality that Wolf rightly criticizes as unworthy of maximal devotion is a kind of idolatry. Saints are not exclusively moral. Since God is a lover of beauty, the divinely inspired artist could also be saintly.

Wolf looks with disfavor on a life of maximal devotion to any ideal, but Adams justifies maximal devotion to God as a way of living a variegated life of excellence. Adams notes that, historically, moral concepts have their origin in religion, and ends his essay by raising the question whether a satisfactory conception of morality can be detached from all reference to a divine source.

One of the merits of Susan Wolf's fascinating and disturbing essay on "Moral Saints"[1] is that it brings out very sharply a fundamental problem in modern moral philosophy. On the one hand, we want to say that morality is of supreme value, always taking precedence over other grounds of choice, and that what is morally best must be absolutely best. On the other hand, if we consider what it would be like really to live in accordance with that complete priority of the moral, the ideal of life that emerges is apt to seem dismally grey and unattractive, as Wolf persuasively argues. I want to present a diagnosis of the problem that differs from Wolf's. Replies to Wolf might be

---

[1] Originally published in *The Journal of Philosophy* 79, 8 (August 1982): 419–439.

offered on behalf of the utilitarian and Kantian moral theories that she discusses, but of them I shall have little to say. My concern here is to see that sainthood, not Kant or utilitarianism, receives its due.

## What Are Saints Like?

The first thing to be said is that there *are* saints—people like St. Francis of Assisi and Gandhi and Mother Teresa—and they are quite different from what Wolf thinks a moral saint would be. In the end I will conclude that they are not exactly *moral* saints in Wolf's sense. But she writes about some of them as if they were, and discussions of moral sainthood surely owe to the real saints much of their grip on our attention. So it will be to the point to contrast the actuality of sainthood with Wolf's picture of the moral saint.

Wolf argues that moral saints will be "unattractive" because they will be lacking in individuality and in the "ability to enjoy the enjoyable in life," and will be so "very, very nice" and inoffensive that they "will have to be dull-witted or humorless or bland." But the real saints are not like that. It is easier to think of St. Francis as eccentric than as lacking in individuality. And saints are not bland. Many have been offended at them for being very, very truthful instead of very, very nice. (Think of Gandhi—or Jesus.) Saints may not enjoy all the same things as other people, and perhaps a few of them have been melancholy; but an exceptional capacity for joy is more characteristic of them. (For all his asceticism, one thinks again of St. Francis.) There are joys (and not minor ones) that only saints can know. And as for attractiveness, the people we think of first as saints were plainly people who were intensely interesting to almost everyone who had anything to do with them, and immensely attractive to at least a large proportion of those people. They have sometimes been controversial, but rarely dull; and their charisma has inspired many to leave everything else in order to follow them.

Wolf may have set herself up, to some extent, for such contrasts, by conceiving of moral sainthood purely in terms of commitment or devotion to moral ends or principles. There are other, less voluntary virtues that are essential equipment for a saint—humility, for instance, and perceptiveness, courage, and a mind unswayed by the voices of the crowd. The last of these is part of what keeps saints from being bland or lacking in individuality.

465

In order to understand how Wolf arrives at her unflattering picture of the moral saint, however, we must examine her stated conception of moral sainthood.

## Wolf's Argument

Wolf states three criteria for moral sainthood; and they are not equivalent. (1) In her third sentence she says, "By *moral saint* I mean a person whose every action is as morally good as possible." (2) Immediately she adds: "a person, that is, who is as morally worthy as can be." Her words imply that these two characterizations amount to the same thing, but it seems to me that the first expresses at most a very questionable test for the satisfaction of the second. The idea that only a morally imperfect person would spend half an hour doing something morally indifferent, like taking a nap, when she could have done something morally praiseworthy instead, like spending the time in moral self-examination, is at odds with our usual judgments and ought not to be assumed at the outset. The assumption that the perfection of a person, in at least the moral type of value, depends on the maximization of that type of value in every single action of the person lies behind much that is unattractive in Wolf's picture of moral sainthood; but I believe it is a fundamental error.

(3) On the next page we get a third criterion: "A necessary condition of moral sainthood would be that one's life be dominated by a commitment to improving the welfare of others or of society as a whole." Here again, while it might be claimed that this is a necessary condition of a person's, or her acts', being as morally worthy as possible, the claim is controversial. It has been held as a moral thesis that the pursuit of our own perfection ought sometimes to take precedence for us over the welfare of others. The utilitarian, likewise, will presumably think that many people ought to devote their greatest efforts to their own happiness and perfection, because that is what will maximize utility. Given a utilitarian conception of moral rightness as doing what will maximize utility, why shouldn't a utilitarian say that such people, and their acts, can be as morally worthy as possible (and thus can satisfy Wolf's first two criteria of moral sainthood) when they pursue their own happiness and perfection? Presumably, therefore, Wolf is relying heavily on her third criterion, as an independent test, when she says that such cases imply "that the

utilitarian would not support moral sainthood as a universal idea."

This third criterion is obviously related to Wolf's conception of morality. Later in her paper she contrasts the moral point of view with "the point of view of individual perfection," which is "the point of view from which we consider what kinds of lives are good lives, and what kinds of persons it would be good for ourselves and others to be." "The moral point of view . . . is the point of view one takes up insofar as one takes the recognition of the fact that one is just one person among others equally real and deserving of the good things in life as a fact with practical consequences, a fact the recognition of which demands expression in one's actions and in the form of one's practical deliberations." And moral theories are theories that offer "answers to the question of what the most correct or the best way to express this fact is."

This account of moral theory and the moral point of view is in clear agreement with Wolf's third criterion of moral sainthood on one central issue: morality, for her, has exclusively to do with one's regard for the good (and perhaps she would add, the rights) of other persons. One's own dignity or courage or sexuality pose *moral* issues for Wolf only to the extent that they impinge on the interests of other people. Otherwise they can be evaluated from the point of view of individual perfection (and she obviously takes that evaluation very seriously) but not from the moral point of view. This limitation of the realm of the moral is controversial, but (without wishing to be committed to it in other contexts) I shall use "moral" and "morality" here in accordance with Wolf's conception.

It might still be doubted whether her third criterion of moral sainthood follows from her definition of the moral point of view. A utilitarian, for reasons indicated above, might argue that for many people a life not "dominated by a commitment to improving the welfare of others or of society as a whole" could perfectly express "recognition of the fact that one is just one person among others equally real and deserving of the good things of life." Dedication to the good of others is not the same as weighing their good equally with one's own. But if the former is not implied by the latter, it is the altruistic dedication that constitutes Wolf's operative criterion of moral excellence (though I suspect she looks to the equal weighing for a criterion of the morally obligatory). I do not wish to quibble about this; for what interests me most in Wolf's paper is what she says about moral devotion, and weighing one's own good equally with the good of others (demanding as that may be) is something less than devotion.

Thus Wolf's three criteria of moral sainthood seem to me to be separable. The second (maximal moral worthiness of the person, rather than the act) probably comes the closest to expressing an intuitive idea of moral sainthood in its most general form. But the other two seem to be her working criteria. I take all three to be incorporated as necessary conditions in Wolf's conception of moral sainthood.

The center of Wolf's argument can now be stated quite simply. It is that in a life perfectly "dominated by a commitment to improving the welfare of others or of society as a whole" there will not be room for other interests. In particular there will not be time or energy or attention for other good interests, such as the pursuit of aesthetic or athletic excellence. The moral saint will not be able to pursue these interests, or encourage them in others, unless "by happy accident" they have an unusual humanitarian payoff. But from the point of view of individual perfection we have to say that some of the qualities that the moral saint is thus prevented from fostering in herself or others are very desirable, and there are commendable ideals in which they have a central place. So "if we think that it is *as* good, or even better for a person to strive for one of these ideals than it is for him or her to strive for and realize the ideal of the moral saint, we express a conviction that it is good not to be a moral saint."

## Sainthood and Religion

While those actual saints whom I have mentioned have indeed been exceptionally devoted to improving the lives and circumstances of other people, it would be misleading to say that their lives have been "dominated by a commitment to improving the welfare of others or of society as a whole." For sainthood is an essentially religious phenomenon, and even so political a saint as Gandhi saw his powerful humanitarian concern in the context of a more comprehensive devotion to God. This touches the center of Wolf's argument, and helps to explain why actual saints are so unlike her picture of the moral saint. Wolf's moral saint sees limited resources for satisfying immense human needs and unlimited human desires, and devotes

468

himself wholly to satisfying them as fully (and perhaps as fairly) as possible. This leaves him no time or energy for anything that does not *have* to be done. Not so the saints. The substance of sainthood is not sheer will power striving like Sisyphus (or like Wolf's Rational Saint) to accomplish a boundless task, but goodness overflowing from a boundless source. Or so, at least, the saints perceive it.

They commonly have time for things that do not *have* to be done, because their vision is not of needs that exceed any possible means of satisfying them, but of a divine goodness that is more than adequate to every need. They are not in general even trying to make their *every action* as good as possible, and thus they diverge from Wolf's first criterion of moral sainthood. The humility of the saint may even require that she spend considerable stretches of time doing nothing of any great importance or excellence. Saintliness is not perfectionism, though some saints have been perfectionistic in various ways. There is an unusual moral goodness in the saints, but we shall not grasp it by asking whether any of their actions could have been morally worthier. What makes us think of a Gandhi, for example, as a saint is something more positive, which I would express by saying that goodness was present in him in exceptional power.

Many saints have felt the tensions on which Wolf's argument turns. Albert Schweitzer, whom many have honored as a twentieth-century saint, was one who felt keenly the tension between artistic and intellectual achievement on the one hand and a higher claim of humanitarian commitment on the other. Yet in the midst of his humanitarian activities in Africa, he kept a piano and spent some time playing it— even before he realized that keeping up this skill would help him raise money for his mission. Very likely that time could have been employed in actions that would have been morally worthier, but that fact by itself surely has no tendency to disqualify Schweitzer from sainthood, in the sense in which people are actually counted as saints. We do not demand as a necessary condition of sainthood that the saint's every act be the morally worthiest possible in the circumstances, nor that he try to make it so.

The religious character of sainthood also helps to explain how the saint can be so self-giving without lacking (as Wolf suggests the Loving Saint must) an interest in his own condition as a determinant of his own happiness. In fact saints have typically been intensely and frankly interested in their own condition, their own perfection, and their own happiness. Without this interest they would hardly have been fitted to lead others for whom they desired perfection and happiness. What enables them to give of themselves unstintedly is not a lack of interest in their own persons, but a trust in God to provide for their growth and happiness.

## Should Everyone Be a Saint?

Even if it can be shown that the life of a Gandhi or a St. Francis is happier and more attractive than Wolf claims that the life of a moral saint would be, we still face questions analogous to some of those she presses. Would it be good if everyone were a saint? Should we all aspire to be saints?

Not everybody *could* be a Gandhi. He himself thought otherwise. "Whatever is possible for me is possible even for a child," he wrote.[2] This is a point on which we may venture to disagree with him. A life like his involves, in religious terms, a vocation that is not given to everyone. Or to put the matter in more secular terms, not all who set themselves to do it will accomplish as much good by humanitarian endeavor as Wolf seems to assume that any utilitarian can. But perhaps some of us assume too easily that we could not be a Gandhi. In all probability there could be more Gandhis than there are, and it would be a very good thing if there were.

Wolf, however, will want to press the question whether there are not human excellences that could not be realized by a Gandhi, or even by someone who seriously aspired to be one, and whether it would not be good for some people to aspire to these excellences instead of aspiring to sainthood. My answer to these questions is affirmative, except for the "instead of aspiring to sainthood." Given the limits of human time and energy, it is hard to see how a Gandhi or a Martin Luther King, Jr., could at the same time have been a great painter or a world-class violinist. Such saints may indeed attain and employ great mastery in the arts of speaking and writing. But there are demanding forms of excellence, in the arts and in science, for example, and also in philosophy, which probably are not compatible with their vocation (and even less compatible with the vocation of a

---

[2]M. K. Gandhi, *Gandhi's Autobiography: The Story of My Experiments with Truth*, trans. Mahadev Desai (Washington, D.C.: Public Affairs Press, 1948), 7.

St. Francis, for reasons of life-style rather than time and energy). And I agree that it is good that some people aspire to those excellences and attain them.

But if it is right to conclude that not everyone should aspire to be a Gandhi or a Martin Luther King or a St. Francis, it may still be too hasty to infer that not everyone should aspire to sainthood. Perhaps there are other ways of being a saint. That will depend, of course, on what is meant by "saint"; so it is time to offer a definition.

If sainthood is an essentially religious phenomenon, as I claim, it is reasonable to seek its central feature (at least for theistic religions) in the saint's relation to God. "Saint" means "holy"—indeed they are the same word in most European languages. Saints are people in whom the holy or divine can be seen. In a religious view they are people who submit themselves, in faith, to God, not only loving Him but also letting His love possess them, so that it works through them and shines through them to other people. What interests a saint may have will then depend on what interests God has, for sainthood is a participation in God's interests. And God need not be conceived as what Wolf would call a "moral fanatic." He is not so limited that His moral concerns could leave Him without time or attention or energy for other interests. As the author of all things and of all human capacities, He may be regarded as interested in many forms of human excellence, for their own sake and not just for the sake of their connection with what would be classified as *moral* concerns in any narrow sense. This confirms the suggestion that Gandhi and Martin Luther King and St. Francis exemplify only certain types of sainthood, and that other types may be compatible with quite different human excellences—and in particular, with a great variety of demanding artistic and intellectual excellences. I do not see why a Fra Angelico or a Johann Sebastian Bach or a Thomas Aquinas could not have been a saint in this wider sense.

Now I suspect that Wolf will not be satisfied with the conclusion that a saint could be an Angelico or a Bach or an Aquinas. And I do not think that the sticking point here will be that the three figures mentioned all dealt with religious subjects. After all, much of Bach's and Aquinas's work is not explicitly religious, and it would be easy to make a case that a saint could have done most of Cézanne's work. The trouble, I rather expect Wolf to say, is that the forms of artistic and intellectual excellence typified by these figures are too sweet or too nice or too wholesome to be the only ones allowed us. There are

471

darker triumphs of human creativity that we also admire; could a saint have produced them?

Not all of them. I admire the art of Edvard Munch, but I certainly grant that most of his work would not have been produced by a saint. I do not think that is a point against the aspiration to sainthood, however, nor even against a desire for universal sainthood. Who knows? Perhaps Munch would have painted even greater things of another sort if he had been a saint. But that is not the crucial point. Perhaps he would have given up painting and done something entirely different. The crucial point is that although I might aspire to Munch's artistic talent and skill, I certainly would not aspire to be a person who would use it to express what he did, nor would I wish that on anyone I cared about. In view not merely of the intensity of unhappiness, but also of the kind of unhappiness that comes to expression in Munch's art, it would be perverse to aspire to it, nobly as Munch expressed it. The lesson to be learned from such cases is that our ethical or religious view of life ought to allow for some ambivalence, and particularly for the appreciation of some things that we ought not to desire.

Van Gogh provides an interesting example of a different sort. There is much in his life to which one would not aspire, and his canvases sometimes express terror, even madness, rather than peace. Yet I would hesitate to say that a saint could not have painted them. The saints have not been strangers to terror, pain, and sadness; and if in Van Gogh's pictures we often see the finite broken by too close an approach of the transcendent, that is one of the ways in which the holy can show itself in human life. Certainly Van Gogh wanted to be a saint; and perhaps, in an unorthodox and sometimes despairing way, he was one.

## Is Morality a Suitable Object of Maximal Devotion?

Wolf's arguments lead her to reject an important received opinion about the nature of morality and about what it means to accept a moral theory—the opinion, namely, that it is "a test of an adequate moral theory that perfect obedience to its laws and maximal devotion to its interests be something we can whole-heartedly strive for in ourselves and wish for in those around us." There are two parts to the received opinion, as it has to do with perfect obedience and with maximal devotion. I cannot see that Wolf's arguments call in question the desirability of perfect obedience to the laws of morality, unless those laws make all good deeds obligatory (as in a rigorous act utilitarianism). Wolf seems on the whole to prefer the view that even nonmoral ideals to which it would be good to aspire ought not to involve the infringement of moral *requirements;* and so she concludes that if (as she has argued) "we have reason to want people to live lives that are not morally perfect, then any plausible moral theory must make use of some conception of supererogation." What she clearly rejects in the received opinion, then, is the desirability of maximal devotion to the interests of morality.

In this I agree with her. We ought not to make a religion of morality. Without proposing, like Kierkegaard and Tillich, to define religion as maximal devotion, I would say that maximal devotion (like sainthood) is essentially religious, or at least that it has its proper place only in religion. Wolf is going too far when she says that "morality itself does not seem to be a suitable object of passion." But maximal devotion is much more than passion. And morality, as Wolf conceives of it, is too narrow to be a suitable object of maximal or religious devotion. Her reason (and one good reason) for thinking this is that a demand for universal maximal devotion to morality excludes too many human excellences.

Religion is richer than morality, because its divine object is so rich. He is not too narrow to be a suitable object of maximal devotion. Since He is lover of beauty, for instance, as well as commander of morals, maximal submission of one's life to Him may in some cases (as I have argued) encompass an intense pursuit of artistic excellence in a way that maximal devotion to the interests of morality, narrowly understood, cannot. Many saints and other religious people, to be sure, have been quite hostile to some of the forms of human endeavor and achievement that I agree with Wolf in prizing. What I have argued is that the breadth of the Creator's interests makes possible a conception of sainthood that does not require this hostility.

There is for many (and not the least admirable) among us a strong temptation to make morality into a substitute for religion, and in so doing to make morality the object of a devotion that is maximal, at least in aspiration, and virtually religious in character. Such a devotion to morality, conceived as narrowly as Wolf conceives of it, would be, from a religious point of view, idolatry. The conclusion to which Wolf's arguments tend is that it would also be, from what she calls "the point of view of individual perfection," oppressive.

On the other hand, the loss of the possibility of sainthood, and of maximal devotion, would be a great loss. Wolf says, "A moral theory that does not contain the seeds of an all-consuming ideal of moral sainthood . . . seems to place false and unnatural limits on our opportunity to do moral good and our potential to deserve moral praise." This seems right, but I do not think it is just our indefinite (not infinite) opportunities and capacities that generate the all-consuming ideal. There are other departments of human life (such as memorization) in which our potential to deserve praise is indefinite but in which it would be bizarre to adopt an all-consuming ideal. The fact is that many of the concepts that we use in morality were developed in a religious tradition; and to tear them loose entirely from a context in which something (distinct perhaps from morality but including it) claims maximal devotion seems to threaten something that is important for the seriousness of morality.

It may not, in other words, be so easy to have a satisfactory conception of morality without religion—that is, without belief in an appropriate object of maximal devotion, an object that is larger than morality but embraces it.[3]

**STUDY QUESTIONS**

1. Adams is accusing Wolf of having caricatured the Moral Saint. Real saints are not like that. What might be Wolf's reply? What do you think of moral saints? What do you think of sainthood as an ideal to be pursued?
2. According to Adams, Wolf has erred in thinking of moral saints as those whose perfection consists in maximizing value in all of their actions. Why is this characterization of the moral saint erroneous?
3. Adams sees the saint as essentially religious. "The religious character of the saint . . . [explains] how the saint can be so self-giving without lacking (as Wolf suggests) an interest in . . . his

---

[3]I wish to thank the Center of Theological Inquiry for fellowship support during the writing of this paper, and Marilyn McCord Adams, for helpful comments on an earlier version.

own happiness." How, in Adams' view, does the religious element make the saint more human and attractive?

4. Many, like Adams, hold that religion is a suitable object of maximal devotion. Adam goes further when he suggests that we cannot have a satisfactory conception of morality that is not grounded in religion. Discuss this contention, and discuss the related contention that anyone maximally devoted to a cause is at bottom "religious."

5. According to Adams, Wolf errs in thinking that the saint must be maximally devoted to being morally perfect. Indeed, Adams says one may be saintly as an artist. Does Adams use the term sainthood too loosely? What is your conception of a saint? Is it closer to Wolf's or to Adams'?

# *Reflections on Gandhi*

### GEORGE ORWELL

George Orwell (1903–1950), British novelist and journalist, was an influential social critic and political analyst. Like Hemingway, Orwell fought in the Spanish Civil War. His best-known novels are *Animal Farm* and *1984*.

George Orwell reviews Mahatma Gandhi's autobiography, using the occasion to appraise Gandhi's saintly nature. Among Gandhi's qualities are physical courage, lack of envy or feeling of superiority, willingness to believe the best of people, freedom from all forms of prejudice. "I believe," says Orwell, "that even Gandhi's worst enemies would admit that he . . . enriched the world simply

REFLECTIONS ON GANDHI From *Shooting an Elephant and Other Essays* by George Orwell. Copyright 1949 by *Partisan Review;* renewed 1977 by Sonia Orwell. Reprinted by permission of Harcourt Brace Jovanovich, Inc.

by being alive." Yet Orwell finds Gandhi not altogether lovable. Orwell rejects the idea that Gandhi was concerned with human welfare in a Western sense. "Gandhi's teachings cannot be squared with the belief . . . that our job is to make life worth living on this Earth. . . . They make sense only on the assumption that the world of solid objects is an illusion to be escaped from."

Gandhi's abstentions were no animal food, no spices, no tobacco, no sexual intercourse, and no close friendships. Orwell notes that the latter is entailed by Gandhi's mission: "To love humanity as a whole, one cannot give one's preference to any individual person."

Orwell believes that Gandhi's abstentions mark the point at which his religious attitudes conflict with ordinary human concerns. Gandhi was prepared even to allow his sick child to die rather than allow the child to transgress vegetarian strictures. Orwell: "There must be some limit to what we will do, and [for Gandhi] the limit is well on this side of chicken broth." This attitude, says Orwell, may be noble, but "it is inhuman."

Yet Orwell finds Gandhi's unrelenting pacificism, his courage, his doctrine of nonviolent resistance altogether admirable. Gandhi's pacificist methods worked well when directed against a society that had a free press and that gave him respectful publicity. Gandhi earns the chief credit for a peaceful end to British rule in India. "[O]ne may reject sainthood as an ideal and therefore feel that Gandhi's basic aims were anti-human . . . but compared with other leading political figures of our time, how clean a smell he has managed to leave behind!"

Saints should always be judged guilty until they are proved innocent, but the tests that have to be applied to them are not, of course, the same in all cases. In Gandhi's case the questions one feels inclined to ask are: to what extent was Gandhi moved by vanity—by the consciousness of himself as a humble, naked old man, sitting on a praying mat and shaking empires by sheer spiritual power—and to what extent did he compromise his own principles by entering politics, which of their nature are inseparable from coercion and fraud? To give a definite answer one would have to study Gandhi's acts and writings in immense detail, for his whole life was a sort of pilgrimage in which every act was significant. But this partial autobiography,[1] which ends in the nineteen-twenties, is strong evidence in his favor, all the more because it covers what he would have called the unregenerate part of his life and reminds one that inside the saint, or near-saint, there was a very shrewd, able person who could, if he had chosen, have been a brilliant success as a lawyer, an administrator, or perhaps even a businessman.

At about the time when the autobiography first appeared I remember reading its opening chapters in the ill-printed pages of some Indian newspaper. They made a good impression on me, which Gandhi himself at that time, did not. The things that one associated with him—home-spun cloth, "soul forces," and vegetarianism—were unappealing, and his medievalist program was obviously not viable in a backward, starving, overpopulated country. It was also apparent that the British were making use of him, or thought they were making use of him. Strictly speaking, as a Nationalist, he was an enemy, but since in every crisis he would exert himself to prevent violence—which, from the British point of view, meant preventing any effective action whatever—he could be regarded as "our man." In private this was sometimes cynically admitted. The attitude of the Indian millionaires was similar. Gandhi called upon them to repent, and naturally they preferred him to the Socialists and Communists who, given the chance, would actually have taken their money away. How reliable such calculations are in the long run is doubtful; as Gandhi himself says, "in the end deceivers deceive only themselves"; but at any rate the gentleness with which he was nearly always handled was due partly to the feeling that he was useful. The British Conservatives only became really angry with him when, as in 1942, he was in effect turning his non-violence against a different conqueror.

But I could see even then that the British officials who spoke of him with a mixture of amusement and disapproval also genuinely liked and admired him, after a fashion. Nobody ever suggested that

___

[1] *The Story of my Experiments with Truth.* By M. K. Gandhi. Translated from the Gujarati by Mahadex Desai. Public Affairs Press.

he was corrupt, or ambitious in any vulgar way, or that anything he did was actuated by fear or malice. In judging a man like Gandhi one seems instinctively to apply high standards, so that some of his virtues have passed almost unnoticed. For instance, it is clear even from the autobiography that his natural physical courage was quite outstanding: the manner of his death was a later illustration of this, for a public man who attached any value to his own skin would have been more adequately guarded. Again, he seems to have been quite free from that maniacal suspiciousness which, as E. M. Forster rightly says in *A Passage to India,* is the besetting Indian vice, as hypocrisy is the British vice. Although no doubt he was shrewd enough in detecting dishonesty, he seems wherever possible to have believed that other people were acting in good faith and had a better nature through which they could be approached. And though he came of a poor middle-class family, started life rather unfavorably, and was probably of unimpressive physical appearance, he was not afflicted by envy or by the feeling of inferiority. Color feeling when he first met it in its worst form in South Africa, seems rather to have astonished him. Even when he was fighting what was in effect a color war, he did not think of people in terms of race or status. The governor of a province, a cotton millionaire, a half-starved Dravidian coolie, a British private soldier were all equally human beings, to be approached in much the same way. It is noticeable that even in the worst possible circumstances, as in South Africa when he was making himself unpopular as the champion of the Indian community, he did not lack European friends.

Written in short lengths for newspaper serialization, the autobiography is not a literary masterpiece, but it is the more impressive because of the commonplaceness of much of its material. It is well to be reminded that Gandhi started out with the normal ambitions of a young Indian student and only adopted his extremist opinions by degrees and, in some cases, rather unwillingly. There was a time, it is interesting to learn, when he wore a top hat, took dancing lessons, studied French and Latin, went up the Eiffel Tower, and even tried to learn the violin—all this was the idea of assimilating European civilization as thoroughly as possible. He was not one of those saints who are marked out by their phenomenal piety from childhood onward, nor one of the other kind who forsake the world after sensational debaucheries. He makes full confession of the misdeeds of his youth, but in fact there is not much to confess. As a frontispiece to the book there is a photograph of Gandhi's possessions at the time of his death. The whole outfit could be purchased for about £5, and Gandhi's sins, at least his fleshly sins, would make the same sort of appearance if placed all in one heap. A few cigarettes, a few mouthfuls of meat, a few annas pilfered in childhood from the maidservant, two visits to a brothel (on each occasion he got away without "doing anything"), one narrowly escaped lapse with his landlady in Plymouth, one out-burst of temper—that is about the whole collection. Almost from childhood onward he had a deep earnestness, an attitude ethical rather than religious, but, until he was about thirty, no very definite sense of direction. His first entry into anything describable as public life was made by way of vegetarianism. Underneath his less ordinary qualities one feels all the time the solid middle-class businessmen who were his ancestors. One feels that even after he had abandoned personal ambition he must have been a resourceful, energetic lawyer and a hardheaded political organizer, careful in keeping down ex-penses, an adroit handler of committees and an indefatigable chaser of subscriptions. His character was an extraordinarily mixed one, but there was almost nothing in it that you can put your finger on and call bad, and I believe that even Gandhi's worse enemies would admit that he was an interesting and unusual man who enriched the world simply by being alive. Whether he was also a lovable man, and whether his teachings can have much value for those who do not accept the religious beliefs on which they are founded, I have never felt fully certain.

Of late years it has been the fashion to talk about Gandhi as though he were not only sympathetic to the Western left-wing movement, but were integrally part of it. Anarchists and pacifists, in particular, have claimed him for their own, noticing only that he was opposed to centralism and State violence and ignoring the other-worldly, anti-humanist tendency of his doctrines. But one should, I think, realize that Gandhi's teachings cannot be squared with the belief that Man is the measure of all things and that our job is to make life worth living on this earth, which is the only earth we have. They make sense only on the assumption that God exists and that the world of solid objects is an illusion to be escaped from. It is worth considering the disciplines which Gandhi imposed on himself and which— though he might not insist on every one of his followers observing every detail—he considered indispensable if one wanted to serve either God or humanity. First of all, no meat-eating, and if possible no animal food in any form. (Gandhi himself, for the sake of his health, had to compromise on milk, but seems to have felt this to be a backsliding.) No alcohol or tobacco, and no spices or condiments even of a vegetable kind, since food should be taken not for its own sake but solely in order to preserve one's strength. Secondly, if possible, no sexual intercourse. If sexual intercourse must happen, then it should be for the sole purpose of begetting children and presumably at long intervals. Gandhi himself, in his middle thirties, took the vow of *brahmacharya,* which means not only complete chastity but the elimination of sexual desire. This condition, it seems, is difficult to attain without a special diet and frequent fasting. One of the dangers of milk-drinking is that it is apt to arouse sexual desire. And finally—this is the cardinal point—for the seeker after goodness there must be no close friendships and no exclusive loves whatever.

Close friendships, Gandhi says, are dangerous, because "friends react on one another" and through loyalty to a friend one can be led into wrong-doing. This is unquestionably true. Moreover, if one is to love God, or to love humanity as a whole, one cannot give one's preference to any individual person. This again is true, and it marks the point at which the humanistic and the religious attitude cease to be reconcilable. To an ordinary human being, love means nothing if it does not mean loving some people more than others. The autobiography leaves it uncertain whether Gandhi behaved in an inconsiderate way to his wife and children, but at any rate it makes clear that on three occasions he was willing to let his wife or a child die rather than administer the animal food prescribed by the doctor. It is true that the threatened death never actually occurred, and also that Gandhi—with, one gathers, a good deal of moral pressure in the opposite direction—always gave the patient the choice of staying alive at the price of committing a sin: still, if the decision had been solely his own, he would have forbidden the animal food, whatever the risks might be. There must, he says, be some limit to what we will do in order to remain alive, and the limit is well on this side of chicken broth. This attitude is perhaps a noble one, but, in the sense which— I think—most people would give to the word, it is inhuman. The essence of being human is that one does not seek perfection, that one *is* sometimes willing to commit sins for the sake of loyalty, that one does not push asceticism to the point where it makes friendly inter-course impossible, and that one is prepared in the end to be defeated and broken up by life, which is the inevitable price of fastening one's love upon other human individuals. No doubt alcohol, tobacco, and so forth, are things that a saint must avoid, but sainthood is also a thing that human beings must avoid. There is an obvious retort to this, but one should be wary about making it. In this yogi-ridden age, it is too readily assumed that "non-attachment" is not only better than a full acceptance of earthly life, but that the ordinary man only rejects it because it is too difficult: in other words, that the average human being is a failed saint. It is doubtful whether this is true. Many people genuinely do not wish to be saints, and it is probable that some who achieve or aspire to sainthood have never felt much temptation to be human beings. If one could follow it to its psycho-logical roots, one would, I believe, find that the main motive for "non-attachment" is a desire to escape from the pain of living, and above all from love, which, sexual or non-sexual, is hard work. But it is not necessary here to argue whether the other-worldly or the humanistic ideal is "higher." The point is that they are incompatible. One must choose between God and Man, and all "radicals" and "progressives," from the mildest liberal to the most extreme anar-chist, have in effect chosen Man.

However, Gandhi's pacifism can be separated to some extent from his other teachings. Its motive was religious, but he claimed also for it that it was a definite technique, a method, capable of producing desired political results. Gandhi's attitude was not that of most West-ern pacifists. *Satyagraha,* first evolved in South Africa, was a sort of non-violent warfare, a way of defeating the enemy without hurting him and without feeling or arousing hatred. It entailed such things as civil disobedience, strikes, lying down in front of railway trains, enduring police charges without running away and without hitting back, and the like. Gandhi objected to "passive resistance" as a trans-lation of *Satyagraha:* in Gujarati, it seems, the word means "firmness in the truth." In his early days Gandhi served as a stretcher-bearer on the British side in the Boer War, and he was prepared to do the same again in the war of 1914–18. Even after he had completely abjured violence he was honest enough to see that in war it is usually neces-sary to take sides. He did not—indeed, since his whole political life centered round a struggle for national independence, he could not—

take the sterile and dishonest line of pretending that in every war both sides are exactly the same and it makes no difference who wins. Nor did he, like most Western pacifists, specialize in avoiding awkward questions. In relation to the late war, one question that every pacifist had a clear obligation to answer was: "What about the Jews? Are you prepared to see them exterminated? If not, how do you propose to save them without resorting to war?" I must say that I have never heard, from any Western pacifist, an honest answer to this question, though I have heard plenty of evasions, usually of the "you're another" type. But it so happens that Gandhi was asked a somewhat similar question in 1938 and that his answer is on record in Mr. Louis Fischer's *Gandhi and Stalin*. According to Mr. Fischer, Gandhi's view was that the German Jews ought to commit collective suicide, which "would have aroused the world and the people of Germany to Hitler's violence." After the war he justified himself: the Jews had been killed anyway, and might as well have died significantly. One has the impression that this attitude staggered even so warm an admirer as Mr. Fischer, but Gandhi was merely being honest. If you are not prepared to take life, you must often be prepared for lives to be lost in some other way. When, in 1942, he urged nonviolent resistance against a Japanese invasion, he was ready to admit that it might cost several million deaths.

At the same time there is reason to think that Gandhi, who after all was born in 1869, did not understand the nature of totalitarianism and saw everything in terms of his own struggle against the British government. The important point here is not so much that the British treated him forbearingly as that he was always able to command publicity. As can be seen from the phrase quoted above, he believed in "arousing the world," which is only possible if the world gets a chance to hear what you are doing. It is difficult to see how Gandhi's methods could be applied in a country where opponents of the régime disappear in the middle of the night and are never heard of again. Without a free press and the right of assembly, it is impossible not merely to appeal to outside opinion, but to bring a mass movement into being, or even to make your intentions known to your adversary. Is there a Gandhi in Russia at this moment? And if there is, what is he accomplishing? The Russian masses could only practice civil disobedience if the same idea happened to occur to all of them simultaneously, and even then, to judge by the history of the Ukraine famine, it would make no difference. But let it be granted that non-violent resistance can be effective against one's own government, or against an occupying power: even so, how does one put it into practice internationally? Gandhi's various conflicting statements on the late war seem to show that he felt the difficulty of this. Applied to foreign politics, pacifism either stops being pacifist or becomes appeasement. Moreover the assumption, which served Gandhi so well in dealing with individuals, that all human beings are more or less approachable and will respond to a generous gesture, needs to be seriously questioned. It is not necessarily true, for example, when you are dealing with lunatics. Then the question becomes: Who is sane? Was Hitler sane? And is it not possible for one whole culture to be insane by the standards of another? And, so far as one can gauge the feelings of whole nations, is there any apparent connection between a generous deed and a friendly response? Is gratitude a factor in international politics?

These and kindred questions need discussion, and need it urgently, in the few years left to us before somebody presses the button and the rockets begin to fly. It seems doubtful whether civilization can stand another major war, and it is at least thinkable that the way out lies through non-violence. It is Gandhi's virtue that he would have been ready to give honest consideration to the kind of question that I have raised above; and, indeed, he probably did discuss most of these questions somewhere or other in his innumerable newspaper articles. One feels of him that there was much that he did not understand, but not that there was anything that he was frightened of saying or thinking. I have never been able to feel much liking for Gandhi, but I do not feel sure that as a political thinker he was wrong in the main, nor do I believe that his life was a failure. It is curious that when he was assassinated, many of his warmest admirers exclaimed sorrowfully that he had lived just long enough to see his life work in ruins, because India was engaged in a civil war which had always been foreseen as one of the by-products of the transfer of power. But it was not in trying to smooth down Hindu-Moslem rivalry that Gandhi had spent his life. His main political objective, the peaceful ending of British rule, had after all been attained. As usual the relevant facts cut across one another. On the other hand, the British did get out of India without fighting, an event which very few observers indeed would have predicted until about a year before it happened. On the other hand, this was done by a Labor government, and it is certain that a Conservative government, especially a government headed by Churchill, would have acted differently. But if, by 1945, there had grown up in Britain a large body of opinion sympathetic to Indian independence, how far was this due to Gandhi's personal influence? And if, as may happen, India and Britain finally settle down into a decent and friendly relationship, will this be partly because Gandhi, by keeping up his struggle obstinately and without hatred, disinfected the political air? That one even thinks of asking such questions indicates his stature. One may feel, as I do, a sort of aesthetic distaste for Gandhi, one may reject the claims of sainthood made on his behalf (he never made any such claim himself, by the way), one may also reject sainthood as an ideal and therefore feel that Gandhi's basic aims were anti-human and reactionary: but regarded simply as a politician, and compared with the other leading political figures of our time, how clean a smell he has managed to leave behind!

## STUDY QUESTIONS

1. Orwell: "Gandhi enriched the world simply by being alive." Why do you think he made people feel this way? Are you acquainted with anyone whose life enriches the *world*?
2. What light does the example of Gandhi cast on the Wolf-Adams controversy? Does it favor either view? Does it favor a third characterization of saintliness?
3. Orwell calls Gandhi "inhuman." In what ways was he inhuman? Are most saints inhuman in those ways? Why, despite that, was Gandhi lovable? Is Gandhi someone to emulate?
4. What is the idea behind nonviolent resistance? Is it always a feasible method? If not, why not?
5. Orwell notes that some have found Gandhi "aesthetically distasteful," that some have rejected sainthood as an ideal, and that some liberal critics have considered Gandhi's basic aims as "antihuman and reactionary." Do you react to Gandhi in any of these ways? If you do, explain and justify your reactions. If you don't, explain why you don't.

## SUGGESTED READINGS

Butler, Joseph. *Five Sermons*, Stuart Brown, Jr., ed. Indianapolis, IN: Bobbs-Merrill, 1950.

MacIntyre, Alasdair. "Egoism and Altruism," Paul Edwards, ed. In *The Encyclopedia of Philosophy*. New York: Macmillan and Free Press, 1967, vol. 2, pp. 462–466.

Nagel, Thomas. *The Possibility of Altruism*. Oxford University Press, 1970.

Nietzsche, Friedrich. *Thus Spake Zarathustra*, Walter Kaufmann, ed. In *The Portable Nietzsche*. New York: Viking Press, 1954.

Olson, Robert. *The Morality of Self-Interest*. New York: Harcourt, Brace and World, 1965.

Rand, Ayn. *The Virtue of Selfishness*. New York: Signet, 1964.

Singer, Peter. *The Expanding Circle: Ethics and Sociobiology*. New York: Farrer, Straus and Giroux, 1981.

## Chapter Six

# MORAL
# EDUCATION

Sooner or later most of us face the problem of what and how to teach a child about moral behavior. Teachers of earlier generations felt free to pass on to children a set of moral precepts and prohibitions; they did not worry about compromising the child's autonomy.

Many teachers today lack confidence in their knowledge of right and wrong. How can one teach what one is not sure of? Even the ethical principles that teachers are prepared to defend are believed by them to be culturally determined. Contemporary teachers see themselves as children of Western culture; they are aware that many of the values they hold dear are not held dear in other cultures. Moreover, they recognize that social norms shift rapidly; behavior deemed wrong in one generation is tolerated and even praised in the next. In this prevailing climate of ethical relativism, moral training appears arbitrary and even presumptuous.

A related problem is the compunction the comtemporary teacher feels in doing anything that smacks of "indoctrination"—a word redolent of the thought conrol and social manipulation that one associates with totalitarian states. Finally, the need to teach *tolerance* of the opinions of others makes the job of teaching values even more difficult; teachers cannot put themselves completely behind the values they are trying to inculcate if they must at the same time show themselves to be tolerant of those who may disapprove heartily of them, or even jeer at them.

The articles of this chapter should be read with such contemporary issues and problems in mind. The first selection presents the classical Aristotelian doctrine on moral education that unself-consciously and unabashedly insists children be trained, habituated, and guided to virtuous behavior. Moral education in the Aristotelian tradition is directed to specific goals. Good behavior is rewarded and reinforced. Vice is punished and discouraged. The character is molded carefully. Tolerance of several points of view and of diversity in moral attitudes was not unknown in Ancient Greece, yet tolerance is not one of the classical virtues. Indeed, tolerance could not be thought of as a primary virtue by anyone who aims to instill a sense of indignation and revulsion at the sight of vice.

Lawrence Kohlberg, a contemporary moral psychologist, argues that directed indoctrination interferes with a child's autonomy and moral development. Kohlberg rejects the Aristotelian tradition in moral education, disparaging it as the old "bag of virtues" approach. He himself avoids ethical relativism by a kind of Platonic insistence that all children are innately moral. Their cognitive and social development consists in an unfolding of their moral potential in a series of stages that ideally culminates in the highest stage of moral understanding: an appreciation of one's duty as a rational moral agent.

George Sher and William J. Bennett reject Kohlberg's arguments against teaching the virtues. They point out that *all* good teaching inculcates belief; in a sense, indoctrination is an inescapable responsibility of the teacher. Sher and Bennett's critique of Kohlberg is, in part, a defense of the traditional Aristotelian approach. Other critics of Kohlberg find him insensitive to different *styles* of moral development. Carol Gilligan, for example, claims that men and women develop morally in different ways. Men tend to adopt a "rights perspective" and women a "caring perspective." The former is more abstract, detached, and impartial; the latter is more concrete, emotional, and personal. Gilligan criticizes Kohlberg for neglecting and undervaluing the moral experience of women.

Allan Bloom ascribes the present malaise in moral education to the pervasive influence of ethical relativism—a doctrine that disparages

487

the idea that any moral principles are objective and universal. The complete ("unprincipled") tolerance of moral diversity is inhospitable to a moral education that could train the student to defend universal and inalienable human rights. In the current relativistic climate, inalienable rights are seen as "Western values"; their rejection by other cultures is tolerantly accommodated. Like Bloom, Christina Sommers believes that the current climate of moral opinion—its relativism, its overvaluing of tolerance—breeds moral apathy and with it, the hope that the government will somehow compensate for the loss of individual moral initiative.

Some recent thinkers believe that the best moral education is a classical education. Ronald Duska argues that the study of great literature helps students find meaning in their lives. Literature trains the passions and the sensibilities. And, *contra* Kohlberg, Duska views moral progress more as an affair of greater passion and sensibility than an affair of greater understanding and wisdom.

James Stockdale tells how his knowledge of history and philosophy helped him survive with dignity eight years of captivity. Any perusal of contemporary essays on moral education immediately suggests that the old question, "Can virtue be taught?" has not gone away. Stockdale's story shows at least that virtue can be learned.

# Habit and Virtue

## ARISTOTLE

A biographical sketch of Aristotle is found on page 181.

How does one become virtuous? According to Aristotle, although we are endowed by nature with the capacity to acquire virtue, we are not virtuous by nature. We become virtuous by performing virtuous acts repeatedly until such acts become "second nature." Legislators, too, seek to promote virtue in citizens by a moral education that habituates citizens to virtuous behavior. This goal is achieved by exposing young people to situations where they may exhibit courage or temperance and by reinforcing such behavior through repetition and reward for creditable performance. Right acts demonstrate moderation. For example, courageous acts avoid the extremes of cowardice on the one side and foolhardiness on the other.

Moral education is compared to training for strength. We become strong by *doing* things that require strength. Similarly, we become virtuous by behaving virtuously until such behavior "stands firm" in us. Pains and pleasures are used as incentives to virtuous behavior during moral training. Later, virtuous behavior becomes pleasurable to us as an end in itself.

Aristotle considers an objection to his view that we become virtuous by behaving virtuously: that it seems we must have been virtuous to begin with. Aristotle replies that our earliest virtuous activity may be somewhat random; the educator identifies the virtuous activity and

HABIT AND VIRTUE From *Nicomachean Ethics* by Aristotle. Translated by Terence Irwin (Indianapolis, IN: Hackett, 1985), pp. 33–40. Reprinted by permission of the publisher.

reinforces it. After the right behavior is reinforced and the wrong behavior is rejected and rendered undesirable, the student has learned to be virtuous automatically. The virtue is internalized; it is no longer a virtue of deed, but of character. Virtuous behavior that stems from character is not random at all, but consists of acts done in the manner that a just or temperate person would do them.

## Virtues of Character in General

### How a Virtue of Character is Acquired

Virtue, then, is of two sorts, virtue of thought and virtue of character. Virtue of thought arises and grows mostly from teaching, and hence needs experience and time. Virtue of character [i.e. of *ēthos*] results from habit [*ethos*]; hence its name "ethical," slightly varied from "*ethos*."

### Virtue comes about, not by a process of nature, but by habituation

Hence it is also clear that none of the virtues of character arises in us naturally.

### (1) What is natural cannot be changed by habituation

For if something is by nature [in one condition], habituation cannot bring it into another condition. A stone, e.g., by nature moves downwards, and habituation could not make it move upwards, not even if you threw it up ten thousand times to habituate it; nor could habituation make fire move downwards, or bring anything that is by nature in one condition into another condition.

Thus the virtues arise in us neither by nature nor against nature, but we are by nature able to acquire them, and reach our complete perfection through habit.

### (2) Natural capacities are not acquired by habituation

Further, if something arises in us by nature, we first have the capacity for it, and later display the activity. This is clear in the case of the senses; for we did not acquire them by frequent seeing or hearing, but already had them when we exercised them, and did not get them by exercising them.

Virtues, by contrast, we acquire, just as we acquire crafts, by having previously activated them. For we learn a craft by producing the same product that we must produce when we have learned it, becoming builders, e.g., by building and harpists by playing the harp; so also, then, we become just by doing just actions, temperate by doing temperate actions, brave by doing brave actions.

### (3) Legislators concentrate on habituation

What goes on in cities is evidence for this also. For the legislator makes the citizens good by habituating them, and this is the wish of every legislator; if he fails to do it well he misses his goal. [The right] habituation is what makes the difference between a good political system and a bad one.

### (4) Virtue and vice are formed by good and bad actions

Further, just as in the case of a craft, the sources and means that develop each virtue also ruin it. For playing the harp makes both good and bad harpists, and it is analogous in the case of builders and all the rest; for building well makes good builders, building badly, bad ones. If it were not so, no teacher would be needed, but everyone would be born a good or a bad craftsman.

It is the same, then, with the virtues. For actions in dealings with [other] human beings make some people just, some unjust; actions in terrifying situations and the acquired habit of fear or confidence make some brave and others cowardly. The same is true of situations involving appetites and anger; for one or another sort of conduct in these situations makes some people temperate and gentle, others intemperate and irascible.

### Conclusion: The importance of habituation

To sum up, then, in a single account: A state [of character] arises from [the repetition of] similar activities. Hence we must display the right activities, since differences in these imply corresponding differences in the states. It is not unimportant, then, to acquire one sort of habit or another, right from our youth; rather, it is very important, indeed all-important.

## What is the right sort of habituation?

### This is an appropriate question, for the aim of ethical theory is practical

Our present inquiry does not aim, as our others do, at study; for the purpose of our examination is not to know what virtue is, but to become good, since otherwise the inquiry would be of no benefit to us. Hence we must examine the right way to act, since, as we have said, the actions also control the character of the states we acquire.

First, then, actions should express correct reason. That is a common [belief], and let us assume it; later we will say what correct reason is and how it is related to the other virtues.

But let us take it as agreed in advance that every account of the actions we must do has to be stated in outline, not exactly. As we also said at the start, the type of accounts we demand should reflect the subject-matter; and questions about actions and expediency, like questions about health, have no fixed [and invariable answers].

And when our general account is so inexact, the account of particular cases is all the more inexact. For these fall under no craft or profession, and the agents themselves must consider in each case what the opportune action is, as doctors and navigators do.

The account we offer, then, in our present inquiry is of this inexact sort; still, we must try to offer help.

### The right sort of habituation must avoid excess and deficiency

First, then, we should observe that these sorts of states naturally tend to be ruined by excess and deficiency. We see this happen with strength and health, which we mention because we must use what is evident as a witness to what is not. For both excessive and deficient exercises ruin strength; and likewise, too much or too little eating or drinking ruins health, while the proportionate amount produces, increases and preserves it.

The same is true, then, of temperance, bravery and the other virtues. For if, e.g., someone avoids and is afraid of everything, standing firm against nothing, he becomes cowardly, but if he is afraid of nothing at all and goes to face everything, he becomes rash. Similarly, if he gratifies himself with every pleasure and refrains from none, he becomes intemperate, but if he avoids them all, as boors do, he becomes some sort of insensible person. Temperance and bravery, then, are ruined by excess and deficiency but preserved by the mean.

The same actions, then, are the sources and causes both of the emergence and growth of virtues and of their ruin; but further, the activities of the virtues will be found in these same actions. For this is also true of more evident cases, e.g. strength, which arises from eating a lot and from withstanding much hard labour, and it is the strong person who is most able to do these very things. It is the same with the virtues. Refraining from pleasures make us become temperate, and when we have become temperate we are most able to refrain from pleasures. And it is similar with bravery; habituation in disdaining what is fearful and in standing firm against it makes us become brave, and when we have become brave we shall be most able to stand firm.

### Pleasure and pain are important in habituation

But [actions are not enough]; we must take as a sign of someone's state his pleasure or pain in consequence of his action. For if someone who abstains from bodily pleasures enjoys the abstinence itself, then he is temperate, but if he is grieved by it, he is intemperate. Again, if he stands firm against terrifying situations and enjoys it, or at least does not find it painful, then he is brave, and if he finds it painful, he is cowardly.

[Pleasures and pains are appropriately taken as signs] because virtue of character is concerned with pleasures and pains.

### Virtue is concerned with pleasure and pain

(1) For it is pleasure that causes us to do base actions, and pain that causes us to abstain from fine ones. Hence we need to have had the appropriate upbringing—right from early youth, as Plato says—to

make us find enjoyment or pain in the right things; for this is the correct education.

(2) Further, virtues are concerned with actions and feelings; but every feeling and every action implies pleasure or pain; hence, for this reason too, virtue is concerned with pleasures and pains.

(3) Corrective treatment [for vicious actions] also indicates [the relevance of pleasure and pain], since it uses pleasures and pains; it uses them because such correction is a form of medical treatment, and medical treatment naturally operates through contraries.

(4) Further, as we said earlier, every state of soul is naturally related to and concerned with whatever naturally makes it better or worse; and pleasures and pains make people worse, from pursuing and avoiding the wrong ones, at the wrong time, in the wrong ways, or whatever other distinctions of that sort are needed in an account.

These [bad effects of pleasure and pain] are the reason why people actually define the virtues as ways of being unaffected and undisturbed [by pleasures and pains]. They are wrong, however, because they speak [of being unaffected] unconditionally, not of being unaffected in the right or wrong way, at the right or wrong time, and the added specifications.

We assume, then, that virtue is the sort of state [with the appropriate specifications] that does the best actions concerned with pleasures and pains, and that vice is the contrary. The following points will also make it evident that virtue and vice are concerned with the same things.

(5) There are three objects of choice—fine, expedient and pleasant—and three objects of avoidance—their contraries, shameful, harmful and painful. About all these, then, the good person is correct and the bad person is in error, and especially about pleasure. For pleasure is shared with animals, and implied by every object of choice, since what is fine and what is expedient appear pleasant as well.

(6) Further, since pleasure grows up with all of us from infancy on, it is hard to rub out this feeling that is dyed into our lives; and we estimate actions as well [as feelings], some of us more, some less, by pleasure and pain. Hence, our whole inquiry must be about these, since good or bad enjoyment or pain is very important for our actions.

(7) Moreover, it is harder to fight pleasure than to fight emotion,

[though that is hard enough], as Heracleitus says. Now both craft and virtue are concerned in every case with what is harder, since a good result is even better when it is harder. Hence, for this reason also, the whole inquiry, for virtue and political science alike, must consider pleasures and pains; for if we use these well, we shall be good, and if badly, bad.

In short, virtue is concerned with pleasures and pains; the actions that are its sources also increase it or, if they are done differently, ruin it; and its activity is concerned with the same actions that are its sources.

### But our claims about habituation raise a puzzle: How can we become good without being good already?

However, someone might raise this puzzle: "What do you mean by saying that to become just we must first do just actions and to become temperate we must first do temperate actions? For if we do what is grammatical or musical, we must already be grammarians or musicians. In the same way, then, if we do what is just or temperate, we must already be just or temperate."

### First reply: Conformity versus understanding

But surely this is not so even with the crafts, for it is possible to produce something grammatical by chance or by following someone else's instructions. To be a grammarian, then, we must both produce something grammatical and produce it in the way in which the grammarian produces it, i.e. expressing grammatical knowledge that is in us.

### Second Reply: Crafts versus virtues

Moreover, in any case what is true of crafts is not true of virtues. For the products of a craft determine by their own character whether they have been produced well; and so it suffices that they are in the right state when they have been produced. But for actions expressing virtue to be done temperately or justly [and hence well] it does not suffice that they are themselves in the right state. Rather, the agent must also be in the right state when he does them. First, he must know [that he is doing virtuous actions]; second, he must decide on

495

them, and decide on them for themselves; and, third, he must also do them from a firm and unchanging state.

As conditions for having a craft these three do not count, except for the knowing itself. As a condition for having a virtue, however, the knowing counts for nothing, or [rather] for only a little, whereas the other two conditions are very important, indeed all-important. And these other two conditions are achieved by the frequent doing of just and temperate actions.

Hence actions are called just or temperate when they are the sort that a just or temperate person would do. But the just and temperate person is not the one who [merely] does these actions, but the one who also does them in the way in which just or temperate people do them.

It is right, then, to say that a person comes to be just from doing just actions and temperate from doing temperate actions; for no one has even a prospect of becoming good from failing to do them.

## Virtue requires habituation, and therefore requires practice, not just theory

The many, however, do not do these actions but take refuge in arguments, thinking that they are doing philosophy, and that this is the way to become excellent people. In this they are like a sick person who listens attentively to the doctor, but acts on none of his instructions. Such a course of treatment will not improve the state of his body; any more than will the many's way of doing philosophy improve the state of their souls.

### STUDY QUESTIONS

1.  Aristotle denies that the virtues are in us by nature. What is there in us that makes it possible for us to acquire the virtues? How do we acquire them?
2.  What does Aristotle mean by saying that actions determine the character of the states that we acquire?
3.  According to Aristotle, the virtues are "preserved by the mean." For example, we become temperate by refraining from extreme pleasures. Explain Aristotle's remark and discuss several other examples of preserving the mean.

4.  Is Aristotle open to the charge that in training a child to be virtuous by habituating it to certain modes of behavior, he is interfering with its autonomy? If not, what *would* constitute an illegitimate interference?
5.  If behaving temperately makes one temperate, it would seem to follow that one must be temperate in order to become temperate. How does Aristotle avoid this paradox?

# The Child as a Moral Philosopher

## LAWRENCE KOHLBERG

Lawrence Kohlberg (1927–1987) was professor of education and social psychology at Harvard University. He wrote numerous articles on cognitive moral development and was director of the Harvard University Center for Moral Development and Education.

The psychologist Lawrence Kohlberg was interested in moral development. Like several other thinkers (see especially Allan Bloom in this chapter), he was concerned with the problems that arise in a relativistic approach to the teaching of values. In this essay Kohlberg says he will "demonstrate that moral education can be free from the charge of cultural relativity and arbitrary indoctrination." The problem of indoctrination cannot be dismissed by insisting that in teaching values the teacher need not indoctrinate students but merely "socialize" them. Nor can the problem of indoctrination be mitigated by confining teachers to the inculcation of "positive" values: for who is to say which values are to be called positive? Kohlberg

THE CHILD AS A MORAL PHILOSOPHER From "Indoctrination v. Relativity in Value Education" in *The Philosophy of Moral Development,* Vol. 1, by Lawrence Kohlberg (New York: Harper & Row/ Chicago: University of Chicago Press, joint publication, 1971). Reprinted by permission of the Estate of Lawrence Kohlberg.

also objects to values clarification, which avoids indoctrination by allowing the teacher to present a smorgasborg of values for the child to choose from. This only confuses the student and renders teachers ineffective as moral educators. (They cannot, for example, persuasively condemn cheating.)

With this background Kohlberg introduces his three-level (six-stage) theory of transcultural moral development. According to Kohlberg all children begin with a preconventional first level in which morality is determined largely by expected punishment and reward, move on to a conventional second level where social norms and need for approval dominate, and eventually proceed to a third level where the individual is self-motivated to adhere to universal moral principles. Good teachers do not indoctrinate; they merely assist students in moving from one stage to the next stage by helping them become conscious of where they currently are and by showing them where they might go next. Such forward movement is brought about by discussing problematic moral situations. For example, children are presented with the Heinz dilemma in which Heinz, who lacks the money to buy a lifesaving drug, obtains it by robbing the druggist. Children are asked whether Heinz did the right thing. Such discussion sharpens children's moral sensibility and also helps move children to a more sophisticated level of moral development.

Thus, Kohlberg's answer to relativism is to argue that in all societies individuals go through the very *same* stages of moral development—though in some cultures the majority of the population are fixed at a conventional level of moral development and have not reached the stage of universal justice. The ideal development goes beyond conventional morality to recognize universal principles of justice and equality.

Although *moral education* has a forbidding sound to teachers, they constantly practice it. They tell children what to do, make evaluations of children's behavior, and direct children's relations in the classrooms. Sometimes teachers do these things without being aware that they are engaging in moral education, but the children are aware of it. For example, my second-grade son told me that he did not want to be one of the bad boys. Asked "Who were the bad boys?" he replied, "The ones who don't put their books back where they belong and get yelled at." His teacher would have been surprised to know that her concerns with classroom management defined for her children what she and her school thought were basic moral values or that she was engaged in value indoctrination.

Most teachers are aware that they are teaching values, like it or not, and are very concerned as to whether this teaching is unjustified indoctrination. In particular, they are uncertain as to whether their own moral opinions should be presented as "moral truths," whether they should be expressed merely as personal opinion or should be omitted from classroom discussion entirely. As an example, an experienced junior high school teacher told us,

> My class deals with morality and right and wrong quite a bit. I don't expect all of them to agree with me; each has to satisfy himself according to his own convictions, as long as he is sincere and thinks he is pursuing what is right. I often discuss cheating this way but I always get *defeated,* because they still argue cheating is all right. After you accept the idea that kids have the right to build a position with logical arguments, you have to accept what they come out with, even though you drive at it ten times a year and they still come out with the same conclusion.

This teacher's confusion is apparent. She believes everyone should "have his own ideas," and yet she is most unhappy if this leads to a point where some of these ideas include the notion that "it's all right to cheat." In other words, she is smack up against the problem of relativity of values in moral education. Using this teacher as an example, I will attempt to demonstrate that moral education can be free from the charge of cultural relativity and arbitrary indoctrination that inhibits her when she talks about cheating.

## Cop-Out Solutions to the Relativity Problem

To begin with, I want to reject a few cop-outs or false solutions sometimes suggested as solving the relativity problem. One is to call moral education *socialization*. Sociologists have sometimes claimed that moralization in the interests of classroom management and maintenance of the school as a social system is a hidden curriculum; that it performs hidden services in helping children adapt to society (Jackson, 1968). They have argued that, since praise and blame on the part of teachers is a necessary aspect of the socialization process, the teacher does not have to consider the psychological and philosophic issues of moral education. In learning to conform to the teacher's expectations and the school rules, children are becoming socialized, they are internalizing the norms and standards of society. I argue in Chapter 2 why this approach is a cop-out. In practice, it means that we call the teacher's yelling at her students for not putting their books away *socialization*. To label it *socialization* does not legitimate it as valid education, nor does it remove the charge of arbitrary indoctrination from it. Basically, this sociological argument implies that respect for social authority is a moral good in itself. Stated in different terms, the notion that it is valid for the teacher to have an unreflective hidden curriculum is based on the notion that the teacher is the agent of the state, the church, or the social system, rather than being a free moral agent dealing with children who are free moral agents. The notion that the teacher is the agent of the state is taken for granted in some educational systems, such as that of the Soviets. However, the moral curriculum is not hidden in Soviet education; it is done explicitly and well as straight indoctrination (Bronfenbrenner, 1968). For the moment, I will not argue what is wrong with indoctrination but will assume that it is incompatible with the conceptions of civil liberties that are central not only to American democracy but to any just social system.

Let us turn now to the second cop-out. This is to rely on vaguely positive and honorific-sounding terms such as "moral values" or "moral and spiritual values." We can see in the following statements how a program called "Teaching Children Values in the Upper Elementary School" (Carr and Wellenberg, 1966) relies on a vague usage of "moral and spiritual values":

> Many of our national leaders have expressed anxiety about an increasing lack of concern for personal moral and spiritual values. Throughout history, nations have sought value systems to help people live congenially. The Golden Rule and the Ten Commandments are examples of such value systems. Each pupil needs to acquire a

foundation of sound values to help him act correctly and make proper choices between right and wrong, truth and untruth. The teacher can develop a sound value system in the following ways:

1. Be a good example.
2. Help young people to assess conflict situations and to gain insight into the development of constructive values and attitudes. Situations arise daily in which pupils can receive praise that will reinforce behavior that exemplified desired values.
3. Show young people how to make generalizations concerning experience through evaluation and expression of desirable values.
4. Help students acquire an understanding of the importance of values that society considers worthwhile.
5. Aid children to uphold and use positive values when confronted by adverse pressure from peers. [p. 11]

The problem, however, is to define these "positive values." We may agree that "positive values" are desirable, but the term conceals the fact that teachers, children, and societies have different ideas as to what constitutes "positive values." Although Carr and Wellenberg cite the Ten Commandments and the Golden Rule as "value systems sought by nations," they also could have used the code of the Hitler or of the communist youth as examples of "value systems sought by nations."

I raise the issue of the "relativity of values" in this context because the words *moral, positive,* and *values* are interpreted by each teacher in a different way, depending on the teacher's own values and standards.

This becomes clear when we consider our third cop-out. This is the cop-out of defining moral values in terms of what I call a "bag of virtues." By a "bag of virtues," I mean a set of personality traits generally considered to be positive. Defining the aims of moral education in terms of a set of "virtues" is as old as Aristotle, who said, "Virtue . . . [is] of two kinds, intellectual and moral. . . . [The moral] virtues we get by first exercising them . . . we become just by doing just acts, temperate by doing temperate acts, brave by doing brave acts."

The attraction of such an approach is evident. Although it is true that people often cannot agree on details of right and wrong or even

501

on fundamental moral principles, we all think such "traits" as honesty and responsibility are good things. By adding enough traits to the virtue bag, we eventually get a list that contains something to suit everyone.

This approach to moral education was widely prevalent in the public schools in the 1920s and 1930s and was called "character education." The educators and psychologists, such as Havighurst and Taba (1949), who developed these approaches defined character as the sum total of a set of "those traits of personality which are subject to the moral sanctions of society."

One difficulty with this approach to moral character is that everyone has his own bag. However, the problem runs deeper than the composition of a given list of virtues and vices. Although it may be true that the notion of teaching virtues, such as honesty or integrity, arouses little controversy, it is also true that a vague consensus on the goodness of these virtues conceals a great deal of actual disagreement over their definitions. What is one person's "integrity" is another person's "stubbornness," what is one person's honesty in "expressing your true feelings" is another person's insensitivity to the feelings of others. This is evident in controversial fields of adult behavior. Student protestors view their behavior as reflecting the virtues of altruism, idealism, awareness, and courage. Those in opposition regard the same behavior as reflecting the vices of irresponsibility and disrespect for "law and order." Although this difficulty can be recognized clearly in college education, it is easier for teachers of younger children to think that their judgments in terms of the bag of virtues are objective and independent of their own value biases. However, a parent will not agree that a child's specific failure to obey an "unreasonable" request by the teacher was wrong, even if the teacher calls the act "uncooperative," as some teachers are prone to do.

I have summarized three cop-outs from the relativity problem and rejected them. Socialization, teaching positive values, and developing a bag of virtues all leave the teacher where she was—stuck with her own personal value standards and biases to be imposed on her students. There is one last cop-out to the relativity problem. That is to lie back and enjoy it or encourage it. In the new social studies, this is called *value clarification*.

As summarized by Engel (in Simon, 1971, p. 902), this position holds that

In the consideration of values, there is no single correct answer, but value clarification is supremely important. One must contrast value clarification and value inculcation. Inculcation suggests that the learner has limited control and hence limited responsibility in the development of his own values. He needs to be told what values are or what he should value.

This is not to suggest, however, that nothing is ever inculcated. As a matter of fact, in order to clarify values, at least one principle needs to be adopted by all concerned. Perhaps the only way the principle can be adopted is through some procedure which might best be termed *inculcation*. That principle might be stated as follows: in the consideration of values there is no single correct answer. More specifically it might be said that the adequate posture both for students and teachers in clarifying values is openness.

Although the basic premise of this value clarification approach is that "everyone has his own values," it is further advocated that children can and should learn (1) to be more aware of their own values and how they relate to their decisions, (2) to make their values consistent and to order them in hierarchies for decisions, (3) to be more aware of the divergencies between their value hierarchies and those of others, and (4) to learn to tolerate these divergencies. In other words, although values are regarded as arbitrary and relative, there may be universal, rational strategies for making decisions that maximize these values. Part of this rational strategy is to recognize that values are relative. Within this set of premises, it is quite logical to teach that values are relative as part of the overall program.

An elaboration of this approach can be found in *Decision Making: A Guide for Teachers Who Would Help Preadolescent Children Become Imaginative and Responsible Decision Makers* (Dodder and Dodder, 1968). In a portion of this book, modern social scientific perspectives are used to develop a curriculum unit entitled "Why Don't We All Make the Same Decisions?" A set of classroom materials and activities are then presented to demonstrate to children the following propositions: (1) we don't all make the same decisions because our values are different; (2) our values tend to originate outside ourselves; (3) our values are different because each of us has been influenced by different important others; and (4) our values are different because each of us has been influenced by a different cultural environment.

The teacher is told to have the children discuss moral dilemmas in such a way as to reveal those different values. As an example, one child might make a moral decision in terms of avoiding punishment, another in terms of the welfare of other people, another in terms of certain rules, another in terms of getting the most for himself. The children are then to be encouraged to discuss their values with each other and to recognize that everyone has different values. Whether or not "the welfare of others" is a more adequate value than "avoiding punishment" is not an issue to be raised by the teacher. Rather, the teacher is instructed to teach only that "our values are different."

Indeed, acceptance of the idea that *all* values are relative does, logically, lead to the conclusion that the teacher should not attempt to teach *any* particular moral values. This leaves the teacher in the quandary of our teacher who could not successfully argue against cheating. The students of a teacher who has been successful in communicating moral relativism will believe, like the teacher, that "everyone has his own bag" and that "everyone should keep doing his thing." If one of these students has learned his relativity lesson, when he is caught cheating he will argue that he did nothing wrong. The basis of his argument will be that his own hierarchy of values, which may be different from that of the teacher, made it right for him to cheat. Although recognizing that other people believe that cheating is wrong, he himself holds the "value" that one should cheat when the opportunity presents itself. If teachers want to be consistent and retain their relativistic beliefs, they would have to concede.

Now I am not criticizing the value clarification approach itself. It is a basic and valuable component of the new social studies curricula, as I have discussed (1973). My point is, rather, that value clarification is not a sufficient solution to the relativity problem. Furthermore, the actual teaching of relativism is itself an indoctrination or teaching of a fixed belief, a belief that we are going to show is not true scientifically or philosophically. . . .

## A Typological Scheme on the Stages of Moral Thought

In other words, I am happy to report that I can propose a solution to the relativity problem that has plagued philosophers for three thousand years. I can say this with due modesty because it did not depend on being smart. It only happened that my colleagues and I were the first people in history to do detailed cross-cultural studies on the development of moral thinking.

The following dilemma should clarify the issue:

*The Heinz Dilemma*

> In Europe, a woman was near death from a very bad disease, a special kind of cancer. There was one drug that the doctors thought might save her. It was a form of radium that a druggist in the same town had recently discovered. The drug was expensive to make, but the druggist was charging ten times what the drug cost him to make. He paid $200 for the radium and charged $2,000 for a small dose of the drug. The sick woman's husband, Heinz, went to everyone he knew to borrow the money, but he could get together only about $1,000, which was half of what it cost. He told the druggist that his wife was dying and asked him to sell it cheaper or let him pay later. But the druggist said, "No, I discovered the drug and I'm going to make money from it." Heinz got desperate and broke into the man's store to steal the drug for his wife.

Should the husband have done that? Was it right or wrong? Is your decision that it is right (or wrong) objectively right, is it morally universal, or is it your personal opinion? If you think it is morally right to steal the drug, you must face the fact that it is legally wrong. What is the basis of your view that it is morally right, then, more than your personal opinion? Is it anything that can be agreed on? If you think so, let me report the results of a National Opinion Research Survey on the question, asked of a representative sample of adult Americans. Seventy-five percent said it was wrong to steal, though most said they might do it.

Can one take anything but a relativist position on the question? By a relativist position, I mean a position like that of Bob, a high school senior. He said, "There's a million ways to look at it. Heinz had a moral decision to make. Was it worse to steal or let his wife die? In my mind, I can either condemn him or condone him. In this case, I think it was fine. But possibly the druggist was working on a capitalist morality of supply and demand."

I went on to ask Bob, "Would it be wrong if he didn't steal it?"

Bob replied, "It depends on how he is oriented morally. If he thinks it's worse to steal than to let his wife die, then it would be wrong what he did. It's all relative; what I would do is steal the drug. I can't say that's right or wrong or that it's what everyone should do."

But even if you agree with Bob's relativism you may not want to go as far as he did. He started the interview by wondering if he could answer because he "questioned the whole terminology, the whole moral bag." He continued, "But then I'm also an incredible moralist, a real puritan in some sense and moods. My moral judgment and the way I perceive things morally changes very much when my mood changes. When I'm in a cynical mood, I take a cynical view of morals, but still, whether I like it or not, I'm terribly moral in the way I look at things. But I'm not too comfortable with it." Bob's moral perspective was well expressed in the late Joe Gould's poem called "My Religion." Brief and to the point, the poem said, "In winter I'm a Buddhist, in the summer I'm a nudist."

Now, Bob's relativism rests on a confusion. The confusion is that between relativity as the social science fact that different people *do* have different moral values and relativity as the philosophic claim that people *ought* to have different moral values, that no moral values are justified for all people.

To illustrate, I quote a not atypical response of one of my graduate students to the same moral dilemma. She said, "I think he should steal it because if there is any such thing as a universal human value, it is the value of life, and that would justify it."

I then asked her, "Is there any such thing as a universal human value?" and she answered, "No, all values are relative to your culture."

She began by claiming that one ought to act in terms of the universal value of human life, implying that human life is a universal value in the sense that it is logical and desirable for all people to respect all human life, that one can demonstrate to other people that it is logical and desirable to act in this way. If she were clear in her thinking, she would see that the fact that all people do not always act in terms of this value does not contradict the claim that all people ought to always act in accordance with it. Because she made this confusion, she ended in total confusion.

What I am going to claim is that if we distinguish the issues of universality as fact and the possibility of universal moral ideals we get a positive answer to both questions. As far as facts go, I claim just the opposite of what Dodder and Dodder (1968) claimed to be basic social science truths. I claim that

1. We often make different decisions and yet have the same basic moral values.

2. Our values tend to originate inside ourselves as we process our social experience.

3. In every culture and subculture of the world, both the same basic moral values and the same steps toward moral maturity are found. Although social environments directly produce different specific beliefs (for example, smoking is wrong, eating pork is wrong), they do not engender different basic moral principles (for example, "consider the welfare of others," "treat other people equally," and so on).

4. Basic values are different largely because we are at different levels of maturity in thinking about basic moral and social issues and concepts. Exposure to others more mature than ourselves helps stimulate maturity in our own value process.

All parents know that the basic values of their children do not come from the outside, from the parents, although many wish they did. For example, at the age of four my son joined the pacifist and vegetarian movement and refused to eat meat because, he said, it is bad to kill animals. In spite of his parents' attempts to dissuade him by arguing about the difference between justified and unjustified killing, he remained a vegetarian for six months. However, he did recognize that some forms of killing were "legitimate." One night I read to him from a book about Eskimo life that included a description of a seal-killing expedition. While listening to the story, he became very angry and said, "You know, there is one kind of meat I would eat, Eskimo meat. It's bad to kill animals so it's all right to eat Eskimos."

This episode illustrates (1) that children often generate their own moral values and maintain them in the face of cultural training, and (2) that these values have universal roots. Every child believes it is bad to kill because regard for the lives of others or pain at death is a natural empathic response, although it is not necessarily universally and consistently maintained. In this example, the value of life led both to vegetarianism and to the desire to kill Eskimos. This latter desire comes also from a universal value tendency: a belief in justice or reciprocity here expressed in terms of revenge or punishment (at higher levels, the belief that those who infringe on the rights of others cannot expect their own rights to be respected).

I quoted my son's response because it is shockingly different from the way you think and yet it has universal elements you will recognize. What is the shocking difference between my son's way of thinking and your own? If you are a psychoanalyst, you will start thinking about oral cannibalistic fantasies and defenses against them and all that. However, that is not really what the difference is at all. You do not have to be cannibalistic to wonder why it is right for humans to kill and eat animals but it is not right for animals or humans to kill and eat humans. The response really shows that my son was a philosopher, like every young child: he wondered about things that most grown-ups take for granted. If you want to study children, however, you have to be a bit of a philosopher yourself and ask the moral philosopher's question: "Why is it all right to kill and eat animals but not humans?" I wonder how many of you can give a good answer. In any case, Piaget started the modern study of child development by recognizing that the child, like the adult philosopher, was puzzled by the basic questions of life: by the meaning of space, time, causality, life, death, right and wrong, and so on. What he found was that the child asked all the great philosophic questions but answered them in a very different way from the adults. This way was so different that Piaget called the difference a difference in stage or quality of thinking, rather than a difference in amount of knowledge or accuracy of thinking. The difference in thinking between you and my son, then, is basically a difference in stage.

My own work on morality started from Piaget's notions of stages and Piaget's notion that the child was a philosopher. Inspired by Jean Piaget's (1948) pioneering effort to apply a structural approach to moral development, I have gradually elaborated over the years a typological scheme describing general stages of moral thought that can be defined independently of the specific content of particular moral decisions or actions. We studied seventy-five American boys from early adolescence on. These youths were continually presented with hypothetical moral dilemmas, all deliberately philosophical, some found in medieval works of casuistry. On the basis of their reasoning about these dilemmas at a given age, we constructed the typology of definite and universal levels of development in moral thought.

The typology contains three distinct levels of moral thinking, and within each of these levels are two related stages. These levels and stages may be considered separate moral philosophies, distinct views of the social-moral world.

We can speak of the children as having their own morality or series of moralities. Adults seldom listen to children's moralizing. If children throw back a few adult clichés and behave themselves, most parents—and many anthropologists and psychologists as well— think that the children have adopted or internalized the appropriate parental standards.

Actually, as soon as we talk with children about morality we find that they have many ways of making judgments that are not "internalized" from the outside and that do not come in any direct and obvious way from parents, teachers, or even peers.

The preconventional level is the first of three levels of moral thinking; the second level is conventional; and the third is postconventional or autonomous. Although preconventional children are often "well behaved" and responsive to cultural labels of good and bad, they interpret these labels in terms of their physical consequences (punishment, reward, exchange of favors) or in terms of the physical power of those who enunciate the rules and labels of good and bad.

This level is usually occupied by children aged four to ten, a fact well known to sensitive observers of children. The capacity of "properly behaved" children of this age to engage in cruel behavior when there are holes in the power structure is sometimes noted as tragic (*Lord of the Flies* and *High Wind in Jamaica*), sometimes as comic (Lucy in *Peanuts*).

The second or conventional level also can be described as *conformist*—but that is perhaps too smug a term. Maintaining the expectations and rules of the individual's family, group, or nation is perceived as valuable in its own right. There is a concern not only with conforming to the individual's social order but in maintaining, supporting, and justifying this order.

The postconventional level is characterized by a major thrust toward autonomous moral principles that have validity and application apart from authority of the groups or people who hold them and apart from the individual's identification with those people or groups.

Within each of these three levels, there are two discernible stages. The following paragraphs explain the dual moral stages of each level just described.

### Definition of Moral Stages

*Preconventional Level*

At this level, the child is responsive to cultural rules and labels of good and bad, right or wrong, but interprets these labels in terms of either the physical or the hedonistic consequences of action (punishment, reward, exchange of favors) or in terms of the physical power of those who enunciate the rules and labels. The level is divided into the following two stages:

### Stage 1. *The Punishment and Obedience Orientation*

The physical consequences of action determine its goodness or badness regardless of the human meaning or value of these consequences. Avoidance of punishment and unquestioning deference to power are valued in their own right.

### Stage 2. *The Instrumental Relativist Orientation*

Right action consists of that which instrumentally satisfies one's needs and occasionally the needs of others. Human relations are viewed in terms like those of the marketplace. Elements of fairness, reciprocity, and equal sharing are present, but they are always interpreted in a physical, pragmatic way. Reciprocity is a matter of "You scratch my back and I'll scratch yours."

*Conventional Level*

At this level, maintaining the expectations of the individual's family, group, or nation is perceived as valuable in its own right, regardless of immediate and obvious consequences. The attitude is not only one of conformity to personal expectations and social order, but of loyalty to it, of actively maintaining, supporting, and justifying the order and of identifying with the people or group involved in it. At this level, there are the following two stages:

### Stage 3. *The Interpersonal Concordance or "Good Boy–Nice Girl" Orientation*

Good behavior is that which pleases or helps others and is approved by them. There is much conformity to stereotypical images of what is majority or "natural" behavior. Behavior is frequently judged by intention—the judgment "he means well" becomes important for the first time. One earns approval by being "nice."

510

## Stage 4. Society Maintaining Orientation

There is an orientation toward authority, fixed rules, and the maintenance of the social order. Right behavior consists of doing one's duty, showing respect for authority, and maintaining the given social order for its own sake.

### Postconventional, Autonomous, or Principled Level

At this level, there is a clear effort to define moral values and principles that have validity and application apart from the authority of the groups or people holding these principles and apart from the individual's own identification with these groups. This level again has two stages:

## Stage 5. The Social Contract Orientation

Right action tends to be defined in terms of general individual rights and in terms of standards that have been critically examined and agreed on by the whole society. There is a clear awareness of the relativism of personal values and opinions and a corresponding emphasis on procedural rules for reaching consensus. Aside from what is constitutionally and democratically agreed on, the right is a matter of personal "values" and "opinion." The result is an emphasis on the "legal point of view," but with an emphasis on the possibility of changing law in terms of rational considerations of social utility (rather than freezing it in terms of Stage 4 "law and order"). Outside the legal realm, free agreement and contract are the binding elements of obligation. This is the "official" morality of the American government and Constitution.

## Stage 6. The Universal Ethical Principle Orientation

Right is defined by the decision of conscience in accord with self-chosen ethical principles appealing to logical comprehensiveness, universality, and consistency. These principles are abstract and ethical (the Golden Rule, the categorical imperative); they are not concrete moral rules such as the Ten Commandments. At heart, these are universal principles of justice, of the reciprocity and equality of human rights, and of respect for the dignity of human beings as individuals.

To understand what these stages mean concretely, let us look at them with regard to two of twenty-five basic moral concepts or

511

aspects used to form the dilemmas we used in our research. One such aspect, for instance, is "motive given for rule obedience or moral action." In this instance, the six stages look like this:

1. Obey rules to avoid punishment.
2. Conform to obtain rewards, have favors returned, and so on.
3. Conform to avoid disapproval and dislike by others.
4. Conform to avoid censure by legitimate authorities and resultant guilt.
5. Conform to maintain the respect of the impartial spectator judging in terms of community welfare.
6. Conform to avoid self-condemnation.

In another of these twenty-five moral aspects, the value of human life, the six stages can be defined thus:

1. The value of human life is confused with the value of physical objects and is based on the social status or physical attributes of the possessor.
2. The value of human life is seen as instrumental to the satisfaction of the needs of its possessor or of other people.
3. The value of human life is based on the empathy and affection of family members and others toward its possessor.
4. Life is conceived as sacred in terms of its place in a categorical moral or religious order of rights and duties.
5. Life is valued both in terms of its relation to community welfare and in terms of life being a universal human right.
6. Human life is sacred—a universal human value of respect for the individual.

I have called this scheme a *typology*. This is because about 67 percent of most people's thinking is at a single stage, regardless of the moral dilemma involved. We call our types *stages* because they seem to represent an invariant development sequence. "True" stages come one at a time and always in the same order.

In our stages, all movement is forward in sequence and does not skip steps. Children may move through these stages at varying speeds, of course, and may be found half in and half out of a particular stage. Individuals may stop at any given stage and at any age, but if they continue to move, they must move in accord with these steps. Moral reasoning of the conventional kind or Stages 3–4, never occurs before the preconventional Stage 1 and Stage 2 thought has taken place. No adult in Stage 4 has gone through Stage 5, but all Stage 5 adults have gone through Stage 4.

Although the evidence is not complete, my study strongly suggests that moral change fits the stage pattern just described.

As a single example of our findings of stage sequence, take the progress of two boys on the aspect "the value of human life." The first boy, Tommy, who had suggested that one should perhaps steal for an important person, is asked, "Is it better to save the life of one important person or a lot of unimportant people?" At age ten, he answers, "All the people that aren't important because one man just has one house, maybe a lot of furniture, but a whole bunch of people have an awful lot of furniture, and some of these poor people might have a lot of money and it doesn't look it."

Clearly Tommy is Stage 1: he confuses the value of a human being with the value of the property he possesses. Three years later (age thirteen), Tommy's conceptions of life's values are most clearly elicited by the question "Should the doctor 'mercy kill' a fatally ill woman requesting death because of her pain?" He answers, "Maybe it would be good to put her out of pain, she'd be better off that way. But the husband wouldn't want it, it's not like an animal. If a pet dies you can get along without it—it isn't something you really need. Well, you can get a new wife, but it's not really the same."

Here his answer is Stage 2: the value of the woman's life is partly contingent on its instrumental value to her husband, who cannot replace her as easily as he can a pet.

Three years later still (age sixteen), Tommy's conception of life's value is elicited by the same question, to which he replies, "It might be best for her, but her husband—it's human life—not like an animal; it just doesn't have the same relationship that a human being does to a family. You can become attached to a dog, but nothing like a human, you know."

Now Tommy has moved from a Stage 2 instrumental view of the woman's value to a Stage 3 view based on the husband's distinctively human empathy and love for someone in his family. Equally clearly, it lacks any basis for a universal human value of the woman's life, which would hold if she had no husband or if her husband did not love her. Tommy, then, has moved step by step through three stages during the age ten to sixteen. Although bright (IQ 120), he is a slow developer in moral judgment.

Let us take another boy, Richard, to show us sequential movement through the remaining three steps. At age thirteen, Richard said about the mercy killing, "If she requests it, it's really up to her. She is in such terrible pain, just the same as people are always putting animals out of their pain," and in general showed a mixture of Stage 2 and Stage 3 responses concerning the value of life. At sixteen, he said, "I don't know. In one way, it's murder, it's not right or privilege of man to decide who shall live and who should die. God put life into everybody on earth and you're taking away something from that person that came directly from God, and you're destroying something that is very sacred, it's in a way part of God and it's almost destroying a part of God when you kill a person. There's something of God in everyone."

Here Richard clearly displays a Stage 4 concept of life as sacred in terms of its place in a categorical moral or religious order. The value of human life is universal; it is true for all humans. It still, however, depends on something else—on respect for God and God's authority; it is not an autonomous human value. Presumably if God told Richard to murder, as God commanded Abraham to murder Isaac, he would do so.

At age twenty, Richard said to the same question, "There are more and more people in the medical profession who think it is a hardship on everyone, the person, the family, when you know they are going to die. When a person is kept alive by an artificial lung or kidney, it's more like being a vegetable than being a human. If it's her own choice, I think there are certain rights and privileges that go along with being a human being. I am a human being, and I have certain desires for life, and I think everybody else does too. You have a world of which you are the center, and everybody else does too, and in that sense we're all equal."

Richard's response is clearly Stage 5, in that the value of life is defined in terms of equal and universal human rights in a context of relativity ("You have a world of which you are the center, and in that sense we're all equal") and of concern for utility or welfare consequences.

At twenty-four, Richard says, "A human life, whoever it is, takes precedence over any other moral or legal value. A human life has inherent value whether or not it is valued by a particular individual. The worth of the individual human being is central where the principles of justice and love are normative for all human relationships."

This young man is at Stage 6 in seeing the value of human life as absolute in representing a universal and equal respect for the human as an individual. He has moved step by step through a sequence culminating in a definition of human life as centrally valuable rather than derived from or dependent on social or divine authority.

In a genuine and culturaly universal sense, these steps lead toward an increased morality of value judgment, where morality is considered as a form of judging, as it has been in a philosophic tradition running from the analyses of Kant to those of the modern analytic or "ordinary language" philosophers. At Stage 6 people have disentangled judgments of—or language about—human life from status and property values (Stage 1); from its uses to others (Stage 2); from interpersonal affection (Stage 3); and so on; they have a means of moral judgment that is universal and impersonal. Stage 6 people answer in moral words such as *duty* or *morally right* and use them in a way implying universality, ideals and impersonality. They think and speak in phrases such as "regardless of who it was" or "I would do it in spite of punishment."

## Universal Invariant Sequence of Moral Development

When I first decided to explore moral development in other cultures, I was told by anthropologist friends that I would have to throw away my culture-bound moral concepts and stories and start from scratch learning a whole new set of values for each new culture. My first try consisted of a brace of villages, one Atayal (Malaysian aboriginal) and the other Taiwanese.

My guide was a young Chinese ethnographer who had written an account of the moral and religious patterns of the Atayal and Taiwanese villages. Taiwanese boys in the ten to thirteen age group were asked about a story involving theft of food: A man's wife is starving to death but the store owner would not give the man any food unless he could pay, and he cannot. Should he break in and steal some food? Why? Many of the boys said, "He should steal the food for his

515

wife because if she dies he'll have to pay for her funeral, and that costs a lot."

My guide was amused by these responses, but I was relieved: they were, of course, "classic" Stage 2 responses. In the Atayal village, funerals were not such a big thing, so the Stage 2 boys said, "He should steal the food because he needs his wife to cook for him."

This means that we have to consult our anthropologists to know what content Stage 2 children will include in instrumental exchange calculations, or what Stage 4 adults will identify as the proper social order. But one certainly does not have to start from scratch. What made my guide laugh was the difference in form between the children's Stage 2 thought and his own, a difference definable independently of particular cultures.

Figures 1.1 and 1.2 indicate the cultural universality of the sequence of stages we have found. Figure 1.1 presents the age trends for middle-class urban boys in the United States, Taiwan, and Mexico. At age ten in each country, the order of use of each stage is the same as the order of its difficulty or maturity.

In the United States, by age sixteen the order is the reverse, from the highest to the lowest, except that Stage 6 is still little used. At age thirteen, the good-boy middle stage (Stage 3) is most used.

The results in Mexico and Taiwan are the same, except that development is a little slower. The most conspicuous feature is that, at the age of sixteen, Stage 5 thinking is much more salient in the United States than in Mexico or Taiwan. Nevertheless, it is present in the other countries, so we know that this is not purely an American democratic construct.

Figure 1.2 shows strikingly similar results from two isolated villages, one in Yucatan, one in Turkey. Although conventional moral thought increases steadily from ages ten to sixteen, it still has not achieved a clear ascendancy over preconventional thought.

Trends for lower-class urban groups are intermediate in the rate of development between those for the middle-class and for the village boys. In the three divergent cultures that I studied, middle-class children were found to be more advanced in moral judgment than matched lower-class children. This was not due to the fact that the middle-class children heavily favored some one type of thought that could be seen as corresponding to the prevailing middle-class pattern. Instead, middle-class and working-class children move

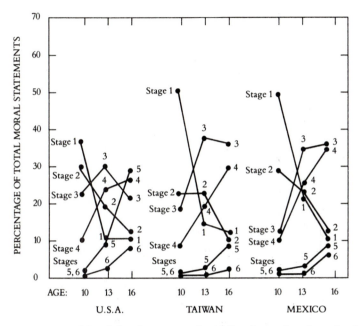

FIGURE I.I   Moral development of middle-class urban boys in the United States, Taiwan, and Mexico. At age ten, the stages are used according to difficulty. At age thirteen, Stage 3 is most used by all three groups. At age sixteen, U.S. boys have reversed the order of age ten stages (with the exception of 6). In Taiwan and Mexico, conventional (3–4) stages prevail at age sixteen, with Stage 5 also little used (Kohlberg, 1968a).

through the same sequences, but the middle-class children move faster and farther.

This sequence is not dependent on a particular religion or on any religion at all in the usual sense. I found no important differences in the development of moral thinking among Catholics, Protestants, Jews, Buddhists, Moslems, and atheists.

In summary, the nature of our sequence is not significantly affected by widely varying social, cultural, or religious conditions. The only thing that is affected is the rate at which individuals progress through this sequence.

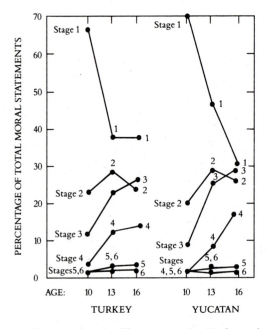

FIGURE I.2    Two isolated villages, one in Turkey, the other in Yucatan, show similar patterns in moral thinking. There is no reversal of order, and conventional (stages 3–4) thought does not gain in a clear ascendancy over preconventional stages at age sixteen (Kohlberg, 1968a).

Why should there be such a universal invariant sequence of development? In answering this question, we need first to analyze these developing social concepts in terms of their internal logical structure. At each stage, the same basic moral concept or aspect is defined, but at each higher stage this definition is more differentiated, more integrated, and more general or universal. When one's concept of human life moves from Stage 1 to Stage 2, the value of life becomes more differentiated from the value of property, more integrated (the value of life enters an organizational hierarchy where it is "higher" than property so that one steals property in order to save life), and more universalized (the life of any sentient being is valuable regardless of status or property). The same advance is true at each stage in the hierarchy. Each step of development, then, is a better cognitive

518

organization than the one before it, one that takes account of every-thing present in the pevious stage but making new distinctions and organizes them into a more comprehensive or more equilibrated structure. The fact that this is the case has been demonstrated by a series of studies indicating that children and adolescents comprehend all stages up to their own, but not more than one stage beyond their own (Rest, 1973). And, importantly, they prefer this next stage.

Moral thought, then, seems to behave like all other kinds of thought. Progress through the moral levels and stages is character-ized by increasing differentiation and increasing integration, and hence is the same kind of progress that scientific theory represents. Like acceptable scientific theory—or like any theory or structure of knowledge—moral thought may be considered partially to generate its own data as it goes along, or at least to expand so as to contain in a balanced, self-consistent way a wider and wider experiential field. The raw data in the case of our ethical philosophies may be consid-ered as conflicts between roles, or values, or as the social order in which people live.

The social worlds of all people seem to contain the same basic structures. All the societies we have studied have the same basic institutions—family, economy, law, government. In addition, how-ever, all societies are alike because they are societies—systems of defined complementary roles. In order to play a social role in the family, school, or society, children must implicitly take the role of others toward themselves and toward others in the group. These role-taking tendencies form the basis of all social institutions. They rep-resent various patternings of shared or complementary expectations.

In the preconventional and conventional levels (Stages 1–4), moral content or value is largely accidental or culture bound. Anything from "honesty" to "courage in battle" can be the central value. But in the higher postconventional levels, Socrates, Lincoln, Thoreau, and Martin Luther King tend to speak without confusion of tongues, as it were. This is because the ideal principles of any social structure are basically alike, if only because there simply are not that many principles that are articulate, comprehensive, and integrated enough to be satisfying to the human intellect. And most of these principles have gone by the name of justice.

I have discussed at some length the culturally universal sequences of stages of moral judgment. I have not entirely clarified how such a sequence helps to resolve relativistic questioning of moral principles, a task taken up in our Chapter 4, "From *Is* to *Ought*." It is easier to clarify how such a sequence helps resolve the dilemma of relativity versus indoctrination in values education. The sequence provides us with a concept of moral development that can be stimulated by education without indoctrination and yet that helps to move student judgment toward more adequate principles.

The way to stimulate stage growth is to pose real or hypothetical dilemmas to students in such a way as to arouse disagreement and uncertainty as to what is right. The teacher's primary role is to present such dilemmas and to ask Socratic questions that arouse student reasoning and focus student listening on one another's reasons.

I noted research by Rest (1973) showing that students prefer the highest stage of reasoning they comprehend but that they do not comprehend more than one stage above their own. As a result, assimilation of reasoning occurs primarily when it is the next stage up from the student's level. Developmental moral discussion thus arouses cognitive-moral conflict and exposes students to reasoning by other students at the next stage above their own.

Using this approach, Blatt and Kohlberg (1975) were able to stimulate one-third of experimental classes of students to advance one stage in a time period in which control classes remained unchanged in moral stage. One year later, the experimental classes retained their relative advance over the control classes.

The developmental approach, first experimentally elaborated by Blatt, is one that any thoughtful classroom teacher may practice. Unlike values clarification, its assumptions are not relativistic but, rather, are based on universal goals and principles. It asks the student for reasons, on the assumption that some reasons are more adequate than others.

The approach differs from indoctrinative approaches because it tries to move student's thinking in a direction that is natural for the student rather than moving the student in the direction of accepting the teacher's moral assumptions. It avoids preaching or didacticism linked to the teacher's authority. . . .

## STUDY QUESTIONS

1. Examine the evidence for Kohlberg's claim that moral development is fundamentally the same in all cultures. Does this amount

to much more than adopting liberal ideas of justice and equality as "the highest stage" and then noting that individuals in some societies do (or aspire to) live by them?

2. Kohlberg claims that no one skips a "stage." Can this be confirmed empirically? How does Kohlberg support his argument for this claim?

3. Kohlberg's highest stages are termed "postconventional." Yet a great deal of morality is conventional and parochial (patriotism, filial and other kinship loyalties), being determined by social position and role and cultural norms. Does Kohlberg escape cultural relativism at the price of downgrading much of the bread-and-butter morality of our conventional daily lives?

4. Kohlberg seems opposed to the usual practices in moral education (e.g., parental and teacher threats, behavior codes, parental/teacher encouragement to cultivate virtues and abjure vice, morally inspiring literature and biographies, a thorough knowledge of the moral traditions of American society). Yet, doesn't a child need just such an "old-fashioned" moral education in order to progress through the first four stages? Discuss.

## REFERENCES

Blatt, M., and L. Kohlberg. "The Effects of Classroom Moral Discussion upon Children's Level of Moral Judgment." *Journal of Moral Education* 4 (1975): 129–61.

Bronfenbrenner, U. "Soviet Methods of Upbringing and Their Effects: A Social-Psychological Analysis." Paper read at conference on Studies of the Acquisition and Development of Values, National Institute of Child Health and Human Development, Washington, D.C., May 23, 1968.

Carr, D. B., and E. P. Wellenberg. *Teaching Children Values*. (Freeport, CA: Honor Your Partner Records, 1966).

Dodder, C., and B. Dodder. *Decision Making: A Guide for Teachers Who Would Help Preadolescent Children Become Imaginative and Responsible Decision Makers*. (Boston: Beacon Press, 1968).

Havighurst, R. J., and H. Taba. *Adolescent Character and Personality*. (New York: Wiley, 1949).

Jackson, P. W. *Life in the Classroom*. (New York: Holt, Rinehart and Winston, 1968).

Kohlberg, L. "Moral Development and the New Social Studies." *Social Education* 37 (1973): 368–75.

Piaget, J. *The Moral Judgment of the Child*. New York: Free Press, 1948. (Originally published 1932.)

Rest, J. "The Hierarchical Nature of Moral Judgment." *Journal of Personality* 41 (1973): 86–109.

Simon, S. "Value-Clarification vs. Indoctrination." *Social Education* 35 (1971): 902.

# *Moral Education and Indoctrination*

## GEORGE SHER and WILLIAM J. BENNETT

George Sher (b. 1942) is professor of philosophy at the University of Vermont. He has written many articles on moral philosophy and metaphysics, and is the author of *Desert*.

William J. Bennett (b. 1943), formally chairman of the National Endowment for the Humanities, most recently was Secretary of Education in the Reagan Administration. (He coauthored this selection prior to being named Secretary of Education.) Bennett has, in addition, taught philosophy at the University of Texas.

George Sher and William Bennett advocate "directive moral education" in which students are explicitly encouraged to accept and to behave in accordance with specific

MORAL EDUCATION AND INDOCTRINATION By George Sher and William J. Bennett. Reprinted from *The Journal of Philosophy*, November 1982, pp. 665–677. Reprinted by permission of the publisher and authors.

principles (e.g., respect for democratic values, treat others as you would like to be treated), and to develop certain traits (e.g., honesty, courage, and self-discipline).

To the objection that directive moral education violates autonomy, Sher and Bennett reply that what really matters is the autonomy of the adult the child will become. Most children cannot be motivated by reason alone. They need such other motives as fear of punishment, parental/teacher approval, desire to imitate a respected model. As mature adults we are capable of understanding the reasons behind a moral principle, and these reasons alone are often sufficient to motivate us. But why, ask Sher and Bennett, should the fact that we are also partly conditioned by childhood training detract from our autonomy? Indeed, moral education helps us to become autonomous. If children develop good moral habits such as truth telling and fairness to others, it will be easier for them to act in accordance with a reasoned morality. "When [good] habits exist in persons who do not appreciate moral reasons, they may be mere facsimiles of virtue. However, when they exist in conjunction *with* an appreciation of reasons, they surely do contribute to moral autonomy."

Sher and Bennett consider the objection that directive moral education violates the American social ideals of tolerance and pluralism. They admit the danger that fanatics might misuse the system, but believe the problem can be avoided if teachers are encouraged to teach only those values that satisfy "high standards of justification," such as fairness, honesty, and consideration for others.

Sher and Bennett also point to a fallacy in pluralism: the pluralist cannot demand that teachers be neutral toward *all* values since pluralism itself is based on the value of tolerance. "If we . . . value toleration, then we must also value the general acceptance of principles that support and further it."

It is now widely agreed that educators have no business inculcating moral views in the classroom. According to many philosophers and educational theorists, all attempts to influence students' moral behavior through exhortation and personal example are indoctrinative and should give way to more discursive efforts to guide children in developing their own values.[1] Yet although the nondirective approach to moral education has become the new orthodoxy, its philosophical underpinnings remain largely unexplored. In particular, the familiar charge that all directive moral education is indoctrinative has not been carefully defended. In this paper, we will argue that no plausible version of it *can* be defended and that adequate moral education must include both directive *and* discursive elements. Because the charge of indoctrination is so unclear, we will not confront it directly. Instead, we will address two closely related claims: that directive moral education (1) violates a student's autonomy, and (2) involves sectarian teaching inappropriate to a pluralistic society. If these complaints can be shown to lack substance, then the charge of indoctrination will carry little weight.

## I

Before discussing the major objections to directive moral education, we must make clearer what such education involves. In particular, we must specify (a) the traits and principles to be taught, and (b) the relevant methods of teaching them, and (c) the positive reasons for adopting such methods.

The traits and principles we have in mind are best illustrated by example. In Talawanda, Ohio, the local school district recently took

---

[1]Thus, for example: "[I]t is . . . wrong to teach ethics by presenting and attempting to inculcate a number of rules or precepts of conduct so as to improve, or at least to alter character, dispositions, or responses. The most effective means for altering responses, and possibly character as well, are those of advertising, propaganda (is there any difference?), indoctrination and brainwashing. These are all objectionable on moral grounds, so one cannot possibly improve character by these means" [Marcus Singer, "The Teaching of Introductory Ethics," *The Monist*, LVIII, 4 (October 1974), p. 617]. "If moral education promotes a definite moral perspective, it tends to be toward indoctrination and the denial of moral autonomy. . . . The problem and the challenge of moral education in our age is to find a middle way which neither indoctrinates young people into one set of moral rules nor gives them the impression that decision making is all a matter of personal opinion" [Robert Hall, "Moral Education Today: Progress, Prospects and Problems of a Field Come of Age," *The Humanist* (November/December 1978), p. 12].

the position that "the schools should help students realize the importance" of principles and traits including:

- Achieving self-discipline, defined as the strength to do what we believe we should do, even when we would rather not do it.
- Being trustworthy, so that when we say we will or will not do something, we can be believed.
- Telling the truth, especially when it hurts us to do so.
- Having the courage to resist group pressures to do what we believe, when alone, that we should not do.
- Using honorable means, those that respect the rights of others, in seeking our individual and collective ends.
- Conducting ourselves, where significant moral behavior is involved, in a manner which does not fear exposure.
- Having the courage to say, "I'm sorry, I was wrong."
- Treating others as we would wish to be treated; recognizing that this principle applies to persons of every class, race, nationality, and religion.
- Doing work well, whatever that work may be.
- Respecting the democratic values of free speech, a free press, freedom of assembly, freedom of religion, and due process of law. Recognizing that this principle applies to speech we abhor, groups we dislike, persons we despise.

Later, we will discuss the degree to which the Talawanda list embodies moral or ideological bias. For now, it suffices to note that the items just listed are close to noncontroversial within our society. They illustrate, but do not exhaust, the traits and principles whose directive teaching we will discuss.

What, exactly, does such teaching involve? Although a full account is again impossible, certain elements stand out. Of these, perhaps the most important is a teacher or administrator's willingness to demonstrate that he himself endorses certain principles—that he accepts them as guides in his own conduct and expects his students to do likewise. This requires that he act as an intentional model of behavior in accordance with the favored principles. It also requires that he explicitly urge his students to develop habits of acting in similar ways and that he express his disapproval, both verbally and through punishment, when his expectations are not met. It is often desirable to explain *why* one should act in the relevant ways, but efforts to influence behavior should not be confined to such explanations. Both encouragement and expressions of disapproval may persist when the proffered reasons are not grasped.

Why should morality be taught in these ways? Quite obviously, any rationale for adopting directive methods must be an instrumental one. The claim must be that, at elementary levels of development, such methods are effective ways of getting children to internalize desirable habits and behave in desirable ways and that, at more advanced levels, the previous application of these methods is necessary for the success of more discursive methods. We believe these claims are supported by recent studies of child and adolescent development and "moral psychology."[2] However, even if all empirical issues remained open, the permissibility of directive moral education would still be worth ascertaining. Even those who are not convinced that such methods work must be interested in learning whether we would be morally permitted to employ them if they did.

## II

Consider, first, the objection that directive moral education violates autonomy. At the core of this objection is a distinction between actions produced by nonrational causes and actions motivated by an awareness of the reasons for performing them. When a child acts to imitate a respected model or in response to exhortation or threat, he is said to be motivated only in the former way. Even if there are good reasons for his action, the very same techniques that have motivated his act could just as well have been used to motivate behavior unsupported by such reasons. Thus, his behavior is evidently *not* produced simply by his appreciation of the reasons for it. Hence, it is said to be neither fully his own nor an appropriate object of moral appraisal.

There is plainly something right about this objection. On any plausible account, an adequate moral education must produce not

---

[2]See especially Norman T. Feather, "Values in Adolescence," and Martin L. Hoffman, "Moral Development in Adolescence," in Joseph Adelson, ed., *The Handbook of Adolescent Psychology* (New York: Wiley, 1980), pp. 247–344.

only a tendency to act rightly, but also a tendency to do so for the right reasons. But, despite its superficial clarity, the objection as stated is both ambiguous and incomplete. It is ambiguous because it does not specify whether the person whose autonomy is violated is the child to whom directive education is administered or the adult whom the child will later become. It is incomplete because it does not explain *how* autonomy is violated in either case.

Whose autonomy is violated by directive moral education? Of the two possible answers, the more straightforward is "the child's." But to this answer, there is a quick rejoinder. However desirable it is to appeal to a person's appreciation of reasons, it surely need not be wrong to influence his behavior in other ways when he cannot respond to reasons alone. But this is manifestly true of young children. With them, appeals to principle simply fail. We must ascend the developmental scale quite far before such appeals promise much success. According to the leading proponent of nondirective moral education, Lawrence Kohlberg, the most common motive for moral action among 13-year-olds is still a desire to avoid disapproval and dislike by others.[3] In Kohlberg's typology, this motive is three full stages away from conscientious aversion to self-reproach. Moreover, in Kohlberg's view, one cannot reach a given stage of moral development without first traversing all the lower stages. Thus, even Kohlberg must acknowledge that, before middle adolescence, most children cannot respond to unadorned appeals to moral reasons. But if so, we do not violate their autonomy when we supplement such appeals with more efficacious influences.

This reply may appear inconclusive; for the opponent of directive moral education can respond by weakening his requirements for autonomy. Instead of contending that moral autonomy requires that one act from moral reasons, he can assert that it requires only that one's motives be those of the highest Kohlbergian level available to one. If so, even a child who acts to satisfy an impersonally construed authority (Kohlberg's level 4) may act significantly more autonomously than one who seeks to imitate a respected elder or to avoid punishment. However, considered by itself, such denatured "autonomy" has little value. Its main significance is pretty clearly to

---

[3]For elaboration, see Kohlberg, *The Philosophy of Moral Development* (New York: Harper & Row, 1981).

pave the way for further moral development. Thus, the response does not really save the claim that directive techniques violate a child's autonomy. If anything, it reinforces the claim that what is violated is the autonomy of the adult whom the child will become.

Put in this second form, the objection no longer presupposes an obviously impossible ideal of autonomy. Unlike children, mature adults often do seem to respond to moral reasons. But why should the previous application of directive techniques be thought to prevent this? It is true that directive techniques use nonrational means to produce desires and character traits that will eventually influence one's adult actions. However, even if an adult *is* motivated by a desire that was originally produced by nonrational means, it still seems possible for his action to be done for good moral reasons. In particular, this still seems possible if his nonrationally produced desire is precisely to act *in accordance with* such reasons. But it is surely just this desire which the sensitive practitioner of directive moral education seeks to instill.

If moral autonomy required only action in accordance with moral reasons, this response would be decisive. However, another strain of thought construes the requirements for autonomy more strictly. On this view, genuine moral autonomy requires not only that an agent act *in accordance with* moral reasons, but also that he *be motivated by* his awareness of them. In Kantian terms, the autonomous agent must be "self-legislating." On this expanded account the effectiveness of a past directive education may again seem threatening to current autonomy. If without his past directive education the agent would not now act as he does, then it is apparently just the desires produced by that education which supply the motivational energy for his current act. But if so, that motivational energy is evidently *not* supplied by his recognition of reasons themselves. His recognition of reasons may *trigger* the motivational energy for his act; but what is triggered is still energy with an independent source. Hence, the requirements for moral autonomy still seem unsatisfied.

With this refinement, we approach the heart of the objection that directive moral education violates autonomy. But although the refinement is familiar, the resulting argument is problematical. Most obviously, it rests on both the obscure metaphor of motivational energy and the undefended requirement that autonomous acts must draw such energy from reasons themselves. But the difficulty goes deeper. Even if its premises were both intelligible and defensible, the argument would be a non sequitur. Although it purports to demonstrate that directive moral education *violates* moral autonomy, it really shows only that such education does not *contribute* to moral autonomy. Far from establishing that directive techniques are pernicious, it at best establishes that they are morally neutral.

For why *should* desires produced by nonrational techniques be thought to prevent one from being motivated by an appreciation of reasons? Is the point merely that anyone subject to nonrationally produced desires would perform his act even if he were *not* motivated by an appreciation of the moral reasons for it? If so, then the most that follows is that his act is motivationally overdetermined. Since this does not negate the motivating force of his appreciation of reasons, it does not undermine his autonomy. Is the point rather that, if one's directively induced desires are required to produce one's action, then the motivation supplied by one's appreciation of reasons is too *weak* to produce it—that the latter motivation requires supplementation? If so, then, without his directive moral education, the agent would not have performed the act at all, and so *a fortiori* would not have performed it autonomously. Here again, nothing suggests that his directive moral education has reduced or violated his autonomy.

Given these considerations, even the strengthened analysis of autonomy does not establish that directive moral education violates one's later autonomy. To show this, one would need two yet stronger premises: that (1) a single act cannot simultaneously be motivated by both the agent's recognition of reasons and a nonrationally induced desire, and (2) when motivation from both sources converges, the motivational energy supplied by the nonrationally induced desire always excludes that supplied by an appreciation of reasons. But although these premises would indeed save the argument, there is little independent basis for them. In ordinary contexts, energy from any number of sources can combine to produce a single result. Hence, given our working metaphor, we must also presume that *motivational* energy from different sources can combine. The presumption must be that the motivating force of reasons does *not* give way when other factors motivate the same act. Moreover, these presumptions are not defeated by any independent theoretical considerations; for no adequate theory of how reasons motivate has yet been proposed.

# III

So far, we have argued that directive moral education need not violate anyone's present or future moral autonomy. This conclusion, if correct, suffices to rebut the first objection to directive education. But more can be said here. Even if autonomy does require motivation by moral reasons, one's past directive education may actually help such autonomy to develop and flourish.

To see how directive education can have this result, recall first that, even if one's grasp of a moral reason does supply one with some impulse to do the right thing, that impulse may be too weak to issue in action. Because of this, its effect may depend on other factors. In particular, that effect may well be increased by one's past directive education. Of course, the desires produced by such education will not contribute to one's moral autonomy if they merely add their weight to the motivation supplied by one's appreciation of reasons. However, and crucially, a past directive education may also augment one's appreciation of reasons in another way. It may neutralize or eliminate what would otherwise be a competing motive, and so may enable one's appreciation of reasons to affect one more strongly. If directive education works this way, it will indeed render the agent more autonomous. Put in terms of our guiding metaphor, its function will be not to provide an additional source of motivational energy, but rather to clear away obstacles so that the energy supplied by reasons can suffice.

How likely is it that directive moral education actually does work in this way? It is not likely to do so always or exclusively. That directive education does not *always* work by eliminating obstacles to moral reasons is shown by the fact that it motivates even very young children and can motivate adults to act immorally. That it rarely works *only* by eliminating such obstacles is suggested by the fact that one's prerational desires seem likely to persist as one matures. But even if a past directive education often affects adults in ways that do not enhance their autonomy, it may simultaneously affect them in other ways as well. Thus, the question is not whether our model is exclusively correct, but only whether it accurately reflects *one* way in which directive moral education often works.

When the question is put this way, we think its answer is clearly yes. It is a psychological commonplace that one's ability to respond to any reason depends on various external considerations. Hunger, anxiety, pain, and fear can all reduce the effect of reasons by diminishing attention to them and by supplying other motives. Thus, eliminatiung these distractions plainly does increase the motivating force of reasons. But if so, then eliminating other distractions seems likely to serve a similar function. Two considerations which most often distract us from moral obligations are preoccupation with our own interests and concern for our own comfort. Hence, one very natural way of increasing the motivating force of moral reasons is to reduce the impact of such distractions. But how better to prevent someone from being unduly distracted by self-interest than by causing him to acquire settled habits of honesty, fair play, and concern for others? Given these habits, one will automatically discount one's selfish interests when they conflict with one's duty. Hence, one will attach proper weight to one's moral obligations as a matter of course. Moreover, how better to ensure that someone will follow his decisions through than by causing him to acquire further habits of diligence, perseverance, and conscientiousness? Given *these* habits, one will not be sidetracked by the blandishments of comfort or inertia. Hence, one's appreciation of reasons will again be rendered more effective.

Given all of this, the traditional content of directive moral education acquires new significance. As the Talawanda list suggests, such education has long aimed at producing the habits just mentioned. These habits are often criticized as poor substitutes for self-conscious and reasoned morality, but we can now see that this criticism misses the point. Far from being alternatives to self-conscious morality, the habits are best understood as indispensible auxiliaries to it. They increase the impact of moral reasons by reducing one's tendency to be diverted. When the habits exist in persons who do not appreciate moral reasons, they may be mere facsimilies of virtue. However, when they exist in conjunction *with* an appreciation of reasons, they surely do contribute to moral autonomy.

## IV

Until now, we have considered only the objection that directive moral education violates the ideal of the morally autonomous agent. However, one may also argue that it violates a related *social* ideal. There is wide agreement that our society should be both tolerant and plural-istic. Instead of stifling disagreements, it should accept and encourage diversity of opinion and should protect unpopular attitudes and beliefs. But a society that officially practices directive moral education seems not to do this. Instead of encouraging diversity, it instills in all children a single "approved" set of values. Far from being neutral, it is unabashedly partisan. Thus, such education may seem flatly incompatible with pluralism and tolerance.

This argument is narrower in scope than its predecessor; for it tells only against the use of directive techniques in public schools. Still, it does seem to animate many charges of indoctrination, and so we must examine it. To see the problems it raises, consider first the premise that society should tolerate and protect diverse values. This premise may mean either that (1) society should not coerce or perse-cute those who already hold unorthodox values, or (2) society should not try to induce people to acquire (or prevent people from acquiring) any values they do not yet hold. Whenever society coerces or perse-cutes those with unpopular values, it provides a disincentive for others to acquire those values. Hence, any violation of (1) is likely to violate (2). However, society may tolerate dissenters while trying to prevent others from acquiring their values. Hence, a violation of (2) does not necessarily violate (1).

Directive moral education neither persecutes anyone nor coerces any adults. When its techniques include punishment, it may be said to coerce children. However, (1) is generally not taken to apply to children, and punishment is in any case theoretically dispensable. Thus, directive moral education need not violate (1). It does violate (2); but that counts against it only if (2) is a proper interpretation of the pluralistic ideal. At first glance, (2) may appear to follow from a more general requirement that unorthodox views should receive a fair hearing. However, this would imply that we owe fair treatment to values as well as persons; and, as John Rawls has noted, such an obligation is highly unlikely.[4] Thus, the more promising strategy is to defend (2) less directly. To do that, one might appeal either to a societal obligation to allow persons to choose their own values or else to the undesirable consequences of inculcating official values. We will argue that neither defense succeeds.

The claim that societal attempts to inculcate values would violate

---

[4] "Fairness to Goodness," *Philosophical Review*, LXXXIV, 4 (October 1975): p. 554.

an obligation to allow people to choose their own values is inherently problematical. In standard cases, people's choices are guided by their values, but here it is precisely one's basic values that are said to *be* chosen. Hence, the relevant choices cannot be grounded in any deeper ' values. But how, then, *are* such choices grounded? Shall we say they have no grounding, but are simply arbitrary? If so, they hardly warrant society's protection. Are they grounded in considerations outside the agent's value system, such as his recognition of independent moral reasons? If so, the complaint against inculcating values must be that it prevents people from *responding* to such reasons. But we already know this is false. The desires and habits produced by directive moral education need not diminish, but may actually enhance, the motivating force of moral reasons. Is the claim, finally, that societally induced desires and habits do allow rational choice of values when they coincide with moral reasons, but prevent it in cases of conflict? If so, the argument is not that it is wrong to inculcate values, but only that society may inculcate the wrong values. Thus construed, the argument appeals to consequences. Hence, having come this far, we may abandon the rubric of choice, and confront the consequentialist approach directly.

The *locus classicus* of consequentialist arguments for tolerance is John Stuart Mill's *On Liberty*.[5] It is true that Mill's main target is not the inculcation of values, but rather intolerance involving coercion and persecution. However, there are also passages where Mill suggests that his arguments *do* extend to education, and presumably *a fortiori* to directive education. Moreover, whatever Mill's own views, any convincing consequentialist argument for (2) is likely to rest on precisely the familiar claims that society is fallible, that genuine challenges to belief enhance understanding, and that diverse practices provide people with a variety of models and "experiments of living." Thus, it is essentially the Millian arguments that we must now consider. Do they show that society should refrain from using nonrational techniques to instill values in its citizens?

We think not. Mill is right to insist that neither anyone's subjective feeling of certainty nor the argeement of society can guarantee the truth of an opinion or the utility of its adoption. However, the warrant for accepting the values of fairness, honesty, and consideration of others is no mere feeling of conviction. Instead, there is good

---

[5]*On Liberty* (Indianapolis: Hackett, 1978).

independent reason to believe that, if any moral propositions are true, propositions enjoining such behavior are among them. Moreover, if the issue turns on social utility, then the warrant for inculcating these values is still more obvious. There is of course a danger that, once any inculcation of values is admitted, dogmatists and fanatics will seek to inculcate values that are *not* well-grounded or useful. However, this danger, though real, is far from decisive. If we can avoid the slippery slope of insisting that *no* values be inculcated, then we can also do so by insisting that society inculcate only values that satisfy high standards of justifiability. This will of course require some exercise of judgment; but that seems unavoidable in any case. As Mill himself remarks, "there is no difficulty in proving any ethical standard whatever to work ill, if we suppose universal idiocy to be conjoined with it."[6]

In view of this, (2) cannot be supported by appealing to human fallibility. But the consequentialist arguments are no better. A person's comprehension of his beliefs and values may indeed be deepened by challenges posed by dissenters, but such challenges are generally not needed to promote either adequate comprehension or tenacious acceptance of moral values. The suggestion that they are is contradicted by common experience. Moreover, even if wide-spread challenges to moral values did bring real benefits, these would be trivial compared to the mischief done by large numbers of people uncommitted to honesty, integrity, or concern for others. Nor, similarly, is it likely that exposure to cruelty, dishonesty, and insensitivity will promote personal development or bring out traits beneficial to others.

These considerations show that directive moral education need not be condemned as incompatible with pluralism. But that point can also be made in another way. It would be self-defeating for pluralists to demand that society be completely neutral toward all values; for the general acceptance of some values is required by pluralism itself. This holds most obviously for the value of toleration, but it is no less true of other values on the Talawanda list. If people were not committed to fairness, cooperation, and trustworthiness, they could hardly maintain a framework within which the rights of the weak

---

[6] *Utilitarianism* (Indianapolis: Hackett, 1979), p. 23.

and unpopular were protected. This may or may not justify the coercive suppression of some views—intolerance in the name of tolerance remains a disputed question of liberalism—but it surely does call for something beyond mere neutrality. If we as a society value toleration, then we must also value the general acceptance of principles that support and further it. Hence, if there is an effective method of advancing such principles which is not otherwise objectionable, we must acknowledge a strong case for adopting it. But precisely this is true of directive moral education. Thus, at least some forms of it seem justified by our commitment to toleration itself.

## V

We have now rejected several familiar arguments against directive moral education. However, in endorsing such education, we do not mean that it should be used to teach every widely accepted moral belief or that it should utilize every effective method of procuring assent. Despite the strong moral component in many issues of economic distribution, foreign policy, and religion, we believe that normative propositions about these matters should generally not be taught directively. And although we believe that fairness and honesty *should* be taught directively, we believe their teaching should not involve immoderate humiliation or pain. But if we are to make such distinctions, we face a difficult further question: why are some forms of directive moral education permissible but others not?

This question is too large for us to answer fully, but some considerations are obviously relevant. To warrant directive teaching, a moral principle must first be clearly and firmly grounded. In addition, it should be simple enough to be comprehended at an early developmental stage, general enough to apply in a variety of situations, and central rather than peripheral to our moral corpus. To be acceptable as a *method* of directive teaching, a practice must neither impair a child's later ability to respond to moral reasons nor violate his rights. In many instances, the satisfaction of these requirements is undisputed. However, if an otherwise eligible principle or method is unacceptable to a conscientious minority, then respect for that minority may itself dictate restraint in directive teaching.

With this we can confront a final objection. It is sometimes said that because directive moral education reflects the prevailing moral climate, it inevitably favors existing practices and institutions. Because it grows out of entrenched attitudes, it is said objectionably to perpetuate the status quo. But we can now see that such worries are overblown. If the principles and habits that are directively taught are strongly justified, central to our evaluative scheme, and of more than parochial application, they are not likely to ratify all aspects of the status quo. Instead, they may well generate considerable dissatisfaction with existing realities. If someone is fair, considers others' interests, and respects democratic values, then he will be highly critical of many existing practices. If he is unmoved by group pressures, he will press his criticism even when it is unpopular. If he respects the truth and disdains dishonorable means, he will abjure self-interested silence. All in all, such a person is unlikely to be passive and indiscriminately accepting. Instead, he is apt vigorously to oppose various existing practices.

This shows that directive moral education need not favor the status quo. But should it ever be used to teach principles that *do* have this effect? To see the problem here, consider some further Talawanda entries:

- Practicing good sportsmanship. Recognizing that although the will to win is important, winning is not all-important.
- Showing respect for the property of others—school property, business property, government property, everyone's property.
- Abstaining from premature sexual experience and developing sexual attitudes compatible with the values of family life.

We believe there is much to be said for each of these. However, each is closely associated with a contested social institution. The first presupposes the legitimacy of competition, the second assumes an economic system which distributes wealth unequally, and the third overtly favors marriage and the family. Alternatives to each institution have been proposed. Does this imply that these principles should not be directively taught?

We believe this question has no simple answer. To decide whether association with an existing institution disqualifies a principle, one must first clarify the nature of the association. Does the principle merely apply *only in the context of* the institution? Or does it, in addition, require that one *accept* it? If acceptance of (say) property or the family is required, must one accept only some form of the institution, or all its current details? If the details need not be accepted, the argument amounts to little. But even if a principle does require full acceptance of an existing institution, the question of its directive teaching is not settled. The main reasons for not directively teaching such principles are to permit full evaluation of alternative institutions and to display respect for persons proposing them. However, despite their relevance, these factors are not always decisive. We saw above that a major determinant of whether a principle should be directively taught is its degree of justification. But if so, then when a principle requires acceptance of a contested institution, we cannot avoid asking how reasonable it is to oppose that institution and how plausible the alternatives are. If these questions are asked, their answers may tip the balance. Hence, directive teaching of principles favoring existing institutions cannot be ruled out.

This of course says little of substance. To evaluate directive teaching about property, sexual behavior, or other matters of controversy, one must say more about a whole range of issues. But that much more must be said is precisely our point. Where directive moral education is concerned, we begin to make progress only when we abandon as sterile the notion of indoctrination and its cognates.

**STUDY QUESTIONS**

1. How do Sher and Bennett reply to the objection that directive moral education violates autonomy? Evaluate their response.
2. What reasons do Sher and Bennett give for their contention that a directive moral education enhances one's moral autonomy? Do you agree?
3. Do you agree with some critics of Sher and Bennett who say that directive moral education violates American social ideals of pluralism and tolerance? Discuss.
4. Sher and Bennett claim that it is self-defeating for pluralists to demand that society be completely neutral toward all values. Do you find their arguments convincing?

# In a Different Voice

## CAROL GILLIGAN

Carol Gilligan (b. 1936) is professor of education in the Graduate School of Education at Harvard University. She has written numerous articles on moral psychology and is the author of *In a Different Voice* (1982).

Carol Gilligan discusses "different ideas about human development, different ways of imagining the human condition, different notions of what is of value in life." She notes that developmental theories in psychology project an ideal that views individual development and maturation as moving away from emotional perspectives toward a stage of impersonal justice in dealing with others. According to Sigmund Freud, this moral ideal is more accessible to men than to women because women are "more often influenced in their judgments by feelings of affection and hostility." But Nancy Chowdorow argues that women are *naturally* more attuned to others and that their moral ideals are defined through (emotional) attachment, rather than impersonal separation. Gilligan develops this theme by arguing that development itself should be redefined to give care and attachment an importance that is lacking in the standard (male) ideal of justice and autonomy.

The neglect of a woman's perspective has given a male bias to the findings of recent research in the psychology of moral education. Gilligan claims that Lawrence

IN A DIFFERENT VOICE Excerpted by permission of the author and publisher from *In a Different Voice* by Carol Gilligan (Cambridge, MA: Harvard University Press). Copyright © 1982 by Carol Gilligan.

538

Kohlberg's six stages of moral development assume the impersonal male "justice perspective," thereby assuring the result that women are morally deficient because of their tendency to understand moral issues in emotional and personal ways. Kohlberg's research, which concentrates on male subjects, concludes that in the highest stages of moral development the individual uses universal impartial ethical principles to justify moral rights. Gilligan argues that this developmental ideal that emphasizes the "rights" perspective over the "care perspective" is biased against women. And indeed Kohlberg "finds" that women are fixed in the earlier stages of moral development as he defines them. A perspective that is sensitive to the ideal of responsibility and caring would do more justice to women and their particular life cycles. "Only when life cycle theorists divide their attention and begin to live with women as they have lived with men will their vision encompass both sexes and their theories become correspondingly more fertile."

In the second act of *The Cherry Orchard,* Lopahin, a young merchant, describes his life of hard work and success. Failing to convince Madame Ranevskaya to cut down the cherry orchard to save her estate, he will go on in the next act to buy it himself. He is the self-made man who, in purchasing the estate where his father and grandfather were slaves, seeks to eradicate the "awkward, unhappy life" of the past, replacing the cherry orchard with summer cottages where coming generations "will see a new life." In elaborating this developmental vision, he reveals the image of man that underlies and supports his activity: "At times when I can't go to sleep, I think: Lord, thou gavest us immense forests, unbounded fields and the widest horizons, and living in the midst of them we should indeed be giants"—at which point, Madame Ranevskaya interrupts him, saying, "You feel the need for giants—They are good only in fairy tales, anywhere else they only frighten us."

Conceptions of the human life cycle represent attempts to order and make coherent the unfolding experiences and perceptions, the changing wishes and realities of everyday life. But the nature of such conceptions depends in part on the position of the observer. The brief excerpt from Chekhov's play suggests that when the observer is a woman, the perspective may be of a different sort. Different judgments of the image of man as giant imply different ideas about human development, different ways of imagining the human condition, different notions of what is of value in life.

At a time when efforts are being made to eradicate discrimination between the sexes in the search for social equality and justice, the differences between the sexes are being rediscovered in the social sciences. This discovery occurs when theories formerly considered to be sexually neutral in their scientific objectivity are found instead to reflect a consistent observational and evaluative bias. Then the presumed neutrality of science, like that of language itself, gives way to the recognition that the categories of knowledge are human constructions. The fascination with point of view that has informed the fiction of the twentieth century and the corresponding recognition of the relativity of judgment infuse our scientific understanding as well when we begin to notice how accustomed we have become to seeing life through men's eyes.

A recent discovery of this sort pertains to the apparently innocent classic *The Elements of Style* by William Strunk and E. B. White. The Supreme Court ruling on the subject of discrimination in classroom texts led one teacher of English to notice that the elementary rules of English usage were being taught through examples which counterposed the birth of Napoleon, the writings of Coleridge, and statements such as "He was an interesting talker. A man who had traveled all over the world and lived in half a dozen countries," with "Well, Susan, this is a fine mess you are in" or, less drastically, "He saw a woman, accompanied by two children, walking slowly down the road."

Psychological theorists have fallen as innocently as Strunk and White into the same observational bias. Implicitly adopting the male life as the norm, they have tried to fashion women out of a masculine cloth. It all goes back, of course, to Adam and Eve—a story which shows, among other things, that if you make woman out of a man, you are bound to get into trouble. In the life cycle, as in the Garden of Eden, the woman has been the deviant.

The penchant of developmental theorists to project a masculine image, and one that appears frightening to women, goes back at least to Freud who built his theory of psychosexual development around the experiences of the male child that culminate in the Oedipus complex. In the 1920s, Freud struggled to resolve the contradictions posed for his theory by the differences in female anatomy and the different configuration of the young girl's early family relationships. After trying to fit women into his masculine conception, seeing them as envying that which they missed, he came instead to acknowledge, in the strength and persistence of women's pre-Oedipal attachments to their mothers, a developmental difference. He considered this difference in women's development to be responsible for what he saw as women's developmental failure.

Having tied the formation of the superego or conscience to castration anxiety, Freud considered women to be deprived by nature of the impetus for a clear-cut Oedipal resolution. Consequently, women's superego—the heir to the Oedipus complex—was compromised: it was never "so inexorable, so impersonal, so independent of its emotional origins as we require it to be in men." From this observation of difference, that "for women the level of what is ethically normal is different from what it is in men," Freud concluded that women "show less sense of justice than men, that they are less ready to submit to the great exigencies of life, that they are more often influenced in their judgements by feelings of affection or hostility."

Thus a problem in theory became cast as a problem in women's development, and the problem in women's development was located in their experience of relationships. Nancy Chodorow, attempting to account for "the reproduction within each generation of certain general and nearly universal differences that characterize masculine and feminine personality and roles," attributes these differences between the sexes not to anatomy but rather to "the fact that women, universally, are largely responsible for early child care." Because this early social environment differs for and is experienced differently by male and female children, basic sex differences recur in personality development. As a result, "in any given society, feminine personality comes to define itself in relation and connection to other people more than masculine personality does."

In her analysis, Chodorow relies primarily on Robert Stoller's studies which indicate that gender identity, the unchanging core of personality formation, is "with rare exception firmly and irreversibly established for both sexes by the time a child is around three." Given that for both sexes the primary caretaker in the first three years of life is typically female, the interpersonal dynamics of gender identity formation are different for boys and girls. Female identity formation takes place in a context of ongoing relationship since "mothers tend to experience their daughters as more like, and continuous with, themselves." Correspondingly, girls, in identifying themselves as female, experience themselves as like their mothers, thus fusing the experience of attachment with the process of identity formation. In contrast, "mothers experience their sons as a male opposite," and boys, in defining themselves as masculine, separate their mothers from themselves, thus curtailing "their primary love and sense of empathic tie." Consequently, male development entails a "more emphatic individuation and a more defensive firming of experienced ego boundaries." For boys, but not girls, "issues of differentiation have become intertwined with sexual issues."

Writing against the masculine bias of psychoanalytic theory, Chodorow argues that the existence of sex differences in the early experiences of individuation and relationship "does not mean that women have 'weaker' ego boundaries than men or are more prone to psychosis." It means instead that "girls emerge from this period with a basis for 'empathy' built into their primary definition of self in a way that boys do not." Chodorow thus replaces Freud's negative and derivative description of female psychology with a positive and direct account of her own: "Girls emerge with a stronger basis for experiencing another's needs or feelings as one's own (or of thinking that one is so experiencing another's needs and feelings). Furthermore, girls do not define themselves in terms of the denial of preoedipal relational modes to the same extent as do boys. Therefore, regression to these modes tends not to feel as much a basic threat to their ego. From very early, then, because they are parented by a person of the same gender . . . girls come to experience themselves as less differentiated than boys, as more continuous with and related to the external object-world, and as differently oriented to their inner object-world as well."

Consequently, relationships, and particularly issues of dependency, are experienced differently by women and men. For boys and men, separation and individuation are critically tied to gender identity since separation from the mother is essential for the development of masculinity. For girls and women, issues of femininity or feminine identity do not depend on the achievement of separation from the mother or on the progress of individuation. Since masculinity is defined through separation while feminity is defined through attachment, male gender identity is threatened by intimacy while female gender identity is threatened by separation. Thus males tend to have difficulty with relationships, while females tend to have problems with individuation. The quality of embeddedness in social interaction and personal relationships that characterizes women's lives in contrast to men's, however, becomes not only a descriptive difference but also a developmental liability when the milestones of childhood and adolescent development in the psychological literature are markers of increasing separation. Women's failue to separate then becomes by definition a failure to develop.

The sex differences in personality formation that Chodorow describes in early childhood appear during the middle childhood years in studies of children's games. Children's games are considered by George Herbert Mead and Jean Piaget as the crucible of social development during the school years. In games, children learn to take the role of the other and come to see themselves through another's eyes. In games, they learn respect for rules and come to understand the ways rules can be made and changed.

Janet Lever, considering the peer group to be the agent of socialization during the elementary school years and play to be a major activity of socialization at that time, set out to discover whether there are sex differences in the games that children play. Studying 181 fifth-grade, white, middle-class children, ages ten and eleven, she observed the organization and structure of their playtime activities. She watched the children as they played at school during recess and in physical education class, and in addition kept diaries of their accounts as to how they spent their out-of-school time. From this study, Lever reports sex differences: boys play out of doors more often than girls do; boys play more often in large and age-heterogeneous groups; they play competitive games more often, and their games last longer than girls' games. The last is in some ways the most interesting finding. Boys' games appeared to last longer not only because they required a higher level of skill and were thus less likely to become boring, but also because, when disputes arose in the course of a game, boys were able to resolve the disputes more effectively than girls: "During the course of this study, boys were seen quarrelling all the time, but not once was a game terminated because of a quarrel and no game was interrupted for more than seven minutes. In the gravest debates, the final word was always, to 'repeat the play,' generally followed by a chorus of 'cheater's proof.'" In fact, it seemed that the boys enjoyed the legal debates as much as they did the game itself, and even marginal players of lesser size or skill participated equally in these recurrent squabbles. In contrast, the eruption of disputes among girls tended to end the game.

Thus Lever extends and corroborates the observations of Piaget in his study of the rules of the game, where he finds boys becoming through childhood increasingly fascinated with the legal elaboration of rules and the development of fair procedures for adjudicating conflicts, a fascination that, he notes, does not hold for girls. Girls, Piaget observes, have a more "pragmatic" attitude toward rules, "regarding a rule as good as long as the game repaid it."

Girls are more tolerant in their attitudes toward rules, more willing to make exceptions, and more easily reconciled to innovations. As a result, the legal sense, which Piaget considers essential to moral development, "is far less developed in little girls than in boys."

The bias that leads Piaget to equate male development with child development also colors Lever's work. The assumption that shapes her discussion of results is that the male model is the better one since it fits the requirements for modern corporate success. In contrast, the sensitivity and care for the feelings of others that girls develop through their play have little market value and can even impede professional success. Lever implies that, given the realities of adult life, if a girl does not want to be left dependent on men, she will have to learn to play like a boy.

To Piaget's argument that children learn the respect for rules necessary for moral development by playing rule-bound games, Lawrence Kohlberg adds that these lessons are most effectively learned through the opportunities for role-taking that arise in the course of resolving disputes. Consequently, the moral lessons inherent in girls' play appear to be fewer than in boys'. Traditional girls' games like jump rope and hopscotch are turn-taking games, where competition is indirect since one person's success does not necessarily signify another's failure. Consequently, disputes requiring adjudication are less likely to occur. In fact, most of the girls whom Lever interviewed claimed that when a quarrel broke out, they ended the game. Rather than elaborating a system of rules for resolving disputes, girls subordinated the continuation of the game to the continuation of relationships.

Lever concludes that from the games they play, boys learn both the independence and the organizational skills necessary for coordinating the activities of large and diverse groups of people. By participating in controlled and socially approved competitive situations, they learn to deal with competition in a relatively forthright manner—to play with their enemies and to compete with their friends—all in accordance with the rules of the game. In contrast, girls' play tends to occur in smaller, more intimate groups, often the best-friend dyad, and in private places. This play replicates the social pattern of primary human relationships in that its organization is more cooperative. Thus, it points less, in Mead's terms, toward learning to take the role of "the generalized other," less toward the abstraction of human relationships. But it fosters the development of the empathy and sensitivity necessary for taking the role of "the particular other" and points more toward knowing the other as different from the self.

The sex differences in personality formation in early childhood that Chodorow derives from her analysis of the mother-child relationship are thus extended by Lever's observations of sex differences in the play activities of middle childhood. Together these accounts suggest that boys and girls arrive at puberty with a different interpersonal orientation and a different range of social experiences.

. . .

"It is obvious," Virginia Woolf says, "that the values of women differ very often from the values which have been made by the other sex." Yet, she adds, "it is the masculine values that prevail." As a result, women come to question the normality of their feelings and to alter their judgments in deference to the opinion of others. In the nineteenth century novels written by women, Woolf sees at work "a mind which was slightly pulled from the straight and made to alter its clear vision in deference to external authority." The same deference to the values and opinions of others can be seen in the judgments of twentieth century women. The difficulty women experience in finding or speaking publicly in their own voices emerges repeatedly in the form of qualification and self-doubt, but also in intimations of a divided judgment, a public assessment and private assessment which are fundamentally at odds.

Yet the deference and confusion that Woolf criticizes in women derive from the values she sees as their strength. Women's deference is rooted not only in their social subordination but also in the substance of their moral concern. Sensitivity to the needs of others and

545

the assumption of responsibility for taking care lead women to attend to voices other than their own and to include in their judgment other points of view. Women's moral weakness, manifest in an apparent diffusion and confusion of judgment, is thus inseparable from women's moral strength, an overriding concern with relationships and responsibilities. The reluctance to judge may itself be indicative of the care and concern for others that infuse the psychology of women's development and are responsible for what is generally seen as problematic in its nature.

Thus women not only define themselves in a context of human relationship but also judge themselves in terms of their ability to care. Women's place in man's life cycle has been that of nurturer, caretaker, and helpmate, the weaver of those networks of relationships on which she in turn relies. But while women have thus taken care of men, men have, in their theories of psychological development, as in their economic arrangements, tended to assume or devalue that care. When the focus on individuation and individual achievement extends into adulthood and maturity is equated with personal autonomy, concern with relationships appears as a weakness of women rather than as a human strength.

The discrepancy between womanhood and adulthood is nowhere more evident than in the studies on sex-role stereotypes reported by Broverman, Vogel, Broverman, Clarkson, and Rosenkrantz. The repeated finding of these studies is that the qualities deemed necessary for adulthood—the capacity for autonomous thinking, clear decision-making, and responsible action—are those associated with masculinity and considered undesirable as attributes of the feminine self. The stereotypes suggest a splitting of love and work that relegates expressive capacities to women while placing instrumental abilities in the masculine domain. Yet looked at from a different perspective, these stereotypes reflect a conception of adulthood that is itself out of balance, favoring the separateness of the individual self over connection to others, and leaning more toward an autonomous life of work than toward the interdependence of love and care.

The discovery now being celebrated by men in mid-life of the importance of intimacy, relationships, and care is something that women have known from the beginning. However, because that knowledge in women has been considered "intuitive" or "instinctive," a function of anatomy coupled with destiny, psychologists have neglected to describe its development. In my research, I have found that women's moral development centers on the elaboration of that knowledge and thus delineates a critical line of psychological development in the lives of both of the sexes. The subject of moral development not only provides the final illustration of the reiterative pattern in the observation and assessment of sex differences in the literature on human development, but also indicates more particularly why the nature and significance of women's development has been for so long obscured and shrouded in mystery.

The criticism that Freud makes of women's sense of justice, seeing it as compromised in its refusal of blind impartiality, reappears not only in the work of Piaget but also in that of Kohlberg. While in Piaget's account of the moral judgment of the child, girls are an aside, a curiosity to whom he devotes four brief entries in an index that omits "boys" altogether because "the child" is assumed to be male, in the research from which Kohlberg derives his theory, females simply do not exist. Kohlberg's six stages that describe the development of moral judgment from childhood to adulthood are based empirically on a study of eighty-four boys whose development Kohlberg has followed for a period of over twenty years. Although Kohlberg claims universality for his stage sequence, those groups not included in his original sample rarely reach his higher stages.

Prominent among those who thus appear to be deficient in moral development when measured by Kohlberg's scale are women, whose judgments seem to exemplify the third stage of his six-stage sequence. At this stage morality is conceived in interpersonal terms and goodness is equated with helping and pleasing others. This conception of goodness is considered by Kohlberg and Kramer to be functional in the lives of mature women insofar as their lives take place in the home. Kohlberg and Kramer imply that only if women enter the traditional arena of male activity will they recognize the inadequacy of this moral perspective and progress like men toward higher stages where relationships are subordinated to rules (stage four) and rules to universal principles of justice (stages five and six).

Yet herein lies a paradox, for the very traits that traditionally have defined the "goodness" of women, their care for and sensitivity to the needs of others, are those that mark them as deficient in moral development. In this version of moral development, however, the conception of maturity is derived from the study of men's lives and reflects the importance of individuation in their development. Piaget, challenging the common impression that a developmental theory is

547

built like a pyramid from its base in infancy, points out that a conception of development instead hangs from its vertex of maturity, the point toward which progress is traced. Thus, a change in the definition of maturity does not simply alter the description of the highest stage but recasts the understanding of development, changing the entire account.

When one begins with the study of women and derives developmental constructs from their lives, the outline of a moral conception different from that described by Freud, Piaget, or Kohlberg begins to emerge and informs a different description of development. In this conception, the moral problem arises from conflicting responsibilities rather than from competing rights and requires for its resolution a mode of thinking that is contextual and narrative rather than formal and abstract. This conception of morality as concerned with the activity of care centers moral development around the understanding of responsibility and relationships, just as the conception of morality as fairness ties moral development to the understanding of rights and rules.

This different construction of the moral problem by women may be seen as the critical reason for their failure to develop within the constraints of Kohlberg's system. Regarding all constructions of responsibility as evidence of a conventional moral understanding, Kohlberg defines the highest stages of moral development as deriving from a reflective understanding of human rights. That the morality of rights differs from the morality of responsibility in its emphasis on separation rather than connection, in its consideration of the individual rather than the relationship as primary, is illustrated by two responses to interview questions about the nature of morality. The first comes from a twenty-five-year-old man, one of the participants in Kohlberg's study:

> [*What does the word morality mean to you?*] Nobody in the world knows the answer. I think it is recognizing the right of the individual, the rights of other individuals, not interfering with those rights. Act as fairly as you would have them treat you. I think it is basically to preserve the human being's right to existence. I think that is the most important. Secondly, the human being's right to do as he pleases, again without interfering with somebody else's rights.
>
> [*How have your views on morality changed since the last interview?*] I think I am more aware of an individual's rights now. I used to be

looking at it strictly from my point of view, just for me. Now I think I am more aware of what the individual has a right to.

Kohlberg cites this man's response as illustrative of the principled conception of human rights that exemplifies his fifth and sixth stages. Commenting on the response, Kohlberg says. "Moving to a perspective outside of that of his society, he identifies morality with justice (fairness, rights, the Golden Rule), with recognition of the rights of others as these are defined naturally or intrinsically. The human's being right to do as he pleases without interfering with somebody else's rights is a formula defining rights prior to social legislation."

The second response comes from a woman who participated in the rights and responsibilities study. She also was twenty-five and, at the time, a third-year law student:

[*Is there really some correct solution to moral problems, or is everybody's opinion equally right?*] No, I don't think everybody's opinion is equally right. I think that in some situations there may be opinions that are equally valid, and one could conscientiously adopt one of several courses of action. But there are other situations in which I think there are right and wrong answers, that sort of inhere in the nature of existence, of all individuals here who need to live with each other to live. We need to depend on each other, and hopefully it is not only a physical need but a need of fulfillment in ourselves, that a person's life is enriched by cooperating with other people and striving to live in harmony with everybody else, and to that end, there are right and wrong, there are things which promote that end and that move away from it, and in that way it is possible to choose in certain cases among different courses of action that obviously promote or harm that goal.

[*Is there a time in the past when you would have thought about these things differently?*] Oh, yeah, I think that I went through a time when I thought that things were pretty relative, that I can't tell you what to do and you can't tell me what to do, because you've got your conscience and I've got mine.

[*When was that?*] When I was in high school. I guess that it just sort of dawned on me that my own ideas changed, and because my own judgment changed, I felt I couldn't judge another person's judgment. But now I think even when it is only the person himself who is going to be affected, I say it is wrong to the extent it doesn't cohere with what I know about human nature and what I know about you, and just from what I think is true about the operation of the universe, I could say I think you are making a mistake.

[*What led you to change, do you think?*] Just seeing more of life, just recognizing that there are an awful lot of things that are common among people. There are certain things that you come to learn pro- mote a better life and better relationships and more personal fulfill- ment than other things that in general tend to do the opposite, and the things that promote these things, you would call morally right.

This response also represents a personal reconstruction of morality following a period of questioning and doubt, but the reconstruction of moral understanding is based not on the primacy and universality of individual rights, but rather on what she describes as a "very strong sense of being responsible to the world." Within this construc- tion, the moral dilemma changes from how to exercise one's rights without interfering with the rights of others to how "to lead a moral life which includes obligations to myself and my family and people in general." The problem then becomes one of limiting responsibili- ties without abandoning moral concern. When asked to describe herself, this woman says that she values "having other people that I am tied to, and also having people that I am responsible to. I have a very strong sense of being responsible to the world, that I can't just live for my enjoyment, but just the fact of being in the world gives me an obligation to do what I can to make the world a better place to live in, no matter how small a scale that may be on." Thus while Kohlberg's subject worries about people interfering with each other's rights, this woman worries about "the possibility of omission, of your not helping others when you could help them."

The issue that this woman raises is addressed by Jane Loevinger's fifth "autonomous" stage of ego development, where autonomy, placed in the context of relationships, is defined as modulating an excessive sense of responsibility through the recognition that other people have responsibility for their own destiny. The autonomous stage in Loevinger's account witnesses a relinquishing of moral di- chotomies and their replacement with "a feeling for the complexity and multifaceted character of real people and real situations." Whereas the rights conception of morality that informs Kohlberg's principled level (stages five and six) is geared to arriving at an objec- tively fair or just resolution to moral dilemmas upon which all ra- tional persons could agree, the responsibility conception focuses instead on the limitations of any particular resolution and describes the conflicts that remain.

Thus it becomes clear why a morality of rights and noninterference may appear frightening to women in its potential justification of indifference and unconcern. At the same time, it becomes clear why, from a male perspective, a morality of responsibility appears inconclusive and diffuse, given its insistent contextual relativism. Women's moral judgments thus elucidate the pattern observed in the description of the developmental differences between the sexes, but they also provide an alternative conception of maturity by which these differences can be assessed and their implications traced. The psychology of women that has consistently been described as distinctive in its greater orientation toward relationships and interdependence implies a more contextual mode of judgment and a different moral understanding. Given the differences in women's conceptions of self and morality, women bring to the life cycle a different point of view and order human experience in terms of different priorities.

The myth of Demeter and Persephone, which McClelland cites as exemplifying the feminine attitude toward power, was associated with the Eleusinian Mysteries celebrated in ancient Greece for over two thousand years. As told in the Homeric *Hymn to Demeter,* the story of Persephone indicates the strengths of interdependence, building up resources and giving, that McClelland found in his research on power motivation to characterize the mature feminine style. Although, McClelland says, "it is fashionable to conclude that no one knows what went on in the Mysteries, it is known that they were probably the most important religious ceremonies, even partly on the historical record, which were organized by and for women, especially at the onset before men by means of the cult of Dionysos began to take them over." Thus McClelland regards the myth as "a special presentation of femine psychology." It is, as well, a life-cycle story par excellence.

Persephone, the daughter of Demeter, while playing in a meadow with her girlfriends, sees a beautiful narcissus which she runs to pick. As she does so, the earth opens and she is snatched away by Hades, who takes her to his underworld kingdom. Demeter, goddess of the earth, so mourns the loss of her daughter that she refuses to allow anything to grow. The crops that sustain life on earth shrivel up, killing men and animals alike, until Zeus takes pity on man's suffering and persuades his brother to return Persephone to her mother.

But before she leaves, Persephone eats some pomegranate seeds, which ensures that she will spend part of every year with Hades in the underworld.

The elusive mystery of women's development lies in its recognition of the continuing importance of attachment in the human life cycle. Woman's place in man's life cycle is to protect this recognition while the developmental litany intones the celebration of separation, autonomy, individuation, and natural rights. The myth of Persephone speaks directly to the distortion in this view by reminding us that narcissism leads to death, that the fertility of the earth is in some mysterious way tied to the continuation of the mother-daughter relationship, and that the life cycle itself arises from an alternation between the world of women and that of men. Only when life-cycle theorists divide their attention and begin to live with women as they have lived with men will their vision encompass the experience of both sexes and their theories become correspondingly more fertile.

**STUDY QUESTIONS**

1. Gilligan speaks of "a consistent observational and evaluative bias" in the way women are viewed. How is this bias manifested in the social and psychological sciences? How is it manifested in general?

2. What is negative about Sigmund Freud's account of women's development? How does Nancy Chodorow correct Freud in a positive way?

3. How do girls and boys characteristically handle disputes? Rules? What general bearing does this have on their individual perspective on morality?

4. What, according to Gilligan, are the peculiar moral strengths of women? What is the distinction between "a morality of rights" and a "morality of responsibility"? How does Gilligan deploy this distinction in criticizing Lawrence Kohlberg?

5. Some feminists have attributed to Gilligan the view that women are by nature morally superior to men. Do you find this to be a reasonable reading of Gilligan's point of view. (Does Gilligan's approach lead to a kind of reverse sexism?)

6. Gilligan sees the male ethic, with its formal emphasis on obligation, as inadequate. Can a similar criticism be reasonably made of an ethic that elevates care and personal commitment over formal obligation?

# Literature and Moral Education

## RONALD DUSKA

Ronald Duska (b. 1937) is professor of philosophy at Rosemont College in Pennsylvania. He has published numerous articles in ethics and is the author of *Moral Development: A Guide to Piaget and Kohlberg* (1973).

Ronald Duska criticizes current moral philosophy, including "applied ethics," charging it with being too formal. The application of formal rules to concrete problems very often does not lead to definitive solutions and even when it does, we are still faced with the question: "Why be moral?"

Duska notes that even formal philosophers implicitly appeal to some ideal of happiness in arriving at solutions to ethical questions. But happiness is not a clearly defined good that we set and pursue. Rather, happiness *accompanies* our activities when we are passionately doing the best we can do "with the hand that has been dealt us."

Passion gives meaning and point to our lives. "No one deeply in love ever asks whether life has meaning." But passion can go wrong. (Witness the tragic consequences of Othello's governing passion, jealousy.) Literature is the

LITERATURE AND MORAL EDUCATION From "What Is Literature to Ethics or Ethics to Literature?" in *Listening: Journal of Religion and Culture*, Winter 1982, by Ronald Duska. Reprinted by permission of the publisher.

primary source for studying the relationship of the passions to happiness and unhappiness. Literature is relevant to ethics in several ways. First and foremost, it shows us how the meaning of our lives is bound up with our passions. Second, it helps to develop our empathy toward others, thereby helping us to become more sensitive, open, and caring persons. Great literature also provides insight into fictional characters: fiction reveals moral truths. Morality has to do with the heart; immorality has to do with insensitivity and lack of care. Thus, literature helps us toward a concrete understanding of "the passionate human being."

Quarry the granite rock with razors, or moor the vessel with a thread of silk; then may you hope with such keen and delicate instruments as human knowledge and human reason to contend against those giants, the passion and pride of man.

John Henry Newman

One can always learn from literature.[1] That statement might offend some purists among contemporary aestheticians who would want to claim that the function of literature as art is to delight and that to use literature for didactic purposes is to abuse it. But the fact remains that literature, good literature, has always been a marvelous teacher. It humanizes us as perhaps nothing else can. Hence the topic of this paper. I want to examine a few ways in which literature aids us in dealing with ethical matters. My conviction, which may appear perverse to some is that in many ways literature contributes more to the clarification of values and the development of morals than ethical theory as it is done today.

I will claim that contemporary ethical theory is inadequate because it rests on an unrealistic picture of human life which largely ignores or misconstrues the role of the passions[2] in constituting a meaningful

---

[1]Under the word "literature" I mean to include for the most part, novels, poems, stories and dramas. I also have in mind good literature, classics if you will, and not things like drugstore novels. I am of course assuming there is a difference between run of the mill literature and good or significant literature.

[2]In this paper I am using the word "passions" rather indiscriminately in a generic sense to include a whole host of areas which would be placed under what psychologists call

human life. Literature, however, expresses or represents in a unique way the passionate sources of human action and consequently shows us what a meaningful human life is in a way that ethics does not. In short, it provides us with what ethical theory does not, content for what has become the formally stringent but largely vacuous enterprise of contemporary ethical theory. I begin with a defense of that claim.

A generation ago, G. E. M. Anscombe requested a moratorium on ethical theory. Since then, Philippa Foot expressed a desire to quit talking about "morality." Rather than acceding to the wishes of these two esteemed philosophers, ethicists have talked and written even more about ethical issues. However, rather than dry as dust discussions of ethical theory or meta-ethics, the talk now revolves around pertinent and substantive ethical issues, often under the name of applied ethics. For my part, instead of teaching about naturalistic fallacies, I now find myself engaged in medical and business ethics, talking about abortion, genetic engineering, corporate responsibility, preferential hiring and a host of other topics. Nevertheless, periodically I ask myself "Why?" Is the kind of discussion carried on about these issues relevant? The topics certainly are relevant, but can this be said of our treatment of them?

The standard move of most "applied ethicists" is to take one of the two canonized ethical theories, either the deontological principles of Kant or Ross, possibly updated by his contemporary disciples and apply them/it to either a class of actions like suicide and abortion or to a particular ethical dilemma. For example, if we address euthanasia or suicide, two problems of the same stripe: either we begin by talking about the duty to oneself or others and the contradictoriness of the taking of a human life to preserve the values of life; or we begin by talking of the rationality of euthanasia or suicide in terms of the consequences of this type of action, and determine whether it is right by deciding whether it will maximize happiness.

One must grant that both of these methods have something to be

---

the affective side of man, i.e., feelings, emotions, attitudes, dispositions, etc. Much of the sorting out of what I have in mind can be found in Robert Solomon's excellent book, *The Passions*, (Doubleday, 1973). The book is partly responsible for some of the directions of this paper, although I would not claim that the paper intentionally follows it, nor would I hold the book responsible for the shortcomings of my thoughts.

said in their favor, for they do show that if certain principles are accepted, certain actions logically follow as appropriate or inappropriate. Nevertheless, for anyone who has ever taught courses in applied ethics, this procedure leaves much to be desired.

What is the problem? First, it seems to be that the application of formal rules to materially concrete problems never leads to definitive solutions. For every answer there is a counter objection and a kind of skepticism is encouraged. Second, even if a definitive solution would be arrived at, a highly unlikely possibility, the question, why do what is prescribed would still remain, i.e., we could still ask, "Why be moral?" "Why do what we have determined that we should?"

There are defenses of these procedures. In a remarkably well written textbook called *Moral Reasoning*, Victor Grassian offers a defense of the study of ethics. According to Grassian, even though the study of ethics will not make us into a good person, it can serve to help us better understand and classify our own moral principles, even refine and change them (one hesitates to ask whether for the better or worse); and it can lead us to a consistent set of principles. Grassian states, at the end of the defense:

> By studying the arguments that philosophers give for their ethical positions and the objections they pose to the view of others, a person's ability to defend his own positions and recognize their shortcomings will itself be sharpened. This is by far the *most important* thing that the study of ethics has to offer.[3]

Marvelous! But with all the sharpening, changing and elimination of shortcomings, something is still missing. What is the good of all this eristic ability if it leads to the sharpening of misguided principles which can be used by a despot or tyrant to justify his behavior? Further, what is the good if it cannot lead to a good person behaving well? What Grassian offers is vaguely reminiscent of what the Sophists offered, is it not?

To give my point more substance let us examine a dilemma found in Grassian's text and demonstrate what ethical theorists are likely to do with it.

---

[3]Victor Grassian, *Moral Reasoning* (Englewood Cliffs, NJ: Prentice Hall, 1981), p. 5.

## A Poisonous Cup of Coffee

> Tom, hates his wife and wanting her dead, puts poison in her coffee, thereby killing her. Joe also hates his wife and would like her dead. One day, Joe's wife accidentally puts poison in her coffee, thinking it's cream. Joe, who happens to be a chemist, has the antidote, but he does not give it to her. Knowing that he is the only one who can save her, he lets her die. Is Joe's failure to act as bad as Tom's action? Why or why not?

It seems fairly obvious that Grassian is using this dilemma to provoke a discussion of the difference (if there is any) between killing and letting die (a distinction that is quite useful in contrasting active and passive euthanasia, among other issues), For that, the dilemma might be pertinent. However, when we look at the questions asked, we cannot help but be frustrated. "Is Joe's failure to act *as bad as* Tom's action?" How would students, confronted with this question, answer it? It requires some sort of calculus to determine quantitatively the relative merits of two reprehensible actions. Presumably the answer would look something like this: From a utilitarian perspective the consequences for the woman are the same. However, Tom is liable to prosecution for homicide whereas it is unlikely that Joe is, and thus it would seem that Tom's action is worse than Joe's because it brings worse consequences. A possible answer from a deontological perspective might be that both actions are equally wrong because they use another person as a means, except that if one distinguishes between killing and letting die, one might say that Joe did not *use* his wife, if using must be an act of commission rather than an omission.

Note what happens. We begin with two obviously immoral acts and then are asked for reasons why one is worse than the other. The reasons are expected to be based on a very general principle, either deontological or consequentialist. The principles quite often conflict, as in cases where good consequences are brought about by immoral means. In that case neither set of reasons is persuasive.

Surely this sort of intellectual rumination is sterile. How, though, did this sort of procedure become so predominant? I suspect that ethicists, under the influence of, or in response to positivism, got locked into a quasi-scientific mode of proceeding, or perhaps more accurately into using an engineering model. If I want to achieve a

557

certain end, I need to perform certain appropriate operations. Given an end, my only problem is to discover acceptable means. Acceptable paths are those which fall within permissible procedures—in ethics the deontological requirements of justice and fairness determine what is acceptable. Thus, we have a goal, find acceptable means, and "Voila!" arrive rigorously at an answer. Unfortunately, deontology does not tell us what to do, only to do it with equity and fairness, while utilitarianism has yet to get clear about what the appropriate ends of man are. However, wouldn't the engineering model work if we could get clear about the ends of man?

If we could find the ends of man and get agreement on them wouldn't my objections lose their force? It is quite fashionable in searching for an end to appeal to a picture or way of life which is held forth as an ideal. In appealing to such an ideal, one attempts to show how one's position on a certain moral issue can be understood in the light of that picture of the ideal life. This sort of appeal is supposed to serve as a justification of one's ethical judgments. We see this in the theory of R. M. Hare when he says, "If pressed to justify a decision completely, we have to give a complete specification of the way of life of which it is a part."[4] Or it can be seen in the theory of P. H. Nowell-Smith, when he says, "Moral philosophy is a practical science; its aim is to answer questions in the form, 'What shall I do?'" But no general answer can be given to this type of question. The most a moral philosopher can do is to paint a picture of various types of life in the manner of Plato and ask which type of life you really want to lead."[5]

It would make the task of this paper quite easy if I were to settle for either of these approaches and say, "Yes. Quite right. Except literature, or fiction if you prefer, is much better at painting pictures than philosophy. Thus, rather than depending on philosophers, let us go to novels and plays and perhaps biographies where we get presentations of specific lives and choose the ones that appeal to us." But there is something amiss. Hare speaks of deciding on a type of life that is completely specified. Who makes choices in that way?

---

[4]R. M. Hare, The Language of Morals (Cambridge, MA: Oxford University Press, 1960), p. 79.

[5]P. H. Nowell-Smith, *Ethics*, (Middlesex: Penguin Books Ltd., 1954), p. 319.

That is simply not what we do.[6] Nowell-Smith speaks of asking what type of life we want, but that is probably not what we do either.[7] Hare and Nowell-Smith attack the problem from the engineer's model. Give me a picture of your goal, (chosen with Hare, and wanted with Nowell-Smith) and then we will figure out what needs to be done to get there. Hare and Nowell-Smith are not the only people who approach ethics in this way. It is a common way of proceeding in ethics. Generally, though, the goal was given the name "Happiness." Suppose, however, we raise some seemingly outrageous questions. Is happiness really the ultimate end of life? Or, if there is an ultimate end, is it the kind philosophers look for?

Happiness is quite often construed as some goal to be pursued or some state to be accomplished as in, "the pursuit of happiness." Often, too, it is thought to be reducible to pleasure or at least the avoidance of pain. It is seen as the goal, the *terminus ad quem* of life. This, however, is precisely the engineering view of life we discussed above.

However, happiness, thus construed, rarely serves as a real goal in life, except according to the anemic views of our engineering friends, the utilitarians. Aristotle's view of happiness, although quite vague and empty in terms of content, seems correct to the extent that he asserts that it is not an end in the sense of a product or a *terminus ad quem* of an activity. Rather it is something that accompanies activity.

---

[6] I am well aware of the dogmatic appearance of this remark. However, even though the point of this section is critical, I am more concerned with presenting an alternative view to this type of approach which Hare and Nowell-Smith offer, than with getting bogged down in what would be important, but nonetheless tedious refutations of their approach. If I would develop an argument, though, it would be to the effect that Hare forgets that human beings make decisions in an historical environmental context and that they have been conditioned by that environment. This results in our having habits and dispositions which partly constitute what we are and limit what we decide upon. We simply do not stand back from our context and make decisions without factors influencing us. A hint of such an argument can be found on pp. 7–9.

[7] As with the claim against Hare, I will not interrupt the presentation of the main point of the paper to develop a sustained argument against Nowell-Smith. However, he ought to recognize that we do not always know what we want and that occurs because our imagination is needed to intend new goals. Sartre makes an argument to this effect in his defense of freedom in *Being and Nothingness*. Note that literature, by giving us imaginative views of new possibilities of living can furnish many new options. It seems it was this sort of thing that Oscar Wilde had in mind when he asserted that "Nature imitates Art."

Anyone who has been disappointed when he has gone out for a good time ought to recognize that one does not seem to be able to "pursue" happiness successfully. This is the hedonistic paradox: those who strive for happiness rarely achieve it, whereas those who pursue other things might find it. Happiness accompanies a life process, but it is not the goal of life in the engineering sense of a goal.

If, however, life is not to be construed as the pursuit of a predetermined goal, how is it to be construed? R. G. Collingwood[8] in writing on art makes a distinction between art and craft that may be helpful. A craft for him is an enterprise where we have a clear goal in mind and where specific steps can be taken to achieve that goal. Collingwood's notion of a craftsman parallels our notion of an engineer. But art is not craft. The true artist does not know his end: he discovers it as he works it out. He works it out through the expressing of his emotions. I would like to suggest that human life is also the working out of our emotions or passions, without a clear notion of where the end is. Thus if ethics or morality concerns itself with the art of living it should do this viewing life as art in Collingwood's sense and not in the sense of art as a craft.

But let us see if the living out of life is really like the working out of an artpiece as Collingwood describes it. When a painter puts a line on the canvas he thereby limits the next line. It can be an indefinite number of lines, but it cannot be just any old line and be appropriate. When an author sketches his character, the character can develop in any number of ways but not just willy-nilly. By page two of *Catcher in the Rye* there are things that Salinger can do with Holden Caulfield, but there are also things he cannot do. To complete the work he must be creative, but creative within the limits set by the opening lines. Just as Salinger creates Caulfield without fully forseeing possible outcomes, we create our lives without fully forseeing possible outcomes. In sum, we do not know where we will end up, but a large part of the working out will depend on where we are. We need to creatively respond to where we are to make our life a finished whole.

There is a contemporary song, "The Gambler," which can also be seen as analogous to human life. One of the verses runs, "No hand's a winner and no hand's a loser" while another runs, "You never count

---

[8]Robin G. Collingwood, *Principles of Art* (London: Oxford University Press, 1938), esp. pp. 128–135.

your money while you're sittin at the table. There'll be plenty time for countin, when the dealin's done." In the game of life, the cards one is dealt and the attitudes one has dictate' what one does to be successful. One can fold with bad cards, or one can bluff. One can lose with good cards or see it through and perhaps win. It depends on what one does with what one gets, and yet there are no guarantees. The point is that in most people's lived existence, the best laid plans go astray. Thus, to view the living of a human life as analogous to the process of an engineer building a bridge or a craftsman making a product is to misconstrue what is involved.

Very well, then, what is involved? To get at that I would like to turn to Camus' treatment of a classical literary figure, Sisyphus. Let us examine the closing lines of Camus' *Myth of Sisyphus*.

> I leave Sisyphus at the foot of the mountain! One always finds one's burden again. But Sisyphus teaches the higher fidelity that negates the gods and raises rocks. He too concludes that *all is well*. This universe henceforth without a master seems to him neither sterile nor futile. Each atom of that stone, each mineral flake of that night filled mountain, in itself form a world. The struggle itself toward the heights is enough to fill a man's heart. One must imagine Sisyphus happy.[9]

Incredible as it sounds, Camus suggests that Sisyphus is happy. This however is in no way the happiness associated with pleasure, but rather a happiness coming from a life that is full. Note that Camus asserts, "The struggle . . . is enough to *fill* a man's heart." Obviously, if we wish to call Sisyphus "happy" in Camus' sense we need to revise our meaning of the concept, since it does not accord with our common understanding of happiness. But let us leave that and recognize that what Camus is doing is approving of Sisyphus because he has made his life *full*. Could we not say that in the midst of a meaningless existence Sisyphus has carved out a meaningful life?

Note further that Sisyphus does not choose his life. His lot is given. "One always finds one's burden again." Further Sisyphus does not get what he wants. He, like the gambler, makes the best of what he gets. Nowell-Smith's "wants" and Hare's "choice" are wrong because life does not proceed the way they imagine. Their

---

[9]Albert Camus, *The Myth of Sisyphus*, translated by Justin O'Brien (New York: Alfred A. Knopf, Inc., 1955).

quasi-scientific engineering model has lead them astray, and to the extent that happiness is construed as an end to be pursued it can serve as a goal for only the most shallow kinds of lives.

But if the craft—engineering model won't do, what will? The clue to this can be found in Sisyphus. Making one's life full seems to be the answer. But if we look at what makes Sisyphus' life full, it seems to be his determination and disposition, those things I would wish to include under the rubric of the passions.

If then the meaningful life is the passionate life, where do we go to find out about it? The best portraits of human passion are found in literature. They are not found in Ethics and some would argue that they are not found in Psychology either. Be that as it may, literature is surely a primary source. Let us claim then that passions are a necessary condition for a full human life, and turn to a piece of literature which not only shows this, but simultaneously depicts the struggle of a person with her passions. I have in mind Amy Lowell's *Patterns*. What this poem teaches us or at least shows us is that we are not automata hooked up to a conveyor belt leading us down the road to happiness. We are individuals in a situation with our passions and we must try to make the best of it. Recall the closing lines.

> In Summer and in Winter I shall walk
> Up and down
> The patterned garden paths
> In my stiff, brocaded gown.
> The Squills and daffodils
> Will give place to pillared roses, and to asters, and to snow.
> I shall go
> Up and down,
> In my gown.
> Gorgeously arrayed,
> Boned and stayed.
> And the softness of my body will be guarded from embrace
> By each button, hook, and lace.
> For the man who should loose me is dead,
> Fighting with the Duke in Flanders,
> In a pattern called a war.
> Christ! What are patterns for?[10]

---

[10]Amy Lowell, *Patterns*, as found in *Best Loved Poems of all Time* (Hallmark, 1971), p. 27.

This is a picture of life, but it is not full. It is empty because it has lost its passion. Lowell's heroine does not stand back objectively and put forth models of the good life. One cannot do that with her own life. She is in the middle of it. Her wants and her passions are removed. What is to be done? The answer is fairly clear . . . new passions must develop. Patterns, rules if you will, are not enough. Could we not also suggest that empty moral rules are also not enough? We learn two things from Lowell. Patterns are not enough to live life. We need to be passionate. No one deeply in love ever asks whether life has meaning. No one passionately engaged in a task asks the question either.

But will just any passions do? Passions may be a necessary condition for a full life, but are they sufficient? Is not something else necessary?

To examine that question I wish to cite some lines from Othello. Note his final speech:

> Soft you; a word or two before you go.
> I have done the state some service, and they know't.
> No more of that. I pray you, in your letters,
> When you shall these unlucky deeds relate,
> Speak of me as I am; nothing extenuate,
> Nor set down aught in malice: then must you speak
> Of one that loved not wisely but too well;
> Of one not easily jealous, but being wrought
> Perplex'd in the extreme; of one whose hand,
> Like the base Indian, threw a pearl away
> Richer than all his tribe; one of whose subdued eyes
> Albeit unused to the melting mood,
> Drops tears as fast as the Arabian trees
> Their medicinal gum. Set you down this;
> And say besides, that in Aleppo once,
> Where a malignant and a turban'd Turk
> Beat a Venetian and traduced the state,
> I took by the throat the circumcised dog,
> And smote him, thus. (Stabs himself.)[11]

Here is without doubt a man living out his passions. Here is a life certainly not seeking happiness. But it is a tragic life. Consequently

---

[11]*Othello*, Act V, scene 2.

it is apparent that passions, though they make life full do not necessarily make for the best life. The passions must be evaluated.

But the evaluation of passions is by no means impossible. Certain passions are appropriate, others not. For example, there are times my anger is inappropriate. There are passions that are destructive. Lowell's heroine's life is empty. We see that. Othello's life is tragic. Why? Because jealousy is a destructive passion, just as is hate. One could even argue that Sisyphus' obstinancy is not the best of passions. Even though it gets him through his burdens it does not allow a life to flower as it might.

We make value judgments about passions easily. Lowell's heroine *needs* a new passion to make her life full. Othello on the other hand does not need more passion; he needs better ones. In some situations passion itself is required and in others some passion *should* have been checked.

The surprising thing is that literature seems to have the ability to show the deficiencies and strengths of the passions. I am not sure I can solve the epistemological question of how this is possible, but it does seem to be a fact. One thought comes to mind though as worth pursuing. If living human life is like doing art in Collingwood's sense, and if there are ways of evaluating art, perhaps we can find some clues for evaluating life in aesthetics. This is not a new suggestion. It was made by Wittgenstein when he said that ethical reasons may well be like aesthetic reasons. Unfortunately, we are not able to develop this theme at this time, not so much for lack of space as for lack of knowing how. Consequently, I leave that as a topic to be pursued at a later time and make some final comments about what I have tried to show.

First, if ethics is irrelevant it is irrelevant because it misconstrues what life is really like, and its procedures for determining what to do fail to take into account the psychology of the passions and the passions' role in making life meaningful. To the extent that literature portrays, imitates or represents human life it shows us that most lives are problematic and, rather than being lives in pursuit of happiness, they are attempts to live out life, perhaps with a hope that we can eke out a bit of happiness along the way, but more importantly in a meaningful way. And, literature shows clearly that the meaning most often comes from the passions.

It should be noted that the encounter with literature can have other benefits. Literature, in allowing us to identify with others, allows us

564

to develop empathy, a requisite for developing our ability to care. It also *shows* us ways of coping *with certain problems* and perhaps even *shows* the shortcomings and flaws of certain lives. All of these contributions are important. Still, the main point of this paper was to claim that literature is relevant to moral considerations because it deals with human beings' inner lives as they are, even if the characters are fictional, whereas ethics deals mainly with rules and maxims that seem so formal that they hardly touch human lives.

If this is so, it is clear that a task needs to be done by ethicists or at least philosophers. We need to begin[12] to deal with the psychology of the passions. Literature, to the extent that it portrays them faithfully, can teach us a great deal about them. Next we need to begin to evaluate them in terms of their potential for making a life good or bad. Literature again provides models. If we do this, we might begin to give our ethical considerations a content they desperately need, and talk about good men in a way that has force.

Let me conclude with a short comment on a few lines written by Stephen King: "If we say that morality proceeds simply from a good heart—which has little to do with ridiculous posturings and happily-ever-afterings—and immorality proceeds from a lack of care, from shoddy observation . . . we may realize we have arrived at a critical stance, one both workable and humane. Fiction is the truth inside the lie."[13]

If morality has to do with the heart, the passionate side of man and immorality with a lack of care, then is it not obvious that we ethicists need to investigate these areas with much more concern? And is it not also obvious that one of the best places to start to understand and experience the passionate human being is in literature?

**STUDY QUESTIONS**

1. What in particular does Duska find wrong with a mainstream theory such as Utilitarianism? Compare Duska's criticism of Utilitarianism with Bernard Williams' critique (see Chapter Two).

---

[12]"Begin" may not be the correct word. As I have indicated Robert Solomon has begun the type of enterprise I have in mind. What we need to do is expand on such work.

[13]Stephen King, "Notes on Horror," *Quest*, June 1981, vol. 5, no. 5, p. 31.

2.  What view of happiness does Duska endorse? How is his con-
    ception of happiness related to the proposition that the meaning-
    ful life is the passionate life?
3.  Duska finds contemporary morality wanting because it ignores
    the passions. MacIntyre finds it wanting because it ignores tra-
    ditions, roles, and historical context. Are they both right? Are
    these critiques of contemporary morality complementary? Or
    would each critic say that the others' views totally miss the point
    of what is wrong with current ethics? What is your own view of
    these two perspectives?
4.  What are the implications of Duska's views for the teaching of
    ethics? Is morality better taught in classes on literature than in
    classes on moral philosophy? How would you devise a curricu-
    lum of moral education that reflected Duska's insights?

# The Closing of the American Mind

### ALLAN BLOOM

Allan Bloom (b. 1930) is a professor on the faculty of the
Committee of Social Thought at the University of Chicago. He is the translator and editor of Plato's *Republic*
and Rousseau's *Emile,* and the author of *Shakespeare's Politics* and *The Closing of the American Mind.*

Allan Bloom is highly critical of the turn taken by American higher education. According to Bloom, the contemporary student enters college equipped with the dogma
that truth is culturally relative. The dogma gives primacy
to tolerance and openness as the most important moral
virtue. The student believes that any claim to absolute

THE CLOSING OF THE AMERICAN MIND From *The Closing of the American Mind* by Allan Bloom (New
York: Simon & Schuster, 1987). Copyright © 1987 by Allan Bloom. Reprinted by permission of
the publisher.

truth can lead to intolerance. Bloom says that this view rejects and undercuts the old ideal that postulated a set of universal truths and inalienable rights for all, regardless of culture. According to the old doctrine, all people have certain rights. According to the new doctrine, this is a Western value judgment that does not have the status of a fact. The fact-value distinction (along with relativism) belongs to the popular philosophy that Bloom inveighs against. Bloom observes that history and the social sciences are deployed to further the new passion for tolerance and relativism. The indiscriminate openness to other cultures goes hand in hand with a growing contempt for our own. We go to the "bazaar of cultures" and find our own wanting. Teachers of openness often are "actively hostile to the Declaration of Independence and the Constitution."

Bloom argues that the new openness and relativism result in a drab conformism. Having no faith in the objective search for a universal good, we drearily create all the lifestyles we want but without any belief in them as truly valuable. Nor is there hope that there are great or wise human beings anywhere who can reveal the truth about life. "Thus what is advertised as a great opening is a great closing."

The ideal is to get along. No one has the truth. No culture is morally superior. "Why fight?" Yet Bloom points out that other cultures do believe in their own superiority and will fight for them. Such ethnocentrism is almost universal, and can be countered only by a belief in universal reason and in natural inalienable rights for all. "Openness used to be the virtue that permitted us to seek the good by using reason. It now means accepting everything."


There is one thing a professor can be absolutely certain of: almost every student entering the university believes, or says he believes, that truth is relative. If this belief is put to the test, one can count on the students' reaction: they will be uncomprehending. That anyone should regard the proposition as not self-evident astonishes them, as though he were calling into question 2 + 2 = 4. These are things you don't think about. The students' backgrounds are as various as America can provide. Some are religious, some atheists; some are to the Left, some to the Right; some intend to be scientists, some humanists or professionals or businessmen; some are poor, some rich. They are unified only in their relativism and in their allegiance to equality. And the two are related in a moral intention. The relativity of truth is not a theoretical insight but a moral postulate, the condition of a free society, or so they see it. They have all been equipped with this framework early on, and it is the modern replacement for the inalienable natural rights that used to be the traditional American grounds for a free society. That it is a moral issue for students is revealed by the character of their response when challenged—a combination of disbelief and indignation: "Are you an absolutist?," the only alternative they know, uttered in the same tone as "Are you a monarchist?" or "Do you really believe in witches?" This latter leads into the indignation, for someone who believes in witches might well be a witchhunter or a Salem judge. The danger they have been taught to fear from absolutism is not error but intolerance. Relativism is necessary to openness; and this is the virtue, the only virtue, which all primary education for more than fifty years has dedicated itself to inculcating. Openness—and the relativism that makes it the only plausible stance in the face of various claims to truth and various ways of life and kinds of human beings—is the great insight of our times. The true believer is the real danger. The study of history and of culture teaches that all the world was mad in the past; men always thought they were right, and that led to wars, persecutions, slavery, xenophobia, racism, and chauvinism. The point is not to correct the mistakes and really be right; rather it is not to think you are right at all.

The students, of course, cannot defend their opinion. It is something with which they have been indoctrinated. The best they can do is point out all the opinions and cultures there are and have been. What right, they ask, do I or anyone else have to say one is better than the others? If I pose the routine questions designed to confute them and make them think, such as, "If you had been a British administrator in India, would you have let the natives under your governance burn the widow at the funeral of a man who had died?," they either remain silent or reply that the British should never have been there in the first place. It is not that they know very much about other nations, or about their own. The purpose of their education is not to make them scholars but to provide them with a moral virtue— openness. . . .

The old view was that, by recognizing and accepting man's natural rights, men found a fundamental basis of unity and sameness. Class, race, religion, national origin or culture all disappear or become dim when bathed in the light of natural rights, which give men common interests and make them truly brothers. The immigrant had to put behind him the claims of the Old World in favor of a new and easily acquired education. This did not necessarily mean abandoning old daily habits or religions, but it did mean subordinating them to new principles. There was a tendency, if not a necessity, to homogenize nature itself.

The recent education of openness has rejected all that. It pays no attention to natural rights or the historical origins of our regime, which are now thought to have been essentially flawed and regressive. It is progressive and forward-looking. It does not demand fundamental agreement or the abandonment of old or new beliefs in favor of the natural ones. It is open to all kinds of men, all kinds of life-styles, all ideologies. There is no enemy other than the man who is not open to everything. . . .

Liberalism . . . the kind that we knew from John Stuart Mill and John Dewey, taught us that the only danger confronting us is being closed to the emergent, the new, the manifestations of progress. No attention had to be paid to the fundamental principles or the moral virtues that inclined men to live according to them. To use language now popular, civic culture was neglected. And this turn in liberalism is what prepared us for cultural relativism and the fact-value distinction, which seemed to carry that viewpoint further and give it greater intellectual weight.

History and social science are used in a variety of ways to overcome prejudice. We should not be ethnocentric, a term drawn from anthropology, which tells us more about the meaning of openness. We should not think our way is better than others. The intention is not so much to teach the students about other times and places as to make them aware of the fact that their preferences are only that— accidents of their time and place. Their beliefs do not entitle them as individuals, or collectively as a nation, to think they are superior to anyone else. John Rawls is almost a parody of this tendency, writing hundreds of pages to persuade men, and proposing a scheme of government that would force them, not to despise anyone. In *A Theory of Justice,* he writes that the physicist or the poet should not look down on the man who spends his life counting blades of grass or performing any other frivolous or corrupt activity. Indeed, he should be esteemed, since esteem from others, as opposed to self-esteem, is a basic need of all men. So indiscriminateness is a moral imperative because its opposite is discrimination. . . .

Sexual adventurers like Margaret Mead and others who found America too narrow told us that not only must we know other cultures and learn to respect them, but we could also profit from them. We could follow their lead and loosen up, liberating ourselves from the opinion that our taboos are anything other than social constraints. We could go to the bazaar of cultures and find reinforcement for inclinations that are repressed by puritanical guilt feelings. All such teachers of openness had either no interest in or were actively hostile to the Declaration of Independence and the Constitution.

The civil rights movement provides a good example of this change in thought. In its early days almost all the significant leaders, in spite of tactical and temperamental differences, relied on the Declaration of Independence and the Constitution. They could charge whites not only with the most monstrous injustices but also with contradicting their own most sacred principles. The blacks were the true Americans in demanding the equality that belongs to them as human beings by natural and political right. This stance implied a firm conviction of the truth of the principles of natural right and of their fundamental efficacy within the Constitutional tradition, which, although tarnished, tends in the long run toward fulfilling those principles. They therefore worked through Congress, the Presidency, and, above all, the Judiciary. By contrast, the Black Power movement that supplanted the older civil rights movement—leaving aside both its excesses and its very understandable emphasis on self-respect and refusal to beg for acceptance—had at its core the view that the Constitutional tradition was always corrupt and was constructed as a defense of slavery. Its demand was for black identity, not universal rights. Not rights but power counted. It insisted on respect for blacks as blacks, not as human beings simply.

Yet the Constitution does not promise respect for blacks, whites, yellows, Catholics, Protestants, or Jews. It guarantees the protection of the rights of individual human beings. This has not proved to be enough, however, to what is perhaps by now a majority of Americans.

The upshot of all this for the education of young Americans is that they know much less about American history and those who were held to be its heroes. This was one of the few things that they used to come to college with that had something to do with their lives. Nothing has taken its place except a smattering of facts learned about other nations or cultures and a few social science formulas. None of this means much, partly because little attention has been paid to what is required in order truly to convey the spirit of other places and other times to young people, or for that matter to anyone, partly because the students see no relevance in any of it to the lives they are going to lead or to their prevailing passions. It is the rarest of occurrences to find a youngster who has been infused by this education with a longing to know all about China or the Romans or the Jews.

All to the contrary. There is an indifference to such things, for relativism has extinguished the real motive of education, the search for a good life. Young Amnericans have less and less knowledge of and interest in foreign places. In the past there were many students who actually knew something about and loved England, France, Germany, or Italy, for they dreamed of living there or thought their lives would be made more interesting by assimilating their languages and literatures. Such students have almost disappeared, replaced at most by students who are interested in the political problems of Third World countries and in helping them to modernize, with due respect to their old cultures, of course. This is not learning from others but condescension and a disguised form of a new imperialism. It is the Peace Corps mentality, which is not a spur to learning but to a secularized version of doing good works.

Actually openness results in American conformism—out there in the rest of the world is a drab diversity that teaches only that values are relative, whereas here we can create all the life-styles we want. Our openness means we do not need others. Thus what is advertised as a great opening is a great closing. No longer is there a hope that there are great wise men in other places and times who can reveal the truth about life—except for the few remaining young people who look for a quick fix from a guru. Gone is the real historical sense of a Machiavelli who wrested a few hours from each busy day in which "to don regal and courtly garments, enter the courts of the ancients and speak with them."

None of this concerns those who promote the new curriculum. The point is to propagandize acceptance of different ways, and indifference to their real content is as good a means as any. It was not necessarily the best of times in America when Catholics and Protestants were suspicious of and hated one another; but at least they were taking their beliefs seriously, and the more or less satisfactory accommodations they worked out were not simply the result of apathy about the state of their souls. Practically all that young Americans have today is an insubstantial awareness that there are many cultures, accompanied by a saccharine moral drawn from that awareness: We should all get along. Why fight? . . .

One of the techniques of opening young people up is to require a college course in a non-Western culture. Although many of the persons teaching such courses are real scholars and lovers of the areas they study, in every case I have seen this requirement—when there are so many other things that can and should be learned but are not required, when philosophy and religion are no longer required—has a demagogic intention. The point is to force students to recognize that there are other ways of thinking and that Western ways are not better. It is again not the content that counts but the lesson to be drawn. Such requirements are part of the effort to establish a world community and train its member—the person devoid of prejudice. But if the students were really to learn something of the minds of any of these non-Western cultures—which they do not—they would find that each and every one of these cultures is ethnocentric. All of them think their way is the best way, and all others are inferior. Herodotus tells us that the Persians thought that they were the best, that those nations bordering on them were next best, that those nations bordering on the nations bordering on them were third best, and so on, their worth declining as the concentric circles were farther from the Persian center. This is the very definition of ethnocentrism. Something like this is as ubiquitous as the prohibition against incest between mother and son.

Only in the Western nations, i.e., those influenced by Greek philosophy, is there some willingness to doubt the identification of the good with one's own way. One should conclude from the study of non-Western cultures that not only to prefer one's own way but to believe it best, superior to all others, is primary and even natural— exactly the opposite of what is intended by requiring students to study these cultures. What we are really doing is applying a Western prejudice—which we covertly take to indicate the superiority of our culture—and deforming the evidence of those other cultures to attest to its validity. The scientific study of other cultures is almost exclusively a Western phenomenon, and in its origin was obviously connected with the search for new and better ways, or at least for validation of the hope that our own culture really is the better way, a validation for which there is no felt need in other cultures. If we are to learn from those cultures, we must wonder whether such scientific study is a good idea. Consistency would seem to require professors of openness to respect the ethnocentrism or closedness they find everywhere else. However, in attacking ethnocentrism, what they actually do is to assert unawares the superiority of their scientific understanding and the inferiority of the other cultures which do not recognize it at the same time they reject all such claims to superiority. They both affirm and deny the goodness of their science. They face a problem akin to that faced by Pascal in the conflict between reason and revelation, without the intellectual intransigence that forced him to abandon science in favor of faith.

The reason for the non-Western closedness, or ethnocentrism, is clear. Men must love and be loyal to their families and their peoples in order to preserve them. Only if they think their own things are good can they rest content with them. A father must prefer his child to other children, a citizen his country to others. That is why there are myths—to justify these attachments. And a man needs a place and opinions by which to orient himself. This is strongly asserted by those who talk about the importance of roots. The problem of getting along with outsiders is secondary to, and sometimes in conflict with, having an inside, a people, a culture, a way of life. A very great narrowness is not incompatible with the health of an individual or a people, whereas with great openness it is hard to avoid decomposition. The firm binding of the good with one's own, the refusal to see a distinction between the two, a vision of the cosmos that has a special place for one's people, seem to be conditions of culture. This is what really follows from the study of non-Western cultures proposed for undergraduates. It points them back to passionate attachment to their own and away from the science which liberates them from it. Science now appears as a threat to culture and a dangerous uprooting charm. In short, they are lost in a no-man's-land between the goodness of knowing and the goodness of culture, where they have been placed by their teachers who no longer have the resources to guide them. Help must be sought elsewhere.

Greek philosophers were the first men we know to address the problem of ethnocentrism. Distinctions between the good and one's own, between nature and convention, between the just and the legal are the signs of this movement of thought. They related the good to the fulfillment of the whole natural human potential and were aware that few, if any, of the nations of men had ways that allowed such fulfillment. They were open to the good. They had to use the good, which was not their own, to judge their own. This was a dangerous business because it tended to weaken wholehearted attachment to their own, hence to weaken their peoples as well as to expose themselves to the anger of family, friends, and countrymen. Loyalty versus quest for the good introduced an unresolvable tension into life. But the awareness of the good as such and the desire to possess it are priceless humanizing acquisitions.

This is the sound motive contained, along with many other less sound ones, in openness as we understand it. Men cannot remain content with what is given them by their culture if they are to be fully human. This is what Plato meant to show by the image of the cave in the *Republic* and by representing us as prisoners in it. A culture is a cave. He did not suggest going around to other cultures as a solution to the limitations of the cave. Nature should be the standard by which we judge our own lives and the lives of peoples. That is why philosophy, not history or anthropology, is the most important human science. Only dogmatic assurance that thought is culture-bound, that there is no nature, is what makes our educators so certain that the only way to escape the limitations of our time and place is to study other cultures. History and anthropology were understood by the Greeks to be useful only in discovering what the past and other peoples had to contribute to the discovery of nature. Historians and anthropologists were to put peoples and their conventions to the test, as Socrates did individuals, and go beyond them.

These scientists were superior to their subjects because they saw a problem where others refused to see one, and they were engaged in the quest to solve it. They wanted to be able to evaluate themselves and others.

This point of view, particularly the need to know nature in order to have a standard, is uncomfortably buried beneath our human sciences, whether they like it or not, and accounts for the ambiguities and contradictions I have been pointing out. They want to make us culture-beings with the instruments that were invented to liberate us from culture. Openness used to be the virtue that permitted us to seek the good by using reason. It now means accepting everything and denying reason's power. The unrestrained and thoughtless pursuit of openness, without recognizing the inherent political, social, or cultural problem of openness as the goal of nature, has rendered openness meaningless. Cultural relativism destroys both one's own and the good. What is most characteristic of the West is science, particularly understood as the quest to know nature and the consequent denigration of convention—i.e., culture or the West understood as a culture—in favor of what is accessible to all men as men through their common and distinctive faculty, reason. Science's latest attempts to grasp the human situation—cultural relativism, historicism, the fact-value distinction—are the suicide of science. Culture, hence closedness, reigns supreme. Openness to closedness is what we teach. . . .

It was always known that there were many and conflicting opinions about the good, and nations embodying each of them. Herodotus was at least as aware as we are of the rich diversity of cultures. But he took that observation to be an invitation to investigate all of them to see what was good and bad about each and find out what he could learn about good and bad from them. Modern relativists take that same observation as proof that such investigation is impossible and that we must be respectful of them all. Thus students, and the rest of us, are deprived of the primary excitement derived from the discovery of diversity, the impulse of Odysseus, who, according to Dante, traveled the world to see the virtues and vices of men. History and anthropology cannot provide the answers, but they can provide the material on which judgment can work.

I know that men are likely to bring what are only their prejudices to the judgment of alien peoples. Avoiding that is one of the main purposes of education. But trying to prevent it by removing the authority of men's reason is to render ineffective the instrument that can correct their prejudices. True openness is the accompaniment of the desire to know, hence of the awareness of ignorance. To deny the possibility of knowing good and bad is to suppress true oppenness. . . .

Error is indeed our enemy, but it alone points to the truth and therefore deserves our respectful treatment. The mind that has no prejudices at the outset is empty. It can only have been constituted by a method that is unaware of how difficult it is to recognize that a prejudice is a prejudice. Only Socrates knew, after a lifetime of unceasing labor, that he was ignorant. Now every high-school student knows that. How did it become so easy? What accounts for our amazing progress? Could it be that our experience has been so impoverished by our various methods, of which oppenness is only the latest, that there is nothing substantial enough left there to resist criticism, and we therefore have no world left of which to be really ignorant? Have we so simplified the soul that it is no longer difficult to explain? To an eye of dogmatic skepticism, nature herself, in all her lush profusion of expressions, might appear to be a prejudice. In her place we put a gray network of critical concepts, which were invented to interpret nature's phenomena but which strangled them and therewith destroyed their own *raison d'être*. Perhaps it is our first task to resuscitate those phenomena so that we may again have a world to which we can put our questions and be able to philosophize. This seems to me to be our educational challenge.

**STUDY QUESTIONS**

1. Explain what Bloom means when he says that to deny the possibility of knowing good and bad is to suppress true openness.
2. According to Bloom, recent education tends to reject natural rights. How?
3. Bloom points out that most cultures are ethnocentric. What conclusion does Bloom draw from this?
4. Bloom blames the popularity of ethical relativism and the fact–value distinction for much of what is wrong about current education. What harm does Bloom see in these doctrines? Do you agree that their popularity is pernicious?

5.  What are the most significant differences between the older style of education favored by Bloom and the newer style that he is criticizing? If you agree that something is badly awry with contemporary education, what do you think should be done? Can one return to the old teaching of the "eternal verities"?

6.  The American Anthropological Association criticized the U.N. Universal Declaration of Human Rights for being "ethnocentric," saying that "Respect for differences between cultures is validated by the scientific fact that no technique of qualitatively evaluating cultures has been discovered." Bloom criticizes this point of view, saying that it undermines the concept of inalienable rights. Bloom and the A.A.A. are diametrically opposed on this issue. Critically examine both positions and state your own conclusions.

# *Where Have All the Good Deeds Gone?*

CHRISTINA SOMMERS

Christina Sommers (b. 1950) teaches philosophy at Clark University in Worcester, Massachusetts. She has written a number of articles on moral philosophy and is Director of the New England Society for Philosophy and Public Affairs.

Sommers contends that social morality is replacing private moral initiative: The modern individual delegates too much moral responsibility to institutions. The literature of the applied ethics movement reflects this change from concern with private morality to concern with public policy by emphasizing public policy issues, such

WHERE HAVE ALL THE GOOD DEEDS GONE? From *Hastings Center Report*, August 1982. © Institute of Society, Ethics and the Life Sciences, 360 Broadway, Hastings-on-Hudson, NY 10706.

as capital punishment and recombinant DNA research,
and neglecting normative ethics in the private sphere.
Sommers maintains that social solutions are not sufficient. We badly need the individual "moral amateur."

Miller House is an old-age home in a well-to-do Boston suburb. As
in many other homes for the elderly, conditions are grim. No matter
how cold it is outside, old men sit downcast on the front porch.
Sometimes one of them wanders over to a nearby fast-food restaurant
where he will sit alone at a table for hours. One resident, Mr. Kelly,
recently slipped out the front door and did not stop walking for three
days. The police picked him up forty miles away, dazed from lack
of sleep and still clutching his cardboard suitcase, and brought
him back.

Mr. Richards, age eighty-four, sleeps more than twenty hours a
day, waking only for meals and cigarette breaks. He hates Miller
House. "I don't like fish cakes," he says. "We have them all the time
and the director makes me eat them."

For the past seven years Miss Pickins, who is ninety-one, has lived
in Miller House. Last year her doctor ordered her to stop smoking.
This upset a daily routine she had enjoyed—coffee and cigarettes in
the lounge downstairs with the men. She became depressed, lost
interest in leaving her room, and now spends most of her time there
alone. The woman who runs the home makes Miss Pickins keep the
sound of her radio so low that she cannot hear it. Once she did not
finish her dessert, and as punishment she no longer gets any. These
little injustices keep her in a constant rage.

Simone de Beauvoir has said, "By the fate it allots to its members
who can no longer work, society gives itself away." Who is to blame
for the fate that has been allotted to Miss Pickins, Mr. Kelly, and Mr.
Richards? It is fashionable to condemn civic agencies and the government. But government agencies are responsible for enforcing standards of cleanliness and safety: should we also require that they meet
standards of good-heartedness and neighborliness? What the Miller
residents need is kindly attention: someone to talk to them, to take an
interest in them, and to mitigate the little cruelties that seem always
to tempt those in charge of helpless people. Should the state pay a

social worker twenty dollars to make sure Miss Pickins gets her dessert? A few concerned neighbors could transform the residence into a much happier place. But that is not going to happen.

One reason, no doubt, is that a lot of people are uncaring and irresponsible, but far more important is the attitude of the responsible private individuals who no longer see themselves as the seat of moral initiative. Good deeds have been given over to experts: the acts that constitute the social morality of our time are being performed by paid professionals in large public agencies. Helping the needy, the sick, and the aged has become an operation whose scale and character leave little room for the virtuous private person. Our ancestors in their idiosyncratic charitable endeavors look like moral amateurs.

Professionals who do use volunteers see them as incipient professionals. The assistant manager of the Greater Boston Red Cross observes: "Volunteers are there but you have to offer them something . . . career benefits and resumé experience." The Children's Museum of Boston offers the potential volunteer entries for a curriculum vitae—a volunteer fund raiser is called a "corporate membership marketing specialist"; someone who helps paint walls, a "maintenance assistant." Since professionals look down on amateurs, executives of social institutions feel forced to counter the stigma of amateurism by conferring on the volunteer a quasi-professional status. The loss of confidence in private moral initiative is part of a general derogation of amateurism, a phenomenon that Christopher Lasch has called the "atrophy of competence."

Is it excessive to say that our society has become more morally passive? After all, the past few decades have seen the growth of liberal ideals and their realization in social programs that have benefited great numbers of people. Also, private moral initiative is not sufficient to guarantee a decent life to citizens in a complex society like our own. Without social security, Medicaid, and board of health regulations, the Miller residents would be much worse off.

The political diversion of moral energies, however, has given rise to a new kind of hypocrisy. It is now possible to consider ourselves morally exemplary simply because we adhere to an enlightened set of social principles. We may vote in accordance with these principles, but they require nothing of us personally: we need never lift a finger to help anyone and we need take no active part in social reform movements. We can even permit ourselves to be ruthless in relations with other people. Because morality has been sublimated into ideology, great numbers of people, the young and educated especially, feel they have an adequate moral identity merely because they hold the "right" views on such matters as ecology, feminism, socialism, and nuclear energy. They may lead narrow, self-indulgent lives, obsessed with their physical health, material comforts, and personal growth, yet still feel a moral advantage over those who actively work to help the needy but who are, in their eyes, ideologically unsound.

The problems that arise from the imbalance of private morality and public policy transcend questions of liberal left versus conservative right. Where the left is directly responsible for the false and the unworkable doctrine that ethics is reducible to public policy, the right wishes to dismantle crucial institutions that protect people's rights to a sustainable existence. Conservatives too believe that one may discharge moral duties by holding and advocating "correct" views on public policy (against busing and gun control, for prayers in the school and the death penalty). If the extreme right proves effective, the indigent will have lost such protection as public policy now provides—and this in a society whose members have lost the will and the way to be their brothers' keeper. Moreover, in any number of situations direct action is simply inappropriate (housing for the elderly or disaster relief are prime examples) and the need for concerted social effort and sound public policy is clear. But being right and effective in social ethics is only half of the moral life; and the growing belief that it is more than half should be combated and dispelled. Courses in ethics might be one place to begin.

A glance at a typical anthology of a college course in ethics reveals that most of what the student will read is directed toward analyzing and criticizing policies on such issues as punishment, recombinant DNA research, abortion, and euthanasia. Since the student is not likely to be personally involved in, say, inflicting the death penalty on anyone, the point is to learn how to form responsible opinions. Inevitably the student gets the idea that applying ethics to modern life is mainly a matter of being for or against some social policy. And since many of the articles read like briefs written for a judge or legislator, before long the student loses sight of him- or herself as a moral agent and begins to think like a proto-jurist or legislator.

The net effect of identifying normative ethics with public policy is to justify the moral passivity of the individual. But private benevolence continues to be badly needed in all areas of social concern. The paid functionaires who have virtually excluded the unpaid, well-meaning person are in no position to replace or repair the bonds that have been weakened by the atrophy of private moral initiative. Intellectuals, too, have lost their nerve. Consider the following, from Simone de Beauvoir's *The Coming of Age:*

> Once we have understood what the state of the aged really is, we cannot satisfy ourselves with calling for a more generous "old age policy," higher pensions, decent housing, and organized leisure. It is the whole system that is at issue and our claim cannot be otherwise than radical—change life itself.

Here is the mysterious and ultimately despairing demand of the contemporary social philosopher who has lost sight of the morally concerned citizen. The concrete need is not for revolutionizing society, perhaps not even for reforming it, but for finding a way to reach people like Miss Pickins and the other residents of Miller House.

## STUDY QUESTIONS

1. Sommers assumes that private persons have a moral responsibility to do something about lonely, needy, elderly people in their community. Do you agree?
2. Isn't it excessive to say that our society has become morally passive? After all, in the past few decades we have seen the implementation of enlightened social policies that have helped unprecedented numbers of people. Is Sommers asking us to return to "the good old days" that were not really all that good?
3. What does Sommers mean by the "moral amateur"?
4. Does Sommers exaggerate the shift from private to social morality? Does she exaggerate the need for more private activity?

# The World of Epictetus

## VICE ADMIRAL JAMES BOND STOCKDALE, USN

James Stockdale (b. 1923) spent ten years in Vietnam, two as a combat naval aviator and eight as a prisoner of war (four years in solitary confinement). He received the Congressional Medal of Honor and, since retiring from the Navy as President of the War College, has pursued the scholarly life. Stockdale has ten honorary degrees, and is currently a Senior Fellow at the Hoover Institution on War, Revolution and Peace. His most recent books are *In Love and War* (1984) and *A Vietnam Experience: Ten Years of Reflection* (1985).

James Stockdale was a senior naval wing commander when he was shot down over North Vietnam in 1965. The article tells of the resources Stockdale found in himself in order to survive the ordeal with his sense of self-respect intact. Not all his fellow prisoners were as internally resourceful. Stockdale reports that he owed a great deal to a classical education that gave him an invaluable perspective on his situation. He learned from literature and from the Bible ( *Job* especially) that life is not fair. The *Enchiridion* of Epictetus taught him to concern himself only with what was within his power. As a prisoner he was physically powerless, and had to learn to control and strengthen his will. He learned that integrity was far more valuable than sleep or food if the latter were

THE WORLD OF EPICTETUS By Vice Admiral James Bond Stockdale, USN. Reprinted from the *Atlantic Monthly*, April 1978. By permission of the author.

obtained from his captors at the price of loss of self-respect. He learned that persons of little learning or philosophy were more vulnerable to brainwashing and the weakness that leads to treasonable betrayal of fellow prisoners. As a result, Stockdale recommends training in history and philosophy for professional soldiers. "In stress situations, the fundamental, the hard core classical subjects, are what serve best."

In 1965 I was a forty-one-year-old commander, the senior pilot of Air Wing 16, flying combat missions in the area just south of Hanoi from the aircraft carrier *Oriskany*. By September of that year I had grown quite accustomed to briefing dozens of pilots and leading them on daily air strikes; I had flown nearly 200 missions myself and knew the countryside of North Vietnam like the back of my hand. On the ninth of that month I led about thirty-five airplanes to the Thanh Hoa Bridge, just west of that city. That bridge was tough; we had been bouncing 500-pounders off it for weeks.

The September 9 raid held special meaning for *Oriskany* pilots because of a special bomb load we had improvised; we were going in with our biggest, the 2000-pounders, hung not only on our attack planes but on our F-8 fighter-bombers as well. This increase in bridge-busting capability came from the innovative brain of a major flying with my Marine fighter squadron. He had figured out how we could jury-rig some switches, hang the big bombs, pump out some of the fuel to stay within takeoff weight limits, and then top off our tanks from our airborne refuelers while en route to the target. Although the pilot had to throw several switches in sequence to get rid of his bombs, a procedure requiring above-average cockpit agility, we routinely operated on the premise that all pilots of Air Wing 16 were above average. I test-flew the new load on a mission, thought it over, and approved it; that's the way we did business.

Our spirit was up. That morning, the *Oriskany* Air Wing was finally going to drop the bridge that was becoming a North Vietnamese symbol of resistance. You can imagine our dismay when we crossed the coast and the weather scout I had sent on ahead radioed back that ceiling and visibility were zero-zero in the bridge area. In the tiny cockpit of my A-4 at the front of the pack, I pushed the button on the throttle, spoke into the radio mike in my oxygen mask, and told the formation to split up and proceed in pairs to the secondary targets I had specified in my contingency briefing. What a letdown.

The adrenaline stopped flowing as my wingman and I broke left and down and started sauntering along toward our "milk run" target: boxcars on a railroad siding between Vinh and Thanh Hoa, where the flak was light. Descending through 10,000 feet, I unsnapped my oxygen mask and let it dangle, giving my pinched face a rest—no reason to stay uncomfortable on this run.

As I glided toward that easy target, I'm sure I felt totally self-satisfied. I had the top combat job that a Navy commander can hold and I was in tune with my environment. I was confident—I knew airplanes and flying inside out. I was comfortable with the people I worked with and I knew the trade so well that I often improvised variations in accepted procedures and encouraged others to do so under my watchful eye. I was on top. I thought I had found every key to success and had no doubt that my Academy and test-pilot schooling had provided me with everything I needed in life.

I passed down the middle of those boxcars and smiled as I saw the results of my instinctive timing. A neat pattern—perfection. I was just pulling out of my dive low to the ground when I heard a noise I hadn't expected—the *boom boom boom* of a 57-millimeter gun—and then I saw it just behind my wingtip. I was hit—all the red lights came on, my control system was going out—and I could barely keep that plane from flying into the ground while I got that damned oxygen mask up to my mouth so I could tell my wingman that I was about to eject. What rotten luck. And on a "milk run"!

The descent in the chute was quiet except for occasional rifle shots from the streets below. My mind was clear, and I said to myself, "five years." I knew we were making a mess of the war in Southeast Asia, but I didn't think it would last longer than that; I was also naive about the resources I would need in order to survive a lengthy period of captivity.

The Durants have said that culture is a thin and fragile veneer that superimposes itself on mankind. For the first time I was on my own, without the veneer. I was to spend years searching through and refining my bag of memories, looking for useful tools, things of value. The values were there, but they were all mixed up with technology, bureaucracy, and expediency, and had to be brought up into the open.

Education should take care to illuminate values, not bury them amongst the trivia. Are our students getting the message that without personal integrity intellectual skills are worthless?

Integrity is one of those words which many people keep in that desk drawer labeled "too hard." It's not a topic for the dinner table or the cocktail party. You can't buy or sell it. When supported with education, a person's integrity can give him something to rely on when his perspective seems to blur, when rules and principles seem to waver, and when he's faced with hard choices of right or wrong. It's something to keep him on the right track, something to keep him afloat when he's drowning; if only for practical reasons, it is an attribute that should be kept at the very top of a young person's consciousness.

The importance of the latter point is highlighted in prison camps, where everyday human nature, stripped bare, can be studied under a magnifying glass in accelerated time. Lessons spotlighted and absorbed in that laboratory sharpen one's eye for their abstruse but highly relevant applications in the "real time" world of now.


In the five years since I've been out of prison, I've participated several times in the process of selecting senior naval officers for promotion or important command assignments. I doubt that the experience is significantly different from that of executives who sit on "selection boards" in any large hierarchy. The system must be formal, objective, and fair; if you've seen one, you've probably seen them all. Navy selection board·proceedings go something like this.

The first time you know the identity of the other members of the board is when you walk into a boardroom at eight o'clock on an appointed morning. The first order of business is to stand, raise your right hand, put your left hand on the Bible, and swear to make the best judgment you can, on the basis of merit, without prejudice. You're sworn to confidentiality regarding all board members' remarks during the proceedings. Board members are chosen for their experience and understanding; they often have knowledge of the particular individuals under consideration. They must feel free to speak their minds. They read and grade dozens of dossiers, and each candidate is discussed extensively. At voting time, a member casts his vote by selecting and pushing a "percent confidence" button, visible only to himself, on a console attached to his chair. When the last member pushes his button, a totalizer displays the numerical average "confidence" of the board. No one knows who voted what.

I'm always impressed by the fact that every effort is made to be fair to the candidate. Some are clearly out, some are clearly in; the borderline cases are the tough ones. You go over and over those in the "middle pile" and usually you vote and revote until late at night. In all the boards I've sat on, no inference or statement in a "jacket" is as sure to portend a low confidence score on the vote as evidence of a lack of directness or rectitude of a candidate in his dealings with others. Any hint of moral turpitude really turns people off. When the crunch comes, they prefer to work with forthright plodders rather than with devious geniuses. I don't believe that this preference is unique to the military. In any hierarchy where people's fates are decided by committees or boards, those who lose credibility with their peers and who cause their superiors to doubt their directness, honesty, or integrity are dead. Recovery isn't possible.

The linkage of men's ethics, reputations, and fates can be studied in even more vivid detail in prison camp. In that brutally controlled environment a perceptive enemy can get his hooks into the slightest chink in a man's ethical armor and accelerate his downfall. Given the right opening, the right moral weakness, a certain susceptibility on the part of the prisoner, a clever extortionist can drive his victim into a downhill slide that will ruin his image, self-respect, and life in a very short time.

There are some uncharted aspects to this, some traits of susceptibility which I don't think psychologists yet have words for. I am thinking of the tragedy that can befall a person who has such a need for love or attention that he will sell his soul for it. I use tragedy with the rigorous definition Aristotle applied to it: the story of a good man with a flaw who comes to an unjustified bad end. This is a rather delicate point and one that I want to emphasize. We had very very few collaborators in prison, and comparatively few Aristotelian tragedies, but the story and fate of one of these good men with a flaw might be instructive.

He was handsome, smart, articulate, and smooth. He was almost sincere. He was obsessed with success. When the going got tough, he decided expediency was preferable to principle.

This man was a classical opportunist. He befriended and worked for the enemy to the detriment of his fellow Americans. He made a tacit deal; moreover, he accepted favors (a violation of the code of conduct). In time, out of fear and shame, he withdrew; we could not get him to communicate with the American prisoner organization.

I couldn't learn what made the man tick. One of my best friends in prison, one of the wisest persons I have ever known, had once been in a squadron with this fellow. In prisoners' code I tapped a question to my philosophical friend: "What in the world is going on with that fink?"

"You're going to be surprised at what I have to say," he meticulously tapped back. "In a squadron he pushes himself forward and dominates the scene. He's a continual fountain of information. He's the person everybody relies on for inside dope. He works like mad; often flies more hops than others. It drives him crazy if he's not liked. He tends to grovel and ingratiate himself before others. I didn't realize he was really pathetic until I was sitting around with him and his wife one night when he was spinning his yarns of delusions of grandeur, telling of his great successes and his pending ascension to the top. His wife knew him better than anybody else; she shook her head with genuine sympathy and said to him: 'Gee, you're just a phony.'"

In prison, this man had somehow reached the point where he was willing to sell his soul just to satisfy this need, this immaturity. The only way he could get the attention that he demanded from authority was to grovel and ingratiate himself before the enemy. As a soldier he was a miserable failure, but he had not crossed the boundary of willful treason; he was not written off as an irrevocable loss, as were the two patent collaborators with whom the Vietnamese soon arranged that he live.

As we American POWs built our civilization, and wrote our own laws (which we leaders obliged all to memorize), we also codified certain principles which formed the backbone of our policies and attitudes. I codified the principles of compassion, rehabilitation, and forgiveness with the slogan: "It is neither American nor Christian to nag a repentant sinner to his grave." (Some didn't like it, thought it seemed soft on finks.) And so, we really gave this man a chance.

Over time, our efforts worked. After five years of self-indulgence he got himself together and started to communicate with the prisoner organization. I sent the message "Are you on the team or not?"; he replied, "Yes," and came back. He told the Vietnamese that he didn't want to play their dirty games anymore. He wanted to get away from those willful collaborators and he came back and he was accepted, after a fashion.

I wish that were the end of the story. Although he came back, joined us, and even became a leader of sorts, he never totally won himself back. No matter how forgiving we were, he was conscious that many resented him—not so much because he was weak but because he had broken what we might call a gentleman's code. In all of those years when he, a senior officer, had willingly participated in making tape recordings of anti-American material, he had deeply offended the sensibilities of the American prisoners who were forced to listen to him. To most of us it wasn't the rhetoric of the war or the goodness or the badness of this or that issue that counted. The object of our highest value was the well-being of our fellow prisoners. He had broken that code and hurt some of those people. Some thought that as an informer he had indirectly hurt them physically. I don't believe that. What indisputably hurt them was his not having the sensitivity to realize the damage his opportunistic conduct would do to the morale of a bunch of Middle American guys with Middle American attitudes which they naturally cherished. He should have known that in those solitary cells where his tapes were piped were idealistic, direct, patriotic fellows who would be crushed and embarrassed to have him, a senior man in excellent physical shape, so obviously not under torture, telling the world that the war was wrong. Even if he believed what he said, which he did not, he should have had the common decency to keep his mouth shut. You can sit and think anything you want, but when you insensitively cut down those who want to love and help you, you cross a line. He seemed to sense that he could never truly be one of us.

And yet he was likable—particularly back in civilization after release—when tension was off, and making a deal did not seem so important. He exuded charm and "hail fellow" sophistication. He wanted so to be liked by all those men he had once discarded in his search for new friends, new deals, new fields to conquer in Hanoi. The tragedy of his life was obvious to us all. Tears were shed by some of his old prison mates when he was killed in an accident that strongly resembled suicide some monhs later. The Greek drama had run its course. He was right out of Aristotle's book, a good man with a flaw who had come to an unjustified bad end. The flaw was insecurity: the need to ingratiate himself, the need for love and adulation at any price.

He reminded me of Paul Newman in *The Hustler*. Newman couldn't stand success. He knew how to make a deal. He was handsome, he was smart, he was attractive to everybody; but he had to have adulation, and therein lay the seed of tragedy. Playing high-stakes pool against old Minnesota Fats (Jackie Gleason), Newman was well in the lead, and getting more full of himself by the hour. George C. Scott, the pool bettor, whispered to his partner: "I'm going to keep betting on Minnesota Fats; this other guy [Newman] is a born loser—he's all skill and no character." And he was right, a born loser—I think that's the message.

How can we educate to avoid these casualties? Can we by means of education prevent this kind of tragedy? What we prisoners were in was a one-way leverage game in which the other side had all the mechanical advantage. I suppose you could say that we all live in a leverage world to some degree; we all experience people trying to use us in one way or another. The difference in Hanoi was the degradation of the ends (to be used as propaganda agents of an enemy, or as informers on your fellow Americans), and the power of the means (total environmental control including solitary confinement, restraint by means of leg-irons and handcuffs, and torture). Extortionists always go down the same track: the imposition of guilt and fear for having disobeyed their rules, followed in turn by punishment, apology, confession, and atonement (their payoff). Our captors would go to great lengths to get a man to compromise his own code, even if only slightly, and then they would hold that in their bag, and the next time get him to go a little further.

Some people are psychologically, if not physically, at home in extortion environments. They are tough people who instinctively avoid getting sucked into the undertows. They never kid themselves or their friends; if they miss the mark they admit it. But there's another category of person who gets tripped up. He makes a small compromise, perhaps rationalizes it, and then makes another one; and then he gets depressed, full of shame, lonesome, loses his willpower and self-respect, and comes to a tragic end. Somewhere along the line he realizes that he has turned a corner that he didn't mean to turn. All too late he realizes that he has been worshiping the wrong gods and discovers the wisdom of the ages: life is not fair.

In sorting out the story after our release, we found that most of us had come to combat constant mental and physical pressure in much the same way. We discovered that when a person is alone in a cell and sees the door open only once or twice a day for a bowl of soup, he realizes after a period of weeks in isolation and darkness that he has to build some sort of ritual into his life if he wants to avoid becoming an animal. Ritual fills a need in a hard life and it's easy to see how formal church ritual grew. For almost all of us, this ritual was built around prayer, exercise, and clandestine communication. The prayers I said during those days were prayers of quality with ideas of substance. We found that over the course of time our minds had a tremendous capacity for invention and introspection, but had the weakness of being an integral part of our bodies. I remembered Descartes and how in his philosophy he separated mind and body. One time I cursed my body for the way it decayed my mind. I had decided that I would become a Gandhi. I would have to be carried around on a pallet and in that state I could not be used by my captors for propaganda purposes. After about ten days of fasting, I found that I had become so depressed that soon I would risk going into interrogation ready to spill my guts just looking for a friend. I tapped to the guy next door and I said, "Gosh, how I wish Descartes could have been right, but he's wrong." He was a little slow to reply; I reviewed Descartes's deduction with him and explained how I had discovered that body and mind are inseparable.

On the positive side, I discovered the tremendous file-cabinet volume of the human mind. You can memorize an incredible amount of material and you can draw the past out of your memory with remarkable recall by easing slowly toward the event you seek and not crowding the mind too closely. You'll try to remember who was at your birthday party when you were five years old, and you can get it, but only after months of effort. You can break the locks and find the answers, but you need time and solitude to learn how to use this marvelous device in your head which is the greatest computer on earth.

Of course many of the things we recalled from the past were utterly useless as sources of strength or practicality. For instance, events brought back from cocktail parties or insincere social contacts were almost repugnant because of their emptiness, their utter lack of value. More often than not, the locks worth picking had been on old schoolroom doors. School days can be thought of as a time when one is filling the important stacks of one's memory library. For me, the golden doors were labeled history and the classics. The historical perspective which enabled a man to take himself away from all the agitation, not necessarily to see a rosy lining, but to see the real nature of the situation he faced, was truly a thing of value.

Here's how this historical perspective helped me see the reality of my own situation and thus cope better with it. I learned from a Vietnamese prisoner that the same cells we occupied had in years before been lived in by many of the leaders of the Hanoi government. From my history lessons I recalled that when metropolitan France permitted communists in the government in 1936, the communists who occupied cells in Vietnam were set free. I marveled at the cycle of history, all within my memory, which prompted Hitler's rise in Germany, then led to the rise of the Popular Front in France, and finally vacated this cell of mine halfway around the world ("Perhaps Pham Van Dong lived here"). I came to understand what tough people these were. I was willing to fight them to the death, but I grew to realize that hatred was an indulgence, a very inefficient emotion. I remember thinking, "If you were committed to beating the dealer in a gambling casino, would *hating* him help your game?" In a pidgin English propaganda book the guard gave me, speeches by these old communists about their prison experiences stressed how they learned to beat down the enemy by being united. It seemed comforting to know that we were united against the communist administration of Hoa Lo prison just as the Vietnamese communists had united against the French administration of Hoa Lo in the thirties. Prisoners are prisoners, and there's only one way to beat administrations. We resolved to do it better in the sixties than they had in the thirties. You don't base system-beating on any thought of political idealism; you do it as a competitive thing, as an expression of self-respect.

Education in the classics teaches you that all organizations since the beginning of time have used the power of guilt; that cycles are repetitive; and that this is the way of the world. It's a naive person who

591

comes in and says, "Let's see, what's good and what's bad?" That's a quagmire. You can get out of that quagmire only by recalling how wise men before you accommodated the same dilemmas. And I believe a good classical education and an understanding of history can best determine the rules you should live by. They also give you the power to analyze reasons for these rules and guide you as to how to apply them to your own situation. In a broader sense, all my education helped me. Naval Academy discipline and body contact sports helped me. But the education which I found myself using most was what I got in graduate school. The messages of history and philosophy I used were simple.

The first one is this business about life not being fair. That is a very important lesson and I learned it from a wonderful man named Philip Rhinelander. As a lieutenant commander in the Navy studying political science at Stanford University in 1961, I went over to philosophy corner one day and an older gentleman said, "Can I help you?" I said, "Yes, I'd like to take some courses in philosophy." I told him I'd been in college for six years and had never had a course in philosophy. He couldn't believe it. I told him that I was a naval officer and he said, "Well, I used to be in the Navy. Sit down." Philip Rhinelander became a great influence in my life.

He had been a Harvard lawyer and had pleaded cases before the Supreme Court and then gone to war as a reserve officer. When he came back he took his doctorate at Harvard. He was also a music composer, had been director of general education at Harvard, dean of the School of Humanities and Sciences at Stanford, and by the time I met him had by choice returned to teaching in the classroom. He said, "The course I'm teaching is my personal two-term favorite—The Problem of Good and Evil—and we're starting our second term." He said the message of his course was from the Book of Job. The number one problem in this world is that people are not able to accommodate the lesson in the book.

He recounted the story of Job. It starts out by establishing that Job was the most honorable of men. Then he lost all his goods. He also lost his reputation, which is what really hurt. His wife was badgering him to admit his sins, but he knew he had made no errors. He was not a patient man and demanded to speak to the Lord. When the Lord appeared in the whirlwind, he said, "Now, Job, you have to shape up! Life is not fair." That's my interpretation and that's the way the book ended for hundreds of years. I agree with those of the opinion that the happy ending was spliced on many years later. If you read it, you'll note that the meter changes. People couldn't live with the original message. Here was a good man who came to unexplained grief, and the Lord told him: "That's the way it is. Don't challenge me. This is my world and you either live in it as I designed it or get out."

This was a great comfort to me in prison. It answered the question "Why me?" It cast aside any thoughts of being punished for past actions. Sometimes I shared the message with fellow prisoners as I tapped through the walls to them, but I learned to be selective. It's a strong message which upsets some people.

Rhinelander also passed on to me another piece of classical information which I found of great value. On the day of our last session together he said, "You're a military man, let me give you a book to remember me by. It's a book of military ethics." He handed it to me, and I bade him goodbye with great emotion. I took the book home and that night started to read it. It was the *Enchiridion* of the philosopher Epictetus, his "manual" for the Roman field soldier.

As I began to read, I thought to myself in disbelief, "Does Rhinelander think I'm going to draw lessons for my life from this thing? I'm a fighter pilot. I'm a technical man. I'm a test pilot. I know how to get people to do technical work. I play golf; I drink martinis. I know how to get ahead in my profession. And what does he hand me? A book that says in part, 'It's better to die in hunger, exempt from guilt and fear, than to live in affluence and with perturbation.'" I remembered this later in prison because perturbation was what I was living with. When I ejected from the airplane on that September morn in 1965, I had left the land of technology. I had entered the world of Epictetus, and it's a world that few of us, whether we know it or not, are ever far away from.

In Palo Alto, I had read this book, not with contentment, but with annoyance. Statement after statement: "Men are disturbed not by things, but by the view that they take of them." "Do not be concerned with things which are beyond your power." "Demand not that events should happen as you wish, but wish them to happen as they do happen and you will go on well." This is stoicism. It's not the last word, but it's a viewpoint that comes in handy in many circumstances, and it surely did for me. Particularly this line:

"Lameness is an impediment to the body but not to the will." That was significant for me because I wasn't able to stand up and support myself on my badly broken leg for the first couple of years I was in solitary confinement.

Other statements of Epictetus took on added meaning in the light of extortions which often began with our captors' callous pleas: "If you are just reasonable with us we will compensate you. You get your meals, you get to sleep, you won't be pestered, you might even get a cellmate." The catch was that by being "reasonable with us" our enemies meant being their informers, their propagandists. The old stoic had said, "If I can get the things I need with the preservation of my honor and fidelity and self-respect, show me the way and I will get them. But, if you require me to lose my own proper good, that you may gain what is no good, consider how unreasonable and foolish you are." To love our fellow prisoners was within our power. To betray, to propagandize, to disillusion conscientious and patriotic shipmates and destroy their morale so that they in turn would be destroyed was to lose one's proper good.

What attributes serve you well in the extortion environment? We learned there, above all else, that the best defense is to keep your conscience clean. When we did something we were ashamed of, and our captors realized we were ashamed of it, we were in trouble. A little white lie is where extortion and ultimately blackmail start. In 1965, I was crippled and I was alone. I realized that they had all the power. I couldn't see how I was ever going to get out with my honor and self-respect. The one thing I came to realize was that if you don't lose integrity you can't be had and you can't be hurt. Compromises multiply and build up when you're working against a skilled extortionist or a good manipulator. You can't be had if you don't take that first shortcut, or "meet them halfway," as they say, or look for that tacit "deal," or make that first compromise.

Bob North, a political science professor at Stanford, taught me a course called Comparative Marxist Thought. This was not an anticommunist course. It was the study of dogma and thought patterns. We read no criticisms of Marxism, only primary sources. All year we read the works of Marx and Lenin. In Hanoi, I understood more about Marxist theory than my interrogator did. I was able to say to that interrogator, "That's not what Lenin said; you're a deviationist."

One of the things North talked about was brainwashing. A psychologist who studied the Korean prisoner situation, which somewhat paralleled ours, concluded that three categories of prisoners were involved there. The first was the redneck Marine sergeant from Tennessee who had an eighth-grade education. He would get in that interrogation room and they would say that the Spanish-American War was started by the bomb within the *Maine,* which might be true, and he would answer, "B.S." They would show him something about racial unrest in Detroit. "B.S." There was no way they could get to him; his mind was made up. He was a straight guy, red, white, and blue, and everything else was B.S.! He didn't give it a second thought. Not much of a historian, perhaps, but a good security risk.

In the next category were the sophisticates. They were the fellows who could be told these same things about the horrors of American history and our social problems, but had heard it all before, knew both sides of every story, and thought we were on the right track. They weren't ashamed that we had robber barons at a certain time in our history; they were aware of the skeletons in most civilizations' closets. They could not be emotionally involved and so they were good security risks.

The ones who were in trouble were the high school graduates who had enough sense to pick up the innuendo, and yet not enough education to accommodate it properly. Not many of them fell, but most of the men that got entangled started from that background.

The psychologist's point is possibly oversimplistic, but I think his message has some validity. A little knowledge is a dangerous thing.

Generally speaking, I think education is a tremendous defense; the broader, the better. After I was shot down my wife, Sybil, found a clipping glued in the front of my collegiate dictionary: "Education is an ornament in prosperity and a refuge in adversity." She certainly agrees with me on that. Most of us prisoners found that the so-called practical academic exercises in how to do things, which I'm told are proliferating, were useless. I'm not saying that we should base education on training people to be in prison, but I am saying that in stress situations, the fundamentals, the hardcore classical subjects, are what serve best.

Theatrics also helped sustain me. My mother had been a drama coach when I was young and I was in many of her plays. In prison I learned how to manufacture a personality and live it, crawl into it, and hold that role without deviation. During interrogations, I'd check the responses I got to different kinds of behavior. They'd get worried when I did things irrationally. And so, every so often, I would play that "irrational" role and come completely unglued. When I could tell that pressure to make a public exhibition of me was building, I'd stand up, tip the table over, attempt to throw the chair through the window, and say, "No way, Goddammit! I'm not doing that! Now, come over here and fight!" This was a risky ploy, because if they thought you were acting, they would slam you into the ropes and make you scream in pain like a baby. You could watch their faces and read their minds. They had expected me to behave like a stoic. But a man would be a fool to make their job easy by being conventional and predictable. I could feel the tide turn in my favor at that magic moment when their anger turned to pleading: "Calm down, now calm down." The payoff would come when they decided that the risk of my going haywire in front of some touring American professor on a "fact-finding" mission was too great. More important, they had reason to believe that I would tell the truth—namely, that I had been in solitary confinement for four years and tortured fifteen times—without fear of future consequences. So theatrical training proved helpful to me.

Can you educate for leadership? I think you can, but the communists would probably say no. One day in an argument with an interrogator, I said, "You are so proud of being a party member, what are the criteria?" He said in a flurry of anger, "There are only four: you have to be seventeen years old, you have to be selfless, you have to be smart enough to understand the theory, and you've got to be a person who innately influences others." He stressed that fourth one. I think psychologists would say that leadership is innate, and there is truth in that. But, I also think you can learn some leadership traits that naturally accrue from a good education: compassion is a necessity for leaders, as are spontaneity, bravery, self-discipline, honesty, and above all, integrity.

I remember being disappointed about a month after I was back when one of my young friends, a prison mate, came running up after a reunion at the Naval Academy. He said with glee, "This is really great, you won't believe how this country has advanced. They've practically done away with plebe year at the Academy, and they've got computers in the basement of Bancroft Hall." I thought, "My God, if there was anything that helped us get through those eight years, it was plebe year, and if anything screwed up that war, it was computers!"

## STUDY QUESTIONS

1. In his years of confinement and torment, Stockdale reverted to the stoic philosophy of Epictetus. Is stoicism primarily a philosophy for critical and extreme situations? If not, how does it apply in ordinary life?

2. How does Stockdale define personal integrity? Does this conform to your idea of personal integrity? How did readings in history and philosophy help Stockdale retain his dignity and integrity under great stress?

3. Discuss the case of the officer who betrayed his fellow prisoners. Stockdale attributes this to a character fault. Could a proper moral education of the kind Stockdale advocates have prevented it?

4. What does Stockdale's article tell us about the importance or unimportance of a formal training in ethics? Is great fiction more valuable for moral development? Compare Stockdale's views on moral education with Duska's.

## SUGGESTED READINGS

Dykstra, Craig. *Vision and Character*. New York: Paulist Press, 1981.

Gilligan, Carol. *In a Different Voice*. Cambridge, MA: Harvard University Press, 1982.

Grimshaw, Jean. *Philosophy and Feminist Thinking*. Minneapolis: University of Minnesota Press, 1986.

Joy, Donald. *Moral Development Foundations*. Nashville: Abingdon Press, 1983.

Kagan, Jerome, ed. *The Emergence of Morality in Children.* Chicago: University of Chicago Press, 1986.

Kohlberg, Lawrence. *Essays on Moral Development,* vols. I and II. San Francisco: Harper and Row, 1981, 1984.

Noddings, Nel. *Caring: A Feminine Approach to Ethics and Moral Education.* Berkeley: University of California Press, 1984.

Parr, Susan Resneck. *The Moral of the Story: Literature, Values, and American Education.* New York: Columbia University Press, 1982.

Sichel, Betty. *Moral Education: Character, Community and Ideals.* Philadelphia: Temple University Press, 1988.

# Chapter Seven

# CHARACTER, DIGNITY, AND SELF-RESPECT

A being capable of wronging another being is a moral agent. A being capable of being wronged by a moral agent is a moral patient. A moral agent has duties; a moral patient has rights.

Any person is at once a moral agent and a moral patient. Consider the notion of self-respect. Respect for oneself as a moral patient is one meaning of self-respect. So understood, to respect oneself is to fulfill the duties one owes to oneself. What does one owe to oneself? Christopher Lasch calls attention to the currently popular assumption—reflected in television commercials that urge us to indulge in certain expensive luxuries because "you owe it to yourself"—that we owe ourselves gratification and pleasure. Lasch is probably right to claim that many people today see self-indulgence as a *moral* duty. All the same, we recognize something slightly ludicrous about refusing to wear or eat something inferior "because I have too much respect for myself."

Contrast this narcissistic idea of self-respect with Kant's idea that the primary self-duty is "the universal duty which devolves upon man of so ordering his life as to be fit for the performance of all moral duties." Kant is still talking of duties to one's ("patient") self. But he claims that morally we owe that self *not* happiness or gratification but self-development as a moral agent. This older ideal of self-obligation is entirely consistent with the concept of virtue-based ethics. The imperative is to become virtuous, to "build character." For Kant, as for the philosophers of virtue, human beings are, in the last analysis, responsible for the kind of person they are (selfish or kind, courageous or cowardly, temperate or self-indulgent). Since virtue is not given to us, we must develop it. Virtue-based ethics' answer to the question "What do we owe to ourselves?" thus (roughly) coincides with Kant's answer: We owe it to ourselves to develop ourselves as moral agents.

Respect for the self as moral patient is one aspect of self-respect. But the self has two aspects and "self-respect" has a second meaning: respect for oneself as moral agent. Persons who consistently behave in an honorable way (discharging their obligations to themselves and others) justifiably can view themselves as moral beings worthy of commendation. Their track record as moral agents is evidence of character, and indeed, respect for one's "agent" self is respect for oneself as a "person of character." Conversely, persons of weak character necessarily lack this form of self-respect. In effect, persons who respect themselves and others as moral patients also will come to respect themselves as moral agents. Kant speaks of this as "noble pride" or "proper self-esteem." Thomas Hill applies the Kantian idea of duty to oneself in finding moral fault with those who defer servilely to others. According to Hill, excessive deference at the expense of oneself betrays a lack of self-respect and an insufficient understanding of what one owes oneself as an autonomous moral agent.

Joan Didion's concept of self-respect also is agent oriented. To have self-respect is to be a person of character with a better-than-average record of acting in accordance with one's principles. Didion stresses that people with the strength of character to achieve this record also are people who accept responsibility for their actions. Thus the tendency to find excuses for oneself indicates a lack of self-respect.

Anthony Quinton's article surveys the vicissitudes of virtue-based ethics in the past few centuries and the changes in conceptions of self-respect and character. Quinton finds that the Victorian emphasis on strength of character is a thing of the past. The transformation Quinton describes can be characterized as a shift of emphasis from the self as an active moral agent to the patient self as a repository of rights, with a corresponding shift in the notion of self-respect. According to Quinton, persons of "character" are persons with the consistent strength of will to apply reason to achieve a long-range gain in situations where they are tempted strongly to forego that gain in favor of immediate satisfactions. Quinton's person of character is the very antithesis of the person Christopher Lasch calls "the new narcissist," a type Lasch finds alarmingly prevalent today.

Lasch, Coles, Didion, and Quinton all deal with the same general phenomenon: Morally speaking, modern men and women see themselves primarily as centers of needs and rights, and only secondarily as centers of obligations and duties. Lasch and Quinton find that a weakening of tradition and social roles accompanies the shift of emphasis to the self as moral patient. Quinton recognizes character, honor, and self-abnegation as currently unfashionable. He believes that each of us must work to reverse this trend. For Coles and Lasch, the new narcissism is socially and morally regressive. Coles is hopeful that character still predominates. Lasch is rather more pessimistic. Robert Coles' "field study" mitigates some of Lasch's negative judgments on the current state of American character. Coles offers much anecdotal evidence that children have an innate sense of dignity and self-respect. Far from being narcissistic, the children Coles observes are unselfish and morally brave.

# Dignity and Self-respect

## IMMANUEL KANT

TRANSLATED BY LOUIS ENFIELD

A biographical sketch of Immanuel Kant is found on page 123.

Moral persons do their duty to themselves as well as others; such persons deserve respect and will rightfully respect themselves. Self-respect is essential to self-worth. For example, says Kant, drunkards fail in their duty to themselves; the result is self-contempt. Similarly, weak persons who constantly find excuses for their moral lapses are contemptible in their own eyes as well as in the eyes of others. Suicide violates self-duty most seriously, since in suicide people use their own free will to destroy themselves as moral agents, thereby using themselves as a means (to avoid pain) and not as an end. Kant denies that we owe ourselves happiness: "Not self-favour but self-esteem" is the principle of self-duty. For Kant, self-respect comes to those who earn it by living a principled life.

## I

By way of introduction it is to be noted that there is no question in moral philosophy which has received more defective treatment than

DIGNITY AND SELF–RESPECT From "Proper Self-respect," and "Duties to Oneself," from *Lectures on Ethics* by Immanuel Kant. Translated by Louis Enfield (New York: Harper & Row, 1963). Reprinted by permission of Methuen and Company Ltd.

that of the individual's duty towards himself. No one has framed a proper concept of self-regarding duty. It has been regarded as a detail and considered by way of an afterthought, as an appendix to moral philosophy, on the view that man should give a thought to himself only after he has completely fulfilled his duty towards others. . . . It was taken for granted that a man's duty towards himself consisted . . . in promoting his own happiness. In that case everything would depend on how an individual determined his own happiness; for our self-regarding duties would consist in the universal rule to satisfy all our inclinations in order to further our happiness. This would, however, militate seriously against doing our duty towards others. In fact, the principle of self-regarding duties is a very different one, which has no connexion with our well-being or earthly happiness. Far from ranking lowest in the scale of precedence, our duties towards ourselves are of primary importance and should have pride of place; for (deferring for the moment the definition of what constitutes this duty) it is obvious that nothing can be expected from a man who dishonours his own person. He who transgresses against himself loses his manliness and becomes incapable of doing his duty towards his fellows. A man who performed his duty to others badly, who lacked generosity, kindness and sympathy, but who nevertheless did his duty to himself by leading a proper life, might yet possess a certain inner worth; but he who has transgressed his duty towards himself, can have no inner worth whatever. Thus a man who fails in his duty to himself loses worth absolutely; while a man who fails in his duty to others loses worth only relatively. It follows that the prior condition of our duty to others is our duty to ourselves; we can fulfil the former only in so far as we first fulfil the latter. Let us illustrate our meaning by a few examples of failure in one's duty to oneself. A drunkard does no harm to another, and if he has a strong constitution he does no harm to himself, yet he is an object of contempt. We are not indifferent to cringing servility; man should not cringe and fawn; by so doing he degrades his person and loses his manhood. If a man for gain or profit submits to all indignities and makes himself the plaything of another, he casts away the worth of his manhood. Again, a lie is more a violation of one's duty to oneself than of one's duty to others. A liar, even though by his lies he does no harm to any one, yet becomes an object of contempt, he throws away his personality; his behaviour is vile, he has transgressed his duty towards himself. We can carry the argument further and say that to accept favours and

603

benefits is also a breach of one's duty to oneself. If I accept favours, I contract debts which I can never repay, for I can never get on equal terms with him who has conferred the favours upon me; he has stolen a march upon me, and if I do him a favour I am only returning a *quid pro quo;* I shall always owe him a debt of gratitude, and who will accept such a debt? For to be indebted is to be subject to an unending constraint. I must for ever be courteous and flattering towards my benefactor, and if I fail to be so he will very soon make me conscious of my failure; I may even be forced to using subterfuge so as to avoid meeting him. But he who pays promptly for everything is under no constraint; he is free to act as he please; none will hinder him. Again, the faint-hearted who complain about their luck and sigh and weep about their misfortunes are despicable in our eyes; instead of sympathizing with them we do our best to keep away from them. But if a man shows a steadfast courage in his misfortune, and though greatly suffering, does not cringe and complain but puts a bold face upon things, to such a one our sympathy goes out. Moreover, if a man gives up his freedom and barters it away for money, he violates his manhood. Life itself ought not to be rated so highly as to warrant our being prepared, in order only not to lose it, to live otherwise than as a man should, i.e. not a life of ease, but so that we do not degrade our manhood. We must also be worthy of our manhood; whatsoever makes us unworthy of it makes us unfit for anything, and we cease to be men. Moreover, if a man offers his body for profit for the sport of others—if, for instance, he agrees in return for a few pints of beer to be knocked about—he throws himself away, and the perpetrators who pay him for it are acting as vilely as he. Neither can we without destroying our person abandon ourselves to others in order to satisfy their desires, even though it be done to save parents and friends from death; still less can this be done for money. If done in order to satisfy one's own desires, it is very immodest and immoral, but yet not so unnatural; but if it be done for money, or for some other reason, a person allows himself to be treated as a thing, and so throws away the worth of his manhood. It is the same with the vices of the flesh (*crimina carnis*), which for that reason are not spoken of. They do no damage to anyone, but dishonour and degrade a man's own person; they are an offence against the dignity of manhood in one's own person. The most serious offence against the duty one owes to oneself is suicide. But why should suicide be so abominable? It is no answer to say "because God forbids it." Suicide is not an abomination because God has forbidden it; it is forbidden by God because it is abominable. If it were the other way about, suicide would not be abominable if it were not forbidden; and I should not know why God had forbidden it, if it were not abominable in itself. The ground, therefore, for regarding suicide and other transgressions as abominable and punishable must not be found in the divine will, but in their inherent heinousness. Suicide is an abomination because it implies the abuse of man's freedom of action: he uses his freedom to destroy himself. His freedom should be employed to enable him to live as a man. He is free to dispose as he pleases of things appertaining to his person, but not of his person; he may not use his freedom against himself. For a man to recognize what his duty is towards himself in this respect is far from easy: because although man has indeed a natural horror of suicide, yet we can argue and quibble ourselves into believing that, in order to rid himself of trouble and misery, a man may destroy himself. The argument makes a strong appeal; and in terms of the rule of prudence suicide may often be the surest and best course; none the less suicide is in itself revolting. The rule of morality, which takes precedence of all rules of reflective prudence, commands apodeictically and categorically that we must observe our duties to ourselves; and in committing suicide and reducing himself to a carcase, man uses his powers and his liberty against himself. Man is free to dispose of his condition but not of his person; he himself is an end and not a means; all else in the world is of value only as a means, but man is a person and not a thing and therefore not a means. It is absurd that a reasonable being, an end for the sake of which all else is means, should use himself as a means. It is true that a person can serve as a means for others (e.g. by his work), but only in a way whereby he does not cease to be a person and an end. Whoever acts in such a way that he cannot be an end, uses himself as a means and treats his person as a thing. . . .

The duties we owe to ourselves do not depend on the relation of the action to the ends of happiness. If they did, they would depend on our inclinations and so be governed by rules of prudence. Such rules are not moral, since they indicate only the necessity of the means for the satisfaction of inclinations, and cannot therefore bind us. The basis of such obligation is not to be found in the advantages we reap from doing our duty towards ourselves, but in the worth of manhood. This principle does not allow us an unlimited freedom in respect of our own persons. It insists that we must reverence humanity in our own person, because apart from this man becomes an object of contempt, worthless in the eyes of his fellows and worthless in himself. Such faultiness is absolute. Our duties towards ourselves constitute the supreme condition and the principle of all morality; for moral worth is the worth of the person as such; our capacities have a value only in regard to the circumstances in which we find ourselves. Socrates lived in a state of wretchedness; his circumstances were worthless; but though his circumstances were so ill-conditioned, yet he himself was of the highest value. Even though we sacrifice all life's amenities we can make up for their loss and sustain approval by maintaining the worth of our humanity. We may have lost everything else, and yet still retain our inherent worth. Only if our worth as human beings is intact can we perform our other duties; for it is the foundation stone of all other duties. A man who has destroyed and cast away his personality, has no intrinsic worth, and can no longer perform any manner of duty.

Let us next consider the basis of the principle of all self-regarding duties.

Freedom is, on the one hand, that faculty which gives unlimited usefulness to all other faculties. It is the highest order of life, which serves as the foundation of all perfections and is their necessary condition. All animals have the faculty of using their powers according to will. But this will is not free. It is necessitated through the incitement of *stimuli,* and the actions of animals involve a *bruta necessitas.* If the will of all beings were so bound to sensuous impulse, the world would possess no value. The inherent value of the world, the *summum bonum,* is freedom in accordance with a will which is not necessitated to action. Freedom is thus the inner value of the world. But on the other hand, freedom unrestrained by rules of its conditional employment is the most terrible of all things. The actions of animals are regular; they are performed in accordance with rules which necessitate them subjectively. Mankind apart, nature is not free; through it all there runs a subjectively necessitating principle in accordance with which everything happens regularly. Man alone is free; his actions are not regulated by any such subjectively necessitating principle; if they were, he would not be free. And what then? If the freedom of man were not kept within bounds by objective rules, the result would be the completest savage disorder. There could then be no certainty that man might not use his powers to destroy himself, his fellows, and the whole of nature. I can conceive freedom as the complete absence of orderliness, if it is not subject to an objective determination. The grounds of this objective determination must lie in the understanding, and constitute the restrictions to freedom. Therefore the proper use of freedom is the supreme rule. What then is the condition under which freedom is restricted? It is the law. The universal law is therefore as follows: Let thy procedure be such that in all thine actions regularity prevails. What does this restraint imply when applied to the individual? That he should not follow his inclinations. The fundamental rule, in terms of which I ought to restrain my freedom, is the conformity of free behaviour to the essential ends of humanity. I shall not then follow my inclinations, but bring them under a rule. He who subjects his person to his inclinations, acts contrary to the essential end of humanity; for as a free being he must not be subjected to inclinations, but ought to determine them in the exercise of his freedom; and being a free agent he must have a rule, which is the essential end of humanity. In the case of animals inclinations are already determined by subjectively compelling factors; in their case, therefore, disorderliness is impossible. But if man gives free rein to his inclinations, he sinks lower than an animal because he then lives in a state of disorder which does not exist among animals. A man is then in contradiction with the essential ends of humanity in his own person, and so with himself. All evil in the world springs from freedom. Animals, not being free, live according to rules. But free beings can only act regularly, if they restrict their freedom by rules. Let us reflect upon the actions of man which refer to himself, and consider freedom in them. These spring from impulse and inclinations or from maxims and principles. It is essential, therefore, that man should take his stand upon maxims and restrain by rules the free actions which relate to himself. These are the rules of his self-regarding duties. For if we consider man in respect of his inclinations and instincts, he is loosed from them and determined by neither. In all nature there is nothing to injure man in the satisfaction of his desires; all injurious things are his own invention, the outcome of his freedom. We need only instance strong drink and the many dishes concocted to tickle his palate. In the unregulated pursuit of an inclination of his own devising, man becomes an object of utter contempt, because his freedom makes it possible for him to turn nature inside out in order to satisfy himself. Let him devise what he pleases for satisfying his desires, so long as he regulates the use of his devices; if he does not, his freedom is his greatest misfortune. It must therefore be restricted, though not by other properties or faculties, but by itself. The supreme rule is that in all the actions which affect himself a man should so conduct himself that every exercise of his power is compatible with the fullest employment of them. Let us illustrate our meaning by examples. If I have drunk too much I am incapable of using my freedom and my powers. Again, if I kill myself, I use my powers to deprive myself of the faculty of using them. That freedom, the principle of the highest order of life, should annul itself and abrogate the use of itself conflicts with the fullest use of freedom. But freedom can only be in harmony with itself under certain conditions; otherwise it comes into collision with itself. If there were no established order in Nature, everything would come to an end, and so it is with unbridled freedom. Evils are to be found, no doubt, in Nature, but the true moral evil, vice, only in freedom. We pity the fortunate, but we hate the vicious and rejoice at their punishment. The conditions under which alone the fullest use of freedom is possible, and can be in harmony with itself, are the essential ends of humanity. It must conform with these. The principle of all duties is that the use of freedom must be in keeping with the essential ends of humanity. Thus, for instance, a human being is not entitled to sell his limbs for money, even if he were offered ten thousand thalers for a single finger. If he were so entitled, he could sell all his limbs. We can dispose of things which have no freedom but not of a being which has free will. A man who sells himself makes himself a thing and, as he has jettisoned his person, it is open to anyone to deal with him as he pleases. Another instance of this kind is where a human being makes himself a thing by making himself an object of enjoyment for some one's sexual desire. It degrades humanity, and that is why those guilty of it feel ashamed. We see, therefore, that just as freedom is the source of virtue which ennobles mankind, so is it also the root of the most dreadful vices—such as, for instance, a *crimen carnis contra naturam,* since it can devise all manner of means to satisfy its inclinations. Some crimes and vices, the result of freedom (e.g. suicide), make us shudder, others are nauseating; the mere mention of them is loathsome; we are ashamed of them because they degrade us below the level of beasts; they are grosser even than suicide, for the mention of suicide makes us shudder, but those other crimes and vices cannot be mentioned without producing nausea. Suicide is the most abominable of the vices which inspire dread and hate, but nausea and contempt indicate a lower level still.

Not self-favour but self-esteem should be the principle of our duties towards ourselves. This means that our actions must be in keeping with the worth of man. There are in us two grounds of action; inclinations, which belong to our animal nature, and humanity, to which the inclinations must be subjected. Our duties to ourselves are negative; they restrict our freedom in respect of our inclinations, which aim at our own welfare. Just as law restricts our freedom in our relations with other men, so do our duties to ourselves restrict our freedom in dealing with ourselves. All such duties are grounded in a certain love of honour consisting in self-esteem; man must not appear unworthy in his own eyes; his actions must be in keeping with humanity itself if he is to appear in his own eyes worthy of inner respect. . . .

## II

Humility, on the one hand, and true, noble pride on the other, are elements of proper self-respect; shamelessness is its opposite. We have reason to have but a low opinion of ourselves as individuals, but as representatives of mankind we ought to hold ourselves in high esteem. In the light of the law of morality, which is holy and perfect, our defects stand out with glaring distinctness and on comparing ourselves with this standard of perfection we have sufficient cause to feel humble. But if we compare ourselves with others, there is no reason to have a low opinion of ourselves; we have a right to consider ourselves as valuable as another. This self-respect in comparison with others constitutes noble pride. A low opinion of oneself in relation to others is no humility; it is a sign of a little spirit and of a servile character. To flatter oneself that this is virtue is to mistake an imitation for the genuine article; it is monk's virtue and not at all natural; this form of humility is in fact a form of pride. There is nothing unjust or unreasonable in self-esteem; we do no harm to another if we consider ourselves equal to him in our estimation. But if we are to pass judgment upon ourselves we must draw a comparison between ourselves and the purity of the moral law, and we then have cause to feel humble. We should not compare ourselves with other righteous men who, like ourselves, model themselves on the moral law. The Gospel does not teach humility, but it makes us humble.

Our self-esteem may arise from self-love and then it is favour and partiality towards ourselves. This pragmatic self-respect in accordance with rules of prudence is reasonable and possible inasmuch as it keeps us in confidence. No one can demand of me that I should humiliate myself and value myself less than others; but we all have the right to demand of a man that he should not think himself superior. Moral self-esteem, however, which is grounded in the worth of humanity, should not be derived from comparison with others, but from comparison with the moral law. Men are greatly inclined to take others as the measure of their own moral worth, and if they find that there are some whom they surpass it gives them a feeling of moral pride; but it is much more than pride if a man believes himself perfect as measured by the standard of the moral law. I can consider myself better than some others; but it is not very much only to be better than the worst, and there is really not much moral pride in that. Moral humility, regarded as the curbing of our self-conceit in face of the moral law, can thus never rest upon a comparison of ourselves with others, but with the moral law. Humility is therefore the limitation of the high opinion we have of our moral worth by comparison of our actions with the moral law. The comparison of our actions with the moral law makes us humble. Man has reason to have but a low opinion of himself because his actions not only contravene the moral law but are also lacking in purity. His frailty causes him to transgress the law, and his weakness makes his actions fall short of its purity. If an individual takes a lenient view of the moral law, he may well have a high opinion of himself and be conceited, because he judges himself by a false standard. The conceptions which the ancients had of humility and all moral virtues were impure and not in keeping with the moral law. The Gospel first presented morality in its purity, and there is nothing in history to compare with it. But if this humility is wrongly construed, harm may result; for it does not bring courage, but the reverse. Conscious of his shortcomings, a man may feel that his actions can never attain to the level of the moral law and he may give up trying, and simply do nothing. Self-conceit and dejection are the two rocks on which man is wrecked if he deviates, in the one direction or the other, from the moral law. On the one hand, man should not despair, but should believe himself strong enough to follow the moral law, even though he himself is not conformable to it. On the other hand, he ought to avoid self-conceit and an exaggerated notion of his powers; the purity of the moral law should prevent him from falling into this pitfall, for no one who has the law explained to him in its absolute purity can be so foolish as to imagine that it is within his powers fully to comply with it. The existence of this safeguard makes the danger of self-conceit less than that of inertia grounded in faith. It is only the lazy, those who have no wish to do anything themselves but to leave it all to God, who interpret their religion thus. The remedy against such dejection and inertia is to be found in our being able to hope that our weakness and infirmity will be supplemented by the help of God if we but do the utmost that the consciousness of our capacity tells us we are able to do. This is the one and indispensable condition on which we can be worthy of God's help, and have a right to hope for it. In order to convince man of his weakness, make him humble and induce him to pray to God for help, some writers have tried to deny to man any good disposition. This can do no good. It is certainly right and proper that man should recognize how weak he is, but not by the sacrifice of his good dispositions, for if he is to receive God's help he must at least be worthy of it. If we depreciate the value of human virtues we do harm, because if we deny good intentions to the man who lives aright, where is the difference between him and the evildoer? Each of us feels that at some time or other we have done a good action from a good disposition and that we are capable of doing so again. Though our actions are all very imperfect, and though we can never hope that they will attain to the standard of the moral law, yet they may approach ever nearer and nearer to it.

**STUDY QUESTIONS**

1. Do you agree with Kant that you have moral duties to yourself? If so, in your opinion, what are they?
2. Do you find Kant's arguments against suicide convincing? Do you agree that suicide is "the most abominable of the vices"?
3. Kant says, "The duties we owe to ourselves do not depend on the relation of the action to the ends of happiness." Is our duty,

then, to make *others* happy? No one happy? What does Kant see
our duty to be?

4. A United States Congressman who was found guilty of accepting "Abscam" bribes pleaded before the judge, "Alcoholism
made me lose my judgment." What would Kant say about this
man's self-respect? In which ways, according to Kant, has this
man failed in his duties to himself?

5. What does Kant mean by "worth"? By self-worth? Why does
our human worth demand reverence? What follows when we
lack a sense of self-worth?

# *Character and Culture*

### ANTHONY QUINTON

Anthony Quinton (b. 1925) is President of Trinity College, Oxford. He is the author of a number of books
including *The Nature of Things* (1973), *Utilitarian Ethics*
(1973), and *Thoughts and Thinkers* (1982).

Quinton describes the decline of the concepts of character
and will over the past hundred years. The person of character "pursues purposes without being distracted by
passing impulses." Character and will are measured by
strength; thus, persons of very weak character are said to
have "no character." As Quinton understands it, character is very much like self-control. He argues that character is the essence of virtue in the classical sense, since
virtuous persons are those persons of reason who pursue
their principled aims without letting passion interfere.
Character in this sense was recently undermined, says
Quinton, by several historical attacks. One came with the
new sexual liberation espoused by some late Victorians

CHARACTER AND CULTURE Reprinted by permission of *The New Republic,* © 1983, The New
Republic, Inc.

and early twentieth-century rationalists (George Bernard Shaw and Bertrand Russell, for example). Another was initiated by estheticists such as Ruskin and Pater. The result is the current permissive morality in both its passive and ecstatic forms (the latter calling for active indulgence of instincts and drives). Both styles are hostile to character and will. The decline of religion is the third factor in the rise of the "characterless self." The religious impulse is transformed into "radical agitation in the interests of various species of underdog." Yet another concern is the current fear of total extinction that creates a climate of living for the moment, "for tomorrow we die." Quinton notes that the literature of modern moral philosophy has neglected character and will, paying far more attention to what people have a right to than to what sort of person they should be. Quinton calls on moral philosophy to redress the imbalance by attending once again to virtue.

In 1973, in "Art, Will and Necessity," Lionel Trilling wrote:

> The concept of the will no longer figures significantly in the systematic psychology of our day. Those of us who are old enough to have been brought up in the shadow of the nineteenth century can recall how important the will was once thought to be in the conduct of the personal life, how confidently our parents and teachers pointed to the practical as well as the moral advantages of having a will of developed strength and discipline. Nothing could be more alien to the contemporary style of rearing and teaching the young. In the nineteenth century the will was a central and controlling topic in psychological and ethical theory—as how could it not be, given an economic system in which the unshakeable resolve of the industrial entrepreneur was of the essence, and given the temperaments of its great cultural figures?

I would like to reopen this question, to inquire what character and will actually are; and then, mindful of the fact that the word "ethics" means different things in the two main English-speaking countries—moral practice here, moral theory in England—I shall consider the declining presence of character and will in actual moral life and their distinctly marginal, even furtive, role in organized thinking about morality.

Character is different from personality. Personality is the style or form of a person's presentation of himself, typically in more or less short-lived encounters. It is, therefore, something that can be put on and taken off more or less at will, like clothing or makeup, the device which makes it possible to be all things to all men for those who want to be so. The derivation of the word from *persona,* a mask, is not evidence, but it is surely symptomatic. Character, by contrast, is something more deeply rooted, not innate or unalterable, but at least a fairly hard-won achievement; character is the reality of which personality is the appearance. I am treating personality here in the sense which it usually has in colloquial speech. Psychologists engaged in the study of what they call personality apply the word much more widely to cover the whole range of a person's dispositions, character and personality colloquially understood being among those dispositions but not exhausting them.

Character is essential or fundamental and not, like personality, a matter of the surface. It is modifiable by teaching and, in a way, by effort, unlike such innate and constitutional things as temperament, tastes, and intellectual power. It is comparatively unspecific, unlike abilities and skills. My main claim is that it is in essence resolution, determination, a matter of pursuing purposes without being distracted by passing impulses. It is something that is measured in terms of its strength. Its strength, indeed, is its existence, for the weaker it is the closer it comes to nonexistence. In that respect it is like the will, as we ordinarily conceive it. To have a will is to have a fairly strong one. To have a very weak will is the next best thing to having no will at all.

Is this a peculiar, idiosyncratic notion of character? It comprises, at any rate, three of the four virtues that Plato took to be most important: prudence, courage, moderation. Insofar as his fourth virtue, justice, is taken to be impartiality or fairness—the power, that is, to resist the promptings of immediate affection or favor—it is also a quality of character. The qualities of character I have mentioned are all dispositions to resist the immediate solicitations of impulse. Prudence is a settled resistance to whim, courage to fear, temperance to greed, justice or selfishness or particular affections. One could add industriousness as resistance to laziness, reliability as resistance to taking the easiest way. They are, generally speaking, ways of deferring gratification, of protecting the achievement of some valued object in the future from being underminded by the pull of lesser objects near at hand.

In the light of these considerations I propose that the idea of character is procedural rather than substantive. It is not a matter of having a particular set of desires alongside the instinctive, impulsive desires we share with other animals. It is the disposition or habit of controlling one's immediate, impulsive desires, so that we do not let them issue in action until we have considered the bearing of that action on the achievement of other, remoter objects of desire. Understood this way, character is much the same thing as self-control or strength of will. Like them it may be used for bad purposes. But one may suspect that only those of the most delightful innate temperament and preferences can achieve much morally without it, and then only if their circumstances are very safe and easy—that is, if all that is required of a moral agent is kindliness.

The cognitive distinguishing mark of the human species is its reasoning power, the ability that we have, conferred by language, to think about what is outside the immediate zone of perception and to work out what to do to produce or prevent future possibilities, contingent on our action, that we find attractive or repellent. Strength of character, by holding in check impulses excited by what is immediately present, allows the cognitive harvest of our reasoning powers to have an effect on what we do. To conceive character in this way is to give an acceptable sense to the idea that reason can and should control the passions.

In the English-speaking world we live and move amid the ruins of Victorian morality, in which character and will occupied an important place. Its central theme was one of strenuous self-discipline. It was itself a reaction against the consciously nonstrenuous morality of the eighteenth century which preceded it, and which was, in its turn, a reversal of the gloomy fanaticism of the seventeenth century and the epoch of the wars of religion. Character and strength of will were not repudiated by the secular good sense of the Augustans. Long-term aims were essential for the rational management of life and for morality, which was seen as an indispensable part of that code of rational living. But the aims now approved were secular and terrestrial, to be pursued by steady and prudent application, not with guilty fanatical enthusiasm. Hume's words for morally desirable qualities of character are representative: they are, he maintained, those that are "agreeable or useful," the properties, we might feel, more of an ideal weekend guest than of a collaborator in some risky and ambitious undertaking.

The morality of the eighteenth century was a relaxed and elegant version of the ideal of life of the Protestant commercial middle class, which had been progressively reconciled to life on this sinful earth by the worldly success that had accrued to its hard word and fore-sight. It was such sober and prudent people who established the first European settlement in North America, people of such moderate outlook as to be capable of using turkey for purposes of celebration. Acquiescing in their own good fortune, they found an emblem, after a century and a half, in Benjamin Franklin, a believer in only the most judicious and economical repression of instinct. By the middle of the nineteenth century an altogether more severe and ascetic ideal of life had replaced his genial accommodation of long-term goals and short-term needs.

The main ingredients of Victorianism are nearly all aspects of an ideal of self-reliance. At the top is industry, in which effort is accompanied by scrupulous workmanship. Honesty and fidelity to promises, so advantageous in the nineteenth-century business world of small enterprises, are seen as required in all people's activities. Waste is deplored, so that opportunity should not be let slip and so that provision is made against ill fortune. Sexuality is narrowly confined within the limits of monogamy. Benevolence is confined to the unfortunate; the merely pitiable do not as such deserve it, since they may be simply failures. Decorum must be maintained, serving as a kind of fireproof matting to keep down smoldering impulses to passion and extravagance.

This morality was overcome by two main lines of attack. The first of them is the rationalism of a group of late nineteenth- and early twentieth-century thinkers who sought to revive the Enlightenment, notably Samuel Butler, George Bernard Shaw, and Bertrand Russell. They attacked Victorian ideas about sex, property, the relations of men to women, and of adults to children; and, consequentially, the decorum that they saw as preserving the moral errors they attacked at one level and the religion they saw as sanctifying them at another. They hoped that a new, more rational morality would free people to perfect themselves. These late-Victorian and Edwardian moral reformers were themselves people of strong character, richly endowed with will. Shaw and Russell were very hard workers; Shaw was physically ascetic above and beyond the call of Victorianism, undefiled by drink, meat, or sexuality.

The other line of attack on Victorianism was, as far as England and no doubt the English-speaking world in general is concerned, an import from continental Europe, particularly France. What I have in mind is a sequence of hedonisms, by no means closely related or sympathetic to each other. To start with, there is the decadence of the 1890s, which, in its politer form, was aestheticism, the Paterian life of intense private sensation. After 1918 the sensations pursued become rougher and more primordial, but there is the same desire to shock and to ridicule older pieties. Vulgar Freudianism, the idea that all inhibition is bad, unhealthy, the cause of neurosis, helped to fill the sails of this pleasure-boat. Just as aestheticism had a kind of rural correlate in the sandal-wearing communities of admirers of Ruskin, given to free love or the drinking of fruit juice, so the rural arm of the hedonism of the 1920s was the instinctualism of D. H. Lawrence, who recruited Freud for his own special uses as did the heroines of Scott Fitzgerald and the early Evelyn Waugh.

In our time everyday morality, emancipated from Victorianism, takes two principal forms, corresponding in their rough and popular way to the two lines of moral reform I have described. The first is the negatively permissive morality whose ideal of life is one of passive consumption, of the more or less inert enjoyment of material and, one might say, recreational satisfactions. An important feature is the unloading onto something called "society" of the duty of ensuring that the means of satisfaction are available at minimal cost and effort, and also of the responsibility for the failures and crimes of individuals. The quality most admired is amiability, a sort of uncritical endorsement of the wants and acts of others, free from all trace of censoriousness.

The second is the ecstatic morality that enjoins the unrestricted indulgence of instinct up to, and even beyond, the limits of ordinary self-preservation. It is less widespread than permissiveness, being largely confined to the young. On this view all frustration or inhibition is bad and unhealthy. Older ideas of the natural goodness of mankind are reanimated, often with the qualification that innocence can survive only in communities sequestered from the corrupting influences of the urban, industrial world. [In this system of thought the freaked-out adolescent takes over the role of Wordsworth's baby as "mighty prophet, seer blest."]

Both moral styles are, even at their best, hostile to character and will. For the permissive, strength of character is tiresome and embarrassing, a source of unnecessary trouble, spoiling things by its imposition of disagreeable restraints, souring the enjoyment of life with irrational guilt. For the ecstatic, strength of character is more like a disease, a neurotic deformation of personality fostered by individualism and to be helped by immersion in a collectivity in which selfhood is dismantled. From a point of view which neither would accept, both are juvenile: permissiveness in its idealization of the style of life of the pampered child, receiving presents and having fun; ecstaticism in its idealization of the wholly uncontrolled or runaway child, living wildly with a gang.

There is a great deal of social commentary and description in which the decline of character and will has been recorded, with and without implied attitudes of welcome or distaste. There is also a great deal of explanatory material to hand, ranging from the influence of theories at one extreme to that of new modes of social organization at the other. Of theories the most relevant are those that affirm the motivation of human conduct by forces that agents are not aware of, above all Freudian psychoanalysis. In particular, the Freudian account of the conscience or superego as the product of aggression turned by the individual against himself through fear of the withdrawal of parental love suggests that obedience to its commands is some sort of self-mutilation. Perhaps Freud did not intend his theory of the superego to have the comprehensively undermining effect that it has had. To argue that conscientiousness or a sense of guilt can be pathologically exaggerated need not show that conscientiousness in general is a sickness, let alone that character or strength of will is. Freud himself was the unashamed possessor of a will of great strength. There is an instructive aspect to his account of conscience in what he says about civilization. Although he sees it as having some qualities of a collective neurosis, he takes the renunciation of instinct it requires to be preferable to the alternative of uncontrolled aggressiveness.

Another factor in the emergence of the characterless self is the decline of religion, or at least its transformation into radical agitation in the interests of various species of underdog. Other features of our times that might be cited in an explanatory way are the prospect of total extinction by nuclear war; the relapse to seventeenth-century levels of brutality in politics, intensified by improved technology; the general disappointment of enlightened liberal expectations as crime has increased at home and despotism abroad, particularly in those parts of the world that have secured political independence from the West. But more to the point, I believe, is the enlargement of the institutions in which people work or with which they are otherwise involved. In the first place, that instills feelings of power-lessness and dependence and so contracts the sphere of action of character and will. Secondly, conscientiousness diminishes when the actions to which it prompts us concern our relations to remote, im-personal organizations rather than concrete individuals.

Whatever the correct explanation may be, there can be no doubt of the fact that a large moral change has taken place in the Western, or at any rate English-speaking, world in the twentieth century. Many would see it as primarily a change in the content of morality, in our conceptions of what actions are right and wrong and of what states of affairs our actions should be morally applied to produce or pre-vent: specifically that hitherto dominant adult males are on the same footing with women and children, and that the supposed rights of those who earn and own should be subordinated to the claims of those who want and need.

What I am suggesting is that such an account of what has hap-pened does not go far enough—that these changes of content or substance are less fundamental than changes of form which have accompanied them and have altered the whole conception of the moral agent. The liberal or progressive proposers of the changes in moral content that have taken place hoped they would provide con-ditions in which the dominated or unfortunate would be free to express their strength of character in achievement previously impos-sible for them. Instead we have witnessed the pervasive decline of character.

Character and will have been very much neglected in modern moral philosophy as well as in life. In fact, philosophers have neglected the subjects far longer—ever since philosophical reflection on morality began to be conducted in an independently rational manner, ab-stracted from, although not necessarily in conflict with, the morality of religion, in the seventeenth century. In the century that followed,

Butler, Hume, and Kant all still concerned themselves with the topic of virtue, which is closely connected with character, since it is partly constitutive of it. But their prime interest was in rightness or duty, which is a property of actions, and only secondarily with the dispositions in agents from which right actions flow.

Since Hume and Kant the topic of virtue has been largely of marginal concern to moral philosophers. Their main concern has been with the question of whether the rightness of acts is intrinsic to them, as Kant and other rationalists like Samuel Clarke supposed, or is a function of the goodness of the consequences which actions of the kind in question can be reasonably expected to produce. Agreeing in general that virtue is the disposition to right action, they have divided into those who see as virtuous only the Kantian motive, which is more or less guaranteed to lead to right action, and those less rigorous thinkers who admit as virtuous any disposition of agents which tends to right action in most cases.

I used to be satisfied with the Humean view. What I now reject in it is the assimilation it makes of virtues in particular and, by implication, of qualities of character in general, to desires, conceived either as settled preferences or as qualities of temperament. Virtues and qualities of character are, I am now convinced, not just given elements in an agent's appetitive constitution, but cultivated and disciplined modes of choice, by which passive appetites are held in check and so brought into contention with longer term purposes. The distinction can be conveniently illuminated by contrasting two ways in which the slightly archaic word "benevolence" can be taken. On the one hand it can be used to refer to a direct appetite or preference for the happiness of others or, again, to settled amiability of temperament. On the other, it can be taken as something more in the nature of a policy, or a principle of giving weight in one's decisions to others' happiness or well-being.

The emphasis was once very different in philosophical reflection on morality. In the classical world the notion of virtue was the primary or fundamental moral notion. The chief question for the moral philosopher, according to Plato and Aristotle, was not so much "what should I do?" asked at some specific juncture, but "how should I live?" or, more exactly, "what sort of person should I be?" Since the early modern period and the resecularization of philosophy the question has become "how am I to find out what I should do?" It is not that that question did not arise for the classical moral thinkers. But the Thrasymachus with whom Socrates argues in the early part of Plato's *Republic* is more a man who does not see that he has a motive for acting justly or rightly than one who is skeptical of conventional beliefs about what it is right or just to do.

Modern moral philosophy, like the rest of philosophy, is inveterately epistemological. And from that point of view, the picking out of certain human dispositions as virtues or morally good qualities of character is secondary. Both Hume and Kant determine the virtuousness of benevolence and fidelity in the one case and conscientiousness in the other by their relation to the independently established moral qualities of actions, that is by their rightness. Cognitively speaking, then, the moral quality of agents is derived from the moral quality of actions. For consequentialists the moral quality of actions is derived in its turn from the value of the states of affairs to which those actions can be reasonably expected to lead.

I have argued that the cognitive pre-occupations of moral philosophers in recent times have led them to ignore virtue, and character generally. It is as if they had seen their task as that of considering the activities of the moral agent in the thick of choice, of the moral critic hoping for some ratification of his critical authority, of the moral disputant involved in disagreement with someone who rejects his moral convictions. There is another perspective from which virtue and character bulk larger. This is the perspective of the moral educator. You have to have some confident idea about what is morally right before you can set about getting people to do it. But it is little use knowing what should be done unless you can get people to do it.

In general outline it seems clear enough that two factors operate in the moral development of the normally brought-up child. The first is simple imitation, the second that pursuit of parental approval which Freud painted in such funereal colors. The fact that virtue and character have such humble beginnings does not undermine or invalidate them. Since we start as minute savages it is inevitable that all our higher achievements should start in some more or less deplorable or undignified Yeatsian rag and bone shop. The fallacy involved in denying that is a curious survival of the pre-Darwinian superstition that the greater cannot come out of the lesser.

Not all development or improvement of character is externally induced. There is such an activity as self-examination; it was a habit for our pious forebears, but we are more likely to be pushed into it by some conspicuous occasion for disgust with ourselves. Morally mature human beings ordinarily acquire certain moral preferences, for courage over cowardice, for equability over petulance. There is no paradox in saying that one can be led by these preferences into the effort of seeking to improve one's character. The fact that in such self-improvement one will need to draw on qualities of character such as determination still does not generate the paradox of using a trait of character to bring itself into existence. The man who says to himself "I really must cultivate more resolution" is in a bit of a fix if he has none whatever. You cannot enter the game with nothing at all or develop the muscle in a missing limb.

There is a weird piece of argument in the ethics of Kant which I always used to ridicule. He said that if nature had intended men to make happiness their overriding end, they would have been fitted out with instincts that led them automatically to it. But, since we have reason, our proper purpose must be something different. I am not yet ready to swallow this whole, but I do now have some sympathy for it. Our instincts are not enough; evolution has organized and modified them, and provided us with a long infancy in which the formation of character can take place. If for no more dignified reason, we should hang on to character for self-defense, as the porcupine does to his prickles or the lobster to his shell.

**STUDY QUESTIONS**

1. Why does Quinton think of character as a hardwon achievement?
2. Character, says Quinton, is a disposition or habit of controlling one's immediate impulsive desires. Does this commit Quinton to the view that even a very immoral person may have a strong character? Do you see a difference between having a strong character and having a good character? Is having a strong character a necessary condition for being a morally good person?
3. What does Quinton mean when he calls the character a "procedural" rather than a "substantive" concept?

4. Quinton criticizes contemporary society for ignoring the traditional virtues by making a cardinal virtue of "amiability"—"a sort of uncritical endorsement of the wants and acts of others." Do you think his criticism is fair?
5. How and why, according to Quinton, has modern philosophy as a discipline neglected character and will?

# On the Nature of Character: Field Notes

## ROBERT COLES

Robert Coles (b. 1929) has been at Harvard University for many years, both as clinician and teacher. He is the author of numerous books including *Children in Crisis* (1967), *The Political Life of Children* (1986), and *The Moral Life of Children* (1986).

Robert Coles' discussion of moral character is anecdotal, consisting primarily of what many students and teachers reported about character and character development. Coles "went into the field" seeking insight into the nature of character. He had grown impatient with the psychologist's approach to character and personality, an approach that focuses mainly on disorders and pathology, and that casts little light on "character building" in the moral sense.

Talking to Ruby Bridges—one of the first black children to challenge school desegregation in the deep South by daily facing up to the wrath of those who lined up to jeer and curse as she entered the school—Coles was convinced further that the "professional" description of

ON THE NATURE OF CHARACTER: FIELD NOTES By Robert Coles. Reprinted from "America's Schools: Portraits and Perspectives," in *Daedalus,* Journal of the American Academy of Arts and Sciences, Fall 1981. By permission of the publisher.

Ruby as culturally deprived and disadvantaged did scant justice to her bravery and strength of character. His contact with children like Ruby Bridges led Coles to distinguish between character and the capacity for moral *thinking*. The latter, for someone like Lawrence Kohlberg, is central to being moral.

In other field studies, Coles spoke to students and teachers in private schools in New England. Here the students were more articulate, but again Coles was pleased to find that they were "not anxious to have all human behavior [reduced to] psychology or psychopathology." Some of those to whom Coles spoke maintained that the study of literature was an important source for the understanding and the building of character. Returning to the South, Coles spoke to teachers and principals of the more disadvantaged schools. Some told him that they helped their students by insisting on responsibility. "Let these kids work hard and better themselves, and be good members of their families . . . and they'll show character . . . But to me character means an active person who is ready to face the world and make a mark on it." Coles was impressed by the importance of religion in the lives of the more disadvantaged children, and he characterizes the Church as "a lifeline that rescues [some] from the culture of narcissism." Coles concludes by citing with approval Kierkegaard's dictum that "morality is character."

In the Harvard College of the decade after the Second World War, Gordon Allport was a significant figure indeed—interested always in connecting the newly influential social sciences to the ethical and religious concerns of earlier social and psychological scholars: William James, of course, and William McDougall, and farther back, J. S. Mill or John Locke. I still remember a lecture of Allport's in 1950 in which he stressed the distinction between character and personality. He was forever anxious to acknowledge Freud's perceptive, trenchant thrusts into the outer precincts of consciousness, while at the same time remind us what Freud could afford to ignore about himself and certain others: a moral center that was, quite simply, *there*. No amount of psychoanalysis, even an interminable stretch of it, Allport cautioned us—drawing on Freud's givens with respect to human development—can provide a strong conscience to a person who has grown up in such a fashion as to become chronically dishonest, mean-spirited, a liar. "Psychoanalysis can provide insight, can help us overcome inhibitions," we were told, "but it was not meant to be an instrument of 'character building.'" I found recently my old college notes, found that sentence. I had put a big question mark above the phrase "character building," as if to say: What is it, really? I had heard the expression often enough in the Boy Scouts, in Sunday School, and, not least, from my somewhat Puritanical parents. They set great store by virtues they referred to as self-discipline, responsibility, honesty (often described as "the best policy"), and not least, the one my mother most commonly mentioned, "good conduct." Could it be that a social *scientist,* in the middle of the twentieth century, was mentioning such qualities in a college lecture—was, in fact, asking us to consider how they might be evaluated in people, with some accuracy and consistency?[1]

At that time such efforts were still being made, notably by Robert Havighurst and Hilda Taba and their colleagues at the University of Chicago.[2] But as I got nearer and nearer to becoming a doctor, then a pediatrician, then a child psychiatrist, I heard less and less about "character" and more and more about "character disorders"—certain elements of psychopathology that many psychoanalysts today connect with the vicissitudes of what is called "psychosexual development."[3] In his early productive years, before he turned fanciful— if not deranged—Wilhelm Reich placed great emphasis on what he called "character reactions," the particular way each person works out his or her psychodynamic fate. "In the main," he once said, "character proves to be a narcissistic defense mechanism."[4] No doubt

---

[1]A good summary of Allport's sensitive moral and psychological writing is found in *Personality: A Psychological Interpretation* (New York: Holt, 1937).

[2]See R. J. Havighurst and H. Taba, *Adolescent Character and Personality* (New York: Wiley, 1949). Also, more recently, R. Havighurst and R. Peck, *The Psychology of Character Development* (New York: Wiley, 1960).

[3]See *Disorders of Character*, by Joseph Michaels (Springfield, Illinois: Thomas, 1955), for a suggestive discussion, with a first-rate bibliography.

[4]Wilhelm Reich, *Character Analysis*, 3d ed. (New York: Farrar, Straus & Giroux, 1972), p. 169.

such a generalization can be helpful; we are brought closer to the subliminal workings of the mind, and to its historic necessities of symbolic expression and self-protection, in the face of turmoil generated from within, never mind the stresses that "life" manages to bring. But at some point, even the most factual-minded or dispassionately "rational" of psychoanalytic observers, anxious to maintain a "value-free" posture, would be tempted to observe that there is more to the assessment of human beings than an analysis (even one "in-depth") of narcissistic defense mechanisms can provide.

Hitler's mechanisms, Stalin's, those of any number of murderers or thieves, surely offered what Reich called a "character armor"—as do, right now, the mechanisms employed by Mother Theresa's unconscious, and that belonging to Dom Helder of Brazil's Recife, or to such among us in America as Robert Penn Warren or Eudora Welty or, until her death recently, Dorothy Day. At some point the issue becomes decidedly moral—or, in today's flat, impoverished language, a "normative matter." If I may call upon Gordon Allport again, "character is personality evaluated," a descriptive notion that may make up, in its everyday usefulness, for whatever is lost so far as "psychodynamic relevance" goes.

How we go about doing that evaluation is a matter of great import. In recent years character has been of little concern for many of us whose interest is mental life, or the social and cultural life of human beings. The very word may suggest a prescientific age; may remind us of pietistic avowals or moralistic banalities many of us have tried to put behind us; may bring up the spectre of a word being used to protect the privileges of the well-born, the powerful—as if what is at issue is etiquette, polish, a certain appearance or manner of talking and carrying oneself. How much fairer, some say, to judge people through their academic performance, or through standardized tests: no risk of subjectivity, not to mention self-serving partiality. Still, it is not only Emerson, in another age, who suggested that "character is higher than intellect," and who observed that "a great soul will be strong to live, as well as strong to think."[5] Walker Percy today reminds us of those "who get all A's and flunk life."[6] And surely, a

---

[5]In his well-known oration, "The American Scholar," delivered before Harvard's Phi Beta Kappa Society on August 31, 1837.

century that has witnessed learned individuals like Jung and Heidegger embrace Nazism, not to mention any number of intellectuals preach uncritically the virtues of Stalinist totalitarianism, is not going to be completely uninterested in such distinctions as the age-old polarity of knowledge as against wisdom.

In my own working life the question of "character" came up in the early 1960s when my wife and I were getting to know the black children who initiated school desegregation in the South, often against high odds—mob violence, even—and the young men and women who made up the nonviolent sit-in movement. I remember the clinical appraisals, psychological histories, and socioeconomic comments I wrote then. I remember my continuing effort to *characterize* those children, those youths—as if one weighty, academically acceptable adjective after another would, in sum, do the job. Ruby was from a "culturally deprived," a "culturally disadvantaged," family. Tessie's grandmother was illiterate. Lawrence was counterphobic, suffering "deep down" from a mix of anxiety and depression. Martha "projected" a lot. George was prone to "reaction-formations." Jim seemed to have a "character disorder," even a "borderline personality." Fred might well become psychotic later on. Meanwhile, these youthful American citizens were walking past grown men and women who were calling them the foulest of names, who were even threatening to kill them—and such hecklers were escaping sociological and psychological scrutiny in the bargain, while any number of judges were ordering "evaluations" by my kind to be done on sit-in students who were violating the (segregationist) laws, and who were thought to be (and eventually declared by doctors to be) "sick" or "delinquent" or "troubled" or "sociopathic" or "psychopathic." A historic crisis had confronted a region politically, and in so doing, had ripped open the political, economic, racial aspects of our manner of judging others—the direct connection between what the Bible calls "principalities and powers," and what in our everyday life is "normal" or "proper" behavior. One day, as I mumbled some statements suffused with the words of psychiatric theory to "explain" a given child's behavior, my wife said, "You are making her sound as

---

[6]Walker Percy, *The Second Coming* (New York: Farrar, Straus & Giroux, 1980). See also his wonderful collection of essays, which take up the same theme again and again, *The Message in the Bottle* (New York: Farrar, Straus & Giroux, 1975).

if she ought to be on her way to a child guidance clinic, but she is walking into a school building—and no matter the threats, she is holding her head up high, even smiling at her obscene hecklers. Last night she even prayed for them!''

It was my wife's judgment that Ruby Bridges, aged six, was demonstrating to all the world *character.* Even if cognitive psychologists were to declare such a child not old enough to make certain recognitions or distinctions; even if other theorists were to find Ruby unable to do very much moral reasoning or analysis; even if still other social scientists or clinicians were to emphasize her severe "problems"— her imitative habits, her fearful responses, her Oedipal tensions, her moments of blind obedience or terror-struck submission; even if she were to demonstrate to any number of curious observers—armed with questions, tests, stories to be analyzed, crayons to be used on drawing paper—certain handicaps, developmental difficulties, emotional impasses or disorders, cognitive blocks, age-related blind spots; nevertheless, she was managing to face those mobs with a quiet, stoic dignity that impressed her teachers, newspaper reporters, and federal marshals (who escorted her each day to and from school). One of her teachers, as a matter of fact, said that she herself could never submit to such a daily scene—suggesting that moral *behavior* is not necessarily the same thing as a capacity for moral *thinking;* that character may not be something one ascertains through questionnaires or through experiments done on a university campus.

Against such vexing theoretical difficulties (which had become for me a matter of continuing astonishment, if not haunting confusion), a chance to talk again with young people in a variety of school situations was most welcome. My wife and I had spent years visiting a number of Atlanta's high schools, though not George Washington Carver School.[7] We had spent a season visiting a high school north of Chicago, though not Highland Park High School.[8] And we have children in the private schools of New England, though not St. Paul's School. I decided to keep trying to gain some sense of the variations

---

[7]See my *Children of Crisis: A Study of Courage and Fear,* vol. I (Boston: Atlantic-Little, Brown, 1967).

[8]See the section, "Schools" in volume 3 of *Children of Crisis: The South Goes North* (Boston: Atlantic-Little, Brown, 1967).

in the moral life of the young by emphasizing that subject in my planned visits to these three schools, in the hope that more and more of what Anna Freud calls "direct observation" (as opposed to eagerly speculative and all too inclusive and unqualified generalizations) will help us to understand where "personality" ends and "character" begins in the mind's life.

The "methodology" is thoroughly simple—a mere beginning in exploration, but perhaps not an altogether futile way to learn something about certain young people. I asked the principals of the two public high schools and the headmaster of the private school to "select two teachers qualified to judge character"; those teachers would, in turn, select four or so students who, they believe, possess "character" or "high character." When the principals of Highland Park and Carver asked what I meant by such a word, such an expression, I replied simply that I was trying to find out precisely *that*. I told each principal that I wanted to speak with all the students chosen together, rather than separately, and that I wanted to meet also with the two teachers together.

I went to St. Paul's School first. The headmaster had arranged for two teachers to select four students, and we met in a classroom a good distance from the headmaster's office. We were, in a sense, free—no classes, no one to interrupt or keep an eye on what was to be a full morning's discussion. I told the students, two young men and two young women, that I wanted to explore the meaning to them of "character," and we were, with no hesitation, off to a sustained inquiry.

The word was not a strange one for these students; they had heard it used repeatedly, they said, though none had ever really stopped to think about its meaning. Early on one of the young women said, "We talk about 'human nature' or 'personality' or 'identity'; I suppose in the past they talked about 'character.'" Yet these students were quite articulate as they sifted and sorted among themselves and their classmates in search of a definition, a way of looking at a particular subject. In no time a whole school was being morally scrutinized: the "jocks," the "beautiful people," the "social butterflies," the "freaks," the "party people," the "grinds," various teachers, and the "goodly heritage," a phrase many who have gone to St. Paul's have heard again and again.

Much time was spent struggling with the question of arrogance, with the temptation of self-importance and self-centeredness—a personal hazard these four were not loath to acknowledge. They were in a school known as one of the best in America. They were, in different ways, doing well there—one academically; one as a scholar-athlete; one for showing concern and compassion for others, near and afar; one as a person trusted and liked by a wide assortment of classmates. Yet they worried that their success was a temptation to "become stuck-up," as one put it. Self-righteousness and self-consciousness were additional hazards—elements likely to shut a person off, making that person less responsive to other people. Gradually, how one responds to others took on high importance. One of the young men put it this way: "I tend to be a private person. I like to take long walks by myself. At times I don't want company. I want to hold onto my individuality. But I like to be with others, too. I like to be a *friend*. I'd like to think that if someone were in trouble, he'd turn to me, and I'd be there, and I'd put that person's trouble above my needs, including taking a solitary walk!"

Other topics came up frequently: the tension between adjustment to the demands of various cliques and the private values a given individual feels to be important—or put differently, the tension between loyalty to one's friends and loyalty to one's own memories, habits, yearnings; the tension between one's competitive side and one's regard for others; and more crudely, the tension between one's wish to win and one's willingness to help others. The word "honesty" was mentioned over and over—an Augustinian examination, done with today's psychological panache: who is "really" honest, and for what "underlying" reasons? Moreover, does it "pay" in this society to be honest all the time? When do honesty and self-effacement turn into "masochism"? When does pride in one's convictions turn into a bullying egotism? If you really do have "a sense of yourself," are you not in danger of being smug, self-serving, all too sure of your own significance? When does popularity reduce one's individuality to the point that one belongs to a herd, has lost a mind of one's own?

Such questions were asked quite earnestly, and always with regard to the matter at hand: the characteristics of character. When pressed by one another (I ended up being, most of the time, a listener), the students offered lists: a person who sticks to a set of principles; a person who can risk unpopularity, yet is commanding enough to

gain the respect of others; a person who has the courage to be himself, herself; a person who is open-minded, who plays fair with
others, who doesn't lie and cheat and, interestingly enough, deceive
himself, herself. These were students who believed such qualities to
be only partially present. These were students, in fact, who had a
decidedly dialectical turn of mind: "You can try to be a better person,
but it's a struggle. You can be humble, and that way, intimidate
people. You can *use* humility. It's hard to know what's genuine in
people. Sometimes people pretend to be something, but they're really
just the opposite. They flip and they flop. I don't like people who are
sanctimonious. They lecture others, and people take it, but it's out
of fear, or there is guilt, and it's being exploited. Every once in a
while, I prefer someone who puts his cards on the table and shows
he's a real pain in the neck to these holier-than-thou types. Character
doesn't mean being a goody-goody person! If you're that kind of
person, there's a lot of meanness, probably, inside you, or competitiveness that you're not letting on about to others. Maybe you don't
know about it yourself!"

These were, obviously, what we would now call a psychologically
sophisticated breed of youth. Yet, they were (thank God!) not anxious to have all human behavior a matter of psychology or psychopathology—or sociology, either: "There are reasons we end up being
one kind of person or another kind of person, but when you actually
*become* that person (when you're nice to others most of the time), then
that's a true achievement. A lot of people *don't* become nice, and it's
no excuse to say you had a bad childhood or you never had the right
luck. I think you have to take your troubles and overcome them!"
The Puritan spirit lives still in the woods of southern New Hampshire, no matter the references—and they were many—to "adolescence," "identity," Sigmund Freud's ideas, the latest notions of what
"motivates" people, what makes us "anxious" or "strung out" or
"ambivalent."

More than anything else, these four youths grappled with what
used to be commonly called "the meaning of life" in philosophy
lectures (before the advent of logical positivism, computers, the li-
bido theory, and a strictly materialist view of life, liberty, the pursuit
of happiness). One of the young men said this toward the end of our
meeting time: "What matters—don't you think?—is what you *do*
with your life. I've tried to be independent, to have my own
thoughts, but to listen to others. I hope to live comfortably, but I

631

hope I won't be greedy and selfish. I don't know what our responsibilities are—to ourselves and our friends and family and neighbors, and to others in places abroad I'll never even see. Even today, this is a big world. What are we supposed to do? We're lucky to be here at St. Paul's. We have such a good life. What do we owe others? Isn't that 'character'—what you decide to do for others, not just yourself?"

The "great suck of self," Walker Percy calls it in *The Second Coming*—the inevitable pull toward our own thoughts, our own wishes, our navels. Adolescence is not the only period of self-absorption, these youths seemed already to know. For them, one is likely to be neither bad nor good. For them, character was no categorical trait. For them, character is not a possession, but something one searches for: a quality of mind and heart one struggles for, sometimes with a bit more success than at other times. Not one of these four wanted to spell out a definition, set down a compulsory series of attributes, offer a list of candidates. One heard from their mouths expressions of confusion, annoyance, vanity, self-satisfaction, self-criticism, self-doubt, self-assurance. One heard, maybe most of all, tentativeness—a reluctance to speak definitively about an aspect of human behavior one student kept describing as "hard to pin down," but also as "important to consider when you're thinking about someone."

The two teachers I met at St. Paul's school, a middle-aged man who taught math, a young woman who taught English, had met, discussed the subject of "character," and added to one another's notions, so that, in the end, there was a final written statement available:

- The aggregate of distinctive qualities belonging to an individual
- Moral vigor or firmness, especially as acquired through self-discipline
- The ability to respond to a setback
- The ability to form an attachment to ideals of a larger community or organization than oneself, and to exert one's influence for the good of the greater body
- The possession of a sense of humor that allows one to see that there is more to life than living
- The ability to be an *individual* in a crowd of *different* people
- A sense of self that has been found through experience
- The ability to allow others to be individuals, even though they may be different

632

- The ability to disagree with others without condemning (or losing respect for) the individual one disagrees with
- A sensitivity toward the feelings of others
- An understanding of the wholeness of other people's personalities or character (even when it is different from one's own)

These were two individuals who had thought long and hard about a vexing subject—whom to chose, and why? A very bright person, involved in many activities, able to speak coherently and easily, headed straight for Harvard, as against a quiet person who defers to the ideas of others in a classroom, does well, but "not all that well," yet in numerous moments seems to reach out for others, not to save them, or turn them into psychiatric cases, but simply "to do a good turn"? A marvelous athlete who also is a leader in many ways during the course of a school year, as against a hardworking youth who is most often self-effacing, yet managed to stand up once or twice on a matter of ethical principle, no matter the risks and the penalties? And surely a host of alternatives, because, as one teacher put it, "when you judge 'character,' you judge the overall person and compare him, or her, to others, and you do so over time, the school year."

In Highland Park, north of Chicago, a somewhat different arrangement had been made. The principal of this suburban high school had selected two teachers, as I requested, but they had picked four students each—seven girls and one boy, interestingly enough. We met in a room across the hall from the principal's office. Twice he asked how we were doing, offered water, tea, coffee—in general, showed a distinct, active interest in our discussions. He himself had thought about the word "character," and as with so many of us, found it a bit puzzling and elusive. So did the students I spent a winter morning with. Several of them said that character had a lot to do with personality; in fact, declared "a good personality" or a "well-rounded person" to be equivalent descriptions to "good character" or "high character." Two young women dissented, however: "Character has to do with honesty. You can be popular, and have a shrink's seal of approval, but not have character!"

We fairly quickly got into a discussion of ethnic and racial tensions—in the school, in our society as a whole. At St. Paul's the cliques were enumerated, as if they threatened individuality, hence character, through the requirements of social cohesion; at Highland Park High School the dominant social divisions, at least for these students, had to do with class and race: Italians and Jews, "working people" and "wealthier people," blacks and whites.

I was given some outspoken lessons in how one's family life affects one's situation in school, and not least, one's character: "It all depends on who you are! Some kids want to go to an Ivy League school; that's all that's on their minds. They put up a good front, to show they have 'character'; they join clubs, and have all these hobbies and interests, so as to impress the teachers and the people who read college applications. Some kids have to work while going to school. They try to get a good deal, a job that pays well. They're making contacts even now for later on. It's built into their 'character' that the world is tough, and you have to know people to get ahead. A lot of the black kids are here because there's a military base in the school district. They come and then they go. It's hard to figure them out. It's in their 'character' to stay away from us whites. There's a lot of tension among us whites. Go into the johns, and you'll see a lot of writing! [I went, and I saw the ethnic slurs.] But a lot of the time we get along pretty well. We've got brainy ones here, headed for college since they were born, and don't get in their way, or else! We've got kids who will work in a store or a factory, and not be ashamed. They see the world different. They take different courses. They have their own code."

The speaker is a wry, outspoken, somewhat detached young woman, bound for college, but "not a fancy one." She is neither Italian nor Jewish, but Anglo-Irish. She had made a certain virtue out of marginality, and the others in the room seemed a bit deferential: "She isn't pushed around by anyone. She's her own person. She can mingle with anyone. She doesn't put on airs with anyone." The associations moved relentlessly from social situation to moral conduct—not the first time, or the last, such a progression would be made for me in the course of this study. "You have to know where the person is coming from," I was told several times. Explain! "Well, if you've got a lot going for you, then you can be more relaxed. True, you can be a tightwad and be rich; but it's easier to be generous if you've got a lot behind you!" On the other hand, one student insisted, "there's still room for being poor and good in this world!"

She persisted: "I know some kids, right in this school, and they're not here now, they weren't chosen to be here, and they're from pretty poor families, compared to others; their fathers just get by, make a living. And they would give you the shirt off their backs, those kids: that's character. And they wouldn't go talking about what they've done, bragging, and showing off—*that's* character! Some people, they know how to play up to the teachers, and they get a big reputation, but what's the *truth* about them? What are they like when no one is looking, and what are they like when no one is listening?"

We touched many bases. Class and character. Egotism and character. Psychology and character. Smartness and character. Motivation and character. Caring and character. Manners and character. To be stuck-up. To be considerate. To be a help when a person needs help—a flat tire, a car ride, a pencil or piece of paper, a loan of money, a sympathetic ear. To take risks, extend oneself to others, brave social pressures. Grade-mongers. Leaders and followers. Hypocrites. People who have one or another veneer. The "way-down-deep truth" of a person. A final test of character: sickness, financial straits, a disaster. Character and mental health.

Part of *Ordinary People* had been made in Highland Park. The students had watched the filming, and they wondered: If one is hurt, bewildered, "seeing a shrink," can one have the "mental peace" to demonstrate character? Consumerism, selfishness—can one defy them, develop "an ability not to be absorbed with objects." And at some interesting and suggestive length: literature as a means of understanding character, as in *To Kill a Mockingbird* (Atticus had character, he was open-minded, stood up for what he believed, no matter the risks and costs, and so was a "moral man"); or as in *Macbeth* (Lady Macbeth was a "bad person," a "bad character"). And politics: Lincoln and Eisenhower and Truman had character; Johnson lacked it, as do Nixon and Carter. "All politicians probably lie," one student observed, "and maybe all people do, but some just keep on lying, and you can't trust them, and you don't like them, and they're just no damn good, and you can tell, after awhile, even if they tell you they pray every other minute! The truth about a person's character eventually comes out, *eventually.*"

Such faith was not universally shared. There was much talk of appearance as against reality: the way people present themselves to others, as opposed to some inner truth about each of us. In contrast

635

to the students at St. Paul's School, these students were distinctly more interested in the relationship between a person's social, economic, ethnic, or racial background—a person's circumstances—and that person's behavior, hence character. And it did come down to that, they all agreed at the end: "You are the way you act—in the long run." What did that qualification mean? Well, it goes like this: "Some people can put on an act. But if you keep your wits, and keep an eye on them, you find out the truth about them. If they're good people, kind to others, not just wrapped up in themselves, you'll find it out. If they're putting on a production, you'll find that out." No one, in that regard, seemed to have any doubts about his or her ultimate psychological acuity—or about the long-run dramatic capacities of one or another individual.

There was, as we were ending, a spirited, occasionally tense discussion of tests, grades, the criteria used by colleges and graduate schools to evaluate people. "I know kids who get all A's, and would murder their parents, their brothers and sisters, if they stood in their way," one youth offered. Yes, but there's plenty of nastiness to go around, others said, even among those who do poorly in school. What *should* various committees of admission do? How *does* one make a fairly accurate moral judgment about a person? Numbers may not tell enough. Multiple choice questions may not do justice to life's strangeness—the ironies and ambiguities, the complexities and inconsistencies and contradictions we all struggle with, though some with more decency and integrity and generosity of spirit than others. But how do we arrive at an estimate of a person's essential kindness with respect to others—in the face of thousands of importunate applicants, each putting on the very best face possible? Don't interviews have *their* hazards, the unpredictable variations of mood and temperament, the nuances of subjectivity which can, alas, of a sudden, amount to outright prejudice? We ended on an eclectic note—the desirability of taking a lot into consideration when accepting people for a job, a place in a college, and yes, when judging that elusive concept "character." The last person to leave the room, the young woman who spoke least, said that she thought "character meant being kind and good, even when there was no one to reward you for being kind and good."

These were students acutely aware of the divisions in this society—as Tillie Olsen put it in her story *O Yes,* the ways we "sort." The two

Highland Park High School teachers were similarly sensitive to issues of "class and caste," as the splits among us have sometimes been
described. Actually, the teachers were themselves a bit split. The
assistant principal, a man, is quite in touch with the more academic
students of the school; whereas the woman teacher is very much
involved with those students who are working at jobs while trying
to get through Highland Park—and who are headed, mostly, for
what many social scientists would call "service jobs," or membership
in the "working class," or the "lower-middle to middle-middle-
class," and on and on. The two did not argue, however; in fact, they
largely echoed the sentiments of their chosen students: "Grades aren't
the whole story, by any means"; and very emphatically, "Character
has something to do with moral life."

Both teachers worried about class—expressed concern, for instance, that "mere etiquette" can deceive, or insisted that human
scoundrels, like wolves, find sheepskins ("social veneer") aplenty to
wear. I heard practically nothing about class-connected deceit at St.
Paul's, a lot about it at Highland Park—and character seemed to
require, everyone agreed, an impressive absence of such a tendency.
Moreover, psychiatry and psychoanalysis were even more prominently mentioned than at St. Paul's—a way of getting to the "deeper
truth" about people, hence to a judgment of their character. (Fallout
from *Ordinary People?*) As already mentioned, disturbed people were
described as less likely to show high character. When I mentioned
Gandhi's personal eccentricities, if not moments of cruelty, vanity,
thoughtlessness, the students were ready, all too ready, to take the
clue, the hint, and write him off as sick. When I reminded them that
he was, yet, a rather impressive moral leader, the students worried
about the burdens placed on his family, and about his own psychiatric ones.

If I had a little trouble persuading this group of students and their
teachers that, neurosis or no neurosis, a person's moral motives can
affect his or her character, they had no trouble letting me know that
a neighborhood, a level of income, the possession of a given nationality, can all affect a person's character. The teachers especially emphasized the distinction between the quietly considerate person, as
against the demonstrative, if not flamboyant, doer of public good
deeds, a performer of sorts. "Some students want to get A in character, too," one teacher said, as we broke off, a reminder that not

637

only can life be unfair, as one American president took pains to remind us, but virtue can be unfairly perceived—when, in truth, sins are being shrewdly masked. As Flannery O'Connor observed, through the comic irony of a title to one of her stories, a good man is hard to find—and maybe, when the pressures are high, almost impossible to take for granted.

At George Washington Carver High School, in Atlanta, Georgia, I had quite another discussion, with the principal ready to point out the extreme hazards to what he called "character formation" well before I saw (in a room that belonged, really, to his office suite) the four children (two boys and two girls) and two teachers (both women, one who teaches math, the other biology). "There is a problem with drugs," he explained. "There is a problem with poverty, with terrible poverty, with welfare homes, with absent fathers, with unemployment all over the place." He gave me a lively lecture of the school's history—once a "dumping ground for school failures," now a "place of hope," much connected to businesses that offer promising black youths a great variety of jobs, a chance "to enter the mainstream," in the principal's words. In time I was able to begin talking with the four selected youths, though not before being told emphatically: "Character is something you have to build, right here in this school, every day. You have to lay down the law, and see that it's enforced. Character means discipline and hard work and looking to the future and getting there!" Of the three school leaders, Carver's principal was the only one to volunteer (or hazard) such an explication.

The students were not averse to this line of reasoning. These were young people who were determined to find jobs, determined to be hard workers, strong parents—and not reluctant to explain why such a commitment was connected to a definition, in their minds, of the word "character": "A lot of us, even here, with the principal and the teachers bearing down every minute on us, have trouble reading and writing. We're not going to college, most of us. We're going to try to get a job and hold onto it! It takes character, I think, to do that—not take the easy way out and drink or use drugs or say the white man is on our backs, so what the devil can we do! To me, character is being stubborn. It's staying in there, it's getting out of a hole, and breathing the fresh air, and not falling down anymore."

My wife and I spent three years in Atlanta, talking with youths such as these—young black men and women trying, in the face of adversity, to forge a better life for themselves. These were more outspoken and self-assured individuals than the ones we got to know in the early 1960s. They were quick to describe themselves as "job-hungry" and as full of determination, willfulness, hopeful anticipation. They were not, though, uninterested in some of the refinements of psychology I had heard discussed in Illinois and New Hampshire: "There's success and success. It's not only getting there, it's how you get there. If you have character, that means you keep trying, no matter how hard it is, and you don't lose your soul while you're doing that. You have to say to yourself, 'I'll go so far and no farther.' You have to draw the line, and if you do, and you can hold to it, you've got character." Nods all around, followed by smiles of recognition as the temptations get mentioned: white devils and black devils who offer serious distractions in the form of drugs and booze, bribes and payoffs, an assortment of "tricks." These are street-smart kids, and they have lots of savvy about Atlanta politics, Atlanta vice, Atlanta hypocrisy, black and white alike. Their moralism and self-conscious, urgently stated rectitude is hard earned, if (they seem to know) not entirely invulnerable.

One pushes the word "character," gets responses connected to hardship, ambition, the requirements of people living on the edge, hence with little interest in metaphysical or metapsychological speculation. Character? Why, J. R. in *Dallas* lacks it, utterly; Dr. King had it, that's for sure. Character? A lot of big shots may seem to have it, but too bad more people don't know who is scratching whose back. On the other hand, there's a woman who works in a Howard Johnson's motel, and she lost her husband from cancer, and she has five kids, and she has two of them out of high school and in good jobs, and the other three are headed that way, and she doesn't stand for any foolishness, *none,* and she takes those kids to church every Sunday, and they pray hard and long, and she has character, in case anyone wants to know! The church—at long last it comes up in a talk about character! Not in a school that bears the name of St. Paul, no less; and not in a school where Catholics and Jews seem ready to square off at each other all day, every day; but in Carver, you bet. Each of these four high-school-age Americans (no fools about getting high or about the demands of the flesh or about the various shortcuts people take) goes to church on Sundays, and if there is reluctance sometimes (the joy of a late sleep), there is, after all, no real choice: "We have to go. Our mother says we have to go, and once we're there, I don't half mind! I like it there. I'll make my kids go, too."

Much talk of "uplift." Much reference to "building" oneself into "a stronger person," getting "on the map." How? There are auto repair shops. There are radio and TV repair shops. There are cosmetology shops. There are dry-cleaning places. There are tailoring and sewing and shoe repair places. There is a big airport, and people work there—on engines if they are on top, otherwise as cleaning people or doing errands, or driving buses and taxis, "lots of things." (No angst about capitalism at Carver!) If you get one of those jobs, and you hold onto it; if you get yourself a girlfriend or a boyfriend, and they become a wife or a husband, and you become a father or a mother, and you "stay with it," and be good to your family, earn them a living, take care of them; if you remain loyal to your church, and pray to God when you're weak; if you don't forget your people, and try to lend a hand to the ones who didn't make it, who stumbled and fell and are hurt and sad and wondering what the point of it all is, and maybe have done wrong, done it too many times—if all that is "inscribed on your soul," then, by God, you have character, and it's important to say "by God," because it's "His grace that does things."

"I'm not as small after church as I am before church," one of these four told me—a lifeline that rescues at least one American, temporarily, from "the culture of narcissism." As for "good manners," they aren't superficial at all; they tell of something very deep down, no matter what so-called depth psychologists have to say, not to mention those who make of them religious figures: "You can tell a person by how he speaks to you. If he's respectful, then he's good; if he gives you the shoulder, then he's bad. I don't care if someone has a lot of bad in him. If he keeps it a secret from the whole world, then he's way out front. If he shows his bad self to everyone, he's putting it on us, man, and it's hard enough without that—another hassle to deal with. My grandmother tells us: 'Keep your mouth shut if there's no good to come out of it. Keep your mischief to yourself. We've all got it—but some of us don't show it off.' She's right; she has character."

Some other virtues that bespeak character: punctuality; how you carry yourself; an ability to laugh, when there's a good excuse for crying or shouting or shaking your fists; how you speak—with clear enunciation of words, so that others may hear you; self-respect, as measured by neatness and choice of clothes, as well as respect for others, as measured by a smile, a please, a thank you; obedience—to your elders, to the law, to your own self-evident ideas of what is right and wrong. "We all stray," said one of the young women, "but if we try hard not to keep repeating ourselves, and if we're not afraid to learn from our mistakes, and if we're willing to work hard, and sacrifice, then we have character." Pieties, all those remarks, the skeptical, psychoanalyzed liberal Yankee muses—fighting off embarrassment, wonder, a touch of awe, and emotional memories of other youths in other Atlanta spots, youths similarly hard-pressed, who managed to "overcome," and youths similarly unwilling to be self-pitying in the face of the severe inequities of this life.

The two teachers—my wife got to know so many very much like these two: tough-minded, outspoken, a touch contemptuous of anyone who wants to offer sympathy, never mind condolences. They are demanding, insistent, forceful women: "Let these kids work hard, and better themselves, and be good members of their families, and they'll show character; that's how, the only way!" And candidly, bluntly, unapologetically: "We chose the best we have to talk with you. We chose the smart ones, the ones who could talk with you and get themselves across. We have others here who would tax your patience and understanding. Maybe they have 'character,' too. I don't think character is the property of the lucky and the smart and the successful, no sir. But to me, character means an active person, who is ready to face the world, and make a mark on it. That's why I chose these kids. They're ready, they're ready to turn their backs on all their troubles, our troubles, and be good—be full of action. 'Never be lazy,' I tell my kids at home, and here in school. There's that expression: going to meet 'the man.' Well, I say we can become 'the man' ourselves. We can take control of our own lives, be our own masters. It may be preachy of me to talk like this, but we've got to pep-talk ourselves, and then *get on with it!* I pray to God—we need His help badly—that more and more of these kids at Carver *will* get on with it."

On the way home, back North again, I took out my books and papers: notes to write, ideas to savor, comparisons to make. There it was, the wonderful message that Kierkegaard gave us over a century ago, the message I often wish a few of us theorists of moral development would keep in constant mind: "Morality is character, character is that which is engraved (χαράσσω); but the sand and the sea have no character and neither has abstract intelligence, for character is really inwardness. Immorality, as energy, is also character; but to be neither moral nor immoral is merely ambiguous, and ambiguity enters into life when the qualitative distinctions are weakened by a gnawing reflection."[9]

He was a great one for leaps, that nineteenth century version of the melancholy (if spiritedly so) Dane. I wondered on my flight home whether he might somewhere in this universe be smiling, be assenting to the message, the slightly hectoring statement delivered by that mathematics teacher, and later by her tough, occasionally *very* tough, principal, who told me that he had "a lot of bad characters" to deal with, but damned if he couldn't "take them on," "turn them around," "convert their wasted energy into useful energy." It all sounded slightly like the noise of strained braggadocio: I'll talk big, and hope for the best. It all sounded exaggerated, romantic—like Kierkegaard. It all sounded pretty good, though, to those four young people and two of their teachers.

**STUDY QUESTIONS**

1. Coles notes that certain learned individuals (Carl Jung, Martin Heidegger among them) embraced Nazism. What moral does Coles draw about the relevant importance of character and intellect? Do you find his point of view persuasive?

2. What does Coles seem to mean by "character"? Explain how Ruby Bridges demonstrated character. Is Coles' notion of character naive? Profound? Discuss.

3. Contrast Coles and Kohlberg on moral development, and assess the relative merits of their approaches.

4. Look over the list of twelve character traits that emerge from the discussion of St. Paul. Choose three that you consider the most important and defend your choices.

---

[9]Søren Kierkegaard, *The Present Age*, translated by Alexander Dru (New York: Harper & Row, 1962), p. 43.

# The New Narcissism

## CHRISTOPHER LASCH

Christopher Lasch (b. 1932) is a professor of history at the University of Rochester. He is the author of a number of books, including *Haven in a Heartless World* (1977) and *The Culture of Narcissism* (1979).

Christopher Lasch describes a new personal ideal that emphasizes living for the moment, and being for oneself. The "new narcissists" feel free to abandon their social roles (for example, as parent or citizen) for the higher purpose of self-fulfillment by self-gratification. The goal of these new individuals is "personal well-being, health, and psychic security." Seeking this goal is incompatible with a direct concern for politics. Nevertheless, Lasch observes that narcissists are sometimes radical politically when the risks give them a sense of well-being and importance. Lasch distinguishes between the nineteenth-century ideal of the rugged individualist and the new individualist ideal. The former were outwardly oriented; they saw the world as a "wilderness to be shaped by [their] own design." Contemporary individualists are self-absorbed; for them, "the world is a mirror." Lasch warns that the new narcissists cannot succeed since the psychic equilibrium of any individual requires "submission to the rules of social intercourse." By denying themselves a social role, narcissists leave themselves open to a sense

THE NEW NARCISSISM Reprinted from *The Culture of Narcissism: American Life in an Age of Diminishing Expectations*, by Christopher Lasch, by permission of W. W. Norton & Company, Inc. Copyright ©1979 by W. W. Norton & Company, Inc.

of inner emptiness. By their self-absorption they live a life of self-gratification in which love plays no part.

## The Waning of the Sense of Historical Time

As the twentieth century approaches its end, the conviction grows that many other things are ending too. Storm warnings, portents, hints of catastrophe haunt our times. The "sense of an ending," which has given shape to so much of twentieth-century literature, now pervades the popular imagination as well. The Nazi holocaust, the threat of nuclear annihilation, the depletion of natural resources, well-founded predictions of ecological disaster have fulfilled poetic prophecy, giving concrete historical substance to the nightmare, or death wish, that avant-garde artists were the first to express. The question of whether the world will end in fire or in ice, with a bang or a whimper, no longer interests artists alone. Impending disaster has become an everyday concern, so commonplace and familiar that nobody any longer gives much thought to how disaster might be averted. People busy themselves instead with survival strategies, measures designed to prolong their own lives, or programs guaranteed to ensure good health and peace of mind.

Those who dig bomb shelters hope to survive by surrounding themselves with the latest products of modern technology. Communards in the country adhere to an opposite plan: to free themselves from dependence on technology and thus to outlive its destruction or collapse. A visitor to a commune in North Carolina writes: "Everyone seems to share this sense of imminent doomsday." Stewart Brand, editor of the *Whole Earth Catalogue,* reports that "sales of the *Survival Book* are booming; it's one of our fastest moving items." Both strategies reflect the growing despair of changing society, even of understanding it, which also underlies the cult of expanded consciousness, health, and personal "growth" so prevalent today.

After the political turmoil of the sixties, Americans have retreated to purely personal preoccupations. Having no hope of improving their lives in any of the ways that matter, people have convinced themselves that what matters is psychic self-improvement: getting in touch with their feelings, eating health food, taking lessons in ballet or belly-dancing, immersing themselves in the wisdom of the East, jogging, learning how to "relate," overcoming the "fear of pleasure." Harmless in themselves, these pursuits, elevated to a program and wrapped in the rhetoric of authenticity and awareness, signify a retreat from politics and a repudiation of the recent past. Indeed Americans seem to wish to forget not only the sixties, the riots, the new left, the disruptions on college campuses, Vietnam, Watergate, and the Nixon presidency, but their entire collective past, even in the antiseptic form in which it was celebrated during the Bicentennial. Woody Allen's movie *Sleeper,* issued in 1973, accurately caught the mood of the seventies. Appropriately cast in the form of a parody of futuristic science fiction, the film finds a great many ways to convey the message that "political solutions don't work," as Allen flatly announces at one point. When asked what he believes in, Allen, having ruled out politics, religion, and science, declares: "I believe in sex and death—two experiences that come once in a lifetime."

To live for the moment is the prevailing passion—to live for yourself, not for your predecessors or posterity. We are fast losing the sense of historical continuity, the sense of belonging to a succession of generations originating in the past and stretching into the future. It is the waning of the sense of historical time—in particular, the erosion of any strong concern for posterity—that distinguishes the spiritual crisis of the seventies from earlier outbreaks of millenarian religion, to which it bears a superficial resemblance. Many commentators have seized on this resemblance as a means of understanding the contemporary "cultural revolution," ignoring the features that distinguish it from the religions of the past. A few years ago, Leslie Fiedler proclaimed a "New Age of Faith." More recently, Tom Wolfe has interpreted the new narcissism as a "third great awakening," an outbreak of orgiastic, ecstatic religiosity. Jim Hougan, in a book that seems to present itself simultaneously as a critique and a celebration of contemporary decadence, compares the current mood to the millennialism of the waning Middle Ages. "The anxieties of the Middle Ages are not much different from those of the present," he writes. Then as now, social upheaval gave rise to "millenarian sects."

Both Hougan and Wolfe inadvertently provide evidence, however, that undermines a religious interpretation of the "consciousness movement." Hougan notes that survival has become the "catchword of the seventies" and "collective narcissism" the dominant disposition. Since "the society" has no future, it makes sense to live only for

645

the moment, to fix our eyes on our own "private performance," to become connoisseurs of our own decadence, to cultivate a "transcendental self-attention." These are not the attitudes historically associated with millenarian outbreaks. Sixteenth-century Anabaptists awaited the apocalypse not with transcendental self-attention but with ill-concealed impatience for the golden age it was expected to inaugurate. Nor were they indifferent to the past. Ancient popular traditions of the "sleeping king"—the leader who will return to his people and restore a lost golden age—informed the millenarian movements of this period. The Revolutionary of the Upper Rhine, anonymous author of the *Book of a Hundred Chapters,* declared, "The Germans once held the whole world in their hands and they will do so again, and with more power than ever." He predicted that the resurrected Frederick II, "Emporer of the Last Days," would reinstate the primitive German religion, move the capital of Christendom from Rome to Trier, abolish private property, and level distinctions between rich and poor.

Such traditions, often associated with national resistance to foreign conquest, have flourished at many times and in many forms, including the Christian vision of the Last Judgment. Their egalitarian and pseudohistorical content suggests that even the most radically otherworldly religions of the past expressed a hope of social justice and a sense of continuity with earlier generations. The absence of these values characterizes the survivalist mentality of the seventies. The "world view emerging among us," writes Peter Marin, centers "solely on the self" and has "individual survival as its sole good." In an attempt to identify the peculiar features of contemporary religiosity, Tom Wolfe himself notes that "most people, historically, have *not* lived their lives as if thinking, 'I have only one life to live.' Instead they have lived as if they are living their ancestors' lives and their offspring's lives. . . ." These observations go very close to the heart of the matter, but they call into question his characterization of the new narcissism as a third great awakening.

## The Therapeutic Sensibility

The contemporary climate is therapeutic, not religious. People today hunger not for personal salvation, let alone for the restoration of an earlier golden age, but for the feeling, the momentary illusion, of personal well-being, health, and psychic security. Even the radicalism of the sixties served, for many of those who embraced it for personal rather than political reasons, not as a substitute religion but as a form of therapy. Radical politics filled empty lives, provided a sense of meaning and purpose. In her memoir of the Weathermen, Susan Stern described their attraction in language that owes more to psychiatry and medicine than to religion. When she tried to evoke her state of mind during the 1968 demonstrations at the Democratic National Convention in Chicago, she wrote instead about the state of her health. "I felt good. I could feel my body supple and strong and slim, and ready to run miles, and my legs moving sure and swift under me." A few pages later, she says: "I felt real." Repeatedly she explains that association with important people made her feel important. "I felt I was part of a vast network of intense, exciting and brilliant people." When the leaders she idealized disappointed her, as they always did, she looked for new heroes to take their place, hoping to warm herself in their "brilliance" and to overcome her feeling of insignificance. In their presence, she occasionally felt "strong and solid"—only to find herself repelled, when disenchantment set in again, by the "arrogance" of those whom she had previously admired, by "their contempt for everyone around them."

Many of the details in Stern's account of the Weathermen would be familiar to students of the revolutionary mentality in earlier epochs: the fervor of her revolutionary commitment, the group's endless disputes about fine points of political dogma, the relentless "self-criticism" to which members of the sect were constantly exhorted, the attempt to remodel every facet of one's life in conformity with the revolutionary faith. But every revolutionary movement partakes of the culture of its time, and this one contained elements that immediately identified it as a product of American society in an age of diminishing expectations. The atmosphere in which the Weathermen lived—an atmosphere of violence, danger, drugs, sexual promiscuity, moral and psychic chaos—derived not so much from an older revolutionary tradition as from the turmoil and narcissistic anguish of contemporary America. Her preoccupation with the state of her psychic health, together with her dependence on others for a sense of selfhood, distinguish Susan Stern from the kind of religious seeker who turns to politics to find a secularized salvation. She needed to establish an identity, not to submerge her identity in a larger cause.

The narcissist differs also, in the tenuous quality of his selfhood, from an earlier type of American individualist, the "American Adam" analyzed by R. W. B. Lewis, Quentin Anderson, Michael Rogin, and by nineteenth-century observers like Tocqueville. The contemporary narcissist bears a superficial resemblance, in his self-absorption and delusions of grandeur, to the "imperial self" so often celebrated in nineteenth-century American literature. The American Adam, like his descendants today, sought to free himself from the past and to establish what Emerson called "an original relation to the universe." Nineteenth-century writers and orators re-stated again and again, in a great variety of forms, Jefferson's doctrine that the earth belongs to the living. The break with Europe, the abolition of primogeniture, and the looseness of family ties gave substance to their belief (even if it was finally an illusion) that Americans, alone among the people of the world, could escape the entangling influence of the past. They imagined, according to Tocqueville, that "their whole destiny is in their own hands." Social conditions in the United States, Tocqueville wrote, severed the tie that formerly united one generation to another. "The woof of time is every instant broken and the track of generations effaced. Those who went before are soon forgotten; of those who will come after, no one has any idea: the interest of man is confined to those in close propinquity to himself."

Some critics have described the narcissism of the 1970s in similar language. The new therapies spawned by the human potential movement, according to Peter Marin, teach that "the individual will is all powerful and totally determines one's fate"; thus they intensify the "isolation of the self." This line of argument belongs to a well-established American tradition of social thought. Marin's plea for recognition of "the immense middle ground of human community" recalls Van Wyck Brooks, who criticized the New England transcendentalists for ignoring "the genial middle ground of human tradition." Brooks himself, when he formulated his own indictment of American culture, drew on such earlier critics as Santayana, Henry James, Orestes Brownson, and Tocqueville. The critical tradition they established still has much to tell us about the evils of untrammeled individualism, but it needs to be restated to take account of the differences between nineteenth-century Adamism and the narcissism of our own time. The critique of "privatism," though it helps to keep alive the need for community, has become more and more misleading as the possibility of genuine privacy recedes. The contemporary American may have failed, like his predecessors, to establish any sort of common life, but the integrating tendencies of modern industrial society have at the same time undermined his "isolation." Having surrendered most of his technical skills to the corporation, he can no longer provide for his material needs. As the family loses not only its productive functions but many of its reproductive functions as well, men and women no longer manage even to raise their children without the help of certified experts. The atrophy of older traditions of self-help has eroded everyday competence, in one area after another, and has made the individual dependent on the state, the corporation, and other bureaucracies.

Narcissism represents the psychological dimension of this dependence. Notwithstanding his occasional illusions of omnipotence, the narcissist depends on others to validate his self-esteem. He cannot live without an admiring audience. His apparent freedom from family ties and institutional constraints does not free him to stand alone or to glory in his individuality. On the contrary, it contributes to his insecurity, which he can overcome only by seeing his "grandiose self" reflected in the attentions of others, or by attaching himself to those who radiate celebrity, power, and charisma. For the narcissist, the world is a mirror, whereas the rugged individualist saw it as an empty wilderness to be shaped to his own design.

In the nineteenth-century American imagination, the vast continent stretching westward symbolized both the promise and the menace of an escape from the past. The West represented an opportunity to build a new society unencumbered by feudal inhibitions, but it also tempted men to throw off civilization and to revert to savagery. Through compulsive industry and relentless sexual repression, nineteenth-century Americans achieved a fragile triumph over the id. The violence they turned against the Indians and against nature originated not in unrestrained impulse but in the white Anglo-Saxon superego, which feared the wildness of the West because it objectified the wildness within each individual. While celebrating the romance of the frontier in their popular literature, in practice Americans imposed on the wilderness a new order designed to keep impulse in check while giving free rein to acquisitiveness. Capital accumulation in its own right sublimated appetite and subordinated the pursuit of self-interest to the service of future generations. In the heat of the struggle to win the West, the American pioneer gave full vent to his rapacity and murderous cruelty, but he always envisioned the result—not without

649

misgivings, expressed in a nostalgic cult of lost innocence—as a peaceful, respectable, churchgoing community safe for his women and children. He imagined that his offspring, raised under the morally refining influence of feminine "culture," would grow up to be sober, law-abiding, domesticated American citizens, and the thought of the advantages they would inherit justified his toil and excused, he thought, his frequent lapses into brutality, sadism, and rape.

Today Americans are overcome not by the sense of endless possibility but by the banality of the social order they have erected against it. Having internalized the social restraints by means of which they formerly sought to keep possibility within civilized limits, they feel themselves overwhelmed by an annihilating boredom, like animals whose instincts have withered in captivity. A reversion to savagery threatens them so little that they long precisely for a more vigorous instinctual existence. People nowadays complain of an inability to feel. They cultivate more vivid experiences, seek to beat sluggish flesh to life, attempt to revive jaded appetites. They condemn the superego and exalt the lost life of the senses. Twentieth-century peoples have erected so many psychological barriers against strong emotion, and have invested those defenses with so much of the energy derived from forbidden impulse, that they can no longer remember what it feels like to be inundated by desire. They tend, rather, to be consumed with rage, which derives from defenses against desire and gives rise in turn to new defenses against rage itself. Outwardly bland, submissive, and sociable, they seethe with an inner anger for which a dense, over-populated, bureaucratic society can devise few legitimate outlets.

The growth of bureaucracy creates an intricate network of personal relations, puts a premium on social skills, and makes the unbridled egotism of the American Adam untenable. Yet at the same time it erodes all forms of patriarchal authority and thus weakens the social superego, formerly represented by fathers, teachers, and preachers. The decline of institutionalized authority in an ostensibly permissive society does not, however, lead to a "decline of the superego" in individuals. It encourages instead the development of a harsh, punitive superego that derives most of its psychic energy, in the absence of authoritative social prohibitions, from the destructive, aggressive impulses within the id. Unconscious, irrational elements in the superego come to dominate its operation. As authority figures in modern society lose their "credibility," the superego in individuals increasingly derives from the child's primitive fantasies about his parents—fantasies charged with sadistic rage—rather than from internalized ego ideals formed by later experience with loved and respected models of social conduct.

The struggle to maintain psychic equilibrium in a society that demands submission to the rules of social intercourse but refuses to ground those rules in a code of moral conduct encourages a form of self-absorption that has little in common with the primary narcissism of the imperial self. Archaic elements increasingly dominate personality structure, and "the self shrinks back," in the words of Morris Dickstein, "toward a passive and primeval state in which the world remains uncreated, unformed." The egomaniacal, experience-devouring, imperial self regresses into a grandiose, narcissistic, infantile, empty self: a "dark wet hole," as Rudolph Wurlitzer writes in *Nog,* "where everything finds its way sooner or later. I remain near the entrance, handling goods as they are shoved in, listening and nodding. I have been slowly dissolving into this cavity."

Plagued by anxiety, depression, vague discontents, sense of inner emptiness, the "psychological man" of the twentieth century seeks neither individual self-aggrandizement nor spiritual transcendence but peace of mind, under conditions that increasingly militate against it. Therapists, not priests or popular preachers of self-help or models of success like the captains of industry, become his principal allies in the struggle for composure; he turns to them in the hope of achieving the modern equivalent of salvation, "mental health." Therapy has established itself as the successor both to rugged individualism and to religion; but this does not mean that the "triumph of the therapeutic" has become a new religion in its own right. Therapy constitutes an antireligion, not always to be sure because it adheres to rational explanation or scientific methods of healing, as its practitioners would have us believe, but because modern society "has no future" and therefore gives no thought to anything beyond its immediate needs. Even when therapists speak of the need for "meaning" and "love," they define love and meaning simply as the fulfillment of the patient's emotional requirements. It hardly occurs to them—nor is there any reason why it should, given the nature of the therapeutic enterprise—to encourage the subject to subordinate his needs and interests to those of others, to someone or some cause or tradition outside himself. "Love" as self-sacrifice or self-abasement, "meaning" as submission to a higher loyalty—these sublimations strike the therapeutic sensibility as intolerably oppressive, offensive to common sense and injurious to personal health and well-being. To liberate humanity from such out-moded ideas of love and duty has become the mission of the post-Freudian therapies and particularly of their converts and popularizers, for whom mental health means the overthrow of inhibitions and the immediate gratification of every impulse.

**STUDY QUESTIONS**

1.  How does the narcissistic self differ from Kant's noble self, Quinton's person of character, or Didion's self-respecting individual?
2.  In 1923, a study known as Middletown recorded the attitudes and practices of citizens in Muncie, Indiana. In 1977, researchers made another study in Muncie, called Middletown III, and were surprised to find that, despite more permissive views on divorce, marijuana, and pornography, students at Muncie High School answered a number of questions exactly the same way their grandparents did in 1923. The majority in both groups, for example, reported that they regarded the Bible as a "sufficient guide for modern life." Does this suggest that Lasch and other pessimistic social critics may be exaggerating the changes that have occurred in American society over the past two decades?
3.  What, for Lasch, is the importance of a sense of tradition and a knowledge of history? What role does their presence or absence play in moral development?

# On Self-respect

## JOAN DIDION

Joan Didion (b. 1934) is a well-known novelist and essay-ist. Her published works include novels such as *Play It as It Lays* (1971) and *A Book of Common Prayer* (1977), and collections of essays titled *Slouching Towards Bethlehem* (1970) and *The White Album* (1979).

What is self-respect and how does one develop it? For Didion, self-respecting persons are persons of character who accept responsibility for their lives and actions. Self-respect requires discipline, the ability to forego immediate gratification, and the ability to take risks and stick to plans. Persons who have these characteristics respect themselves. Persons who lack them live with a certain self-contempt and a contempt for those who uncritically admire them.

Once, in a dry season, I wrote in large letters across two pages of a notebook that innocence ends when one is stripped of the delusion that one likes oneself. Although now, some years later, I marvel that a mind on the outs with itself should have nonetheless made painstaking record of its every tremor, I recall with embarrassing clarity the flavor of those particular ashes. It was a matter of misplaced self-respect.

I had not been elected to Phi Beta Kappa. This failure could scarcely have been more predictable or less ambiguous (I simply did

ON SELF-RESPECT Reprinted by permission of Farrar, Straus and Giroux, Inc. "On Self-Respect" from *Slouching Towards Bethlehem* by Joan Didion. Copyright ©1961, 1968 by Joan Didion.

not have the grades), but I was unnerved by it; I had somehow thought myself a kind of academic Raskolnikov, curiously exempt from the cause-effect relationships which hampered others. Although even the humorless nineteen-year-old that I was must have recognized that the situation lacked real tragic stature, the day that I did not make Phi Beta Kappa nonetheless marked the end of something, and innocence may well be the word for it. I lost the conviction that lights would always turn green for me, the pleasant certainty that those rather passive virtues which had won me approval as a child automatically guaranteed me not only Phi Beta Kappa keys but happiness, honor, and the love of a good man; lost a certain touching faith in the totem power of good manners, clean hair, and proven competence on the Stanford-Binet scale. To such doubtful amulets had my self-respect been pinned, and I faced myself that day with the nonplused apprehension of someone who has come across a vampire and has no crucifix at hand.

Although to be driven back upon oneself is an uneasy affair at best, rather like trying to cross a border with borrowed credentials, it seems to me now the one condition necessary to the beginnings of real self-respect. Most of our platitudes notwithstanding, self-deception remains the most difficult deception. The tricks that work on others count for nothing in that very well-lit back alley where one keeps assignations with oneself: no winning smiles will do here, no prettily drawn lists of good intentions. One shuffles flashily but in vain through one's marked cards—the kindness done for the wrong reason, the apparent triumph which involved no real effort, the seemingly heroic act into which one had been shamed. The dismal fact is that self-respect has nothing to do with the approval of others—who are, after all, deceived easily enough; has nothing to do with reputation, which, as Rhett Butler told Scarlet O'Hara, is something people with courage can do without.

To do without self-respect, on the other hand, is to be an unwilling audience of one to an interminable documentary that details one's failings, both real and imagined, with fresh footage spliced in for every screening. *There's the glass you broke in anger, there's the hurt on X's face; watch now, this next scene, the night Y came back from Houston, see how you muff this one.* To live without self-respect is to lie awake some night, beyond the reach of warm milk, phenobarbital, and the sleeping hand on the coverlet, counting up the sins of commission and omission, the trusts betrayed, the promises subtly broken, the gifts irrevocably wasted through sloth or cowardice or carelessness. However long we postpone it, we eventualy lie down alone in that notoriously uncomfortable bed, the one we make ourselves. Whether or not we sleep in it depends, of course, on whether or not we respect ourselves.

To protest that some fairly improbable people, some people who *could not possibly respect themselves,* seem to sleep easily enough is to miss the point entirely, as surely as those people miss it who think that self-respect has necessarily to do with not having safety pins in one's underwear. There is a common superstitution that "self-respect" is a kind of charm against snakes, something that keeps those who have it locked in some unblighted Eden, out of strange beds, ambivalent conversations, and trouble in general. It does not at all. It has nothing to do with the face of things, but concerns instead a separate peace, a private reconciliation. Although the careless, suicidal Julian English in *Appointment in Samarra* and the careless, incurably dishonest Jordan Baker in *The Great Gatsby* seem equally improbable candidates for self-respect, Jordan Baker had it, Julian English did not. With that genius for accommodation more often seen in women than in men, Jordan took her own measure, made her own peace, avoided threats to that peace: "I hate careless people," she told Nick Carraway. "It takes two to make an accident."

Like Jordan Baker, people with self-respect have the courage of their mistakes. They know the price of things. If they choose to commit adultery, they do not then go running, in an access of bad conscience, to receive absolution from the wronged parties; nor do they complain unduly of the unfairness, the undeserved embarrassment, of being named co-respondent. In brief, people with self-respect exhibit a certain toughness, a kind of moral nerve; they display what was once called *character,* a quality which, although approved in the abstract, sometimes loses ground to other, more instantly negotiable virtues. The measure of its slipping prestige is that one tends to think of it only in connection with homely children and United States senators who have been defeated, preferably in the primary, for reelection. Nonetheless, character—the willingness to accept responsibility for one's own life—is the source from which self-respect springs.

Self-respect is something that our grandparents, whether or not they had it, knew all about. They had instilled in them, young, a certain discipline, the sense that one lives by doing things one does not particularly want to do, by putting fears and doubts to one side, by weighing immediate comforts against the possibility of larger, even intangible, comforts. It seemed to the nineteenth century admirable, but not remarkable, that Chinese Gordon put on a clean white suit and held Khartoum against the Mahdi; it did not seem unjust that the way to free land in California involved death and difficulty and dirt. In a diary kept during the winter of 1846, an emigrating twelve-year-old named Narcissa Cornwall noted coolly: "Father was busy reading and did not notice that the house was being filled with strange Indians until Mother spoke about it." Even lacking any clue as to what Mother said, one can scarcely fail to be impressed by the entire incident: the father reading, the Indians filing in, the mother choosing the words that would not alarm, the child duly recording the event and noting further that those particular Indians were not, "fortunately for us," hostile. Indians were simply part of the *donnée*.

In one guise or another, Indians always are. Again, it is a question of recognizing that anything worth having has its price. People who respect themselves are willing to accept the risk that the Indians will be hostile, that the venture will go bankrupt, that the liaison may not turn out to be one in which *every day is a holiday because you're married to me*. They are willing to invest something of themselves; they may not play at all, but when they do play, they know the odds.

That kind of self-respect is a discipline, a habit of mind that can never be faked but can be developed, trained, coaxed forth. It was once suggested to me that, as an antidote to crying, I put my head in a paper bag. As it happens, there is a sound physiological reason, something to do with oxygen, for doing exactly that, but the psychological effect alone is incalculable; it is difficult in the extreme to continue fancying oneself Cathy in *Wuthering Heights* with one's head in a Food Fair bag. There is a similar case for all the small disciplines, unimportant in themselves; imagine maintaining any kind of swoon, commiserative or carnal, in a cold shower.

But those small disciplines are valuable only insofar as they represent larger ones. To say that Waterloo was won on the playing fields of Eton is not to say that Napoleon might have been saved by a crash program in cricket; to give formal dinners in the rain forest would be pointless did not the candlelight flickering on the liana call forth deeper, stronger disciplines, values instilled long before. It is a kind of ritual, helping us to remember who and what we are. In order to remember it, one must have known it.

To have that sense of one's intrinsic worth which constitutes self-respect is potentially to have everything: the ability to discriminate, to love and to remain indifferent. To lack it is to be locked within oneself, paradoxically incapable of either love or indifference. If we do not respect ourselves, we are on the one hand forced to despise those who have so few resources as to consort with us, so little perception as to remain blind to our fatal weaknesses. On the other, we are peculiarly in thrall to everyone we see, curiously determined to live out—since our self-image is untenable—their false notions of us. We flatter ourselves by thinking this compulsion to please others an attractive trait: a gist for imaginative empathy, evidence of our willingness to give. Of *course* I will play Francesca to your Paolo, Helen Keller to anyone's Annie Sullivan: no expectation is too misplaced, no role too ludicrous. At the mercy of those we cannot but hold in contempt, we play roles doomed to failure before they are begun, each defeat generating fresh despair at the urgency of divining and meeting the next demand made upon us.

It is the phenomenon sometimes called "alienation from self." In its advanced stages, we no longer answer the telephone, because someone might want something; that we could say *no* without drowning in self-reproach is an idea alien to this game. Every encounter demands too much, tears the nerves, drains the will, and the specter of something as small as an unanswered letter arouses such disproportionate guilt that answering it becomes out of the question. To assign unanswered letters their proper weight, to free us from the expectations of others, to give us back to ourselves—there lies the great, the singular power of self-respect. Without it, one eventually discovers the final turn of the screw: one runs away to find oneself, and finds no one at home.

**STUDY QUESTIONS**

1. Do you agree with Didion's claim that self-respect has nothing to do with the approval of others?
2. Didion defines character as willingness to accept responsibility

for your life. Can persons of character be self-righteous? Hypo-critical? Self-excusers? Why does Didion think that being a self-excuser is inconsistent with having self-respect? Can you imagine people, ruthless criminals, for example, who accept responsibility for their actions, but can nevertheless be said to have no character or self-respect?

3. Didion says self-respect is a "discipline," or "a habit of mind that can never be faked, but can be developed [and] trained . . ." How might someone develop more self-respect?

4. What, according to Didion, is the cost of living without self-respect?

5. Do you think most people are more concerned about their good reputation or their self-respect? Which is harder to live without?

# *Servility and Self-respect*

## THOMAS E. HILL, JR.

A biographical sketch of Thomas E. Hill, Jr. is found on page 293.

According to Thomas Hill, servility is a moral defect. He discusses three servile types: The Uncle Tom, The Self-Deprecator, and the Deferential Wife.

The Uncle Tom is exploited by white people but "does not feel he has the right to expect anything better." The Self-Deprecator is not oppressed externally, but constantly shrinks from giving voice to his own preferences; his self-contempt invites exploitation and humiliation by others. The Deferential Wife tends to count her own interests as relatively unimportant. "No one is trampling

SERVILITY AND SELF-RESPECT By Thomas E. Hill, Jr. First published in *Monist*, Journal of the Department of Philosophy, University of California at Los Angeles, vol. 57, no. 1. By permission of the publisher.

on her rights, she says; for she is quite glad and proud to serve her husband as she does."

Each servile type is morally defective. But why is servility to be condemned? All are lacking self-respect; yet utilitarian grounds do not explain what is wrong with this. It may even be that The Uncle Tom's sufferings are balanced by the pleasures he gives to his master. The Deferential Wife may be taking perverse pleasure in her own submissiveness. The Self-Deprecator may be masochistic and derive pleasure from humiliation.

According to Hill, the morally objectionable feature the three types share is their failure to acknowledge and to respect their personal rights. The Uncle Tom implicitly denies that he is the moral equal of those who exploit him. The Deferential Wife appears voluntarily to have waived her rights in consenting to defer to her husband's demands. It may be, says Hill, that "her consent has been coerced by her lack of viable options open to women in her society." Hill then argues for the following thesis: Disregard for one's own rights is objectionable on Kantian grounds, which require one to respect the moral law by respecting all persons including oneself. "The objection to the servile person . . . is that he does not satisfy the basic requirement to respect morality."

Several motives underlie this paper. In the first place, I am curious to see if there is a legitimate source for the increasingly common feeling that servility can be as much a vice as arrogance is. There seems to be something morally defective about the Uncle Tom and the submissive housewife; and yet, on the other hand, if the only interests they sacrifice are their own, it seems that we should have no right to complain. Secondly, I have some sympathy for the now unfashionable view that each person has duties to himself as well as to others. It does seem absurd to say that a person could literally violate his own rights or owe himself a debt to gratitude, but I suspect that the classic defenders to duties to oneself had something different in mind. If there are duties to oneself, it is natural to expect that a duty to avoid being servile would have a prominent place among them. . . .

# I

Three examples may give a preliminary idea of what I mean by *servility*. Consider, first, an extremely deferential black, whom I shall call the *Uncle Tom*. He always steps aside for white men; he does not complain when less qualified whites take over his job; he gratefully accepts whatever benefits his all-white government and employers allot him, and he would not think of protesting its insufficiency. He displays the symbols of deference to whites, and of contempt towards blacks: he faces the former with bowed stance and a ready "Sir" and "Ma'am"; he reserves his strongest obscenities for the latter. Imagine, too, that he is not playing a game. He is not the shrewdly prudent calculator, who knows how to make the best of a bad lot and mocks his masters behind their backs. He accepts without question the idea that, as a black, he is owed less than whites. He may believe that blacks are mentally inferior and of less social utility, but that is not the crucial point. The attitude which he displays is that what he values, aspires for, and can demand is of less importance than what whites value, aspire for, and can demand. He is far from the picture book's carefree, happy servant, but he does not feel that he has a right to expect anything better.

Another pattern of servility is illustrated by a person I shall call the *Self-deprecator*. Like the Uncle Tom, he is reluctant to make demands. He says nothing when others take unfair advantage of him. When asked for his preferences or opinions, he tends to shrink away as if what he said should make no difference. His problem, however, is not a sense of racial inferiority but rather an acute awareness of his own inadequacies and failures as an individual. These defects are not imaginary: he has in fact done poorly by his own standards and others'. But, unlike many of us in the same situation, he acts as if his failings warrant quite unrelated maltreatment even by strangers. His sense of shame and self-contempt makes him content to be the instrument of others. He feels that nothing is owed him until he has earned it and that he has earned very little. He is not simply playing a masochist's game of winning sympathy by disparaging himself. On the contrary, he assesses his individual merits with painful accuracy.

A rather different case is that of the *Deferential Wife*. This is a woman who is utterly devoted to serving her husband. She buys the clothes *he* prefers, invites the guests *he* wants to entertain, and makes love whenever *he* is in the mood. She willingly moves to a new city in order for him to have a more attractive job, counting her own friendships and geographical preferences insignificant by comparison. She loves her husband, but her conduct is not simply an expression of love. She is happy, but she does not subordinate herself as a means to happiness. She does not simply defer to her husband in certain spheres as a trade-off for his deference in other spheres. On the contrary, she tends not to form her own interests, values, and ideals; and, when she does, she counts them as less important than her husband's. She readily responds to appeals from Women's Liberation that she agrees that women are mentally and physically equal, if not superior, to men. She just believes that the proper role for a woman is to serve her family. As a matter of fact, much of her happiness derives from her belief that she fulfills this role very well. No one is trampling on her rights, she says; for she is quite glad, and proud, to serve her husband as she does.

Each one of these cases reflects the attitude which I call servility.[1] It betrays the absence of a certain kind of self-respect. What I take this attitude to be, more specifically, will become clearer later on. It is important at the outset, however, not to confuse the three cases sketched above with other, superficially similar cases. In particular, the cases I have sketched are not simply cases in which someone refuses to press his rights, speaks disparagingly of himself, or devotes himself to another. A black, for example, is not necessarily servile because he does not demand a just wage; for, seeing that such a demand would result in his being fired, he might forbear for the sake of his children. A self-critical person is not necessarily servile by virtue of bemoaning his faults in public; for his behavior may be merely a complex way of satisfying his own inner needs quite independent of a willingness to accept abuse from others. A woman need not be servile whenever she works to make her husband happy and prosperous; for she might freely and knowingly choose to do so from

---

[1]Each of the cases is intended to represent only one possible pattern of servility. I make no claims about how often these patterns are exemplified, nor do I mean to imply that only these patterns could warrant the labels "Deferential Wife," "Uncle Tom," etc. All the more, I do not mean to imply any comparative judgments about the causes or relative magnitude of the problems of racial and sexual discrimination. One person, e.g. a self-contemptuous woman with a sense of racial inferiority, might exemplify features of several patterns at once; and, of course, a person might view her being a woman the way an Uncle Tom views his being black, etc.

love or from a desire to share the rewards of his success. If the effort did not require her to submit to humiliation or maltreatment, her choice would not mark her as servile. There may, of course, be grounds for objecting to the attitudes in these cases; but the defect is not servility of the sort I want to consider. It should also be noted that my cases of servility are not simply instances of deference to superior knowledge or judgment. To defer to an expert's judgment on matters of fact is not to be servile; to defer to his every wish and whim is. Similarly, the belief that one's talents and achievements are comparatively low does not, by itself, make one servile. It is no vice to acknowledge the truth, and one may in fact have achieved less, and have less ability, than others. To be servile is not simply to hold certain empirical beliefs but to have a certain attitude concerning one's rightful place in a moral community.

## II

Are there grounds for regarding the attitudes of the Uncle Tom, the Self-Deprecator, and the Deferential Wife as morally objectionable? Are there moral arguments we could give them to show that they ought to have more self-respect? None of the more obvious replies is entirely satisfactory.

One might, in the first place, adduce utilitarian considerations. Typically the servile person will be less happy than he might be. Moreover, he may be less prone to make the best of his own socially useful abilities. He may become a nuisance to others by being overly dependent. He will, in any case, lose the special contentment that comes from standing up for one's rights. A submissive attitude encourages exploitation, and exploitation spreads misery in a variety of ways. These considerations provide a *prima facie* case against the attitudes of the Uncle Tom, the Deferential Wife, and the Self-deprecator, but they are hardly conclusive. Other utilities tend to counterbalance the ones just mentioned. When people refuse to press their rights, there are usually others who profit. There are undeniable pleasures in associating with those who are devoted, understanding, and grateful for whatever we see fit to give them—as our fondness for dogs attests. Even the servile person may find his attitude a source of happiness, as the case of the Deferential Wife illustrates. There may be comfort and security in thinking that the hard choices must be made by others, that what I would say has little to do with what ought to be done. Self-condemnation may bring relief from the pangs of guilt even if it is not deliberately used for that purpose. On balance, then, utilitarian considerations may turn out to favor servility as much as they oppose it.

For those who share my moral intuitions, there is another sort of reason for not trying to rest a case against servility on utilitarian considerations. Certain utilities seem irrelevant to the issue. The utilitarian must weigh them along with others, but to do so seems morally inappropriate. Suppose, for example, that the submissive attitudes of the Uncle Tom and the Deferential Wife result in positive utilities for those who dominate and exploit them. Do we need to tabulate *these* utilities before conceding that servility is objectionable? The Uncle Tom, it seems, is making an error, a moral error, quite apart from consideration of how much others in fact profit from his attitude. The Deferential Wife may be quite happy; but if her happiness turns out to be contingent on her distorted view of her own rights and worth as a person, then it carries little moral weight against the contention that she ought to change that view. Suppose I could cause a woman to find her happiness in denying all her rights and serving my every wish. No doubt I could do so only by nonrational manipulative techniques, which I ought not to use. But is this the only objection? My efforts would be wrong, it seems, not only because of the techniques they require but also because the resultant attitude is itself objectionable. When a person's happiness stems from a morally objectionable attitude, it ought to be discounted. That a sadist gets pleasure from seeing others suffer should not count even as a partial justification for his attitude. That a servile person derives pleasure from denying her moral status, for similar reasons, cannot make her attitude acceptable. These brief intuitive remarks are not intended as a refutation of utilitarianism, with all its many varieties; but they do suggest that it is well to look elsewhere for adequate grounds for rejecting the attitudes of the Uncle Tom, the Self-deprecator, and the Deferential Wife.

. . .

### III

Why, then, is servility a moral defect? There is, I think, another sort of answer which is worth exploring. The first part of this answer must be an attempt to isolate the objectionable features of the servile person; later we can ask why these features are objectionable. As a step in this direction, let us examine again our three paradigm cases. The moral defect in each case, I suggest, is a failure to understand and acknowledge one's own moral rights. I assume, without argument here, that each person has moral rights. Some of these rights may be basic human rights; that is, rights for which a person needs only to be human to qualify. Other rights will be derivative and contingent upon his special commitments, institutional affiliations, etc. Most rights will be *prima facie* ones; some may be absolute. Most can be waived under appropriate conditions; perhaps some cannot. Many rights can be forfeited; but some, presumably, cannot. The servile person does not, strictly speaking, violate his own rights. At least in our paradigm cases he fails to acknowledge fully his own moral status because he does not fully understand what his rights are, how they can be waived, and when they can be forfeited.

The defect of the Uncle Tom, for example, is that he displays an attitude that denies his moral equality with whites. He does not realize, or apprehend in an effective way, that he has as much right to a decent wage and a share of political power as any comparable white. His gratitude is misplaced; he accepts benefits which are his by right as if they were gifts. The Self-deprecator is servile in a more complex way. He acts as if he has forfeited many important rights which in fact he has not. He does not understand, or fully realize in his own case, that certain rights to fair and decent treatment do not have to be earned. He sees his merits clearly enough, but he fails to see that what he can expect from others is not merely a function of his merits. The Deferential Wife *says* that she understands her rights vis-à-vis her husband, but what she fails to appreciate is that her consent to serve him is a valid waiver of her rights only under certain conditions. If her consent is coerced, say, by the lack of viable options for women in her society, then her consent is worth little. If socially fostered ignorance of her own talents and alternatives is responsible for her consent, then her consent should not count as a fully legitimate waiver of her right to equal consideration within the marriage. All the more, her consent to defer constantly to her husband is not a legitimate setting aside of her rights if it results from her mistaken belief that she has a moral duty to do so. (Recall: "The *proper* role for a woman is to serve her family.") If she believes that she has a *duty* to defer to her husband, then, whatever she may say, she cannot fully understand that she has a *right* not to defer to him. When she says that she freely gives up such a right, she is confused. Her confusion is rather like that of a person who has been persuaded by an unscrupulous lawyer that it is legally incumbent on him to refuse a jury trial but who nevertheless tells the judge that he understands that he has a right to a jury trial and freely waives it. He does not really understand what it is to have and freely give up the right if he thinks that it would be an offense for him to exercise it.

Insofar as servility results from moral ignorance or confusion, it need not be something for which a person is to blame. . . . Suppose, however, that our servile persons come to know their rights but do not substantially alter their behavior. Are they not still servile in an objectionable way?

. . .

The answer, I think, should depend upon why the deferential role is played. If the motive is a morally commendable one, or a desire to avert dire consequences to oneself, or even an ambition to set an oppressor up for a later fall, then I would not count the role player as servile. The Uncle Tom, for instance, is not servile in my sense if he shuffles and bows to keep the Klan from killing his children, to save his own skin, or even to buy time while he plans the revolution. Similarly, the Deferential Wife is not servile if she tolerates an abusive husband because he is so ill that further strain would kill him, because protesting would deprive her of her only means of survival, or because she is collecting atrocity stories for her book against marriage. If there is fault in these situations, it seems inappropriate to call it *servility*. The story is quite different, however, if a person continues in his deferential role just from laziness, timidity, or a desire for some minor advantage. He shows too little concern for his moral status as a person, one is tempted to say, if he is willing to deny it for a small profit or simply because it requires some effort and courage to affirm it openly. A black who plays the Uncle Tom merely to gain an advantage over other blacks is harming them, of course; but he is also displaying disregard for his own moral position as an equal among human beings. Similarly, a woman throws away her rights too lightly if she continues to play the subservient role because she is used to it or is too timid to risk a change. A Self-deprecator who readily accepts what he knows are violations of his rights may be indulging his peculiar need for punishment at the expense of denying something more valuable. In these cases, I suggest, we have a kind of servility independent of any ignorance or confusion about one's rights. The person who has it may or may not be blameworthy, depending on many factors; and the line between servile and nonservile role playing will often be hard to draw. Nevertheless, the objectionable feature is perhaps clear enough for present purposes: it is a willingness to disavow one's moral status, publicly and systematically, in the absence of any strong reason to do so.

. . .

## IV

The objectionable feature of the servile person, as I have described him, is his tendency to disavow his own moral rights either because he misunderstands them or because he cares little for them. The question remains: why should anyone regard this as a moral defect? After all, the rights which he denies are is own. He may be unfortunate, foolish, or even distasteful; but why *morally* deficient? One sort of answer, quite different from those reviewed earlier, is suggested by some of Kant's remarks. Kant held that servility is contrary to a perfect nonjuridical duty to oneself.[2] To say that the duty is perfect is roughly to say that it is stringent, never overridden by other considerations (e.g., beneficence). To say that the duty is nonjuridical is to say that a person cannot legitimately be coerced to comply. Although Kant did not develop an explicit argument for this view, an argument can easily be constructed from materials which reflect the spirit, if not the letter, of his moral theory. The argument which I have in mind is prompted by Kant's contention that respect for persons, strictly speaking, is respect for moral law.[3] If taken as a claim about

---

[2]See Immanuel Kant, *The Doctrine of Virtue*, Part II of *The Metaphysics of Morals*, ed. by M. J. Gregor (New York: Harper & Row, 1964), pp. 99–103; Prussian Academy edition, vol. VI, pp. 434–37.

[3]Immanuel Kant, *Groundwork of the Metaphysics of Morals*, ed. by H. J. Paton (New York: Harper & Row, 1964), p. 69; Prussian Academy edition, vol. IV, p. 401; *The Critique of Practical Reason*, ed. by Lewis W. Beck (New York: Bobbs-Merrill, 1956), pp. 81, 84; Prussian Academy edition, vol. V, pp. 78, 81. My purpose here is not to interpret what Kant meant but to give a sense to his remark.

all sorts of respect, this seems quite implausible. If it means that we respect persons only for their moral character, their capacity for moral conduct, or their status as "authors" of the moral law, then it seems unduly moralistic. My strategy is to construe the remark as saying that at least one sort of respect for persons is respect for the rights which the moral law accords them. If one respects the moral law, then one must respect one's own moral rights; and this amounts to having a kind of self-respect incompatible with servility.

The premises for the Kantian argument, which are all admittedly vague, can be sketched as follows:

*First,* let us assume, as Kant did, that all human beings have equal basic human rights. Specific rights vary with different conditions, but all must be justified from a point of view under which all are equal. Not all rights need to be earned, and some cannot be forfeited. Many rights can be waived but only under certain conditions of knowledge and freedom. These conditions are complex and difficult to state; but they include something like the condition that a person's consent releases others from obligation only if it is autonomously given, and consent resulting from underestimation of one's moral status is not autonomously given. Rights can be objects of knowledge, but also of ignorance, misunderstanding, deception, and the like.

*Second,* let us assume that my account of servility is correct; or, if one prefers, we can take it as a definition. That is, in brief, a servile person is one who tends to deny or disavow his own moral rights because he does not understand them or has little concern for the status they give him.

*Third,* we need one formal premise concerning moral duty, namely, that each person ought, as far as possible, to respect the moral law. In less Kantian language, the point is that everyone should approximate, to the extent that he can, the ideal of a person who fully adopts the moral point of view. Roughly, this means not only that each person ought to do what is morally required and refrain from what is morally wrong but also that each person should treat all the provisions of morality as valuable—worth preserving and prizing as well as obeying. One must, so to speak, take up the spirit of morality as well as meet the letter of its requirements. To keep one's promises, avoid hurting others, and the like, is not sufficient; one should also

667

take an attitude of respect towards the principles, ideals, and goals of morality. A respectful attitude towards a system of rights and duties consists of more than a disposition to conform to its definite rules of behavior; it also involves holding the system in esteem, being unwilling to ridicule it, and being reluctant to give up one's place in it. The essentially Kantian idea here is that morality, as a system of equal fundamental rights and duties, is worthy of respect, and hence a completely moral person would respect it in word and manner as well as in deed. And what a completely moral person would do, in Kant's view, is our duty to do so far as we can.

The assumptions here are, of course, strong ones, and I make no attempt to justify them. They are, I suspect, widely held though rarely articulated. In any case, my present purpose is not to evaluate them but to see how, if granted, they constitute a case against servility. The objection to the servile person, given our premises, is that he does not satisfy the basic requirement to respect morality. A person who fully respected a system of moral rights would be disposed to learn his proper place in it, to affirm it proudly, and not to tolerate abuses of it lightly. This is just the sort of disposition that the servile person lacks. If he does not understand the system, he is in no position to respect it adequately. This lack of respect may be no fault of his own, but it is still a way in which he falls short of a moral ideal. If, on the other hand, the servile person knowingly disavows his moral rights by pretending to approve of violations of them, then, barring special explanations, he shows an indifference to whether the provisions of morality are honored and publicly acknowledged. This avoidable display of indifference, by our Kantian premises, is contrary to the duty to respect morality. The disrespect in this second case is somewhat like the disrespect a religious believer might show towards his religion if, to avoid embarrassment, he laughed congenially while nonbelievers were mocking the beliefs which he secretly held. In any case, the servile person, as such, does not express disrespect for the system of moral rights in the obvious way by violating the rights of others. His lack of respect is more subtly manifested by his acting before others as if he did not know or care about his position of equality under that system.

The central idea here may be illustrated by an analogy. Imagine a club, say, an old German dueling fraternity. By the rules of the club, each member has certain rights and responsibilities. These are the same for each member regardless of what titles he may hold outside the club. Each has, for example, a right to be heard at meetings, a right not to be shouted down by the others. Some rights cannot be forfeited: for example, each may vote regardless of whether he has paid his dues and satisfied other rules. Some rights cannot be waived: for example, the right to be defended when attacked by several members of the rival fraternity. The members show respect for each other by respecting the status which the rules confer on each member. Now one new member is careful always to allow the others to speak at meetings; but when they shout him down, he does nothing. He just shrugs as if to say, "Who am I to complain?" When he fails to stand up in defense of a fellow member, he feels ashamed and refuses to vote. He does not deserve to vote, he says. As the only commoner among illustrious barons, he feels that it is his place to serve them and defer to their decisions. When attackers from the rival fraternity come at him with swords drawn, he tells his companions to run and save themselves. When they defend him, he expresses immense gratitude—as if they had done him a gratuitous favor. Now one might argue that our new member fails to show respect for the fraternity and its rules. He does not actually violate any of the rules by refusing to vote, asking others not to defend him, and deferring to the barons, but he symbolically disavows the equal status which the rules confer on him. If he ought to have respect for the fraternity, he ought to change his attitude. Our servile person, then, is like the new member of the dueling fraternity in having insufficient respect for a system of rules and ideals. The difference is that everyone ought to respect morality whereas there is no comparable moral requirement to respect the fraternity.

The conclusion here is, of course, a limited one. Self-sacrifice is not always a sign of servility. It is not a duty always to press one's rights. Whether a given act is evidence of servility will depend not only on the attitude of the agent but also on the specific nature of his moral rights, a matter not considered here. Moreover, the extent to which a person is responsible, or blameworthy, for his defect remains an open question. Nevertheless, the conclusion should not be minimized. In order to avoid servility, a person who gives up his rights must do so with a full appreciation for what they are. A woman, for example, may devote herself to her husband if she is uncoerced, knows what she is doing, and does not pretend that she has no decent alternative. A self-contemptuous person may decide not to press various unforfeited rights but only if he does not take the attitude that he is too rotten to deserve them. A black may demand less than is due to him provided he is prepared to acknowledge that no one has a right to expect this of him. Sacrifices of this sort, I suspect, are extremely rare. Most people, if they fully acknowledged their rights, would not autonomously refuse to press them.

An even stronger conclusion would emerge if we could assume that some basic rights cannot be waived. . . .

Even if there are no specific rights which cannot be waived, there might be at least one formal right of this sort. This is the right to some minimum degree of respect from others. No matter how willing a person is to submit to humiliation by others, they ought to show him some respect as a person. By analogy with self-respect, as presented here, this respect owed by others would consist of a willingness to acknowledge fully, in word as well as action, the person's basically equal moral status as defined by his other rights. To the extent that a person gives even tacit consent to humiliations incompatible with this respect, he will be acting as if he waives a right which he cannot in fact give up. To do this, barring special explanations, would mark one as servile.

. . .

Kant suggests that duties to oneself are a precondition of duties to others. On our account of servility, there is at least one sense in which this is so. Insofar as the servile person is ignorant of his own rights, he is not in an adequate position to appreciate the rights of others. Misunderstanding the moral basis for his equal status with others, he is necessarily liable to underestimate the rights of those with whom he classifies himself. On the other hand, if he plays the servile role knowingly, then, barring special explanation, he displays a lack of concern to see the principles of morality acknowledged and respected and thus the absence of one motive which can move a moral person to respect the rights of others. In either case, the servile person's lack of self-respect necessarily puts him in a less than ideal position to respect others. Failure to fulfill one's duty to oneself, then, renders a person liable to violate duties to others. This, however, is a consequence of our argument against servility, not a presupposition of it.

**STUDY QUESTIONS**

1. Hill considers servility to be a moral flaw. Yet, traditionally, meekness has been one of the Christian virtues. Is Hill at odds with this tradition? If so, do you find the traditional conception defective? Or is Hill missing something?

2. Hill suggests that the deferential wife who consents to being deferent may nevertheless have been coerced by the lack of viable options open to women. In that case, we may discount her consent as not freely given. Do social conditions coerce consent? And if they do, is it fair to consider the women so coerced to be morally defective?

3. The author of *Uncle Tom's Cabin* thought of Uncle Tom as a moral hero. So did the millions of her readers. Yet today we appear ready to think of Uncle Tom in an entirely different light. Are we morally more sophisticated than the people of the nineteenth century? (Consider also such "deferential wives" as Dorothea Casaubon in George Eliot's *Middlemarch* or Mrs. Ramsey in Virginia Woolf's *To the Lighthouse.*)

4. According to Hill, the servile person does not satisfy the basic requirement to respect morality. How does Hill arrive at this position?

5. Do you know of someone of superior moral character who, nevertheless, seems to fit Hill's descriptions of one who is excessively self-effacing and deferential. How do you square your perception of this person with the arguments presented here for thinking of him or her as someone who does not respect morality?

**SUGGESTED READINGS**

Bellah, Robert *et al.*, eds. *Individualism and Commitment in American Life.* New York: Harper & Row, 1984.

Goffman, Erving. *The Presentation of Self in Everyday Life.* New York: Doubleday, 1979.

Hochschild, Arlie. *The Managed Heart.* Los Angeles: University of California Press, 1984.

Kant, Immanuel. *Lectures on Ethics,* trans. Louis Enfield. New York: The Century Company, 1930.

Lasch, Christopher. *The Culture of Narcissism*. New York: Norton, 1979.

Rorty, Amelie. *The Identities of Persons*. Berkeley and Los Angeles: University of California Press, 1976.

Sennett, Richard. *The Fall of Public Man*. New York: Alfred A. Knopf, 1977.

Williams, Bernard. *Moral Luck*. Cambridge, MA: Cambridge University Press, 1981.

Yankelovich, Daniel. *New Rules: Searching for Fulfillment in a World Turned Upside Down*. New York: Random House, 1981.

## Chapter Eight

# MORALITY AND THE FAMILY

What is happening to the family? We can find the answer by looking at the change in attitudes and practices regarding filial relations, parental authority, the status of women, and divorce—changes that have destabilized traditional family ties.

Several authors in Chapter Eight see contemporary irreverence toward traditional family norms as socially pernicious. Rabbi Norman Lamm is concerned with the family as an institution that guarantees the survival of moral and religious traditions. Christina Sommers tries to show that many contemporary moral philosophers contribute to a climate of opinion that undermines the network of moral obligations that bind the members of a family. Rebecca West discusses the effect of divorce on children and considers whether prohibiting divorce would be wise. Implicit in the articles of Lamm, Sommers, and Lin Yutang is the conviction of a need to preserve the family's integrity as a social institution of great value for civilization. Thus they tend to subordinate such other moral considerations as the desirability of allowing family members a great deal of individual freedom to the wider concern of preserving the family itself.

In contrast, Jane English represents the many contemporary philosophers who aim to liberate individuals from family practices they view as oppressive. For example, according to English we only owe our parents those duties we owe to good friends in general. No friendship, no obligations.

Lin Yutang, following Confucius and Mencius, would find the views that English expresses altogether unacceptable and inhumane. In the Chinese tradition, feelings of gratitude and respect for one's parents rank highly among the moral virtues. Lin Yutang points out that filial regard for parents and grandparents does not come naturally; it must be "taught by culture." Yutang finds Western society sadly lacking in the kind of acculturation that assures its members a dignified old age.

Trebilcot and Wasserstrom are more directly concerned with the "gender system," which they consider "sexist" and unfair to women. They argue for replacing the basic institutions that reinforce gender differences by a new social arrangement in which sexual difference plays no social or legal role. In such an "androgynous" or "assimilationist" society, the family as we know it would have no legal status and would not necessarily be the primary social unit within which children are reared. Wasserstrom and Trebilcot are radical feminist philosophers. Sommers' critique of philosophers hostile to the family defends a more liberal and less radical feminism than is currently popular.

# On Growing Old Gracefully

~~~

LIN YUTANG

Lin Yutang (1895–1976) was a novelist and a philosopher. He is the author of a number of books, including *The Importance of Living* (1937) and *The Wisdom of China and India* (1955).

Lin Yutang describes the Chinese family system's treatment of old people and contrasts it with Western norms and attitudes. He notes that we need strong cultural norms to assure respect for parents, grandparents, and older people in general. "A natural man loves his children, but a cultured man loves his parents." Chinese deference and respect for age contrasts sharply with Western attitudes, where we view growing old as almost disgraceful and expect old people not to "interfere" in the family's home life.

The Chinese family system, as I conceive it, is largely an arrangement of particular provision for the young and the old, for since childhood and youth and old age occupy half our life, it is important that the young and the old live a satisfactory life. It is true that the young are more helpless and can take less care of themselves, but on the other hand, they can get along better without material comforts than the old people. A child is often scarcely aware of material hardships,

ON GROWING OLD GRACEFULLY From *The Importance of Living* by Lin Yutang (William Heinemann Ltd., 1931). Reprinted with the permission of Mrs. Lin Yutang.

with the result that a poor child is often as happy as, if not happier than, a rich child. He may go barefooted, but that is a comfort, rather than a hardship to him, whereas going barefooted is often an intolerable hardship for old people. This comes from the child's greater vitality, the bounce of youth. He may have his temporary sorrows, but how easily he forgets them. He has no idea of money and no millionaire complex, as the old man has. At the worst, he collects only cigar coupons for buying a pop-gun, whereas the dowager collects Liberty Bonds. Between the fun of these two kinds of collection there is no comparison. The reason is the child is not yet intimidated by life as all grown-ups are. His personal habits are as yet unformed, and he is not a slave to a particular brand of coffee, and he takes whatever comes along. He has very little racial prejudice and absolutely no religious prejudice. His thoughts and ideas have not fallen into certain ruts. Therefore, strange as it may seem, old people are even more dependent than the young because their fears are more definite and their desires are more delimited.

Something of this tenderness toward old age existed already in the primeval consciousness of the Chinese people, a feeling that I can compare only to the Western chivalry and feeling of tenderness toward women. If the early Chinese people had any chivalry, it was manifested not toward women and children, but toward the old people. That feeling of chivalry found clear expression in Mencius in some such saying as, "The people with grey hair should not be seen carrying burdens on the street," which was expressed as the final goal of a good government. Mencius also described the four classes of the world's most helpless people as: "The widows, widowers, orphans, and old people without children." Of these four classes, the first two were to be taken care of by a political economy that should be so arranged that there would be no unmarried men and women. What was to be done about the orphans Mencius did not say, so far as we know, although orphanages have always existed throughout the ages, as well as pensions for old people. Every one realizes, however, that orphanages and old age pensions are poor substitutes for the home. The feeling is that the home alone can provide anything resembling a satisfactory arrangement for the old and the young. But for the young, it is to be taken for granted that not much need be said, since there is natural parental affection. "Water flows downwards and not upwards," the Chinese always say, and therefore the affection for parents and grandparents is something that stands more in need of being taught by culture. A natural man loves his children, but a cultured man loves his parents. In the end, the teaching of love and respect for old people became a generally accepted principle, and if we are to believe some of the writers, the desire to have the privilege of serving their parents in their old age actually became a consuming passion. The greatest regret a Chinese gentleman could have was the eternally lost opportunity of serving his old parents with medicine and soup on their deathbed, or not to be present when they died. For a high official in his fifties or sixties not to be able to invite his parents to come from their native village and stay with his family at the capital, "seeing them to bed every night and greeting them every morning," was to commit a moral sin of which he should be ashamed and for which he had constantly to offer excuses and explanations to his friends and colleagues. This regret was expressed in two lines by a man who returned too late to his home, when his parents had already died:

> The tree desires repose, but the wind will not stop;
> The son desires to serve, but his parents are already gone.

It is to be assumed that if man were to live this life like a poem, he would be able to look upon the sunset of his life as his happiest period, and instead of trying to postpone the much feared old age, be able actually to look forward to it, and gradually build up to it as the best and happiest period of his existence. In my efforts to compare and contrast Eastern and Western life, I have found no differences that are absolute except in this matter of the attitude towards age, which is sharp and clearcut and permits of no intermediate positions. The differences in our attitude towards sex, toward women, and toward work, play, and achievement are all relative. The relationship between husband and wife in China is not essentially different from that in the West, nor even the relationship between parent and child. Not even the ideas of individual liberty and democracy and the relationship between the people and their ruler are, after all, so very different. But in the matter of our attitude toward age, the difference is absolute, and the East and West take exactly opposite points of view. This is clearest in the matter of asking about a person's age or telling one's own. In China, the first question a person asks the other on an official call, after asking about his name and surname is, "What is your glorious age?" If the person replies apologetically that he is twenty-three or twenty-eight, the other party generally comforts him by saying that he has still a glorious future, and that one day he may become old. But if the person replies that he is thirty-five or thirty-eight, the other party immediately exclaims with deep respect, "Good luck!"; enthusiasm grows in proportion as the gentleman is able to report a higher and higher age, and if the person is anywhere over fifty, the inquirer immediately drops his voice in humility and respect. That is why all old people, if they can, should go and live in China, where even a beggar with a white beard is treated with extra kindness. People in middle age actually look forward to the time when they can celebrate their fifty-first birthday, and in the case of successful merchants or officials, they would celebrate even their forty-first birthday with great pomp and glory. But the fifty-first birthday, or the half-century mark, is an occasion of rejoicing for people of all classes. The sixty-first is a happier and grander occasion than the fifty-first and the seventy-first is still happier and grander, while a man able to celebrate his eighty-first birthday is actually looked upon as one specially favored by heaven. The wearing of a beard becomes the special prerogative of those who have become grandparents, and a man doing so without the necessary qualifications, either of being a grandfather or being on the other side of fifty, stands in danger of being sneered at behind his back. The result is that young men try to pass themselves off as older than they are by imitating the pose and dignity and point of view of the old people, and I have known young Chinese writers graduated from the middle schools, anywhere between twenty-one and twenty-five, writing articles in the magazines to advise what "the young men ought and ought not to read," and discussing the pitfalls of youth with a fatherly condescension.

This desire to grow old and in any case to appear old is understandable when one understands the premium generally placed upon old age in China. In the first place, it is a privilege of the old people to talk, while the young must listen and hold their tongue. "A young man is supposed to have ears and no mouth," as a Chinese saying goes. Men of twenty are supposed to listen when people of thirty are talking, and these in turn are supposed to listen when men of forty are talking. As the desire to talk and to be listened to is almost universal, it is evident that the further along one gets in years, the better chance he has to talk and to be listened to when he goes about in society. It is a game of life in which no one is favored, for everyone has a chance of becoming old in his time. Thus a father lecturing his son is obliged to stop suddenly and change his demeanor the moment the grandmother opens her mouth. Of course he wishes to be in the grandmother's place. And it is quite fair, for what right have the young to open their mouth when the old men can say, "I have crossed more bridges than you have crossed streets!" What right have the young got to talk?

In spite of my acquaintance with Western life and the Western attitude toward age, I am still continually shocked by certain expressions for which I am totally unprepared. Fresh illustrations of this attitude come up on every side. I have heard an old lady remarking that she has had several grandchildren, but, "It was the first one that hurt." With the full knowledge that American people hate to be thought of as old, one still doesn't quite expect to have it put that way. . . .

I have no doubt that the fact that the old men of America still insist on being so busy and active can be directly traced to individualism carried to a foolish extent. It is their pride and their love of independence and their shame of being dependent upon their children. But among the many human rights the American people have provided for in the Constitution, they have strangely forgotten about the right to be fed by their children, for it is a right and an obligation growing out of service. How can any one deny that parents who have toiled for their children in their youth, have lost many a good night's sleep when they were ill, have washed their diapers long before they could talk and have spent about a quarter of a century bringing them up and fitting them for life, have the right to be fed by them and loved and respected when they are old? Can one not forget the individual and his pride of self in a general scheme of home life in which men are justly taken care of by their parents and, having in turn taken care of their children, are also justly taken care of by the latter? The Chinese have not got the sense of individual independence because the whole conception of life is based upon mutual help within the home; hence there is no shame attached to the circumstance of one's being served by his children in the sunset of one's life. Rather it is considered good luck to have children who can take care of one. One lives for nothing else in China.

In the West, the old people efface themselves and prefer to live alone in some hotel with a restaurant on the ground floor, out of consideration for their children and an entirely unselfish desire not to interfere in their home life. But the old people have the right to interfere, and if interference is unpleasant, it is nevertheless natural, for all life, particularly the domestic life, is a lesson in restraint. Parents interfere with their children anyway when they are young, and the logic of noninterference is already seen in the results of Behaviorists, who think that all children should be taken away from their parents. If one cannot tolerate one's own parents when they are old and comparatively helpless, parents who have done so much for us, whom else can one tolerate in the home? One has to learn self-restraint anyway, or even marriage will go on the rocks. And how can the personal service and devotion and adoration of loving children ever be replaced by the best hotel waiters?

The Chinese idea supporting this personal service to old parents is expressly defended on the sole ground of gratitude. The debts to one's friends may be numbered, but the debts to one's parents are beyond number. Again and again, Chinese essays on filial piety mention the fact of washing diapers, which takes on significance when one becomes a parent himself. In return, therefore, is it not right that in their old age, the parents should be served with the best food and have their favorite dishes placed before them? The duties of a son serving his parents are pretty hard, but it is sacrilege to make a comparison between nursing one's own parents and nursing a stranger in a hospital. For instance, the following are some of the duties of the junior at home, as prescribed by Tu Hsishih and incorporated in a book of moral instruction very popular as a text in the old schools:

> In the summer months, one should, while attending to his parents, stand by their side and fan them, to drive away the heat and the flies and mosquitoes. In winter, he should see that the bed quilts are warm enough and the stove fire is hot enough, and see that it is just right by attending to it constantly. He should also see if there are holes or crevices in the doors and windows, that there may be no draft, to the end that his parents are comfortable and happy.

> A child above ten should get up before his parents in the morning, and after the toilet go to their bed and ask if they have had a good night. If his parents have already gotten up, he should first curtsy to them before inquiring after their health, and should retire with another curtsy after the question. Before going to bed at night, he should prepare the bed, when the parents are going to sleep, and stand by

until he sees that they have fallen off to sleep and then pull down the bed curtain and retire himself.

Who, therefore, wouldn't want to be an old man or an old father or grandfather in China?

This sort of thing is being very much laughed at by the proletarian writers of China as "feudalistic," but there is a charm to it which makes any old gentlemen inland cling to it and think that modern China is going to the dogs. The important point is that every man grows old in time, if he lives long enough, as he certainly desires to. If one forgets this foolish individualism which seems to assume that an individual can exist in the abstract and be literally independent, one must admit that we must so plan our pattern of life that the golden period lies ahead in old age and not behind us in youth and innocence. For if we take the reverse attitude, we are committed without our knowing to a race with the merciless course of time, forever afraid of what lies ahead of us—a race, it is hardly necessary to point out, which is quite hopeless and in which we are eventually all defeated. No one can really stop growing old; he can only cheat himself by not admitting that he is growing old. And since there is no use fighting against nature, one might just as well grow old gracefully. The symphony of life should end with a grand finale of peace and serenity and material comfort and spiritual contentment, and not with the crash of a broken drum or cracked cymbals.

## STUDY QUESTIONS

1. Describe Lin Yutang's account of how the West and the East treat their elderly people.

2. Yutang asks, "How can any one deny that parents who have toiled for their children . . . have lost many a good night's sleep when they were ill, have washed their diapers . . . and have spent about a quarter of a century bringing them up . . . have the right to be fed by them and loved and respected when they are old?" Do you agree with him? Do you feel a moral obligation to care for your parents when they are old?

3. How does Yutang distinguish between debts of friendship and debts to parents? Do you see a fundamental difference between the two?

4.  Does Yutang criticize Western mores fairly? Or does he fail to understand the kind of individualism that characterizes human relations in our society? Some say the price for deference to the aged is a feeling of obligation that may interfere with our sense of independence. Do you agree with this?

# What Do Grown Children Owe Their Parents?

## JANE ENGLISH

Jane English (1947–1978), who taught philosophy at the University of North Carolina, Chapel Hill, wrote several articles and edited a number of books in the area of practical ethics. She died tragically at 31 in an expedition on the Matterhorn.

Jane English argues that grown children have no filial obligations. She distinguishes between relations based on reciprocal favors and relationships of friendship. Both involve duties, but English argues that friendship and its duties ought to be the norm governing the relationship of grown children and parents. Filial obligation is not required per se; it is the result of friendship rather than a debt owed for services rendered. Thus obligations to parents exist "just so long as friendship exists."

WHAT DO GROWN CHILDREN OWE THEIR PARENTS? © *Having Children: Philosophical and Legal Reflections on Parenthood,* edited by Onora O'Neill and William Ruddick (New York: Oxford University Press, 1979).

What do grown children owe their parents? I will contend that the answer is "nothing." Although I agree that there are many things that children *ought* to do for their parents, I will argue that it is inappropriate and misleading to describe them as things "owed." I will maintain that parents' voluntary sacrifices, rather than creating "debts" to be "repaid," tend to create love or "friendship." The duties of grown children are those of friends and result from love between them and their parents, rather than being things owed in repayment for the parents' earlier sacrifices. Thus, I will oppose those philosophers who use the word "owe" whenever a duty or obligation exists. Although the "debt" metaphor is appropriate in some moral circumstances, my argument is that a love relationship is not such a case.

Misunderstandings about the proper relationship between parents and their grown children have resulted from reliance on the "owing" terminology. For instance, we hear parents complain, "You owe it to us to write home (keep up your piano playing, not adopt a hippie lifestyle), because of all we sacrificed for you (paying for piano lessons, sending you to college)." The child is sometimes even heard to reply, "I didn't ask to be born (to be given piano lessons, to be sent to college)." This inappropriate idiom of ordinary language tends to be obscure, or even to undermine, the love that is the correct ground of filial obligation.

## 1. Favors Create Debts

There are some cases, other than literal debts, in which talk of "owing," though metaphorical, is apt. New to the neighborhood, Max barely knows his neighbor, Nina, but he asks her if she will take in his mail while he is gone for a month's vacation. She agrees. If, subsequently, Nina asks Max to do the same for her, it seems that Max has a moral obligation to agree (greater than the one he would have had if Nina had not done the same for him), unless for some reason it would be a burden far out of proportion to the one Nina bore for him. I will call this a *favor*: when A, at B's request, bears some burden for B, then B incurs an obligation to reciprocate. Here the metaphor of Max's "owing" Nina is appropriate. It is not literally a debt, of course, nor can Nina pass this IOU on to heirs, demand payment in the form of Max's taking out her garbage, or sue Max.

Nonetheless, since Max ought to perform one act of similar nature and amount of sacrifice in return, the term is suggestive. Once he reciprocates, the debt is "discharged"—that is, their obligations revert to the condition they were in before Max's initial request.

Contrast a situation in which Max simply goes on vacation and, to his surprise, finds upon his return that his neighbor has mowed his grass twice weekly in his absence. This is a voluntary sacrifice rather than a favor, and Max has no duty to reciprocate. It would be nice for him to volunteer to do so, but this would be supererogatory on his part. Rather than a favor, Nina's action is a friendly gesture. As a result, she might expect Max to chat over the back fence, help her catch her straying dog, or something similar—she might expect the development of a friendship. But Max would be chatting (or whatever) out of friendship, rather than in repayment for mown grass. If he did not return her gesture, she might feel rebuffed or miffed, but not unjustly treated or indignant, since Max has not failed to perform a duty. Talk of "owing" would be out of place in this case.

It is sometimes difficult to distinguish between favors and non-favors, because friends tend to do favors for each other, and those who exchange favors tend to become friends. But one test is to ask how Max is motivated. Is it "to be nice to Nina" or "because she did $x$ for me"? Favors are frequently performed by total strangers without any friendship developing. Nevertheless, a temporary obligation is created, even if the chance for repayment never arises. For instance, suppose that Oscar and Matilda, total strangers, are waiting in a long checkout line at the supermarket. Oscar, having forgotten the oregano, asks Matilda to watch his cart for a second. She does. If Matilda now asks Oscar to return the favor while she picks up some tomato sauce, he is obligated to agree. Even if she had not watched his cart, it would be inconsiderate of him to refuse, claiming he was too busy reading the magazines. He may have had a duty to help others, but he would not "owe" it to her. But if she had done the same for him, he incurs an additional obligation to help, and talk of "owing" is apt. It suggests an agreement to perform equal, reciprocal, canceling sacrifices.

## 2. The Duties of Friendship

The terms "owe" and "repay" are helpful in the case of favors, because the sameness of the amount of sacrifice on the two sides is important; the monetary metaphor suggests equal quantities of sacrifice. But friendship ought to be characterized by *mutuality* rather than reciprocity: friends offer what they can give and accept what they need, without regard for the total amounts of benefits exchanged. And friends are motivated by love rather than by the prospect of repayment. Hence, talk of "owing" is singularly out of place in friendship.

For example, suppose Alfred takes Beatrice out for an expensive dinner and a movie. Beatrice incurs no obligation to "repay" him with a goodnight kiss or a return engagement. If Alfred complains that she "owes" him something, he is operating under the assumption that she should repay a favor, but on the contrary his was a generous gesture done in the hopes of developing a friendship. We hope that he would not want her repayment in the form of sex or attention if this was done to discharge a debt rather than from friendship. Since, if Alfred is prone to reasoning in this way, Beatrice may well decline the invitation or request to pay for her own dinner, his attitude of expecting a "return" on his "investment" could hinder the development of a friendship. Beatrice should return the gesture only if she is motivated by friendship.

Another common misuse of the "owing" idiom occurs when the Smiths have dined at the Joneses' four times, but the Joneses at the Smiths' only once. People often say, "We owe them three dinners." This line of thinking may be appropriate between business acquaintances, but not between friends. After all, the Joneses invited the Smiths not in order to feed them or to be fed in turn, but because of the friendly contact presumably enjoyed by all on such occasions. If the Smiths do not feel friendship toward the Joneses, they can decline future invitations and not invite the Joneses; they owe them nothing. Of course, between friends of equal resources and needs, roughly equal sacrifices (though not necessarily roughly equal dinners) will typically occur. If the sacrifices are highly out of proportion to the resources, the relationship is closer to servility than to friendship.[1]

Another difference between favors and friendship is that after a friendship ends, the duties of friendship end. The party that has sacrificed less owes the other nothing. For instance, suppose Elmer

---

[1] *Cf.* Thomas E. Hill, Jr., "Servility and Self-respect," *Monist* 57 (1973). Thus, during childhood, most of the sacrifices will come from the parents, since they have most of the resources and the child has most of the needs. When children are grown, the situation is usually reversed.

donated a pint of blood that his wife Doris needed durng an operation. Years after their divorce, Elmer is in an accident and needs one
pint of blood. His new wife, Cora, is also of the same blood type. It
seems that Doris not only does not "owe" Elmer blood, but that she
should actually refrain from coming forward if Cora has volunteered
to donate. To insist on donating not only interferes with the new-
lyweds' friendship, but it belittles Doris and Elmer's former relationship by suggesting that Elmer gave blood in hopes of favors returned
instead of simply out of love for Doris. It is one of the heart-rending
features of divorce that it attends to quantity in a relationship previously characterized by mutuality. If Cora could not donate, Doris's
obligation is the same as that for any former spouse in need of blood;
it is not increased by the fact that Elmer similarly aided her. It *is*
affected by the degree to which they are still friends, which in turn
may (or may not) have been influenced by Elmer's donation.

In short, unlike the debts created by favors, the duties of friendship
do not require equal quantities of sacrifice. Performing equal sacrifices does not cancel the duties of friendship, as it does the debts of
favors. Unrequested sacrifices do not themselves create debts, but
friends have duties regardless of whether they requested or initiated
the friendship. Those who perform favors may be motivated by
mutual gain, whereas friends should be motivated by affection.
These characteristics of the friendship relation are distorted by talk
of "owing."

## 3. Parents and Children

The relationship between children and their parents should be one of
friendship characterized by mutuality rather than one of reciprocal
favors. The quantity of parental sacrifice is not relevant in determining what duties the grown child has. The medical assistance grown
children ought to offer their ill mothers in old age depends upon the
mothers' need, not upon whether they endured a difficult pregnancy,
for example. Nor do one's duties to one's parents cease once an equal
quantity of sacrifice has been performed, as the phrase "discharging
a debt" may lead us to think.

Rather, what children ought to do for their parents (and parents
for children) depends upon (1) their respective needs, abilities,
and resources and (2) the extent to which there is an ongoing friendship between them. Thus, regardless of the quantity of childhood

sacrifices, an able, wealthy child has an obligation to help his needy parents more than does a needy child. To illustrate, suppose sisters Cecile and Dana are equally loved by their parents, even though Cecile was an easy child to care for, seldom ill, while Dana was often sick and caused some trouble as a juvenile delinquent. As adults, Dana is a struggling artist living far away, while Cecile is a wealthy lawyer living nearby. When the parents need visits and financial aid, Cecile has an obligation to bear a higher proportion of these burdens than her sister. This results from her abilities, rather than from the quantities of sacrifice made by the parents earlier.

Sacrifices have an important causal role in creating an ongoing friendship, which may lead us to assume incorrectly that it is the sacrifices that are the source of obligation. That the source is the friendship instead can be seen by examining cases in which the sacrifices occurred but the friendship, for some reason, did not develop or persist. For example, if a woman gives up her newborn child for adoption, and if no feelings of love ever develop on either side, it seems that the grown child does not have an obligation to "repay" her for her sacrifices in pregnancy. For that matter, if the adopted child has an unimpaired love relationship with the adoptive parents, he or she has the same obligations to help them as a natural child would have.

The filial obligations of grown children are a result of friendship, rather than owed for services rendered. Suppose that Vance married Lola despite his parents' strong wish that he marry within their religion, and that as a result, the parents refuse to speak to him again. As the years pass, the parents are unaware of Vance's problems, his accomplishments, the birth of his children. The love that once existed between them, let us suppose, has been completely destroyed by this event and thirty years of desuetude. At this point, it seems, Vance is under no obligation to pay his parents' medical bills in their old age, beyond his general duty to help those in need. An additional, filial obligation would only arise from whatever love he may still feel for them. It would be irrelevant for his parents to argue, "But look how much we sacrificed for you when you were young," for that sacrifice was not a favor but occurred as part of a friendship which existed at the time but is now, we have supposed, defunct. A more appropriate message would be, "We still love you, and we would like to renew our friendship."

I hope this helps to set the question of what children ought to do for their parents in a new light. The parental argument, "You ought to do *x* because we did *y* for you," should be replaced by, "We love you and you will be happier if you do *x*," or "We believe you love us, and anyone who loved us would do *x*." If the parents' sacrifice had been a favor, the child's reply, "I never asked you to do *y* for me," would have been relevant; to the revised parental remarks, this reply is clearly irrelevant. The child can either do *x* or dispute one of the parents' claims: by showing that a love relationship does not exist, or that love for someone does not motivate doing *x*, or that he or she will not be happier doing *x*.

Seen in this light, parental requests for children to write home, visit, and offer them a reasonable amount of emotional and financial support in life's crises are well founded, so long as a friendship still exists. Love for others does call for caring about and caring for them. Some other parental requests, such as for more sweeping changes in the child's lifestyle or life goals, can be seen to be insupportable, once we shift the justification from debts owed to love. The terminology of favors suggests the reasoning, "Since we paid for your college education, you owe it to us to make a career of engineering, rather than becoming a rock musician." This tends to alienate affection even further, since the tuition payments are depicted as investments for a return rather than done from love, as though the child's life goals could be "bought." Basing the argument on love leads to different reasoning patterns. The suppressed premise, "If A loves B, then A follows B's wishes as to A's lifelong career" is simply false. Love does not even dictate that the child adopt the parents' values as to the desirability of alternative life goals. So the parents' strongest available argument here is, "We love you, we are deeply concerned about your happiness, and in the long run you will be happier as an engineer." This makes it clear that an empirical claim is really the subject of the debate.

The function of these examples is to draw out our considered judgments as to the proper relation between parents and their grown children, and to show how poorly they fit the model of favors. What is relevant is the ongoing friendship that exists between parents and children. Although that relationship developed partly as a result of parental sacrifices for the child, the duties that grown children have to their parents result from the friendship rather than from the sacrifices. The idiom of owing favors to one's parents can actually be destructive if it undermines the role of mutuality and leads us to think in terms of quantitative reciprocal favors.

**STUDY QUESTIONS**

1. How does English distinguish between duties created by debts and duties created by friendship?
2. Do you agree with English that filial obligation is not owed for services rendered, but instead results from friendship? How would Lin Yutang react to this view?
3. In some states, law requires children of poor elderly people to contribute to their support. Do you think English would argue for or against this? Do you support legislation of this kind?
4. Can we criticize English for advocating a "minimalist ethic" according to which no duties of self-sacrifice or altruism apply outside one's small circle of friends—all people, even family members, are moral strangers unless one voluntarily "contracts" an obligation?
5. How might English account for the moral duty many people feel to take care of not only their own elderly parents, but needy elderly people in general?

# Traditional Jewish Family Values

## NORMAN LAMM

Rabbi Norman Lamm (1927), president of Yeshiva University, is the author of *Faith and Doubt* (1971) and *The Good Society* (1974).

Lamm presents an idealized model of the traditional Jewish family and contrasts it with the average contemporary Jewish family. The traditional family is much more rigorously organized, its members' roles are strictly defined, and, consequently, the family itself is more important as an institution. This results in greater intimacy and a strong sense of mutual obligation, for example, to the elderly who are esteemed as authoritative. Members of the traditional family practice a great deal of restraint and forebearance, emphasizing duty, rather than rights. Finally, the family sees itself as part of a more general community of Jewish families that is, in turn, part of a continuous tradition and history. The traditional family is religious and committed to carrying on a Jewish tradition. This, says Lamm, gives it further cohesiveness.

Lamm argues for the importance of the "benevolent authority" that parents exercise, an authority all the more effective because the higher authority of God qualifies it. According to Lamm, a family that lacks a central authority cannot be cohesive. The children of such families tend

TRADITIONAL JEWISH FAMILY VALUES From *Jewish Consciousness-raising*. Edited by Norman Linzer. © 1973 by the Board of Jewish Education of Greater New York. Reprinted by permission of the copyright holder.

to be confused and disoriented. Lamm warns that we are
losing our sense of commitment to tradition in a world
without faith and cannot replace it simply by recognizing
how badly we need it.

. . . I am going to set up a contrast between two arbitrarily designed
models, one of a traditional and the other of a modern Jewish home.
My excuse is that I am not aiming at sociological accuracy but at
clarity of exposition. First, the idealized version of the traditional
Jewish home is characterized by a high degree of intimacy, of love,
of devotion, usually non-demonstrative. The husband normally is a
monogamist and the wife is satisfied to be at home. As opposed to
this, contemporary parents are more remote. They are encouraged
to follow their own interests. The mother is told that she should not
allow her life to be wrapped up entirely in her children and in
her home, but should find outside interests. The father, when he
comes back from the office, seeks out a peer group or other kinds of
involvements. As a result, the parents seek their own particular levels
of interest, or areas of interest, and are removed from the nexus of
the home.

Second, in traditional Jewish homes there is a special esteem for
age, which is cherished for its own sake. Of course, this goes back to
the Biblical commandments of "Honor thy father and mother" and
honor for the teacher and elder, but sociologically speaking, it is not
so much a revealed norm as a lived value. The traditional home likely
as not included an extended family larger than the nuclear family.
Most Jewish children grew up in the presence of a grandfather or a
grandmother, some kind of living relic of the past, and developed a
natural respect and reverence for age not because of any specific
function of the elderly, but because age itself was valued. Compare
that now to the contemporary emphasis on youth and youthfulness,
especially in America but all over the Western world as well. That
the focus of our culture is the young is often revealed in some of the
inanities of the Jewish community organizations and its press. We are
so geared to the young that when we want to decide the great questions of the day, we send out a researcher to take a statistical analysis
of what high school sophomores are thinking, because that represents "the wave of the future" which ought, by implication, to determine our stand, not only with regard to dress and speech but even

with regard to policy, religion, etc. I am presenting a caricature, of course (although I have certain specific incidents in mind), but it does contain the kernel of a true reflection of the quality of life in America.

Third, in this idealized picture of the traditional Jewish home, there were more or less well defined roles for father and mother. Probably, this was not only true for the Jewish home: it was the case for general culture in which Jews found themselves in pre-modern or pre-contemporary times. A little boy knew what was expected of him when he became a big boy and a big man, and a little girl knew the role into which she was emerging and for which, therefore, she ought to be striving. This clear role definition is increasingly absent in the contemporary home, where there occurs a great deal of blurring and interchanging of roles, with consequent functional chaos when it comes to identifying the roles of father and mother as separate and distinct from each other.

Fourth, the traditional Jewish home emphasized the value of self-restraint, of renunciation, "Thou shalt not." The modern home, in our pop-culture, regards "Thou shalt not" as an excessive inhibition which can harm the emotions and mentality of the growing child. Morally, the modern home is characterized much more by permissiveness than by renunciation and restraint. Perhaps one can best describe the difference between the traditional Jewish home and the modern Jewish home by the polarity of duty and right. The traditional home emphasized duty. What am I supposed to do? What must I do? The modern Jewish home is more a matter of rights: the children's right, the wife's right, the mother's right, the father's right. Everyone has his or her rights, and in this competition of rights a balance has to be struck and a harmony established so that everyone gets his due. The emphasis is not on the contribution that I must make, but rather on what my fair share is, what my rights are.

Finally, in the traditional Jewish home there is understood and presupposed a commitment by all members of the family to a goal or a source that transcends the family. There is some kind of transcendent commitment which binds the members of the family. This transcendent commitment is usually some aspect of, or combination of aspects of, the Jewish tradition—the Jewish people, Jewish law, Jewish religion, God, Torah. The modern home lacks the axiological or ideological cohesiveness. If a religious or nationalistic commitment is present, it is not considered particularly important. It never really plays a central role in the life of the family. Again I ask you not to charge me with being unscientific. I am setting up models, and not insisting, of course, that every modern family follows one path or every traditional family the other.

The five elements, for the purpose of our discussion, may be reduced to three more basic issues: love, authority, and commitment.

## Love

Let us begin with the first one, love. The traditional Jewish family structure is disintegrating. As time goes on and assimilation increases, you find that the whole pattern I have described as the paradigm of a Jewish family that we have inherited from the past, is falling apart. We are experiencing an accelerated decentralization of the family as a result of the various centrifugal forces which tend to pull the family apart. As it is wrenched out of the context of a stable, self-sufficient Jewish community life, the family begins to disintegrate at the edges. Eventually, the community as a whole follows suit. Furthermore, modern goals such as the desideratum of self-fulfillment and self-realization, which really are basic and important values for moderns, tend to polarize individuals in the family. They diminish the virtues of self-sacrifice, of loyalty, of restraint which had previously acted as centripetal forces in favor of the family unit. If I must seek my self-fulfillment and my self-realization, I will find that that often conflicts with what I might otherwise consider my specific duties to my parents, to my wife, to my children, to the family as a whole. . . .

Now, in the highly structured traditional Jewish family, especially the patriarchal one, where there is a clear source of authority (which we shall discuss in more detail later), the family enforces a practical conformity with its norms and its ideological commitment. Sometimes, however, the traditional Jewish family, in enforcing this ideological pattern, this whole routine of life for all its members, overuses its discipline which overwhelms the element of love. In this model we have set up the traditional Jewish family, love and devotion were ever-present, but so was discipline, which guaranteed family cohesion. But sometimes it happened that the discipline was too strong, so that it became rigid, thus diminishing the element of love, warmth, spontaneity, and the sense of intimacy. That is why you find sometimes that within Orthodox families—especially in the modern or contemporary period—there is a rigidity and a defensiveness against the "outside world" that was not true when the entire community was more or less traditional. Often an Orthodox family in our days finds itself on the defensive as a cognitive minority and develops a kind of "man the ramparts" psychology, and even philosophy, that undergirds it. It is not always the healthiest thing for the development of a family's solidarity to feel that they are living in a beleagured fortress. Sometimes it helps, sometimes it doesn't. But because of it, parents in a truly Orthodox family will sometimes be harsh with children—overly harsh—neglecting, in this sense, some of the wisdom of their own tradition.

This wisdom can best be recapitulated in a famous story told of the founder of the Hasidic movement, the Besht (Rabbi Israel Baal Shem Tov.) A father once came to him to complain that his son was going off on the wrong path and leaving Jewish morality and Jewish religious practice. He said to the Rabbi, "What can I do? He is destroying my life, he is destroying everything I've stood for." The Besht answered in three words: *"Love him more."* Instead of bearing down on him, love him more. And with love you probably can achieve a great deal more than by cracking the whip. If you are overly harsh, if you are overly insistent upon conformity to standards that you have inherited which you cherish, then this kind of strictness can be counter-productive.

## Authority

The center of gravity in the family makes it a family and not just a group of biologically related people who happen to live under the same roof. The father is usually the source of authority in the traditional Jewish family, but not always. Sometimes it is the mother. In a number of very pious families today in this country, as in the *shtetl,* a young husband will spend several years of intensive study in a *Kollel,* a school of advanced Talmudic research. If he was a great or at least a good scholar, he usually was the source of authority. It sometimes happened that the father who went off to study was not quite that competent and never amounted to much. In that case, the mother, who had much less education and was sometimes illiterate, often was, by virtue of her own gut wisdom, the real and effective head of the family. (One can cite similar instances of a secularized version of this pattern. There are young men in modern, non-religious families who go off to graduate school with their fellowships and scholarships to earn their degrees, while the working wife is the one who really is the "smart" one and runs the family.) However, as a rule it is the father who represented the patriarchal communal authority for his particular family. In the discussion that is now to follow, if I used the term "father," you may easily substitute "mother" if the particular family circumstances call for it. He or she is the one person who above all other represents authority for the entire family. . . .

This father in the traditional Jewish family is an *authority*. He is not a "pal" to his children. He does not run the family along the lines of a participatory democracy where every important problem is taken to a vote with children possessing one-man, one-vote rights equally with father and mother. In this family you do not find the contemporary penchant for an unconscious divination of the future by a reverential observation of the "younger set." Here, then, is no assumption that, since the future is always an improvement over the present, a higher point in inevitable "progress," therefore, children possess some intuitive wisdom to which parents must make obeisance. Not here do you find the phenomenon of treating children as the brokers of the peer group, who actually inform parents how to be "with it" and run things. Often, as you are well aware, the failure of parents to exercise discipline is not really a sign of their love for their children, but rather a disguise for their fundamental lack of concern. If I don't genuinely care for my child, then I will act like a "pal," let him do as he wishes, and delude myself into thinking that in this manner he will think better of me. But with such an attitude, the role of the authority in the family is eroded. This liberal posture, and in radical circles, this conscious and deliberate egalitarianism, represents a frontal attack on the structure of the family by gutting its source and focus of authority.

One must bear in mind that the authority of parents in traditional Judaism was never considered absolute, even in Biblical days. The father was not acknowledged as a kind of petty tyrant who could do with his family as he liked. He was, to follow the metaphor, a constitutional monarch. . . . The father was not the absolute sovereign of that family. This Biblical and Rabbinic teaching must be compared to the then contemporary or even later cultures. In the Grecian and

Roman times, a father had the legal right to put a child to death for disobedience. In Greece, a child who was weak and therefore a drain on the family's finances could be taken up to a mountain and left to die. This was accepted as normal and legitimate practice by parents. Not so in Judaism, where *a* source of authority does not imply *absolute* authority. Only God is absolute authority. Parental direction had to be benevolent, and even loving, giving the family its reference point and its structure.

This description of the exercise of benevolent authority and discipline in the traditional Jewish family is, of course, idealized. It was not always so effective. There was apparently always present in Jewish life the phenomenon of Jewish overindulgence of children. Let me illustrate this with two interesting examples from Jewish literature and history. The universality of this proclivity for excessive forbearance by Jewish parents is given fascinating testimony in the following passage:

> There is yet one other evil disease regarding raising children that is not practiced by other people. A child sits at the table with his father and mother and he is the first to stretch forth his hand to partake of the food. He thus grows up arrogant, without fear or culture or refinement, acting as if his father and mother were friends or siblings. By the time he is 8 or 9 years old and his parents wish to correct their earlier mistakes, they no longer are able to, for his childish habits have already become second nature . . .

> Another bad and bitter practice: Parents take a child to school, and in front of the child, warn the teacher not to punish him. When the child hears this, he no longer pays attention to his school work and his disobedience grows worse. This was not the practice of our ancestors. In their days, if a child came crying to his father or mother and told of being punished by a teacher, they would send along the child a gift to the teacher and congratulate the teacher . . .

Modern though it sounds, this complaint comes from *Tzeror Hachayyim* by Rabbi Mosheh Hagiz, over 220 years ago. Two centuries ago, in the pre-modern period, Jewish parents were already indulgent, so this Jewish syndrome is older than the modern period.

Let us cite one more passage, this time advice by a German Jew on the desirable method of raising children.

A man should begin to train his children in the service of God and in good character when they are yet very young. He must be careful not to permit his love for them to indulge them and permit them to do whatever they wish. . . . However, he must be very careful not to frighten them unnecessarily, lest the child be driven to harm himself. . . . Every parent must judge his child's individual personality and treat him accordingly. Also, if a parent is always angry, the child will come to despise him and pay no more attention to his approach than to a barking dog.

This frank and intelligent advice comes from *Yosef Ometz* of 350 years ago. It is worth listening to him closely. It summarizes, in a way, 3,000 years of cumulative Jewish experience. It is the frequent absence of this combined love and authority, which equals intelligent discipline, that bedevils so many families today.

## Commitment

After love and authority, our third and final element for discussion is: commitment. The father in this idealized Jewish traditional family is not only the visible and present focus of authority for the children, but he is also a symbol, the representative and refractor of a Higher Authority. . . . The father effectively acts as the psychological focus for the child of an authority greater than the father himself. He is a surrogate, a broker, of a kind of authority that is beyond the family itself. The father as authority is not self-contained and, in traditional Judaism, he is not self-authenticating. There is a higher authority which legitimates the role of the father. The father is only the broker of this higher authority of God, Torah, Judaism, tradition. The father grounds his authority in the sanction of the Transcendent to which father and son and mother and daughter are all mutually committed. This sanction of the father's authority (or, if you will, the authority of his authority) is the cement of commitment that helped bind the family and make of it a cohesive, well-structured unit. The child knows: if I am angry at my father and I want to rebel, I may hate him; I may even have a death wish for him. But I know all along that there is something beyond father; he is not the ultimate ground of authority, and some day I will be the continuation of my own family because all of us are bound to something much higher.

The focus of the commitment must be beyond the father or

whoever happens to be the authority in that family, in order for the family to be united by this commitment.

Thus, this religious commitment is a necessary but not sufficient condition for the reconstitution of family life. Most Jewish homes today are fundamentally non-Jewish. ("Ethnic Jewishness" is totally irrelevant in this respect.) Those Jewish values which do survive, however you want to describe them, are the fortuitous results of a cultural lag. When the fundamental commitment has spent itself, the accompanying phenomena tend to continue for a while: but you can't draw endlessly on that spent capital. Take a minor example: education. Most of us have or had parents whose formal education was less than the one that we possess. Why? The answer is: the Jewish drive for education. A Jewish boy and a Jewish girl must get an education. We, in turn, give this value to our children. But I don't know how much longer this is going to continue, not only because the counter-culture makes a virtue a nonachievement rather than achievement, but because our whole impulse for education—to take this one Jewish value—derives from a religious commitment. It is not primarily a sociological phenomenon—the way for the immigrants to get out of the sweatshops. The original inclination comes from the *Mitzvah* of *Talmud Torah,* the religious commandment to study the Torah. This purely religious norm later became secularized, turning from "Torah" to "education," and that meant how to be a doctor or a lawyer or a professor. But when you cut off the major commitment—the religious commitment—all its derivative Jewish values can continue only by virtue of a cultural lag. Alone, these values have only limited endurance and must soon vanish.

## Prescription

So much for analysis. Let us now turn to prescription. Unfortunately, I believe I have a much better grasp of what's wrong than I have any ability to prescribe for it. But since the theme assigned to me requires prescription as well, I shall try my hand and hope the medicine I offer you is at least somewhat effective. I feel that the best approach is the indirect one. Let me follow my outline with a slight change, and discuss authority first.

For a family to be cohesive, to be healthy, there has to be a source—a focus of authority. A totally shared authority is inadequate because it is unfocused; it means that no one really knows what's going on. Children under such conditions become confused, not knowing whom to turn to. . . . When I say authority, I hope I will not be misunderstood. I am not speaking of the petty tryant who pulls at his suspenders and says "I'm boss because I wear the pants in the family." I refer, rather, to an intelligent, enlightened attitude where there is, within rational psychological limits, a division of labor, a division of responsibility, and a division of authority, but where at least there is some kind of grouping around a center.

Of course, there are special problems with fatherless families. What does one do in a family made fatherless through death or divorce or separation or abandonment? Here I believe one ought to begin to search out a surrogate father. Either mother must learn how to assert authority or, if she is constitutionally unable to do so, there has to be some way for her children to find a father-model, whether it be a teacher or someone else who can firmly assert moral responsibility and moral authority. Granted, this is easier said than done.

Love. If it doesn't exist, the family situation seems almost hopeless, because of personal, psychological, and sociocultural reasons. Even the minimum effort that would be necessary to support it under such conditions appears to me to be heroic. The problem is complicated nowadays by the fact that the nuclear family in contemporary Jewish life is largely divorced from the extended family, and it is the extended family which tends to retain Judaism's social and moral norms longer than the solitary nuclear family. When a unit consisting of father and mother and children are pulled out of the context of the larger Jewish group, it will tend to lose any traditional values much more quickly than a continuing Jewish neighborhood will lose those same values even if they are already suffering the attrition of assimilation. The Jewish community as a whole has, of course, undergone assimilatory erosion, but I think that the great move to suburbia which came about during the '50s was the beginning of a precipitate abandonment of the whole Jewish nexus, which was a core of the residue of Jewish values. In other words, upper social mobility spelled for us a very sudden downward trend in psychological stability and religious continuity.

Finally, let us turn to the theme of commitment. In the absence of any genuine inner religious commitment in a Jewish family, we must seek some external idea or cause which can attract and centralize the commitment of the individual members of the family. I am a great believer in the fact that the focus of family cohesiveness must be transcendent and not immanent. It cannot be the family for the family's sake. It just doesn't work in the kind of society in which we live, with all its centrifugal pulls. It has got to be something beyond the family to which all members, or most members of the family, are mutually committed.

## Conclusions

. . . You say: what can we do? My answer is: we are facing a terribly messy situation. It is the universal condition of man today—of man without God, of man without faith, without an awareness of transcendence, man who feels terribly endangered by the gaping existential void within him, by the threat of meaninglessness which is aggravated by the ubiquitous awareness of death. You just cannot fill the transcendental void by values which we sit down and artificially create. There is no way out. To be honest, either we choose the real thing, or we are in despair. We cannot in one hour or in one lifetime ever hope to devise an adequate substitute for religious faith; in any event, according to my own commitments, substitutes are called—idols.

The Jewish family was strong not when it discussed values but when it lived them. It began to disintegrate when it substituted cocktails for *kiddush* and tuxedo for *tallit*. Traditional Jewish wholesomeness was grounded in a spiritual commitment, in a sublime web of ritual acts invested with both metaphysical significance and nostalgic and historic recollection, so that individuals were both synchronically and diachronically part of a people—a people called a *mishpachah* (family) at its very founding by Abraham. These are not just disembodied "values" or artificial "rituals," but part of a living organism, which gave life and vitality to the family and a sense of validity to its members, despite the ubiquitous domestic problems to which Jews, like all humans, are heir.

### STUDY QUESTIONS

1. Lamm gives several criteria of family integrity. In your opinion, are these specific to the traditional Jewish family or are they more

general? For example, would a cohesive Catholic or Protestant family satisfy *these* conditions or some others? Specify them.
2. According to Lamm, commitment to the authority of God is an important ingredient in the cohesive family. How, in your opinion, does such commitment contribute to a family's integrity? Is commitment to God an *essential* ingredient?
3. Assuming Lamm is right, how, if in any way, can we create the conditions necessary for stable families? Lamm himself points out that we cannot do this artifically. Are there natural ways?
4. If Lamm's criteria for the close-knit family are indeed too stringent for modern times, is the rapid decline of the family as an institution inevitable?

# *Divorce*

## REBECCA WEST

Rebecca West (1892–1982) was one of the foremost figures in twentieth-century Anglo-American intellectual life. Her work, which includes fiction, criticism, biography, history, and travel reporting, is admired for its wit, eloquence, and intellectual power.

In her essay on divorce, Rebecca West assumes that the family is a vital institution. This raises a question: Should we preserve the family by outlawing divorce even at the cost of individual happiness? West's answer is a qualified no. She describes the harmful effects of divorce on children, effects of a "radiating kind, likely to travel down and down through the generations, such as few would care to have on their consciences." Conversely, she notes that, sometimes, remaining with a brutal parent can be

DIVORCE From *The London Daily Express*, 1930. Reprinted by permission of A. D. Peters & Co. Ltd.

even more harmful. West also argues in favor of the right
to divorce because countries that do not allow it are often
oppressive and sexually hypocritical.

The way one looks at divorce depends on the way one looks at a much
broader question.

Is the mental state of humanity so low that it is best to lay down
invariable rules for it which have been found to lead to the greatest
happiness of the greatest number, and insist that everyone keep them
in spite of the hardship necessarily inflicted on certain special cases,
thus dragooning the majority into compulsory happiness? Or is it so
high that it is safe to lay down rules which will admit of variation for
different people in different circumstances, when it seems to them
these variations can secure their happiness?

If one agrees with the first view, then one is bound to disapprove
altogether of divorce. If one agrees with the second, then one is bound
to approve of legislation which enables unhappily married persons
to separate and remarry.

Though I have the kind of temperament that hates to own failure
and would never wish to break a marriage I had made, I regard
divorce laws as a necessary part of the arrangements in a civilized
State. This is the result of my experience of life in countries where
there is practically no divorce, and in countries where divorce is
permissible on grounds of varying latitude.

Superficially the case against divorce is overwhelming: and indeed
it should never be forgotten, least of all by those who approve of
divorce as a possibility. Getting a divorce is nearly always as cheerful
and useful an occupation as breaking very valuable china. The divorce of married people with children is nearly always an unspeak-
able calamity. It is only just being understood, in the light of modern
psychological research, how much a child depends for its healthy
growth on the presence in the home of both its parents. This is not a
matter of its attitude to morals; if divorce did nothing more than
make it accustomed to the idea of divorce, then no great harm would
be done. The point is that if a child is deprived of either its father or
its mother it feels that it has been cheated out of a right. It cannot be
reasoned out of this attitude, for children are illogical, especially

where their affections are concerned, to an even greater degree than ourselves. A child who suffers from this resentment suffers much more than grief: he is liable to an obscuring of his vision, to a warping of his character. He may turn against the parent to whom the courts have given him, and regard him or her as responsible for the expulsion of the other from the home. He may try to compensate himself for what he misses by snatching everything else he can get out of life, and become selfish and even thievish. He may, through yearning for the unattainable parent, get himself into a permanent mood of discontent, which will last his life long and make him waste every opportunity of love and happiness that comes to him later.

If either parent remarries, the child may feel agonies of jealousy. What is this intruder coming in and taking affection when already there is not as much as there ought to be? This is an emotion that is felt by children even in the case of fathers and mothers who have lost their partners by death: as witness the innumerable cases of children who come up before the Juvenile Courts and prove on examination to have committed their offences as acts of defiance against perfectly inoffensive and kindly step-parents. It is felt far more acutely in the case of parents whose relationships have been voluntarily severed, who have no excuse of widowhood or widowerhood to justify the introduction of a new partner. This, of course, need not always happen. One of the happiest homes I can think of is the second venture of a man and a woman who both divorced their first partners as a result of conduct that poisoned not only their lives but their children's: it is one of the most cheerful sights I know to see their combined family of four children realizing with joy and surprise that actually they can have a family life like other people. But that man and that woman are not only kindly people, they are clever people. They handle the children with extreme sensitiveness to the issues involved. More commonly the situation for the child is not completely salved.

In fact, people with children who divorce husbands or wives because they are troublesome are likely to find themselves saddled with rather more discontent than they hoped to escape. And the new trouble is of a radiating kind, likely to travel down and down through the generations, such as few would care to have on their consciences.

As for the divorce of childless married couples, there is of course a matter of infinitely less social significance. If it is regarded too lightly it cheats a lot of them out of their one chance of happiness. A man and woman marry each other because they represent to each other the types they have always found attractive and about which they have spun innumerable romantic dreams. They then grow disappointed with each other because they insist on being themselves, the human beings they happened to be born, instead of the dreamed-of types. If they stay together it may in time penetrate to each that the other may not have the qualities of the imagined one, but may have real and valuable virtues which are much more useful; and a very kindly feeling of attachment may develop. But if a couple break up during the first shock of disappointment they are certain to go off and immediately find other people who resemble the dreamed-of types, marry them, and go through the same process of disillusionment, ending in another separation. Thus a whole group of people will be involved in sterile and inharmonious excitements which will waste the very short time we are given to establish ourselves in fruitful and harmonious relationships.

Against these considerations, of course, we have to reckon that although the consequences of being the child of divorced parents are heavy, they are sometimes not so heavy as the consequences of being a child brought up in close propinquity and at the mercy of a brutal and vicious parent. We have also to admit that in the case of a childless couple there may be reasons why a divorce may become as essential to a human being's continued existence as food or air. There is infidelity, there is drunkenness, there is, above all, cruelty, not only of the body but of the mind. No one who has not been through it can know the full horror of being tied to a man who craves war instead of peace, whose love is indistinguishable from hate. The day that is poisoned from its dawn by petty rages about nothing, by a deliberate destruction of everything pleasant: the night that is full of fear, because it is certain that no one can suffer all this without going mad, and if one goes mad there will be nobody to be kind; these are things to which no human being should have a life sentence.

But brutal and vicious parents are in a minority. Human nature is not so bad as all that. The opponents of divorce are therefore justified when they ask if it is not dangerous to give the victims of this minority the power to free themselves from these burdens that cannot be borne, when that power will inevitably be available to those who want to free themselves from burdens that they only think cannot be borne. For human beings are stupid; they do not know what is best for them, they certainly will not use that power wisely. If the majority is to suffer unnecessarily from these facilities for divorce, would it not be better to withdraw and let the minority fend for itself?

I do not think so. Because there is another element involved; and that is the general attitude of the community toward sex. That seems to be invariably less sane where there is no divorce than where there is. What makes humanity stupid is that it will act on certain mad fairy-tales about life which it refuses to outgrow, and its attitude to sex determines all these mad fairy-tales.

The lack of divorce corrupts the community's attitude to sex for several reasons. First of all, it deprives marriage of all standards. If one cannot be penalized for failure in an activity, and the prizes for success in it are of a highly rarefied and spiritual nature, the baser man will regard it as a go-as-you-please affair. The man who knows that he can commit adultery without the slightest check from society will have to be a very high type if he does not come to the conclusion that, since society is so indifferent to it, adultery must be a trivial matter. But his natural jealousy will not permit him to think like that of his wife's adultery. That he will punish in all of the very extensive ways which are open to him through his economic power.

Thus there starts the fictitious system of morality which, instead of regarding sexual conduct as a means to an end, and that end the continuance of the species in the most harmonious conditions, places purely arbitrary values on different sexual entities and plays a game with them like Mah-Jong. Since a man's adultery does not matter and a woman's adultery does, it follows that a man's whole sexual life is without moral significance, and a woman's sexual life is portentous with it. Whenever you have no divorce laws you must have the double standard of morality. Consequently a large part of the male sex, as much as is not controlled by idealism, roves about the world trying with complete impunity to persuade the female sex to a course of action which, should the female comply, leads them to disaster. The seducer, it must be noted, has an enormous advantage in countries where there is no divorce. Even in England, we sometimes come across a Don Juan who has the luck to have a wife who will not divorce him, and note how useful he finds this in persuading ladies that he loves them. He can so safely say that he would marry them if he could, without danger that his bluff will be called. Every

Don Juan enjoys this advantage in a country where there is no divorce. Illegitimate births follow which—because of the arbitrary distinction between the sexes—are not robbed of their sting as they are in the countries where divorce is possible by laws that guarantee the offspring its maintenance, but result in the persecution of mother and child.

In fact, sex is associated with cruelty in countries where there is no divorce, as it is in the institution of prostitution: this also flourishes wherever there is this double standard of morality. No illicit love affair, where both parties are exercising free choice, can possibly do the community as much harm as the traffic between the prostitute and her client. That a woman should be held in contempt for submitting to the same physical relationship that is the core of marriage degrades marriage, and all women, and all men; and the greater the contempt she is held in the more she becomes genuinely contemptible. For as she sinks lower she becomes more and more a source of disease, and more and more a brutalized machine. It is in countries where there is no divorce that the prostitute is most firmly established as the object of extra-marital adventures and is most deeply despised.

One can test this by its converse if one goes to a library and turns up old comic papers and plays, particularly farces. As the law and society began to sanction divorce, and impressed on the public a sense of moral obligation, this ceased to be the case.

It is one of the most important things in the world that people should have a sane and kindly outlook on sex; that it should not be associated with squalor and cruelty. Because divorce makes it clear to the ordinary man and woman that they must behave well in the married state or run the risk of losing its advantages, it does impress on them some rudiments of a sane attitude towards sex. It therefore lifts up the community to a level where happy marriages, in which the problem of our human disposition to cruelty and jealousy is satisfactorily solved, are much more likely to occur.

**STUDY QUESTIONS**

1. Rebecca West says that "people with children who divorce husbands or wives because they are troublesome are likely to find themselves saddled with rather more discontent than they hoped

to escape. And the new trouble is of a radiating kind, likely to travel down and down through the generations, such as few would care to have on their consciences." Can West be consistent in permitting divorce, given her views on its ill effects?

2. Why does West believe that lack of divorce has a corrupting effect on society? Do you agree that the human cost of permitting divorce is lower than the cost of outlawing it?

3. West notes that children suffer from the effects of divorce through several generations. If this is so, wouldn't prohibiting divorce be morally right in those cases where one or both parents do not brutalize the children? Why, after all, should parents be allowed to inflict a divorce on their innocent children?

# Sex Roles and the Ideal Society

## RICHARD WASSERSTROM

Richard Wasserstrom (b. 1936) is professor of philosophy at the University of California at Santa Cruz. He has served as President of the American Philosophical Association (Pacific Division), and is the author of numerous articles and books in ethics and social philosophy. Among his books are *War and Morality* (1970) and *Philosophy and Social Issues* (1980).

Richard Wasserstrom argues for a society that incorporates the "assimilationist ideal." In the assimilationist society, whether one is male or female signifies no more than whether one is blue-eyed or brown-eyed. "[N]o political rights or social institutions, practices and norms would mark the physiological differences between males

SEX ROLES AND THE IDEAL SOCIETY Excerpted from *Philosophy and Social Issues* by Richard Wasserstrom (Notre Dame, IN: University of Notre Dame Press, 1980), pp. 23–41.

and females as important. . . . Bisexuality, not hetero-sexuality or homosexuality would be the typical intimate, sexual relationship in the ideal society that was assimila-tionist in respect to sex."

Wasserstrom considers and rejects a number of popular arguments against assimilationism. To the objection that gender role differences are to some extent determined by biological differences, Wasserstrom replies that apart from childbearing, all major roles and functions are de-termined socially; for example, child rearing could be assigned without regard for sex. To the argument that this would be "unnatural," Wasserstrom replies that all social arrangements are in one sense unnatural, and that we are morally bound to institute arrangements that will give everyone, male or female, equality of opportunity and personal autonomy. The attempt to keep the status quo is conservative and illiberal. To the argument that the universality of gender roles suggests that they serve vital human purposes, Wasserstrom replies that no such pur-poses have ever been demonstrated and that the univer-sality of sexual differentiation in respect to social roles is, anyway, morally irrelevant since such differentiation usu-ally keeps women in subordinate positions; morally we should rectify this state of affairs by instituting the appro-priate assimilationist reforms.

Wasserstrom considers the argument that children are better raised by women. Even if this is so, Wasserstrom argues that it is objectionable to assign to women an oner-ous burden that involves a disproportionate share of what is unpleasant, unsatisfying, unrewarding work.

Wasserstrom points out that many of the objections to assimilationism overlook the fact that one's sex is not a matter of choice, while the choice of social arrangements and reforms that we can institute is ours to make as moral and socially responsible beings. A nonassimilationist so-ciety cannot be viewed plausibly as a good or just society. So we must work for the assimilationist ideal.

. . . [O]ne conception of a nonracist society is that which is captured by what I shall call the assimilationist ideal: a nonracist society would be one in which the race of an individual would be the functional equivalent of the eye color of individuals in our society today. In our society no basic political rights and obligations are determined on the basis of eye color. No important institutional benefits and burdens are connected with eye color. Indeed, except for the mildest sort of aesthetic preferences, a person would be thought odd who even made private, social decisions by taking eye color into account. It would, of course, be unintelligible, and not just odd, were a person to say today that while he or she looked blue-eyed, he or she regarded himself or herself as really a brown-eyed person. Because eye color functions differently in our culture than does race, there is no analogue to passing for eye color. Were the assimilationist ideal to become a reality, the same would be true of one's race. In short, according to the assimilationist ideal, a nonracist society would be one in which an individual's race was of no more significance in any of these three areas than is eye color today.

What is a good deal less familiar is an analogous conception of the good society in respect to sexual differentiation—one in which an individual's sex were to become a comparably unimportant characteristic. An assimilationist society in respect to sex would be one in which an individual's sex was of no more significance in any of the three areas than is eye color today. There would be no analogue to transsexuality, and, while physiological or anatomical sex differences would remain, they would possess only the kind and degree of significance that today attaches to the physiologically distinct eye colors persons possess.

It is apparent that the assimilationist ideal in respect to sex does not seem to be as readily plausible and obviously attractive here as it is in the case of race. In fact, many persons invoke the possible realization of the assimilationist ideal as a reason for rejecting the Equal Rights Amendment and indeed the idea of women's liberation itself. The assimilationist ideal may be just as good and just as important an ideal in respect to sex as it is in respect to race, but it is important to realize at the outset that this appears to be a more far-reaching proposal when applied to sex rather than race and that many more persons think there are good reasons why an assimilationist society in respect to sex would not be desirable than is true for the comparable racial ideal. Before such a conception is assessed, however, it will be useful to provide a somewhat fuller characterization of its features.

To begin with, it must be acknowledged that to make the assimilationist ideal a reality in respect to sex would involve more profound and fundamental revisions of our institutions and our attitudes than would be the case in respect to race. On the institutional level we would, for instance, have to alter significantly our practices concerning marriage. If a nonsexist society is a society in which one's sex is no more significant than eye color in our society today, then laws which require the persons who are getting married to be of different sexes would clearly be sexist laws.

More importantly, given the significance of role differentiation and ideas about the psychological differences in temperament that are tied to sexual identity, the assimilationist ideal would be incompatible with all psychological and sex-role differentiation. That is to say, in such a society the ideology of the society would contain no proposition asserting the inevitable or essential attributes of masculinity or feminity; it would never encourage or discourage the ideas of sisterhood or brotherhood; and it would be unintelligible to talk about the virtues or the disabilities of being a woman or a man. In addition, such a society would not have any norms concerning the appropriateness of different social behavior depending upon whether one were male or female. There would be no conception of the existence of a set of social tasks that were more appropriately undertaken or performed by males or by females. And there would be no expectation that the family was composed of one adult male and one adult female, rather than, say, just two adults—if two adults seemed the appropriate number. To put it simply, in the assimilationist society in respect to sex, persons would not be socialized so as to see or understand themselves or others as essentially or significantly who they were or what their lives would be like because they were either male or female. And no political rights or social institutions, practices, and norms would mark the physiological differences between males and females as important.

Were sex like eye color, these kinds of distinctions would make no sense. Just as the normal, typical adult is virtually oblivious to the eye color of other persons for all significant interpersonal relationships, so, too, the normal, typical adult in this kind of nonsexist society would be equally as indifferent to the sexual, physiological differences of other persons for all significant interpersonal relationships. Bisexuality, not heterosexuality or homosexuality, would be the typical intimate, sexual relationship in the ideal society that was assimilationist in respect to sex. . . .

. . . [T]here appear to be very few, if any, respects in which the ineradicable, naturally occurring differences between males and females *must* be taken into account. The industrial revolution has certainly made any of the general differences in strength between the sexes capable of being ignored by the good society for virtually all significant human activities. And even if it were true that women are naturally better suited than men to care for and nurture children, it is also surely the case that men can be taught to care for and nurture children well. Indeed, the one natural or biological fact that seems *required* to be taken into account is the fact that reproduction of the human species requires that the fetus develop *in utero* for a period of months. Sexual intercourse is not necessary, for artificial insemination is available. Neither marriage nor the nuclear family is necessary either for conception or child rearing. Given the present state of medical knowledge and what might be termed the natural realities of female pregnancy, it is difficult to see why any important institutional or interpersonal arrangements are constrained to take the existing biological differences as to the phenomenon of *in utero* pregnancy into account.

But to say all this is still to leave it a wholly open question to what degree the good society *ought* to build upon any ineradicable biological differences, or to create ones in order to construct institutions and sex roles which would thereby maintain a substantial degree of sexual differentiation. . . .

The point that is involved here is a very general one that has application in contexts having nothing to do with the desirability or undesirability of maintaining substantial sexual differentiation. It has to do with the fact that humans possess the ability to alter their natural and social environment in distinctive, dramatic, and unique ways. An example from the nonsexual area can help bring out this too seldom recognized central feature. It is a fact that some persons born in human society are born with congenital features such that they cannot walk or walk well on their legs. They are born naturally crippled or lame. However, humans in our society certainly possess the capability to devise and construct mechanical devices and institutional arrangements which render this natural fact about some persons relatively unimportant in respect to the way they and others will live together. We can bring it about, and in fact are in the process of bringing it about, that persons who are confined to wheelchairs can move down sidewalks and across streets because the curb stones at corners of intersections have been shaped so as to accommodate the passage of wheelchairs. And we can construct and arrange buildings and events so that persons in wheelchairs can ride elevators, park cars, and be seated at movies, lectures, meetings, and the like. Much of the environment in which humans live is the result of their intentional choices and actions concerning what that environment shall be like. They can elect to construct an environment in which the natural incapacity of some persons to walk or walk well is a major difference or a difference that will be effectively nullified vis-à-vis the lives that they, too, will live.

Nonhuman animals cannot do this in anything like the way humans can. A fox or an ape born lame is stuck with the fact of lameness and the degree to which that will affect the life it will lead. The other foxes or apes cannot change things. This capacity of humans to act intentionally and thereby continuously create and construct the world in which they and others will live is at the heart of what makes studies of nonhuman behavior essentially irrelevant to and for most if not all of the normative questions of social, political, and moral theory. Humans can become aware of the nature of their natural and social environment and then act intentionally to alter the environment so as to change its impact upon or consequences for the individuals living within it. Nonhuman animals cannot do so. This difference is, therefore, one of fundamental theoretical importance. At the risk of belaboring the obvious, what it is important to see is that the case against any picture of the good society of an assimilationist sort—if it is to be a defensible critique—ought to rest on arguments concerned to show why some other ideal would be preferable; it cannot plausibly rest in any significant respect upon the claim that the sorts of biological differences typically alluded to in contexts such as these require that the society not be assimilationist in character.

There are, though, several other arguments based upon nature, or the idea of the "natural" that also must be considered and assessed. First, it might be argued that if a way of doing something is natural, then it ought to be done that way. Here, what may be meant by "natural" is that this way of doing the thing is the way it would be done if culture did not direct or teach us to do it differently. It is not clear, however, that this sense of "natural" is wholly intelligible; it supposes that we can meaningfully talk about how humans would behave in the absence of culture. And few if any humans have ever lived in such a state. Moreover, even if this is an intelligible notion, the proposal that the natural way to behave is somehow the appropriate or desirable way to behave is strikingly implausible. It is, for example, almost surely natural, in this sense of "natural," that humans would eat their food with their hands, except for the fact that they are, almost always, socialized to eat food differently. Yet, the fact that humans would naturally eat this way, does not seem in any respect to be a reason for believing that that is thereby the desirable or appropriate way to eat food. And the same is equally true of any number of other distinctively human ways of behaving.

Second, someone might argue that substantial sexual differentiation is natural not in the sense that it is biologically determined nor in the sense that it would occur but for the effects of culture, but rather in the sense that substantial sexual differentiation is a virtually universal phenomenon in human culture. By itself, this claim of virtual universality, even if accurate, does not directly establish anything about the desirability or undesirability of any particular ideal. But it can be made into an argument by the addition of the proposition that where there is a widespread, virtually universal social practice or institution, there is probably some good or important purpose served by the practice or institution. Hence, given the fact of substantial sex-role differentiation in all, or almost all, cultures, there is on this view some reason to think that substantial sex-role differentiation serves some important purpose for and in human society.

This is an argument, but it is hard to see what is attractive about it. The premise which turns the fact of sex-role differentiation into any kind of a strong reason for sex-role differentiation is the premise of conservatism. And it is no more or less convincing here than elsewhere. There are any number of practices or institutions that are typical and yet upon reflection seem without significant social purpose. Slavery was once such an institution; war perhaps still is. . . .

To put it another way, the question that seems fundamentally to be at issue is whether it is desirable to have a society in which sex-role differences are to be retained in the way and to the degree they are today—or even at all. The straightforward way to think about the question is to ask what would be good and what would be bad about a society in which sex functioned like eye color does in our society;

or alternatively, what would be good and what would be bad about a society in which sex functioned in the way in which religious identity does today; or alternatively, what would be good and what would be bad about a society in which sex functioned in the way in which it does today. We can imagine what such societies would look like and how they might work. It is hard to see how thinking about answers to this question is substantially advanced by reference to what has typically or always been the case. If it is true, for instance, that the sex-role-differentiated societies that have existed have tended to concentrate power and authority in the hands of males, have developed institutions and ideologies that have perpetuated that concentration, and have restricted and prevented women from living the kinds of lives that persons ought to be able to live for themselves, then this, it seems to me, says far more about what may be wrong with any strongly nonassimilationist ideal than does the conservative premise say what may be right about any strongly nonassimilationist ideal. . . .

One strong, affirmative moral argument on behalf of the assimilationist ideal is that it does provide for a kind of individual autonomy that a substantially nonassimilationist society cannot provide. The reason is because any substantially nonassimilationist society will have sex roles, and sex roles interfere in basic ways with autonomy. The argument for these two propositions proceeds as follows.

Any nonassimilationist society must have some institutions and some ideology that distinguishes between individuals in virtue of their sexual physiology, and any such society will necessarily be committed to teaching the desirability of doing so. That is what is implied by saying it is nonassimilationist rather than assimilationist. And any substantially nonassimilationist society will make one's sexual identity an important characteristic so that there will be substantial psychological, role, and status differences between persons who are male and those who are female. That is what is implied by saying that it is substantially nonassimilationist. Any such society will necessarily have sex roles, a conception of the places, characteristics, behaviors, etc., that are appropriate to one sex or the other but not both. That is what makes it a *sex* role.

Now, sex roles are, I think, morally objectionable on two or three quite distinct grounds. One such ground is absolutely generic and applies to all sex roles. The other grounds are less generic and apply only to the kinds of sex roles with which we are familiar and which

714

are a feature of patriarchal societies, such as our own. I begin with the more contingent, less generic objections.

We can certainly imagine, if we are not already familiar with, societies in which the sex roles will be such that the general place of women in that society can be described as that of the servers of men. In such a society individuals will be socialized in such a way that women will learn how properly to minister to the needs, desires, and interests of men; women and men will both be taught that it is right and proper that the concerns and affairs of men are more important than and take precedence over those of women; and the norms and supporting set of beliefs and attitudes will be such that this role will be deemed the basic and appropriate role for women to play and men to expect. Here, I submit, what is objectionable about the connected set of institutions, practices, and ideology—the structure of the prevailing sex role—is the role itself. It is analogous to a kind of human slavery. The fundamental moral defect—just as is the case with slavery—is not that women are being arbitrarily or capriciously assigned to the social role of server, but that such a role itself has no legitimate place in the decent or just society. As a result, just as in the case with slavery, the assignment on *any* basis of individuals to such a role is morally objectionable. A society arranged so that such a role is a prominent part of the structure of the social institutions can be properly characterized as an *oppressive* one. It consigns some individuals to lives which have no place in the good society, which restrict unduly the opportunities of these individuals, and which do so in order improperly to enhance the lives and opportunities of others.

But it may be thought possible to have sex roles and all that goes with them without having persons of either sex placed within a position of general, systemic dominance or subordination. Here, it would be claimed, the society would not be an oppressive one in this sense. Consider, for example, the kinds of sex roles with which we are familiar and which assign to women the primary responsibilities for child rearing and household maintenance. It might be argued first that the roles of child rearer and household maintainer are not in themselves roles that could readily or satisfactorily be eliminated from human society without the society itself being deficient in serious, unacceptable ways. It might be asserted, that is, that these are roles or tasks that simply must be filled if children are to be raised in a satisfactory way. Suppose this is correct, suppose it is granted that society would necessarily have it that these tasks would have to be done. Still, if it is also correct that, relatively speaking, these are unsatisfying and unfulfilling ways for humans to concentrate the bulk of their energies and talents, then, to the degree to which this is so, what is morally objectionable is that if this is to be a *sex* role, then women are unduly and unfairly allocated a disproportionate share of what is unpleasant, unsatisfying, unrewarding work. Here the objection is the degree to which the burden women are required to assume is excessive and unjustified vis-à-vis the rest of society, i.e., the men. Unsatisfactory roles and tasks, when they are substantial and pervasive, should surely be allocated and filled in the good society in a way which seeks to distribute the burdens involved in a roughly equal fashion.

Suppose, though, that even this feature were eliminated from sex roles, so that, for instance, men and women shared more equally in the dreary, unrewarding aspects of housework and child care, and that a society which maintained sex roles did not in any way have as a feature of that society the systemic dominance or superiority of one sex over the other, there would still be a generic moral defect that would remain. The defect would be that any set of sex roles would necessarily impair and retard an individual's ability to develop his or her own characteristics, talents, capacities, and potential life-plans to the extent to which he or she might desire and from which he or she might derive genuine satisfaction. Sex roles, by definition, constitute empirical and normative limits of varying degrees of strength—restrictions on what it is that one can expect to do, be, or become. As such, they are, I think, at least prima facie objectionable.

To some degree, all role-differentiated living is restrictive in this sense. Perhaps, therefore, all role differentiation in society is to some degree troublesome, and perhaps all strongly role-differentiated societies are objectionable. But the case against sex roles and the concomitant sexual differentiation they create and require need not rest upon this more controversial point. For one thing that distinguishes sex roles from many other roles is that they are wholly involuntarily assumed. One has no choice about whether one shall be born a male or female. And if it is a consequence of one's being born a male or a female that one's subsequent emotional, intellectual, and material development will be substantially controlled by this fact, then it is necessarily the case that substantial, permanent, and involuntarily assumed restraints have been imposed on some of the most central factors concerning the way one will shape and live one's life. The point to be emphasized is that this would necessarily be the case, even in the unlikely event that substantial sexual differentiation could be maintained without one sex or the other becoming dominant and developing oppressive institutions and an ideology to support that dominance and oppression. Absent some far stronger showing than seems either reasonable or possible that potential talents, abilities, interests, and the like are inevitably and irretrievably distributed between the sexes in such a way that the sex roles of the society are genuinely congruent with and facilitative of the development of those talents, abilities, interests, and the like that individuals can and do possess, sex roles are to this degree incompatible with the kind of respect which the good or the just society would accord to each of the individual persons living within it. It seems to me, therefore, that there are persuasive reasons to believe that no society which maintained what I have been describing as *substantial* sexual differentiation could plausibly be viewed as a good or just society.

**STUDY QUESTIONS**

1.  What does Richard Wasserstrom mean by the "Assimilationist Ideal"? What reasons does he give for aspiring to it and for working to realize it?
2.  Wasserstrom says that "bisexuality, not heterosexuality or homosexuality, would be the typical intimate, sexual relationship in the ideal society that was assimilationist in respect to sex." Why does bisexuality become the ideal form of sexual intimacy for Wasserstrom? If you disagree with him, where do you think his argument goes wrong?
3.  How does Wasserstrom respond to the following arguments against assimilationism: (1) sexual differentiation is natural and (2) sexual differentiation is a universal phenomenon in human culture.
4.  Wasserstrom claims that sex roles are harmful because they interfere with individual freedom and autonomy. Could it be argued that the sexual differentiation between men and women enriches people's lives and that an "assimilated" (fully androgynous) society would be alienating and demoralizing for most people?

# Two Forms of Androgynism

## JOYCE TREBILCOT

Joyce Trebilcot (b. 1933) styles herself "a feminist lesbian philosopher." She is coordinator of Women's Studies
at Washington University and is the editor of *Mothering:
Essays in Feminist Theory* (1984). A collection of her work,
entitled *In Process: Radical Lesbian Essays*, is to be published in 1989.

Androgyny, the sharing of male and female characteristics, is a biological term that has been redefined by many
feminist thinkers to apply to men and women who reject
the assignment of masculine and feminine roles along
sexual lines. Joyce Trebilcot distinguishes between sex
("biological difference") and gender ("psychosocial difference"). The androgynous person rejects the idea that
gender roles should correspond to sexual difference.

Trebilcot distinguishes two kinds of androgyny and
discusses the virtues of each. The *monoandrogynist* holds
that males and females should cultivate the best characteristics of *both* sexes and that *both* sexes should perform
masculine and feminine roles. Thus everyone should
strive to be nurturant and assertive, and everyone should
perform tasks that usually are associated with a given sex.
If one is living with someone, then one will share the
responsibility for, say, housework, child care, car repairs,

TWO FORMS OF ANDROGYNISM By Joyce Trebilcot. Reprinted from the *Journal of Social Philosophy*,
January 1977. By permission of Villanova University and the author.

snow shoveling, and the like. By contrast, the *polyandrogynist* advocates a variety of options that would allow a man or a woman to adopt a purely feminine or masculine role. Both varieties of androgyny seek to break the connection between sex and gender as a social ideal, but the polyandrogynist argues that, as a matter of individual choice, one might still opt for a lifestyle that follows the conventional pattern. Trebilcot examines several arguments favoring monoandrogyny, but in the end concludes that polyandrogynism should be promoted as the ideal because it is freer and more flexible.

Traditional concepts of women and men, of what we are and should be as females and males, of the implications of sex for our relationships to one another and for our places in society, are not acceptable. But what models, if any, should we adopt to replace them? In this paper I consider just two of the alternatives discussed in recent literature—two versions of androgynism.

In discussing these two views I follow the convention of distinguishing between sex (female and male) and gender (feminine and masculine). Sex is biological, whereas gender is psychosocial. Thus, for example, a person who is biologically female may be—in terms of psychological characteristics or social roles—feminine or masculine, or both.

Although what counts as feminine and masculine varies among societies and over time, I use these terms here to refer to the gender concepts traditionally dominant in our own society. Femininity, on this traditional view, has nurturing as its core: it centers on the image of woman as mother, as provider of food, warmth, and emotional sustenance. Masculinity focuses on mastery: it comprises the notion of man struggling to overcome obstacles, to control nature, and also the notion of man as patriarch or leader in society and the family.

The first form of androgynism to be discussed here takes the word "androgyny" literally, so to speak. In this word the Greek roots for man (*andros*) and woman (*gynē*) exist side by side. According to the first form of androgynism, both feminine and masculine characteristics should exist "side by side" in every individual: each woman and man should develop personality traits and engage in activities traditionally assigned to only one sex. Because this view postulates a single ideal for everyone, I call it monoandrogynism, or, for brevity, *M*.

Monoandrogynism, insofar as it advocates shared roles, is now official policy in a number of countries. For example, the Swedish government presented a report to the United Nations in 1968 specifying that in Sweden, "every individual, regardless of sex, shall have the same practical opportunities not only for education and employment but also fundamentally the same responsibility for his or her own financial support as well as shared responsibility for child upbringing and housework."[1]

Closer to home, Jessie Bernard, in her discussion of women's roles, distinguishes the one-role view, according to which woman's place is in the home; the two-role pattern, which prescribes a combination of the traditional housewife-mother functions and work outside the home; and what she calls the "shared-role ideology" which holds "that children should have the care of both parents, that all who benefit from the services supplied in the household should contribute to them, and that both partners should share in supporting the household."[2]

Caroline Bird in her chapter "The Androgynous Life" writes with approval of role-sharing. She also suggests that the ideal person "combines characteristics usually attributed to men with characteristics usually attributed to women."[3] The psychological dimension of *M* is stressed by Judith M. Bardwick. In her essay "Androgyny and Humanistic Goals, or Goodbye, Cardboard People," she discusses a view according to which the ideal or "healthy" person would have traits of both genders. "We would then expect," she says, "both nurturance and competence, openness and objectivity, compassion and competitiveness from both women and men, as individuals, according to what they were doing."[4]

---

[1] Official Report to the United Nations on the Status of Women in Sweden, 1968. Quoted in Rita Liljeström, "The Swedish Model," in Georgene H. Seward and Robert C. Williamson, eds., *Sex Roles in Changing Society* (New York: Random House, 1970), p. 200.

[2] Jessie Bernard, *Women and the Public Interest* (Chicago: Aldine, 1971); and idem, *The Future of Marriage* (New York: Bantam Books, 1972). The quotation is from the latter book, p. 279.

[3] Caroline Bird, *Born Female* (New York: Pocket Books, 1968), p. xi.

The work of these and other writers provides the basis for a normative theory, *M*, which prescribes a single ideal for everyone: the person who is, in both psychological characteristics and social roles, both feminine and masculine.

The second form of androgynism shares with the first the principle that biological sex should not be a basis for judgments about the appropriateness of gender characteristics. It differs from the first, however, in that it advocates not a single ideal but rather a variety of options including "pure" femininity and masculinity as well as any combination of the two. According to this view, all alternatives with respect to gender should be equally available to and equally approved for everyone, regardless of sex. Thus, for example, a female might acceptably develop as a completely feminine sort of person, as both feminine and masculine in any proportion, or as wholly masculine. Because this view prescribes a variety of acceptable models, I call it polyandrogynism, or *P*.[5]

Constantina Safilios-Rothschild supports *P* in her recent book *Women and Social Policy*. In this work she makes a variety of policy recommendations aimed at bringing about the liberation of both sexes. Liberation requires, she says, that individuals live "according to their wishes, inclinations, potentials, abilities, and needs rather than according to the prevailing stereotypes about sex roles and sex-appropriate modes of thought and behavior." Some persons, she adds, "might *choose* to behave according to their sex's stereotypic . . . patterns. But some women and some men may *choose,* if they are so inclined, to take options in some or all of the life sectors now limited to the opposite sex."[6]

Carolyn Heilbrun's work also suggests *P*. In *Toward a Recognition of Androgyny* she writes, "The ideal toward which I believe we should

---

[4]Judith M. Bardwick, "Androgyny and Humanistic Goals, or Goodbye, Cardboard People," in Mary Louise McBee and Kathryn A. Blake, eds., *The American Woman: Who Will She Be?* (Beverly Hills, CA: Glencoe Press, 1974), p. 61.

[5]"Monoandrogynism" and "polyandrogynism" are perhaps not very happy terms, but I have been unable to find alternatives which are both descriptive and non-question-begging. In an earlier version of this paper I used "A₁" and "A₂" but these labels are not as perspicuous as "M" and "P." Mary Anne Warren in "The Ideal of Androgyny" (unpublished) refers to "the strong thesis" and "the weak thesis," but this terminology tends to prejudice judgment as to which view is preferable. Hence, I use "M" and "P."

[6]Constantina Safilios-Rothschild, *Women and Social Policy* (Englewood Cliffs, NJ: Prentice-Hall 1974), p. 7; emphasis hers.

move is best described by the term 'androgyny.' This ancient Greek word . . . defines a condition under which the characteristics of the sexes, and the human impulses expressed by men and women, are not rigidly assigned. Androgyny seeks to liberate the individual from the confines of the appropriate." Androgyny suggests, Heilbrun says, "a full range of experience open to individuals who may, as women, be aggressive, as men, tender; it suggests a spectrum upon which human beings choose their places without regard to propriety or custom."[7]

This second form of androgynism focuses on a variety of options rather than on the single model of the part-woman/part-man (that is, of the androgyne in the classic sense). It is appropriate, however, to extend the term "androgynism" to apply to it; for, like $M$, it seeks to break the connection between sex and gender.

For both forms of androgynism, the postulated ideals are best construed so as to exclude aspects of traditional gender concepts which are morally objectionable. Femininity should not be taken to include, for example, weakness, foolishness, or incompetence. Similarly, tendencies such as those to authoritarianism and violence should be eliminated from the concept of masculinity. Most importantly, aspects of the gender concepts which prescribe female submissiveness and male domination (over women and over other men) must, on moral grounds, be excluded from both the single ideal advocated by $M$ and the range of options recommended by $P$.

Either form of androgyny may, in the long run, lead to major changes in human attributes. It is often suggested that the androgyne is a person who is feminine part of the time and masculine part of the time. But such compartmentalization might be expected to break down, so that the feminine and masculine qualities would influence one another and be modified. Imagine a person who is at the same time and in the same respect both nurturant and mastery-oriented, emotional and rational, cooperative and competitive, and so on. I shall not undertake here to speculate on whether this is possible, or, if it is, on how such qualities might combine. The point is just that androgyny in the long run may lead to an integrating of femininity and masculinity that will yield new attributes, new kinds of

---

[7]Carolyn Heilbrun, *Toward a Recognition of Androgyny* (New York: Harper & Row, 1973), pp. 7–8.

personalities. The androgyne at this extreme would perhaps be not part feminine and part masculine, but neither feminine nor masculine, a person in whom the genders disappear.

I turn now to the question of which of these two forms of androgynism is more acceptable. I am not concerned here to evaluate these positions in relation to other alternatives (for example, to the traditional sexual constitution of society or to matriarchy).[8] For the sake of this discussion, I assume that either $M$ or $P$ is preferable to any alternative, and that the problem is only to decide between them. Let us first consider this problem not as abstract speculation, and not as a problem for some distant society, but rather as an immediate issue for our own society. The question is then: Which form of androgynism is preferable as a guide to action for us here and now?

Suppose we adopt $M$. Our task then is to provide opportunities, encouragement, and perhaps even incentives for those who are now feminine to be also masculine, and conversely. Suppose, on the other hand, that we adopt $P$. Our task is to create an environment in which, without reference to sex, people choose among all (moral) gender alternatives. How can this best be accomplished? What is required, clearly, is that the deeply-entrenched normative connection between sex and gender be severed. Virtually everyone now, in formulating preferences for the self and in judging the appropriateness of gender characteristics for others, at least on some occasions takes it, consciously or otherwise, that the sex of the individual in question is a relevant consideration: that one is female tends to count in favor of a feminine trait and against a masculine one, and conversely. In order to break this connection, it must be shown that masculinity is acceptable for females and femininity for males. There must, then, be opportunities, encouragement, and perhaps even incentives for gender-crossing. But this is what is required by $M$. Hence, under present conditions, the two forms of androgynism prescribe the same course of action—that is, the promotion of gender-crossing.

The question "Which form of androgynism is preferable here and

---

[8] My current view is that we should work for the universal realization of women's values; but that is another paper. (For some arguments against the use of the term "androgyny" in feminist theory, see, for example, Mary Daly, "The Qualitative Leap beyond Patriarchal Religion," *Quest: A Feminist Quarterly*, vol. 1, no. 4 [Spring 1975], pp. 29 *ff.*; and Janice Raymond, "The Illusion of Androgyny," *Quest*, vol. 2, no. 1 [Summer 1975].)

now?" then, is misconstrued. If one is an androgynist of either sort, what one must do now is seek to break the normative connection between sex and gender by bringing about gender-crossing. However, once the habit of taking sex as a reason for gender evaluation is overcome, or is at least much weaker and less widespread than it is today, then the two forms of androgynism do prescribe different courses of action. In particular, on $M$ "pure" gender is condemned, but on $P$ it is accepted. Let us consider, then, which version of androgynism is preferable for a hypothetical future society in which femininity and masculinity are no longer normatively associated with sex.

The major argument in favor of $P$ is, of course, that because it stipulates a variety of acceptable gender alternatives it provides greater gender freedom than $M$. Now, freedom is a very high priority value, so arguments for $M$ must be strong indeed. Let us consider, then, two arguments used to support $M$ over $P$—one psychological, one ethical.

The psychological argument holds that in a society which is open with respect to gender, many people are likely to experience anxiety when faced with the need, or opportunity, to choose among different but equally acceptable gender models. Consider the words of Judith M. Bardwick:

> People need guidelines, directions that are agreed upon because they help each individual to know where one ought to go, how one can get there, and how far one is from one's goal. It is easier to sustain frustration that comes from knowing how far you are from your objective or what barriers are in your way than it is to sustain the anxiety that comes from not being sure about what you want to do or what others want you to do. It will be necessary, then, to develop new formulations by which people will guide their lives.[9]

Bardwick says that anxiety "comes from not being sure about what you want to do or what others want you to do." But in a society of the sort proposed by $P$, the notion that one should seek to please others in deciding among gender models would be rejected; ideally "what others want you to do" in such a society is to make your own decisions. Of course there is still the problem of not being sure about what *you* want to do. Presumably, under $P$, people would provide

---

[9]Bardwick, *op. cit.*, p. 50.

one another with help and support in finding suitable life-styles. Nevertheless, it could be that for some, choosing among alternatives would be anxiety-producing. On the other hand, under $M$, the lack of approved alternatives could produce frustration. Hence, the argument from anxiety should be paired with an argument from frustration. In $M$, socialization is designed to make everyone androgynous (in ways similar, perhaps, to those which have traditionally produced exclusive femininity and masculinity in our own society), and frustration is part of the cost. In $P$, socialization is directed toward enabling people to perceive, evaluate, and choose among alternatives, and there is a risk of anxiety. We are not now in a position to decide whether the frustration or the anxiety is worse, for there are no data on the numbers of people likely to suffer these emotions nor on the extent of the harm that they are likely to do. Hence, neither the argument from anxiety nor the argument from frustration is of any help in deciding between the two forms of androgynism.

I turn now to a more persuasive argument for $M$, one which claims that androgyny has universal value. This argument supports $M$ not, as the argument from anxiety does, because $M$ prescribes some norm or other, but rather because of the content of the norm. The argument holds that both traditional genders include qualities that have human value, qualities that it would be good for everyone to have. Among the elements of femininity, candidates for universal value are openness and responsiveness to needs and feelings, and being gentle, tender, intuitive, sensitive, expressive, considerate, cooperative, compassionate. Masculine qualities appealed to in this connection include being logical, rational, objective, efficient, responsible, independent, courageous. It is claimed, then, that there are some aspects of both genders (not necessarily all or only the ones I have mentioned) which are desirable for everyone, which we should value both in ourselves and in one another. But if there are aspects of femininity and masculinity which are valuable in this way—which are, as we might call them, virtues—they are *human* virtues, and are desirable for everyone. If Smith is a better person for being compassionate or courageous, then so is Jones, and never mind the sex of Smith or Jones. Hence, the argument concludes, the world envisioned by $M$, in which everyone or nearly everyone is both feminine and masculine, is one in which life for everyone is more rewarding than the world advocated by $P$, in which some people are of only one gender; therefore we should undertake to bring about $M$.

The argument claims, then, that both genders embody traits that it would be valuable for everyone to have. But how is this claim to be tested? Let us adopt the view that to say that something is valuable for everyone is, roughly, to say that if everyone were unbiased, well-informed, and thinking and feeling clearly, everyone would, in fact, value it. As things are now, it is difficult or impossible to predict what everyone would value under such conditions. But there is an alternative. We can seek to establish conditions in which people do make unbiased, informed, etc., choices, and see whether they then value both feminine and masculine traits.

But this reminds us, of course, of the program of $P$. $P$ does not guarantee clear thought and emotional sensitivity, but it does propose an environment in which people are informed about all gender options and are unbiased with respect to them. If, in this context, all or most people, when they are thinking clearly, etc., tend to prefer, for themselves and others, both feminine and masculine virtues, we will have evidence to support the claim that androgyny has universal value. (In this case, $P$ is likely to change into $M$.) On the other hand, if "pure" gender is preferred by many, we should be skeptical of the claim that androgyny has universal value. (In this case we should probably seek to preserve $P$.) It appears, then, that in order to discover whether $M$ is preferable to $P$, we should seek to bring about $P$.

In summary, we have noted the argument from freedom, which supports $P$; arguments from anxiety and frustration, which are indecisive; and the argument from universal value, whose analysis suggests the provisional adoption of $P$. As far as I know, there are no additional major arguments which can plausibly be presented now for either side of the issue. Given, then, the problem of deciding between $M$ and $P$ without reference to other alternatives, my tentative conclusion is that because of the great value of freedom, and because in an atmosphere of gender-freedom we will be in a good position to evaluate the major argument for $M$ (that is, the argument from the universal value of androgyny), $P$ is preferable to $M$.

Of course all we have assumed about the specific nature of the hypothetical society for which we are making this judgment is that the connection between sex and gender would be absent, as would be the unacceptable components of traditional gender concepts, particularly dominance and submission. It might be, then, that particular social conditions would constitute grounds for supporting *M* rather than *P*. For example, if the society in question were hierarchical with leadership roles tightly held by the predominantly masculine individuals, and if leaders with feminine characteristics were more likely to bring about changes of significant value (for example, eliminating war or oppression), it could reasonably be argued that *M*, in which everyone, including leaders, has both feminine and masculine characteristics, would be preferable to *P*. But such conditions are only speculative now.

**STUDY QUESTIONS**

1. What importance does the distinction between sexual difference and gender difference play in feminist thinking? To which difference is the recommendation for an androgynous lifestyle relevant?
2. Trebilcot believes that one should be free to choose one's gender "without regard to propriety or custom." Are there morally sound reasons that she may be overlooking for giving importance to propriety and custom in choosing a gender role? Is gender role really a matter of choice?
3. What moral arguments support the adoption of androgyny as a social ideal?
4. What is monoandrogyny? Polyandrogny? What are the arguments for adopting the former as an individual ideal?
5. Is the ideal of androgyny distasteful to you? If it is, can you defend your aversion to it from the arguments that seem to show it to be an ideal that would mitigate sexist injustice?

# Philosophers Against the Family*

## CHRISTINA SOMMERS

A biographical sketch of Christina Sommers is found on page 577.

Christina Sommers points out that recent moral philosophy neglects the family and tends even to be actively hostile to it. Hostility to such a basic institution as the family is part of a radical social philosophy that seeks the reform of social arrangements that are seen to be unjust or inimical to individual freedom. Sommers distinguishes between direct and indirect criticisms of the family by social philosophers.

The direct criticisms are exemplified by many feminist thinkers who view the family as the bastion of a "gender system" that oppresses women. The more radical feminists argue for an androgynous or assimilationist social system that would do away with all institutions in which sex difference plays a role. Sommers criticizes these radical feminists for being ideologically inflexible and for paying little attention to what women actually want. And she points out that the feminist attack on the family is

*This paper is part of a project funded by an NEH Fellowship for College Teachers. Earlier versions were read at a conference at the University of Minnesota, "Ethics: The Personal Turn," and at the Philosopher's Forum at Long Island University. I received helpful criticism on both occasions. For the unabridged version of this paper, see Hugh LaFollette and George Graham, eds., *Person to Person* (Philadelphia, PA: Temple University Press), forthcoming.

irresponsible in not attending to the human costs of instituting the proposed ideal. Sommers suggests that what we need is a liberal feminism more in tune with the grassroots aspirations of women.

The indirect criticisms undermine the family by holding to a "volunteerist theory" of obligation that excludes the "special duties." According to most contemporary moral philosophers, no obligation is binding that is not grounded in a voluntary commitment. Since we do not choose our parents, brothers, sisters, and the like, and since we only rarely assume special responsibilities with respect to them in a voluntary or explicit way, it would follow that we have no special moral obligations to any of our kin. Sommers argues that this theory of obligation undermines the network of mutual obligations that characterizes the family and its members. She points out that philosophers accept the volunteerist theory and use it to deny a moral basis for filial and other obligations that have not been voluntarily assumed. According to Sommers, the volunteerist theory is a popular dogma that is altogether inadequate as a way of understanding our obligations to those close to us.

Much of what commonly counts as personal morality is measured by how well we behave within family relationships. We live our moral lives as son or daughter to this mother and that father, as brother or sister to this sister or brother, as father or mother, grandfather, granddaughter to this boy or girl or that man or woman. These relationships and the moral duties defined by them were once popular topics of moral casuistry; but when we turn to the literature of recent moral philosophy, we find little discussion of what it means to be a good son or daughter, a good mother or father, a good husband or wife, a good brother or sister.

Modern ethical theory concentrates on more general topics. Perhaps the majority of us who involve ourselves with ethics accept some version of Kantianism or Utilitarianism, yet these mainstream doctrines are better designed for telling us about what we should do as persons in general than about our special duties as parents or children or siblings. We believe, perhaps, that such universal theories can account fully for the morality of special relations. In any case, modern ethics is singularly silent on the bread and butter issues of personal morality in everyday life. However, silence is only part of it. With the exception of marriage itself, family relationships are a biological given. The contemporary philosopher is, on the whole, actively unsympathetic to the idea that we have *any* duties defined by relationships into which we have not voluntarily entered. We do not, after all, choose our parents or siblings. And even if we do choose to have children, this is not the same as choosing, say, our friends. Because the special relationships that constitute the family as a social arrangement are, in this sense, not voluntarily assumed, many moralists feel bound in principle to dismiss them altogether. The practical result is that philosophers are to be found among those who are contributing to an ongoing disintegration of the traditional family. In what follows I shall expose some of the philosophical roots of the current hostility to family morality. My own view that the ethical theses underlying this hostility are bad philosophy will be made evident throughout the discussion.

## 1. The Moral Vantage

Social criticism is a heady pastime to which philosophers are professionally addicted. One approach, Aristotelian in method and temperament, is antiradical, though it may be liberal, and approaches the task of needed reform with a prima facie respect for the norms of established morality. It is conservationist and cautious in its recommendations for change. It is, therefore, not given to such proposals as abolishing the family or abolishing private property and, indeed, does not look kindly on such proposals from other philosophers. The antiradicals I am concerned about are not those who would be called Burkean. I shall call them liberal but this use of "liberal" is somewhat perverse since, in my stipulative use of the term, a liberal is a philosopher who advocates social reform but always in a conservative spirit. My liberals share with Aristotle the conviction that the traditional arrangements have great moral weight and that common opinion is a primary source of moral truth. A good modern example is Henry Sidgwick with his constant appeal to Common Sense. But philosophers like John Stuart Mill, William James, and Bertrand Russell also can be cited. On the other hand, because no radical can be called a liberal in my sense, many so-called liberals could be excluded perversely. Thus when John Rawls toys with the possibility of abolishing the family because kinship bias is a force inimical to equality of opportunity, he is no liberal.

The more exciting genre of social criticism is not liberal-Aristotelian but radical and Platonist in spirit. Its vantage is external or even supernal to the social institutions it has placed under moral scrutiny. Plato was as aware as anyone could be that what he called the cave was social reality. One reason for calling it a cave was to emphasize the need, as he saw it, for an external, objective perspective on established morality. Another consideration in calling it a cave was his conviction that common opinion was benighted, and that reform could not be accomplished except by substantial "consciousness raising" and enlightened social engineering. Plato's supernal vantage made it possible for him to look on social reality in somewhat the way the Army Corps of Engineers looks upon a river that must have its course changed and its waywardness tamed. In our own day much social criticism of a Marxist variety has taken this radical approach to social change. And, of course, much contemporary feminist philosophy is radical.

Some philosophers are easily classifiable as radical or liberal. John Locke is clearly a liberal, Leon Trotsky is clearly a radical. I remarked a moment ago that there is a radical strain in Rawls. But it is a strain only: Rawls' attitude to social reality is not, finally, condescending. On the other hand, much contemporary social criticism is radical in temper. In particular, I shall suggest that the prevailing attitude toward the family is radical and not liberal. And the inability of mainstream ethical theory to come to grips with the special obligations that family members bear to one another contributes to the current disregard of the commonsense morality of the family cave. We find, indeed, that family obligations are criticized and discounted precisely because they do not fit the standard theories of obligation. If I am right, contemporary ethics is at a loss when it comes to dealing with parochial morality; but few have acknowledged this as a defect to be repaired. Instead the common reaction has been: if the family does not fit my model of autonomy, rights, or obligations, then so much the worse for the family.

To illustrate this, I cite without comment recent views on some aspects of family morality.

1. Michael Slote[1] maintains that any child capable of supporting itself is "morally free to opt out of the family situation." To those who say that the child should be expected to help his needy parents for a year or two out of reciprocity or fair play, Slote responds:

   > The duty of fair play presumably exists only where past benefits are voluntarily accepted . . . and we can hardly suppose that a child has voluntarily accepted his role in family . . . life.[2]

2. Virgina Held[3] wants traditional family roles to be abolished and she recommends that husbands and wives think of themselves as roommates of the same sex in assigning household and parental tasks. (She calls this the "Roommate Test.") To the objection that such a restructuring might injure family life, she replies that similar objections were made when factory workers demanded overtime pay.

3. The late Jane English[4] defended the view that adult children owe their parents no more than they owe their good friends. "[A]fter friendship ends, the duties of friendship end." John Simmons[5] and Jeffrey Blustein[6] also look with suspicion upon the idea that there is a debt of gratitude to the parents for what, in any case, they were duty bound to do.

4. Where Slote argues for the older child's right to leave, Howard Cohen[7] argues for granting that right to young children who still need parental care. He proposes that

---

[1]Michael Slote, "Obedience and Illusions," in Onora O'Neill and William Ruddick, eds., *Having Children* (New York: Oxford, 1979), p. 320.

[2]Slote, p. 230.

[3]Virginia Held, "The Obligations of Mothers and Fathers," in Joyce Trebilcot, ed., *Mothering: Essays in Feminist Theory* (Totowa, NJ: Rowman and Allanheld, 1983), pp. 7–20.

[4]Jane English, "What Do Grown Children Owe Their Parents?" in O'Neill and Ruddick, *op. cit.*, pp. 351–56.

[5]John Simmons, *Moral Principles and Political Obligation* (Princeton, NJ: Princeton University Press, 1979), p. 162.

[6]Jeffrey Blustein, *Parents and Children: The Ethics of the Family* (New York: Oxford, 1982), p. 182.

[7]Howard Cohen, *Equal Rights for Children* (Totowa, NJ: Rowman and Littlefield, 1980), p. 66.

every child be assigned a "trusted advisor" or agent. If the child wants to leave his parents, his agent will be charged with finding alternative caretakers for him.

The philosophers I have cited are not atypical in their dismissive attitude to commonsense morality or in their readiness to replace the parochial norms of the family cave with practices that would better approximate the ideals of human rights and equality. A theory of rights and obligations that applies generally to moral agents is, in this way, applied to the family with the predictable results that the family system of special relations and non-contractual special obligations is judged to be grossly unfair to its members.

## 2. Feminism and the Family

I have said that the morality of the family has been relatively neglected. The glaring exception to this is, of course, the feminist movement. Although the movement is complex, I am confined primarily to its moral philosophers, of whom the most influential is Simone de Beauvoir. For de Beauvoir, a social arrangement that does not allow all its participants full autonomy is to be condemned. De Beauvoir criticizes the family as an unacceptable arrangement since, for women, marriage and childbearing are essentially incompatible with their subjectivity and freedom:

> The tragedy of marrige is not that it fails to assure woman the promised happiness . . . but that it mutilates her; it dooms her to repetition and routine . . . At twenty or thereabouts mistress of a home, bound permanently to a man, a child in her arms, she stands with her life virtually finished forever.[8]

For de Beauvoir the tragedy goes deeper than marriage. The loss of subjectivity is unavoidable as long as human reproduction requires the woman's womb. De Beauvoir starkly describes the pregnant woman who ought to be a "free individual" as a "stockpile of colloids, an incubator, an egg."[9] And as recently as 1977 she compared childbearing and nurturing to slavery.[10]

---

[8] Simone de Beauvoir, *The Second Sex*, tr. H. M. Parshley (New York: Random House 1952), p. 534.

[9] De Beauvoir, p. 553.

[10] De Beauvoir, "Talking to De Beauvoir," *Spare Rib* (March 1977), p. 2.

It would be a mistake to say that de Beauvoir's criticism of the family is outside the mainstream of Anglo-American philosophy. Her criterion of moral adequacy may be formulated in continental existentialist terms, but its central contention is generally accepted: who would deny that an arrangement that systematically thwarts the freedom and autonomy of the individual is *eo ipso* defective? What is perhaps a bit odd to Anglo-American ears is that de Beauvoir makes such scant appeal to ideals of fairness and equality. For her, it is the loss of autonomy that is decisive.

De Beauvoir is more pessimistic than most feminists she has influenced about the prospects for technological and social solutions. But implicit in her critique is the ideal of a society in which sexual differences are minimal or nonexistent. This ideal is shared by many contemporary feminist philosophers. The views of Richard Wasserstrom, Ann Ferguson, Carol Gould, and Alison Jaggar are representative.

Wasserstrom's approach to social criticism is Platonist in its hypothetical use of a good society. The ideal society is nonsexist and "assimilationist."[11] Social reality is scrutinized for its approximation to this ideal and criticism is directed against all existing norms. Take the custom of having sexually segregated bathrooms: whether this is right or wrong "depends on what the good society would look like in respect to sexual differentiation." The key question in evaluating any law or arrangement in which sex difference figures is: "What would the good or just society make of (it)?"[12]

Thus the supernal light shines on the cave, revealing its moral defects. *There*, in the ideal society, gender in the choice of lover or spouse would be of no more significance than eye color. *There* the family would consist of adults but not necessarily of different sexes and not necessarily in pairs. *There* we find equality ensured by a kind of affirmative action which compensates for disabilities. If women are somewhat weaker than men, or if they are subject to lunar disabilities, then this must be compensated for. (Wasserstrom compares women to persons with congenital defects for whom the good society makes special arrangements.) Such male-dominated sports as

---

[11]Richard Wasserstrom, *Philosophy and Social Issues* (Notre Dame, IN: University of Notre Dame Press, 1980), p. 26.

[12]Wasserstrom, p. 23.

wrestling and football will there be eliminated and marriage, as we know it, will not exist. "Bisexuality, not heterosexuality or homo-sexuality, would be the typical intimate, sexual relationship in the ideal society that was assimilationist in respect to sex."[13]

Other feminist philosophers are equally confident about the need for sweeping change. Ann Ferguson wants a "radical reorganization of child rearing." She recommends communal living and a de-emphasis on biological parenting. In the ideal society "[l]ove rela-tionships, and the sexual relationships developing out of them, would be based on the individual meshing-together of androgynous human beings."[14] Carol Gould argues for androgyny and for abolishing legal marriage. She favors single parenting, co-parenting and communal parenting. The only arrangement she opposes emphatically is the traditional one where the mother provides primary care for the chil-dren.[15] Alison Jaggar, arguing for a "socialist feminism," wants a society that is both classless and genderless. She looks to the day of a possible transformation of such biological functions as insemination, lactation, and gestation "so that one woman could inseminate an-other . . . and . . . fertilized ova could be transplanted into women's or even men's bodies." This idea is partly illustrated in a science fiction story that Jaggar praises in which "neither sex bears children, but both sexes, through hormone treatments, suckle them . . ."[16] To those of us who find this bizarre, Jaggar replies that this betrays the depth of our prejudice in favor of the "natural" family.

Though they differ in detail, the radical feminists hold to a com-mon social ideal that is broadly assimilationist in character and in-imical to the traditional family. Sometimes it seems as if the radical feminist simply takes the classical Marxist eschatology of the

---

[13]Wasserstrom, p. 26.

[14]Ann Ferguson, "Androgyny as an Ideal for Human Development," in *Feminism and Philosophy*, eds. M. Vetterling-Braggin, F. Elliston and J. English (Totowa, NJ: Row-man and Littlefield, 1977), pp. 45–69.

[15]Carol Gould, "Private Rights and Public Virtues: Woman, the Family and Democ-racy," in *Beyond Domination*, ed. Carol Gould (Totowa, NJ: Rowman and Allanheld, 1983), pp. 3–18.

[16]Alison Jaggar, "Human Biology in Feminist Theory: Sexual Equality Reconsi-dered," in Gould, *op. cit.*, p. 41. Jaggar is serious about the possibility and desirability of what she calls the "transformation of sexuality," which is elaborated in her book *Feminist Politics and Human Nature* (Totowa, NJ: Rowman and Allanheld, 1983), p. 132.

Communist Manifesto and substitutes "gender" for "class." Indeed, the feminist and the old-fashioned Marxist do have much in common. Both see their caves as politically divided into two warring factions: one oppressing, the other oppressed. Both see the need of raising the consciousness of the oppressed group to its predicament and to the possibility of removing its shackles. Both look forward to the day of a classless or genderless society. Both deny the value and naturalness of tradition. Both believe that people and the institutions they inhabit are as malleable as Silly Putty. And both groups are zealots, paying little attention to the tragic personal costs to be paid for the revolution they wish to bring about. The feminists tell us little about that side of things. To begin with, how will the benighted myriads in the cave who do not wish to "mesh together" with other androgynous beings be reeducated? And how are children to be brought up in the gender-less society? Plato took great pains to explain his methods: would the new methods be as thoroughgoing? Unless these questions can be given plausible answers, the supernal attack on the family must always be irresponsible. The appeal to the just society justifies nothing until it can be shown that the radical proposals do not have monstrous consequences. That has not been shown. Indeed, given the perenially dubious state of the social sciences, it is precisely what *cannot* be shown.

Any social arrangement that falls short of the assimilationist ideal is labeled "sexist." It should be noted that this characteristically feminist use of the term "sexist" differs significantly from its popular or literal sense. Literally, and popularly, "sexism" connotes unfair discrimination. But in its extended philosophical use it connotes discrimination, period. Wasserstrom and many feminists trade on the popular pejorative connotations of sexism when they invite us to be antisexist. Most liberals are antisexist in the popular sense. But to be antisexist in the technical, radical philosophical sense is not merely to be opposed to discrimination against women; it is to be *for* what Wasserstrom calls the assimilationist ideal. The antisexist philosopher opposes any social policy that is nonandrogynous, objecting, for example, to legislation that allows for maternity leave. As Alison Jaggar remarks: "We do not, after all, elevate 'prostate leave' into a special right of men."[17] From being liberally opposed to sexism, one

---

[17]Alison Jaggar, "On Sex Equality," in *Sex Equality*, ed. Jane English (Englewood Cliffs, NJ: Prentice-Hall, 1977), p. 102.

may in this way be led insensibly to a radical critique of the family whose ideal is assimilationist and androgynous. For it is very clear that the realization of the androgynous ideal is incompatible with the survival of the family as we know it.

The neological extension of such labels as "sexism," "slavery," and "prostitution" is a feature of radical discourse. The liberal too sometimes calls for radical solutions to social problems. Some institutions are essentially unjust. To "reform" slavery or a totalitarian system of government is to eliminate them. Radicals trade on these extreme practices in characterizing other practices. They may, for example, characterize low wages as "slave" wages and the workers who are paid them as "slave" laborers. Taking these descriptions seriously may start one on the way to treating a free-labor market system as a "slave system" that, in simple justice, must be overthrown and replaced by an alternative system of production. The radical feminist typically explains that, "existentially," women, being treated by men as sex objects, are especially prone to bad faith and false consciousness. Marxist feminists see them as part of an unawakened and oppressed economic class. Clearly we cannot call on a deluded woman to cast off her bonds before we have made her aware of her bondage. So the first task of freeing the slave woman is dispelling the thrall of a false and deceptive consciousness. One must "raise" her consciousness to the "reality" of her situation. (Some feminists acknowledge that it may in fact be too late for many of the women who have fallen too far into the delusions of marriage and motherhood. But the educative process can save many from falling into the marriage and baby trap.)

In this sort of rhetorical climate nothing is what it seems. Prostitution is another term that has been subjected to a radical enlargement. Alison Jaggar believes that a feminist interpretation of the term "prostitution" is badly needed and asks for a "philosophical theory of prostitution." Observing that the average woman dresses for men, marries a man for protection, and so forth, she says: "For contemporary radical feminists, prostitution is the archetypal relationship of women to men."[18]

Of course, the housewife Jaggar has in mind might be offended at the suggestion that she herself is a prostitute, albeit less well paid and

---

[18]Alison Jaggar, "Prostitution," in Marilyn Pearsell, ed., *Women and Values: Reading in Recent Feminist Philosophy* (Belmont, CA: Wadsworth, 1986), pp. 108–121.

less aware of it than the professional street prostitute. To this the radical feminist reply is (quoting Jaggar):

> [I]ndividuals' intentions do not necessarily indicate the true nature of what is going on. Both men and woman might be outraged at the description of their candlelit dinner as prostitution, but the radical feminist argues this outrage is due simply to the participants' failure or refusal to perceive the social context in which their dinner date occurs.[19]

Apparently, this failure or refusal to perceive affects most women. Thus we may even suppose that the majority of women who have been treated to a candlelit dinner by a man prefer it to other dining alternatives they have experienced. To say that these preferences are misguided is a hard and condescending doctrine. It would seem that most feminist philosophers are not overly impressed with Mill's principle that there can be no appeal from a majority verdict of those who have experienced two alternatives.

The dismissive feminist attitude to the widespread preferences of women takes its human toll. Most women, for example, prefer to have children and those who have them rarely regret having them. It is no more than sensible, from a utilitarian standpoint, to take note of such widespread preferences and to take it seriously in planning one's own life. But a significant number of women discount this general verdict as benighted, taking more seriously the idea that the reported joys of motherhood are exaggerated and fleeting, if not altogether illusory. These women tell themselves and others that having babies is a trap to be avoided. But for many women childlessness has become a trap of its own, somewhat lonelier than the more conventional traps of marriage and babies. Some come to find their childlessness regrettable; this sort of regret is common to those who flout Mill's reasonable maxim by putting the verdict of ideology over the verdict of human experience.

## 3. Feminists Against Femininity

It is a serious defect of American feminism that it concentrates its zeal on impugning femininity and feminine culture at the expense of the grass roots fight against economic and social injustices to which

---

[19]Jaggar, "Prostitution," p. 117.

women are subjected. As we have seen, the radical feminist attitude to the woman who enjoys her femininity is condescending or even contemptuous. Indeed, the contempt for femininity reminds one of misogynist biases in such philosophers as Kant, Rousseau, and Schopenhauer, who believed that femininity was charming but incompatible with full personhood and reasonableness. The feminists deny the charm, but they too accept the verdict that femininity is weakness. It goes without saying that an essential connection between femininity and powerlessness has not been established by *either* party.

By denigrating conventional feminine roles and holding to an assimilationist ideal in social policy, the feminist movement has lost its natural constituency. The actual concerns, beliefs, and aspirations of the majority of women are not taken seriously *except* as illustrations of bad faith, false consciousness, and successful brainwashing. What women actually want is discounted and reinterpreted as to what they (have been led to) *think* they want ("a man," "children"). What most women *enjoy* (male gallantry, candlelit dinners, sexy clothes, makeup) is treated as an obscenity (prostitution).

As the British feminist, Janet Radcliffe Richards, says:

> Most women still dream about beauty, dress, weddings, dashing lovers, domesticity and babies . . . but if feminists seem (as they do) to want to eliminate nearly all of these things—beauty, sex conventions, families and all—for most people that simply means the removal of everything in life which is worth living for.[20]

Radical feminism creates a false dichotomy between sexism and assimilation, as if there were nothing in between. This view ignores completely the middle ground in which a woman can be free of oppression and nevertheless feminine in the sense abhorred by many feminists. For women are simply not waiting to be freed from the particular chains the radical feminists are trying to sunder. The average woman enjoys her femininity. She wants a man, not a roommate. She wants children and the time to care for them. When she enters the work force, she wants fair opportunity and equal treatment. These are the goals that women actually have, and they are not easily attainable. But they will never be furthered by an elitist radical movement that views the actual aspirations of women as the product of a

---

[20]Janet Radcliffe Richards, *The Skeptical Feminist* (Middlesex, England: Penguin Books, 1980), pp. 341–42.

false consciousness. There is room for a liberal feminism that would work for reforms that would give women equal opportunity in the workplace and in politics, but would leave unimpugned the basic institutions that women want and support, i.e., marriage and motherhood. Such a feminism is already in operation in some European countries. But it has been obstructed here in the United States by the ideologues who now hold the seat of power in the feminist movement.[21]

In characterizing and criticizing American feminism, I have not taken into account the latest revisions and qualifications of a lively and variegated movement. There is a kind of "Feminism of the Week" that one cannot hope to keep abreast of short of divorcing all other concerns. The best one can do for present purposes is attend to central theses and arguments that bear on the feminist treatment of the family. Nevertheless, even for this limited purpose it would be wrong to omit discussion of an important turn taken by feminism in the past few years. I have in mind the recent literature on the theme that there is a specific female ethic that differs from the male ethic in being more "concrete," less rule oriented, more empathic and "caring," and more attentive to the demands of a particular context.[22] The kind of feminism that accepts the idea that women differ from men in approaching ethical dilemmas and social problems from a "care perspective" is not oriented to androgyny as a positive ideal. Rather it seeks to develop a special female ethic and to give it greater practical scope.

The stress on context might lead one to think that these feminists are more sympathetic to the family as the social arrangement that shapes the moral development of women since the family is the context for many of the moral dilemmas that women actually face. However, one sees as yet no attention being paid to the fact that feminism itself is a force working against the preservation of

---

[21]See Sylvia Ann Hewlett, *A Lesser Life: The Myth of Woman's Liberation in America* (New York: William Morrow, 1986).

[22]See, for example, Carol Gilligan, *In a Different Voice* (Cambridge, MA: Harvard University Press, 1982); Eva Kittay and Diana Meyers, eds., *Women and Moral Theory* (Totowa, NJ: Rowman and Littlefield, 1987); Lawrence Blum, *Friendship, Altruism and Morality* (London: Routledge & Kegan Paul, 1980); Jean Grimshaw, *Philosophy and Feminist Thinking* (Minneapolis, MN: University of Minnesota Press, 1986); Nel Noddings, *Caring: A Feminine Approach to Ethics and Moral Education* (Berkeley, CA: University of California Press, 1984).

the family. Psychologists like Carol Gilligan and philosophers like Lawrence Blum concentrate their attention on the moral quality of caring relationships, yet these relationships themselves are not viewed in their concrete embedment in any formal social or institutional arrangement.

It should also be said that some feminists are moving away from the earlier hostility to motherhood.[23] Here, too, one sees the weakening of the positive assimilationist ideal in the acknowledgment of a primary gender role. However, childrearing is not seen primarily within the context of the family but as a special relationship between mother and daughter or (more awkwardly) between mother and son, a relationship that effectively excludes the male parent. And the new celebration of motherhood remains largely hostile to traditional familial arrangements.

It is too early to say whether a new style of nonassimilationist feminism will lead to a mitigation of the feminist assault on the family or even on femininity. In any case, the recognition of a female ethic of care and responsibility is hardly inconsistent with a social ethic that values the family as a vital (perhaps indispensable) institution. And the recognition that women have their own moral style may well be followed by a more accepting attitude toward the kind of femininity that some feminists currently reject. One may even hope to see the "holier than thou" aspects of feminism fade into a relaxed recognition that both sexes have their distinctive graces and virtues. Such a feminism would not be radical but liberal.

## 4. The Indirect Attack

The philosophers I shall now discuss do not criticize the family directly; in some cases they do not even mention the family. However, each one holds a view that subverts, ignores, or denies the special moral relations that characterize the family and are responsible for its functioning. And if they are right, family morality is a vacuous subject.

Judith Thomson maintains that an abortion may be permissible even if the fetus is deemed a person from the moment of conception,[24]

---

[23]See, for example, Joyce Trebilcot, ed., *Mothering: Essays in Feminist Theory* (Totowa, NJ: Rowman and Allanheld, 1984).

[24]Judith Thomson, "A Defense of Abortion," in *Philosophy and Public Affairs*, vol. 1, no. 1, 1972.

for in that case being pregnant would be like having an adult surgically attached to one's body. And it is arguable that if one finds oneself attached to another person, one has the right to free oneself even if such freedom is obtained at the price of the other person's death by, say, kidney failure. I shall, for purposes of this discussion, refer to the fetus as a prenatal child. I myself do not think the fetus is a person from the moment of conception. Nor does Thomson. But here we are interested in her argument for the proposition that abortion of a prenatal child/person should be permissible.

Many have been repelled by Thomson's comparison of pregnancy to arbitrary attachment. Thomson herself is well aware that the comparison may be bizarre. She says:

> It may be said that what is important is not merely the fact that the fetus is a person, but that it is a person for whom the woman has a special kind of responsibility issuing from the fact that she is its mother.[25]

To this Thomson replies: "Surely we do not have any such 'special responsibility' for a person unless we have assumed it, explicitly or implicitly." If the mother does not try to prevent pregnancy, does not obtain an abortion, but instead gives birth to it and takes it home with her, then, at least implicitly, she has assumed responsibility for it.

One might object that although pregnancy is a state into which many women do not enter voluntarily, it is nevertheless a state in which one has some responsibility to care for the prenatal child. Many pregnant women do feel such a prenatal responsibility, and take measures to assure the prenatal child's survival and future health. But here one must be grateful to Professor Thomson for her clarity. A mother who has not sought pregnancy deliberately bears *no* special responsibility to her prenatal child. For she has neither implicitly nor explicitly taken on the responsibility of caring for it. For example, the act of taking the infant home from the hospital implies voluntary acceptance of such responsibility. By choosing to take it with her, the mother undertakes to care for the infant and no longer has the right to free herself of the burden of motherhood at the cost of the child's life.

---

[25]Thomson, p. 64.

The assumption, then, is that there are no noncontractual obligations or special duties defined by the kinship of mother to child. As for social expectations, none are legitimate in the morally binding sense unless they are underpinned by an implicit or explicit contract freely entered into. If this assumption is correct, sociological arrangements and norms have no moral force unless they are voluntarily accepted by the moral agent who is bound by them. I shall call this the "volunteer theory of moral obligation." It is a thesis that is so widely accepted today that Thomson saw no need to argue for it.

Michael Tooley's arguments in defense of infanticide provide another solid example of how a contemporary philosopher sidetracks and ultimately subverts the special relations that bind the family.[26] Tooley holds that being sentient confers the prima facie right not to be treated cruelly, and that possession of those characteristics that make one a person confers the *additional* right to life. Tooley then argues that infants lack these characteristics and so may be painlessly killed. In reaching this conclusion, Tooley's sole consideration is whether the infant intrinsically possesses the relevant "right-to-life-making characteristic" of personality—a consideration that abstracts from any right to care and protection that the infant's relation to its parents confers on it causally and institutionally. For Tooley, as for Thomson, the relations of family or motherhood are morally irrelevant. So it is perhaps not surprising that one finds nothing in the index under "family," "mother," or "father" in Tooley's book on abortion and infanticide.

Howard Cohen is concerned strictly with the rights of persons irrespective of the special relations they may bear to others.[27] Just as Thomson holds that the mother's right to the free unencumbered use of her body is not qualified by any special obligations to her child, so Cohen holds that the child's right to a no-fault divorce from its parents cannot be diminished because of the special relation it bears to them. Where Thomson is concerned with the overriding right of the mother, Cohen is concerned with the right of the child. Yet all three philosophers agree that the right of a child is not less strong than the right of any adult. Indeed, Thomson compares the unborn

---

[26]Michael Tooley, "Abortion and Infanticide," in *Philosophy and Public Affairs*, vol. 2, no. 1, 1972.

[27]Howard Cohen, *Equal Rights for Children*, chs. V and VI.

child to a fully grown adult and Tooley holds that any person—be it child, adult, or sapient nonhuman—is equal in rights.

Our three philosophers are typical in holding that any moral requirement is either a general duty incumbent on everyone or else a specific obligation voluntarily assumed. Let us call a requirement a *duty* if it devolves on the moral agents whether or not they have voluntarily assumed it. (It is, for example, a duty to refrain from murder.) And let us call a requirement an *obligation* only if it devolves on certain moral agents but not necessarily on all moral agents. (One is, for example, morally obligated to keep a promise.) According to our three philosophers, all duties are general in the sense of being requirements on all moral agents. Any moral requirement that is *specific* to a given moral agent must be grounded in his or her voluntary commitment. Thus, there is no room for any special requirement on a moral agent that has not been assumed voluntarily by that agent. In other words, *there are no special duties*. This is what I am calling the volunteer theory of obligation. According to the voluntaristic thesis, all duties are general and only those who volunteer for them have any obligations toward them.

This thesis underlies Cohen's view that the child can divorce its parents. For it is unnecessary to consider whether the child has any special duties to the parents that could conflict with the exercise of its right to leave them. It underlies Thomson's view that the woman who had not sought pregnancy has no special responsibility to her unborn child and that any such responsibility that she may later have is assumed implicitly by her voluntary act of taking it home with her. In underlies Tooley's psychobiological method for answering the moral question of infanticide by determining the right-making characteristics of personhood: all we need to know about the neonate is whether or not it possesses the psychological characteristics of personhood. If it does, then it has a right to life. If it does not, then it is not a person and thus may be killed painlessly. It is unnecessary to consider the question of whether the child has a special relation to anyone who may have a "special responsibility" to see to the child's survival.

What I am calling the volunteer thesis is a confidently held thesis of many contemporary Anglo-American philosophers. It is easy to see that the thesis is contrary to what Sidgwick called Common Sense. For it means that there is no such thing as filial duty per se, no such thing as the special duty of mother to child, and generally no such thing as a morality of special family or kinship relations. All of which is contrary to what people think. For most people think that we do owe special debts to our parents even though we have not voluntarily assumed our obligations to them. Most people think that what we owe to our own children does not have its origin in any voluntary undertaking, explicit or implicit, that we have made to them. And, "preanalytically," many people believe that we owe special consideration to our siblings even at times when we may not *feel* very friendly to them. But if there are no special duties, then most of these prima facie requirements are misplaced and without moral force, and should be looked upon as archaic survivals to be ignored in assessing our moral obligations.

The idea that to be committed to an individual is to have made a voluntarily implicit or explicit commitment to that individual is generally fatal to family morality. For it looks upon the network of felt obligation and expectation that binds family members as a sociological phenomenon that is without presumptive moral force. The social critics who hold this view of family obligation usually are aware that promoting it in public policy must further the disintegration of the traditional family as an institution. But whether they deplore the disintegration or welcome it, they are bound in principle to abet it.

It may be that so many philosophers have accepted the voluntaristic dogma because of an uncritical use of the model of promises as the paradigm for obligations. If all obligations are like the obligation to keep a promise, then indeed they could not be incumbent on anyone who did not undertake to perform in a specified way. But there is no reason to take promises as paradigmatic of obligation. Indeed, the moral force of the norm of promise-keeping must itself be grounded in a theory of obligations that moral philosophers have yet to work out.

A better defense of the special duties would require considerably more space than I can give it here.[28] However, I believe the defense of special duties is far more plausible than rival theories that reject special duties. My primary objective has been to raise the strong suspicion that the volunteer theory of obligation is a dogma that is

---

[28]For a defense of the special duties not assumed voluntarily, see Christina Sommers, "Filial Morality," *The Journal of Philosophy*, no. 8, August 1986.

very probably wrong and misconceived, a view that is certainly at odds with common opinion.

Once we reject the doctrine that a voluntary act by the person concerned is a necessary condition of special obligation, we are free to respect the commonsense views that attribute moral force to many obligations associated with kinship and other family relationships. We may then accept the family as an institution that defines many special duties but that is nevertheless imperfect in numerous respects. Nevertheless, we still face the choice of how, as social philosophers, we are to deal with these imperfections. That is, we have the choice of being liberal or conservative in our attitude toward reform.

Burkean conservatives would change little or nothing, believing that the historical development of an institution has its own wisdom. They oppose utopian social engineering, considering it altogether immoral in the profound sense of destroying the very foundations of the special duties. But Burkeans also oppose what Karl Popper called "piecemeal social engineering," which seeks to remedy unjust practices without destroying the institution that harbors them. For Burkeans believe, on empirical grounds, that reform is always dangerous: that reform usually has unforseen consequences worse than the original injustices sought to be eliminated. Thus, conservatives are much like environmental conservationists in their attitude toward an ecological system: their general advice is extreme caution or hands off.

Liberals are more optimistic about the consequences of reform. Like conservatives, they believe that the norms of any tradition or institution not essentially unjust have prima facie moral force. All of which means we can rely on our common-sense beliefs that the system of expectations within the family is legitimate and should be respected. The liberal will acknowledge that a brother has the right to expect more help from a brother than from a stranger and not just because of what he has done for him lately. And the case is the same for all traditional expectations that characterize family members. On the other hand, there may be practices within the family that are systematically discriminatory and unfair to certain members. Unlike conservatives, liberals are prepared to do some piecemeal social engineering to eliminate injustice in the family.

It should be said that the appeal to common sense or common opinion is not final. For common sense often delivers conflicting verdicts on behavior. But a commonsense verdict is strongly presumptive. For example, there is the common belief that biological mothers have a special responsibility to care for their children, even their unwanted children. One *takes* this as presumptive evidence of an *objective* moral responsibility on the part of the mother. Note that the "verdict" of common sense is not really a verdict at all. Rather, it is evidence of a moral consideration that *must* enter into the final verdict on what to do and how to behave. Thomson ignores common sense when she asserts that the mother of a child, born or unborn, has no special responsibility to it unless she has in some way voluntarily assumed responsibility for it. Now, to say that a pregnant woman may have a moral responsibility to her unborn child does not entail that abortion is impermissible. For there are other common-sense considerations that enter here and other responsibilities that the mother may have (to her other children, to herself) that may conflict and override the responsibility to the fetus. So common sense is often not decisive. One may say that a commonsense opinion is symptomatic of a prima facie duty or liberty, as the case may be. Yet it still remains for the casuist to determine the *weight* of the duty in relation to other moral considerations that also may have the support of common sense. Politically and morally, lack of respect for common sense fosters illiberalism and elitism. Here we have the radical temper that often advocates actions and policies wildly at odds with common opinion—from infanticide to male lactation, from no-fault divorce on demand for children to the "roommate test" for marital relationships.

## 5. The Broken Family

In the final section we look at certain of the social consequences of applying radical theory to family obligation. I have suggested that, insofar as moral philosophers have any influence on the course of social history, their influence has recently been in aid of institutional disintegration. I shall now give some indication of how the principled philosophical disrespect for common sense in the area of family morality has weakened the family and how this affects the happiness of its members. Although much of what I say here is fairly well known, it is useful to say it in the context of an essay critical of the radical way of approaching moral philosophy. For there are periods in history when the radical way has great influence. And it is worth seeing what happens when Plato succeeds in Syracuse.

The most dramatic evidence of the progressive weakening of the family is found in the statistics on divorce. Almost all divorce is painful and most divorce affects children. Although divorce does not end but merely disrupts the life of a child, the life it disrupts is uncontroversially the life of a person who can be wronged directly by the actions of a moral agent. One might, therefore, expect that philosophers who carefully examine the morality of abortion also would carefully examine the moral ground for divorce. But here, too, the contemporary reluctance of philosophers to deal with the special casuistry of family relations is evidenced. For example, there are more articles on euthanasia or on recombinant DNA research than on divorce.

Each year there are another million and a quarter divorces in the United States affecting over one million children. The mother is granted custody in ninety percent of the cases, although legally it is no longer a matter of course. There is very persuasive evidence that children of divorced parents are affected seriously and adversely. Compared with children from intact families, they are referred more often to school psychologists, are more likely to have lower IQ and achievement test scores, are arrested more often, and need more remedial classes.[29] Moreover, these effects show little correlation to economic class. Children in the so-called latency period (between six and twelve) are the most seriously affected. In one study of children in this age group, one-half the subjects showed evidence of a "consolidation into troubled and conflicted depressive behavior patterns."[30] Their behavior patterns included "continuing depression and low self-esteem, combined with frequent school and peer difficulties."

One major cause for the difference between children from broken and intact families is the effective loss of the father. In the *majority* of cases the child has not seen the father within the past year. Only one child in six has seen his or her father in the past week; only 16 percent have seen their fathers in the past month; 15 percent see them once a year; the remaining 52 percent have had no contact at all for the past year. Although 57 percent of college educated fathers see their

---

[29]Lenore Weitzman, *The Divorce Revolution: The Unexpected Social and Economic Consequences for Women and Children in America* (New York: The Free Press, 1985).

[30]A. Skolnick and J. Skolnick, eds., *Family in Transition* (Boston: Little Brown, 1929), p. 452.

children at least once a month, their weekly contact is the same as for all other groups (one in six).[31]

It would be difficult to demonstrate that the dismissive attitude of most contemporary moral philosophers to the moral force of kinship ties and conventional family roles has been a serious factor in contributing to the growth in the divorce rate. But that is only because it is so difficult in general to demonstrate how much bread is baked by the dissemination of philosophical ideas. It is surely fair to say that the emphasis on autonomy and equality, when combined with the philosophical denigration of family ties, may have helped to make divorce both easy and respectable, thereby facilitating the rapid change from fault-based to no-fault divorce. If contemporary moralists have not caused the tide of family disintegration, they are avidly riding it. On the other side, it is not difficult to demonstrate that there is very little in recent moral philosophy that could be cited as possibly contributing to *stemming* the tide.

In the past two decades there has been a celebrated resurgence of interest in applied or practical ethics. It would appear, however, that the new enthusiasm for getting down to normative cases does not extend to topics of personal morality defined by family relationships. Accordingly, the children who are being victimized by the breakdown of the family have not benefited from this. Indeed, we find far more concern about the effect of divorce on children from philosophers a generation or two ago when divorce was relatively rare than we find today. Thus, Bertrand Russell writes:

> [H]usband and wife, if they have any love for their children, will so regulate their conduct as to give their children the best chance of a happy and healthy development. This may involve, at times, very considerable self-repression. And it certainly requires that both should realize the superiority of the claims of children to the claims of their own romantic emotions.[32]

And while Russell is not opposed to divorce, he believes that children place great contraints on it.

---

[31]Weitzman, p. 259.

[32]Bertrand Russell, *Marriage and Morals* (New York: Liveright, 1929), p. 236.

> . . . parents who divorce each other, except for grave cause, appear to
> me to be failing their parental duty.[33]

Discerning and sensitive observers of a generation ago did not need masses of statistics to alert them to the effects of divorce on children. Nor did it take a professional philosopher (citing statistics gathered by a professional sociologist) to see that acting to dissolve a family must be evaluated morally primarily in terms of what such action means for the children.

Writing in the *London Daily Express* in 1930, Rebecca West says:

> The divorce of married people with children is nearly always an un-
> speakable calamity. It is only just being understood . . . how much a
> child depends for its healthy growth on the presence in the home of
> both its parents. . . . The point is that if a child is deprived of either
> its father or its mother it feels that it has been cheated out of a right.[34]

West describes the harmful effects of divorce on children as effects of "a radiating kind, likely to travel down and down through the generations, such as few would care to have on their consciences."

I have quoted West in some fullness because her remarks contrast sharply with what one typically finds in contemporary college texts. In a book called *Living Issues in Ethics,* the authors discuss unhappy parents and the moral questions they face in contemplating divorce.

> We believe that staying together for the sake of the children is worse
> than the feelings and adjustment of separation and divorce.[35]

Further on the authors give what they feel to be a decisive reason for this policy:

> Remaining together in an irreconcilable relationship violates the norm
> of interpersonal love.

One of the very few philosophers to discuss the question of divorce and its consequences for children is Jeffrey Blustein in his book, *Parents and Children.* Blustein looks with equanimity on the priority of personal commitment to parental responsibility, pointing out that

---

[33]Russell, p. 238.

[34]Rebecca West, *London Daily Express*, 1930

[35]R. Nolan and F. Kirkpatrick, eds., *Living Issues in Ethics* (Belmont, CA: Wadsworth, 1983), p. 147.

750

The traditional view . . . that the central duties of husband and wife are the . . . duties of parenthood is giving way to a conception of marriage as essentially involving a serious commitment between two individuals as individuals.[36]

Blustein also tells us (without telling us how he knows it) that children whose parents are unhappily married are worse off than if their parents were divorced.

Indeed it could be argued that precisely on account of the childen the parents' unhappy marriage should be dissolved. . . .[37]

The suggestion that parents who are unhappy should get a divorce "for the sake of the children" is *very* contemporary.

To my knowledge, no reliable study has yet been made that compares children of divorced parents to children from intact families whose parents do not get on well together. So I have no way of knowing whether the claims of these authors are true or not. Moreover, because any such study would be compromised by certain arbitrary measures of parental incompatibility, one should probably place little reliance on them. It is, therefore, easy to see that contemporary philosophers are anxious to jump to conclusions that do not render implausible the interesting view that the overriding question in considering divorce is the compatibility of the parents, and that marital ties should be dissolved when they threaten or thwart the personal fulfillment of one or both the marital partners.

These philosophers set aside special duties and replace them with an emphasis on friendship, compatibility, and interpersonal love among family members. However, this has a disintegrative effect. That is to say, if what one owes to members of one's family is largely to be understood in terms of feelings of personal commitment, definite limits are placed on what one owes. For as feelings change, so may one's commitments. The result is a structure of responsibility within the family that is permanently unstable.

I have, in this final section, illustrated the indifference of contemporary philosophers to the family by dwelling on their indifference to the children affected by divorce. Nevertheless, I hope it is clear that nothing I have said is meant to convey that I oppose divorce. I

---

[36]Blustein, *Parents and Children*, p. 230.

[37]Blustein, p. 232.

do not. Neither Russell nor West nor any of the sane and compassionate liberal thinkers of the recent past opposed divorce. They simply did not play fast and loose with family mores, did not encourage divorce, and pointed out that moralists must insist that the system of family obligations is only partially severed by a divorce that cuts the marital tie. Morally, as well as legally, the obligations to the children remain as before. Legally, this is still recognized. But in a moral climate where the system of family obligation is given no more weight than can be justified in terms of popular theories of deontic volunteerism, the obligatory ties are too fragile to survive the personal estrangements that result from divorce. It is, therefore, to be expected that parents (especially fathers) will be off and away doing their own thing. And the law is largely helpless.

I have no special solutions to the tragedy of economic impoverishment and social deprivation that results from the weakening of family ties. I believe in the right of divorce and do not even oppose no-fault divorce. I do not know how to get back to the good old days when moral philosophers had the common sense to acknowledge the moral weight of special ties and the courage to condemn those who failed in them—the days when, in consequence, the *climate* of moral approval and disapproval was quite different from what it is today. I do not know how to make fathers ashamed of their neglect and inadvertent cruelty. What I do know is that moral philosophers should be paying far more attention to the social consequences of their views than they are. It is as concrete as taking care that what one says will not affect adversely the students whom one is addressing. If what students learn from us encourages social distintegration, then we are responsible for the effects this may have on their lives and on the lives of their children. This then is a grave responsibility, even graver than the responsibility we take in being for or against something as serious as euthanasia or capital punishment—since most of our students will never face these questions in a practical way.

I believe then that responsible moral philosophers are liberal or conservative but not radical. They respect human relationships and traditions and the social environment in which they live as much as they respect the natural environment and its ecology. They respect the family. William James saw the rejection of radicalism as central to the pragmatist way of confronting moral questions.

> [Experience] has proved that the laws and usages of the land are what yield the maximum of satisfaction. . . . The presumption in cases of

conflict must always be in favor of the conventionally recognized good. The philosopher must be a conservative, and in the construction of his casuistic scale must put things most in accordance with the customs of the community on top.[38]

A moral philosophy that does not give proper weight to the customs and opinions of the community is presumptuous in its attitude and pernicious in its consequences. In an important sense it is not a moral philosophy at all. For it is humanly irrelevant.

## STUDY QUESTIONS

1. Briefly explain Sommers' distinction between Aristotelian and Platonic social criticism. What bearing does the distinction have on the feminist debate?
2. Is Sommers' suggestion that radical feminists are unsympathetic to "femininity" fair? Can *any* effective feminist movement accept standards of femininity that seem to view women as the "weaker vessel?"
3. Critically discuss Sommers' criticism of "consciousness raising."
4. How does Sommers characterize the moral philosophers' indirect attack on the family? Give examples of how the integrity of the family is undermined by the indirect attack.
5. Give arguments for and against the doctrine that an obligation to a particular person must be one that is assumed voluntarily. Do you accept the "volunteerist" theory? If not, why not?

## SUGGESTED READINGS

Becker, Gary. *A Treatise on the Family*. Cambridge, MA: Harvard University Press, 1981.

Berger, Brigitte and Peter. *The War over the Family: Capturing the Middle Ground*. New York: Doubleday, 1983.

Bernard, Jessie. *The Future of Motherhood*. New York: Penguin, 1975.

---

[38]William James, "The Moral Philosopher and the Moral Life", in *Essays in Pragmatism* (New York: Hafner, 1948), p. 80.

Blustein, Jeffrey. *Parents and Children. The Ethics of the Family.* Oxford University Press, 1983.

Chodorow, Nancy. *The Reproduction of Mothering: Psychoanalysis and Sociology of Gender.* Los Angeles: University of California Press, 1978.

Daniels, Norman. *Am I My Parent's Keeper?: An Essay on Justice Between the Young and the Old.* Oxford University Press, 1987.

Lamm, Norman, ed. *The Good Society: Jewish Ethics in Action.* New York: Viking Press, 1974.

McKee, Patrick. *Philosophical Foundations of Gerontology.* New York: Human Sciences Press, 1982.

Nicholson, Linda. *Gender and History: The Limits of Social Theory in the Age of the Family.* New York: Columbia University Press, 1988.

O'Neil, Onora, and William Ruddick, eds. *Having Children: Philosophical and Legal Reflections on Parenthood.* New York: Oxford University Press, 1979.

Russell, Bertrand. *Marriage and Morals.* New York: Liveright Publishing Corp., 1929.

Scruton, Roger. *Sexual Desire: A Moral Philosophy of the Erotic.* New York: Macmillan, 1986.

Shils, Edward. *Tradition.* Chicago: University of Chicago Press, 1981.

Trebilcot, Joyce, ed. *Mothering: Essays in Feminist Theory.* Totowa, NJ: Rowman and Allanheld, 1984.

Vetterling-Braggin, Mary, ed. *"Femininity," "Masculinity," and "Androgyny": A Modern Philosophical Discussion.* Totowa, NJ: Rowman and Allanheld, 1982.

# Chapter Nine

# MORALITY AND SOCIETY

One striking development in contemporary moral philosophy is the increasing attention we pay to specific practical questions in social ethics. Is abortion right or wrong? Are physicians ever authorized to give lethal injections to dying, pain-ridden patients who request their own death? Do animals have moral rights? The practical ethics movement originated in the late sixties when philosophers began to participate in national debates on such issues as free speech, civil disobedience, capital punishment, euthanasia, and abortion. The recent interest in applying ethical theory to practical social problems is not a novel development, for philosophers since Plato and Aristotle continuously have concerned themselves with questions of everyday morality. The period between 1940 and 1970 is something of a historical exception. During those post-World War II decades, Western philosophy became increasingly analytical and methodologically rigorous. Clarification and theory were of primary concern; applied ethics was secondary. Although this interest in theory and method has not waned, in the past fifteen years philosophers have reentered

755

the arena of applied ethics with a vengeance. Consider what social philosopher Michael Walzer says about the new popularity of applied ethics:

> . . . [W]hen in our books and college courses we argue about distributive justice, killing in war, deception in politics, medical ethics . . . we are . . . engaged in a common human activity . . . temporarily discontinued at American universities at some cost. Now it is apparently about to be resumed. . . . It presses us back toward older moralities, or forward to newer ones, in which personal choice and utilitarian calculation are subjected to the discipline of public philosophy.

The essays in Chapter Nine deal primarily with broad social questions. Here morality is somewhat impersonal since, in the main, our actions are not directed to persons with whom we are acquainted. Nevertheless, as the debate on the question of whether and how much to sacrifice for famine relief shows, there is a clearly personal side to the ethical question of what to do about the multitudes whom we shall never know, but who need our help. Peter Singer maintains that readers themselves have a serious moral obligation to do all they can to fight world hunger. Garrett Hardin argues that international famine relief can be responsible for a cycle of increasing misery. In effect, Hardin argues, a well-meaning and good-hearted moralist like Singer may do far more harm than good.

John Arthur claims that even if Singer is right about the overall utility of famine relief, it still is not our duty to do without luxuries in order to help distant strangers. Common morality does not make such demands on ordinary human beings, and common morality is reasonable in this respect since "morality is not for angels." But Murdoch and Oaten do not agree that the demands are excessive. And they find serious fault with Hardin's empirical arguments that famine relief is counterproductive.

One broad area of social morality is political. In a democratic society, the views of the electorate often are decisive in the formation of policies regarding a host of questions of domestic and foreign policy. Policies on abortion, capital punishment, war, famine aid (by government action), human rights here and in foreign countries, all have their moral dimensions, and citizens are called upon to form morally responsible positions on them in order to support policies they deem worthy. Here the questions are not so much what one is personally to do but of civic responsibility in supporting the right causes politically, thereby influencing the government to do the right thing. And again, as with all important and concrete issues, one must contend with disagreements over facts and values. One of the vexing dilemmas concerns the question of moral constraints on democratic governments that, like all democratic governments, are committed to furthering the national interest. This question comes dramatically to the fore when, as often happens, our government gives aid to a friendly power whose domestic political system is undemocratic. Such autocratic governments are often under attack by forces seeking to overthrow them, but who are hostile to the United States. In some cases, the United States is accused of actively subverting progressive governments and of installing and supporting right-wing dictatorships to assure itself that the government in power will be amenable to furthering United States interests. Here there often are sharp disagreements about the facts as well as the policy. The articles by Douglas MacLean, Jeane Kirkpatrick, Jean-François Revel, and Michael Walzer all reflect an informed and concerned social conscience—but they also show how volatile is the issue of political morality when it bears on public policy pertaining to the national interest. Finally, anyone who reads the accounts of what many callous governments are inflicting on their own people cannot fail to gain the impression that even today, despite the formal acceptance of *The Universal Declaration of Human Rights*, an official respect of fundamental liberties may well be the historical exception rather than the rule.

# Famine, Affluence, and Morality

## PETER SINGER

A biographical sketch of Peter Singer is found on page 436.

Singer describes the mass starvation in many parts of the world and argues that affluent persons are morally obligated to contribute part of their time and income toward alleviating hunger. He assumes that passivity, when people are able to act to prevent evil, is morally wrong. Nowadays we can help people over great distances; instant communication and air travel have transformed the world into a "global village." If, says Singer, bystanders see a child drowning in a shallow pond, they ought to save that child even if it means muddying their clothes. Failure to do so is gross moral negligence. Singer compares the citizens of the affluent West to these bystanders.

As I write this, in November 1971, people are dying in East Bengal from lack of food, shelter, and medical care. The suffering and death that are occurring there now are not inevitable, not unavoidable in any fatalistic sense of the term. Constant poverty, a cyclone, and a civil war have turned at least nine million people into destitute refugees; nevertheless, it is not beyond the capacity of the richer nations

FAMINE, AFFLUENCE, AND MORALITY From *Philosophy and Public Affairs*, vol. 1, no. 3 (Spring 1972). Copyright © 1972 by Princeton University Press. Reprinted by permission of Princeton University Press.

to give enough assistance to reduce any further suffering to very small proportions. The decisions and actions of human beings can prevent this kind of suffering. Unfortunately, human beings have not made the necessary decisions. At the individual level, people have, with very few exceptions, not responded to the situation in any significant way. Generally speaking, people have not given large sums to relief funds; they have not written to their parliamentary representatives demanding increased government assistance; they have not demonstrated in the streets, held symbolic fasts, or done anything else directed toward providing the refugees with the means to satisfy their essential needs. At the government level, no government has given the sort of massive aid that would enable the refugees to survive for more than a few days. Britain, for instance, has given rather more than most countries. It has, to date, given £14,750,000. For comparative purposes, Britain's share of the nonrecoverable development costs of the Anglo-French Concorde project is already in excess of £275,000,000, and on present estimates will reach £400,000,000. The implication is that the British government values a supersonic transport more than thirty times as highly as it values the lives of the nine million refugees. Australia is another country which, on a per capita basis, is well up in the "aid to Bengal" table. Australia's aid, however, amounts to less than one-twelfth of the cost of Sydney's new opera house. The total amount given, from all sources, now stands at about £65,000,000. The estimated cost of keeping the refugees alive for one year is £464,000,000. Most of the refugees have now been in the camps for more than six months. The World Bank has said that India needs a minimum of £300,000,000 in assistance from other countries before the end of the year. It seems obvious that assistance on this scale will not be forthcoming. India will be forced to choose between letting the refugees starve or diverting funds from her own development program, which will mean that more of her own people will starve in the future.[1]

These are the essential facts about the present situation in Bengal. So far as it concerns us here, there is nothing unique about this situation except its magnitude. The Bengal emergency is just the

---

[1]There was also a third possibility: that India would go to war to enable the refugees to return to their lands. Since I wrote this paper, India has taken this way out. The situation is no longer that described above, but this does not affect my argument, as the next paragraph indicates.

latest and most acute of a series of major emergencies in various parts of the world, arising both from natural and from man-made causes. There are also many parts of the world in which people die from malnutrition and lack of food independent of any special emergency. I take Bengal as my example only because it is the present concern, and because the size of the problem has ensured that it has been given adequate publicity. Neither individuals nor governments can claim to be unaware of what is happening there.

What are the moral implications of a situation like this? In what follows, I shall argue that the way people in relatively affluent countries react to a situation like that in Bengal cannot be justified; indeed, the whole way we look at moral issues—our moral conceptual scheme—needs to be altered, and with it, the way of life that has come to be taken for granted in our society.

In arguing for this conclusion I will not, of course, claim to be morally neutral. I shall, however, try to argue for the moral position that I take, so that anyone who accepts certain assumptions, to be made explicit, will, I hope, accept my conclusion.

I begin with the assumption that suffering and death from lack of food, shelter, and medical care are bad. I think most people will agree about this, although one may reach the same view by different routes. I shall not argue for this view. People can hold all sorts of eccentric positions, and perhaps from some of them it would not follow that death by starvation is in itself bad. It is difficult, perhaps impossible, to refute such positions, and so for brevity I will henceforth take this assumption as accepted. Those who disagree need read no further.

My next point is this: if it is in our power to prevent something bad from happening, without thereby sacrificing anything of comparable moral importance, we ought, morally, to do it. By "without sacrificing anything of comparable moral importance" I mean without causing anything else comparably bad to happen, or doing something that is wrong in itself, or failing to promote some moral good, comparable in significance to the bad thing that we can prevent. This principle seems almost as uncontroversial as the last one. It requires us only to prevent what is bad, and not to promote what is good, and it requires this of us only when we can do it without sacrificing anything that is, from the moral point of view, comparably important. I could even, as far as the application of my argument to the Bengal emergency is concerned, qualify the point so as to make it: if it is in our power to prevent something very bad from happening, without thereby sacrificing anything morally significant, we ought, morally, to do it. An application of this principle would be as follows: if I am walking past a shallow pond and see a child drowning in it, I ought to wade in and pull the child out. This will mean getting my clothes muddy, but this is insignificant, while the death of the child would presumably be a very bad thing.

The uncontroversial appearance of the principle just stated is deceptive. If it were acted upon, even in its qualified form, our lives, our society, and our world would be fundamentally changed. For the principle takes, firstly, no account of proximity or distance. It makes no moral difference whether the person I can help is a neighbor's child ten yards from me or a Bengali whose name I shall never know, ten thousand miles away. Secondly, the principle makes no distinction between cases in which I am the only person who could possibly do anything and cases in which I am just one among millions in the same position.

I do not think I need to say much in defense of the refusal to take proximity and distance into account. The fact that a person is physically near to us, so that we have personal contact with him, may make it more likely that we *shall* assist him, but this does not show that we *ought* to help him rather than another who happens to be further away. If we accept any principle of impartiality, universalizability, equality, or whatever, we cannot discriminate against someone merely because he is far away from us (or we are far away from him). Admittedly, it is possible that we are in a better position to judge what needs to be done to help a person near to us than one far away, and perhaps also to provide the assistance we judge to be necessary. If this were the case, it would be a reason for helping those near to us first. This may once have been a justification for being more concerned with the poor in one's own town than with famine victims in India. Unfortunately for those who like to keep their moral responsibilities limited, instant communication and swift transportation have changed the situation. From the moral point of view, the development of the world into a "global village" has made an important, though still unrecognized, difference to our moral situation. Expert observers and supervisors, sent out by famine relief organizations or permanently stationed in the famine-prone areas, can direct our aid to a refugee in Bengal almost as effectively as we could get it to someone in our own block. There would seem, therefore, to be no possible justification for discriminating on geographical grounds.

There may be a greater need to defend the second implication of my principle—that the fact that there are millions of other people in the same position, in respect to the Bengali refugees, as I am, does not make the situation significantly different from a situation in which I am the only person who can prevent something very bad from occurring. Again, of course, I admit that there is a psychological difference between the cases; one feels less guilty about doing nothing if one can point to others, similarly placed, who have also done nothing. Yet this can make no real difference to our moral obligations. Should I consider that I am less obliged to pull the drowning child out of the pond if on looking around I see other people, no further away than I am, who have also noticed the child but are doing nothing? One has only to ask this question to see the absurdity of the view that numbers lessen obligation. It is a view that is an ideal excuse for inactivity; unfortunately most of the major evils—poverty, overpopulation, pollution—are problems in which everyone is almost equally involved.

The view that numbers do make a difference can be made plausible if stated in this way: if everyone in circumstances like mine gave £5 to the Bengal Relief Fund, there would be enough to provide food, shelter, and medical care for the refugees; there is no reason why I should give more than anyone else in the same circumstances as I am; therefore I have no obligation to give more than £5. Each premise in this argument is true, and the argument looks sound. It may convince us, unless we notice that it is based on a hypothetical premise, although the conclusion is not stated hypothetically. The argument would be sound if the conclusion were: if everyone in circumstances like mine were to give £5, I would have no obligation to give more than £5. If the conclusion were so stated, however, it would be obvious that the argument has no bearing on a situation in which it is not the case that everyone else gives £5. This, of course, is the actual situation. It is more or less certain that not everyone in circumstances like mine will give £5. So there will not be enough to provide the needed food, shelter, and medical care. Therefore by giving more than £5 I will prevent more suffering than I would if I gave just £5.

It might be thought that this argument has an absurd consequence. Since the situation appears to be that very few people are likely to give substantial amounts, it follows that I and everyone else in similar circumstances ought to give as much as possible, that is, at least up to the point at which by giving more one would begin to cause serious suffering for oneself and one's dependents—perhaps even beyond this point to the point of marginal utility, at which by giving more one would cause oneself and one's dependents as much suffering as one would prevent in Bengal. If everyone does this, however, there will be more than can be used for the benefit of the refugees, and some of the sacrifice will have been unnecessary. Thus, if everyone does what he ought to do, the result will not be as good as it would be if everyone did a little less than he ought to do, or if only some do all that they ought to do.

The paradox here arises only if we assume that the actions in question—sending money to the relief funds—are performed more or less simultaneously, and are also unexpected. For if it is to be expected that everyone is going to contribute something, then clearly each is not obliged to give as much as he would have been obliged to had others not been giving too. And if everyone is not acting more or less simultaneously, then those giving later will know how much more is needed, and will have no obligation to give more than is necessary to reach this amount. To say this is not to deny the principle that people in the same circumstances have the same obligations, but to point out that the fact that others have given, or may be expected to give, is a relevant circumstance: those giving after it has become known that many others are giving and those giving before are not in the same circumstances. So the seemingly absurd consequence of the principle I have put forward can occur only if people are in error about the actual circumstances—that is, if they think they are giving when others are not, but in fact they are giving when others are. The result of everyone doing what he really ought to do cannot be worse than the result of everyone doing less than he ought to do, although the result of everyone doing what he reasonably believes he ought to do could be.

If my argument so far has been sound, neither our distance from a preventable evil nor the number of other people who, in respect to that evil, are in the same situation as we are, lessens our obligation to mitigate or prevent that evil. I shall therefore take as established the principle I asserted earlier. As I have already said, I need to assert it only in its qualified form: if it is in our power to prevent something very bad from happening, without thereby sacrificing anything else morally significant, we ought, morally, to do it.

The outcome of this argument is that our traditional moral categories are upset. The traditional distinction between duty and charity cannot be drawn, or at least, not in the place we normally draw it. Giving money to the Bengal Relief Fund is regarded as an act of charity in our society. The bodies which collect money are known as "charities." These organizations see themselves in this way—if you send them a check, you will be thanked for your "generosity." Because giving money is regarded as an act of charity, it is not thought that there is anything wrong with not giving. The charitable man may be praised, but the man who is not charitable is not condemned. People do not feel in any way ashamed or guilty about spending money on new clothes or a new car instead of giving it to famine relief. (Indeed, the alternative does not occur to them.) This way of looking at the matter cannot be justified. When we buy new clothes not to keep ourselves warm but to look "well-dressed" we are not providing for any important need. We would not be sacrificing anything significant if we were to continue to wear our old clothes, and give the money to famine relief. By doing so, we would be preventing another person from starving. It follows from what I have said earlier that we ought to give money away, rather than spend it on clothes which we do not need to keep us warm. To do so is not charitable, or generous. Nor is it the kind of act which philosophers and theologians have called "supererogatory"—an act which it would be good to do, but not wrong not to do. On the contrary, we ought to give the money away, and it is wrong not to do so.

I am not maintaining that there are no acts which are charitable, or that there are no acts which it would be good to do but not wrong not to do. It may be possible to redraw the distinction between duty and charity in some other place. All I am arguing here is that the present way of drawing the distinction, which makes it an act of charity for a man living at the level of affluence which most people in the "developed nations" enjoy to give money to save someone else from starvation, cannot be supported. It is beyond the scope of my argument to consider whether the distinction should be redrawn or abolished altogether. There would be many other possible ways of drawing the distinction—for instance, one might decide that it is good to make other people as happy as possible, but not wrong not to do so.

Despite the limited nature of the revision in our moral conceptual scheme which I am proposing, the revision would, given the extent of both affluence and famine in the world today, have radical implications. These implications may lead to further objections, distinct from those I have already considered. I shall discuss two of these.

One objection to the position I have taken might be simply that it is too drastic a revision of our moral scheme. People do not ordinarily judge in the way I have suggested they should. Most people reserve their moral condemnation for those who violate some moral norm, such as the norm against taking another person's property. They do not condemn those who indulge in luxury instead of giving to famine relief. But given that I did not set out to present a morally neutral description of the way people make moral judgments, the way people do in fact judge has nothing to do with the validity of my conclusion. My conclusion follows from the principle which I advanced earlier, and unless that principle is rejected, or the arguments shown to be unsound, I think the conclusion must stand, however strange it appears. . . .

The second objection to my attack on the present distinction between duty and charity is one which has from time to time been made against utilitarianism. It follows from some forms of utilitarian theory that we all ought, morally, to be working full time to increase the balance of happiness over misery. The position I have taken here would not lead to this conclusion in all circumstances, for if there were no bad occurrences that we could prevent without sacrificing something of comparable moral importance, my argument would have no application. Given the present conditions in many parts of the world, however, it does follow from my argument that we ought, morally, to be working full time to relieve great suffering of the sort that occurs as a result of famine or other disasters. Of course, mitigating circumstances can be adduced—for instance, that if we wear ourselves out through overwork, we shall be less effective than we would otherwise have been. Nevertheless, when all considerations of this sort have been taken into account, the conclusion remains: we ought to be preventing as much suffering as we can without sacrificing something else of comparable moral importance. This conclusion is one which we may be reluctant to face. I cannot see, though, why it should be regarded as a criticism of the position for which I have argued, rather than a criticism of our ordinary standards of behavior. Since most people are self-interested to some degree, very few of us are likely to do everything that we ought to do. It would, however, hardly be honest to take this as evidence that it is not the case that we ought to do it. . . .

The conclusion reached earlier [raises] the question of just how much we all ought to be giving away. One possibility, which has already been mentioned, is that we ought to give until we reach the level of marginal utility—that is, the level at which, by giving more, I would cause as much suffering to myself or my dependents as I would relieve by my gift. This would mean, of course, that one would reduce oneself to very near the material circumstances of a Bengali refugee. It will be recalled that earlier I put forward both a strong and a moderate version of the principle of preventing bad occurrences. The strong version, which required us to prevent bad things from happening unless in doing so we would be sacrificing something of a comparable moral significance, does seem to require reducing ourselves to the level of marginal utility. I should also say that the strong version seems to me to be the correct one. I proposed the more moderate version—that we should prevent bad occurrences unless, to do so, we had to sacrifice something morally significant— only in order to show that even on this surely undeniable principle a great change in our way of life is required. On the more moderate principle, it may not follow that we ought to reduce ourselves to the level of marginal utility, for one might hold that to reduce oneself and one's family to this level is to cause something significantly bad to happen. Whether this is so I shall not discuss, since, as I have said, I can see no good reason for holding the moderate version of the principle rather than the strong version. Even if we accepted the principle only in is moderate form, however, it should be clear that we would have to give away enough to ensure that the consumer society, dependent as it is on people spending on trivia rather than giving to famine relief, would slow down and perhaps disappear entirely. There are several reasons why this would be desirable in itself. The value and necessity of economic growth are now being questioned not only by conservationists, but by economists as well.[2] There is no doubt, too, that the consumer society has had a distorting effect on the goals and purposes of its members. Yet looking at the

---

[2]See, for instance, John Kenneth Galbraith, *The New Industrial State* (Boston, 1967); and E. J. Mishan, *The Costs of Economic Growth* (London, 1967).

matter purely from the point of view of overseas aid, there must be a limit to the extent to which we should deliberately slow down our economy; for it might be the case that if we gave away, say, forty percent of our Gross National Product, we would slow down the economy so much that in absolute terms we would be giving less than if we gave twenty-five percent of the much larger GNP that we would have if we limited our contribution to this smaller percentage.

I mention this only as an indication of the sort of factor that one would have to take into account in working out an ideal. Since Western societies generally consider one percent of the GNP an acceptable level for overseas aid, the matter is entirely academic. Nor does it affect the question of how much an individual should give in a society in which very few are giving substantial amounts.

It is sometimes said, though less often now than it used to be, that philosophers have no special role to play in public affairs, since most public issues depend primarily on an assessment of facts. On questions of fact, it is said, philosophers as such have no special expertise, and so it has been possible to engage in philosophy without committing oneself to any position on major public issues. No doubt there are some issues of social policy and foreign policy about which it can truly be said that a really expert assessment of the facts is required before taking sides or acting, but the issue of famine is surely not one of these. The facts about the existence of suffering are beyond dispute. Nor, I think, is it disputed that we can do something about it, either through orthodox methods of famine relief or through population control or both. This is therefore an issue on which philosophers are competent to take a position. The issue is one which faces everyone who has more money than he needs to support himself and his dependents, or who is in a position to take some sort of political action. These categories must include practically every teacher and student of philosophy in the universities of the Western world. If philosophy is to deal with matters that are relevant to both teachers and students, this is an issue that philosophers should discuss.

Discussion, though, is not enough. What is the point of relating philosophy to public (and personal) affairs if we do not take our conclusions seriously? In this instance, taking our conclusion seriously means acting upon it. The philosopher will not find it any easier than anyone else to alter his attitudes and way of life to the extent that, if I am right, is involved in doing everying that we ought to be doing. At the very least, though, one can make a start. The philosopher who does so will have to sacrifice some of the benefits of the consumer society, but he can find compensation in the satisfaction of a way of life in which theory and practice, if not yet in harmony, are at least coming together.

**STUDY QUESTIONS**

1. Do you accept Singer's conclusion that you *personally* have a serious moral obligation to do something about world hunger? If not, where do you think his argument goes wrong?
2. Briefly outline Singer's argument. Name two of the strongest objections we can raise against his position. How do you think he would reply to them?
3. If Singer is right, then what we regard as charity is really moral duty. Does this set too high a standard for most people to follow?
4. For utilitarians like Singer the *consequences* of an action determine its moral character. The consequences of not sending food to starving people are the same as sending them poisoned food: In both cases the people die. Are you guilty of the moral equivalent of murder?

# World Hunger and Moral Obligation: The Case Against Singer

### JOHN ARTHUR

John Arthur is professor of philosophy at Tennessee State University. He has published numerous articles and anthologies in areas of ethics and social philosophy.

John Arthur criticizes what he calls "Singer's greater moral evil rule," according to which we ought to sacrifice our own interests if that will result in a greater net welfare to others. (For example, we should all do without luxuries to help those who are starving in Ethiopia.) Singer's premise is the equality of interests: Like amounts of suffering or happiness are of equal moral significance no matter who is experiencing them.

Arthur objects that Singer ignores the part of our common moral code that recognizes rights and deserts as determinants of duty. We have rights to our own lives, to our body parts, to the fruits of our labor—and these qualify our obligations to help others. Arthur denies that others have the *right* to our property whenever our property can reduce their misery without undue sacrifice on our part. "We are . . . entitled to invoke our own rights

WORLD HUNGER AND MORAL OBLIGATION: THE CASE AGAINST SINGER By John Arthur. Excerpted from "Equality, Entitlements and the Distribution of Income." © 1984 by John Arthur. Reprinted by permission.

as justification for our not giving to distant strangers." On the other hand, our moral code does recognize that our *own* children do have rights against us for food and protection.

Rights are one kind of entitlement that qualifies the duty of benevolence. Another is *desert*. We deserve the fruits of our labors. Our common morality does encourage benevolence "especially when it is a friend or someone we are close to geographically, and when the cost is not significant. But it also gives weight to rights and deserts, so we are not usually obligated to give to strangers . . ."

But perhaps Singer can be seen as advocating a reasonable *reform* of our present moral code. Perhaps we, who are in fortunate circumstances, should ignore our current entitlements and *change* our ways. Arthur argues that a call for reform is *un*reasonable and morally suspect. Moral codes are not made for angels, but for human beings with their subjective biases in favor of those close to them. Moreover, ignoring rights and deserts suggests a lack of respect for other persons. So Arthur concludes that our present moral code (that Singer judges to be overly selfish) *is* morally reasonable and in need of no reform in the direction suggested by Singer.

## Introduction

My guess is that everyone who reads these words is wealthy by comparison with the poorest millions of people on our planet. Not only do we have plenty of money for food, clothing, housing, and other necessities, but a fair amount is left over for far less important purchases like phonograph records, fancy clothes, trips, intoxicants, movies, and so on. And what's more we don't usually give a thought to whether or not we ought to spend our money on such luxuries rather than to give it to those who need it more; we just assume it's ours to do with as we please.

Peter Singer, "Famine, Affluence, and Morality" argues that our assumption is wrong, that we should not buy luxuries when others are in severe need. But [is he] correct? . . .

He first argues that two general moral principles are widely accepted, and then that those principles imply an obligation to eliminate starvation.

The first principle is simply that "suffering and death from lack of food, shelter and medical care are bad." Some may be inclined to think that the mere existence of such an evil in itself places an obligation on others, but that is, of course, the problem which Singer addresses. I take it that he is not begging the question in this obvious way and will argue from the existence of evil to the obligation of others to eliminate it. But how, exactly, does he establish this? The second principle, he thinks, shows the connection, but it is here that controversy arises.

This principle, which I will call the greater moral evil rule, is as follows:

> If it is in our power to prevent something bad from happening, without thereby sacrificing anything of comparable moral importance, we ought, morally, to do it.[1]

In other words, people are entitled to keep their earnings only if there is no way for them to prevent a greater evil by giving them away. Providing others with food, clothing, and housing would generally be of more importance than buying luxuries, so the greater moral evil rule now requires substantial redistribution of wealth.

Certainly there are few, if any, of us who live by that rule, although that hardly shows we are *justified* in our way of life; we often fail to live up to our own standards. Why does Singer think our shared morality requires that we follow the greater moral evil rule? What arguments does he give for it?

He begins with an analogy. Suppose you came across a child drowning in a shallow pond. Certainly we feel it would be wrong not to help. Even if saving the child meant we must dirty our clothes, we would emphasize that those clothes are not of comparable significance to the child's life. The greater moral evil rule thus seems a natural way of capturing why we think it would be wrong not to help.

---

[1] Singer also offers a "weak" version of this principle which, it seems to me, is *too* weak. It requires giving aid only if the gift is of *no* moral significance to the giver. But since even minor embarrassment or small amounts of happiness are not completely without moral importance, this weak principle implies little or no obligation to aid, even to the drowning child.

But the argument for the greater moral evil rule is not limited to Singer's claim that it explains our feelings about the drowning child or that it appears "uncontroversial." Moral equality also enters the picture. Besides the Jeffersonian idea that we share certain rights equally, most of us are also attracted to another type of equality, namely that like amounts of suffering (or happiness) are of equal significance, no matter who is experiencing them. I cannot reasonably say that, while my pain is no more severe than yours, I am somehow special and it's more important that mine be alleviated. Objectivity requires us to admit the opposite, that no one has a unique status which warrants such special pleading. So equality demands equal consideration of interests as well as respect for certain rights.

But if we fail to give to famine relief and instead purchase a new car when the old one will do, or buy fancy clothes for a friend when his or her old ones are perfectly good, are we not assuming that the relatively minor enjoyment we or our friends may get is as important as another person's life? And that a form of prejudice; we are acting as if people were not equal in the sense that their interests deserve equal consideration. We are giving special consideration to ourselves or to our group, rather like a racist does. Equal consideration of interests thus leads naturally to the greater moral evil rule.

## Rights and Desert

Equality, in the sense of giving equal consideration to equally serious needs, is part of our moral code. And so we are led, quite rightly I think, to the conclusion that we should prevent harm to others if in doing so we do not sacrifice anything of comparable moral importance. But there is also another side to the coin, one which Singer ignore[s]. . . . This can be expressed rather awkwardly by the notion of entitlements. These fall into two broad categories, rights and desert. A few examples will show what I mean.

All of us could help others by giving away or allowing others to use our bodies. While your life may be shortened by the loss of a kidney or less enjoyable if lived with only one eye, those costs are probably not comparable to the loss experienced by a person who will die without any kidney or who is totally blind. We can even imagine persons who will actually be harmed in some way by your not granting sexual favors to them. Perhaps the absence of a sexual partner would cause psychological harm or even rape. Now suppose that you can prevent this evil without sacrificing anything of comparable importance. Obviously such relations may not be pleasant, but according to the greater moral evil rule that is not enough; to be justified in refusing, you must show that the unpleasantness you would experience is of equal importance to the harm you are preventing. Otherwise, the rule says you must consent.

If anything is clear, however, it is that our code does not *require* such heroism; you are entitled to keep your second eye and kidney and not bestow sexual favors on anyone who may be harmed without them. The reason for this is often expressed in terms of rights; it's your body, you have a right to it, and that weighs against whatever duty you have to help. To sacrifice a kidney for a stranger is to do more than is required, it's heroic.

Moral rights are normally divided into two categories. Negative rights are rights of noninterference. The right to life, for example, is a right not to be killed. Property rights, the right to privacy, and the right to exercise religious freedom are also negative, requiring only that people leave others alone and not interfere.

Positive rights, however, are rights of recipience. By not putting their children up for adoption, parents give them various positive rights, including rights to be fed, clothed, and housed. If I agree to share in a business venture, my promise creates a right of recipience, so that when I back out of the deal, I've violated your right.

Negative rights also differ from positive in that the former are natural; the ones you have depend on what you are. If lower animals lack rights to life or liberty it is because there is a relevant difference between them and us. But the positive rights you may have are not natural; they arise because others have promised, agreed, or contracted to give you something.

Normally, then, a duty to help a stranger in need is not the result of a right he has. Such a right would be positive, and since no contract or promise was made, no such right exists. An exception to this would be a lifeguard who contracts to watch out for someone's children. The parent whose child drowns would in this case be doubly wronged. First, the lifeguard should not have cruelly or thoughtlessly ignored the child's interests, and second, he ought not to have violated the rights of the parents that he help. Here, unlike Singer's case, we can say there are rights at stake. Other bystanders also act wrongly by cruelly ignoring the child, but unlike the lifeguard they do not violate anybody's rights. Moral rights are one factor to be weighed, but we also have other obligations; I am not claiming that rights are all we need to consider. That view, like the greater moral evil rule, trades simplicity for accuracy. In fact, our code expects us to help people in need as well as to respect negative and positive rights. But we are also entitled to invoke our own rights as justification for not giving to distant strangers or when the cost to us is substantial, as when we give up an eye or kidney. . . .

Desert is a second form of entitlement. Suppose, for example, an industrious farmer manages through hard work to produce a surplus of food for the winter while a lazy neighbor spends his summer fishing. Must our industrious farmer ignore his hard work and give the surplus away because his neighbor or his family will suffer? What again seems clear is that we have more than one factor to weigh. Not only should we compare the consequences of his keeping it with his giving it away; we also should weigh the fact that one farmer deserves the food, he earned it through his hard work. Perhaps his deserving the product of his labor is outweighed by the greater need of his lazy neighbor, or perhaps it isn't, but being outweighed is in any case not the same as weighing nothing!

Desert can be negative, too. The fact that the Nazi war criminal did what he did means he deserves punishment, that we have a reason to send him to jail. Other considerations, for example the fact that nobody will be deterred by his suffering, or that he is old and harmless, may weigh against punishment and so we may let him go; but again that does not mean he doesn't still deserve to be punished.

Our moral code gives weight to both the greater moral evil principle and entitlements. The former emphasizes equality, claiming that from an objective point of view all comparable suffering, whoever its victim, is equally significant. It encourages us to take an impartial look at all the various effects of our actions; it is thus forward-looking. When we consider matters of entitlement, however, our attention is directed to the past. Whether we have rights to money, property, eyes, or whatever, depends on how we came to possess them. If they were acquired by theft rather than from birth or through gift exchange, then the right is suspect. Desert, like rights, is also backward-looking, emphasizing past effort or past transgressions which now warrant reward or punishment.

Our commonly shared morality thus requires that we ignore neither consequences nor entitlements, neither the future results of our action nor relevant events in the past. It encourages people to help others in need, especially when it's a friend or someone we are close to geographically, and when the cost is not significant. But it also gives weight to rights and desert, so that we are not usually obligated to give to strangers. . . .

But unless we are moral relativists, the mere fact that entitlements are an important part of our moral code does not in itself justify such a role. Singer . . . can perhaps best be seen as moral reformer advocating the rejection of rules which provide for distribution according to rights and desert. Certainly the fact that in the past our moral code condemned suicide and racial mixing while condoning slavery should not convince us that a more enlightened moral code, one which we would want to support, would take such positions. Rules which define acceptable behavior are continually changing, and we must allow for the replacement of inferior ones.

Why should we not view entitlements as examples of inferior rules we are better off without? What could justify our practice of evaluating actions by looking backward to rights and desert instead of just to their consequences? One answer is that more fundamental values than rights and desert are at stake, namely fairness, justice, and respect. Failure to reward those who earn good grades or promotions is wrong because it's *unfair;* ignoring past guilt shows a lack of regard for *justice;* and failure to respect rights to life, privacy, or religious choice suggests a lack of *respect for other persons.*

Some people may be persuaded by those remarks, feeling that entitlements are now on an acceptably firm foundation. But an advocate of equality may well want to question why fairness, justice, and respect for persons should matter. But since it is no more obvious that preventing suffering matters than that fairness, respect, and justice do, we again seem to have reached an impasse.

The lesson to be learned here is a general one: The moral code it is rational for us to support must be practical; it must actually work. This means, among other things, that it must be able to gain the support of almost everyone.

But the code must be practical in other respects as well. I have emphasized that it is wrong to ignore the possibilities of altruism, but it is also important that a code not assume people are more unselfish than they are. Rules that would work only for angels are not the ones it is rational to support for humans. Second, an ideal code cannot assume we are more objective than we are; we often tend to rationalize when our own interests are at stake, and a rational person will also keep that in mind when choosing a moral code. Finally, it is not rational to support a code which assumes we have perfect knowledge. We are often mistaken about the consequences of what we do, and a workable code must take that into account as well. . . .

It seems to me, then, that a reasonable code would require people to help when there is no substantial cost to themselves, that is, when what they are sacrificing would not mean *significant* reduction in their own or their families' level of happiness. Since most people's savings accounts and nearly everybody's second kidney are not insignificant, entitlements would in those cases outweigh another's need. But if what is at stake is trivial, as dirtying one's clothes would normally be, then an ideal moral code would not allow rights to override the greater evil that can be prevented. Despite our code's unclear and sometimes schizophrenic posture, it seems to me that these judgments are not that different from our current moral attitudes. We tend to blame people who waste money on trivia when they could help others in need, yet not to expect people to make large sacrifices to distant strangers. An ideal moral code thus might not be a great deal different from our own.

**STUDY QUESTIONS**

1. What is Singer's greater moral evil rule and why does Arthur object to it?
2. What is the status of the common moral code in Arthur's moral system? How does Arthur deploy the moral code to undermine Singer's general position that utilitarian considerations override parochial loyalties and interests?
3. How does Arthur classify rights? Why is the child's right to parental protection and food a "positive right"? How does Arthur's conception of rights preclude the view that needy but distant strangers have the right to our benevolence?
4. Arthur says "Our commonly shared morality requires that we ignore neither consequences nor entitlements." Is it fair to say that Singer ignores entitlements?

# Lifeboat Ethics: The Case Against Helping the Poor

## GARRETT HARDIN

Garrett Hardin (b. 1921) is a professor of biology at the University of California at Santa Barbara. He is the author of several books, including *The Limits of Altruism: An Ecologist's View of Survival* (1977) and *Naked Emperors: Essays of a Taboo-Stalker* (1982).

Activists concerned with world hunger claim that the earth is like a "spaceship" whose passengers each have an equal claim to its scarce resources. Hardin rejects the spaceship metaphor, pointing out that a spaceship operates under *one* captain; he prefers to think of the world as consisting of several different lifeboats. Some are quite well stocked and well maintained, and carry a safe number of passengers; others are ill equipped, chaotic, disease ridden, and so overcrowded that passengers constantly fall overboard. Hardin asks, What should the passengers on the wealthy boats do when they see refugees from the poor boats swimming their way? Let them all come aboard and allow the boat to sink? Take a few and eliminate the boat's safety margin? Or allow no one in and guard against boarding parties? Hardin recommends the latter. He not only argues that we should not let the

LIFEBOAT ETHICS: THE CASE AGAINST HELPING THE POOR From *Psychology Today*, September 1974. Reprinted by permission of the author.

world's poor into our own advantaged countries; he also recommends that we be very careful about sending massive aid to countries suffering from extreme poverty and famine. Well-intentioned food programs may lead to dangerous population increase and a corresponding escalation of misery.

Environmentalists use the metaphor of the earth as a "spaceship" in trying to persuade countries, industries, and people to stop wasting and polluting our natural resources. Since we all share life on this planet, they argue, no single person or institution has the right to destroy, waste, or use more than a fair share of its resources.

But does everyone on earth have an equal right to an equal share of its resources? The spaceship metaphor can be dangerous when used by misguided idealists to justify suicidal policies for sharing our resources through uncontrolled immigration and foreign aid. In their enthusiastic but unrealistic generosity, they confuse the ethics of a spaceship with those of a lifeboat.

A true spaceship would have to be under the control of a captain, since no ship could possibly survive if its course were determined by committee. Spaceship Earth certainly has no captain; the United Nations is merely a toothless tiger, with little power to enforce any policy upon its bickering members.

If we divide the world crudely into rich nations and poor nations, two thirds of them are desperately poor, and only one third comparatively rich, with the United States the wealthiest of all. Metaphorically each rich nation can be seen as a lifeboat full of comparatively rich people. In the ocean outside each lifeboat swim the poor of the world, who would like to get in, or at least to share some of the wealth. What should the lifeboat passengers do?

First, we must recognize the limited capacity of any lifeboat. For example, a nation's land has a limited capacity to support a population and as the current energy crisis has shown us, in some ways we have already exceeded the carrying capacity of our land.

## I. Adrift in a Moral Sea

So here we sit, say fifty people in our lifeboat. To be generous, let us assume it has room for ten more, making a total capacity of sixty. Suppose the fifty of us in the lifeboat see 100 others swimming in the water outside, begging for admission to our boat or for handouts. We have several options: We may be tempted to try to live by the Christian ideal of being "our brother's keeper," or by the Marxist ideal of "to each according to his needs." Since the needs of all in the water are the same, and since they can all be seen as "our brothers," we could take them all into our boat, making a total of 150 in a boat designed for sixty. The boat swamps, everyone drowns. Complete justice, complete catastrophe.

Since the boat has an unused excess capacity of ten or more passengers, we could admit just ten more to it. But which ten do we let in? How do we choose? Do we pick the best ten, the neediest ten, "first come, first served"? And what do we say to the ninety we exclude? If we do let an extra ten into our lifeboat, we will have lost our "safety factor," an engineering principle of critical importance. For example, if we don't leave room for excess capacity as a safety factor in our country's agriculture, a new plant disease or a bad change in the weather could have disastrous consequences.

Suppose we decide to preserve our small safety factor and admit no more to the lifeboat. Our survival is then possible, although we shall have to be constantly on guard against boarding parties.

While this last solution clearly offers the only means of our survival, it is morally abhorrent to many people. Some say they feel guilty about their good luck. My reply is simple: "Get out and yield your place to others." This may solve the problem of the guilt-ridden person's conscience, but it does not change the ethics of the lifeboat. The needy person to whom the guilt-ridden person yields his place will not himself feel guilty about his good luck. If he did, he would not climb aboard. The net result of conscience-stricken people giving up their unjustly held seats is the elimination of that sort of conscience from the lifeboat.

This is the basic metaphor within which we must work out our solutions. Let us now enrich the image, step by step, with substantive additions from the real world, a world that must solve real and pressing problems of overpopulation and hunger.

The harsh ethics of the lifeboat become even harsher when we consider the reproductive differences between the rich nations and the poor nations. The people inside the lifeboats are doubling in numbers every eighty-seven years; those swimming around outside are doubling, on the average, every thirty-five years, more than twice as fast as the rich. And since the world's resources are dwindling, the difference in prosperity between the rich and the poor can only increase.

As of 1973, the U.S. had a population of 210 million people, who were increasing by 0.8 percent per year. Outside our lifeboat, let us imagine another 210 million people (say the combined populations of Colombia, Ecuador, Venezuela, Morocco, Pakistan, Thailand, and the Philippines), who are increasing at a rate of 3.3 percent per year. Put differently, the doubling time for this aggregate population is twenty-one years, compared to eighty-seven years for the U.S.

## II. Multiplying the Rich and the Poor

Now suppose the U.S. agreed to pool its resources with those seven countries, with everyone receiving an equal share. Initially the ratio of Americans to non-Americans in this model would be one-to-one. But consider what the ratio would be after eighty-seven years, by which time the Americans would have doubled to a population of 420 million. By then, doubling every twenty-one years, the other group would have swollen to 354 billion. Each American would have to share the available resources with more than eight people.

But, one could argue, this discussion assumes that current population trends will continue and they may not. Quite so. Most likely the rate of population increase will decline much faster in the U.S. than it will in the other countries, and there does not seem to be much we can do about it. In sharing with "each according to his needs," we must recognize that needs are determined by population size, which is determined by the rate of re-production, which at present is regarded as a sovereign right of every nation, poor or not. This being so, the philanthropic load created by the sharing ethic of the spaceship can only increase.

## III. The Tragedy of the Commons

The fundamental error of spaceship ethics, and the sharing it requires, is that it leads to what I call "the tragedy of the commons." Under a system of private property, the men who own property recognize their responsibilities to care for it, for if they don't they will eventually suffer. A farmer, for instance, will allow no more cattle in a pasture than its carrying capacity justifies. If he overloads it, erosion sets in, weeds take over, and he loses the use of the pasture.

If a pasture becomes a commons open to all, the right of each to use it may not be matched by a corresponding responsibility to protect it. Asking everyone to use it with discretion will hardly do, for the considerate herdsman who refrains from overloading the commons suffers more than a selfish one who says his needs are greater. If everyone would remain himself, all would be well; but it takes only one less than everyone to ruin a system of voluntary restraint. In a crowded world of less than perfect human beings, mutual ruin is inevitable if there are no controls. This is the tragedy of the commons.

One of the major tasks of education today should be the creation of such an acute awareness of the dangers of the commons that people will recognize its many varieties. For example, the air and water have become polluted because they are treated as commons. Further growth in the population or per capita conversion of natural resources into pollutants will only make the problem worse. The same holds true for the fish of the oceans. Fishing fleets have nearly disappeared in many parts of the world, technological improvements in the art of fishing are hastening the day of complete ruin. Only the replacement of the system of the commons with a responsible system of control will save the land, air, water, and oceanic fisheries.

## IV. The World Food Bank

In recent years there has been a push to create a new commons called a world food bank, an international depository of food reserves to which nations would contribute according to their abilities and from which they would draw according to their needs. This humanitarian proposal has received support from many liberal international groups, and from such prominent citizens as Margaret Mead, U.N. Secretary General Kurt Waldheim, and Senators Edward Kennedy and George McGovern.

A world food bank appeals powerfully to our humanitarian impulses. But before we rush ahead with such a plan, let us recognize where the greatest political push comes from, lest we be disillusioned later. Our experience with the "Food for Peace program," or Public Law 480, gives us the answer. This program moved billions of dollars worth of U.S. surplus grain to food-short, population-long countries during the past two decades. But when P.L. 480 first became law, a headline in the business magazine *Forbes* revealed the real power behind it: "Feeding the World's Hungry Millions: How It Will Mean Billions for U.S. Business."

And indeed it did. In the years 1960 to 1970, U.S. taxpayers spent a total of $7.9 billion on the Food for Peace program. Between 1948 and 1970, they also paid an additional $50 billion for other economic-aid programs, some of which went for food and food-producing machinery and technology. Though all U.S. taxpayers were forced to contribute to the cost of P.L. 480, certain special interest groups gained handsomely under the program. Farmers did not have to contribute the grain; the Government, or rather the taxpayers, bought it from them at full market prices. The increased demand raised prices of farm products generally. The manufacturers of farm machinery, fertilizers, and pesticides benefited by the farmers' extra efforts to grow more food. Grain elevators profited from storing the surplus until it could be shipped. Railroads made money hauling it to ports, and shipping lines profited from carrying it overseas. The implementation of P.L. 480 required the creation of a vast Government bureaucracy, which then acquired its own vested interest in continuing the program regardless of its merits.

## V. Extracting Dollars

Those who proposed and defended the Food for Peace program in public rarely mentioned its importance to any of these special interests. The public emphasis was always on its humanitarian effects. The combination of silent selfish interests and highly vocal humanitarian apologists made a powerful and successful lobby for extracting money from taxpayers. We can expect the same lobby to push now for the creation of a world food bank.

However great the potential benefit to selfish interests, it should not be a decisive argument against a truly humanitarian program. We must ask if such a program would actually do more good than harm, not only momentarily but also in the long run. Those who propose the food bank usually refer to a current "emergency" or "crisis" in terms of world food supply. But what is an emergency? Although they may be infrequent and sudden, everyone knows that emergencies will occur from time to time. A well-run family, company, organization, or country prepares for the likelihood of accidents and emergencies. It expects them, it budgets for them, it saves for them.

782

## VI.  Learning the Hard Way

What happens if some organizations or countries budget for accidents and others do not? If each country is solely responsible for its own well-being, poorly managed ones will suffer. But they can learn from experience. They may mend their ways, and learn to budget for infrequent but certain emergencies. For example, the weather varies from year to year, and periodic crop failures are certain. A wise and competent government saves out of the production of the good years in anticipation of bad years to come. Joseph taught this policy to Pharaoh in Egypt more than 2,000 years ago. Yet the great majority of the governments in the world today do not follow such a policy. They lack either the wisdom or the competence, or both. Should those nations that do manage to put something aside be forced to come to the rescue each time an emergency occurs among the poor nations?

"But it isn't their fault!" some kindhearted liberals argue. "How can we blame the poor people who are caught in an emergency? Why must they suffer for the sins of their government?" The concept of blame is simply not relevant here. The real question is, What are the operational consequences of establishing a world food bank? If it is open to every country every time a need develops, slovenly rulers will not be motivated to take Joseph's advice. Someone will always come to their aid. Some countries will deposit food in the world food bank, and others will withdraw it. There will be almost no overlap. As a result of such solutions to food shortage emergencies, the poor countries will not learn to mend their ways, and will suffer progressively greater emergencies as their populations grow.

## VII.  Population Control the Crude Way

On the average, poor countries undergoe a 2.5 percent increase in population each year; rich countries, about 0.8 percent. Only rich countries have anything in the way of food reserves set aside, and even they do not have as much as they should. Poor countries have none. If poor countries received no food from the outside, the rate of their population growth would be periodically checked by crop failures and famines. But if they can always draw on a world food bank in time of need, their population can continue to grow unchecked, and so will their "need" for aid. In the short run, a world food bank may diminish that need, but in the long run it actually increases the need without limit.

Without some system of worldwide food sharing, the proportion of people in the rich and poor nations might eventually stabilize. The over-populated poor countries would decrease in numbers, while the rich countries that had room for more people would increase. But with a well-meaning system of sharing, such as a world food bank, the growth differential between the rich and the poor countries will not only persist, it will increase. Because of the higher rate of population growth in the poor countries of the world, 88 percent of today's children are born poor, and only 12 percent rich. Year by year the ratio becomes worse, as the fast-reproducing poor outnumber the slow-reproducing rich.

A world food bank is thus a commons in disguise. People will have more motivation to draw from it than to add to any common store. The less provident and less able will multiply at the expense of the abler and more provident, bringing eventual ruin upon all who share in the commons. Besides, any system of "sharing" that amounts to foreign aid from the rich nations to the poor nations will carry the taint of charity, which will contribute little to the world peace so devoutly desired by those who support the idea of a world food bank.

As past U.S. foreign-aid programs have amply and depressingly demonstrated, international charity frequently inspires mistrust and antagonism rather than gratitude on the part of the recipient nation.

## VIII. Chinese Fish and Miracle Rice

The modern approach to foreign aid stresses the export of technology and advice, rather than money and food. As an ancient Chinese proverb goes: "Give a man a fish and he will eat for a day; teach him how to fish and he will eat for the rest of his days." Acting on this advice, the Rockefeller and Ford Foundations have financed a number of programs for improving agriculture in the hungry nations. Known as the "Green Revolution," these programs have led to the development of "miracle rice" and "miracle wheat," new strains that offer bigger harvests and greater resistance to crop damage. Norman Borlaug, the Nobel Prize-winning agronomist who, supported by the Rockefeller Foundation, developed "miracle wheat," is one of the most prominent advocates of a world food bank.

Whether or not the Green Revolution can increase food production as much as its champions claim is a debatable but possibly irrelevant point. Those who support this well-intended humanitarian effort should first consider some of the fundamentals of human ecology. Ironically, one man who did was the late Alan Gregg, a vice president of the Rockefeller Foundation. Two decades ago he expressed strong doubts about the wisdom of such attempts to increase food production. He likened the growth and spread of humanity over the surface of the earth to the spread of cancer in the human body, remarking that "cancerous growths demand food; but, as far as I know, they have never been cured by getting it."

## IX. Overloading the Environment

Every human born constitutes a draft on all aspects of the environment: food, air, water, forests, beaches, wildlife, scenery, and solitude. Food can, perhaps, be significantly increased to meet a growing demand. But what about clean beaches, unspoiled forests, and solitude? If we satisfy a growing population's need for food, we necessarily decrease its per capita supply of the other resources needed by men.

India, for example, now has a population of 600 million, which increases by 15 million each year. This population already puts a huge load on a relatively impoverished environment. The country's forests are now only a small fraction of what they were three centuries ago, and floods and erosion continually destroy the insufficient farmland that remains. Every one of the 15 million new lives added to India's population puts an additional burden on the environment, and increases the economic and social costs of crowding. However humanitarian our intent, every Indian life saved through medical or nutritional assistance from abroad diminishes the quality of life for those who remain, and for subsequent generations. If rich countries make it possible, through foreign aid, for 600 million Indians to swell to 1.2 billion in a mere twenty-eight years, as their current growth rate threatens, will future generations of Indians thank us for hastening the destruction of their environment? Will our good intentions be sufficient excuse for the consequences of our actions?

My final example of a commons in action is one for which the public has the least desire for rational discussion—immigration.

Anyone who publicly questions the wisdom of current U.S. immigration policy is promptly charged with bigotry, prejudice, ethnocentrism, chauvinism, isolationism, or selfishness. Rather than encounter such accusations, one would rather talk about matters, leaving immigration policy to wallow in the crosscurrents of special interests that take no account of the good of the whole or the interests of posterity.

Perhaps we still feel guilty about things we said in the past. Two generations ago the popular press frequently referred to Dagos, Wops, Polacks, Chinks, and Krauts in articles about how America was being "overrun" by foreigners of supposedly inferior genetic stock. But because the implied inferiority of foreigners was used then as justification for keeping them out, people now assume that restrictive policies could only be based on such misguided notions. There are other grounds.

## X. A Nation of Immigrants

Just consider the numbers involved. Our Government acknowledges a new inflow of 400,000 immigrants a year. While we have no hard data on the extent of illegal entries, educated guesses put the figure at about 600,000 a year. Since the natural increase (excess of births over deaths) of the resident population now runs about 1.7 million per year, the yearly gain from immigration amounts to at least 19 percent of the total annual increase, and may be as much as 37 percent if we include the estimate for illegal immigrants. Considering the growing use of birth-control devices, the potential effect of educational campaigns by such organizations as Planned Parenthood Federation of America and Zero Population Growth, and the influence of inflation and the housing shortage, the fertility rate of American women may decline so much that immigration could account for all the yearly increase in population. Should we not at least ask if that is what we want?

For the sake of those who worry about whether the "quality" of the average immigrant compares favorably with the quality of the average resident, let us assume that immigrants and nativeborn citizens are of exactly equal quality, however one defines that term. We will focus here only on quantity; and since our conclusions will depend on nothing else, all charges of bigotry and chauvinism become irrelevant.

## XI. Immigration vs. Food Supply

World food banks *move food to the people,* hastening the exhaustion of the environment of the poor countries. Unrestricted immigration, on the other hand *moves people to the food,* thus speeding up the destruction of the environment of the rich countries. We can easily understand why poor people should want to make this latter transfer, but why should rich hosts encourage it?

As in the case of foreign-aid programs, immigration receives support from selfish interests and humanitarian impulses. The primary selfish interest in unimpeded immigration is the desire of employers for cheap labor, particularly in industries and trades that offer degrading work. In the past, one wave of foreigners after another was brought into the U.S. to work at wretched jobs for wretched wages. In recent years the Cubans, Puerto Ricans, and Mexicans have had this dubious honor. The interests of the employers of cheap labor mesh well with the guilty silence of the country's liberal intelligentsia. White Anglo-Saxon Protestants are particularly reluctant to call for a closing of the doors to immigration for fear of being called bigots.

But not all countries have such reluctant leadership. Most educatated Hawaiians, for example, are keenly aware of the limits of their environment, particularly in terms of population growth. There is only so much room on the islands, and the islanders know it. To Hawaiians, immigrants from the other forty-nine states present as great a threat as those from other nations. At a recent meeting of Hawaiian government officials in Honolulu, I had the ironic delight of hearing a speaker, who like most of his audience was of Japanese ancestry, ask how the country might practically and constitutionally close its doors to further immigration. One member of the audience countered: "How can we shut the doors now? We have many friends and relatives in Japan that we'd like to bring here some day so that they can enjoy Hawaii too." The Japanese-American speaker smiled sympathetically and answered: "Yes, but we have children now, and someday we'll have grandchildren too. We can bring more people here from Japan only by giving away some of the land that we hope to pass on to our grandchildren some day. What right do we have to do that?"

At this point, I can hear U.S. liberals asking: "How can you justify slamming the door once you're inside? You say that immigrants

787

should be kept out. But aren't we all immigrants, or the descendants of immigrants? If we insist on staying, must we not admit all others?" Our craving for intellectual order leads us to seek and prefer symmetrical rules and morals: a single rule for me and everybody else; the same rule yesterday, today, and tomorrow. Justice, we feel, should not change with time and place.

We Americans of non-Indian ancestry can look upon ourselves as the descendants of thieves who are guilty morally, if not legally, of stealing this land from its Indian owners. Should we then give back the land to the now living American descendants of those Indians? However morally or logically sound this proposal may be, I, for one, am unwilling to live by it and I know no one else who is. Besides, the logical consequence would be absurd. Suppose that, intoxicated with a sense of pure justice, we should decide to turn our land over to the Indians. Since all our wealth has also been derived from the land, wouldn't we be morally obliged to give that back to the Indians too?

## XII. Pure Justice vs. Reality

Clearly, the concept of pure justice produces an infinite regression to absurdity. Centuries ago, wise men invented statutes of limitations to justify the rejection of such pure justice, in the interest of preventing continual disorder. The law zealously defends property rights, but only relatively recent property rights. Drawing a line after an arbitrary time has elapsed may be unjust, but the alternatives are worse.

We are all the descendants of thieves, and the world's resources are inequitably distributed. But we must begin the journey to tomorrow from the point where we are today. We cannot remake the past. We cannot safely divide the wealth equitably among all peoples so long as people reproduce at different rates. To do so would guarantee that our grandchildren, and everyone else's grandchildren, would have only a ruined world to inhabit.

To be generous with one's own possessions is quite different from being generous with those of posterity. We should call this point to the attention of those who, from a commendable love of justice and equality, would institute a system of the commons, either in the form of a world food bank, or of unrestricted immigration. We must convince them if we wish to save at least some parts of the world from environmental ruin.

Without a true world government to control reproduction and the use of available resources, the sharing ethic of the spaceship is impossible. For the foreseeable future, our survival demands that we govern our actions by the ethics of a lifeboat, harsh though they may be. Posterity will be satisfied with nothing less.

**STUDY QUESTIONS**

1. Explain the difference between a "lifeboat ethic" and a "spaceship ethic." Defend one or the other.
2. Hardin sees a difference between "reality" and "pure justice." Do you agree?
3. The third-century theologian Tertullian wrote, "The scourges of pestilence, famine, wars, and earthquakes have come to be regarded as a blessing to overcrowded nations, since they serve to prune away the luxuriant growth of the human race." How would Hardin and Singer respond to this remark? With whom do you agree most?

# Population and Food: Metaphors and the Reality

## WILLIAM W. MURDOCH
## and ALLAN OATEN

William Murdoch (b. 1939) is professor of biology at the University of California at Santa Barbara. He has written numerous articles on population, ecology, and famine. He is the author of *The Poverty of Nations: Population, Hunger and Development* (1980).

Allan Oaten is professor of biology at the University of California at Santa Barbara. He has published in the areas of population control and environmentalism.

William Murdoch and Allan Oaten seek to show that Hardin's arguments against famine relief to poor third-world nations are unsound. One mechanism of relief is the proposed world food bank from which needy nations could draw. Hardin had argued that such a resource is a "commons"—people usually deplete a commons without adding to it—that would have the effect of increasing the populations of the poorer nations, eventually bringing disaster to rich and poor alike. Hardin had also argued that aid does not give rise to better birth control; on the contrary, it makes it easy for the poor to continue to

POPULATION AND FOOD: METAPHORS AND THE REALITY By William W. Murdoch and Allan Oaten. Excerpted from *BioScience,* September 9, 1975, pp. 561–567. Copyright 1975 by The American Institute of Biological Sciences. Reprinted by permission of the publisher and the authors.

propagate and thereby to exacerbate the problem that aid is meant to resolve.

According to Murdoch and Oaten, Hardin fails to see that the richer countries in many ways are responsible for the cycle of poverty in the third world. They encourage cash crops instead of food crops; they support repressive rulers for political reasons; they enforce trade policies that exploit the resources of poor countries and do little to help them feed themselves. All this contributes to the endemic state of poverty and to the cycle of famine in the third world. If such policies were revised, the poor nations would be better able to help themselves.

Murdoch and Oaten strongly advocate famine relief. They are unimpressed by Hardin's commons and lifeboat metaphors. And they note, *contra* Hardin, that in some third-world countries birth rates are falling. This occurs when a population is sufficiently well off to enjoy increased literacy, to have some reasonable confidence in the future, and when women enjoy improved status and gain access to birth-control information. None of these events occur, however, in conditions of starvation. Murdoch and Oaten believe that making health education and jobs available to the lowest income groups are prerequisites for a decline in birth rates. They conclude, from the evidence considered, that "The policies dictated by a sense of decency are also the most realistic and rational."

## Misleading Metaphors

[Hardin's] "lifeboat" article actually has two messages. The first is that our immigration policy is too generous. This will not concern us here. The second, and more important, is that by helping poor nations we will bring disaster to rich and poor alike:

> Metaphorically, each rich nation amounts to a lifeboat full of comparatively rich people. The poor of the world are in other, much more crowded lifeboats. Continuously, so to speak, the poor fall out of their lifeboats and swim for a while in the water outside, hoping to be admitted to a rich lifeboat, or in some other way to benefit from the "goodies" on board. What should the passengers on a rich lifeboat do?

> This is the central problem of "the ethics of a lifeboat." (Hardin, 1974, p. 561)[1]

Among these so-called "goodies" are food supplies and technical aid such as that which led to the Green Revolution. Hardin argues that we should withhold such resources from poor nations on the grounds that they help to maintain high rates of population increase, thereby making the problem worse. He forsees the continued supplying and increasing production of food as a process that will be "brought to an end only by the total collapse of the whole system, producing a catastrophe of scarcely imaginable proportions" (p. 564).

Turning to one particular mechanism for distributing these resources, Hardin claims that a world food bank is a commons—people have more motivation to draw from it than to add to it; it will have a ratchet or escalator effect on population because inputs from it will prevent population declines in over-populated countries. Thus "wealth can be steadily moved in one direction only, from the slowly-breeding rich to the rapidly-breeding poor, the process finally coming to a halt only when all countries are equally and miserably poor" (p. 565). Thus our help will not only bring ultimate disaster to poor countries, but it will also be suicidal for us.

As for the "benign demographic transition" to low birth rates, which some aid supporters have predicted, Hardin states flatly that the weight of evidence is against this possibility.

Finally, Hardin claims that the plight of poor nations is partly their own fault: "wise sovereigns seem not to exist in the poor world today. The most anguishing problems are created by poor countries that are governed by rulers insufficiently wise and powerful." Establishing a world food bank will exacerbate this problem: "slovenly rulers" will escape the consequences of their incompetence—"Others will bail them out whenever they are in trouble"; "Far more difficult than the transfer of wealth from one country to another is the transfer of wisdom between sovereign powers or between generations" (p. 563).

What arguments does Hardin present in support of these opinions? Many involve metaphors: lifeboat, commons, and ratchet or escalator. These metaphors are crucial to his thesis, and it is, therefore, important for us to examine them critically.

---

[1] G. Hardin, 1974, "Living on a Lifeboat," *BioScience*, vol. 24, pp. 561–68.

The lifeboat is the major metaphor. It seems attractively simple, but it is in fact simplistic and obscures important issues. As soon as we try to use it to compare various policies, we find that most relevant details of the actual situation are either missing or distorted in the lifeboat metaphor. Let us list some of these details.

Most important, perhaps, Hardin's lifeboats barely interact. The rich lifeboats may drop some handouts over the side and perhaps repel a boarding party now and then, but generally they live their own lives. In the real world, nations interact a great deal, in ways that affect food supply and population size and growth, and the effect of rich nations on poor nations has been strong and not always benevolent.

First, by colonization and actual wars of commerce, and through the international marketplace, rich nations have arranged an exchange of goods that has maintained and even increased the economic imbalance between rich and poor nations. Until recently we have taken or otherwise obtained cheap raw material from poor nations and sold them expensive manufactured goods that they cannot make themselves. In the United States, the structure of tariffs and internal subsidies discriminates selectively against poor nations. In poor countries, the concentration on cash crops rather than on food crops, a legacy of colonial times, is now actively encouraged by western multinational corporations (Barraclough 1975).[2] Indeed, it is claimed that in famine-stricken Sahelian Africa, multinational agribusiness has recently taken land out of food production for cash crops (Transnational Institute 1974).[3] Although we often self-righteously take the "blame" for lowering the death rates of poor nations during the 1940s and 1950s, we are less inclined to accept responsibility for the effects of actions that help maintain poverty and hunger. Yet poverty directly contributes to the high birth rates that Hardin views with such alarm.

Second, U.S. foreign policy, including foreign aid programs, has favored "pro-Western" regimes, many of which govern in the interests of a wealthy elite and some of which are savagely repressive.

---

[2]G. Barraclough, 1975, "The Great World Crisis I, *The New York Revue of Books*, vol. 21, pp. 20–29.

[3]Transitional Institute, 1974, *World Hunger: Causes and Remedies* (Washington: Institute for Policy Studies).

Thus, it has often subsidized a gross maldistribution of income and has supported political leaders who have opposed most of the social changes that can lead to reduced birth rates. In this light, Hardin's pronouncements on the alleged wisdom gap between poor leaders and our own, and the difficulty of filling it, appear as a grim joke: our response to leaders with the power and wisdom Hardin yearns for has often been to try to replace them or their policies as soon as possible. Selective giving and withholding of both military and non-military aid has been an important ingredient of our efforts to maintain political leaders we like and to remove those we do not. Brown (1974b),[4] after noting that the withholding of U.S. food aid in 1973 contributed to the downfall of the Allende government in Chile, comments that "although Americans decry the use of petroleum as a political weapon, calling it 'political blackmail,' the United States has been using food aid for political purposes for twenty years—and describing this as 'enlightened diplomacy.'"

Both the quantity and the nature of the supplies on a lifeboat are fixed. In the real world, the quantity has strict limits, but these are far from having been reached (University of California Food Task Force 1974).[5] Nor are we forced to devote fixed proportions of our efforts and energy to automobile travel, pet food, packaging, advertising, corn-fed beef, "defense" and other diversions, many of which cost far more than foreign aid does. The fact is that enough food is now produced to feed the world's population adequately. That people are malnourished is due to distribution and to economics, not to agricultural limits (United Nations Economic and Social Council 1974).[6]

Hardin's lifeboats are divided merely into rich and poor, and it is difficult to talk about birth rates on either. In the real world, however, there are striking differences among the birth rates of the poor countries and even among the birth rates of different parts of single countries. These differences appear to be related to social conditions (also absent from lifeboats) and may guide us to effective aid policies.

---

[4]L. R. Brown, 1974b, *By Bread Alone* (New York: Praeger).

[5]University of California Food Task Force, 1974, *A Hungry World: The Challenge to Agriculture* (University of California, Division of Agricultural Sciences).

[6]United Nations Economic and Social Council, "Assessment: Present Food Situation and Dimensions and Causes of Hunger and Malnutrition in the World" (New York: Economic Conference, May 8, 1974), p. 65.

Hardin's lifeboat metaphor not only conceals facts, but misleads about the effects of his proposals. The rich lifeboat can raise the ladder and sail away. But in real life, the problem will not necessarily go away just because it is ignored. In the real world, there are armies, raw materials in poor nations, and even outraged domestic dissidents prepared to sacrifice their own and others' lives to oppose policies they regard as immoral.

No doubt there are other objections. But even this list shows the lifeboat metaphor to be dangerously inappropriate for serious policy making because it obscures far more than it reveals. Lifeboats and "lifeboat ethics" may be useful topics for those who are shipwrecked; we believe they are worthless—indeed detrimental—in discussions of food-population questions.

The ratchet metaphor is equally flawed. It, too, ignores complex interactions between birth rates and social conditions (including diets), implying as it does that more food will simply mean more babies. Also, it obscures the fact that the decrease in death rates has been caused at least as much by developments such as DDT, improved sanitation, and medical advances, as by increased food supplies, so that cutting out food aid will not necessarily lead to population declines.

The lifeboat article is strangely inadequate in other ways. For example, it shows an astonishing disregard for recent literature. The claim that we can expect no "benign demographic transition" is based on a review written more than a decade ago (Davis 1963).[7] Yet, events and attitudes are changing rapidly in poor countries: for the first time in history, most poor people live in countries with birth control programs; with few exceptions, poor nations are somewhere on the demographic transition to lower birth rates (Demeny 1974);[8] the population-food squeeze is now widely recognized, and governments of poor nations are aware of the relationship. Again, there is a considerable amount of evidence that birth rates can fall rapidly in poor countries given the proper social conditions (as we will discuss later); consequently, crude projections of current population growth rates are quite inadequate for policy making.

---

[7]K. Davis, 1963, "Population," *Scientific American*, vol. 209, pp. 62–71.

[8]P. Demeny, 1974, "The Populations of the Underdeveloped Countries," *Scientific American*, vol. 231, pp. 149–159.

## The Tragedy of the Commons

Throughout the lifeboat article, Hardin bolsters his assertions by reference to the "commons" (Hardin 1968).[9] The thesis of the commons, therefore, needs critical evaluation.

Suppose several privately owned flocks, comprising 100 sheep altogether, are grazing on a public commons. They bring in an annual income of $1.00 per sheep. Fred, a herdsman, owns only one sheep. He decides to add another. But 101 is too many: the commons is overgrazed and produces less food. The sheep lose quality and income drops to 90¢ per sheep. Total income is now $90.90 instead of $100.00. Adding the sheep has brought an overall loss. But Fred has gained: *his* income is $1.80 instead of $1.00. The gain from the additional sheep, which is his alone, outweighs the loss from overgrazing, which he shares. Thus he promotes his interest at the expense of the community.

This is the problem of the commons, which seems on the way to becoming an archetype. Hardin, in particular, is not inclined to underrate its importance: "One of the major tasks of education today is to create such an awareness of the dangers of the commons that people will be able to recognize its many varieties, however disguised" (Hardin 1974, p. 562) and "All this is terribly obvious once we are acutely aware of the pervasiveness and danger of the commons. But many people still lack this awareness . . ." (p. 565).

The "commons" affords a handy way of classifying problems: the lifeboat article reveals that sharing, a generous immigration policy, world food banks, air, water, the fish populations of the ocean, and the western range lands are, or produce, a commons. It is also handy to be able to dispose of policies one does not like and "only a particular instance of a class of policies that are in error because they lead to the tragedy of the commons" (p. 561).

But no metaphor, even one as useful as this, should be treated with such awe. Such shorthand can be useful, but it can also mislead by discouraging thought and obscuring important detail. To dismiss a proposal by suggesting that "all you need to know about this proposal is that it institutes a commons and is, therefore, bad" is to assert that the proposed commons is worse than the original

---

[9]G. Hardin, 1968, "The Tragedy of the Commons," *Science*, vol. 162, pp. 1243–48.

problem. This might be so if the problem of the commons were, indeed, a tragedy—that is, if it were insoluble. But it is not.

Hardin favors private ownership as the solution (either through private property or the selling of pollution rights). But, of course, there are solutions other than private ownership; and private ownership itself is no guarantee of carefully husbanded resources.

One alternative to private ownership of the commons is communal ownership of the sheep—or, in general, of the mechanisms and industries that exploit the resource—combined with communal planning for management. (Note, again, how the metaphor favors one solution: perhaps the "tragedy" lay not in the commons but in the sheep. "The Tragedy of the Privately Owned Sheep" lacks zing, unfortunately.) Public ownership of a commons has been tried in Peru to the benefit of the previously privately owned anchoveta fishery (Gulland 1975).[10] The communally owned argiculture of China does not seem to have suffered any greater over-exploitation than that of other Asian nations.

Another alternative is cooperation combined with regulation. For example, Gulland (1975) has shown that Antarctic whale stocks (perhaps the epitome of a commons since they are internationally exploited and no one owns them) are now being properly managed, and stocks are increasing. This has been achieved through cooperation in the International Whaling Commission, which has by agreement set limits to the catch of each nation.

In passing, Hardin's private ownership argument is not generally applicable to nonrenewable resources. Given discount rates, technology substitutes, and no more than an average regard for posterity, privately owned nonrenewable resources, like oil, coal and minerals, are mined at rates that produce maximum profits, rather than at those rates that preserve them for future generations. . . .

## Birth Rates: An Alternative View

Is the food-population spiral inevitable? A more optimistic, if less comfortable, hypothesis, presented by Rich (1973)[11] and Brown

---

[10]J. Gulland, 1975, "The Harvest of the Sea," in W. W. Murdoch, ed., *Environment: Resources, Pollution and Society* (Sunderland, MA: Sinauer Associates), pp. 167–189.

[11]W. Rich, 1973, "Smaller Families through Social and Economic Progress" (Washington: Overseas Development Council Monograph #7).

(1974a),[12] is increasingly tenable: contrary to the "ratchet" projection, population growth rates are affected by many complex conditions beside food supply. In particular, a set of socioeconomic conditions can be identified that motivate parents to have fewer children; under these conditions, birth rates can fall quite rapidly, sometimes even before birth control technology is available. Thus, population growth can be controlled more effectively by intelligent human intervention that sets up the appropriate conditions than by doing nothing and trusting to "natural population cycles."

These conditions are: parental confidence about the future, an improved status of women, and literacy. They require low infant mortality rates, widely available rudimentary health care, increased income and employment, and an adequate diet above subsistence levels. Expenditure on schools (especially elementary schools), appropriate health services (especially rural paramedical services), and agricultural reform (especially aid to small farmers) will be needed, and foreign aid can help here. It is essential that these improvements be spread across the population; aid can help here, too, by concentrating on the poor nations' poorest people, encouraging necessary institutional and social reforms, and making it easier for poor nations to use their own resources and initiative to help themselves. It is *not* necessary that per capita GNP be very high, certainly not as high as that of the rich countries during their gradual demographic transition. In other words, low birth rates in poor countries are achievable long before the conditions exist that were present in the rich countries in the late 19th and early 20th centuries.

Twenty or thirty years is not long to discover and assess the factors affecting birth rates, but a body of evidence is now accumulating in favor of this hypothesis. Rich (1973) and Brown (1974a) show that at least 10 developing countries have managed to reduce their birth rates by an average of more than one birth per 1,000 population per year for periods of 5 to 16 years. A reduction of one birth per 1,000 per year would bring birth rates in poor countries to a rough replacement level of about 16/1,000 by the turn of the century, though age distribution effects would prevent a smooth population decline. We have listed these countries in Table 1, together with three other

---

[12]L. R. Brown, 1974a, *In the Human Interest* (New York: W. W. Norton).

TABLE I    *Declining Birth Rates and per Capita Income in Selected Developing Countries* These are crude birth rates, uncorrected for age distribution. [13]

| | | Births/1,000/Year | | |
| | | Avg. annual decline in crude birth rate | Crude birth rate 1972 | $ per capita per year 1973 |
| Country | Time span | | | |
|---|---|---|---|---|
| Barbados | 1960–69 | 1.5 | 22 | 570 |
| Taiwan | 1955–71 | 1.2 | 24 | 390 |
| Tunisia | 1966–71 | 1.8 | 35 | 250 |
| Mauritius | 1961–71 | 1.5 | 25 | 240 |
| Hong Kong | 1960–72 | 1.4 | 19 | 970 |
| Singapore | 1955–72 | 1.2 | 23 | 920 |
| Costa Rica | 1963–72 | 1.5 | 32 | 560 |
| South Korea | 1960–70 | 1.2 | 29 | 250 |
| Egypt | 1966–70 | 1.7 | 37 | 210 |
| Chile | 1963–70 | 1.2 | 25 | 720 |
| China | | | 30 | 160 |
| Cuba | | | 27 | 530 |
| Sri Lanka | | | 30 | 110 |

nations, including China, that are poor and yet have brought their birth rates down to 30 or less, presumably from rates of over 40 a decade or so ago.

These data show that rapid reduction in birth rates is possible in the developing world. No doubt it can be argued that each of these cases is in some way special. Hong Kong and Singapore are relatively rich; they, Barbados, and Mauritius are also tiny. China is able to exert great social pressure on its citizens; but China is particularly significant. It is enormous; its per capita GNP is almost as low as India's; and it started out in 1949 with a terrible health system. Also, Egypt, Chile, Taiwan, Cuba, South Korea, and Sri Lanka are quite large, and they are poor or very poor (Table 1). In fact, these examples represent an enormous range of religion, political systems, and

---

[13]M. S. Teitelbaum, 1975, "Relevance of Demographic Transition Theory for Developing Countries," *Science*, vol. 188, pp. 420–25.

geography and suggest that such rates of decline in the birth rate can be achieved whenever the appropriate conditions are met. "The common factor in these countries is that the *majority* of the population has shared in the economic and social benefits of significant national progress. . . . [M]aking health, education and jobs more broadly available to lower income groups in poor countries contribute[s] significantly toward the motivation for smaller families that is the prerequisite of a major reduction in birth rates" (Rich 1973).

. . . As a disillusioning quarter-century of aid giving has shown, the obstacles of getting aid to those segments of the population most in need of it are enormous. Aid has typically benefitted a small rich segment of society, partly because of the way aid programs have been designed but also because of human and institutional factors in the poor nations themselves (Owens and Shaw 1972).[14] With some notable exceptions, the distribution of income and services in poor nations is extremely skewed—much more uneven than in rich countries. Indeed, much of the population is essentially outside the economic system. Breaking this pattern will be extremely difficult. It will require not only aid that is designed specifically to benefit the rural poor, but also important institutional changes such as decentralization of decision making and the development of greater autonomy and stronger links to regional and national markets for local groups and industries such as cooperative farms.

Thus, two things are being asked of rich nations and of the United States in particular: to increase nonmilitary foreign aid, including food aid, and to give it in ways, and to governments, that will deliver it to the poorest people and will improve their access to national economic institutions. These are not easy tasks, particularly the second, and there is no guarantee that birth rates will come down quickly in all countries. Still, many poor countries have, in varying degrees, begun the process of reform, and recent evidence suggests that aid and reform together can do much to solve the twin problems of high birth rates and economic underdevelopment. The tasks are far from impossible. Based on the evidence, the policies dictated by a sense of decency are also the most realistic and rational.

---

[14]E. Owens and R. Shaw, 1972, *Development Reconsidered* (Lexington, MA: Heath & Co.).

**STUDY QUESTIONS**

1. How do Murdoch and Oaten seek to undermine Hardin's life-boat analogy? What do they find wrong with the "commons" argument?
2. Both Hardin and his critics contend that they are the more realistic. Who impresses you as the more realistic of the protagonists in this controversy?
3. Murdoch and Oaten maintain that Hardin overlooks the extent of the richer nations' responsibility in causing third-world problems. Is the account of this responsibility exaggerated? Assuming it is accurate and fair, how does that fact bear on the question of the feasibility of famine relief? For example, how is it relevant to the question of establishing a world food bank?

# *Moral Constraints on Foreign Policy*

DOUGLAS MACLEAN

Douglas MacLean (b. 1946) is director of the Center for Philosophy and Public Policy at the University of Maryland, where he also teaches courses in applied ethics.

MacLean believes the United States should refrain from aiding countries that violate human rights. Critics of a policy that makes foreign aid conditional on human rights reform maintain that "moralistic constraints" are a self-defeating luxury that harm the national interest.

MORAL CONSTRAINTS ON FOREIGN POLICY From "Constraints, Goals, and Moralism in Foreign Policy" in Peter G. Brown and Douglas MacLean, eds. *Human Rights & U.S. Foreign Policy* (Lexington, MA: Lexington Books-D. C. Heath and Company, 1979). Reprinted by permission of the copyright holder.

801

But MacLean counters that it is wrong to refrain from introducing considerations of rights into our international relations because the United States government is a moral agent bound by the democratic ideals of the American people. MacLean argues that objecting to rights constraints is like objecting to rules of war that prohibit barbaric practices, and that adhering to such rules could also be said to harm the national interest. Moreover, MacLean denies that an active policy of promoting human rights is actually detrimental to the national interest. To the contrary, although complicity in the abuse of human rights may achieve some short-term benefits, it usually is harmful in the long term.

Governments that violate the rights of their own populations often deny that people have the right not to be interfered with; the idea of human rights is said to be a Western ideal not shared by the entire world. Thus some critics of constraint argue that when we introduce moral considerations in international dealings, we are being culturally chauvinistic in taking for granted that our values are best. MacLean rejects this form of ethical relativism, noting that human rights have been accepted internationally (see *The Universal Declaration on Human Rights* in Chapter Two).

Opposing rights constraints on foreign policy is not only shortsighted, it is morally indefensible. Looking the other way when a "friendly" government tortures its own citizens is like looking the other way when a neighbor abuses a child. Dealing with such governments in a "normal" way makes us passively complicit in their actions. We lose moral credibility and eventually our own best interest as a nation suffers.

The common fate of ideals that reach Washington these days, it seems to me, is not death by corruption but rather death by sophistication. The affairs of government, we are told, should be handled discreetly, by experts. "[F]oreign policy is not a matter of objectives, it is a matter of strategy." Even our most basic values should not rigidly constrain the experts who play the games of global strategy as they administer our foreign policy. According to former secretary of state Henry Kissinger, human rights should not be a "vocal objective" of foreign policy. This is the view I wish to challenge.

The human rights movement began in the U.S. Congress in 1973, several years before Jimmy Carter was elected president and announced that human rights would be a major concern of his administration. It comes as no shock to learn that, in the early days, congressional attempts to use the human rights issue in order to exert some control over U.S. foreign policy were vigorously opposed by the Ford-Kissinger administration. What is more surprising is that every human rights bill brought before the Congress since President Carter took office has been just as vigorously opposed by his administration, and for remarkably similar reasons.

The Congress has been rather explicit in its human rights legislation. Section 502B of the Foreign Assistance Act, for example, says that "a principal goal of the foreign policy of the United States shall be to promote the increased observance of internationally recognized human rights by all countries." This act goes on to order that security assistance not be provided to countries whose governments violate these rights. It also orders the president to

> formulate and conduct international security assistance programs of the United States in a manner which will promote and advance human rights and avoid identification of the United States, through such programs, with governments which deny to their people internationally recognized human rights and fundamental freedoms . . .

The Congress has clearly expressed its concern for both practices that violate human rights in other countries and American responsibility for and complicity in those practices.

Henry Kissinger consistently doubted whether such human rights legislation was an appropriate expression of either concern. Acknowledging that "it is our obligation as the world's leading democracy to dedicate ourselves to assuring freedom for the human spirit," he went on to warn:

> But responsibility compels also a recognition of our limits. Our alliances . . . serve the cause of peace by strengthening regional and world security. If well conceived, they are not favors to others but a recognition of common interest. They should be withdrawn when

803

those interests change; they should not, as a general rule, be used as leves to extort a standard of conduct or to punish acts with which we do not agree.

Apparently, Dr. Kissinger did not think that promoting human rights should be a principal goal of foreign policy. He certainly did not think that Congress had any business passing laws that would firmly constrain U.S. involvement with governments that violate human rights:

> We have generally opposed attempts to deal with sensitive international human rights issues through legislation, not because of the moral view expressed, which we share, but because legislation is almost always too inflexible, too public, and too heavyhanded a means to accomplish what it seeks.

I would like to address both the criticism that the existing human rights amendments are too inflexible and the criticism that promoting respect for human rights ought not be a principal goal of U.S. foreign policy. These are the most frequent criticisms brought against the current administration's human rights policy and against the human rights legislation. They are also heard more and more frequently as the costs of a serious human rights policy become more obvious. . . . [T]he growing chorus, critical of enforcing the strong human rights provisions in foreign assistance legislation, tells us to leave this task to the experts. They can decide how best to realize this end on a case-by-case basis, unhampered by rigid principles.

If the position of these critics were simply that all that matters is the end result, and not the means of achieving it, the discussion could end right here. This view is obviously morally unacceptable and requires no further discussion. However, the criticism might instead be intended to claim only that human rights amendments are ineffective or self-defeating ways of achieving the goal of promoting respect for human rights in other countries. A "dirty hands" argument might further be invoked, to the effect that the goal of avoiding complicity in the wrongdoing of other governments is a moral luxury that it would be wrong to indulge. A challenge to such a position should ideally show both that it is not wrong to avoid complicity and that the human rights amendments do not interfere with the goal of promoting respect for human rights. This is what I shall argue presently. The challenge need not be a proof—mine is not—but only an argument that makes clear that the burden of justification falls on the side of the critics, and that the burden amounts to more than the familiar appeals to the complexity of foreign relations.

## Obeying Constraints

At least part of the justification of the human rights provisions is an appeal to the goal of removing U.S. responsibility for the human rights abuses of other governments. Our government is a moral agent which, like all moral agents, is bound by some moral requirements. There are constraints on the way a government can conduct its foreign policy. This simply means that a government is not allowed to do whatever it wants, disregarding the effects of its actions on people outside its borders.

The reasons for acknowledging limits on a government's actions are similar to the justifications offered for laws of war; without saying very much about national goals or the reasons for existing policies, we can still determine limits on how to attain those goals. We can even acknowledge that our policymakers ought to view the world of nations as a highly competitive arena in which the different parties pursue the goals of their own national security and domestic economic prosperity, realizing that this struggle consists to some considerable degree in gaining a relative advantage over others. Still, large numbers of people are affected by what our government does, and this fact places limits on what our policies can be. We cannot appropriate land or people as suits us. The justification for this does not have to be based on any agreement or contract that exists between our government and the other peoples of the world. In order to argue that certain values must be respected universally by our own government's activities, it is sufficient to appeal to the agreement that exists between *us* and our government. That agreement presupposes a consensus among our own citizens about certain ideals, such as that all people are equal and that every human being is entitled to certain liberties. Our government must respect such ideals, because its authority is granted partly for that purpose. Even though it is true that our government does not assume nearly the same responsibilities to foreign peoples as it does to its own citizens, certain ways of treating any human being are nevertheless inconsistent with our own ideals. Although it is fashionable to speak about universal human rights, for the purposes of justifying moral constraints on our own government's policies, we can instead appeal to the rights of U.S. citizens to have certain ideals respected and even affirmed by their government. We are not, for the moment, taking this to mean that our government must promote those ideals abroad, only that it is bound to respect them and not to violate them in its actions and policies where it represents the nation.

Thus, to say that moral ideals place constraints on how our government can act means at least that some of the moral beliefs that are basic to our justification of our own political institutions, in particular those that establish rights and liberties extending to all people, must be applied consistently to all of our government's activities. It has not been given the authority, under normal circumstances, to act otherwise. If these ideals define the rules of legitimate governmental activity, I can see no reason not to embody them in laws and make them public. The question of strategy does not even arise here, for the goal we are now considering is that of prohibiting the U.S. government from engaging in morally unacceptable activities. Our Bill of Rights is a public and inflexible document that aims in part to constrain the activities of the government that affect our fellow citizens. The human rights laws simply function in a similar way to protect all people from our government's activities, where we believe all people equally deserve and need protection. Enforceable laws alone can achieve this goal. To argue that the experts who administer foreign policy should police themselves as they see fit is to demand more trust from our citizens than it is reasonable for them to give. . . .

It is argued that maintaining our foreign assistance programs gives us leverage for continuing to affect the policies of other governments. If we terminate those programs because of moral constraints on our own actions, thereby keeping our hands clean, we lose our leverage and our ability to help people who are suffering under repressive regimes. This argument has been made recently about countries where we have terminated assistance, especially Chile. It is claimed to be important to maintain our involvement in those countries if we have any hope of making things better, and it is wrong to ignore this fact by placing moral constraints on our own actions and policies, because by working within rigid constraints we bring about worse consequences than by ignoring constraints. In such cases, different moral goals conflict with one another.

Where we are responsible for a repressive regime's very existence, this pragmatic argument is thinly disguised hypocrisy, but it is a serious question whether one ought to act on principle when one is aware that the consequences of such a policy are worse than they would be if the principles were ignored. The best response to this dilemma attempts to avoid it. Where a regime *needs* our aid, we have leverage, and by constraining our own programs for giving aid, in order to remove our own complicity in wrongdoings, we use that leverage in the most effective way. If another government is not dependent on our aid, then we have little leverage, if any at all, and thus we have no justification for supporting them and accepting some of the responsibility for their wrongs. Some people will argue that in diplomatic forums leverage does not work in this straightforward way, and that we must maintain our complicity while working for gradual change. At this point, however, the burden of proof is with the advocates of this view to show that loosening the moral constraints on our own policies is the only effective way of decreasing the suffering in the world because of another government's violating human rights. Even then, it remains to be shown that relaxing the moral constraints would be the right thing to do.

A parallel response can be made about arms sales, except that here the costs of constraining our activities can be significantly higher. How should we respond to the threat of higher costs? Moral rules are not absolutely binding, and they can bend in the face of extraordinary circumstances. Yet when a plea is made to sell helicopters to Argentina or sophisticated airplanes to Iran, in spite of the dismal human rights records in those countries, the economic issues are sometimes the only ones cited. All too often the moral issues are ignored, as if any economic cost were enough to set aside all other values. Strong human rights amendments—public and inflexible rules (but with their permissible exceptions explicitly included, as they now are)— may at least be able to remedy this inexcusable blindness.

Do the constraints imposed by the human rights amendments generally threaten other (and perhaps nonmoral) national interests? Of course there will be costs in some cases, but I believe the human rights amendments can in general be defended strictly on grounds of prudence. A tacit agreement between us and our government justifies but also limits governmental authority, giving to the government the responsibility for protecting human rights domestically. Many of these rights are ways of constraining social interference, including that of the government itself, in the lives of individuals. These rights express a moral ideal, that individuals should be allowed to exercise as much autonomy as is possible and reasonable in pursuing their own lives. Our rights are not merely ways of protecting us from harm, for we would want to be able to claim our rights even if those in power were completely benevolent. This view about the importance of rights may not be universally shared, but perhaps it is not necessary to appeal to this moral ideal in order to justify the practice of constraining governmental authority. That practice may be seen instead as the condition necessary to secure full support for a government, without which it might not have any authority at all. Thus, one important reason for protecting human rights is to promote the social stability that results when a government operates with general approval and support.

Now, a government that prohibits all dissent, that arrests and tortures its opposition, secures its authority in a way that is not naturally stable and self-reinforcing. It is unreasonable to think that such practices are based ultimately on principle; they are instead deemed necessary for maintaining control. They are bound to be unpopular practices which are resorted to anyway because the use of force and terror are needed to secure authority for an unpopular government. If the government had popular support, it could allow dissent and would not have to engage in practices that make itself vulnerable to worldwide criticism. Whatever stability these practices gain for a regime is linked to the practices and the fear they generate. They must continue to be employed successfully. As the regime becomes less popular among its own people, the chances increase that it will be overthrown whenever this becomes possible. These regimes may become increasingly dependent on outside aid to finance the unpopular programs aimed at suppressing their own citizens. We ally ourselves with such governments, therefore, at some risk and perhaps at some cost; for if they lose control we stand to lose whatever advantage we sought to gain by allying ourselves with them in the first place.

The conclusion to draw from these considerations is that if we want to use our foreign assistance programs to gain influence in the countries we aid, it is prudent to ally ourselves with popular regimes wherever this is possible. Realistically, however, such reasoning carries limited weight because the argument has a limited application.

A tyrannical regime, especially with outside aid, may be able to tolerate the costs of oppression and unpopularity for a long time, long enough, for instance, to serve our ends. Furthermore, the argument assumes that popular regimes are likely not to violate (what we take to be) human rights because they do not have to. Although the argument gives reasons for thinking that this is generally true, exceptions can and do occur. This only shows that agents are not always prudent, or else that morality and prudence can conflict.

The "experts" who oppose the human rights amendment may pick up on this "realistic" suggestion to argue the merits of making decisions on a case-by-case basis. Nevertheless, recent cases can be cited (for example, Cambodia, Vietnam, Greece) where U.S. attempts to gain influence by supporting repressive regimes have backfired. We have shown a disturbing tendency in our pragmatic foreign policy to back the wrong horse, and when some current crises are resolved, they are likely to show that we have made the wrong bets again in Nicaragua and Iran.

## Promoting Other Goals

Turning now to consider the other, more publicized goal of the human rights movement, promoting respect for human rights by *other* governments, we confront a different set of objections. Some charge that this goal itself is indefensible, accusing the human rights movement of being moralistic or morally imperialistic for imposing American values abroad. . . .

To be moralistic is to be more than a very moral person, it is to make morality into a cause in an objectionable way. Although moralism usually applies to the practice of trying to make other people moral, there is also another sense in which a person can be moralistic. We sometimes think a person is moralistic who is unusually conscious about following moral principles in his or her own actions. We must not confuse this person with a person who is unusually moral, who could not harm a flea. A moralistic person makes morality itself a goal; he or she lets moral principles override even laudable natural tendencies. Thus, moralism in a person can be directed toward others, or it can be directed toward oneself. A moralistic person, especially when the moralism is self-directed, is mildly obsessive, and even though he or she may be harmless (though perhaps a bit cold or calculating), we do not normally think moralism is a good thing.

The human rights movement appears to its critics to be moralistic in both of the ways just described. It embodies self-directed moralism by making moral principles explicit goals of policy, in order to meet our own moral constraints, and it embodies crusading moralism by including in those goals the promotion of our moral values in other countries.

We have now isolated the issues that must be confronted in defending the strong human rights legislation against its critics. What are a government's positive duties? Do moralistic policies ask too much of nations in the same way and for the same reasons as they ask too much of individuals? I shall begin by responding to the charge of self-directed moralism. . . .

It is by overextending the analogy of governments with individuals that the promotion of human rights as a principal goal of a government's interaction with other governments appears excessively moralistic. If moralism is excessive, and if it interferes with our other goals as a nation, then it is wrong. But the analogy between a government and an individual human being is not complete enough to support this type of criticism. It is not reasonable to expect governments and persons to fulfill their responsibilities in the same way. A better way to extend the analogy would be to see a government as like a person, but a socially retarded one, who *can* do what he should, but only with effort and only in an entirely self-conscious way.

The charge of crusading moralism involves different issues, which raise questions about sovereignty and about the autonomy of individual nations and cultures to determine their own values. I shall begin responding to them by considering a case that involves only individuals.

Suppose someone has conclusive evidence that his neighbors are beating one of their children. This child is helpless, the parents show no signs of stopping the practice, and the other children—the only other members of the household—are too confused and frightened and perhaps too weak to do anything about it themselves. What is the knowledgeable neighbor's duty in such a case? It is obvious, I think, that for him to do nothing would be seriously wrong. Even though it is in some sense a family matter, this goes far beyond anything that could be dismissed as strictly as domestic concern. The knowledgeable neighbor might have legitimate qualms about barging in and rescuing the child, not the least of which might be a reasonable fear for his own safety. (We might even imagine that the child's father owns the store in which this man works so that it involves a serious risk for him even to mention it directly.) Fortunately, he has another alternative open to him; he may report the matter to the local police. They are able to take care of such matters, and to protect the informer's anonymity. He has an obligation at least to do this. If the neighbor happened also to be paying this family's rent, or giving them the food they need, or providing them with an automobile, he might by virtue of this more involved relationship have additional obligations to exert leverage on his own to stop the brutality.

How is this different from a case in which our government knows that another government is seriously violating the rights of its citizens? Child-beating is not just wrong, it is against the law; and socially sanctioned enforcement mechanisms carry out the law. These enforcement agencies do not exist on an international level, except in very weak and rudimentary forms. The offending father could not claim that child-beating is nobody else's business, for even if no individual neighbor has a legal duty to intervene, the police certainly do. And the neighbor has a moral, if not a legal, duty to inform the police that they are needed. Suppose that the father said he did not see anything so bad about his actions—that he thought this was the only way to instill discipline in a unruly child—and for that reason it is wrong of other people to impose their values on him. He is in fact mistaken about child-rearing, but that is not the essential point; what he did is both wrong and against the law, and the law applies to him. The wrongness of his act does not lie in what his neighbors simply happen to believe. The social consensus which makes it wrong, and which determines the values of society, is supported by social institutions and by common belief, as well as by facts about what causes harm or suffering. If a government made a similar claim about torturing its citizens, no matter how ridiculous the claim is, there is an important difference, since there is no comparable broader society of which that government is a part.

Such differences between these cases rest on two closely related claims. The first is that some moral principles apply to all the members of a society because they are the society's values. If this claim is to be noncontroversial, then in a broader sense it must apply to only those values that it would be extremely unlikely that anyone in the society would in fact deny. They must be such that if somebody does in fact deny them, we have more reason to wonder about the person than about the value. The second claim is that these values might not apply to all nations or societies, because individual societies are not organized and determined by any broader structure as the citizens within each society are.

The larger issue involved here is that of ethical relativism, the claim that no moral values are universal because all values are culturally determined and cultures are different. To my knowledge, however, it has never been demonstrated that cultures are in fact different enough to make the logical possibility of relativism into a moral thesis with any application. Regardless, the debate about moral relativism is simply not relevant here, for we could accept relativism as the correct moral theory and still rebut the charge that our foreign policy embodies crusading moralism. We need only to recognize that there are some positive duties, that somebody ought to come to the aid of the victims of oppressive governments. There is no question about evaluating types of governments and imposing the type we happen to like on other nations or cultures, not unless torturing and detaining political dissidents without trial are essential to some types of government that a culture supports.

Perhaps this is unfair to the critics of the human rights movement. After all, they are not committed to ignoring torture wherever it occurs in the world. The charge of crusading moralism does not have to rely on ethical relativism and does not have to deny that our nation has positive duties, even though some of the criticism of the legislation seems to imply these claims. The objection that the legislation is moralistic really questions whether the strong and explicit language of the laws—that one of our country's "principal goals" is to "promote increased observance" of certain values—is justifiable.

It is important to remember that the rights in question have been recognized by nearly all nations and have the status of international law. That status, however, is different from a status of domestic law in crucial respects. There is no comparable enforcement mechanism, no international police force with anywhere near the power or authority of domestic police.

The lack of a strong multilateral enforcement mechanism may not be a weakness of international law at all; there may be good reasons for not allowing such a police force to be formed. How would the scope of its authority be determined? To whom would it be accountable?

Most likely, some forms of multilateral enforcement of international law are possible and desirable, but to the extent that these are not sufficient means of enforcement the burden falls to individual governments to do what they can. Individual governments are working in a setting different from the setting of individuals within a society, and they must assume different sorts of responsibilities and duties. Because of the lack of socially sanctioned enforcement mechanisms at an international level, nations must assume the moral burden of using what leverage they can to enforce international law. Rigid provisions for action, built explicitly into a nation's laws, as in 502B, appear in this light to be reasonable ways to meet this requirement. If this means moralism in the international arena is necessary for the enforcement of international law, then there is nothing wrong with this kind of moralism.

Objections to the human rights legislation are increasing and the current laws will almost certainly be revised. My claim is that there is nothing wrong in principle with the stand the Congress has taken, and the question of the best strategy for promoting respect for human rights is an open one. There are other important considerations to keep in mind, as the critics often assert. The one I have emphasized is the legitimate goal of constraining what our government may do as it pursues the national interest.

**STUDY QUESTIONS**

1. Kissinger notes that the State Department has "generally opposed attempts to deal with sensitive international human rights issues through legislation, not because of the moral view expressed which we share, but because legislation is almost always too inflexible, too public and too heavyhanded a means to accomplish what it seeks." How does MacLean respond to these points? Do you find MacLean's response adequate? Discuss.

2. MacLean maintains that aiding a government that violates the rights of its citizens is like being in complicity with a neighbor that abuses a child. Is his analogy appropriate? In general, is it morally appropriate to judge a nation as one would judge an individual person?

3. MacLean talks of three cases (Cambodia, Greece, Vietnam) "where U.S. attempts to support repressive regimes have backfired." Discuss two such cases, analyzing his contention that generally an amoral expediency is counterproductive.
4. How do critics who favor constraint legislation deal with the point that because such legislation reflects Western values it is overly moralistic and culturally chauvinistic?

# Dictatorships and Double Standards

JEANE KIRKPATRICK

Jeane Kirkpatrick (b. 1926) is professor of government at Georgetown University. She was U.S. Ambassador to the United Nations from 1981–1985. *Dictatorships and Double Standards* (1981) is but one work among numerous articles and books Kirkpatrick has published.

Many countries under autocratic rule are politically friendly to the United States. Although internally there are elements that seek to overthrow the government, more often than not these revolutionary forces are Marxist (as in Nicaragua) and sometimes theocratic (as in Iran). In any such confrontation, liberal Americans tend to empathize with those seeking to oust the autocrats in power. They question the morality and wisdom of continuing to aid the incumbent government, and often they have "actually assisted the coming to power of new regimes in which ordinary people enjoy fewer freedoms and less personal security than under the previous autocracy—regimes moreover hostile to American interests and

DICTATORSHIPS AND DOUBLE STANDARDS By Jeane Kirkpatrick. Excerpt reprinted from *Commentary*, November 1979. By permission of the publisher and the author. All rights reserved.

policies." Jeane Kirkpatrick accuses President Jimmy Carter of having pursued a liberal policy of this kind, a policy that helps to depose a friendly ruler (the Shah, Samoza) and to install a regime hostile to America.

The liberals that Kirkpatrick speaks of are said by her to hold several beliefs:

1. that there are in fact democratic alternatives to the autocratic government they dislike;
2. that the status quo cannot be maintained;
3. that the ensuing government (albeit a Marxist one) must be preferable to the one in place.

Kirkpatrick believes that these three assumptions are generally false and that many liberal Americans tend to believe in them because of their "innocent conviction that it is possible to democratize governments anywhere, anytime, under any circumstances."

Kirkpatrick points out that most societies under autocratic regimes lack "the appropriate political culture" for quick democratic reform. Although a gradual reform may now be in progress in some countries (Brazil, Taiwan), a rapid democratic revolution is not to be hoped for as a general rule.

Given this state of affairs, Kirkpatrick argues that we should recognize that traditional right-wing authoritarian governments, however distasteful and harmful to the general population, are nevertheless generally *less* repressive than the revolutionary regimes that replace them. She cites Vietnam, Cambodia, and North Korea as examples of the latter. She also notes that China has been more repressive than Taiwan and North Korea more repressive than South Korea. Kirkpatrick points to the streams of refugees from the countries that have achieved their left-wing revolutions.

Traditional autocracies are repressive but in ways that respect local traditions, institutions, and the age-old habits of the population. True, such societies have masses of poor and those in power are very rich—but they create no refugees. Kirkpatrick argues that U.S. policy should encourage gradual democratization of such friendly

815

> right-wing autocracies but avoid such efforts at times
> "when the government is fighting for its life against vio-
> lent adversaries" who are usually anti-American. Kirk-
> patrick does not believe that her position is antiliberal or
> lacking in idealism. "Liberal idealism need not be identi-
> cal with masochism and need not be incompatible with
> the defense of freedom and the national interest."

The failure of the Carter administration's foreign policy is now clear
to everyone except its architects, and even they must entertain private
doubts, from time to time, about a policy whose crowning achievement has been to lay the groundwork for a transfer of the Panama
Canal from the United States to a swaggering Latin dictator of Cas-
troite bent. In the thirty-odd months since the inauguration of
Jimmy Carter as President there has occurred a dramatic Soviet military build-up, matched by the stagnation of American armed forces,
and a dramatic extension of Soviet influence in the Horn of Africa,
Afghanistan, Southern Africa, and the Caribbean, matched by a
declining American position in all these areas. The U.S. has never
tried so hard and failed so utterly to make and keep friends in the
Third World.

As if this were not bad enough, in the current year the United
States has suffered two other major blows—in Iran and Nicaragua—
of large and strategic significance. In each country, the Carter administration not only failed to prevent the undesired outcome, it actively
collaborated in the replacement of moderate autocrats friendly to
American interests with less friendly autocrats of extremist persuasion. It is too soon to be certain about what kind of regime will
ultimately emerge in either Iran or Nicaragua, but accumulating
evidence suggests that things are as likely to get worse as to get better
in both countries. The Sandinistas in Nicaragua appear to be as
skillful in consolidating power as the Ayatollah Khomeini is inept,
and leaders of both revolutions display an intolerance and arrogance
that do not bode well for the peaceful sharing of power or the establishment of constitutional governments, especially since those leaders
have made clear that they have no intention of seeking either.

. . . [N]o problem of American foreign policy is more urgent
than that of formulating a morally and strategically acceptable, and
politically realistic, program for dealing with non-democratic

governments who are threatened by Soviet-sponsored subversion. In the absence of such a policy, we can expect that the same reflexes that guided Washington in Iran and Nicaragua will be permitted to determine American actions from Korea to Mexico—with the same disastrous effects on the U.S. strategic position. (That the administration has not called its policies in Iran and Nicaragua a failure—and probably does not consider them such—complicates the problem without changing its nature.)

There were, of course, significant differences in the relations between the United States and each of these countries during the past two or three decades. Oil, size, and proximity to the Soviet Union gave Iran greater economic and strategic import than any Central American "republic," and closer relations were cultivated with the Shah, his counselors, and family than with President Somoza, his advisers, and family. Relations with the Shah were probably also enhanced by our approval of his manifest determination to modernize Iran regardless of the effects of modernization on traditional social and cultural patterns (including those which enhanced his own authority and legitimacy). And, of course, the Shah was much better looking and altogether more dashing than Somoza; his private life was much more romantic, more interesting to the media, popular and otherwise. Therefore, more Americans were more aware of the Shah than of the equally tenacious Somoza.

But even though Iran was rich, blessed with a product the U.S. and its allies needed badly, and led by a handsome king, while Nicaragua was poor and rocked along under a long-tenure president of less striking aspect, there were many similarities between the two countries and our relations with them. Both these small nations were led by men who had not been selected by free elections, who recognized no duty to submit themselves to searching tests of popular acceptability. Both did tolerate limited opposition, including opposition newspapers and political parties, but both were also confronted by radical, violent opponents bent on social and political revolution. Both rulers, therefore, sometimes invoked martial law to arrest, imprison, exile, and occasionally, it was alleged, torture their opponents. Both relied for public order on police forces whose personnel were said to be too harsh, too arbitrary, and too powerful. Each had what the American press termed "private armies," which is to say, armies pledging their allegiance to the ruler rather than the "constitution" or the "nation" or some other impersonal entity.

In short, both Somoza and the Shah were, in central ways, traditional rulers of semi-traditional societies. Although the Shah very badly wanted to create a technologically modern and powerful nation and Somoza tried hard to introduce modern agricultural methods, neither sought to reform his society in the light of any abstract idea of social justice or political virtue. Neither attempted to alter significantly the distribution of goods, status, or power (though the democratization of education and skills that accompanied modernization in Iran did result in some redistribution of money and power there).

Both Somoza and the Shah enjoyed long tenure, large personal fortunes (much of which were no doubt appropriated from general revenues), and good relations with the United States. The Shah and Somoza were not only anti-Communist, they were positively friendly to the U.S., sending their sons and others to be educated in our universities, voting with us in the United Nations, and regularly supporting American interests and positions even when these entailed personal and political cost. The embassies of both governments were active in Washington social life, and were frequented by powerful Americans who occupied major roles in this nation's diplomatic, military, and political life. And the Shah and Somoza themselves were both welcome in Washington, and had many American friends.

Though each of the rulers was from time to time criticized by American officials for violating civil and human rights, the fact that the people of Iran and Nicaragua only intermittently enjoyed the rights accorded to citizens in the Western democracies did not prevent successive administrations from granting—with the necessary approval of successive Congresses—both military and economic aid. In the case of both Iran and Nicaragua, tangible and intangible tokens of U.S. support continued until the regime became the object of a major attack by forces explicitly hostile to the United States.

But once an attack was launched by opponents bent on destruction, everything changed. The rise of serious, violent opposition in Iran and Nicaragua set in motion a succession of events which bore a suggestive resemblance to one another and a suggestive similarity to our behavior in China before the fall of Chiang Kai-shek, in Cuba before the triumph of Castro, in certain crucial periods of the Vietnamese war, and, more recently, in Angola. In each of these countries, the American effort to impose liberalization and democratization on a government confronted with violent internal opposition not only failed, but actually assisted the coming to power of new regimes in which ordinary people enjoy fewer freedoms and less personal security than under the previous autocracy—regimes, moreover, hostile to American interests and policies.

The pattern is familiar enough: an established autocracy with a record of friendship with the U.S. is attacked by insurgents, some of whose leaders have long ties to the Communist movement, and most of whose arms are of Soviet, Chinese, or Czechoslovak origin. The "Marxist" presence is ignored and/or minimized by American officials and by the elite media on the ground that U.S. support for the dictator gives the rebels little choice but to seek aid "elsewhere." Violence spreads and American officials wonder aloud about the viability of a regime that "lacks the support of its own people." The absence of an opposition party is deplored and civil-rights violations are reviewed. Liberal columnists question the morality of continuing aid to a "rightist dictatorship" and provide assurances concerning the essential moderation of some insurgent leaders who "hope" for some sign that the U.S. will remember its own revolutionary origins. Requests for help from the beleaguered autocrat go unheeded, and the argument is increasingly voiced that ties should be established with rebel leaders "before it is too late." The President, delaying U.S. aid, appoints a special emissary who confirms the deterioration of the government position and its diminished capacity to control the situation and recommends various measures for "strengthening" and "liberalizing" the regime, all of which involve diluting its power.

The emissary's recommendations are presented in the context of a growing clamor for American disengagement on grounds that continued involvement confirms our status as an agent of imperialism, racism, and reaction; is inconsistent with support for human rights; alienates us from the "forces of democracy"; and threatens to put the U.S. once more on the side of history's "losers." This chorus is supplemented daily by interviews with returning missionaries and "reasonable" rebels.

As the situation worsens, the President assures the world that the U.S. desires only that the "people choose their own form of government"; he blocks delivery of all arms to the government and undertakes negotiations to establish a "broadly based" coalition headed by a "moderate" critic of the regime who, once elevated, will move quickly to seek a "political" settlement to the conflict. Should the incumbent autocrat prove resistant to American demands that he step aside, he will be readily overwhelmed by the military strength of his opponents, whose patrons will have continued to provide sophisticated arms and advisers at the same time the U.S. cuts off military sales. Should the incumbent be so demoralized as to agree to yield power, he will be replaced by a "moderate" of American selection. Only after the insurgents have refused the proffered political solution and anarchy has spread throughout the nation will it be noticed that the new head of government has no significant following, no experience at governing, and no talent for leadership. By then, military commanders, no longer bound by loyalty to the chief of state, will depose the faltering "moderate" in favor of a fanatic of their own choosing.

In either case, the U.S. will have been led by its own misunderstanding of the situation to assist actively in deposing an erstwhile friend and ally and installing a government hostile to American interests and policies in the world. At best we will have lost access to friendly territory. At worst the Soviets will have gained a new base. And everywhere our friends will have noted that the U.S. cannot be counted on in times of difficulty and our enemies will have observed that American support provides no security against the forward march of history. . . .

[T]he Carter administration brought to the crises in Iran and Nicaragua several common assumptions each of which played a major role in hastening the victory of even more repressive dictatorships than had been in place before. These were, first, the belief that there existed at the moment of crisis a democratic alternative to the incumbent government; second, the belief that the continuation of the status quo was not possible; third, the belief that any change, including the establishment of a government headed by self-styled Marxist revolutionaries, was preferable to the present government. Each of these beliefs was (and is) widely shared in the liberal community generally. Not one of them can withstand close scrutiny.

Although most governments in the world are, as they always have been, autocracies of one kind or another, no idea holds greater sway in the mind of educated Americans than the belief that it is possible to democratize governments, anytime, anywhere, under any circumstances. This notion is belied by an enormous body of evidence based on the experience of dozens of countries which have attempted with more or less (usually less) success to move from autocratic to democratic government. Many of the wisest political scientists of this and previous centuries agree that democratic institutions are especially difficult to establish and maintain—because they make heavy demands on all portions of a population and because they depend on complex social, cultural, and economic conditions.

Two or three decades ago, when Marxism enjoyed its greatest prestige among American intellectuals, it was the economic prerequisites of democracy that were emphasized by social scientists. Democracy, they argued, could function only in relatively rich societies with an advanced economy, a substantial middle class, and a literate population, but it could be expected to emerge more or less automatically whenever these conditions prevailed. Today, this picture seems grossly over-simplified. While it surely helps to have an economy strong enough to provide decent levels of well-being for all, and "open" enough to provide mobility and encourage achievement, a pluralistic society and the right kind of political culture—and time— are even more essential.

In his essay on *Representative Government,* John Stuart Mill identified three fundamental conditions which the Carter administration would do well to ponder. These are: "One, that the people should be willing to receive it [representative government]; two, that they should be willing and able to do what is necessary for its preservation; three, that they should be willing and able to fulfill the duties and discharge the functions which it imposes on them."

Fulfilling the duties and discharging the functions of representative government make heavy demands on leaders and citizens, demands for participation and restraint, for consensus and compromise. It is not necessary for all citizens to be avidly interested in politics or well-informed about public affairs—although far more widespread interest and mobilization are needed than in autocracies. What *is* necessary is that a substantial number of citizens think of themselves as participants in society's decision-making and not simply as subjects bound by its laws. Moreover, leaders of all major sectors of the society must agree to pursue power only by legal means, must eschew (at least in principle) violence, theft, and fraud, and must accept defeat when necessary. They must also be skilled at finding and creating common ground among diverse points of view and interests, and correlatively willing to compromise on all but the most basic values.

In addition to an appropriate political culture, democratic government requires institutions strong enough to channel and contain conflict. Voluntary, non-official institutions are needed to articulate and aggregate diverse interests and opinions present in the society. Otherwise, the formal governmental institutions will not be able to translate popular demands into public policy.

In the relatively few places where they exist, democratic governments have come into being slowly, after extended prior experience with more limited forms of participation during which leaders have reluctantly grown accustomed to tolerating dissent and opposition, opponents have accepted the notion that they may defeat but not destroy incumbents, and people have become aware of government's effects on their lives and of their own possible effects on government. Decades, if not centuries, are normally required for people to acquire the necessary disciplines and habits. In Britain, the road from the Magna Carta to the Act of Settlement, to the great Reform Bills of 1832, 1867, and 1885, took seven centuries to traverse. American history gives no better grounds for believing that democracy comes easily, quickly, or for the asking. A war of independence, an unsuccessful constitution, a civil war, a long process of gradual enfranchisement marked our progress toward constitutional democratic government. The French path was still more difficult. Terror, dictatorship, monarchy, instability, and incompetence followed on the revolution that was to usher in a millennium of brotherhood. Only in the 20th century did the democratic principle finally gain wide acceptance in France and not until after World War II were the principles of order and democracy, popular sovereignty and authority, finally reconciled in institutions strong enough to contain conflicting currents of public opinion.

Although there is no instance of a revolutionary "socialist" or Communist society being democratized, right-wing autocracies do sometimes evolve into democracies—given time, propitious economic, social, and political circumstances, talented leaders, and a strong indigenous demand for representative government. Something of the kind is in progress on the Iberian peninsula and the first steps have been taken in Brazil. Something similar could conceivably have also occurred in Iran and Nicaragua if contestation and participation had been more gradually expanded.

But it seems clear that the architects of contemporary American foreign policy have little idea of how to go about encouraging the liberalization of an autocracy. In neither Nicaragua nor Iran did they realize that the only likely result of an effort to replace an incumbent autocrat with one of his moderate critics or a "broad-based coalition" would be to sap the foundations of the existing regime without moving the nation any closer to democracy. Yet this outcome was entirely predictable. Authority in traditional autocracies is transmitted through personal relations: from the ruler to his close associates (relatives, household members, personal friends) and from them to people to whom the associates are related by personal ties resembling their own relation to the ruler. The fabric of authority unravels quickly when the power and status of the man at the top are undermined or eliminated. The longer the autocrat has held power, and the more pervasive his personal influence, the more dependent a nation's institutions will be on him. Without him, the organized life of the society will collapse, like an arch from which the keystone has been removed. The blend of qualities that bound the Iranian army to the Shah or the national guard to Somoza is typical of the relationships—personal, hierarchical, non-transferable—that support a traditional autocracy. The speed with which armies collapse, bureaucracies abdicate, and social structures dissolve once the autocrat is removed frequently surprises American policy-makers and journalists accustomed to public institutions based on universalistic norms rather than particularistic relations.

The failure to understand these relations is one source of the failure of U.S. policy in this and previous administrations. There are others. In Iran and Nicaragua (as previously in Vietnam, Cuba, and China) Washington overestimated the political diversity of the opposition—especially the strength of "moderates" and "democrats" in the opposition movement; underestimated the strength and intransigence of radicals in the movement; and misestimated the nature and extent of American influence on both the government and the opposition.

Confusion concerning the character of the opposition, especially its intransigence and will to power, leads regularly to downplaying the amount of force required to counteract its violence. In neither Iran nor Nicaragua did the U.S. adequately appreciate the government's problem in maintaining order in a society confronted with an ideologically extreme opposition. Yet the presence of such groups was well known. . . .

What *is* the function of foreign policy under these conditions? It is to understand the processes of change and then, like Marxists, to align ourselves with history, hoping to contribute a bit of stability along the way. And this, administration spokesmen assure us, is precisely what we are doing. The Carter administration has defined the U.S. national interest in the Third World as identical with the putative end of the modernization process. Vance put this with characteristic candor in a recent statement when he explained that U.S. policy vis-à-vis the Third World is "grounded in the conviction that we best serve our interest there by supporting the efforts of developing nations to advance their economic well-being and preserve their political independence." Our "commitment to the promotion of constructive change worldwide" (Brzezinski's words) has been vouchsafed in every conceivable context.

But there is a problem. The conceivable contexts turn out to be mainly those in which non-Communist autocracies are under pressure from revolutionary guerrillas. Since Moscow is the aggressive, expansionist power today, it is more often than not insurgents, encouraged and armed by the Soviet Union, who challenge the status quo. The American commitment to "change" in the abstract ends up by aligning us tacitly with Soviet clients and irresponsible extremists like the Ayatollah Khomeini or, in the end, Yasir Arafat.

Inconsistencies are a familiar part of politics in most societies. Usually, however, governments behave hypocritically when their principles conflict with the national interest. What makes the inconsistencies of the Carter administration noteworthy are, first, the administration's moralism—which renders it especially vulnerable to charges of hypocrisy; and, second, the administration's predilection for policies that violate the strategic and economic interests of the United States. The administration's conception of national interest borders on doublethink: it finds friendly powers to be guilty representatives of the status quo and views the triumph of unfriendly groups as beneficial to America's "true interests."

This logic is quite obviously reinforced by the prejudices and preferences of many administration officials. Traditional autocracies are, in general and in their very nature, deeply offensive to modern American sensibilities. The notion that public affairs should be ordered on the basis of kinship, friendship, and other personal relations rather than on the basis of objective "rational" standards violates our conception of justice and efficiency. The preference for stability rather than change is also disturbing to Americans whose whole national experience rests on the principles of change, growth, and progress. The extremes of wealth and poverty characteristic of traditional societies also offend us, the more so since the poor are usually *very* poor and bound to their squalor by a hereditary allocation of role. Moreover, the relative lack of concern of rich, comfortable rulers for the poverty, ignorance, and disease of "their" people is likely to be interpreted by Americans as moral dereliction pure and simple. The truth is that Americans can hardly bear such societies and such rulers. Confronted with them, our vaunted cultural relativism evaporates and we become as censorious as Cotton Mather confronting sin in New England.

But if the politics of traditional and semi-traditional autocracy is nearly antithetical to our own—at both the symbolic and the operational level—the rhetoric of progressive revolutionaries sounds much better to us; their symbols are much more acceptable. One reason that some modern Americans prefer "socialist" to traditional autocracies is that the former have embraced modernity and have adopted modern modes and perspectives, including an instrumental, manipulative, functional orientation toward most social, cultural, and personal affairs; a profession of universalistic norms; an emphasis on reason, science, education, and progress; a deemphasis of the sacred; and "rational," bureaucratic organizations. They speak our language.

Because socialism of the Soviet/Chinese/Cuban variety is an ideology rooted in a version of the same values that sparked the Enlightenment and the democratic revolutions of the 18th century; because it is modern and not traditional; because it postulates goals that appeal to Christian as well as to secular values (brotherhood of man, elimination of power as a mode of human relations), it is highly congenial to many Americans at the symbolic level. Marxist revolutionaries speak the language of a hopeful future while traditional autocrats speak the language of an unattractive past. Because left-wing revolutionaries invoke the symbols and values of democracy— emphasizing eglitarianism rather than hierarchy and privilege, liberty rather than order, activity rather than passivity—they are again and again accepted as partisans in the cause of freedom and democracy.

Nowhere is the affinity of liberalism, Christianity, and Marxist socialism more apparent than among liberals who are "duped" time

825

after time into supporting "liberators" who turn out to be totalitarians, and among Left-leaning clerics whose attraction to a secular style of "redemptive community" is stronger than their outrage at the hostility of socialist regimes to religion. In Jimmy Carter— egalitarian, optimist, liberal, Christian—the tendency to be repelled by frankly non-democratic rulers and hierarchical societies is almost as strong as the tendency to be attracted to the idea of popular revolution, liberation, and progress. Carter is, *par excellence,* the kind of liberal most likely to confound revolution with idealism, change with progress, optimism with virtue. . . .

The President continues to behave . . .—not like a man who abhors autocrats but like one who abhors only right-wing autocrats.

In fact, high officials in the Carter administration understand better than they seem to the aggressive, expansionist character of contemporary Soviet behavior in Africa, the Middle East, Southeast Asia, the Indian Ocean, Central America, and the Caribbean. But although the Soviet/Cuban role in Grenada, Nicaragua, and El Salvador (plus the transfer of MIG-23's to Cuba) had already prompted resumption of surveillance of Cuba (which in turn confirmed the presence of a Soviet combat brigade), the President's eagerness not to "heat up" the climate of public opinion remains stronger than his commitment to speak the truth to the American people. His statement on Nicaragua clearly reflects these priorities:

> It's a mistake for Americans to assume or to claim that every time an evolutionary change takes place in this hemisphere that somehow it's a result of secret, massive Cuban intervention. The fact in Nicaragua is that the Somoza regime lost the confidence of the people. To bring about an orderly transition there, our effort was to let the people of Nicaragua ultimately make the decision on who would be their leader—what form of government they should have.

This statement, which presumably represents the President's best thinking on the matter, is illuminating. Carter's effort to dismiss concern about military events in this specific country as a manifestation of a national proclivity for seeing "Cuban machinations" under every bed constitutes a shocking effort to falsify reality. There was no question in Nicaragua of "evolutionary change" or of attributing such change to Castro's agents. There was only a question about the appropriate U.S. response to a military struggle in a country whose location gives it strategic importance out of proportion to its size or strength.

But that is not all. The rest of the President's statement graphically illustrates the blinding power of ideology on his interpretation of events. When he says that "the Somoza regime lost the confidence of the people," the President implies that the regime had previously rested on the confidence of "the people," but that the situation had now changed. In fact, the Somoza regime had never rested on popular will (but instead on manipulation, force, and habit), and was not being ousted by it. It was instead succumbing to arms and soldiers. However, the assumption that the armed conflict of Sandinistas and Somozistas was the military equivalent of a national referendum enabled the President to imagine that it could be, and should be, settled by the people of Nicaragua. For this pious sentiment even to seem true the President would have had to be unaware that insurgents were receiving a great many arms from other non-Nicaraguans; and that the U.S. had played a significant role in disarming the Somoza regime.

The President's mistakes and distortions are all fashionable ones. His assumptions are those of people who want badly to be on the progressive side in conflicts between "rightist" autocracy and "leftist" challenges, and to prefer the latter, almost regardless of the probable consequences.

To be sure, neither the President, nor Vance, nor Brzezinski *desires* the proliferation of Soviet-supported regimes. Each has asserted his disapproval of Soviet "interference" in the modernization process. But each, nevertheless, remains willing to "destabilize" friendly or neutral autocracies without any assurance that they will not be replaced by reactionary totalitarian theocracies, totalitarian Soviet client states, or worst of all, by murderous fanatics of the Pol Pot variety.

The foreign policy of the Carter administration fails not for lack of good intentions but for lack of realism about the nature of traditional versus revolutionary autocracies and the relation of each to the American national interest. Only intellectual fashion and the tyranny of Right/Left thinking prevent intelligent men of good will from perceiving the *facts* that traditional authoritarian governments are less repressive than revolutionary autocracies, that they are more susceptible of liberalization, and that they are more compatible with U.S. interests. The evidence on all these points is clear enough.

Surely it is now beyond reasonable doubt that the present governments of Vietnam, Cambodia, Laos are much more repressive than those of the despised previous rulers; that the government of the People's Republic of China is more repressive than that of Taiwan, that North Korea is more repressive than South Korea, and so forth. This is the most important lesson of Vietnam and Cambodia. It is not new but it is a gruesome reminder of harsh facts.

From time to time a truly bestial ruler can come to power in either type of autocracy—Idi Amin, Papa Doc Duvalier, Joseph Stalin, Pol Pot are examples—but neither type regularly produces such moral monsters (though democracy regularly prevents their accession to power). There are, however, *systemic* differences between traditional and revolutionary autocracies that have a predictable effect on their degree of repressiveness. Generally speaking, traditional autocrats tolerate social inequities, brutality, and poverty while revolutionary autocracies create them.

Traditional autocrats leave in place existing allocations of wealth, power, status, and other resources which in most traditional societies favor an affluent few and maintain masses in poverty. But they worship traditional gods and observe traditional taboos. They do not disturb the habitual rhythms of work and leisure, habitual places of residence, habitual patterns of family and personal relations. Because the miseries of traditional life are familiar, they are bearable to ordinary people who, growing up in the society, learn to cope, as children born to untouchables in India acquire the skills and attitudes necessary for survival in the miserable roles they are destined to fill. Such societies create no refugees.

Precisely the opposite is true of revolutionary Communist regimes. They create refugees by the million because they claim jurisdiction over the whole life of the society and make demands for change that so violate internalized values and habits that inhabitants flee by the tens of thousands in the remarkable expectation that their attitudes, values, and goals will "fit" better in a foreign country than in their native land.

The former deputy chairman of Vietnam's National Assembly from 1976 to his defection early in August 1979, Hoang Van Hoan, described recently the impact of Vietnam's ongoing revolution on that country's more than one million Chinese inhabitants:

> They have been expelled from places they have lived in for generations.
> They have been dispossessed of virtually all possessions—their lands,

their houses. They have been driven into areas called new economic zones, but they have not been given any aid.

How can they eke out a living in such conditions reclaiming new land? They gradually die for a number of reasons—diseases, the hard life. They also die of humiliation.

It is not only the Chinese who have suffered in Southeast Asia since the "liberation," and it is not only in Vietnam that the Chinese suffer. By the end of 1978 more than six million refugees had fled countries ruled by Marxist governments. In spite of walls, fences, guns, and sharks, the steady stream of people fleeing revolutionary utopias continues.

There is a damning contrast between the number of refugees created by Marxist regimes and those created by other autocracies: more than a million Cubans have left their homeland since Castro's rise (one refugee for every nine inhabitants) as compared to about 35,000 each from Argentina, Brazil, and Chile. In Africa more than five times as many refugees have fled Guinea and Guinea Bissau as have left Zimbabwe Rhodesia, suggesting that civil war and racial discrimination are easier for most people to bear than Marxist-style liberation.

Moreover, the history of this century provides no grounds for expecting that radical totalitarian regimes will transform themselves. At the moment there is a far greater likelihood of progressive liberalization and democratization in the governments of Brazil, Argentina, and Chile than in the government of Cuba; in Taiwan than in the People's Republic of China; in South Korea than in North Korea; in Zaire than in Angola; and so forth.

Since many traditional autocracies permit limited contestation and participation, it is not impossible that U.S. policy could effectively encourage this process of liberalization and democratization, provided that the effort is not made at a time when the incumbent government is fighting for its life against violent adversaries, and that proposed reforms are aimed at producing gradual change rather than perfect democracy overnight. To accomplish this, policymakers are needed who understand how actual democracies have actually come into being. History is a better guide than good intentions.

A realistic policy which aims at protecting our own interest and assisting the capacities for self-determination of less developed nations will need to face the unpleasant fact that, if victorious, violent insurgency headed by Marxist revolutionaries is unlikely to lead to anything but totalitarian tyranny. Armed intellectuals citing Marx and supported by Soviet-bloc arms and advisers will almost surely not turn out to be agrarian reformers, or simple nationalists, or democratic socialists. However incomprehensible it may be to some, Marxist revolutionaries are not contemporary embodiments of the Americans who wrote the Declaration of Independence, and they will not be content with establishing a broad-based coalition in which they have only one voice among many.

It may not always be easy to distinguish between democratic and totalitarian agents of change, but it is also not too difficult. Authentic democratic revolutionaries aim at securing governments based on the consent of the governed and believe that ordinary men are capable of using freedom, knowing their own interest, choosing rulers. They do not, like the current leaders in Nicaragua, assume that it will be necessary to postpone elections for three to five years during which time they can "cure" the false consciousness of almost everyone.

If, moreover, revolutionary leaders describe the United States as the scourge of the 20th century, the enemy of freedom-loving people, the perpetrator of imperialism, racism, colonialism, genocide, war, then they are not authentic democrats or, to put it mildly, friends. Groups which define themselves as enemies should be treated as enemies. The United States is not in fact a racist, colonial power, it does not practice genocide, it does not threaten world peace with expansionist activities. In the last decade especially we have practiced remarkable forbearance everywhere and undertaken the "unilateral restraints on defense spending" recommended by Brzezinski as appropriate for the technetronic era. We have also moved further, faster, in eliminating domestic racism than any multiracial society in the world or in history.

For these reasons and more, a posture of continuous self-abasement and apology vis-à-vis the Third World is neither morally necessary or politically appropriate. No more is it necessary or appropriate to support vocal enemies of the United States because they invoke the rhetoric of popular liberation. It is not even necessary or appropriate for our leaders to forswear unilaterally the use of military force to counter military force. Liberal idealism need not be identical with masochism, and need not be incompatible with the defense of freedom and the national interest.

**STUDY QUESTIONS**

1. It is part of being moral to be socially responsible and sensitive to peoples all over the world. This sort of responsibility is especially felt by those who live well and under good governments. Assuming this to be so, what is the general import of Kirkpatrick's article? How does it affect the possibility of helping the poor and oppressed in foreign countries?

2. What does Kirkpatrick seem to mean by the "national interest"? She appears to be suggesting that we pursue the national interest even where this helps keep oppressive governments in power. Is national self-interest an adequate justification for this policy?

3. Kirkpatrick claims that her views are not incompatible with liberal idealism. Do you agree? Discuss.

4. Has Kirkpatrick appeared to have accurately characterized the beliefs of liberals? If she has, do her conclusions follow that aid should be continued to friendly right-wing dictatorships?

5. Does Kirkpatrick's view toward the fate of the underprivileged populations in the autocracies of which she speaks strike you as callous? If so, what would be your personal constructive approach to helping such populations? Consider also Kirkpatrick's arguments that "reform" could lead to disintegration and even greater oppression.

6. Do you agree with Kirkpatrick that Americans are foolish to believe it is possible to democratize governments anytime, anywhere, and under any circumstances? Discuss.

# *Why Democracies Fail*

## JEAN-FRANÇOIS REVEL

Jean-François Revel (b. 1924) is a French journalist and philosopher. He is the author of several books including a multivolume history of philosophy, *Without Marx or Jesus*, and *How Democracies Perish* (1983).

Jean-François Revel is dismayed by the destructive and unfair criticisms that liberal citizens of Western democracies direct against their own governments, especially in the United States. The criticism are destructive because they play into the hands of the arch rival of Western democracy, the Soviet Union. Such criticisms sap our will to stand up for the forces that are friendly to the West. Such criticisms are unfair because the moral faults of the United States are relatively minor in light of what happens when U.S. policy fails and left-wing totalitarian governments come to power.

International communism helps to orchestrate Western self-criticism. In third-world countries, international communism "uses peoples' aspirations to well-being, freedom, dignity and independence to eliminate the democracies."

Revel carefully analyzes the particular style of destructive self-criticism that is fashionable among liberal intellectuals in the West. A major technique is to admit the existence of Communist crimes and failures but instantly

WHY DEMOCRACIES FAIL Excerpted from *How Democracies Perish* by Jean-François Revel. Translated by William Byran. Translation © copyright 1984 by Doubleday, a division of Bantam, Doubleday, Dell Publishing Group, Inc. Reprinted by permission of the publisher.

to match these by "equivalent" crimes committed by the democratic West. "Communism is now absolved not because it never sins but because the democracies sin as grievously." Revel shows how the critics of democracies use tortuous reasoning to conclude that the democracies are *at least* as responsible as the communists for the evils of the world. Moreover, the communist world is deemed less guilty since the sufferings by communists are considered to be temporary lapses on the way to a utopian society.

According to Revel, the worst excesses and horrors of the left come from its utopian zeal. In Cambodia nearly one-third of the population was slaughtered systematically by a handful of ideologues who sought to purify their society of all capitalist traces. However, left-wing utopian radicalism is attractive to the poor and ignorant in many countries who have no idea of what the attempt to achieve a utopian society portends for them.

Revel pleads for the Western liberals to be alert to the damage they cause by their acts of balancing and equating the evils of the two rival worlds. By denouncing capitalist misdeeds, Western liberals help stir dissension and sometimes successful revolution in the democratic world. Of course, such is not the case in the totalitarian camp, where effective dissension is precluded by the full control of all communication. And once achieved, a totalitarian revolution can never be undone. "The communist world is seriously challenged only from the outside—and then how flabbily!" Revel warns that to continue to lump the evils of the two worlds together "is to send democracies to their graves."

Self-criticism is one of the vital springs of democratic civilization and one of the reasons for its superiority over all other systems. But constant self-condemnation, often with little or no foundation, is a source of weakness and inferiority in dealing with an imperial power that has dispensed with such scruples. Believing it is always right, even when the facts say it's wrong, is as blinding and weakening to a society as to an individual. But assuming it is always wrong, whatever the truth may be, is discouraging and paralyzing. Not only do the democracies today blame themselves for sins they have not committed, but they have formed the habit of judging themselves by ideals so inaccessible that the defendants are automatically guilty. It follows that a civilization that feels guilty for everything it is and does and thinks will lack the energy and conviction to defend itself when its existence is threatened. Drilling into a civilization that it deserves defending only if it can incarnate absolute justice is tantamount to urging that it let itself die or be enslaved.

For this is really what's at stake. Exaggerated self-criticism would be a harmless luxury of civilization if there were no enemy at the gate condemning democracy's very existence. But it becomes dangerous when it portrays its mortal enemy as always being in the right. Extravagant criticism is a good propaganda device in internal politics. But if it is repeated often enough, it is finally believed. And where will the citizens of democratic societies find reasons to resist the enemy outside if they are persuaded from childhood that their civilization is merely an accumulation of failures and a monstrous imposture?

. . .

When the West tries to protect archaic regimes or those of "modernistic authoritarians" like the Shah of Iran from disintegration or attempts to restrain their abuses, it cannot help seeming to defend the right against the left, the past against the future, the billionaires against the poverty-stricken masses. The fact that when the Communist left overturns the right it brings with it rampant famine, the camps and the boat people, that it is the left of Cambodian genocide and Khomeini's firing squads, never works as a *preventive*. If the West tries to pressure an archaic regime into becoming more liberal, either it is accused of "interference" by outraged nationalists or its well-meaning proselytizing shoves the country into unforeseeable chaos, as exemplified by the Islamic revolution in Iran. And while the ayatollahs' bloody terror may now be partly anti-Communist, for essentially religious reasons, the Kremlin knows very well that in the long run, when the brink of the pit of anarchy is reached, Iran may topple into the Soviet camp, but it is unlikely ever again to tip back over into the free world.

The Soviet Union's advantage over the free world is that neither world opinion nor, of course, its own muzzled public expects it to preach to its allies before associating with them or to hold on to its satellites by any way but sheer force; it is not even required to provide enough food for the peoples it absorbs into its imperial system.

But "international opinion"—the phrase describes part of the free countries' public opinion plus Soviet propaganda—will not accept violation of the rules of democracy by the West's friends. Even when such countries as Taiwan, South Korea, Malaysia and Singapore develop thriving economies that most other nations in the Third World envy and that would bring cries of admiration from the Western left if they blossomed under Soviet banners, they are not appreciated. For they have curtailed their citizens' freedom. The socialist regimes, of course, have obliterated freedom without even achieving comparable prosperity.

The hostility toward the United States inspired in men of goodwill by the horrors of the Vietnamese War is understandable. Yet we now see that the regime that won the war, with help from the Russians, the Chinese and world opinion, was the worst possible for the Vietnamese, for their neighbors, for the independence of Vietnam and the countries around it, for human rights and an adequate standard of living, and for peace in the area. Had the United States won, South Vietnam would doubtless have been subjected to the "imposed democracy" experienced in Japan after World War II—and which has not done too badly by the Japanese. But the Russians would probably have maintained terrorism there and a prosperous South Vietnam would be disturbed by demonstrations against "imperialist domination" and for "the liberation of Vietnam." The demonstrations would spread to the rest of the world, especially to the United States.

International communism uses peoples' aspirations to well-being, freedom, dignity and independence to eliminate the democracies. It is not afterward compelled to satisfy these aspirations; it merely safeguards its own political and strategic interests. The free world, on the other hand, seems not to have the right to consider *its* own political and strategic interests unless it has first fulfilled all the other conditions—has instituted social justice, political democracy and economic prosperity. It is very practiced at this and tries to meet the terms whenever it can.

When the democracies do take on a reactionary regime as an ally, it is not at all because they prefer such governments or even because they need it to realize their primary objective. This contradiction is a source of perpetual trouble; it makes the democracies vulnerable to hostile propaganda and is often a prelude to the worst kind of political upheavals. Whenever possible, the West much prefers that the countries on which its security depends be democratic. Unfortunately, this is not always possible. . . .

Almost throughout the twentieth century, the politically cross-eyed left in the democracies has unsheathed its fury only against the crimes of the capitalist world. Around 1970, the amnesia that periodically rejected unsavory disclosures about the Communist world began to show cracks. Telltale scars remained after each new cleansing absolution. Soon the mass of facts grew too dense to deny out of hand. This is when the lumping-together hoax was devised.

It consists of admitting the existence of Communist crimes and failures provided these can instantly be matched by equivalents in the capitalist world. Binary obsession, apocalyptic symmetry, mania for linkage, fussy egalitarianism—all working to see to it that both pans of the scale hold exactly balanced doses of horror. They are zealously checked and, when necessary, readjusted with a sly flick of the finger to maintain their absolute equilibrium. Communism is now absolved not because it never sins but because the democracies sin as grievously.

In this new dialectical game, everyone is free, without necessarily being dishonest, to retail the misdeeds and ailings of totalitarian communism, but on condition that we hasten to present their capitalist twins. Any derogation from the rule is immediately vilified as "selective indignation" and earns the cheat the severe censure of impartial players. A serene mind is obliged, as soon as it observes a flaw or social sore behind the iron, bamboo, sable, sugarcane or coconut-palm curtains, to scramble to find the thug charged with seeing to it that a matching canker is pinpointed on this side of the silver curtain, in the capitalist sphere.

The lumping-together technique is really just the modern way to routinize communism and grant it a plenary indulgence. When everyone is equally guilty, no one is, with the possible exception of capitalism, which does not, after all, have the same excuses to plead as a rival that will not share its concern for building a more just society.

For example, a doctrinally pure French socialist, Louis Mermaz,

President of the National Assembly since 1981, replied to a reporter's question about the gulags, "I am as horrified as you are by the gulags, which are a perversion of communism. But I ask that you also condemn that monstrosity of the capitalist system: hunger throughout the world that kills fifty million people each year, thirty million of them children."[1] The retort, remarkable for its speed, is less so for its objectivity. For the parallel is only apparent: the gulags are a "perversion" of communism, but famine, according to the Socialist leader, is a product of the basic nature of capitalism. And while the magic of parallelism makes the Communist sin almost venial, that of capitalism remains mortal. Indeed, absolution is usually a one-way grant—to forgive the horrors of communism. It seems unlikely that, if questioned on famine in the world, Mermaz would have replied with a diatribe against the gulags; he would have protested violently against the shocking malnutrition of some of our fellow humans, and he would have been right. That the gulags exist does not make Third World poverty any less morally intolerable. But by what sorcery is the reverse true?

Besides, the magician was using phony statistics. As demographers know, some fifty million people die in the world every year. They can't all die of starvation, and three fifths of them can't be children. The fight against infant mortality in the poor countries has reduced its incidence, which is why their populations are increasing. Nutritionists estimate the number of deaths annually due to malnutrition at 10 percent of the total, *and this includes the Communist countries,* which slightly weakens the indictment of capitalism. Starvation deaths in the Communist world may be better hidden, but the victims are just as dead as any others. Mao's successors have confirmed what demographers had already determined from their study of Chinese population patterns: that some sixty million Chinese died of starvation in 1960–70. . . .

Historically, capitalism has in fact rid Europe of the periodic famines that plagued it until the middle of the eighteenth century, as they now do in the less developed countries. It has even begun to relieve starvation in some of the poorer countries, India and Brazil, for example, which now export foodstuffs. Much, enormously much remains to be done everywhere before all mankind can enjoy the

---

[1] The statement was made during radio station Europe 1's "Press Club" program on July 5, 1981.

high nutritional standard that not even the capitalist West reached until the nineteenth century. But this problem has nothing whatever to do with the question at issue: the deliberate creation by an organized political regime of a repressive concentration-camp system that doubles as a system of government.

Whatever conclusions we may come to on these matters, the truth is that the lumping-together process is designed to make evil relative—which, in the last analysis, means to excuse it. The procedure also implies tailor-made interpretations of available data, and this must lead to error and prevarication: you cannot artifically equate events and faults that are rarely comparable without jerryrigging the facts.

When a political-science professor entitles his article on El Salvador "A Western Cambodia?"[2] not even the question mark saves it from being a soothing balm to many of his readers. The genocide by the Khmer Rouge Communists in Cambodia daubed socialism with a stain that no socialist laundering, however "perverted," can wash away. By suggesting, even tentatively, that the West is saddling itself with a Cambodia in Latin America, the article restores the balance. Communism is not the only guilty party. Everybody back to square one. The weakness in this Solomonic impartiality lies in the author's almost total ignorance of the situation in El Salvador or his refusal to learn about it. It is not discounting the deaths there to point out that, fortunately, there have been far fewer of them in Cambodia. Moreover, seldom have two historical situations been more different than the genocide in Cambodia and the civil war in El Salvador.

In Cambodia, a fourth to a third of the population was methodically exterminated by a handful of ideologists who aimed to purify their society by restricting it to people who knew nothing about capitalism, money, consumption or culture. We sometimes forget to cite one of the most effective of the many ways mankind has found to commit suicide: utopia. This has no part in the Salvadoran civil war, which, if we can speak this way of human suffering, had far more "classic" causes. Again, no one is trying here to minimize or excuse or accuse, only to understand. But this is precisely what we are prevented from doing by obsessive attempts to use El Salvador

---

[2]By Maurice Duverger in *Le Monde*, 15 January 1981.

as a rag to wipe away the stain of Cambodia. And that of Afghanistan, another case with which the Central American problem cannot be compared. The stubborn pursuit of equivalences has led some excellent politicians to willfully neglect available information about El Salvador. Hence their disappointment at the fact that elections there have been held as regularly as possible, under close international observation; their chagrin has been deepened by the results of these elections, for which the voters have turned out in force to show unequivocally that the rebels have only minority support in the tiny country. This is mortifying. No one likes to see his theories upset by the facts; the tendency is to avoid this by deforming those facts still more. Example: the Socialist International, meeting in Bonn, rejected the election held in El Salvador on March 28, 1982, as "manipulated." Whatever else might be said about that election, it is for once impossible to allege it was faked. If it had been, the incumbent government would not have been defeated. . . .

[M]ost people in the democracies and the "nonaligned" nations sincerely believe the United States alone was responsible for the military coup d'état against Socialist President Salvador Allende in September 1973; especially important is the fact that *non*-Communist opinion believes it (for the real Communists, the professionals, know perfectly well what really happened). They further believe that the United States single-handedly supports and maintains Pinochet in power, blocking any chance for a return to democracy in Chile just as, again, the Soviets are propping up Jaruzelski in Poland and Karmal in Afghanistan. As usual, the West loses by the comparison, but in Chile it was in a non-win situation anyway.

When the military coup got under way, Allende, who was already guilty of a number of illegalities and who was opposed by the majority of Chileans, could only hang on to power by suspending the Chilean constitution and modeling his regime on Castro's—something he had long since been heading toward. Had he succeeded, Chile would have entered the Soviet orbit while the West looked on impotently as its sphere of influence shrank. When he lost, the West was blamed for his fall. And because the Army won the final shoot-out when it took Allende's Castroists by surprise, the West lost on different grounds: it was charged with having

assassinated a democracy and its President, which discredits its alleged fight against totalitarianism.[3]

As a rule, then, if the Soviets succeed in taking over a country, they
score a net gain; if they destabilize it but fail to control it and cannot
install a client dictator there, the story is that they were defeated by a
"rightist plot" and the democracies are seen as reactionaries. Why is
the West so viewed? Because of a widespread sophism that identifies
the forces holding communism in check in any country as invariably
being creatures of the West, particularly of the United States. Either
the democracies lose the battle on the ground or they lose on the
propaganda front, which includes their own public opinion; this
inevitably weakens them and paves the totalitarians' way to future
victories.

A dictatorship like Pinochet's is infinitely more useful to the Soviet
Union than a bland, Western-style democracy. It is the most valuable
of allies because the Communists' bête noire, their worst enemy, is a
capitalistic, welfare democracy that works reasonably well. A rightist dictatorship is a redoubtable weapon for the Soviets to wield in
subverting the democracies everywhere in the world: if they succeed
in their subversion, they rack up another satellite; if they fail, they
have at least created the conditions for a rightist dictatorship that, for
years afterward, their propagandists can throw in the West's face.
What makes this weapon so effective is that these dictatorships *really
are* evil; the Soviet Union has only to insist that they exist by the will
and design of the free world[4]. . . .

Although I have come to believe that a capitalist society does far
less harm than totalitarian systems do, I want to assume for purposes

---

[3]A referendum, for which machinery existed in the constitution, could have settled
the conflict between the majority of the population and the "illegalists" who favored
outright radicalization of the regime and who pushed Allende toward Castroism. All
through 1972 and most of 1973 the President refused to call a referendum because he
knew he would lose it. When he finally made up his mind to it, on September 10,
1973, it was too late. The coup d'état took place September 11.

[4]During the summer of 1983 Augusto Pinochet's autocratic power began to be seriously shaken by political opponents and street demonstrations. In spite of a callous
and bloody repression Pinochet was unable to completely curb the wave of protest and
the move of the country toward change. The process of return to democracy had
begun in Chile. These events show once more the difference between the "classical"
dictatorships of the military-fascist type and the true totalitarian systems. The former
must, sooner or later, accept a process of liberalization or be overthrown from within.
The latter is devoid of any capability of self-transformation to a democratic regime
and is much better equipped to resist and suppress any kind of internal opposition.

of demonstration that they are equally guilty. My aim is not to prove that either of the two worlds is better than the other but to show how and why one of them is devouring the other—never mind now whether for better or worse. And I conclude that even the assumption of equal weight for the failures, errors and crimes committed in both worlds automatically grants an advantage to the totalitarian side.

The reason for this is that any denunciation of capitalist misdeeds stirs dissension, crises, dispute, sometimes rebellion and revolution in the democratic world. Such is not the case in the totalitarian camp. Even supposing all things equal—which they are not—the capitalist world comes under ceaseless attack from within and without. The Communist world is seriously challenged only from outside, and then how flabbily! Because of the effectiveness of its totalitarian instruments of defense, communism far more easily suppresses domestic challenges, usually has little difficulty in parrying those from abroad, and, most important, never has to deal with both at once, which is its key formula for undermining the West. Thus, for its smallest weakness, for any flaw of which the totalitarians are equally guilty, democracy pays twice the basic price that Communist dictatorships pay. To lump them together, then, is to send the democracies to their grave.

**STUDY QUESTIONS**

1. Compose a discussion between a right-wing critic of the Soviet Union and a liberal American, seeking to be fair to both sides. What characteristic moves does the critic make? What characteristic moves does the liberal apologist make? Now discuss what Revel makes of the discussion.
2. Compare Revel's critique of the liberal left with that of Jeane Kirkpatrick. Are they essentially the same? How do they differ?
3. Revel obviously thinks that looking for utopia is dangerous, yet admits the world is imperfect. What kind of criticism and reform *would* be acceptable to Revel?

# Totalitarianism vs. Authoritarianism

## MICHAEL WALZER

Michael Walzer (b. 1935) is professor of social science at the Institute for Advanced Study at Princeton University. Prior to this appointment, Walzer was a member of the faculty of the Government Department at Harvard University. Among his books are *Just and Unjust Wars* (1977), *Radical Principles* (1980), and *Interpretation and Social Criticism* (1987).

Calling them "cold warriors," Michael Walzer challenges such right-wing critics as Jeane Kirkpatrick and Jean-François Revel, who distinguish sharply between authoritarian governments that do not intervene in the traditional routines (including religion) of the citizens and totalitarian governments characteristic of communist regimes. One supposed difference is that totalitarian regimes never revert to anything less repressive than they are. Another difference concerns the level of brutality and oppression. According to the right, totalitarian brutality is worse, as attested by the stream of refugees from the communist countries. But Walzer argues that the distinction between authoritarian and totalitarian systems is being misused.

Walzer believes that in many communist countries the possibility of transition is there; he does not agree that

TOTALITARIANISM VS. AUTHORITARIANISM By Michael Walzer. Excerpted from *The New Republic,* July 1981, pp. 4–11. © 1981 by The New Republic, Inc. Reprinted by permission of the publisher.

totalitarianism is irreversible. According to Walzer, the hard-line assumption that totalitarian and authoritarian governments are necessarily different is mistaken. Walzer says we should condemn totalitarian regimes *and* also refuse to support authoritarianism; we should always remain aware of those who suffer under either sort of tyranny.

. . . We know that the free world includes a large number of brutal and repressive regimes. These are "our" dictatorships, many of which, to the naked eye, don't look all that different from "theirs." But the new cold warriors of the 1980s want to draw the line exactly as it was drawn in the 1950s. So they have dug deeper into the original theory, looking for richer conceptual plunder. And indeed, as the theory was worked out by writers like Hannah Arendt and Carl Friedrich, totalitarianism was not contrasted with freedom. There was, after all, nothing new about unfree government. Most states through most of human history have been unfree; most still are. Totalitarianism was a radically new kind of unfreedom, a new species of the genus "tyrannus," different from all the others. This was the difference on which the theorists focused their attention, and it played a part too in political debates among small groups of leftist intellectuals struggling to understand Stalinist terror. But it was a difference largely ignored in the official ideology of the cold war.

Now, however, it has been taken up by the new cold war ideologists, led, for the moment, by our representative to the United Nations. Yes, they say, many of our allies are tyrants and always have been. But these are ordinary, old-fashioned tyrants. The real enemy, the present danger, is totalitarianism, that is, communism. And for the sake of the struggle against communism, we must make our peace with tyranny. Authoritarian regimes in South Korea or Guatemala or Argentina are not so bad when compared with Russia or North Vietnam or Cuba. (China, with which, it appears, we must also make our peace, tends to get overlooked in these discussions.) We must not allow moralistic qualms about routine oppression—the tyrants ye always have with you—to get in the way of our outrage at what is truly new and truly dangerous. Compared to the cold war rhetoric of the 1950s, this sort of talk represents, I suppose, a more

843

sophisticated appropriation of the original theory. It is not, however, a less corrupt one.

The original theory still has genuine value. Totalitarianism is indeed a new kind of tyranny, not entirely without precedent in the long history of tyranny, but new nonetheless. Partly its novelty consists in nothing more than a radical improvement in bureaucratic and police control, the introduction of a more advanced technology of surveillance: old tyranny with new machinery. One of the most frightening features of Orwell's *1984* was the two-way television screen. But machines are of little use without the will to use them, and what is most novel and most important about totalitarianism is the peculiarly modern ambition of its leaders: to control everything, to wipe out not merely opposition, but every form of difference, recalcitrance, hesitation, private doubt, and caution, to create an entirely new order and even a new kind of human being. Hence the need to penetrate every aspect of social life, religion, culture, and family, to seize every secondary association, to supervise all communication between persons, all movement between places, all thought and all feeling. Older tyrannies were marked by a more limited ambition. Their leaders wanted simply to stay in power, to enjoy the fruits of power for as long as possible. They were a danger to rivals and opponents, but private life, traditional routines, passive minorities were generally (not always) safe from their interventions.

That is the key distinction and it remains, to my mind, a useful guide to 20th-century politics. But it can't just be applied mechanically, dividing the world, for totalitarianism is an "ideal type," a picture of horrifying perfection never quite achieved in fact, while authoritarianism is a catchall category. The idea of totality bears the marks of its discovery in the immediate aftermath of the Holocaust and in the last years of Stalin's personal rule. The concentration camp, Hannah Arendt wrote, is the model of totalitarian control. The Hitler and Stalin regimes come as close as regimes have ever come to realizing that model, but even they realized it for some, not for all, of their subjects. And if we set aside the Soviet Union, where Stalinism remains today a regime-in-reserve, it is clear that all the other examples of post-World Warr II Communist and fascist governments are failed totalitarianisms. They don't measure up to Arendt's standard, they fall short of Orwell's brilliant science fiction, their terror isn't total. Between these regimes and others sorts of tyranny it isn't easy to draw a sharp line. And it is sheer willfulness, ideological relentlessness, to insist that this line, once it is worked out, will conform to the cold war division between East and West.

Consider now the two major moral/political arguments of the new cold warriors. I'll take them from Jeane Kirkpatrick's *Commentary* article ("Dictatorships and Double Standards," November 1979), a particularly good example of contemporary ideology, even if it isn't, or just because it isn't, a particularly good article. The first of these is an argument about political possibility. Communist totalitarianism brings with it a long, dark night. "There is no instance of a revolutionary 'socialist' or Communist society being democraticized," writes Kirkpatrick. Our own tyrants, by contrast, are sometimes replaced by democratic regimes—though it is always important for the stability of the new democracy that the replacement take place *very slowly*. Kirkpatrick doesn't discuss what might be called the reverse replacement rate. In fact, I'm afraid, the decline of democracy in the free world is rather more noticeable than its slow advance. In any case, this is a false distinction. Hungary, Czechoslovakia, and Poland probably would be democratic states today were it not for the Red Army. The Red Army is a threat to human freedom, but communism, in these states at least, is an ugly but not a powerful political system. There is nothing in its internal mechanics that rules out a democratic transformation. Assuming that the Russians don't intervene—an unlikely but analytically necessary assumption—the prospects for democracy are probably better, certainly no worse, in much of Eastern Europe than, to cite some of Kirkpatrick's odder examples, in Argentina, Brazil, South Korea, and Zaire. In all these cases, social structure and political culture are far more important than the current regime in shaping the long-term evolution.

The second argument is about relative brutality. Old-fashioned tyrannies, according to Kirkpatrick, because they don't set out to transform their societies, do much less damage to them. They tolerate existing patterns of misery and injustice, but at least they don't create new ones. And their subjects are accustomed to the old patterns, have long ago adjusted to them and learned how to survive. Hence "such societies create no refugees." This is the "damning contrast" between Communist regimes and "other autocracies." The massive refugee population of the modern world is largely a creation of Communist totalitarianism. It would be nice—not for the refugees but for the ideological peace of mind of the rest of us—if this were true. But it isn't true. The refugees who fled Hungary in 1956 or Afghanistan in 1980 were fleeing the Red Army, not domestic oppression. The million Cubans who have reached our shores since the 1960s probably could be matched by a million Haitians, were the latter given a comparable welcome. And the largest single group of refugees since World War II was produced by Pakistani repression in East Bengal, which was nothing if not old-fashioned. Certainly there are Communist states that fit Kirkpatrick's account. East Germany and Cambodia are different but equally clear-cut examples. But the line she draws is a fabrication.

The contrast between totalitarian and authoritarian regimes is a conceptual contrast, not a practical one. It doesn't conform to, nor does it justify, our actual alliances. It doesn't make Kissinger's Pakistani "tilt" of 1971 smell any better. It doesn't rule out economic (or even military) cooperation with Communist China. One can't pull politics or morality out of a theoretical hat. That sort of thing is always a trick. Theory, *once we have it right,* does nothing more than shape our perceptions, guide our understanding; within the framework it provides, choices still have to be made.

The hardest choice, and the one for the sake of which the new cold war ideology has been worked out, is simply this: an authoritarian regime, old-fashioned, brutal, repressive, allied to the West, is threatened by a revolutionary movement some of whose leaders have totalitarian ambitions and/or Russian connections. What should we do? The claim of the new cold warriors is that the liberal impulse in all such cases is to support the revolutionaries or at least to desert at the first opportunity the authoritarian regime. And what they want instead is the opposite policy, a steadfast commitment to the regime, because totalitarianism is the greater danger, the irreversible transformation, and so on.

But this is to turn policy into a reflex of ideology (disguised as theory). There just isn't going to be one answer in cases like the one I've described, and to act as if there is one answer—we get it right or wrong, we win or lose—is the beginning of political disaster. Often we can't do anything at all. Or rather, our choice is the same choice that the Russians have faced again and again in Eastern Europe: send in the troops or let the local conflict take its course. But let's assume that there is room, some limited room, for political maneuver (economic aid, military supply, diplomatic pressure, and so on). Then, obviously, the direction of our maneuvers will have to be determined by the shape of the terrain. How much popular support does the regime have? How much capacity for change? Who are the rebels and what is their "cause"? What sorts of alliances have they already made and how stable are those alliances? What are our own strategic interests in the area? That last question is generally taken to mean we should align ourselves with the established regime. In fact, however, if there really are strategic interests, and if we take them seriously, then it would seem to follow that we should line up as early as possible with the side most likely to win, so long as there is a real chance of keeping the winners out of the Russian camp. It is characteristic of the new cold warriors that they would support authoritarian governments both when it is in our interests to do so and also when it isn't—so that one is led to suspect that they just support authoritarian governments. In any case, there probably are such governments that we ought on balance to help. Otherwise, we could hardly have any relations at all with third world states. And there probably are oppositionists and revolutionaries whom we ought on balance to help too.

Rarely, however, in any part of the third world, are there going to be old or new regimes, governments, or movements to which we should be ideologically committed. We don't have to become apologists for the internal policies of our allies. What we owe them at most is critical support. Foreign policy is always a double business: we have to pursue our interests and we have to defend our values. In the long run, we hope that these two efforts come together, but at any given moment there are conflicts and contradictions. Maybe it is in our interest to support, say, the present South Korean regime. But we must also, for the sake of our values, maintain some critical distance from it. And that kind of argument doesn't work only for right-wing regimes. After 1960, it was in our interest that Cuban communism develop in, say, a Yugoslav rather than a Bulgarian direction, and we might have accomplished that, or at least assisted in it, through some sort of economic cooperation. But cooperation would have been no excuse for a failure to criticize Castro's dictatorship, the repression of dissidents, the campaign against homosexuals, and so on.

A policy of this kind assumes that there is no long, dark night, no thousand-year Reich, no totalitarian transformation that is proof against political opposition and social change. That has to be, I think, the working assumption of any sane diplomacy. The new cold

847

warriors exploit what we might think of as the apocalyptic features of the theory of totalitarianism. And in the 20th century it is difficult to avoid some engagement with, some hard contemplation of, apocalypse. In political terms that means that there have been and will be again regimes so evil that the only moral stand one can adopt toward them is absolute opposition. But what policies follow from that moral stand? Surely Stalin's was one such regime, and yet we fought with Stalin against the Nazis. Even evil has its degrees. We must hope—we can reasonably believe—that it also has its duration.

In the third world, at any rate, there is not likely to be much permanence—no sustained development toward modernity and liberty, but also very few stable or solidly established tyrannies. No doubt many of the tyrants will have totalitarian ambitions; the rhetoric of revolution is now the *lingua franca* of the third world. But that only means that there will be many failed totalitarianisms. Whether these failures will be bloodier than the "other autocracies" is a question unlikely to find a yes or no answer. Some of them will and some won't. For our part, we can and should maintain a steady hostility toward every sort of totalitarian ambition. But that is no reason for supporting the "other autocracies" or excusing their bloodiness. We can make the alliances we have to make on both sides of this shadowly line, and we can condemn when we must the internal policies of our allies. I understand, of course, that there are serious diplomatic difficulties involved in any such policy—much discussed and never overcome during the Carter years. But it is a worse policy to refuse altogether to confront those difficulties. The real danger, *the present danger,* of the new cold war ideology is that it will drive us into alliances that our material defense does not require and rule out the outspokenness that the defense of our values does require. And all this for the sake of a misunderstood and badly applied political theory!

But perhaps I overestimate the power of theory (it is a common professional mistake). One might detect among contemporary cold warriors a sneaking sympathy for "traditional autocrats [who] leave in place existing allocations of wealth, power, status, and other resources. . . ." On the far left, there is often similar sympathy for revolutionaries who upset those allocations, even if they do so only in order to establish a new tyranny—and this view, too, has its theoretical rationale. But I would propose a different sympathy: for

848

the tortured dissidents, the imprisoned oppositionists, the threatened minorities, all the "disappeared" and murdered men and women of all the tyrannies, old and new. And we don't need a political theory to explain why we should keep these people always in the forefront of our consciousness, their names on the tip of our tongues.

## STUDY QUESTIONS

1. Compose a three-way debate with Walzer on one side and Kirkpatrick and Revel on the other. Who, in your view, comes off best?

2. Both Kirkpatrick and Revel refer to the genocide in Cambodia; Walzer mentions it but does not dwell on what happened there. Does Walzer give reasonable grounds for not treating this as a decisive indication that totalitarianism is very much worse than authoritarianism?

3. Do Walzer's criticisms also apply to Revel? How would Revel view Walzer's theses? Would Revel see them as obscuring the issue facing democracies and thereby weakening their necessary resolve to face the threat of totalitarianism? Would Revel think of Walzer as naive? Dangerous? Reasonable?

4. Do you agree with Walzer's conclusion that humanitarianism and not ideology (left or right) should guide our foreign policy?

## SUGGESTED READINGS

Aiken, William and Hugh La Follette, eds. *World Hunger and Moral Obligation.* Englewood Cliffs, NJ: Prentice-Hall, 1977.

Brown, Peter G. and Douglas MacLean. *Human Rights and U.S. Foreign Policy.* Lexington, MA: Lexington Press, 1979.

Lucas, George R., and Thomas W. Ogletree, eds. *Lifeboat Ethics: The Moral Dilemma of World Hunger.* New York: Harper and Row, 1976.

Narveson, Jan, ed. *Moral Issues.* Oxford University Press, 1983.

Shue, Henry. *Basic Rights: Subsistence, Affluence and U.S. Foreign Policy.* Princeton: Princeton University Press, 1980.

Singer, Peter. *Practical Ethics.* Cambridge, MA: Cambridge University Press, 1979.

D 1
E 2
F 3
G 4
H 5
I 6
J 7